ACHE LIFE HISTORY

FOUNDATIONS OF HUMAN BEHAVIOR
An Aldine de Gruyter Series of Texts and Monographs

SERIES EDITORS
Sarah Blaffer Hrdy, *University of California, Davis*
Monique Borgerhoff Mulder, *University of California, Davis*

ACHE LIFE HISTORY

The Ecology and Demography of a Foraging People

KIM HILL and A. MAGDALENA HURTADO

ALDINE DE GRUYTER

New York

About the Authors

Kim Hill is Associate Professor of Anthropology, University of New Mexico. He received his Ph.D. from the University of Utah, and has been the recipient of ten L.S.B. Leakey Foundation Grants. Dr. Hill's field work in Mexico and South America spans more than nineteen years, including a cumulative 53 months with the Ache in Paraguay. His research is widely published in edited volumes and major journals.

A. Magdalena Hurtado is Assistant Professor of Anthropology, University of New Mexico, where she is also Research Director for the New Mexico Medical Treatment Effectiveness Research Center for Ethnic Populations for the School of Medicine. Dr. Hurtado's field work covers more than eleven years in South America, including concentration on the Ache in Paraguay. Her writings are widely published in major journals.

ALDINE DE GRUYTER
A division of Walter de Gruyter, Inc.
200 Saw Mill River Road
Hawthorne, New York 10532

This publication is printed on acid free paper

Library of Congress Cataloging-in-Publication Data
Hill, Kim, 1953–
    Ache life history : the ecology and demography of a foraging
people / Kim Hill and A. Magdalena Hurtado.
        p. cm.
    Includes bibliographical references (p.   ) and index.
    ISBN 0-202-02036-3 (cloth : alk. paper) 0-202-02037-1 (paper : alk. paper).
    1. Guayaki Indians—Population. 2. Indians of South America—
Paraguay. I. Hurtado, A. Magdalena. II. Title.
F2679.2.G9H55 1995
304.6'08998'30892—dc20   95-18065
                                                       CIP

Manufactured in the United States of America

10 9 8 7 6 5 4 3 2 1

For Don and Mary, Luis and Inés

Contents

Preface

The principles of life history research in hunter-gatherer populations explored in this book were put together in piecemeal fashion over many years. Some are buried in seemingly impenetrable math problems and others are afterthoughts to empirical observations. Our aim always has been to weave together the diverse threads of life history concepts and behavioral research methods using data on Ache hunter-gatherers. Simply put, we have labored to tie difficult concepts in life history theory to the basic goals of human behavioral ecology in anthropology. However, the motivation behind the fieldwork that made this manuscript possible germinated not in life history theory but in a personal search for a satisfying explanation of human behavioral variation.

We have worked together on the issues outlined in this book for fourteen years, but at the beginning there are two different stories to tell. Kim started as a graduate student in molecular biology at UCSD but left that field when he became dissatisfied with a life of laboratory work. During his last month at UCSD he signed up for a Peace Corps program in Paraguay called "Indigenous Community Development." Before leaving for Paraguay, Kim spent several days at the library reading about Paraguayan Indians. The book *Genocide in Paraguay* by Richard Arens had the most lasting impression. It described the near extermination of the Ache Indians of Paraguay. We would later learn that the material was highly inaccurate, but it instilled a desire to meet the Ache. Little did Kim imagine at that time that the Ache would become lifelong friends who would help to answer both personal and scientific questions.

Kim was determined to see the Ache and learn about their nomadic ways of life. Rumors in Paraguay about the Ache being mysterious forest cannibals, with white skin, full beards, and regularly practicing polyandry and homosexuality, were all the more enticing. Although most of the rumors turned out to be exaggerated or unfounded, they fanned the fires of motivation to meet the Ache and learn of their lives. Kim arrived at the Manduvi mission run by the Divine Word order of the Catholic Church on January 1, 1978, and began his work as a Peace Corps volunteer. During all of 1978 and part of 1979 he lived with the Ache and spent a good deal of time with them on forest treks as well as participating in daily life at the mission.

Kim's year with the Ache had a greater impact on him than he ever could have imagined. The experience called into question every assumption he had about what people should and should not do, and about how people should live and interact. He had spent months at a time rarely seeing another non-Ache person. He saw children born and watched people die. He became close friends with people who had known killing and death all their lives and seemed to show indifference to events that he found shocking. He became an intimate participant in group life where people openly discuss sexual topics and don't censor their conversations in front of children or members of the opposite sex. Blatant public sexual flirtation was the norm. He lived with people who went naked for much of their lives and had no particular shame concerning the human body. Property was never really private, and sharing was the most important aspect of the behavioral code. Bragging and self-aggrandizement were considered repugnant, and privacy was absolutely nonexistent. Moodiness was countered by teasing the offending party. Social pressure and "shame" kept everyone in check and led to an unquestioned behavioral conformity. Among the Ache there were no revolutionaries, no visionaries, and no rebels. Joking and happy-go-lucky demeanor were universal, and physical touching was an important part of every social interaction— between friends of the same, or opposite, sex. Men and women seemed comfortable in each other's presence regardless of whether they were friends, lovers, potential lovers, kin, young, old, or middle-aged. In short, the Ache were indeed very different from any people he had ever known.

After Kim left the Peace Corps he began to think about graduate training in anthropology. Near the end of his stay in Paraguay he had met David Maybury-Lewis, chair of the anthropology department of Harvard University and director of Cultural Survival. Maybury-Lewis had advised Kim not to attend graduate school in anthropology, stating that "only people who want it more than anything else in the world should consider anthropology as a career." Despite this realistic advice, Kim began graduate school at Columbia University in 1980. The last few months before graduate school Kim also rediscovered a lost interest in biology, as anthropological questions began to look more and more similar to issues in behavioral biology that he had studied years before.

In 1979, Kim had taken an anthropology course from Kristen Hawkes at the University of Utah. Kristen was a fantastic teacher with a keen sense of "the important questions" in anthropology. She had explored a variety of theoretical perspectives as a cultural anthropologist. Her interest in economics had driven her to sit in on biology courses about foraging theory taught by Eric Charnov. As a biology student Kim had also known Charnov, and now both Kim and Kristen began to investigate the field of animal behavioral ecology as a model for applying evolutionary biology to the study of human culture. Behavioral ecology differed somewhat from sociobiology in that it placed less emphasis on genetic evolution of social behavior and more emphasis on phenotypic plasticity and adaptive facultative response patterns.

By the beginning of 1980 both Kim and Kristen were committed to exploring evolutionary biology and its implications for human behavior. Kim knew little about anthropology but a good deal about biology. Nevertheless it was Kristen who chose the first research problem, motivated by models in behavioral ecology. Kristen wanted to test some ideas derived from optimal foraging theory (OFT) in biology, and she wanted to carry out the test on a data set specifically collected for this purpose. Kim's contribution was the choice of field site. He had told Kristen about the Ache, and she had come to realize that the Ache might indeed offer a good opportunity to test the optimal diet model, a central model in foraging theory at that time. From March through July 1980 Kristen and Kim spent several months in Paraguay doing treks into the forest with the Ache and collecting foraging data.

The year Kim began graduate school at Columbia University, he met two people who were to become his most important research colleagues. Hilly Kaplan had come to Columbia from the University of Pennsylvania, where he was studying communication. Before long he and Kim began to plan a research project to study Ache food sharing. Magdalena Hurtado was a Venezuelan student who had come to the United States to train in anthropology in order to help solve some very practical and difficult problems among Venezuelan indigenous groups: poverty and social malaise that accompanied incorporation in international politics and economics. Because the prevailing paradigms failed to provide systematic means to formulate and test ideas, she turned to alternatives within a few months of entering graduate school at Columbia. At the time, she felt that behavioral ecology offered the most promise for solving the problems she wanted to address.

Magdalena learned, however, that specific applications of evolutionary theory were far from apparent. It took several years of postdoctoral training in epidemiology and biostatistics for her to make this interdisciplinary link. Hilly was very involved in her early work, and together they worked on modeling constraints in female foraging decisions that were overlooked by optimal foraging models. Later Magdalena's efforts encouraged the team to think about complex relationships between ecology, parental investment decisions, juvenile mortality, and morbidity. This served as the substantive bridge between basic and applied research that Magdalena had ultimately wanted to cross.

In September of 1981, Magdalena, Hilly, and Kim traveled to Paraguay to study food sharing, time allocation, and foraging patterns among the Ache and to collect some of the data used in this book. Kristen joined us in January and was accompanied by Kevin Jones, an archaeologist. It was a great year, and the memories of our base camp and the fun times that we had spring up whenever we all get together. The most unfortunate incident of the year was an automobile accident, which sent Jones back to the United States. When Magdalena, Hilly, and Kim returned to the states they transferred to the University of Utah to work with Kristen.

In 1983 Hilly and Kim spent two months doing a survey of the Mashco-Piro nomads in the Manu National Park in Peru. Collecting data from several other societies kept the research team from fixating on a single group of people. In subsequent years we (the co-authors) spent about twenty-five months working with other native groups in Peru and Venezuela. Hilly spent about the same amount of time in Peru and Botswana with new research associates, and Kristen teamed up with Jim O'Connell and Nick Blurton Jones to carry out many months of fieldwork with the Hadza of Tanzania and additional trips to collect data on the !Kung of Botswana.

In September of 1984, Hilly, Magdalena, and Kim returned to the Ache together for the last time. Also on this trip were Kevin Jones, who had been injured in the 1982 accident, and Heather Dove, who was interested in child development. Kim and Magdalena quickly discovered the difficulties of having a 15-month-old infant in the field. Karina, our daughter, was loved and spoiled by the Ache, but keeping her healthy and happy under very primitive field conditions was extremely difficult.

In 1987 Kim and Magdalena returned to the Ache again. This time our daughter was four years old, and she had spent many months in the field in Peru and Venezuela. We were able to accomplish a great deal, enjoy ourselves, and have our whole family together. It was the ideal fieldwork situation. During that year, Magdalena became heavily involved in working on the demographic study that Kim had begun years earlier. We decided to write a book on Ache demographic patterns. Between 1985 and 1988 we also spent a considerable amount of time in the field working with the Hiwi foragers of Venezuela. The comparison between the Hiwi and the Ache provided many insights about foraging people that are expressed in these pages.

In 1991, Magdalena trained in epidemiology as a William T. Grant Foundation Faculty Scholar at the University of Michigan's School of Public Health. Her training contributed new and rigorous research design and statistical methodology to all our subsequent work together, including this book. The log-linear models that predominate in our analyses were unknown to us throughout graduate school. Their importance and power for research in behavioral ecology is now evident.

Between 1989 and early 1995 Kim returned alone to the Ache seven more times. On most of these trips he lived in the hut of one of our Ache friends, slept in a bed with family members, and ate meals with the household. These experiences gave him a chance to get back in touch with the Ache after seven years of doing fieldwork while maintaining our own separate base camp. The conditions were very difficult at times, but in the absence of his wife and family the insights gained made the discomfort worthwhile. In these years Kim was able to talk late into the night with some of our closest friends and learn the very private details of their lives and their concerns. He heard children crying from hunger and saw the deaths of some good friends—events that reminded us again not to romanticize this way of life that we had learned to respect. These final years have also included new students and new experiences. Doug Jones carried out a project with us to study Ache opinions of attractiveness, and Richard Bribiescas visited the Ache with us to study male reproductive function using salivary hormone profiles. Interviews with Ache men and women on these topics gave us new insights into the Ache mating game and have influenced some of the analyses presented in this book.

Finally, in 1989 and 1991 we were able to give two of our closest friends something that we would have never believed possible. In 1978 Bepurangi and Membogi told us that their sister had died a few weeks after first contact in 1972. Two of her small children had survived and had been adopted by Americans. They wanted us to locate the Ache children and bring them back for a visit. We tried to explain that the United States was an enormous country and that there was no chance of us finding their relatives, but we promised to try. We did not even have the last name of the family that had adopted the children. All we knew is that they were Peace Corps volunteers who had worked at the National Gua-yaki (Ache) Reservation for a short time in the early 1970s. To make a long story short, through a combination of lucky breaks and steady investigation we located the two Ache orphans, who by 1989 were fully grown adults. Chevugi and Tykuarangi, brother and sister, were both hesitant but eventually agreed to accompany us on a visit to the Ache.

Chevugi visited his people in 1989 and his sister Tykuarangi followed two years later. We know that the visits were emotionally exhausting as the sights and sounds and smells of a lost life, buried deep in their memory, came back to them. Both trips included a lot of crying and a lot of joy. We were able to fulfill a promise to Membogi and Bepurangi that we had made more than ten years earlier, and for Chevugi and Tykuarangi hopefully it will bring a new appreciation of their past. In a way, this book is for people like Chevugi and Tykuarangi, who are looking for some clues into their own past and trying to sort out some difficult questions. For us, this book is the culmination of a long struggle to understand the dimensions of a human past that we all share in common.

Acknowledgments

First, we would like to thank the Ache for the most incredible hospitality that we have ever experienced in our many years of fieldwork with several different ethnic groups. They put up with years of tedious questions about their personal lives that they must have thought silly or obnoxious at times. For the most part they genuinely seemed to enjoy talking about their relatives, spouses, children, and grandchildren. Unlike many groups, the Ache have no taboo against discussing the deceased and often seemed pleased to provide intimate details of the lives of their deceased parents, siblings, and grandparents. Some of the Ache who provided us shelter in their homes or with whom we spent a good deal of time outside work hours became special friends and contributed crucial insights into the topics we discuss in this book. We especially want to thank Pedro Bepurangi and Agustina Buachugi, Martin Achipurangi and Antonia Javagi, Enrique Tykuarangi and Margarita Chachupurangi, Lorenzo Kuchingi and Loreta Kuaregi, Roque Chachugi and Facunda Membopurangi, Chito Membogi and Lucia Bepurangi, Antonio Kuachingi and Antonia Byvangi, Carlos Bejyvagi and Teresa Bepurangi, and Roberto Tykuarangi and Petrona Tatugi. Each of these couples became our close friends and helped us with daily life and our struggle of raising our children in the field. Pedro Javagi and Julio Kuaregi worked with us for months to correct errors in the data set and provide more details on ages and dates of events. To all the Ache, who will probably never read this book or care about the details we report in it, we hope that the results of this study will be positive and in some small way make it easier to deal with the changes that have been thrust upon you. *Ore Achepe bygatuete vyvy, ore javevaty Ache, ore eji eko jueche.*

This study spans fourteen years of data collection and nearly five years of writing. Many people provided help, advice, encouragement, and intellectual support during that period. Most importantly we wish to thank Kristen Hawkes and Hilly Kaplan, our closest collaborators, who worked with the Ache for several years and provided a continuous stream of important theoretical feedback. Kristen's keen eye and healthy skepticism of commonly held ideas about hunter-gatherers has been critical in forcing us to search for rigorous methods that can differentiate between alternative explanations of patterns we observed. Hilly Kaplan lived with us in the field on many occasions both in Paraguay and Peru throughout the 1980s and has always been the best possible colleague and a great friend in the field and back in the states. He collected some of the data reported in this study and spent thousands of hours discussing models, preliminary results, and suggesting new analyses. His ideas about fertility variation and kinship effects are heavily incorporated into Chapters 12 and 13.

Our faculty colleagues at the University of Michigan and the University of New Mexico have also been instrumental in the development of many ideas in this book. In particular we wish to thank our colleagues in the Evolution and Human Behavior Program at Michigan, Richard Alexander, David Buss, Warren Holmes, Bobbi Low, John Mitani, Barb Smuts, and Richard Wrangham, as well as our colleagues in the Human Evolutionary Ecology program at New Mexico, Suzie Alvarado, Jim Boone, Jane Lancaster, and Hillard Kaplan. Students in both programs also provided a good deal of advice and criticism, especially John Bock, Charles Keckler, Doug Jones, Joe Manson, Susan Perry, Richard Sosis, and all the graduate students who participated in our life history seminars over the past several years. Richard Bribiescas, Doug Jones, and Kevin Jones all initiated research with the Ache while we were working on this project, which has helped to clarify Ache spatial use, economics, mate choice criteria, and male reproductive strategies.

Nick Blurton Jones, Monique Borgerhoff Mulder, Tom Fricke, Henry Harpending, Alan Rogers, and David Tracer all read pieces of the book in its early stages and provided valuable written feedback. Monique made detailed comments on the entire final draft. Sara Hrdy commented on the finished manuscript as well as providing encouragement throughout the project. Nancy Howell also provided important comments.

For help with life history concepts we wish to thank Ric Charnov and Alan Rogers, who pointed us in a variety of interesting directions and provided important guidance at various points. Dan Promislow provided useful comments on several chapters. Charnov also deserves special thanks for his input into our graduate training and for showing us the power of evolutionary ecology for making sense out of human variation.

Our interest in anthropological demography was stimulated by the pioneering work of Nancy Howell, and our interest in evolutionary approaches to the use of demographic data was inspired by Napoleon Chagnon. Richard Lee's early work on the !Kung was the basis for our decision to work with modern hunter-gatherers and our theoretical focus on ecology. Subsequent forager studies carried out by the Harvard Ituri Project and the Hadza research team provided us with important ideas as well as wonderful colleagues. Those not yet mentioned include Bob Bailey, Jim O'Connell, Nadine Peacock, and Peter Ellison. Indeed, Peter Ellison's reproductive ecology group was responsible for much of our interest in the evolutionary biology of fertility variation.

Frequent interaction with a variety of colleagues in human evolutionary ecology through the years has affected our thinking about topics discussed in this book. Among those not yet mentioned are Gillian Bentley, Laura Betzig, Robert Boyd, Liz Cashdan, Martin Daly, Irv DeVore, Ray Hames, Henry Harpending, Barry Hewlett, Bill Irons, Renee Pennington, Joan Silk, Eric Smith, Holly

Smith, Don Symons, Paul Turke, Barb Smuts, Virginia Vitzhum, Margo Wilson, Bruce Winterhalder, and Carol Worthman.

Other friends and colleagues made important contributions to our work. Sherry Ortner and Dick Ford of the University of Michigan were extremely supportive of our efforts and helped make it possible for us to acquire new analytical skills in demography, statistics, and epidemiology. They also provided Kim with one paid semester of leave to work on this book. Debra Graddick made many of the bureacratic complications of academia less time consuming for us. Erik Trinkaus and Jane Lancaster at the University of New Mexico were very helpful in providing the atmosphere needed to complete this project in the midst of a cross-country move. We are deeply grateful to June-el Piper for her conscientious and outstanding editorial assistance, and to Richard Koffler and Arlene Perazzini for their enthusiastic encouragement. K. G. Anderson generously assisted us in constructing the index with meticulous care under considerable time pressure. We would also like to thank David Waynforth for preparing Tables 1.1, 1.2 and 14.1, and Meredith Mahony for help with bibliographic entries.

Funding for research and analyses presented here came from many sources. The L. S. B. Leakey Foundation provided us with two grants and a fellowship. The University of Michigan provided one year of funding and the University of New Mexico gave us two small grants for completing this work. Most importantly the National Science Foundation (grant BNS 86-13186) provided money to finish data collection and begin the analyses presented here.

Finally, we wish to thank many people for their hospitality in Paraguay over the years. Graciela Ocariz and Oscar Centurion were instrumental in getting us permission to work with the Ache year after year and providing institutional support and friendship. They also showed a genuine concern for the welfare of Paraguayan native peoples that was encouraging to us when our spirits sagged after observing sad events of persecution. Bjarne Fostervold has been our most dependable friend and helper year after year. He and his wife Rosalba have always made us feel completely at home regardless of the inconvenience we have imposed on them. Fathers Alejandro Pytell, Wayne Robbins, and Benjamin Remiorz of the Divine Word order of the Catholic Church were gracious hosts who provided logistic support as well as welcome friendship. Ruth Sammons of New Tribes missions was always extremely generous with her Ache linguistic material. Chalo Vega Cañete of Curuguaty put us up in his house dozens of times and never complained when we showed up at odd hours of the night, filthy from a long trip and accompanied by a truckload of Ache who were ravenous. He became our closest friend near the field site and the one person in the remote countryside who always treated the Ache like human beings. His insightful analyses of differences between American and Paraguayan culture helped us to feel more comfortable when problems arose that we did not understand.

To all these people and many more who must remain unnamed, we owe a huge debt of gratitude. We hope that the completion of this study after so many years of promise will repay that debt in some small way.

Membogi in his house, July 1989.

1

Life History and Demography

The small group of women froze in mid-step just for a moment. "Kwiiiit . . . be quiet." Then, they heard it again. Faintly in the distance was a sound that seemed like a bloodcurdling scream. Suddenly, pandemonium broke loose in the forest camp. Younger women shrieked and moaned as children scampered up nearby trees and began to wail rhythmically. "Aiei, Aiei, Aiei." Infants in baby slings bawled as their mothers roughly jolted them while slinging off their carrying baskets and dropping them to the ground. Old women scowled and scolded and shouted in the direction of the men. "Get over there quick, he is screaming." There was heated discussion. Was that a scream? Who could it have been?

They heard the rustling of leaves across the lagoon and hollered out, "Who are you? Who let out the shriek of a jaguar attack?" "I'm Membogi," came back the reply. "Was it my brother who screamed?" Then, as they heard no more sounds the group slowly became calm again. Perhaps it was just the wind whistling through the bamboo.

As the day ended and the hunters converged on the small camp the women had laid out, a dreadful awareness came over Membogi. All the hunters but one were accounted for. Membogi's older brother Achipurangi was missing.

The next day Kuchingi began to track Achipurangi from where he was last seen. After a few hours he found a guan that had been shot and left, along with all of Achipurangi's arrows. The hunter's bow was nowhere to be found. He picked up the fresh trail of a tapir and followed it along. Perhaps Achipurangi had shot the tapir and then left his arrows behind in order to crawl along the ground tracking it. Then Kuchingi came upon a startling sign. Large jaguar tracks were laid down on top of the tapir trail and what looked like the path Achipurangi had made in the vegetation while tracking the tapir. Maybe the jaguar had killed the tapir, jaguars often kill tapirs. Perhaps Achipurangi shot the tapir and then the jaguar came along behind too. Maybe the jaguar had bitten the tapir first and then Achipura tracked it down, hoping to finish it off. Then maybe the jaguar found him. Maybe after tracking the tapir Achipurangi turned back and then found the jaguar coming along behind in the same tracks. Kuchingi returned to the guan and roasted it in a fire. When Kuchingi started back he found many jaguar tracks only minutes old by a large stream. Then a bird was flushed out very close and made a cry of alarm. Kuchingi was sure the jaguar was very nearby; he ran back to the camp. The Ache never found Achipurangi's body.

Back in camp, Pirajugi sobbed as the children hit her with sticks and lengths of

vine. "Hit her," commanded the old women firmly. "Hit her good—hit her."
"That's enough," countered some of the older men. Pirajugi was their godchild.
She was the one whose essence they had helped form by providing meat to her
mother when she was in the womb. She was the one whom they had named, and
they would defend her as was the custom. Pirajugi was only seventeen years old
and Achipurangi had been her first husband. Her belly was large with his child
soon to be born.[1]

The small band was camped near the banks of the Jejui Guasu, a large muddy
meandering river that had created swamps and oxbow lagoons along its banks
through millennia of tropical rainstorms and relentless wandering through the flat
sandy alluvial soils of what had once been a huge inland lake. The band would
not be able to cross the river now because it had recently flooded after three days
of rain. Last time they had tried to cross in a flood, Chejugi's baby had fallen in
the water and was swept away while Chejugi looked on helplessly. Neither she
nor any other adult in the band could swim.

It began to rain again. Normally the band would have begun to construct palm
leaf shelters and stayed put for the rest of the day, but now everyone wanted to
move, to distance themselves from the danger and from their sadness. Women and
children were nervous and on their guard to avoid any provocation of the men,
particularly the older men who had the scars on their backs that meant they had
killed. Men were bylla, *they had "lost their essence of humanness" because of the*
death, and they might fly into a fit of violence at the slightest provocation. The
people plodded through the rain and mud until dark and then made camp. A fire
was lit in the dry hollow of a large tree since no other dry tinder could be found.
The men cut brush from the surrounding thickets with an old broken machete they
had stolen from a woodcutter's camp. Hurriedly they built a circular corral of
brush around the camp. The jaguar would be heard if it approached during the
night.

The leader of the small band was Tall-Bywangi and his wife Pikygi was the
sister of Pirajugi. They were not present when Achipurangi disappeared. They
had left the band to go off by themselves for a few days. Living in the same band
at that time was one of their brothers, Javagi. Membogi, Achipurangi's brother,
was not yet fully adult, so he slept at the fire of his sister Chevugi, and her
husband Kanjegi-the-bearded-one. Kuchingi was there along with his wife
Kuaregi, and her old mother Kanegi. Kuaregi's brother, Betapagi, was almost
twenty-five years old but had no wife, so he slept at his sister's fire. Also present
were Kanje-the-stabber (he had run his wife through with his hardwood bow),
Grandpa Bepurangi, Pirajugi's father Brikugi, and a half-dozen others. The band
was small, about nine men and seven women, plus a few adolescents and children. A much larger group of Ache was camped a short distance up the river. The
leader of that group was Kravachingi-the-killer. He had earned his name by

mortally wounding two men in club fights and from the several children he had killed in order to bury them with a deceased companion.

Early the next morning Tall-Bywangi's group packed up and set out in the direction of the larger camp. There had been much bickering and scolding through the night, as men and women tried to assign blame for the tragedy. Kravachingi-the-killer would be enraged when he heard the news and might demand a club fight. Only Membogi and Pirajugi said nothing.

The band moved for two days, and when they arrived at the site of the larger camp it was abandoned. Kravachingi-the-killer had crossed the river before the rains, and his band was far to the south, toward the place where parrots came to eat mud. In that same direction enemies with rock-shooting-thunder had recently killed Ache. Kravachingi's group would move quickly and quietly until they reached the bamboo forest. Tall-Bywangi's band continued to move about on the north side of the river, making a new campsite each night. Every day or two they saw tracks of the jaguar that had devoured Achipurangi. Jaguars often followed Ache bands for days, but one that had recently killed was a serious concern. People were edgy and the hunters seldom strayed far from the band.

Pirajugi married Betapagi after a few days. He had talked sweetly to her every day, bringing her palm hearts and asking if he could sleep at her fire. He stayed near her late at night, whispering jokes and stories long after other band members had dozed off. At first she refused him. He was ugly and a lackluster hunter. But other band members began to pressure her, insisting that she should remarry. She finally relented but continued to be plagued by the question that had haunted her since the day Achipurangi died. Betapagi would bring her baby into the world, but was he a willing father to another man's child?

Pirajugi didn't have to wait long for the answer. Her baby was born in camp a few days later, and all the Ache examined it carefully. Young children crowded close to watch the birth and touch the baby as their mothers rebuked them and pushed them away. Every man of the band was present except Betapagi, who had departed with his bow as soon as his new wife began to show signs of labor pain.

The baby was small and had very little hair on its head. The Ache felt little affection for children born without hair. No woman volunteered to cradle the baby while the mother recovered from the birth. No man stepped forward to cut the umbilical cord. The signs were clear, and it took only Kuchingi's verbal suggestion to settle the point. "Bury the child," he said. "It is defective, it has no hair." "Besides, it has no father. Betapagi does not want it. He will leave you if you keep it." Pirajugi said nothing, and the old woman Kanegi began to dig silently with a broken bow stave. The child and placenta were placed in the hole and covered with red sandy soil. A few minutes later the Ache packed up their belongings and Grandpa Bepurangi began to break a trail through the undergrowth with his unstrung bow. Pirajugi was tired, but she had nothing to carry, so she was able to keep up without difficulty. Women cried softly as they walked through the forest. "Ooooooh Kuajy maiecheve. . . ." "Our parents and grandparents who took care of us. . . .

That night it rained hard, and it rained much of the next day. People remained in camp and cut nearby palm trees to extract the edible fiber, which was full of starch.

Pirajugi ate only palm hearts and rested. Betapagi brought some palm fiber for his new wife to eat but then set off to probe the area for armadillo or paca burrows. The following day the sky cleared and the men were off early to hunt. They set off, doubling back down the same trail from where they had come, back towards the spot where Pirajugi had given birth. In a short time they reappeared, panting and gasping, and they conversed excitedly. The dead baby was gone. The jaguar had come during the rain and dug it up. It had been eaten, along with the placenta. The men were agitated. They wanted to cross the large river immediately and join the larger group to the south. Everyone agreed, and a trail was cut in the direction of the river. The men hunted nearby as the band made slow progress through a bog filled waist deep with water from the recent rain, and children stayed especially close to their mothers. It would not be possible to cross the river, and the jaguar continued to follow the band, always just out of sight.

The band stopped in a high spot and made a camp. They cut saplings and brush to make a thick corral around their chosen spot. If the jaguar came at night it would make plenty of noise and give them time to prepare. Kanjegi-the-bearded-one went further out into the forest looking for branches. Suddenly he shrieked and ran back to camp. The jaguar had attacked him, but somewhat timidly, and he had managed to escape. His shoulder was bleeding. The men continued their work on the brush corral and nobody went out to hunt.

For two days the Ache remained in their brush corral. Nobody hunted, and little food was found in the area. Children cried from hunger. They had been sleeping in trees since the day Kanjegi-the-bearded-one was attacked. That night the camp was quiet. Little game had been killed, so children dozed off early, and the men did not joke or sing. The moon was small, and the forest was as black as the inner reaches of a deep cave. Everyone was sleeping soundly when the night resounded with an awful shriek. Pirajugi let out a high-pitched squeal and was silent. The men fanned up the flames on their fires and women and children began to cry. Some children climbed into nearby trees and their mothers stood just below. Then as the flames danced higher they saw the source of commotion. A large female jaguar stood in the bushes at the edge of the camp with Pirajugi's body dangling from her mouth. Pirajugi's skull had been neatly pierced and she was lifeless. A roar went up as men and women bellowed at the top of their lungs and men rattled their bows and arrows. Some men took aim to shoot, but the jaguar dropped her prey and escaped into the night.

The band was spooked. They spoke in hushed tones of Achipurangi's words. Only days before he disappeared he had said to his wife, "I had a dream that I will not come back again. I will eat your unborn child and then I will eat you. I will not return." Now Achipurangi's dream had come true. It was exactly as he had told his wife. Others began to speculate that the jaguar was the same one they had raised as a cub. That one had been freed when it became too large, but it had no fear of people. It used to follow along behind the band as a cub, just as this one was doing now.

The next day the Ache remained in their brush corral. Grandmother Kanegi told her son-in-law Kuchingi, "Tonight there will be a very tiny slice of the moon. Wait in a tree and shoot the jaguar." That night they took extraordinary precautions. Brush was cut and piled high in a large circle around the campsite. Extra firewood was cut, and flames were fanned high through the night. Kuchingi did wait in a tree high above camp with his bow and arrows. If the jaguar returned he would have a good chance to shoot it.

The night grew long and the Ache began to doze off, one by one. Most were snoring deeply. Only Kuchingi, perched uncomfortably on a limb of the tree above camp, kept watch. Suddenly, he heard a rustling sound and saw the body of an old female jaguar. Kuchingi quickly took aim and shot with a bladed large-game arrow. The jaguar let out a blowing grunt as it was hit. It jerked in uncontrolled spasms for a moment, and then, snapping the arrow shaft with one quick blow of its paw, ran off into the darkness.

The next morning the men pursued the jaguar's tracks for a few hundred meters and then returned to the camp. Kuchingi had dreamed that the jaguar was dead, and nobody wished to track it. The people all went out to collect philodendron fruit. They were starving and brought back baskets piled high with the fruit. Then, all the Ache bundled up their belongings and crossed the large river on a log that was cut across the river. Vines were strung along above the log in order to provide a handhold that swayed and swung with the weight of each grasping hand but provided some stability to complement the slippery foothold that could be gotten along the submerged parts of the log.

It was January of 1962. The small band would soon find Kravachingi-the-killer, and the safety of a larger camp. Despite their anxiety, Kravachingi-the-killer did not demand a club fight. Javagi, brother of Pirajugi, was not yet married but would soon find a wife. Kanjegi-the-bearded-one's wife Chevugi gave birth to a boy a few months later, and Membogi underwent a puberty ceremony in which he had his lip pierced for a lip plug. He would go on to marry and have children of his own, but the jaguar that killed his brother would haunt his memory even after he abandoned the forest and entered the confusing world of the white man.

One moonless night in July 1989 as we listened to this story for at least the fifth time, it took on new dimensions.[2] We had finished some of the analyses presented in this book and knew that the story was not necessarily representative of a typical week in the forest. We had heard the story several times in the past twelve years of working with the Ache, a newly contacted group of hunter-gatherers in Paraguay, and we would hear it again in the summers of 1990 and 1994 after most of this book had been written. It had been told to us by Kuchingi, his wife Kuaregi, Betapagi, and Javagi, the brother of Pirajugi. It was a true story, but now as we listened to Membogi, we still marveled at the details—details that honestly capture a way of life because they are real and describe events that actually took place not too many years ago, but details that also mislead the naive listener and distort the common patterns that characterize life among the Ache. The average Ache man or woman does not get eaten by a jaguar, and most children are not buried alive. Nonetheless, these things do happen occasionally and have important influences on many other aspects of Ache life, from foraging tactics to marriage patterns to mythology. In particular, the rates at which adults and children die from unavoidable causes may be a key to understanding the timing of events in the life course. But to make this connection we must leave the domain of storytelling and enter the domain of scientific theory and data analyses.

WHY STUDY LIFE HISTORY AND DEMOGRAPHY?

Listening to the above story, undergraduate students in our classes have asked a series of insightful questions. How often do people really get killed by jaguars? Is infanticide common? Do many people survive to old age? Do women generally have babies when they are only seventeen years old? Do women marry men much older than themselves? How many men are killers—or are killed by others? Did the Ache always live in such small groups? Do women remarry so quickly when they are widowed or left by their husband?

The questions go on and on, but they all have one thing in common. Although they are inspired by stories and accounts such as the one presented here, *they cannot be answered by telling more anecdotes.* Only a large body of carefully collected facts and statistical analyses can provide the information that these curious students desire.

Questions concerning comparisons with our own life are also commonly asked by undergraduates. Do the Ache have a higher murder rate than we do? Do they get married younger? Do they divorce as often as Americans do? To answer these questions requires not only statistical data concerning the patterns in the United States but equivalent measurements for Ache society.

Students also ask questions of a less descriptive nature. Why do the Ache have so many children? Why don't the Ache have more children? Why do they begin reproducing so young? Why do they undergo menopause at about the same age as American women? Why do men experience higher mortality than women, just like in the United States? These types of questions can never be answered through simple statistical comparison. They require a theory of life history traits that explains similarity and variation in human groups around the world.

Fertility and mortality rates in human societies are traits that are correctly perceived as biological in nature. Women become pregnant after their bodies reach adult size and begin a complex hormonal cycle that allows them to conceive. Babies are born after sperm and eggs unite to produce new life. Infants die at high rates mainly as a result of exposure and susceptibility to other biological organisms. Old people become increasingly frail as their physiological machinery begins to operate less effectively. Nevertheless, a variety of environmental and social factors clearly can and do affect the probability of dying or giving birth through time.

Perhaps of even greater interest to anthropologists is the possibility that these "biological" parameters also constrain the "cultural" patterns of the people they study. This connection formed the basis of the anthropological field of cultural ecology in the first half of the twentieth century. Cultural materialism (Harris 1979), another anthropological paradigm, has also assumed that biological constraints placed strong limits on cultural possibilities. Beginning in the late 1970s, however, anthropologists and biologists became increasingly aware that "biology" and "culture" interact in ways that make the two interdependent. The most extreme example of this trend to unify biology and culture is the emerging field of human evolutionary ecology, a perspective in which "biology" and "culture" are seen as inseparable.

Regardless of one's view about the culture-biology connection, all anthropologists must recognize that a society's demographic parameters have important implications. Even the most symbolically oriented of anthropologists, should have some interest in demographic information. For example, from the story presented at the beginning of this chapter it should come as no surprise that the Ache have many myths about jaguars and about floods. So do other South American natives, who are also subject to jaguar attack and sometimes stranded in tremendous floods. Tapirs, peccaries, giant armadillos, giant otters, capybaras, and deer are all large and impressive South American mammals, yet among the Ache, jaguars are more important mythologically than all the others combined. This is very probably due to the fact that jaguars can and do kill the Ache. Given the number of jaguar paintings on the walls of Mayan ruins, one might also speculate that jaguars killed a significant number of Mayan hunters long before Columbus visited the new world. Although the details and mechanisms of interaction between demography, behavior, and symbolic conceptualization of the world are far from simple, the point remains that demographic parameters almost certainly affect other aspects of people's lives.

In addition to the indirect effects of demographic patterns on the culture or behavior of a population, the mortality and fertility parameters themselves have direct unavoidable implications for members of a society. Here are a few examples:

1. High birth rates and low death rates are indicators of rapid growth. Such a situation may imply a relatively recent change in the conditions that affect fertility and mortality, because high growth rates result in impossible population densities over a long period of time. Thus observations of rapid population growth probably mean that something very different and new has recently taken place in the environment of a study population. Unless major population crashes are also typical of a study population, high fertility and low mortality cannot be found among traditional peoples living "as they always have, and where they always have, without outside influence.

2. High mortality rates among adults should lead to certain types of flexible social systems. These systems must allow for easy remarriage. Children must be

easily incorporated into families that include individuals other than both biological parents (since both are unlikely to survive simultaneously), and alliances may be expected to be found between unrelated adults since many individuals will have no surviving close relatives.

    3.   High fertility rates should generally be associated with low mobility in primitive societies, since it is difficult to carry more than one child. High fertility may also be associated with low levels of female subsistence labor, or subsistence tasks of only a certain character, since child care often competes for a mother's time with other resource-producing activities.

Hypothetical examples of the influence of demographic parameters on other aspects of human society are countless. Thus, ecologically oriented anthropologists have developed considerable interest in demographic studies of isolated peoples. Demographic patterns (called "life history characteristics" by biologists) are seen as constraints within which other behavioral outcomes develop. Fertility and mortality resulting from alternative behavioral patterns can also be considered the "causal" reason why some behaviors but not others are commonly adopted by a population of individuals. Thus, in scientific jargon, demographic patterns are important as the independent variables for researching a wide variety of topics.

Finally, researchers who are interested in the demographic parameters themselves are interested in the demography of primitive populations. Why and how fertility and mortality rates vary are fascinating topics of inquiry that have recently led to considerable specialization in the study of particular details of mortality and fertility patterns. In this book we present less detail and smaller sample sizes than a demographer or an epidemiologist might prefer, but our treatment of demographic parameters within the context of modern evolutionary biology and life history theory provides some important insights that should be refreshing to those who have sensed that higher level theory is needed to make sense of commonly observed patterns.

Demographers and epidemiologists, for example, have discovered considerable variation in absolute levels of mortality and fertility among most of the world's noncontracepting populations. These data are primarily derived from studies of industrialized or developing nation states with many common experiences. Although the absolute levels of mortality and fertility often reflect poverty, malnutrition, etc., the *shape* of the curves that describe mortality and fertility rates as a function of age are generally quite similar in noncontracepting populations. Thus, two simple questions have frequently been asked: (1) Is there evidence that curves representing age-specific mortality and fertility rates in traditional populations are characterized by fundamentally different *shapes* from those that characterize most of the modern populations of the world? (2) Is there evidence that the *absolute levels* of mortality or fertility fall outside the range of those measured in modern populations of the world? If no new and unique patterns are found amongst isolated traditional peoples, perhaps we can draw some general conclusions about the life history parameters of our species. If significant variation is discovered, however, we can use that variation to develop and test specific models about the determinants of human life history variation.

The field of anthropological demography is concerned with issues such as why one society's fertility or mortality pattern differs from that observed in another society. In recent years, one of the most active debates has been over variations in absolute levels of female fertility through time and across space— why some groups that do not use contraception show much lower female fertility levels than those that are possible for humans and observed in other noncontracepting groups (e.g., Howell 1979; Campbell and Wood 1991). Another debate concerns the nature of the survivorship curve among humans. Howell (1979) has suggested that a relatively uniform pattern of age specific mortality characterizes human populations. Pennington and Harpending (1993) have argued against this viewpoint using new data and techniques. Other issues, though not as popular, can easily be imagined. For example, do any primitive societies show very low levels of mortality, similar to those that characterize many modern state societies? If not, why not? Why are population sex-ratios in primitive societies often strongly skewed? Are there large differences in the rates of mortality due to homicide and violence among societies whose members are not controlled by state intervention and a formal legal system? Are the ages at onset and termination of reproduction fairly constant across human societies? And probably most important of all, is there any theory that allows us to explain the timing and rate of these events in the lives of individuals? Can information about other mammals tell us something about our own species, or should we focus only on human experience as has been the tradition in the fields of population studies and demography.

These questions lead directly to an important body of biological study called *life history theory.* Life history concerns the timing of development, reproductive events, and mortality through the life course, and the optimal solutions to such problems as length of gestation, how large offspring should be at birth, how long to lactate, when to start reproduction, how many young to produce at a time, how long to wait between births, and when to stop reproducing. In short, life history theory provides the theoretical framework within which to develop and test models in animals and plants about the same parameters that are studied by demographers and epidemiologists in humans. To date, few demographers and epidemiologists have discovered the body of theory that not only predicts the types of patterns they commonly find but actually provides explanations for such patterns. More surprising still is the fact that primate life histories have probably been examined more thoroughly than those of any other mammal (e.g., Harvey and Clutton-Brock 1985), yet studies of the demography/life history our own species have proceeded essentially in complete ignorance of this body of biological inquiry. We believe that the long historical separation between the social sciences, which specialize in human studies, and the biological sciences departments, which focus on the life history of all other living organisms, has been detrimental to both fields.

The study of demography in foraging populations is particularly relevant to understanding the evolved life history characteristics of our own species. Only in the past 10,000 years have humans begun to live in larger, more complex, socioeconomically stratified societies. The fossil record shows that all significant morphological evolution of our species took place in a band-level foraging context. It is likely that most of our physiological machinery evolved under similar circumstances. Neural mechanisms responsible for behavioral tendencies and trends are also likely to have evolved primarily in a context of foraging lifestyles. This means that the adaptive functional significance of human life history traits is more likely to be illuminated in studies of modern foragers than from populations living in modern environments, which often include new and novel constraints to our species.

In this book we provide answers to some of the questions of interest to students who as yet know little about anthropology, life history theory, or the lives of traditional peoples. However, the majority of the book is dedicated to issues that arise from detailed anthropological comparison of traditional societies and the demographic variation that takes place within them. The studies presented here are motivated by an interest in the utility of evolutionary theory for understanding human behavioral patterns, and a curiosity about human evolution. These topics helped to focus fourteen years of data collection and analyses, and the long process of writing and revising this monograph.

We initially began to collect demographic data on the Ache because we wanted to know something about hunter-gatherers. Howell (1979:3) had pointed out that despite her comprehensive study of the !Kung, many more similar studies would be necessary in order to "describe the population processes of the universe of contemporary hunter-gatherers." Later, we became more interested in causal models to explain observed fertility and mortality patterns in any human population, and the implications of such patterns for generating other behavioral trends. Recently we have become interested in understanding to what extent human life history characteristics are typical or atypical of mammals in general, and how our species may have diverged from our pongid relatives to become characterized by a very unique mammalian life history. This topic is treated only superficially in this book but underlies much of the organization of data presentation and focuses some of the analyses.

Thus the issues that organized our research with the Ache and subsequent data analyses can be broken into three major categories, with overlap among them:

1.   How do the demographic parameters that characterize the Ache compare with those of other hunting and gathering populations, and other unacculturated technologically primitive peoples? How do they compare with those of other

isolated native South American populations? What can account for the observed differences, and how do mortality and fertility rates of these small groups compare with those commonly reported in modern peasant and industrial populations?

2.   What are the biological implications of Ache patterns of mortality and fertility? How and why could such "life history parameters" evolve, and what are some of the implications of these patterns for other cultural and behavioral observations? Can we show that particular life history patterns are currently being maintained by natural selection and are thus adaptive? Are models derived from life history theory useful for explaining the differences in fertility and mortality parameters that characterize different groups of individuals, and can the sensitivity to fertility and mortality outcomes, favorable or unfavorable, be used to predict some human behavioral patterns under different circumstances?

3.   What are the implications of the Ache demographic parameters for understanding hominid evolution? Do our data support speculations from paleo-demographic studies, and can general patterns be modeled in a way that will allow us to project these findings into the past? Do the fertility and mortality patterns of other foragers in combination with the new Ache data allow us to put reasonable limits on earlier hominid demographic patterns?

Despite these lofty organizational guides to data collection and analyses, and our own anxiousness to get directly at the heart of burning theoretical issues in anthropology and biology, much of the present study will be dedicated to more mundane issues of a descriptive nature. This is absolutely crucial since little is known about fertility and mortality in human foraging populations, and methods that have been developed during the course of our study must be specified in detail before tests of theoretical issues can be evaluated. We have in particular emphasized the presentation of tabulated data from this study to enable useful future comparisons and to permit the type of collaborative scrutiny that will advance the field of inquiry. We are extremely sensitive to the unique nature of our data base and the difficulty of collecting similar data in a rapidly modernizing world where the hunter-gatherer lifestyle may become extinct during our own lifetime. Thus, above all we aim to present detailed accurate descriptive data on the life history experiences of one of the last well-studied groups of human foragers.

THE ORGANIZATION OF THIS BOOK

This book is organized into three parts. Chapters 2–4 present background information on the Ache and detailed descriptions of the study population, sampling scheme, data collection methods, and analytical methods employed. Chapters 5–9 present descriptive analyses on mortality and fertility patterns during the pre-contact period, the period of contact upheaval, and the past fifteen years when the Ache were living for a good part of the time on reservation settlements. Finally, Chapters 10–13 present tests of models drawn from life history theory and human evolutionary ecology. These chapters may be difficult for some readers not familiar with evolutionary biology, logistic regression, or mathematical modeling. We have tried to explain all concepts that are not common knowledge to first-year graduate students in behavioral biology, but have aimed these chapters to graduate students in anthropology who are familiar with evolutionary biology and human behavior. Readers without this background may wish to consult some of the references cited in the next section. In the remainder of this chapter we provide a theoretical overview of evolutionary ecology as applied to humans, and life history theory. We conclude this chapter with an assessment of the relationship between life history theory and human demography. This final section summarizes the main goal of this book, which is to encourage all readers with a strong interest in either of these two fields to appreciate the contributions that each field can make to the other.

HUMAN EVOLUTIONARY ECOLOGY

In this book we draw explicitly from evolutionary biology and from a knowledge of mammalian mortality and fertility patterns, and the factors that affect them, in order to make "biological sense" out of the observed Ache demographic patterns. As evolutionary biologists, we are specifically concerned with the functional significance of the traits being observed. In other words we take the parameters that we have measured as design features of the organism (Williams 1966) and want to know, for example, "why a population of individuals shows the fertility and mortality profile that they do (rather than feasible alternative patterns), and what are the implications of such patterns for other behaviors that characterize that population." We assume that demographic patterns are produced by the sum of individual behaviors, and that behaviors, just like morphological and physiological traits, are phenotypes of the organism. We recognize that organisms are generally expected to show behavioral phenotypes that maximize their genetic contribution to the gene pool (fitness).

The expectation of fitness maximization for phenotypic traits is a logical deduction of natural selection acting under simple circumstances with plenty of time and variation. As Darwin pointed out, any biological trait that (1) showed heritable variation and (2) was associated with differential reproduction would always evolve through natural selection. We recognize that other forces of biological change (e.g., drift) may at times be more important than natural selection, and many useful hypothetical adaptations may never arise owing to lack of appropriate genetic variation. In addition, some traits are expected to be the inevitable side effects of other desirable traits due to genetic or phenotypic pleiotropy, but in general, most organisms should come to be characterized by phenotypes that result in higher fitness than would be characteristic of other feasible alternative phenotypes. We also recognize, however, that natural selection may often produce phenotypic "rules of thumb" that approximate perfect adaptive phenotypes under most conditions and require much less costly biological machinery than would be needed to achieve a perfect adaptive fit to the environment. In any case, the expectation that phenotypes should be approximately optimal (i.e., fitness maximizing) is a useful starting point for learning about biological design function (Parker and Maynard Smith 1990).

The assumption that behavior can be treated just like morphology, physiology, or any other organism phenotype is based on the realization that all behaviors are produced by organic components of the body. The central nervous system, the peripheral nervous system, hormones, blood chemistry, muscles, etc., all act in sequence and in concert to produce behavioral patterns. All these organic components are in turn produced by proteins for which instructions are encoded on the DNA sequence of an organism. Changes in DNA sequences can therefore directly affect behavioral patterns, and thus all behaviors and behavioral tendencies have a heritable component (although a particular behavioral variation may not be heritable). More important, basic goals and desires which motivate behavioral decisions are themselves a product of the central nervous system and therefore must be affected by natural selection.

Because fertility and mortality rates are biological characteristics, we can expect that in general the observed patterns will be adaptive unless relevant environmental constraints have recently changed. Specifically, humans should have evolved fertility and mortality patterns that lead to highest contribution to the future gene pool, *given the constraints provided by general human morphological, physiological, and social characteristics, and the environments in which our species lives.* Future contribution to the gene pool can come from direct reproduction or from helping kin who are likely to share genes that will be passed on (Hamilton 1964). The fitness derived from individual and kin components of reproduction constitutes what is referred to as "inclusive fitness."

From an evolutionary perspective, we might also expect that differences in mortality and fertility rates between individuals and groups will often represent adaptive *responses* of individuals who find themselves experiencing particular circumstances. In such cases the phenotypes themselves are not genetically encoded, but the ability to respond correctly under each different circumstance must be heritable and evolve by natural selection. This adaptive response pattern is generally referred to as a *reaction norm*. Reaction norms that produce phenotypic variation with ecological variation are expected to be adaptive because they are based in the organic machinery of the body and are therefore heritable. Reaction norms can characterize morphological, physiological, or behavioral traits. Indeed, because it is defined as rapid phenotypic change in response to the environment, behavior is virtually always characterized by a reaction norm. We assume that most of the life history traits described in this study are the result of evolved reaction norms (both physiological and behavioral) interacting with the peculiarities of the Ache ecological situation. It is important to note clearly that under this framework demographic phenotypes themselves are not expected to be heritable, but the range of phenotypes that characterize a range of social or physical environments (the reaction norm) is expected to be heritable. A clear understanding of phenotypic plasticity, as produced by reaction norms, has important ramifications for all studies of human social behavior, since much of what we call culture may simply be the result of evolved reaction norms in varying contexts. Cultural variation under these conditions will *not* be genetically determined but will be adaptive, a fact which most early anthropological critiques of human evolutionary ecology failed to appreciate (e.g., Harris 1979; Kitcher 1985; Sahlins 1976). The validity of this view of human social behavior can only be determined empirically, and early studies suggest this approach is a fruitful way to study human behavior (e.g., Borgerhoff Mulder 1991; Smith and Winterhalder 1992).

The perspective outlined above can be labeled "adaptationist." An adaptationist expects to find that biological characteristics usually maximize the inclusive fitness of the individuals exhibiting them, relative to any other realistic alternatives that might arise and be "tried" through evolutionary time. Inclusive fitness can only be maximized in a particular context, however, and the organism often has little control over the context itself. Thus organisms are expected to make the best of the world they inherit and adopt behaviors that result in the highest fitness given the social and environmental constraints that act upon them. When many different environments (social or physical) characterize the range of a species, each may lead to a different suite of traits that will maximize inclusive fitness only in its own particular context. We expect that this general principle underlies much human behavioral variation.

Nevertheless, in this book the adaptationist perspective is not meant to describe the real relationship between behavior and inclusive fitness; instead it is employed to make sense out of the observed phenotypic variation. This means, for example, that even though we assume that human fertility patterns are "adaptive," we should not be surprised to find patterns that do not maximize individual inclusive fitness in particular situations. However, in attempting to assess how closely the observed pattern comes to that which *would* result in highest fitness, we will learn a great deal about how individual fertility is constrained by social and environmental ecology, and why some individuals are unable to achieve the optimal (fitness-maximizing) fertility pattern. Demographic outcomes tell us how well certain behaviors fit certain ecologies and give us a precise measure of that fit in the same currency in which natural selection operates. Evolutionary ecology then, is the study of how environmental and social factors affect the phenotypic patterns of individuals and populations, starting with the assumption that most phenotypic variation represents an adaptation to the constraints experienced by individuals.

If behaviors, like other phenotypes, are the result of genes and environmental input both during development and in the immediate time frame of observation, then differences between observed phenotypes for any two organisms or populations can be due exclusively to genetic differences, environmental differences, or both. This means that observed differences in phenotypes may or may not have a heritable component. Since evolution can only act on phenotypic differences that are heritable, this distinction is crucial. Behavioral variation between populations that is exclusively the product of differential environmental exposure cannot be directly attributed to natural selection. This realization has led many anthropologists to assume incorrectly that most human behavior is not affected by natural selection and cannot be adaptive. In fact, nothing could be further from the truth. Most phenotypes of living organisms are flexible and can be modified by the environment in ways that make them *more* adaptive, even though the phenotypes themselves are not heritable.

How can phenotypic variation between two groups of individuals be completely due to environment, not heredity, and yet represent a biologically "adaptive" response? The answer is best illustrated using well-studied cases in human physiology. Humans show a variety of flexible phenotypic responses that are clearly adaptive to the individuals exhibiting them, such as increased metabolic rate in cold environments; changes in body proportions due to temperature; increased red blood cell concentration, greater lung size, and smaller body size at high altitudes; and smaller body size and slower growth rates at low levels of food intake (Frisancho 1981). For many of these examples it is now known that observed differences between populations are primarily due to environmental exposure, not genetic differences. In other words, *the phenotypic variation itself is not heritable.* On the other hand, these flexible phenotypic responses are almost certainly biologically adaptive. This is true because the *ability to respond* to environmental variation has evolved and is heritable. Specifically, our bodies have evolved the ability to perceive the relevant environmental cues (oxygen concentration, temperature, etc.) and respond in ways that result in higher fitness in each environment. These evolved response patterns are what we referred to above as "reaction norms."

The situation for behavioral phenotypic response is directly analogous. Different behavioral patterns are not the result of genetic differences, yet the ability to respond behaviorally in the appropriate environment has probably evolved. Indeed, it is easy to imagine that variants having the ability to "perceive" the specific constraints of the environment and behave in a way that resulted in greater ultimate genetic contribution to the future gene pool would rapidly replace the descendants of a population of organisms that showed behavioral inflexibility (if the costs of perception were not too high). The "perception" of relevant constraints and fitness payoffs need not be conscious, although in some cases organisms may be aware of their own knowledge of relevant information. Humans, just like many other organisms, seem to process and store information about the world without necessarily being aware that the information has been processed or used in behavioral decisions. Indeed, there is good evidence that humans unconsciously store the very types of information that we present in this book (fertility and mortality rates and covariates) without realizing that they do so (see Hasher and Zacks 1984).

Fertility and mortality are aspects of human life that are fundamentally biological. Proximate causes of both can be understood at the cellular and molecular level as the result of particular biochemical reactions in the body. However, the ultimate causes of fertility and mortality *variation* are more complex. They include environmental input, social input, and physiological input from the bodies of the individuals in a population. These same parameters affect the fertility and mortality patterns of most other socially living organisms and have been widely studied by behavioral biologists. Environmental challenges often lead to single (or a few) optimal solutions to a specific life history problem. Such problems are generally modeled using optimization or maximization techniques (Parker and Maynard Smith 1990). Decreasing temperature, for example, may favor the evolution of increasing periods of parental gestation, which are ultimately balanced by the costs imposed by carrying a larger and larger fetus. A single optimal gestation period may evolve.

Social challenges are somewhat more complex, since the social environment may react to the evolved tactics of individuals in ways that make them no longer adaptive. Anthropologists, and sometimes demographers, have been particularly interested in the way that social input, the common patterns of behavior in a society, can affect fertility and mortality. Often, however, social scientists have assumed that such input negates the fundamentally biological character of these parameters. In this book we recognize that social input is essentially biological in nature since it is composed of multiple behavioral adaptations of individual conspecifics. Nevertheless, social constraints are much more complex than environmental ones and generally require game theory modeling (Maynard Smith 1982) in order to develop predictive explanatory models. It is important to recognize that optimal (e.g., evolutionarily stable) behavioral patterns of social interaction may lead to low survival and reproductive rates for all members of a population. Such outcomes must still be considered adaptive if no alternative behavioral pattern would result in higher fitness for the individuals who employed it.

Following this logic, we expect human behavior to be generally adaptive across a wide variety of circumstances that do not vary too much from those experienced in our evolutionary history. More precisely put, the descendants of those who had nervous systems that did not respond correctly to ecological constraints (environmental or social) would be replaced by the descendants of those who had inherited nervous systems that did respond correctly. A simple demographic example can be provided. Suppose that a human population was characterized by female fertility physiology that was insensitive to whether or not conditions were favorable for reproduction. A new mutant that allowed women's bodies to perceive whether conditions were favorable, and conceive only during favorable periods, might be rapidly favored by natural selection, since much wasted reproductive effort would be avoided. This tendency to rear offspring in favorable periods could arise through physiological sensitivity to social or environmental stress, or it might arise through the conscious ability to decide when to avoid reproduction (through abstinence, contraception, abortion, infanticide, etc.). It could also be associated with cultural beliefs about the appropriate times for reproduction. The precise mechanism matters less than the functional outcome.

The realization that flexible adaptive phenotypic responses are likely to be very advantageous provides impetus to search for them in humans. This type of research, guided by an evolutionary perspective, is new to the social sciences. Connecting observations with theoretically derived expectations and with observed patterns in other living creatures will lead to an exciting new era of interest in demography. This perspective is also fundamentally different from the inductive and descriptive mathematical manipulations that have characterized much of human demography in the past, because it is vitally concerned with ultimate *explanations* of the observed patterns. Much of recent anthropological demography has emphasized the development of hazards models to describe life history parameters. While we appreciate the importance of hazards models *as a methodological tool* (and we use them abundantly throughout this book), we also recognize that they do not constitute theory, nor can they ever substitute for a theoretical understanding of why life history parameters vary the way that they do.

We strongly reject the notion that "The development of similar [hazards] models for all the proximate determinants [of fertility] is currently the principal theoretical goal of this whole line of research [i.e., anthropological demography]" (Wood 1990:230). Hazards models of fertility and mortality cannot represent any "theoretical" goal, since such models simply redescribe observed phenomena and establish the statistical significance of associations. Instead, we suggest that the ultimate theoretical goal of anthropological demography should be a complete *explanation* of why certain demographic patterns are expressed (see below). This includes an explanation of why some demographic parameters are related to a variety of other demographic, environmental, and social factors, and why the relationships take the form they do (i.e., the slope and shape of such relationships).

Many of the controversial issues that an evolutionary perspective raises are well outside the focus of this book. Nevertheless, it is important to stress that a consistent "adaptationist" perspective underlies all the analyses in this book. The descriptive parameters that we present were chosen because they characterize important aspects of the inclusive fitness of individuals in the population. The hypotheses that are tested are directly derived from evolutionary behavioral biology and are generally pointed at testing whether the observed patterns for subgroups of individuals make adaptive sense. Finally, all the parameters together will be considered as an adaptive complex that could vary. The timing and frequency of events such as births and deaths lead to the "life history" that characterizes the population. Since many life history parameters are often interconnected (e.g., rapid maturation and early reproduction is correlated with shorter life span across living organisms), we will examine whether the complex of traits that lead to the life history of the study population makes adaptive sense.

LIFE HISTORY THEORY

Life history traits consist of age-specific schedules of mortality and fecundity, and the traits that are directly the result of these schedules (life span, age at first reproduction, etc.) or are in some direct way connected to them (growth, body size, developmental trajectory, etc.). Developmental biologist J. T. Bonner (1965) noted that the ultimate description of an organism is not just a description of the adult phase, but that of its whole life cycle. Thus the life history of an organism can be thought of as a complete description of that organism. With such a grand view of life history, it is not surprising that life history theory is complex and still underdeveloped relative to some areas of evolutionary biology (like foraging theory or sex allocation theory, for example). Nevertheless a considerable amount is known about the way that life history traits correlate with each other and are constrained into possible sets of relationships that are repeatedly observed regardless of phylogenetic affiliation. The conditions that lead to the tremendous diversity of observed life histories have been investigated in increasing detail in the past 10–15 years (see Charnov 1993; Lessells 1991; Roff 1992; and Stearns 1992 for reviews). We use life history theory to organize the descriptive data presented in this book and dedicate several chapters near the end of the book to tests of hypotheses derived from this field. Here we present a short overview of the theory. Detailed consideration of particular models is presented in Chapters 11–13, where models derived from the theory are tested with Ache data.

The basic tenet of life history theory which logically flows from the laws of thermodynamics is the principle of allocation, which states simply that energy used for one purpose cannot be used for another. As organisms proceed through their life cycle they harvest energy from the environment and invest it in various life functions. Decisions about how to invest energy are made at the molecular, physiological, and behavioral levels, and in general we should expect natural selection to result in optimal allocation patterns given relevant constraints. These patterns result in the life history of an organism. Natural selection may be expected to result in genetically evolved life histories that lead to higher fitness than other feasible alternatives (subject to genetic and ontogenetic constraints). Selection may also result in reaction norms that facultatively adjust life history traits in ways that are adaptive to a wide variety of circumstances. Both types of life history predictions have been extensively examined in a variety of organisms from plants and invertebrates to mammals.

Energy harvested during the life cycle can be used for maintenance and repair of the soma, growth, storage, or reproduction. Since the energy used for one purpose cannot be used for another purpose, living organisms face a series of trade-offs. The two most fundamental trade-offs that are at the center of all life history theory are the trade-off between current and future reproduction, and the trade-off between number and fitness of offspring produced. Genetic trade-offs in life history traits are also widely reported, but careful inspection suggests that such trade-offs generally represent molecular examples of the principle of energy allocation (e.g., Kirkwood and Rose 1991). Thus, genes that have indirect effects on a variety of traits (pleiotropy) are expected to produce such effects through the principle of allocation and the energetic costs of prior phenotypic expression.

The trade-off between current and future reproduction has generally been referred to as the "cost of reproduction" (Williams 1966). Careful experimental manipulation and genetic studies have shown a reduction in survival or fertility following higher reproductive effort among many animals (see Lessells 1991 for a review). Such costs are nearly impossible to measure using natural variation in a population because of phenotypic correlations between life history traits, which are expected because individuals who are in better condition will often show both higher early reproductive rates and higher subsequent survival or fertility through time. This means that adequate measures of the cost of reproduction require sophisticated experimental or genetic manipulation (Bell and Koufopanou 1986). A good estimate of the reproductive cost function is critical for modeling optimal life history trajectories for any organism or set of conditions. This raises some serious problems for human biologists (see Chapter 12). The cost of reproduction should be difficult to assess in humans because of the inability to selectively breed for particular traits or carry out experimental manipulations of reproductive effort. Nevertheless, some natural experiments can provide useful information when subjects do not self-select into high and low reproductive effort groups. Sophisticated multivariate analyses may also allow us to use comparative samples and partial out the effects of phenotypic correlation in order to obtain estimates of the cost of reproduction.

One useful tool for investigating life history traits is the reproductive value equation developed by Fisher (1930). Reproductive value (V) at age x is defined as the expected contribution to the population gene pool (measured in units of currently existing offspring) from age x onward. The discrete-time version of this equation that is generally employed in studies with real data is

$$V_x = \sum_{y=x}^{\infty} \frac{l_y}{l_x} m_y e^{-r(y-x+1)} \tag{1.1}$$

where V_x is reproductive value at age x, m_x and l_x are fertility at age x and survivorship to age x, respectively, and r is the instantaneous growth rate of the population. Note that l_y/l_x is the probability of surviving to age y given survival to age x. If one disaggregates this equation into current reproduction and residual reproductive value (Williams 1966) the "cost of reproduction" trade-off is well captured by the two terms on the right side of the equality, which represent current and future reproduction:

$$V_x = m_x e^{-r} + \sum_{y=x+1}^{\infty} \frac{l_y}{l_x} m_y e^{-r(y-x+1)} \tag{1.2}$$

It is readily apparent that effort expended on current reproduction m_x must be accompanied by a concomitant decrease in future survival (l_y/l_x) or future fertility (m_y); otherwise selection would favor infinitely high fertility at each age. Instead, the optimal value of m_x depends on the exact quantitative relationship between current fertility and the components of residual reproductive value. The optimal solution also depends partially on the population growth rate, a point we will return to below.

The second trade-off implied by the principle of allocation is that between number and fitness of offspring produced. Simply put, with the same reproductive effort, a parent can produce many cheap offspring who may have a low chance of surviving and successfully finding a mate, or fewer high-quality offspring who experience higher survivorship and may have higher fertility once they reach adulthood. We can think of m_x in equation 1.2 as the optimal solution to this trade-off. A simple solution to the offspring quality–offspring quantity trade-off can be illustrated as a function of E, total energy that can be invested in offspring, and N, the number of offspring born. $S_{E/N}$, is the survivorship to adulthood given E/N energy investment per offspring, and $V_{\alpha,E/N}$, the reproductive value at adulthood of offspring who receive E/N investment. Parents maximize their fitness, w, by producing the number of offspring that will maximize the number of offspring who survive to adulthood times the reproductive value of those offspring at adulthood. Thus if

$$w = [NS_{E/N}V_{\alpha,E/N}] \tag{1.3}$$

individual fitness will be maximized when the product of these three terms is maximized, and parental investment decisions (physiological or behavioral) should reflect this trade-off. The optimal solution to this trade-off can be determined empirically if S and V_α are measured as a function of N, or the optimal solution can be derived analytically using calculus if the S and V_α functions of N are known.

Experimental manipulation in animals has shown that this trade-off does in fact characterize some parental investment decisions (Clutton-Brock 1991; Lessells 1991). As with the previously discussed trade-off, however, natural variation in parental investment per offspring (offspring size, clutch size, interbirth interval) cannot be used to estimate the relationship between investment and offspring fitness. Parents who have more resources available are likely to produce both more offspring and higher-quality offspring simultaneously, and the problem of phenotypic correlation again arises. When parental quality has been carefully controlled, whether through manipulation of already existing brood size or controlled feeding, the trade-off between offspring number and fitness is easily demonstrated (e.g., Gustafsson and Sutherland 1988; Wilson 1989, cited in Lessells 1991).

Time Preferences

The first trade-off in life history theory, that between current and future reproduction, leads to an interesting set of biological problems that are in many ways analogous to discounting in the economics of interest rate theory (see Rogers 1994). Should an organism take a small gain now or wait for a larger gain in the future? Should an organism take a small cost now to avoid paying a larger cost later on? Intuitively we know that this depends on how much greater the benefit or cost would be at the later point in time, and on the probability that the benefit or cost will be realized.

In life history theory, trade-offs between current and future gain are central to all aspects of understanding phenotypic variation. The principle of allocation (above) implies that all current investment in reproduction will entail a future cost in survival or fertility. The true impact of future costs is determined by the extrinsic mortality curve, and the population's growth rate. When survival is low, future costs are unlikely to be paid by most individuals and thus should be discounted accordingly. When population growth is rapid, future reproduction will contribute a lower proportion to the gene pool, whereas currently produced offspring will themselves contribute to the growing gene pool. Thus, current reproduction is often worth more (in fitness units) than future reproduction.

The mathematics of time discounting are fairly simple and straightforward. If the probability of dying between times x and $x + 1$ is q_x, the probability of still being alive at any time x is $\prod_{x=0}^{x-1} (1 - q_x)$. Since $\prod_{x=0}^{x-1} (1 - q_x)$ is defined as l_x, the probability of being alive at age x, then l_y/l_x is the probability that an individual who has survived to age x will survive to age y (the product terms from age 0 to age x will cancel out of the numerator and the denominator, leaving only the product terms from ages x to y in the numerator). This probability that an individual will survive to experience future benefits therefore gives the value of any future benefit relative to a current one. Note that in the disaggregated reproductive value equation (eq. 1.2), the value of future reproduction at each time y is discounted by the probability of survival to that age. Thus, for example, when an organism faces the evolutionary trade-off between current and future reproduction in a nongrowing population, the decision should take into account the potential effect of the investment on m_x or $\Sigma(l_y/l_x)m_y$ and favor whichever term will lead to the greatest increase. Organisms that have a low chance of surviving into the future should invest more heavily in current fertility than organisms that have a high probability of survival to future breeding opportunities. Whether or not an individual should make a short-term sacrifice for long-term gain is an empirical issue. Thus, for example, if reproductive investment can result in 1 offspring at time x, or 3 offspring at time y, the decision should be made in favor of time y only if the individual has greater than a $1/3$ probability of surviving from time x to y.

A second form of time preference occurs in expanding or contracting populations. An individual who produces O offspring in a population of N individuals will make a proportional contribution of $1/2 O/N$ to the gene pool. If reproduction does not take place until a later point in time and the population is growing, the individual will contribute less to the gene pool since the total number of individuals in the population (the denominator) is greater. Population size at time zero is related to population size at time t by the equation $N_t = N_o e^{rt}$, where r is the instantaneous rate of increase. This means that the proportional contribution to the future gene pool relative to the current contribution will be

$$\frac{1/2 O \,/\, N}{1/2 O \,/\, N e^{rt}} \qquad \text{or} \qquad e^{-rt} \tag{1.4}$$

In order to compensate for this effect, future offspring are always discounted in value relative to currently produced offspring (see eq. 1.3) and selection will always favor earlier reproduction in growing populations (when all else is equal). Thus selection may strongly favor investment in immediate fitness benefits (e.g., early reproduction) either because mortality rates are high or because population growth rates are high.

The implications for human behavior outside the economic arena have not been fully appreciated by most social scientists (Hill 1993; Rogers 1994). The implications for the fields of medicine, public health, and public policy making are enormous, yet their exploration has barely begun (for an exception see Williams and Nesse 1991). People may be quite willing to engage in behaviors that provide small immediate benefits even if huge costs are likely to be incurred at a later point in the life span (e.g., smoking, drinking, high salt or high fat diets, criminal behavior). Similarly they may not be willing to incur small costs in the present in order to avoid much higher costs at a later point (exercise, educational investment, conservation of resources, saving, etc.). As biologists we can expect natural selection to design a central nervous system that makes such decisions. The public policy implications may be depressing but should be taken into account. Life history theory and the principle of time preference can often make sense of what seem like irrational decisions that involve linked costs and benefits spread over long periods of time.

Theory of Mortality Variation

Mortality rates may be higher in some individuals than others for four different sets of "ultimate" reasons: (1) because they face greater environmental hazards; (2) because they have lesser intrinsic ability to resist negative consequences of exposure to those hazards; (3) because they have fewer resources to reduce exposure and its consequences; or (4) because they choose to allocate fewer of their resources to survival and instead allocate resources to alternative life history goals (e.g., growth, storage, fertility). More proximate causes of mortality belong to one or more of these ultimate sets. Explanations of mortality should not only describe the relationship between each of these constraints and observable mortality, they should offer reasons *why* the individuals in question are not able or willing to avoid hazards, acquire more resources, or allocate them differently. Such a perspective implies that mortality rates are at least partially under the control of the individuals who experience them and that individuals may sometimes *choose* to experience higher mortality rates than the minimum possible. This perspective contrasts sharply with the common view in the social/health sciences, which is based on an unstated and unverified assumption that individuals will always choose to maximize their own (or their offspring's) survival through the entire life span, and that lower than maximum survival when observed is only due to lack of resources or information needed to alleviate health hazards.

The model described above predicts that environmental hazard levels should be associated with higher or lower mortality in a straightforward fashion. It also suggests that individuals who have the ability to acquire more resources to combat environmental exposure, illness, and disease should show higher survival. In particular, juveniles who are better nourished and grow faster should survive at higher rates. This expectation is met for a variety of insects, fish, and reptiles (see Lessells 1991) and is a common finding in comparative or experimental studies with mammals (Table 1.1). Not surprisingly, studies of human populations also show that higher food intake results in better survivorship during childhood (Chapter 10). Nevertheless, the relationship between resource *allocation patterns* (e.g., life history decisions) and survival has proven much more difficult to establish. This is because the trade-off costs of increased survival can only be detected between individuals when hazard exposure, inherent resistance, and available resources are held constant. For example, individuals characterized by higher fertility should experience lower offspring survival than those with lower fertility because the resources expended on producing one offspring cannot be expended on increasing the survival of another. The trade-off may be impossible to detect or measure accurately, however, in a population where some individuals have more resources than others. Such individuals may show both higher fertility and higher offspring survival, and thus a positive rather than a negative correlation between life history outcomes. Indeed, with positively sloped but diminishing gain functions between resources and fertility, offspring survival, and adult survival, an individual with more resources will generally maximize fitness by expending the additional resources to affect *all three* of these parameters! Thus individuals with more resources should have higher survival, higher fertility, and higher offspring survival than those with fewer resources.

Since life history theory predicts a series of negative correlations between different life history traits as the result of allocation trade-offs in energy expenditure, but differential resource access predicts positive correlations between life history traits, it is quite difficult to perform an adequate test of life history theory predictions. In humans, the most likely solution to this problem will involve sophisticated multivariate nonlinear regression models, in which the effects of allocation decisions can be measured after exposure, resistance, and resource availability have been statistically controlled. That is the strategy we employ in Chapters 10 and 12.

Theory of Fertility Variation

Fertility is expected to vary between individuals for reasons similar to those that produce mortality variation. Long-term fertility of some females may be lower than the population mean because (1) they experience significantly fewer copulations; (2) they have lesser intrinsic ability to turn resources into offspring; (3) they have fewer resources to convert into offspring; or (4) they choose to allocate fewer of their resources to reproduction and instead allocate resources to alternative life history goals (e.g., growth, storage, somatic maintenance, somatic repair, parental investment). As we suggested for mortality variation, the goal of researchers working on fertility issues should be to establish the factors that affect fertility and to explain why fertility is expected to be sensitive to those factors, as well as explaining the precise character (slope and shape) of the relationship. These issues are explored in Chapters 10–12.

Modern fertility studies also contain a good deal of political content that we believe can be redirected by using a life history perspective. Fertility is a hot social topic because of an increasing awareness that population growth is one of the most serious problems facing the world today, and that our species is doomed to an ever-decreasing standard of living in the long run if we do not discover ways to curb rampant population growth. For these reasons, many population studies researchers are motivated in their quest for discovering key fertility determinants in order to "help" populations regulate their growth rates. This applied perspective has sometimes been associated with a repression of ideas that are believed to interfere with the goal of population control. In particular, any interpretation of data that has suggested that people might consciously *opt* for high fertility or early reproduction when it could be avoided has met swift rejection by the population studies establishment. The dogmatic rejection of the notion that well-informed individuals might opt for high fertility is not consistent with life history theory, which instead emphasizes that fertility variation represents a flexible adaptive response to conditions in which zero population growth is not expected to be a goal of decision makers.

Suggestions that high or early fertility are not always due to ignorance or high infant mortality have also been quickly denounced. Such a perspective must be abandoned if we hope to explain, for example, why fertility is both early and high on Native American reservations, where infant mortality rates are currently very low (e.g., Howard 1991). Adherents of the traditional viewpoint have been forced to take the condescending position that women in such populations simply "don't know what is best for them." Life history theorists instead assume that these women are well informed and intelligent and simply choose high fertility because of the character of their socioecological environment. Finally, the possibility of a link between nutrition and fertility has often been frowned upon because it is believed that the establishment of such a connection would lead to reduced food aid to the developing world, where population growth is greatest (e.g., Bongaarts 1980). Although we can appreciate the concern of these researchers, there is good reason to expect a food-fertility link in humans. Many studies show a clear link between food and fertility in other mammals that share a similar reproductive physiology (Table 1.2). Theory suggests that all organisms should be efficient at turning food into genetic contribution, and many human studies do provide good evidence for a food-fertility link (Chapter 10). We do not believe that the denial of such a link because of political concerns is a productive way to solve world population problems.

Thus, many population studies researchers have adhered to an ideological position which presumes that people in the developing world have high fertility either because they are forced to (in order to overcome infant mortality rates, or lack of contraception) or because they are too ignorant to realize that it would be in their best interest to reduce their fertility (thus stressing the importance of family planning propaganda, etc.). Unfortunately, this view is not consistent with the way natural selection can be expected to design the central nervous system and human priorities. We recognize that modern fertility patterns are extremely complex and do not fit simple fitness maximization models (e.g., Kaplan 1994; Kaplan et al. 1995). Nevertheless, we believe that life history theory, because of its emphasis on the evolutionary forces that produced human goals, provides scientists with a unique opportunity to understand worldwide fertility variation rather than simply advocate particular patterns. Details of a life history approach to fertility are provided in Chapters 10–12.

Some Additional Life History Issues

Life Span.   Senescence is a progressive increase in age-specific mortality even when conditions for survival are ideal. Rates of senescence among mammals vary considerably. Humans show a doubling of the adult mortality rate every eight years, whereas adult mortality rates in mice double every 120 days (Austad 1993a). Appropriate time discounting shows that large costs may be incurred late in the life span if smaller fitness gains can be experienced early in the life span by incurring the later costs. This is one likely explanation of why organisms get old and deteriorate near the end of the normal adult life span (Charlesworth 1980; Williams 1957). The idea that some genes which produce positive phenotypes at one point in time could later be responsible for damaging traits is called "antagonistic pleiotropy." We might imagine, for example, that the same genes that produce beneficial strengthening of arterial walls early in life ultimately produce hardening of the arteries later in life. With a constant mortality rate, however, fewer and fewer individuals will live to a particular age, and deleterious effects that express themselves at ages when few individuals are likely to be alive are simply not under strong negative selection (Charlesworth 1980). If the same gene that produces a small gain in early fitness leads to a complete collapse of a major organ system late in life, it may still be favored by selection. Thus antagonistic pleiotropy may lead to physiological deterioration and senescence. The antagonistic pleiotropy theory of senescence is complemented by a second, called the "disposable soma" theory (Kirkwood and Rose 1991). The proponents of the disposable soma theory point out that a certain energy budget must be dedicated to somatic maintenance and repair in order for an organism to survive indefinitely. Without sufficient repair, molecular and physiological systems will deteriorate and ultimately become nonfunctional. Kirkwood and Rose (1991) have developed a mathematical model of the energy budget trade-off between maintenance and reproduction and conclude that under conditions very common to living organisms, natural selection will favor allocating less energy to maintenance than is necessary for indefinite survival. Thus most organisms might be expected to "reproduce themselves to death" through lower than necessary energy expenditure on somatic maintenance.

Theories of senescence suggest that rates of senescence will be directly related to the extrinsic adult mortality rate. Extrinsic mortality is death from causes that cannot be avoided by the normal range of behavioral or physiological counter-strategies open to an organism. This means that organisms exposed to high rates of mortality from certain types of predation, accidents, environmental fluctuations, or other unavoidable factors should show more rapid physiological senescence. This prediction is supported by one recent study on opossums living on islands (without predators) and on the mainland in the southeastern United States (Austad 1993b). Theories of senescence also imply an evolved trade-off between reproduction and life span, which cannot be eliminated when extrinsic hazards of mortality are artificially removed. This prediction is supported by studies showing that selection for longevity leads to decreased reproductive function (e.g., Luckinbill et al. 1987; Rose 1984). In addition, numerous studies show that selection for increased fertility results in reduced life span (e.g., Bell and Koufopanou 1986), and in some cases the act of mating itself is sufficient to decrease survival even when no offspring are produced (Fowler and Partridge 1989). It is particularly interesting to note that sterilized individuals from species as diverse as fruit flies (Maynard Smith 1958) to cats and humans (Bronson 1981; Hamilton 1965; Hamilton and Mestler 1969) show longer life spans than animals with intact reproductive function.

Age at Maturity. Models of optimal age at sexual maturity have been among the most successful life history models for predicting actual values of a trait in natural populations (e.g., Charnov 1989; Gross 1985; Kozlowski 1992; Roff 1986; Stearns and Crandall 1981; Taylor and Gabriel 1992). All these models have several assumptions in common. First, they assume that energy put into growth cannot be used in reproduction, and vice versa. Thus, growth is impeded or halted by a shift allocating resources to reproductive function. Second, they assume that growth (body size) positively affects reproductive value. Third, they all assume that each time-unit delay in reproduction is associated with a lower probability of survival. Thus, organisms face a trade-off between continued growth with a concomitant increase in reproductive value, and an ever-decreasing probability of surviving to reproduce. If an individual waits one more year before maturity, energy can be used in growth, which will result in larger body size and higher reproductive value at the age of maturity. However, each year delay decreases the probability that the individual will survive to reproductive age. These same assumptions are also required in order to explain why organisms grow at all.

It is easy to develop a simple model of optimal timing of first birth based on only these assumptions. If age at first reproduction is α, S_α is survival to that age, and V_α is the reproductive value at that age, then

$$V_0 = S_\alpha V_\alpha \qquad (1.5)$$

Let's assume that natural selection will maximize the expected lifetime reproductive output of individuals at birth, V_0. If the increase in V_α is proportional to weight at α, and it takes time to grow, an organism is faced with a trade-off between beginning reproduction at a lower V_α but a higher S_α or waiting some time period during which growth takes place but as a result S_α will be lower. The organism faces a trade-off between reproductive value and survivorship, and it should be selected to begin reproduction at an age that will maximize the product of juvenile survivorship and reproductive value at maturity. The optimal solution to this trade-off can be specified mathematically as the point where $(d \log V_\alpha)/d_\alpha$ equals $(-d \log S_\alpha)/d_\alpha$, or when the proportional increase in reproductive value with age is exactly matched by the proportional decrease in survival with age. By definition, $(-d \log S_\alpha)/d_\alpha$ is the instantaneous mortality rate at age α. If reproductive value is proportional to body size, as it seems to be for many organisms, and if we assume that excess energy is completely diverted from growth to reproduction at age α the optimal age at first reproduction is the point where the proportional growth rate (grams gained per gram body weight) is equal to the adult mortality rate!

Although all organisms have a maximum body size that is determined by the metabolic expenditure and energy harvest functions of body size, the theory predicts that many organisms should stop growth well before their theoretical asymptote and that the growth halt may be quite abrupt if the growth rate is steep near age α. This pattern is widely observed among living organisms and is referred to as *determinate growth*. Knowing the time of first reproduction (α) and the growth function with respect to time also allows one to predict observed adult body size. Thus the model not only explains age at maturity but also mean adult body size, if feeding niche and growth rates are taken as givens. This type of simple model has been tested on a variety of organisms with good success (Charnov 1989; Roff 1986, 1992; Stearns 1992). As predicted by the models, temporarily increased adult mortality rates have been shown to lead to earlier ages of sexual maturity in a variety of organisms from invertebrates to mammals (e.g., Boyce 1981; Minchella and Loverde 1981; see below). Most interestingly, several experimental studies show that animals can react to indirect cues of the adult mortality hazard to speed up their maturation rates (e.g., Skelly and Werner 1990). For some aquatic animals, the mere presence of chemical substances associated with predators or predatory action is enough to result in earlier age of sexual maturity (Crowl and Covich 1990). These findings have obvious implications for the interpretation of data suggesting that human females may reach sexual maturity at younger ages under a variety of stressful conditions (see Belsky et al. 1991).

Any parameter that affects reproductive value through time may be substituted for the growth function in order to predict optimal time of first reproduction. In humans, for example, much energy is stored extrasomatically, and such factors as education which influence income throughout the life span may affect V_α and may be more appropriate than body size for predicting optimal age at commencement of reproduction. Indeed, the use of contraception to delay first reproduction among high socioeconomic status (SES) American women who use educational opportunities to increase adult incomes can be modeled easily using this same framework (note that lower mortality rates of high SES American women would also favor delayed reproduction). Body size, however, may be a good indicator of proportional increases in reproductive value in many traditional societies, and a model based on that assumption does quite well for predicting age at first birth among the Ache (see Chapter 11).

Optimal Fertility Rate, Interbirth Interval. Lack (1947) was the first biologist to model the trade-off between number of offspring produced and the fitness of those offspring. The tendency for an intermediate brood size to lead to highest number of surviving offspring has often been called the "Lack effect" by evolutionary biologists. With a given energy budget for reproduction, parents are forced to partition resources in ways that affect the survivorship and future fertility of their offspring. Animals studies have provided strong confirmation that such a trade-off does exist when total parental effort is carefully controlled (Gustafsson and Sutherland 1988; Wilson 1989, cited in Lessells 1991). Subsequent theoretical exploration suggests that this trade-off is often complicated by parent-offspring conflict (Godfray and Parker 1991), which may lead to a brood size outcome far from the predicted parental optimum. Optimal brood size is also likely to be affected by the brood's cost in residual parental reproductive value (Charnov and Krebs 1974) and the effects of stochastic variation on clutch size and the fitness gain curve (Godfray and Ives 1988). Thus, there are many reasons for not expecting an exact fit between the predicted optimum brood size (or interbirth interval) and the observed optimal brood size in real populations when models are based on the trade-off between clutch size and offspring survival alone.

Surprisingly, however, one human study has provided support for the simple version of the Lack trade-off between offspring number and fitness. Blurton Jones (1986) measured success rates at raising children to adulthood for different birth intervals among the !Kung. He reported that the birth interval that led to the highest number of surviving offspring for !Kung parents was also the most common birth interval in the population. This study was the first to apply evolutionary logic and an optimality approach to the issue of human fertility, but the results must be evaluated cautiously for several reasons. First, it is unclear whether the optimum fertility rate should also be the most commonly observed fertility rate in real populations (Borgerhoff Mulder 1992a). Second, most recent modifications of Lack's model explicitly recognize that all parental residual reproductive value, as well as offspring fitness, is traded off against current fertility. Models that assume a trade-off only between offspring quantity and quality should overestimate the optimal fertility rate.

A primary concern regarding the !Kung study is the problem of phenotypic correlation (see Chapter 12). Significant resource variation and differences in maternal condition would probably lead to women with the shortest birth intervals showing higher than average offspring survival and the highest fitness in the population. Only those parents who make a strategic error (in evolutionary terms) should show lower offspring survival associated with shorter birth intervals. Indeed, mathematical studies of parental investment decisions suggest that survival and fertility will usually vary positively because of parental allocation decisions that take into account the marginal rate of substitution between these two fitness components (e.g., Kaplan et al. 1995). These reservations are supported by empirical studies with birds showing that often it is *not* possible to measure a Lack effect without experimentally manipulating brood size (Gustafsson and Sutherland 1988). Thus, we should carefully examine any human study that claims to show a negative relationship between fertility and survivorship in natural populations, or a relationship strong enough to suggest higher fitness for women with modal interbirth intervals. Many studies have failed to find such an effect (e.g., Palloni and Millman 1986; Pennington and Harpending 1993; Wolfers and Scrimshaw 1975).

Menopause.   The fact that human females cease to reproduce when they still have a high probability of surviving for many years represents a rare pattern among mammals and is probably absent in all other primates under natural conditions (Hill and Hurtado 1991; Paveleka and Fedigan 1991; see also Caro et al. 1995). The fact that fifty-year-old women have virtually no remaining reproductive function but can expect to live for many more years presents an interesting challenge to life history theory. Several evolutionary biologists have suggested that such a pattern could be favored by kin selection if older females were able to use energy more efficiently by increasing the reproductive success of their close relatives than they could by attempting to produce additional offspring of their own (Alexander 1974; Gaulin 1980; Hamilton 1966; Hawkes et al. 1989; Trivers 1972; Williams 1957). A recent test of this hypothesis (Hill and Hurtado 1991) failed to find evidence that menopause could be maintained through kin selection in one group of hunter-gatherers. A reconsideration, however, leads us to question whether the test was adequate (Hill and Hurtado 1995).

Perhaps a trade-off between early and late reproductive function can explain why human (and some other mammalian) females lose reproductive function long before the end of their life span. For example, Peter Ellison (personal communication) has proposed that the human female trait of producing all viable oocytes before birth and storing them in arrested metaphase throughout the life span (semelgametogenesis) may be a mechanism to reduce the accumulation of mutations that take place with cell division. This same mechanism leads to the depletion of viable oocytes, which are necessary for reproduction. Presumably the gains in fitness early in life outweigh the later costs of reproductive senescence. Among mammals, only baleen whales and elephants appear to reproduce at ages greater than fifty years, and both are large enough to contain ovaries with a higher number of viable oocytes at birth. Some species of whales, but not elephants, are also characterized by life spans similar to that of humans. Whether or not all mammalian females are characterized by semelgametogenesis is unknown, but since humans have an exceptionally long life span for their body size it would not be surprising if humans are one of the few species to run out of oocytes during adulthood. Nevertheless, reliable data also suggest that females of several toothed whale species undergo reproductive senescence at about age forty even though their mortality hazard is still low at that age, and females regularly live for 80+ years (Marsh and Kasuya 1986; Olesiuk et al. 1990). In addition, natural selection could only act to counter rapid senescence and death after menopause if postmenopausal females continue to increase the fitness of their genetic relatives. Thus, a coherent evolutionary model of menopause still remains a serious challenge for life history theory.

A General Model of Life History

A consensus developing among some life history theorists suggests that ex-trinsic adult mortality rates in combination with the juvenile growth rate may be the most important initial variables in limiting the feasible set of life history parameters that would maximize the fitness of an organism (see Harvey and Nee 1991). The extrinsic adult mortality rates are due to unavoidable predation, environmental hazards, and other factors not related to the reproductive effort of the organism. A good example would be the jaguar attack described at the beginning of this chapter. In organisms whose reproductive value is a function of body size, the adult mortality rate and the allometric growth constant will allow prediction of optimal age and size at maturity. In combination with energy harvest and expenditure rates as a function of body size, this information will lead to predictions of optimal reproductive effort. The function that relates off-spring fitness to parental investment should predict both optimal size at birth and the fertility rate that will maximize fitness when reproductive effort is specified. Finally, in stable populations birth and death rates must balance, so juvenile mortality rates are determined by the difference between fertility and the adult mortality function. Thus, the adult mortality hazard in combination with growth rates and a series of functions relating investment patterns to fitness can in theory be used to predict most life history parameters for any organism. This can be shown schematically as a relatively simple causal chain (Figure 1.1).

If we drastically simplify life history for organisms whose reproductive value at maturity is proportional to body size at maturity, we need only investigate the growth rate and the optimal parental investment patterns to estimate age-specific fertility and mortality schedules from the adult mortality function. We should not conclude that all major life history issues have been resolved. First, the above scheme does not easily address the trade-off between current and future repro-duction, which has been central to life history theory. Indeed, energy allocated to reproductive effort in the above model is assumed to be determined by the difference between energy harvest rates and metabolic "requirements" at the optimal adult body size. The model thus assumes that estimates of metabolic costs are straightforward and those costs are a biological "given" of the organism. In reality, however, metabolic costs are expected to reflect the optimal partitioning of energy into activity, growth, current reproduction, storage, somatic repair, and maintenance. Thus metabolic requirement is a complicated topic whose outcome itself should be partially determined by the extrinsic adult mortality rate (Kirkwood and Rose 1991).

Despite the complexity of human demographic patterns, there is reason for optimism. Models derived from life history theory have proven very successful at explaining demographic patterns in organisms as diverse as bacteria, plants, and large mammals (Roff 1992; Stearns 1992). Applying life history to the demographic patterns of our species should enable us to *explain* such patterns rather than simply describe them with mathematical models.

DEMOGRAPHY AND LIFE HISTORY

After this discussion of the application of life history theory to issues of human demography and development it is important to clarify once again the distinction between description and explanation and between inductively discovered patterns of covariation and theory. We recognize that demographers, human biologists, and social scientists have made important contributions through the accurate description of fertility, mortality, growth, and developmental patterns, but an explanation of *why* the patterns take the character they do is absent from these fields. In particular, mathematical modeling by demographers has provided a wealth of data on the shape of the human mortality and fertility functions as well as a good deal of information on relationships between these functions and other socioecological variables. Most of these models simply redescribe observable patterns, however, and thus do not constitute an explanation for them (see Pennington and Harpending 1993 for a similar viewpoint). An explanatory model must include not only a good description of a pattern or relationship, but an explanation of *why* those patterns exist and why they take the particular form that they do (and not some other feasible form). This type of explanatory modeling is missing from most demographic and developmental studies of human life history and is in fact the major contribution that can be provided by evolutionary biology.

We define theory as *a set of principles regarding causal connections between variables that explains what should be observed and why, and that unites previously unconnected observations in a common framework while making new predictions about previously unstudied relationships in a fashion that can withstand the scrutiny of empirical observation.* It is our assessment that no "theory" as such exists in the fields that have traditionally been dedicated to describing human life history traits. Researchers from the "proximate determinants" school of fertility or mortality variation have established some facts about the relationship between environmental and behavioral patterns and outcomes, but they do not have any clear theory that addresses why the relationship between these patterns exists and why they take the form they do. For example, why should there be a relationship between nursing patterns and fertility, and why should that relationship take the mathematical form that it does (and not some other form)? What other variables (genetic, physiological, environmental, etc.) should also affect fertility, and in what precise form?

Given the topics covered by life history theory one might logically expect human demographic studies to be a subset of life history studies in general, with active interchange between demographers and biologists. This has not been the case, since most human demographers are either unaware of life history theory altogether or reject biological models as inapplicable to *Homo sapiens*. Equally perplexing is the fact that biologists seem oblivious to the enormous quantities of data on human life history parameters. The lack of communication is unfortunate since biologists and human demographers have much to learn from each other. Because of phylogenetic association, humans show features of reproductive physiology and aging that are common to other mammals. Treating them as a separate and unique case is not biologically justifiable. Demographers could rapidly increase their understanding of these patterns if they familiarized themselves with the nonhuman literature.

For example, in a graduate class on demography taught at a prominent American university in 1989 we heard a professor comment that observed demographic patterns of higher mortality among adult males relative to adult females and later age at first reproduction among males were *cultural characteristics of modern western societies* that could not be easily explained. Such a statement demonstrates very little background in anthropology or basic mammalian biology. These traits are found not only in virtually all nonwestern human societies, but also among most other mammals as well. The expectation of such traits can be derived from sexual selection theory, which dates back to Darwin (1859), and empirical tests of the basis for these predictions have shown the theory to be extremely robust and powerful, leading to a good understanding of these as well as a variety of other sexually dimorphic life history traits.

The fact that well-educated biologists ignore data on humans is also curious. More data on age-specific mortality and fertility schedules and associated parameters are available for humans than for all other mammals combined, and sample sizes in human studies often exceed those in mammalian studies by three or four orders of magnitude. Life history theorists struggle with mammalian data sets on dozens to a few hundred individuals when they could access human data with sample sizes in the hundreds of thousands to millions. Demographers have collected data on almost all of the relevant parameters for testing important aspects of life history theory, yet biologists continue to employ inadequate data sets from a handful of mammalian species.

The best way to illustrate how both human demographers and life history theorists could contribute to each other's work is with an example from the work of two excellent anthropological demographers. Wood and Smouse (1982) developed a sophisticated mathematical model for detecting and describing density-dependent effects on human vital rates. They used the model to demonstrate that among the Gainj of Papua New Guinea during the 1970s, increased population density led to an increase in the mortality rates of small children and postreproductive individuals, but not to an increase in adult mortality rates or a significant change in fertility rates. Wood and Smouse were interested in *how* population density is "regulated" among primitive human groups, and they satisfactorily demonstrated that among the Gainj, population density is probably regulated more through varying childhood mortality than any other single factor. Wood and Smouse conclude their study by stating that their finding is only applicable to the Gainj case, however: "We do not wish to prejudice future results at this stage by arguing that either fertility or mortality is inherently more likely to be implicated in population regulation."

The main reason that Wood and Smouse were reluctant to generalize about how density might effect demographic parameters in other human populations is because they had no theoretical basis from which to derive such expectations. Biologists have also spent a good deal of time studying density-dependent effects on vital rates. Among mammals, increasing density and associated resource competition and nutritional stress generally lead to a predictable sequence of responses to the resulting resource deficiencies: (1) increased juvenile mortality; (2) increased age of sexual maturity; (3) decreased natality; and (4) increased adult mortality (see Eberhart 1977; Fowler 1981, 1987). Theoretical models have been developed to explain why this hierarchy of responses should be found among iteroparous mammals, and under what conditions a different set of density-dependent responses would be expected (see Charnov 1986, 1991). Thus biologists, unlike demographers, are in a position to speculate about future results based both on a solid empirical pattern and ultimately on theoretically derived models that explain *why* the observed pattern should be found. Theoretical biologists focus on the ultimate explanation of an observed trait and have incorporated the theory of evolution by natural selection into their understanding of demographic variation. Yet none of the biologists has incorporated the human data into their discussion, nor have they considered how postreproductive individuals might be affected by density-dependent resource shortages (as did Wood and Smouse). Thus both the human demographers and the biologists have something to gain from increased interaction.

The need for theory in demography and human demographic data in life history studies is an underlying theme throughout this book. An emphasis on this point is explicitly the goal of Chapters 10–13, where we test some life history predictions with varying degrees of success that will hopefully stimulate a new generation of research.

SUMMARY

This book systematically investigates the fertility and mortality patterns of Ache hunter-gatherers in Paraguay. Stories about Ache life are instructive but can be misleading without a statistical analyses of life events. Cross-cultural comparisons as well as predictive models require specific quantitative data analyses in order to answer interesting questions about how the Ache differ from other groups of people and why differences or similarities might occur. Anthropological demography can be a fascinating field of inquiry if the implications of demographic parameters for other cultural patterns are carefully considered. Since fertility and mortality are essentially biological traits, a background in evolutionary biology is necessary in order to make sense out of observed similarities and differences in demographic parameters. Life history theory in biology has been developed to explain the timing of development, fertility, and mortality schedules for living organisms. Human demography and the biological study of life history are essentially the same enterprise—in which only the organisms of study differ—yet very little interaction has taken place between these two fields. Increased collaboration and communication between groups is desirable and perhaps inevitable as social scientists shift their focus from describing to explaining human fertility and mortality variation, and biologists begin to incorporate human data into their generalizations of life processes on this planet.

NOTES

1.   Translation of Ache tape-recorded statements or documents originally written in Spanish appear throughout this book. Ache statements come from our own work as well as that of Ruth Sammons, an evangelical missionary with New Tribes Missions who published a translation of several Ache texts in 1978. All Ache quotes are derived from our own tapes unless otherwise stated. Our own interjections, used to provide context but not part of the original text, are shown in brackets.

2.   We have heard many different versions of this story and taped it at least three times. Not surprisingly, the details vary from version to version. The version given here is a composite of that from Membogi and others.

Table 1.1. Food Intake and Juvenile Mortality in Selected Mammals

Species, sample size	Reference	Type of study	Finding
Yellow baboon (*Papio cynocephalus*) *n* = 17 infants	Altmann 1991	wild	greater energy and protein shortfall in diet led to higher infant mortality
Japanese macaque (*Macaca fuscata*) *n* = 320 infants	Watanabe and Mori 1992	observation on provisioned group	infant mortality increased when provisioning was withdrawn
House cat (*felis cattus*) *n* = 2414 infants	Olovson 1986	captive experiment	increased fat in diet lowered infant mortality
Pig *n* = 848 mothers	Cromwell et al. 1982	captive experiment	feed-supplemented sows had lower infant mortality than controls
Pig *n* = 85 litters	Cieslak et al. 1983	captive experiment	sows fed perinatal fat supplement had higher infant survival than controls
Pig *n* = 96 litters	Seerley	captive experiment	increased fat in diet lowered infan. mortality
Mouse *N* = 42 litters	Smart and silence 1977	captive experiment	mice fed 40% of ad libitum diet had higher infant mortality than controls

Table 1.2. Food Intake and Fertility in Selected Mammals

Species *sample size*	*Reference*	*Type of* *study*	*Outcome* *variable*	*Finding*
Savanna baboon (*Papio anubis*) *n* = 19 females	Bercovitch and Strum 1993	wild	age at repro- ductive matu- rity	age at first sexual swel- ling delayed with low food availability
Rhesus macaque (*Macaca mulatta*) *n* = 15 females	Schwartz et al. 1988	captive ex- periment	age at repro- ductive matu- rity	lower percent of calories from fat delays menarche
Cow *n* = 477 females	Milagres et al. 1979	experiment on domestic animals	age at repro- ductive matu- rity	lower body weight at age 1 predicts late first calv- ing
House mouse (*Mus musculus* *domesticus*) *n* = 10 females	Hamilton and Bronson 1985	captive ex- periment	age at repro- ductive matu- rity	food-restricted mice had slower development of reproductive system than controls fed ad libitum
Sheep *n* = 18 females	Prasad et al. 1993	experiment on domestic animals	age at repro- ductive matu- rity	sheep fed 80% fewer cal- ories and protein had lat- er onset of puberty than controls
Japanese macaque (*Macaca fuscata*) *n* = 895 fem. yr.	Watanabe and Mori 1992	observation on pro- visioned group	age at first birth, IBI, mean birth rate	mean birth rate decreased when provisioning was withdrawn; IBI and age at first birth increased
Japanese macaque (*Macaca fuscata*) *n* = 282 fem. yr.	Sugiyama and Ohsawa 1982	observation on pro- visioned group	mean birth rate and ASFR	birth rate and ASFR de- creased when provision- ing was withdrawn
Yellow baboon (*Papio cyno-* *cephalus*) *n* = 6 females	Altmann 1991	wild	number of offspring and length of re- productive lifespan	individuals with greater energy and protein short- fall in diet had fewer off- spring and shorter reproductive span
Lab mouse *n* = 70 females	Smart and Silence 1977	experiment on domestic animals	probability of conception	mice fed 40% of ad libi- tum diet were less likely to produce a litter
House cat *n* = 70 females	Olovson 1986	observation on domestic animals	annual birth rate	lower fat content in diet reduced annual number of litters per cat
Cow *n* = 337 females	Lemenager et al. 1980	experiment on domestic animals	probability of conception	low-energy winter diet led to reduced probability of conception

(continued)

Table 1.2.   (continued)

Species sample size	*Reference*	*Type of study*	*Outcome variable*	*Finding*
Red deer $n = 3157$ females	Albon et al. 1983	wild	probability of conception	lower body weight deer less likely to have embryo and corpus lutea after mating season
White-tailed deer $n = 49$ females	Verme 1965	experiment on captive animals	litter size	low feed-level deer had smaller litters than high feed-level group
Pig $n = 40$ females	Lodge and Hardy 1968	experiment on domestic animals	litter size	doubling feed allowance increased litter size
House cat $n = 70$ females	Olovson 1986	observation on domestic animals	litter size	lower fat content in diet reduced litter size
Lab mouse $n = 47$ females	Smart and Silence 1977	experiment on domestic animals	litter size	mice fed 40% of ad libitum diet had smaller litters
Pig $n = 75$ females	Seerley et al. 1981	experiment on domestic animals	litter size	high-fat diet increased litter size
Cow $n = 62$ females	Belows and Short 1978	experiment on domestic animals	IBI	IBI longer for cows on low feed level than for cows on high feed level
Opossum (*D. marsupialis, virginiana*) $n = 116$ females	Sundquist and Eisenberg 1993	wild-provisioned vs. non-prov.	inter-birth interval	IBI between first and second litters shorter for provisioned females than for controls
Rhesus macaque (*Macaca mulatta*) $n = 31$ females	Kohrs et al. 1976	experiment on captive animals	proportion of live births	females on low protein diet had lower proportion of live births to miscarriages and stillbirths than controls
Squirrel monkey (*Saimiri sciureus*) $n = 66$ females	Manocha and Long 1977	experiment on captive animals	proportion of live births	females on low protein diet had lower proportion of live births to miscarriages and stillbirths than controls

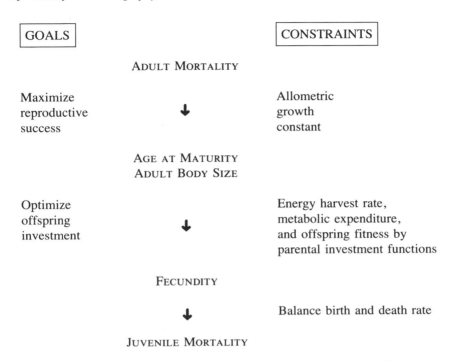

Figure 1.1. A causal chain of life history variables among female mammals (adapted from Harvey and Nee 1991, after Charnov 1991).

Ache hunter on a forest trek in 1982 listens for monkeys.

2

The Ache

The Ache are a small population of native inhabitants of eastern Paraguay who distinguish themselves from other indigenous Paraguayan groups on the basis of linguistic and behavioral patterns and material culture. They are referred to as "Guayaki" by other Guarani native populations and Paraguayan nationals, as well as in many early historical and anthropological accounts. Because the Ache find the term "Guayaki" offensive (it has derogatory connotations), and because all Ache groups refer to themselves as "Ache," we have chosen to employ that term in all publications. (Practical orthographies, and the Ache themselves, spell their name without any syllabic emphasis, and we have chosen to follow their lead.) Clastres (1972a, 1972b), who studied the Ypety and Yvytyruzu groups of Ache in the early 1960s, has provided good ethnographic accounts of the Ache.

The Ache language is affiliated with the Tupi-Guarani linguistic family. Although the current Ache vocabulary includes many words used by native Guarani-speaking groups in the seventeenth century, there are regular phonetic changes, important differences in grammatical structure, and differences in accent that have made the two languages mutually unintelligible to modern monolingual speakers of Ache or Guarani. The Ache language also includes a large vocabulary of words specific to forest life that have no recorded Guarani equivalent in modern or historical dictionaries.

All Ache groups in recent times lived entirely from hunting animals and gathering plant and insect resources (Bertoni 1941; Clastres 1972b). During the four hundred years since the first arrival of the Spaniards, the Ache have engaged in only hostile relations with outsiders. They did not trade, intermarry, or visit with any of the Guarani Indian groups, and there is no clear evidence that they have ever experienced amicable relations with any other ethnic population in Paraguay. The Ache lived in small bands, generally composed of 15–70 individuals, and moved camp frequently. Several bands were often closely affiliated and comprise a larger unit that we call a "group." This term corresponds to what the Ache refer to as *irondy* or "those who are customarily our people/brothers," as opposed to *Ache irolla* or "Ache who are not our people." Four distinct "groups" of Ache existed in the second half of the twentieth century, just before permanent contact with outsiders.

AREA OVERVIEW

The Ache live in the southwestern part of what is generally referred to as the Eastern Brazilian Highlands. This area lies south of the Amazon tropical forest basin. Because of its ecological peculiarities and the fact that archaeological and ethnographic information suggests some regional continuities, the Eastern Brazilian Highlands is generally treated separately from the Amazon Basin in most overviews of South American ethnology and prehistory. The area is generally drier and higher than the Amazon Basin, and most of the rivers flow to the Atlantic, or to the Rio de la Plata, rather than to the Amazon. Portions of the northwestern part of the Eastern Brazilian Highlands are grassland savanna whereas most of the southern part is covered by the Atlantic coastal rain forest. The Alto Parana area of eastern Paraguay, where the Ache live, has been covered by tropical forest since before the end of the most recent glaciation (Hester 1966; Prance 1982). According to ethnographic accounts the Eastern Brazilian Highlands seem to have been populated at the time of contact by two major linguistic groups: tribes of the Macro-Ge family and tribes of the Tupi-Guarani family (Steward 1949). The tribes of the Macro-Ge group were typically quite dependent on hunting and gathering, with most tribes also involved to some extent in maize agriculture. Ge peoples typically left their villages to trek for several months of the year, subsisting primarily on forest resources. Some of these groups had no pottery at the time of contact and lived as band-level hunter-gatherers (e.g., the Botocudo [Metraux 1946]; the Kaingang [Henry 1941]), while others showed the typical seminomadic economic pattern (e.g., Nambicuara [Levi-Strauss 1948]; Xavante [Maybury-Lewis 1967]). The Tupi-Guarani, on the other hand, were typical Amazonian tropical forest horticulturists. They relied on bitter manioc as their primary staple, had a well-developed pottery technology, were oriented to the major rivers and Atlantic coastal areas, and generally lived in larger and more permanent villages than their Ge-speaking neighbors (Metraux 1948). To understand Ache history it is important to recognize that a general cultural trait of the Tupi-Guarani groups was the subjugation of conquered groups. Instead of extermination through conquest, the expanding Tupi-Guarani simply made slaves and servants of whole villages and moved in with their foes after vanquishing them in battle (Susnik 1979–1980). Oral traditions of both Ache and Guarani populations suggest this may once have been the relationship between the two tribes. By the time of Spanish conquest, however, the Ache had no interaction with Guarani groups. Because the Tupi-Guarani groups arrived late in the area, it is generally assumed that the currently surviving Macro-Ge groups are direct descendants of the inhabitants who lived in the Eastern Brazilian Highlands before the Tupi-Guarani invasion (Steward 1946).

PREHISTORY OF EASTERN PARAGUAY

Humans probably first arrived in North America between 14,000 to 20,000 years ago and reached southern South America by about 12,000 years ago (Roosevelt 1991:112; Salzano 1988:4; Willey 1971:29). The earliest well-accepted sites with artifacts and bone in clear stratigraphic position are from Venezuela and Argentina and date to 14,000 to 12,000 BP (MacNeish 1973). A date from an even earlier site (20,000 BP) in Peru is not well accepted by New World archaeologists but suggests the possibility of even earlier human occupation. Archaeological sites are abundant in the Eastern Brazilian Highlands beginning about 10,000 BP (Willey 1971:26–69). This was once believed to antedate evidence for humans in the Amazon Basin by many thousands of years (Willey 1971:394–428), but recent evidence suggests that this may not be true (Roosevelt 1991). The first archaeological evidence of native peoples in eastern Paraguay is represented by the "Altoparanese industry" of crude flake tools (Mayntzhusen 1928; Menghim 1957) found in many sites near the Parana River. Assemblages of this lithic type are located throughout the areas inhabited by the Ache in the twentieth century and are not too different from those found in preceramic Amazonian sites (Roosevelt 1991:112). The lithic tools in these assemblages have been generally interpreted as cutting tools for working wood, bone, and other material, rather than projectile points or weapons (Willey 1971:61–65). Interestingly, there is evidence from as early as 9,000 BP for stone axes or celts virtually identical to those used by the Ache (Hurt 1964). During the twentieth century (and even up to 1993) the Ache have used celts to extract palm fiber, insect larvae, and honey. The Altoparanense flake industry is dated to approximately 10,000 BP (Lanning and Patterson 1967). Thus, this industry represents a Paleoindian hunter-gatherer phase of human occupation that lasted for about 10,000 years in eastern Paraguay following the end of the most recent glacial phase. Although no current evidence would allow us to conclude that the Ache are the direct descendants of these early people, that possibility must be considered, especially in light of the extreme genetic differences between the Ache and any of the other Paraguayan native groups (see below).

Although root crop horticulture appears to have been practiced as early as 5,000 to 3,000 BP in some areas of lowland South America, it arrived considerably later in the Eastern Brazilian Highlands. In fact, there is *no* good evidence of manioc cultivation before the arrival of the Tupi-Guarani into the area at around AD 500 (Willey 1971:435–452). At that time the typical Amazonian manioc-fish-game economic complex was probably well established in most tropical forest areas, and large floodplain chiefdoms with economies based on maize farming and fishing were probably flourishing in a variety of savanna sites throughout Amazonia (Roosevelt 1980, 1991). Whether or not maize-based economies were present in eastern Paraguay before the arrival of the root crop complex is unknown. In eastern Paraguay, swidden manioc horticulture may have been brought by an earlier wave of Arawakan immigrants (Susnik 1983) but was probably introduced about AD 1000 when the Guarani from the headwaters of the Araguaya, Xingu, Arinos, and Paraguay rivers, began to migrate into the region, coming downstream along the Parana and Paraguay rivers and replacing many local populations (Susnik 1979–1980). This migration/conquest was still taking place to some extent during the Spanish conquest and was one of the reasons why the Guarani so quickly allied themselves with the Spaniards against other local native populations. At the time of European conquest, eastern Paraguayan native populations were primarily dependent on bitter manioc as their main staple, and regional complexity, village size, and ethnohistoric documents suggest that several small chiefdoms and confederations probably existed among the Guarani of the Paraguay Basin. Some time after the Spanish conquest, local Guarani populations switched to a sweet manioc–based economy, and higher-level political structures were obliterated, leaving only small autonomous villages like those present throughout much of tropical Amazonia today.

ETHNOHISTORY

Asuncion, the capital of Paraguay, was founded in 1524. At the time the Spaniards first explored the Paraguay and Parana rivers, there were two major populations in eastern Paraguay and nearby areas of Brazil: Guarani-speaking canoeist-horticulturists and Ge (Kaingang)-speaking forager-horticulturists (Susnik 1979–1980:9–65). In addition to these two main population blocks there were unidentifiable "wild" or "forest" tribes whose ethnolinguistic affiliation is not well known (Lozano 1873–1874) but who were often referred to as "Caaigua." The Ache were usually classified with these latter groups by early writers. Their ethnohistory has already been discussed in some detail by Melia and Munzel (1973), and Bertoni (1941) published a bibliography of works that mention the Ache. Chase-Sardi (1989) has also compiled a bibliography of Ache studies, incorporating more recent publications, but additional information is useful in order to contextualize the Ache of the twentieth century, who are the subjects of the present study.

Groups identified as Caaigua (a generic term meaning "forest people" in Guarani) were located on the east side of the Parana River (in present-day Brazil) and south toward the Uruguay River (in present-day Argentina). Some of the Caaigua groups may have been Ache (see Melia et al. 1973; Susnik 1979–1980), but the detailed descriptions of these groups also provide examples of cultural patterns and material goods (Techo 1897) not found in any group more recently identified as Ache. These Caaigua groups were usually later identified as nomadic foraging populations affiliated with the Southern Ge linguistic family, or maize farming–trekking groups of Kaingang who inhabited most of the Parana forested region east of the river (see Metraux 1946).The Caaigua are generally described by early writers in very negative terms:

> The customs and demeanor of the caaiguas are the most barbaric that have been discovered in America. Their name in the Guarani language means "wild people" and that they are, in spirit, in their condition, and in every way. . . . Their capacity for reason was so low, that they can barely be differentiated from animals; They are more like animals on two feet than men with a soul. . . . They are so lacking in intelligence that they don't even produce anything to eat, everything they have is gotten from fishing or hunting, when they are lucky enough to get something in the forest or the river; Most of them however, feed themselves with worms, snakes, rats, ants, or some similar critters that don't require any effort to obtain. They stubbornly pursue monkeys, with the ease as if they were monkeys themselves, jumping from tree to tree with a strange agility; Just like those creatures, they carry their children the same way, and if one [a monkey] falls from the tree, from his flesh the caaiguas make a splendid banquet. Wild honey is their favorite delicacy, and honey water their ambrosia that heats them such that they can resist the cold of winter (Lozano 1873–1874:412–414, our translation).

The earliest published mention of a group that is indisputably Ache comes from Jesuit missionary chronicles of the seventeenth and eighteenth centuries, which summarize earlier Jesuit explorations (Lozano 1873–1874; also see Melia and Munzel 1973 for review). During that time, various groups of Ache (called "Guayagui‘) were reported to live in the forests west of the Parana River between the Guaira falls on the north and the dense strip of Jesuit missions in the south near Encarnacion. They were first contacted along the Acaray river by Padre Jose de Insuarralde in the 1630s and 1640s. These Ache were frequently hunted by Guarani Indians and missionaries, and some of the southernmost groups were temporarily incorporated into Jesuit missions near Encarnacion. Some Northern Ache bands *still* lived in the headwaters of the Acaray River when they were contacted in 1972–1973; thus these groups had inhabited the same general area for at least 350 years. Descriptions from the 1600s differ little from those of the twentieth century.

> Only slightly less barbaric [than the caaiguas] is the guachagui nation, although easier to tame. They live in the lands called Ibaroti where the reduccion of "Jesus" was originally founded [near the mouth of the Acaray River]. Their language, although different from Guarani, and which is spoken with a certain tone as if they were singing, can be easily understood by the Guarani natives. Their weapons are very large bows of about two varas [meters], arrows proportional to the bow of about one and a half varas, and a long club.
> With their arrows being so long, they shoot them with great accuracy, but if by chance some day they are without meat, they have the foresight to domesticate a few peccaries and raise other tame animals called "guatis" [coatis] that they kill to

eat when they don't find anything else edible in the forest. They go completely naked, men and women, except that they cover their backs with a piece of woven material to guard against thorns. Around their neck the men wear a long necklace of animal teeth which they prefer over metal tools in order to make their weapons.

The women adorn themselves with strings of certain fruits called aguai, *without missing in the slightest the diamond jewels that greed leads people to desire, but they do have the vanity of their sex, they thus appear to show off with their aguais, the highest class and beauty. In order to open the trees from which they extract bee hives, or to split the palms whose pith they eat, they make use of very pointed stone axes that work with such force that it would seem they were iron.*

They all have small eyes; their lips are perforated in order to introduce the "tembeta" which is a colored stone or carved stick which makes them quite ugly; but, from their point of view it is the one ornament that enhances their appearance; and even though this seems right, it is more based on perception than reality. The men shave themselves from the front to the middle of the head, and the back hairs they let grow a bit long; but the women, not a hair do they allow on their head from the time they marry, and from their hair they weave a braid that their husbands wrap around their left wrist, I don't know if to keep their marital love alive or as a defense so that they are not injured by their bowstring.

Sometimes they have civil wars amongst themselves; and the most common reason is because of stealing the women of others, because there are few of them, and the number of men is greater (than that of women), something that is certainly rare in these Eastern Indies. The one who is fortunate enough that a daughter is born to him, is very careful in raising her, because through her he will become the head [leader] of others; being the inviolate law of the guayaguis that a son-in-law must follow his father in law, and become part of his family, because among them they have no chiefs, only that the brothers and sons-in-law get together in a group and recognize their father or father-in-law as the leader; but the power that he enjoys over others is very limited, since each lives according to his own whims.

Almost everyone thinks that this is a nation originating from some fugitive group of the Guarani, and this is based on the fact that the language is a corruption of Guarani, differing only in that it lacks the initial prefixes used in that language. That is how it was described by Padre Jose de Insurralde, an eminent authority on the Guarani language, that having been three times in three years to gather that group on a mission, on the first expedition he didn't understand the Guayaguis, but after considering carefully the vocabulary he noticed that it was the same as Guarani except the first letters were missing; he spoke it like that on the two following expeditions and understood, and was understood in turn by the Guayaguis. But, an argument used by others against the common origin [of the Ache and Guarani] is the fact that they don't recognize chiefs and they don't make use of the Paraguayan yerba, that is so abundant in their area.

In religious matters they make no errors, nor superstitions, nor do they worship any objects, but they have a simple knowledge of only one true God, creator of heaven and earth and some reluctant traces of a belief that the wicked are punished with flames and fire, which causes them some fear. . . . And seeing or sensing strangers in their country they flee quickly without allowing one to speak with them, because they believe either that they are going to be killed, or they are being sought in order to steal their women, like they do to each other, and for this reason, if there is time, the first thing they do is find a safe refuge, taking along their children to the most hidden and obscured places; but if they are caught off guard, they don't concern themselves with anything except their own safety, leaving in the hands of strangers their women, daughters and sons, in a manner that, in order to make them Christians it seems as if they are among those of which the Evangelist said "compelle intrare."

With this goal then the ancient Christians of our missions would go out to hunt these wild people, and the manner of hunting them was as follows: In the open forest the guayaguis have a wide trail on which they move during the day, and by night they enclose themselves in a brush corral to sleep together, where the women and children have their little camp guarded by an old man, while the men go out to search for food. It is necessary for the Guarani who go to search for them to carry on their back all their equipment and provisions until they are able to find that wide trail where they determine in which direction the tracks are headed, and continue along to look for the mentioned corrals; when they find fires still burning it is a certain sign that the guayaguis slept there the previous night.

Here they leave their supplies and arm themselves with bow, arrows, a rope and a big stick, bow and arrow. They soon find the heathens, [the weapons] are not used, but only to win their respect; the rope and the stick, yes [are used]: the rope in order to tie up the adults, in order to ensure that they don't flee, and the stick in order to deflect the long arrows and the clubs that the less timid guayaguis, once they see that they are surrounded, will use to defend themselves. Thus armed the Christians move out in two lines in which they go along forming a long procession preceded by a spy that makes a signal with his hands when they are near the corral of the heathens.

They surround the corral and sleep with watchmen; at the crack of dawn the sneak up on the camp very quietly and suddenly attack the guayaguis who awake in the hands of those they imagine to be enemies; and in order that they don't escape in the commotion, or perhaps to defend themselves, they get carried away with excessive force, they tie them up with the rope they had brought, they search for the children who tend to hide in the forest, especially searching the highest trees where they climb, and when these matters are taken care of they sit with them very lovingly, giving them food and dressing them in order that they can appear decently in front of others. With these demonstrations of affection they slowly lose their fear, bury their false apprehension and return to themselves (*Lozano 1873–1874:415–421, our translation*).

The earliest ethnohistoric reports are generally in agreement that the "forest people," unlike their Guarani neighbors, did not practice horticulture but instead lived from hunting wild game and collecting fruits and insects. One report does mention a group of "Guayagui" who apparently planted small patches of corn, which were harvested before they fully ripened.

Although they roam like nomads through the forest searching for wild honey, fruits and animals to eat, they also plant small corn patches; nevertheless, they

don't harvest much because they like to eat it young, before it matures, corn which
around here is called "choclo" (Lozano 1873–1874:416, our translation).

The author does not clarify whether the description refers to a specific group of Ache who were "missionized" by the Jesuits or to an "unacculturated" forest group. Since the description comes from Lozano's direct observations, and Lozano states that he observed "missionized" Ache firsthand (Lozano 1873–1874:421), either interpretation is possible. In almost three hundred publications about the Ache by more than one hundred different authors (Chase-Sardi 1989), *no other ethnohistoric account or direct observation provides evidence that the Ache ever cultivated gardens.* Most ethnographic descriptions are in fact adamant that the Ache knew nothing about cultivation (e.g., Bertoni 1941:9; Clastres 1972b:144), and the Ache themselves are quite clear about the fact that nobody in living memory, nor any of their real (known) ancestors, ever planted gardens. When asked why they didn't make gardens before contact they simply say, "We didn't know how." This explanation is not literally true, however, since some Ache adults were captured and later released after having worked in Paraguayan gardens as laborers.

After the expulsion of the Jesuits from Paraguay in 1768, no reliable information on the Ache is available until the end of the nineteenth century. Around that time, many new sources of information about the Ache become available (e.g., La Hitte and Ten Kate 1897; Mayntzhusen 1912, 1920, 1945; Vellard 1939). In his work, published posthumously, Bertoni (1941) recognizes several independent subpopulations of Ache living in the forests east of the mountainous "Cordilleras" and west of the Parana River in Paraguay (Figure 2.1). Much of this area was heavily depopulated during the slave raids at Jesuit missions in the seventeenth and eighteenth centuries. During that time, as many as 300,000 Guarani may have been killed or enslaved by the Brazilian "mamelucos" (Metraux 1948). In the late nineteenth century the war of the Triple Alliance against Paraguay resulted in the death of about two-thirds of the entire Paraguayan population (Bertoni and Gorham 1973). This depopulation of eastern Paraguay probably allowed for the rapid expansion of the Northern Ache population described in this book. Like the Guarani before them, the Ache were relentlessly pursued by slave traders and attacked by Paraguayan frontiersmen from the time of the conquest right up until peaceful contact (Chase-Sardi 1971; Melia et al. 1973).

By the early twentieth century the southernmost groups of Ache who had lived near the Jesuit missions were either integrated into the local population or were extinct. Around 1908, a wealthy immigrant landholder, Federico Mayntzhusen, contacted a small group of Ache near the mouth of the Tembey River in the state of Itapua. These Ache lived on a ranch near present-day Capitan Meza for about ten years, but when Mayntzhusen was forced to return to Germany, members of this small group either dispersed among Paraguayans, returned to the forest, or went extinct. After Mayntzhusen's time, all subsequent reports of Ache bands place them north of the San Rafael mountain range. These populations remained hostile and isolated throughout the first half of the twentieth century.

Starting around the turn of the century, the history of recent and current Ache groups can be determined using published reports and Ache accounts. At the time of peaceful contact in the late twentieth century there were four independent populations of Ache. The largest of these, the Northern Ache, roamed in an area of about 18,500 km^2 between the Sierra de San Joaquin near the village of Carajao and the Parana River (Figure 2.1). Their range was bounded on the north by the Sierra de Mbaracayu and on the south by the newly built road between Coronel Oviedo and Ciudad del Este. In the early part of the century the Northern Ache lived mainly around the San Joaquin Mountains, but in the 1930s they merged with another small group of Ache who lived toward the headwaters of the Itambey and Acaray rivers. Most Northern Ache then inhabited the headwaters of the Jejui River, making occasional forays out to the San Joaquin Mountains and toward the Parana River. The northern group of Ache numbered about 550 individuals in 1970 before recent contact and are the subject of the present study.[1]

The other three Ache populations were all quite small at the time of first peaceful contact. A group of about sixty individuals were cut off from the Northern Ache in the late 1930s after the new road to Ciudad del Este was built and extensive colonization began. This group took refuge south of Caaguazu and east of Villarica, in the Yvytyruzu Mountains, and is referred to as the "Yvytyruzu group." Another group of Ache inhabited the eastern Yvytyruzu range and the headwaters of the Monday River. They numbered only thirty-two individuals at contact and are currently referred to as the "Ypety group."[2] Finally, the fourth group of Ache, called the "Ñacunday group," lived along the middle section of the Ñacunday and Yñaro rivers and numbered about thirty individuals at contact in 1976.

During the 1940s and 1950s the Ypety and Yvytyruzu groups were constantly harassed and attacked by Paraguayan colonists. In 1959, a member of the Ypety group, who had been enslaved and later escaped into the forest, brought most of his Ypety band to live at the ranch of a patron who had treated him well, Jesus Manuel Pereira. Later, the entire Ypety group joined Pereira's camp. Pereira made use of the Ypety Ache to track down and capture two Yvytyruzu Ache in 1962. These captives were pampered and later released to help bring in the others of their group (Chase-Sardi 1971; Clastres 1972b; Hill 1983b). During this contact Pereira personally visited the Yvytyruzu Ache in the forest and convinced them to walk to his ranch to live with him. By 1963 Pereira had convinced all the Ache of these two groups to live under his "protection," and he was given a government post and a salary in order to administer a newly created "reservation." Between 1963 and 1968, about half of the members of the Yvytyruzu and Ypety groups died from contact-related respiratory infections. Both the Ypety and Yvytyruzu Ache were the subjects of extensive linguistic and ethnographic studies by Susnik, Cadogan, and Clastres in the early sixties.

In 1968 Pereira moved the Ache reservation north into the San Joaquin hills to a place called Cerro Moroti (Figure 2.1) in order to attract the Northern Ache. In that same year the dirt road between Coronel Oviedo and Saltos de Guaira was finished. This road bisected the traditional home range of the Northern Ache and led to increasingly hostile contacts between the Northern Ache and Paraguayan nationals. Pereira was actively encouraged to "pacify" the Ache. For two years, he and the Ache who lived under his protection searched for Northern Ache bands without making direct contact. Finally, in November of 1970, the process of extracting the Northern Ache from their forest home range began. We have heard numerous retellings of the first contact event from our Northern Ache informants. A summary of that event follows:

Some Ache from the Cerro Moroti reservation were hunting in the forest. An Ache man from the Ypety group who was digging a tegu lizard out of its burrow was shot in the buttocks with an arrow by a hunter from the uncontacted Northern Ache. The Northern Ache band was moving their camp from one area to another and had discovered the intruders in their home range. The brother of the man who was shot chased the enemy archer and soon discovered a whole camp of women and children who ran in panic at his arrival. He fired his shotgun in the air and captured a woman who froze in fear when she heard the explosion from the weapon. That woman was taken to the Cerro Moroti reservation and treated well. A few months later she led a mixed group of Ypety and Yvytyruzu Ache into the forest to find her band. They located the band quickly, and after some discussion, all but one family in that band of Northern Ache agreed to visit the Cerro Moroti reservation. Kravachingi, the one man who chose *not* to leave the forest, told his siblings that he would go search for other close relatives and then bring them all to the Cerro Moroti reservation. This "surrender" to "foreign Ache" was accomplished primarily due to the fact that members of the Northern Ache were closely related to some members of the Yvytyruzu group who already lived at the Cerro Moroti reservation (some members of each group were full siblings). The older individuals in each group had known each other as adolescents. The Northern Ache band that made first peaceful contact was led by Kuareijugi and consisted of thirty-six individuals.[3]

After this initial contact with the Ache, extracting the remaining forest bands was a relatively simple task. The Paraguayan government wanted to pacify the hostile Ache, and Pereira hoped to control as many Ache as possible. Pereira's income was almost a direct function of how many Indians he had under his control. He was paid to administer the reservation and was given money and supplies according to the size of the reservation population. Most of these resources were embezzled and used to support Pereira's frequent drinking binges. The Ache had their own reasons for wanting to bring group members into the reservation (see below). Thus, all three interested parties collaborated to bring additional Ache to the reservation settlement.

By the end of 1970 Pereira had developed a successful method of bringing new Ache groups to his reservation. This consisted of sending out friends and relatives of the forest bands, convincing them to walk out to the nearest road, and then sending a truck to pick them up. *In no case* were armed parties sent out, nor was there any violence or physical coercion involved. Almost as many Ache stayed in the forest as the number that decided to "visit" the reservation (see Chapter 5). Ache informants emphatically deny previous reports that individuals were forcibly captured and brought to the reservation (Arens 1976; Melia et al. 1973; Munzel 1973, 1974, 1976; see Hill 1983a for a rebuttal). There is little doubt, however, that strong social pressure and social coercion were occasionally employed. The bands remaining in the forest throughout this time were led by the most powerful men in the entire northern group, however, and many of those Ache simply refused to leave the forest. They were never "captured," despite common knowledge of their location, and almost all subsequently died without ever leaving the forest.

Many members of Kuareijugi's band died at the Cerro Moroti reservation in 1971, primarily from respiratory infections. By March of 1972, Pereira had located recent signs of another band along the road from Curuguaty to Saltos de Guaira and sent several Ache led by Kanegi (who was given the Spanish name Rafael) into the forest to contact that band. The forest band that Kanegi found was quite large, as they had recently gathered for a club fight. Here is one short account of that event (translated from a taped conversation, April 1978):

Kim Hill:	How did the white people see you?
Bepurangi:	They saw our trail, where it crossed the road. Then they sent word to *apa bujagi* [Pereira], "Here there have been Ache." Then Ache came to where we were.
KH:	Then what? Kanegi found you?
B:	Then we talked together.
KH:	How did he find you?
B:	He came along the trail to the camp. Grandmother was bringing water. Then he grabbed her by the arm [to scare her as a joke, he explains], Grandmother cried then, she cried. We had gone hunting with the older men, then we came back to the camp and he (Kanegi) was waiting. Grandfather yelled to us, old grandfather.
KH:	What did he say?
B:	The Ache eaters [the Ypety group] have come. Like that he said it.
KH:	Then what did you think?

> *B:*   Like this (he yelled). "To take us away, they will take us."
>   We will be taken we thought. [At this time the Northern Ache
>   already knew from the reports of Kravachingi mentioned
>   above that other members of their group had gone away in
>   December 1970 with members of the Ypety group.]
> *KH:* To take you to eat you? [The Ypety group were cannibals.]
> *B:*   Yes. Then at that place were some of our people. They said,
>   "No they won't eat you." Then we weren't afraid. We were
>   really hungry in the jungle [because they were living in a
>   very large group, traveling to the club fight]. Then we went in
>   the truck (to the reservation).

About three-fourths of the Ache gathered in the forest camp at that time were convinced that they should accompany Kanegi to the reservation, and about ninety of them arrived in a truck on March 8, 1972. The remaining Ache dispersed throughout the forest, spreading the news that Northern Ache from Kuareijugi's band had visited "enemy outsiders" and returned to the forest to take others with them. After this contact, the same technique was used again and again to bring new bands of Northern Ache to the Cerro Moroti reservation between 1972 and 1974. Many of these contacts, however, were not instigated by Pereira (who was fired and then later arrested in 1973), but by the Ache themselves, and perhaps evangelical missionaries who replaced Pereira as the administrators of the reservation. In fact, many Ache insist (contrary to previous accusations; cf. Arens 1976; Munzel 1974, 1976) that Pereira himself discouraged the rapid attempt to contact all forest bands of Ache. "Kanegi took us to the white people's house. There the Ache all died. Pereira was really angry. 'Why are you in such a hurry to bring all the Ache for no reason?' (he said). 'Don't hurry, take your time,' he used to say. Pereira was really angry [that the Ache went back to make more contacts]" (translated from an interview with Kuchingi taped in November 1984).

Although assigning the motivation for this wholesale "surrender" to people who had traditionally been enemies of the Northern Ache is complicated, it appears that groups often came to the reservation with the intention of visiting relatives, because of curiosity, or because of illnesses sweeping through the forest population. Most mention that the frequent hostile encounters with Paraguayans in the forest had driven them to desire a peaceful relationship with their more powerful neighbors. "I was brave [not afraid of non-Indians]. I didn't want to live in the forest. If we stay in the forest we will all be killed (they said). Let's go to the non-Indians (they said)" (translated from an interview with Kuchingi taped in November 1984). In addition, the abundance of food at the reservation was greatly exaggerated as a means of "convincing" forest groups to visit.

Individual Ache were motivated to "bring in" their kinsmen for a variety of reasons. Many young acculturated Ache men used this opportunity to steal the wives of the less acculturated forest-living men. Young men also sought to dominate the older men who had been politically powerful in the forest. At the reservation, the traditional power structure was turned upside down. Teenage boys and young men who adapted rapidly to new customs, technology, and language quickly used their new political and economic leverage to their advantage over the older men. This ultimately gave young men more wives and children than they had been able to acquire in the forest (Chapter 9). Finally, some Ache brought in relatives from the forest because they thought it might be safer to live at the reservation. Although the reservations had problems, no Ache who lived there was ever shot by a Paraguayan in the types of skirmishes that had been common throughout the past several hundred years on the Paraguayan forest frontier.

Whatever the reasons for the initial contact and assimilation of Northern Ache bands into the Cerro Moroti reservation, the ultimate outcome was disastrous. All new arrivals became sick soon after their first exposure to reservation Ache, and mortality was extremely high in some cases. Informants report that sometimes illness would strike a forest band literally within hours of the arrival of Ache from the reservation (although this seems medically unlikely, Ache informants insisted that it was true). These virgin soil epidemics of respiratory disease resulted in tremendous mortality both in the forest and at the reservation in 1972 and 1973 (see Chapters 5 and 6).

Forest bands aware of the danger occasionally tried to avoid contact. In one case, Kravachingi, the man who had fled with his family from the initial contact in 1970, pleaded with his brother (Kanegi) from the reservation *not* to approach the forest band where Kravachingi had taken refuge. Another brother in the forest band, Byvangi, threatened to shoot his own brother if he approached. Kanegi, fresh from the reservation, had come to lead the band to the road in order to load them on a truck that would take them to Cerro Moroti. Byvangi held his brother at bay on the trail with a drawn bow and demanded that he return without entering the forest camp. After a few tense minutes other Ache in the forest band convinced Byvangi not to harm his younger brother, and Kanegi spent a few days with the band.

This band (like several others) decided not to accompany Kanegi back to Cerro Moroti, and instead set off north in search of other forest Ache. Kravachingi had told them that the enemy Ache from the Ypety group that he had seen in November 1970 "were hideously ugly and repulsive." Kanegi could not convince his brother's band to visit the reservation and see for themselves that this was not true. Almost everyone in Kravachingi's new forest band died in the jungle near the Jejui Mi River, and the Ache report that "king vultures blackened the skies above their camps." Because all the adults were ill at the time, none of the dead were buried, and the trail was littered with corpses as stragglers attempted to follow the band each time it moved. Many weak and dying Ache were eaten alive by vultures in a death that the Ache describe as most horrifying.

Because of this possibility, sick Ache often asked to be buried alive before the band moved on. The tearful description by one close friend of how he buried his mother alive during this epidemic, so the vultures would not pick her eyes out when she was left behind, is probably the saddest and most moving story we have ever heard. Modern parallels to assisted suicide among terminally ill old people in our own country allow us to appreciate the emotional stress of such circumstances.

The situation at the reservation was not much better than in the forest. Members of newly contacted bands sickened and died within days of their arrival. Other individuals, who had survived the initial epidemic associated with their own contact, often caught the illness from newly arriving Ache and then died a year or two after they themselves had first left the forest. Saddest of all, children who were perfectly healthy throughout the epidemics (data in Chapter 5 show that mainly the adults were susceptible to the initial respiratory epidemics) would slowly starve and finally succumb through weakness to a new wave of epidemics. Because the adult population was unable to acquire food, and Pereira and other reservation caretakers never provided adequate supplies to feed the population, hunger and malnutrition plagued the children and the recovering adults and contributed significantly to the ever-increasing death rate at the reservation.

During the confusion of the contact and epidemic period, Manuel Pereira was arrested for embezzling resources meant for the Ache. He served a short jail sentence and was released (partially due to a personal plea from some Ypety Ache on his behalf). The German anthropologist Mark Munzel, who had witnessed the chaos and death of the 1972 contact, began to publish reports of "genocide" of the Ache and he was evicted from Paraguay. The Cerro Moroti reservation was informally turned over to American evangelical missionaries (New Tribes Mission), who remained until recently. Between 1972 and 1974 hundreds of Ache left the reservation and wandered through eastern Paraguay. Some returned to the forest, only to be contacted again. Others were sold, or coerced into working without wages on Paraguayan farms and ranches. Others worked of their own free will among friendly Paraguayan communities and moved from farm to farm at whim. The Paraguayan government took no steps to protect this naive and vulnerable population, and almost every individual was victimized in some way. Although, it is extremely difficult to piece together the history of contact during this confusing period, we believe that six different contacts took place between April 1972 and January 1975. All of these contacts were initially carried out by the Ache themselves, but they were often strongly encouraged by Pereira or New Tribes Mission personnel. In one case, a forest band, led by previously contacted Ache guides, walked 80 km through the forest to arrive directly at the ranch where Pereira lived when he was released from jail.

In 1974, Catholic missionaries (of the Divine Word order) set up a new mission/reservation much closer to the Parana River. This mission, designed to collect the dispersed Ache living on ranches and farms near Curuguaty, was moved to a place called Manduvi and later to the Jejui Guasu River at a place now called Chupa Pou (Figure 2.1). At Manduvi the final two contacts of independent forest-living Northern Ache were carried out. Both were planned and executed by the Ache without the knowledge of any outsiders. The first, in August of 1975, brought thirty-nine Ache from the Itambey River directly into the Manduvi camp. These were the surviving remnants of two bands that had been decimated in the forest by the epidemics of 1973. Unfortunately about half of these individuals died because of a lapse in medical attention at the Manduvi mission. The second contact, which took place in 1978, was the only contact of Northern Ache that did not result in excessive mortality.

In early 1978 Kim Hill had been informed by the Ache that a previously uncontacted band was living in the forest far to the north near a town called Ygatimi. He had hoped to visit this band in the forest after he could speak fluent Ache and understood the general patterns of forest life. Unfortunately, two Ache men working with Paraguayan woodcutters were told that residents of Ygatimi were angry that their gardens were frequently raided and were planning an attack against the band. The Ache men apparently decided to remove the band from the forest "for their own safety." In April of 1978 three Ache men from the Manduvi mission entered the forest at the Guarani Indian colony of Mboi Jagua and in two days had located the forest band and convinced them to leave the forest. This band consisted of twenty-four individuals. They walked to Mboi Jagua, a Guarani Indian village where one family of Ache was living, and waited for a truck to take them to Manduvi. In the mean time, German evangelical missionaries provided them with medical care and some clothing. The German missionaries encouraged the new Ache to stay, while the Ache from Manduvi encouraged them to join that mission. Eventually the band split in two.

During the first few months after this contact, Hill had the opportunity to observe firsthand the disastrous effects of first contact. All the newly contacted Ache at Manduvi became ill, and the older adults became gravely ill with pneumonia. Hill, along with mission personnel, provided medical treatment and food for several months. Eventually all but one small girl recovered. She subsequently died of pneumonia in a hospital. The German missionaries also provided careful attention to the group of Ache who stayed at Mboi Jagua, and again, only one small child died.

The first peaceful contact with the Ñacunday group of Ache was also carefully executed. Rolf Fostervold, a Protestant missionary who had hoped to work with the Northern Ache, heard rumors in the late 1970s about another group of Ache further to the south. The Fostervold family moved down near the Ñacunday River, and in 1976 after tracking a forest band with the help of an Ypety Ache, they were able to talk with a few members of the frightened group. Fostervold, through his interpreter, told the Ache that he would return in a boat along the Ñacunday River on a certain day and asked them to wait there. On the appointed day as he rounded a bend on the river he encountered the entire band of twenty-eight individuals sitting on the beach. These Ache were apparently motivated to make peaceful contact because they had been terrorized by the surrounding Paraguayan population and were rapidly diminishing in number. In addition, one old man in the band had previously spent some time with outsiders and was not afraid of the missionaries. Again, careful medical attention resulted in the death of only one small child. This contact experience, along with Hill's observations in 1978, leaves little doubt that most of the Ache could have been saved from the virgin soil epidemics that killed almost half the population in the 1960s and 1970s if they had been given complete medical attention and food supplementation.

CURRENT SITUATION

Currently the Ache live in five major mission/reservation settlements (Figure 2.1). In July 1989 the first settlement, Puerto Barra, consisted of 37 Ñacunday Ache, 1 Northern Ache, and 1 Ypety Ache living at the confluence of the Yñaro and the Ñacunday rivers. The second settlement, called Ypetymi, consisted of 33 Ypety Ache, 14 Yvytyruzu Ache, 28 Northern Ache, and 15 Ache children with parents from two different groups (mixed) living near the headwaters of the Ypety, a tributary of the Monday River. The third settlement is the Cerro Moroti reservation in the San Joaquin hills near Cecilio Baez. It contained 150 Northern Ache, 35 Yvytyruzu Ache, 7 Ypety Ache, and 35 mixed Ache children in 1989. The fourth settlement is the Chupa Pou community on the Jejui Guasu River near the town of Ygatimi. Including surrounding satellite groups, Chupa Pou had a population of 285 Northern Ache, 5 Yvytyruzu Ache, and 5 mixed Ache children. A fifth small community of Ache at Arroyo Bandera consisted of 34 Northern Ache in June of 1989. Although 1989 was the last year that we carried out a complete census of the population, we have visited each of these groups more recently. The most notable shift in population has been a migration out of the Cerro Moroti settlement to Chupa Pou and then out of Chupa Pou to Arroyo Bandera. This trend indicates movement away from the more developed areas of eastern Paraguay and in the direction of the more remote forested areas.

Each of the original four Ache groups has maintained some degree of autonomy. The Yvytyruzu and Northern Ache groups have mixed significantly, but this is not surprising since they are closely related historically and genealogically. The Ypety group was originally shunned by its neighbors because they practiced cannibalism and were the long-standing enemies of the northern groups (they are stilled called *Ache ua,* "those who eat Ache"). They in turn considered themselves superior to their enemies, the Northern and Yvytyruzu Ache, because they were more acculturated and "civilized" (see Clastres 1972a). These barriers have only begun to disappear in the past few years, and young people who are now looking for a spouse do not seem to be concerned with which group of Ache a potential mate comes from (but they are still strongly prejudiced against marrying non-Ache). The Ñacunday Ache have been historically isolated from the other three groups and were unaware of their existence prior to contact. Nevertheless, two marriages between Ñacunday men and Northern Ache women have taken place recently. As of 1994 there was only one marriage between an Ache and Guarani Indian, and only one marriage between an Ache and a Paraguayan. Thus, the Ache are essentially a closed breeding population.

In parallel with their historical connections or isolation, strong cultural variation is observed among the four groups of Ache. The Northern and Yvytyruzu Ache, who only split in the 1930s, are culturally identical but show slight variations in vocabulary and accent. The Yvytyruzu Ache, despite being a subgroup of the Northern Ache, show a much lower incidence of light skin color (a trait the Ache are widely known for in Paraguay) than the other three groups. This is probably due to a founder effect producing genetic drift. The Ypety and Yñaro Ache have slightly different facial features and body types, which allow the Northern Ache (and us) to recognize them immediately. Both also speak dialects that are somewhat difficult for Northern Ache to understand if they haven't heard it before. The Ypety group shows a very high incidence of light skin color, male baldness, and a heavy beard pattern, traits that traditionally set all the Ache groups apart from other Paraguayan Indians (see below). The Ypety group not only practiced regular cannibalism through 1963 (see Clastres 1974) but also showed other cultural differences from the Northern Ache groups. Mythology and rituals seem more elaborately developed in the Ypety group (some Northern Ache informants concur with this), but surprisingly these Ache did not practice club fighting, a ritual of extreme importance among the northern groups. Musical instruments are more elaborate among the Ypety Ache, and the singing style is noticeably different.

The Ñacunday Ache show the highest evidence of outside influence in their culture. They sing in several different melodic styles that are not found in any of the other three Ache groups, and they have more elaborate technology, including metal-tipped arrows and hunting traps. They alone drink the *yerba mate* tea that is commonly consumed by Guarani Indians and Paraguayan peasants. They also speak the most divergent dialect of Ache. These factors indicate a long period of separation between this group and the other Ache, perhaps combined with some previous outside contact. Interestingly, the oldest living member of this group has recounted a story of riding in a motorboat on the Parana River when he was a boy.

MODERN ECOLOGICAL STUDIES

Between 1980 and 1990 the Ache were the focus of a large research project that began at the University of Utah. This project has resulted in nearly thirty publications focusing on ecological studies of the Ache. Since demographic processes represent the long-term outcomes of human interaction under both environmental and social constraints, much of this information is critical for understanding why the Ache fertility and mortality patterns are different from those found in other populations, and also for explaining why the Ache patterns show the types of internal variations that they do. In relevant sections on fertility and mortality, we will refer to specific findings from this previous research, but many readers may prefer to read the primary sources for themselves. For that reason we provide a complete bibliography on previous research. The publications, divided according to topic, are as follows:

Diet, foraging models, hunting and gathering	Hawkes 1987, 1990; Hawkes and Hill 1982; Hawkes et al. 1982, 1985; Hill 1983a, 1988; Hill and Hawkes 1983; Hill et al. 1984, 1987
Time allocation	Hill et al. 1985; Hurtado 1985; Hurtado et al. 1985, 1992
Food sharing	Hawkes 1991; Kaplan 1983; Kaplan and Hill 1985b; Kaplan et al. 1984, 1990
Reproductive strategies	Hill and Kaplan 1988a, 1988b; Kaplan and Hill 1985a
Ethnoarchaeology	Jones 1983, 1984
Child development	Kaplan and Dove 1987
Mission settlement activities	Hawkes et al. 1987
General	Hill 1983b; Hill and Hurtado 1989

BIOLOGICAL AND GENETIC AFFINITY

The Ypety and Yvytyruzu groups of Ache were the subject of several anthropometric, biomedical, and genetic studies in the 1960s (e.g., Brown et al. 1974, 1975; Clastres 1972a; Manrique Castañeda 1966; Matson et al. 1968; Miraglia and Saguier Negrete 1969; Moreno Azorero 1966) because of the widespread Paraguayan belief that they represented a separate race of Indians with some affinities to Europeans. No biomedical or genetic studies have yet been conducted on the Northern Ache who made peaceful contact more recently. The light skin, hair and eye color, abundant body hair, thick beards, and distinct male baldness patterns of the Ache, as well as their striking facial features, have been reported in almost every scientific and popular article ever written about the group. Indeed some popular writers had concluded that the Ache were descendants of Vikings or shipwrecked sailors during early European exploration. This is curious since the close neighbors of the Ache generally concede that the Ache look Japanese rather than European, and the Ache themselves often confuse

Japanese colonists for distant Ache groups when they travel. Other authors have noted that the Ache exhibit a series of traits suggesting extreme tropical forest adaptation, including especially short stature, relatively long arms and short legs, flat nostrils, and a radio/humeral index greater than that measured in any other human group (e.g., La Hitte and Ten Kate 1897; Saguier Negrete et al. 1968; Miraglia 1969, 1973). Based on anthropometric measurements Miraglia (1969) and Saguier Negrete et al. (1968) go so far as to call them an "arboreal race."

More recent genetic studies have in fact concluded that the Ache are physically and genetically dissimilar to most other South American Indians studied but they show no evidence of any European or African admixture. Specifically, Salzano (1988:158) shows that the Ache are one of only eleven out of a total of fifty-eight well-studied native South American groups that show no evidence of Old World admixture. He further shows that they are strikingly dissimilar to their neighbors for the genetic allele Le (Salzano 1988:167), which is generally correlated with latitude in most South American native populations. A dendrogram of the fifty-eight South American Indian groups puts the Ache at the top of the tree, *most distant from all other South American Indians*, along with one other group (the Parakaña) who live 2,500 kilometers away near the Para River but are also Tupi-Guarani speakers and are also characterized by light skin and heavy beards (Salzano 1988:186, pl. 3)! The Siriono/Yuqui, another group of Guarani-speaking hunter-gatherers who are in many ways ethnically similar to the Ache (see Holmberg 1969; Stearman 1989) are another early branch on the dendrogram. The Caingang, which many early writers had associated culturally with the Ache, are in the middle of the dendrogram and do not share a recent common genetic history with them.

Other writers have also emphasized the genetic uniqueness of the Ache (e.g., Brown et al. 1974), but recent authors have cautioned that dendrograms produced thus far do not provide useful information on the evolutionary history of South Amerind populations (e.g., Black 1991). The lack of evidence of significant genetic inflow from neighboring Guarani populations makes it doubtful that any peaceful long-term interaction took place between the Ache and their Guarani neighbors in recent times; however, the fact that the Ache speak a language that is not too different from seventeenth-century Guarani suggests some social contact or historical affinity. In order to resolve these conflicting pieces of evidence, more detailed genetic studies will be needed.

Finally, data on immunological patterns suggest that the Ache have had little or no contact with outsiders in the recent past. Specifically, Brown et al. (1975) show that the Ache are one of the few groups in the world that show virtually no HI immune response to BK and JC papioviruses, and that the few positive individuals show the lowest immune titers to those viruses of any group in a medium-sized world sample (including other remote populations from South America and Malaysia). Since antibodies to human papioviruses are ubiquitous in most human societies, and immune response is rapidly acquired during childhood, the data suggest the Ache *were probably not in physical contact with other Paraguayan groups* (nationals or indigenous populations) in recent times. In short, available data suggest that the Ache were genetically and socially isolated from all neighboring populations for a long period of time prior to recent contact in the latter twentieth century.

ECOLOGY OF EASTERN PARAGUAY

Because this book contains only analyses of demographic patterns among the Northern Ache group, the remainder of the information we present will be specific to that group and the area in which they reside. The Northern Ache, until contact, roamed in an area of about 18,500 km² between 24 and 25.5 degrees south latitude and between 54.5 and 56.5 degrees west longitude. Aerial photos from the mid 1960s show about 90% of the area to be covered with mature forest and the remaining 10% with savanna grassland meadows. In the 1970s and 1980s vast tracts of the forest were cleared for agriculture and cattle ranching. This deforestation was accelerated near the end of the 1980s when the Paraguayan government began to allow expropriation of lands that were not in "rational use." The definition of rational land use in Paraguay does not include any activities that leave mature forest uncut. Most of the Northern Ache core area lies in the headwaters of two major drainage systems, the Acaray River, which flows east to the Parana, and the Jejui River, which flows west to the Paraguay. The headwater streams in the Ache area are generally no more than 20–30 m across and only a meter or two deep, but during long periods of intense rain they can flood to become more than a kilometer wide in some places.

Eastern Paraguay is characterized by gentle rolling hills composed of soft sedimentary rock and weathered basalt, interspersed with low flat valleys. Elevation ranges from 150 to 300 m in the Northern Ache home range. Because the river systems drain old sediments or basalt outcrops, the silt is poor in nutrients and rivers are not especially productive (this is particularly true of the Parana clear water drainage).

Seasonality in eastern Paraguay is marked primarily by temperature change. Some weather data for the Northern Ache area are presented by Hill et al. (1984). Temperatures range from a mean daily average of 27 degrees centigrade in January to 17 degrees in June and July. Mean high and low temperatures show a range between 24 and 33 degrees (high) and between 9 and 21 degrees (low), with extreme daily high temperatures reaching about 38 degrees and extreme daily lows of 2–3 degrees below zero and several days of hard frost each year. Humidity has exceeded 90% in all months of the year (Bertoni and Gorham 1973), although short spells of very dry weather can occur. The humidity, in combination with the temperature pattern, results in very uncomfortably hot and humid weather during part of the year, especially in December and January, and some very cold and damp days throughout May, June, and July. Only the coldest weather represents a serious threat to health. On some days the Ache sit by campfires until 10 AM and return early in the afternoon to the warmth of their hearths. Nights in which the temperature drops below freezing are extremely unpleasant (the Ache sleep naked by the fire), and a hard frost in the treetops the next morning sometimes elicits a comment that many capuchin monkeys have probably frozen to death during the night. Unlike most lowland South American native populations, the Ache are familiar with ice. Hunters who fail to return at night and sleep in the forest without fire are in danger of death from exposure if they are caught out on a very cold night. The cold dry weather in August often leads to tremendous leaf fall in which canopy and exposed understory trees and shrubs may completely shed their leaves for about a month.

Rainfall is characterized by statistically evident wet (October to February) and dry (June to September) seasons, but precipitation is quite erratic, varying considerably from year to year. On the basis of thirty-four years of weather data from the Parana forest, Bertoni and Gorham (1973) conclude that almost any month of the year can be the wettest or driest in a particular year. Total annual rainfall ranges from about 1,700 to 2,000 mm in a west to east gradient of increasing rainfall. October shows peak average monthly rainfall with 225 mm, while August is the driest with a mean of 100 mm. Rainfall influences the distribution of important food resources by affecting flowering and fruiting patterns in the forest, but it also affects the Ache directly, because they generally do not hunt or move campsite on days of heavy rainfall. Three or more days of continuous rain can result in serious food stress.

The botanical community of the Northern Ache area is representative of the rapidly diminishing Selva Alto Parana formation of the almost extinct Atlantic coastal rain forest of Brazil. In the western part of the Ache range this botanical community slowly merges with the Selva Central formation of Paraguay. The area is mainly covered with neotropical semideciduous evergreen forest. Ecologically the Northern Ache home range is part of the Brazilian Rain Forest Biogeographic Province, or Warm Humid Temperate Brazilian Forest Life Zone (Fundacion Moises Bertoni 1987). A commercial assessment of the upper Jejui watershed, in the very center of the traditional Ache home range, found 81.5% of the area to be "productive commercial forest," almost equally distributed between high, low, and intermediate primary forest. About 5% of the area was assessed as "inaccessible montane forest," 10.5% as "riparian forest," and the remaining 4% as "shrub savanna" and "grass savanna." The high proportion of forest with good commercial potential is typical in eastern Paraguay and explains why so much of the forest has been cut in the past thirty years. Our own transects with Ache guides suggest a slightly different forest breakdown according to Ache categories. While recording vegetation type according to Ache forest categories along 900 person-kilometers of linear transect, we found fifty-four forest types distinguished by Ache hunters. Types of high forest made up 69% of the total; low and intermediate forest accounted for 11%; and poorly drained areas, 20%.

Only one study of woody plant densities has been carried out in the upper Jejui watershed. In 1987 a team of four botanists and two Ache assistants led by S. Keel and the late A. Gentry recorded all plants with a diameter at breast height (dbh) greater than 2.5 cm on a variety of transects that added up to a total of 1,000 m² in the northeast corner of the Mbaracayu reserve in the upper Jejui watershed. These detailed transects suggest that much of the forest is mature primary forest (Keel 1987). This is confirmed by the high density of large lianas > 2.5 cm dbh, including many examples > 10 cm dbh. In the sample, 382 woody plants with > 2.5 cm dbh were recorded. These trees represented more than eighty species in sixty genera and thirty-one families. Strikingly, 103 individuals were lianas, making this one of the richest liana sites in the neotropics. Three of the genera encountered, *Jacaratia, Campomanesia,* and *Citrus,* produce fruits that are quite important in the Ache economy. A few others produce less important fruits, and *Holocalyx* is used for making arrow points.

While these forest transects are useful for in-depth characterization of a small portion of the forest, they fail to uncover many important and common species in the upper Jejui area because of the limited area they cover. Most important to the Ache are the edible palms, *Syagrus (Arrecastrum) romanzolfianum* and *Acromia totai (sclerocarpa),* which produce edible fiber, growing shoots, fruits, and nuts, and are used to make bows, carrying baskets, shelters, and a variety of other tools. Neither of these species was reported in the Keel and Gentry study. We have counted these palms at an average density of approximately 35 per hectare in ground transects. In addition, some of the most important fruits in the Ache diet come from species not encountered at all in the Keel and Gentry study (e.g., *Rheedia brasiliense* and *Eugenia pungens*). Finally, the scale of the botanical study is not completely relevant to Ache foragers, who cover an average of 12 km per day while foraging and may travel out for more than 100 km before turning back. Like other human foragers, the Ache tend to target high-quality patches of resources that are extremely widely dispersed relative to the scale at which most tropical biologists work. Large areas of the upper Jejui watershed are dominated by bamboo either in the understory or the middle story, and we have observed immense areas of low scrub forest with understory dominated by bromeliads. None of these patterns can be discerned from small-scale forest inventory.

The mammalian fauna in eastern Paraguay has been the subject of many inventory studies, but none has attempted to determine absolute or relative densities of the entire array of large mammals. During extended collections in the 1970s, Myers et al. (1995) counted 134 species of mammals that probably live in eastern Paraguay. Ninety-one of the species on the list are bats, small rodents, or opossums and are never hunted by the Ache. The remaining forty-three species of large nonvolant mammals counted by Myers et al. include several that we have never seen, and the list does not include several that we have observed while hunting with the Ache. We have observed or heard reliable reports (from Ache hunters) concerning thirty-seven species of large mammals (not including bats, rodents, and opossums). A preliminary assessment of relative and absolute densities of some mammals can be obtained from 42 focal man-follows and 10 transect-days in which we recorded every large vertebrate ($\geq$ .5 kg) encountered during diurnal travel. Those data can be compared with other neotropical mammalian encounter rates reported using standard census methods (e.g., Emmons 1984) as well as one study done near Manu Park, Peru (Alvard 1993), which also reports encounter rates of native hunters.

The faunal community in eastern Paraguay is rich but does not show the high species diversity of more tropical lowland South American forests. For example, although Barro Colorado Island (BCI) in Panama supports five species of primates, and Manu National Park in Peru is inhabited by fourteen sympatric species of primates, the upper Jejui region is home for only two primate species. The two mammalian genera showing the highest biomass in BCI, *Bradypus* and *Cholepus,* are totally absent from eastern Paraguay. Other commonly observed genera on BCI also missing from the Ache forests are *Proechymys, Sciurus,* and *Cyclopes.* Reptiles and birds are also less diverse in eastern Paraguay than in other South American forests. There is only one or two species of caiman, two species of rarely encountered turtles, and about three hundred species of birds in the Ache territory. On the other hand, eastern Paraguay is home for many rare tropical animals that are now endangered in other places, such as giant otters, jaguars, bush dogs, giant armadillos, and macaws. These data point to the often unappreciated conclusion that considerable diversity in forest types and composition exists within lowland South America.

Mammals most commonly hunted by the Ache include white-lipped and collared peccaries, tapir, deer, pacas, agoutis, armadillos, capuchin monkeys, capybara, and coatis. Game transects suggest that most of these common mammals are present in lower densities in eastern Paraguay than has been found in other well-studied neotropical forests. For example, we tentatively estimate that the biomass of the species listed above totals about 400 kg/km in the forest where the Ache hunt, but on Barro Colorado Island in Panama the same species show almost twice the total biomass (Eisenberg and Thorington 1973). In combination with higher species diversity, this estimate means that well-studied neotropical forests such as BCI and Manu Park appear to have from two to seven times the mammalian biomass than is found in eastern Paraguay.

Community structure comparisons are even more informative. First, arboreal folivores are extremely rare in the upper Jejui watershed relative to densities reported for Barro Colorado Island in Panama (Eisenberg and Thorington 1973) or a variety of South American forest sites (Emmons 1984). The upper Jejui area has no sloths, and howler monkeys are very rare—probably because of the yearly leaf drop, which may be sufficiently severe to eliminate these species.

Second, the upper Jejui area probably has the highest concentration of terrestrial insectivore-omnivores of any South American forest, with extremely high densities of armadillos and coatis. Indeed, comparison with Alvard (1993) shows diurnal encounter rates of both to be more than an order of magnitude higher in upper Jejui than in the Manu region, and this agrees with our impressions from hunting in both areas. Third, the encounter rate with *Cebus* in the upper Jejui region is equal to or greater than that found elsewhere despite the lack of other primates. Fourth, *Agouti paca* may be more common in upper Jejui than most other sites, whereas *Dasyprocta* is much rarer in the upper Jejui region. Fifth, *Tajassu pecari* may be present at higher densities than *T. tajacu* in the upper Jejui region, whereas the opposite is often true in other South American forests. This conclusion is tentative, however, since *T. pecari* covers large distances and can migrate into and out of regions much larger than those censused in most other studies. (Paraguay data cover 226 km, including one transect extending 60 km, whereas much of the data cited in biological studies come from a trail network not more than 1–2 km distant from a central research station.)

The large data base on Ache game killed during sample days over a five-year period supports this general picture. *Cebus* is the most important game species numerically, whereas *Cebus, Dasypus,* and *T. pecari* contribute about equally in weight. Next in importance come *Nasua, Agouti, Mazama,* and *T. tajacu,* with all other species being considerably less important. In comparisons of the upper Jejui region with other neotropical forests it is tempting to speculate about the impact of nonnative *Citrus,* which were imported into the region by Jesuits in the seventeenth century and were subsequently scattered throughout the primary forest by monkeys and rodents. These feral oranges, which fruit throughout much of the year, may be responsible for the high densities of *Cebus, Agouti,* and *T. pecari,* all of which feed heavily on its fruit.

Regardless of the low absolute mammalian biomass, the Paraguayan forest is not unfavorable for human hunters because some of the most common animals are also highly vulnerable to human predation. Most of the Paraguayan fauna is made up of terrestrial and easy to hunt species. Armadillos, pacas, and coatis, which make up a good part of the Ache diet, can all be hunted without any weapon at all! Armadillos, which are highly accessible to human hunters, are also present at higher densities in Paraguay than in any other South American forest reported thus far. In contrast, much of the animal biomass in other South American forests is composed of nocturnal rodents and arboreal herbivores, which can be difficult to locate because of their inactivity during the day. Thus, without an in-depth study of the human use of a particular forest, it may be difficult to predict whether any given tropical forest represents a "plentiful" environment for human hunters and gatherers.

In summary, the environment of eastern Paraguay is characterized by a primary forest that includes a diversity of plant and animal resources which are the basis of Ache subsistence. Temperature rather than rainfall is the major marker of seasonal change, and the Paraguayan forest seems to show lower species diversity and mammalian biomass than that found in more tropical regions of the New World. Nevertheless, the species that are found in Paraguay are exceptionally vulnerable to human predation; thus resources may be effectively more "abundant" for humans than they are in other tropical areas.

FOREST LIFE

Daily life among forest-living Ache was (and still is) centered around the food quest. Ache informants report that daily life prior to outside contact was very similar to the patterns that we have observed during the past fifteen years on extended forest treks, with the possible exception that the forest economy may have included a greater reliance on palm products than is currently indicated by forest treks. Men hunt for about seven hours per day, pursuing mammalian game and collecting honey when it is available. Men provided about 87% of the calories in the diet on forest treks that we monitored, and most of these calories came from meat (Hill et al. 1984). The primary hunting weapon is a bow and arrow of impressive dimensions, but men also kill many smaller animals by hand (Hill and Hawkes 1983). Women often extract the fiber from palm trees, as well as gather assorted fruits and insect larvae, spending about two hours per day collecting food on forest days that we monitored (Hurtado et al. 1985). Women also carry the family's possessions, children, and pets in woven palm carrying baskets, spending an additional two hours per day moving camp. Most of their activities during the day center around the care of young and highly vulnerable infants and children, which constrains their subsistence effort considerably (Hurtado 1985; Hurtado et al. 1992).

Men sometimes spend a few hours during the day traveling with the women's group, carrying young children or breaking the trail through the forest. Usually, however, they set off in a small group to search for game (Hill et al. 1985). Although men and women separate during the day, they always come together in the late afternoon. At that time food acquired throughout the day is prepared and widely shared among band members. Hunters very rarely eat from their own kills; the meat is shared very evenly among other adult members of the band, who then pass portions on to children (Kaplan and Hill 1985a). Collected resources are also shared with band members, but redistribution of gathered items is less extensive than the redistribution of game and honey. After cooking and consuming food, evening is often the time of singing and joking. Eventually band members drift off to sleep, with one or two nuclear families around each fire. The next day the food quest begins again. Our direct observations indicate that camp is likely to be moved almost every day, but informant reports suggest that before contact some Ache bands may have camped for one to two weeks in a spot before moving on, depending on the season, habitat, and particular band in question.

Bands were autonomous economic and residential units. They often formed around a core bilocal kin group and one or two important men, whose names might be used to describe the band (e.g., Tayjangi's band or Betapagi's band). Before contact, bands had a median of about fifty individuals, with camp composition on single days varying from 3 to 160 individuals (Hill and Hurtado 1989). Since the Northern Ache population consisted of about 550 individuals just prior to contact, at any point in time there must have been about eleven different residential bands. Before contact, band members often dispersed into small, temporary, family-group camps for a day or two before reforming. Adult men and sometimes their wives would forage in distant areas (8–15 km away), leaving children and older kin at a base camp for a day or two. Grandparents would frequently serve as baby-sitters on these occasions (see Chapter 13). Resources from these day outings would then be transported back to the central camp, and the band might then move to a new area and begin the pattern anew. Bands generally camped within a few hours walk of the nearest neighboring band but sometimes might range fifty or a hundred kilometers from the nearest neighboring band for a few months. Sometimes a messenger would be sent to invite a neighboring band to join them for a short time to consume large kills, such as a tapir or many peccaries. Ritual events such as club fights and initiation ceremonies might bring together up to half of the adults in the entire Northern Ache group. Band membership was highly flexible, with band size and composition generally changing every few months, but core kin groups often stayed together for years. Bands were composed of closely related kin as well as individuals who reported that they resided together because they were "friends." A random sample of precontact residential camp composition shows extremely flexible membership, with not one camp of the 104 censused (by retrospective interview) showing the same membership composition. Nevertheless, some consistencies in band composition are obvious to casual inspection, especially the tendency for large sib groups of both sexes to remain together along with their spouses and some affinal kin.

Much of forest life was taken up with the daily subsistence patterns described above. In the past, as now, however, other events of importance occasionally took place. Births and deaths, the subject of this book, were important events, even though they happened infrequently. Many of the ritual aspects of Ache births and deaths have been described by Clastres (1972a). At the time of birth a mother often remains in camp and is helped by older men and women, who hold and massage her body during labor. Births are thus public events, and often every man, woman, and child in a band witnesses the birth. When the child emerges, the new mother sits by herself at the edge of camp, buries the placenta, and rests. In the mean time, a previously designated woman holds the child in her lap and washes it gently. She is called the *tapare,* a label implying a godmother-type relationship, and she is responsible for much of the child's care during its first few days of life and retains a special relationship with the mother and the child throughout her life. The tapare is supposed to provide assistance to the child when it is needed, and anecdotal accounts suggest that she will sometimes adopt her godchild if the child's mother dies.

Along with the tapare, a single man has also been designated to have a special relationship to the child. This man, called *mondoare*, cuts the umbilical cord of the child with a bamboo knife. He is expected to provide for his godchild in times of need, and again, specific anecdotal accounts show that he sometimes adopts his godchild if the parents die (Chapter 13). Finally, other individuals who lift and hold the child, or wash it in the first few minutes after birth, are designated as *upiare*, "those who lifted it," and they too take on a godparent-like relationship as described above, though apparently not as strongly. Two or three days after the birth, the new parents and all the godparents are washed with the bark of a large vine in order to purify them after the exposure to human blood. Godparents were required to cut many palms and provide a large supply of palm hearts to the new mother. After a birth the band would camp in one place for several weeks, and male lip-piercing ceremonies would often be performed at this time.

Another important nonkin relationship is that between adult men and the children whose *bykua* or "essence of human life" they provide. Successful hunters will offer specific game animals to a pregnant woman, in order to give a bykua to her unborn child. She cooks the animal and it is shared among band members. All men who provide such game enter into a godfather-type relationship with the child like that described above. In addition, one or more of these men ultimately give the child its name. When the child is born the mother chooses a name from amongst the animals that have been provided to her for the child's bykua. She generally chooses the largest, rarest, or most frequently eaten animal during the last few months of her pregnancy, or an animal associated with a very notable event (such as the time ten coatis were killed on one day). That name usually stays with the child throughout its life, though occasionally names are changed, and a very small number of the Northern Ache have two or more names (the Ñacunday Ache all have multiple bykua names). Often the men who provide the bykua for a child are also likely to have engaged in sexual relations with its mother, and because of their status as men who provided the bykua they are allowed to take revenge on anyone perceived as responsible for any harm that befalls the child.

If a child dies, regardless of whether the death is due to sickness or unavoidable accident (such as being struck by lightning), women begin to weep, and a young child is instructed to hit the mother. "Why did you let your baby die?" the child will ask. Those who are godparents to the child often become quite upset and hit the mother as well. Occasionally, a man who is a *mondoare*, *upiare*, or *bykuare* will challenge the father of the dead child to a club fight to "get revenge" for the child. Dead children are buried in a small hole with no ceremony.

Adult deaths are mourned by the entire band, but close relatives who cry more than a few minutes are severely chastised. If the dead adult was well liked he or she will be buried in an upright sitting position in a hole about 2.5 m deep. Often the arms and legs of the deceased are bound in a fetal position. Once the body is positioned in the grave, close relatives and children are scolded not to watch as dirt is thrown in as quickly as possible. Generally a large palm hut is built above the grave. The band departs and does not return to the area for some time because of fears about the spirit's desire to take others along with it in death, or cause other harm. Later, when an animal is killed that has the same name as a well-loved Ache who has died, the women of the band will sit next to the dead prey and cry, remembering their relatives and friends who had its name. Names of dead individuals are not taboo and are frequently mentioned in daily conversation. If an adult who died was particularly old, ugly, mean, low status, or otherwise disliked, or if the death was particularly violent and unpleasant, the cadaver is burned in an enormous fire, and the site is abandoned. This practice is believed to free or drive out the revenge-seeking spirit of the dead individual, which might harbor a grudge against living Ache. This custom is mythologically linked to the origins of cannibalism among the Ypety Ache, who simply ate the cooked flesh of such cadavers and broke open the skulls to liberate the vengeful spirit rather than cremating the body completely.

One Ache custom associated with the death of adult males had extremely important demographic consequences prior to contact. After death, important men were often buried along with living small children. The sacrificed children, referred to as *chape*, were usually girls who were under five years of age but also included male children and sometimes children as old as about twelve years. Several of the dozens of accounts we recorded concerning sacrificial deaths included events in which an ill child or one with an injury or birth defect was buried. Occasionally a very old or sick adult would also volunteer to be buried with the deceased man. This practice was thought to appease the dead man's angry spirit so he would not attempt to take another living adult with him into death.

Informant accounts indicate that sometimes the dying man called for a specific child to accompany him in the grave (often one of his own daughters), but more often, other band members decided which child to bury alive, after the death had occurred. Mothers sometimes volunteered their small infants, but most mothers that we interviewed admitted being very upset when one of their children was killed. Fathers, too, occasionally volunteered their own children, although informants hint that some men knew ahead of time that the child would be rescued by another close relative (thus a "sacrificial offering" did not always represent a sincere offering). Informants insist that many of the child victims were orphaned or defective and unlikely to be cared for effectively. They admit a strong negative feeling toward children with no father who would "be constantly begging for food." Almost any child could be saved, even after being chosen, if an adult came forward "to defend the child," and offered to take care of the child and raise it to adulthood. Many of our informants recalled being dragged to a graveside, only to be saved by a godparent, aunt, or grandparent, after their father had died. Not surprisingly the memories of these traumatic events seem etched into their memories for life. This ritual child homicide, which is well described by Clastres (1972a), has noticeable effects on the sex ratio of certain age classes, as well as a significant impact on overall child mortality rates. A quantitative description of this pattern is presented in Chapter 13.

Two important ritual events have an impact on the lives of forest-dwelling Ache, and they have important implications for demographic studies. First are the puberty ceremonies. At her first menses, a girl would be treated as a newborn child—she was held, lifted, massaged, and washed by adults of both sexes, who then took on a ritual relationship with the girl. The men with whom she had sexual relations prior to menarche (most girls had sexual intercourse before menarche) were also washed at this time. The girl was then covered from head to foot with woven mats and forced to lie or sit still for several days, or weeks (we have never observed this in the forest, as seclusion now takes place inside a house for about two weeks). The girl was not allowed to show her face or uncover herself during this time. She could only walk if she needed to perform bodily functions, and she was required to adhere to a few minor food taboos. After this period of isolation, the girl underwent a scarification rite. An older man using a sharp object (broken glass in recent times) would cut parallel lines in the back, legs, arms, buttocks, and stomach of the girl, while she lay horizontally holding the trunk of a felled palm. This experience was extremely painful (the cuts are about one-quarter to one-half inch deep), and most women admitted that they cried during the process. After the cuts were made, charcoal dust was rubbed into the wound. When the scars healed they left long sets of parallel lines with a bluish tint from the charcoal.

Boys underwent initiation when they were between fourteen and about eighteen years old (some claim to have been much older). This rite consisted of first perforating the lower lip for a lip plug, and later scarification like that described for girls. The lip perforation often accompanied the birth of a child, or the first menses of a girl, and individuals who experienced these events together were called *kmanove,* or "those who suffered together." Sometimes, however, two to eight boys of the correct age would be gathered together specifically for the purpose of the lip piercing ritual. After the lower lip was punctured with a sharp bone, a small piece of bamboo was introduced to keep the hole from healing over. The boys were not allowed to eat any food for several days, and boiling water was constantly applied to their wound so it would not become infected (one boy in our sample died of infection after lip piercing). The boys were kept in a tall palm hut made for the ritual, and a mock or real club fight often followed the lip perforation. In this club fight, the boys were approached by older men with clubs, and the one who perforated each boy's lip "defended" him against the others in mock battle. Later, when their lips had healed, the boys wore long pointed labrets made of wood or bone. Adult men rarely, if ever, wore lip plugs, an observation that incorrectly led some early ethnographers to assume that the Ache were rapidly and forcibly deculturated after contact.

The initiation ceremony was an extremely important rite of passage because it marked the point at which boys were "allowed" to have sexual relations, marry, and were subject to club fighting challenges. Although most adolescent boys were anxious for the sexual privileges (which they may have been enjoying covertly for some time), all men we interviewed were apprehensive about club fights when they were newly initiated. For this reason, some boys tried to wait as long as possible before being initiated, and some fathers withheld their sons from the rite, claiming they were still too young (the fathers also did not want their sons to marry at a young age according to several informants). After boys were initiated they generally left their parent's band and went to reside for some time period with the man who had pierced their lip and with their *kmanove*. Since this period was usually followed by a period of residence with a new bride's family following early marriages, the male initiation often marked the end of a boy's residence with his nuclear family, if it had not in fact effectively ended earlier.

The second major ritual event in Ache society was the club fight. Club fights could be "organized" or happen spontaneously. Before contact there was no other socially sanctioned form of aggression between Ache men who were *irondy* or "of the same people." Even now, Ache men do not yell at, argue with, or scold each other in a confrontational manner, and they never hit or shove each other. Indeed, we have never observed a scuffle between Ache men in seventeen years of work with them. No member of the same group was ever allowed to shoot another group member with an arrow under any circumstances, but anyone not in the group, including other Ache, could be shot on sight. In the twentieth century we know of only one case in which this cultural rule was broken. Club fights were the sole allowable form of male confrontation. Thus, for example, if a man caught another man in a liaison with his wife, he could either ignore the event, beat his wife, or challenge the opponent to a club fight. Spontaneous club fights were immediate outbursts of anger over a serious event. They almost always involved a wife's infidelity. Occasionally men also reported spontaneous club fights when members of unfriendly bands accidentally encountered each other in the forest.

Organized club fights were more common than spontaneous ones in Ache history and had an impact on almost every Ache who lived in the forest. They were described as dreadfully awesome by all informants—men, women, and children. When the few simulated and mock club fights that we witnessed in recent years got temporarily out of control they were indeed terrifying. Organized club fights were often called to exact revenge for an event that could be "blamed" on some individual or individuals. If children were captured or killed by Paraguayans, or killed in any freak accident (such as lightning striking, or a tree falling), a relative, a man who had provided the essence, or a godparent of the child might call for a club fight in order to avenge the child's death. The death of an important adult very often led to an organized club fight. In addition, older and powerful adult males would sometimes call club fights "just because they wanted/liked to." Informants admit that in addition to calling club fights in order to avenge the victim of an accident, club fighting was organized by big men so that each man could "display one's strength . . . to show how strong we are."

In order to bring together the 10–15 bands that might be scattered as far as 100 km apart, runners were sent out with the message that a club fight was to be held at some location. Not all bands attended, and some purposely avoided the event. Nevertheless, usually close to half the Northern Ache group would attend a single "organized" club fight. The camp would sometimes grow to include 300–400 people. Bands generally camped about 100 m apart. Those hosting the club fight would clear an area the size of a football field down to bare earth. All roots, trunks, and stumps were completely removed. During this time each adult man began making his club, a two-meter-long hardwood bat with sharp edges on two sides. Clubs were decorated with a charcoal and beeswax mixture in a pattern with a variety of spots and stripes.

When the fighting area was cleared, old men would be sent to each band to inform the others that the next morning the fight would begin. During this time, each man paid close attention to the gossip in order to determine who his enemies might be. Young men and newly initiated adolescents were particularly concerned, as they might be challenged if they had made enemies. Most boys who had not engaged in blatant sexual affairs with an older man's wife or insulted another man indirectly might participate in their first few club fights without serious combat. Eventually, however, every man made enemies.

On the morning of combat, men painted themselves black and stuck white vulture feathers on their body, using a mixture of honey and charcoal. Each band entered the arena with a deafening roar as men stared at each other, huddled together, and worked each other into a frenzy with low throaty growls. Bands might line up temporarily, but as new bands began to arrive in the clearing from different directions, the procession soon broke into chaos. Men dashed across the clearing, seeking out their enemies and uttering low howls that sent chills up the spine. The clubs were swung directly overhead and brought crashing down on skulls, collarbones, arms, and other vulnerable parts of the anatomy. Sometimes a man's worst enemy was from his own band, and men soon turned on their neighbors. The fight would become a free-for-all with only two rules: Hit any man that you dislike; and help defend your close kin and friends. Fathers, sons, and brothers often stayed close together to form powerful coalitions. Sometimes, however, personal friendship alliances temporarily outweighed kin obligations, and a brother would rush off to help a friend, leaving the other sibling vulnerable. Seeing such an opportunity, an enemy of the two brothers might then viciously attack the lone brother, who until that time had been part of a coalition too powerful to challenge. This in turn might provoke an unrelated ally of the lone brother to come rushing to his aid.

Club fights usually lasted until there were almost no men left standing, perhaps from 8 AM until 3 PM, without formal breaks or rests. Children watched from high in the trees surrounding the field of combat. Women with small infants screamed and ran at the approach of men, who could seriously injure a child by swinging wildly without paying attention to bystanders. Women without infants would often rush into the fray to defend their male kin. These women might grab and hold the club of a man trying to hit their brother, son, or father (it does not seem they defended husbands very often). Not all men showed the admirable courage expected. Some would run and hide from the outset, and almost all would prudently retreat if sufficiently outnumbered. Men who displayed blatant cowardice were scolded, especially by the old women.

When the club fight finally ended, animosities were supposed to be forgotten. More often, however, newer and stronger animosities were generated as the result of the battle. Men who had no enemies would suddenly find themselves badly disposed towards those they had seen hit their father or brothers. Immediately after the club fight all the women sat in a circle weeping, while male kin hit them with their hands and with sticks. During the days after the club fight everyone would suffer from hunger. Most men were injured and sore, with broken bones and flesh wounds. Some women, too, might be seriously hurt. Only the healthy women were able to provide food. They would bring palm fiber and other collected resources, but after a few days the huge camp would deplete nearby resources. All informants describe this as a miserable time, when children were constantly crying from fear and hunger and the camp was filled with the moans of injured combatants.

In the first few days some men might die, but most recovered, even if their skulls had been split after a direct hit. Many Ache men have multiple large dents in their skulls, evidence of past fights and their ability to recover. As men recovered, they began to hunt again. Soon the camp would be full of meat and the misery forgotten. This was a pleasant social time, when people could renew old acquaintances with people they may not have seen for years. Individuals assessed the composition of various bands to determine if a switch would be desirable. Some adults might abandon their spouses and set off with new ones. Young men and women carried out secret meetings, becoming lovers and sometimes initiating a marriage. Adolescent children became aware of potential mates, flirting and teasing with each other. After six weeks or so of recovery, the bands would set off again, each in a different direction. "I'm headed for fish creek," one old man would say. His offspring and brother and several other unrelated families would accompany him. "I'm going back to where I cut many palms, over by the parrot mud lick," another would announce. "They must be loaded with fat larvae, and that is what I want to eat now."

Another man might say nothing, but just sneak off with his wife and a few others, hoping not to attract the attention of his wife's new lover, who might attempt to come along. Some people would leave with one band and then return the next day after changing their mind. Eventually, all the Ache had to choose. The individuals with whom one left might be the only Ache seen for many months. This was a crucial decision since anything could happen. "Suppose my husbands dies," a woman might think. "Who will I be stuck living with then, and who will defend my children?" These considerations must have loomed important in the mind of each individual. Each time two bands met and parted, a decision could be made, but at club fights there were many new options.

Thus in many ways club fights were the most important social events of Ache forest life. They caused deaths, but also built friendships. They allowed men to assess the value of the alliances they had been cultivating, and also the strengths and weaknesses of their competitors. They allowed women to evaluate men according to the criteria of strength, bravery, agility, and alliance connections. Finally, they provided the only opportunity for members of the entire group of Northern Ache to get to know each other and learn about potential mates. Large planned club fights were not frequent events, usually taking place only once every two to three years. Nevertheless, the six weeks or so that the bands were camped together could in many ways be considered the most critical periods of their life.

It is very likely that the "cultural" patterns described in this section ultimately both constrain and were constrained by the patterns of births and deaths that will be presented in later chapters. Indeed, understanding the types of factors that affect fertility and mortality outcomes provides much of the information necessary to "imagine" some of what individual Ache men, women, and children must have been concerned about during important social events such as puberty rites and club fights. Behavioral observations allow us to assess how they reacted to those concerns.

RESERVATION LIFE

After contact the Northern Ache continued to forage frequently in the forest, sometimes staying for weeks or months at a time. In the early years of our study (1977–1980) the Ache did very little work at the permanent settlements and spent long periods of time in the forest, hunting and gathering. For example, in 1978 one group of Ache spent five and a half months in the forest without visiting a mission settlement. Later that year Hill spent another forty-seven days in the forest with a group of about fifty people. Nevertheless, the Ache have now developed a new set of options and a new lifestyle at reservation settlements. The Chupa Pou colony, where most of the data in this study were collected, had a school, sometimes a health clinic, a small store, and a soccer field, in 1989. The mission is run by Catholic missionaries of the Divine Word order. In 1989 one priest, one seminary student, and a schoolteacher resided at the mission.

Through time, younger Ache have learned slash-and-burn agriculture and raise some domestic animals. This change has been very gradual, but now in the late 1980s the Ache have essentially become a settlement/trekking population, with an economic pattern similar to that described for many South American horticulturists (e.g., Mekranoti [Werner 1983]; Akwe Xavante [Maybury-Lewis 1967]; Yanomamo [Good 1989]). Random spot checks of the population at the Chupa Pou mission between 1980 and 1989 show that the population spent about 37% of all days trekking in the forest in 1980, 25% in 1982, 21% in 1984 and 1985, 18% in 1987, and only 12% during the short 1989 field session. In 1992, however, there was a renewed emphasis on foraging, with one band spending more than a month in the forest during our field period. In 1993, when the Ache received temporary title to a new piece of land adjoining their reservation, a small group of about nine families moved to the remotest corner of the reservation and was living completely off foraging during the time that we visited. Trekking in the forest away from the large settlements is now common primarily during particular seasons of the year. In seasons when gardening tasks demand daily labor, the Ache rarely leave the settlement for overnight trips. During these periods, nighttime tree stand hunting near the settlement has become increasingly common. This technique was never observed in 1980–1982, but by 1989 the man in whose house Hill lived went out on 28% of the sample days for night hunting; only 11% of sample days were spent on overnight forest trips, and 39% of sample days were characterized by short day hunts lasting from two to six hours.

While time spent in the forest has diminished and then increased over the past decade, the size of horticultural gardens has increased and then diminished. In 1980 the entire population had only about 5 hectares under cultivation. By 1982 this total had risen to about 25 hectares, and in 1989 there were about 81.5 hectares under active cultivation (Renshaw 1989). By 1992 total garden size was cut back to perhaps only 40 hectares. During the 1989 peak, cleared land amounted to about 1 hectare for every 3.6 individuals. The majority of the cultivated land in 1989 was planted in cotton (24 hectares), an inedible cash crop. Major edible cultigens were manioc (12.5 hectares) and maize (26 hectares). The emphasis on cash cropping has fluctuated a good deal in recent years. After a series of bad years near the end of the 1980s and early 1990s we observed much smaller gardens in 1992 and 1993, virtually no cash cropping, and a renewed interest in foraging as an important economic activity.

Equally important changes have taken place in the wage labor economy. In 1980 only a handful of Ache could count to ten, and only about five teenage boys made cash purchases at a nearby Paraguayan store during the entire year. By 1982 most families spent some cash earned from wage labor, handicrafts, or selling forest products (mainly animal skins). This amounted to about $6.50 per family per month according to records of the only two stores within walking distance (Hawkes et al. 1987). By 1989 the Ache had begun to run their own cooperative store, and the cash flow was impressive, even by rural Paraguayan standards. Although the population had been essentially broke through 1987, in late 1988 they received legal title to their reservation. This prompted a spree of selling off all the valuable timber on the land, resulting in a cash glut by the time Hill visited in May–July 1989. People were well dressed, had new houses and radios, and spent considerable money on food at the cooperative store. Although we do not have data on expenditures we would estimate that monthly cash expenditures were about 4–5 times higher than what we observed in 1982. Some individual Ache men spent close to $30 in a single day on food, gambling, and soft drinks for friends.

In July of 1990 the boom had ended and the Ache were back to living as small-scale horticulturists. The cooperative store had gone broke (prior store workers were dismissed for embezzlement but had nothing to show for their "gains") and very few Ache made significant purchases during that month. Two years later a systematic assessment of familial net worth revealed a startling result. The Chupa Pou and Arroyo Bandera Ache in 1992 had a net worth of only about $12 per nuclear family, including all housing materials, store-bought tools, clothing, food, livestock, and miscellaneous items as well as the value of all traditional tools and handicrafts in each house. This was lower than the net worth of the same people thirteen years earlier when we finished our first field session with them. Simply put, the Ache have not accumulated any property whatsoever since the late 1970s and continue to be (along with some other indigenous groups) the poorest people in Paraguay.

Social changes have accompanied these slow economic changes. The political structure has shifted such that very young men now wield the greatest influence in the community. Since the late 1980s there is also a pattern of increasing political dominance by Ache who lived for some time with Paraguayans as children. These Ache, called *berupuare* or "those who come from the Para-guayans," are generally more educated, politically astute, and aggressive than the Ache who never lived with Paraguayans. They are also more likely to form alliances with missionaries, Indian rights workers, government officials, and others in order to leverage their way into power at the current reservations. Older men still lead most forest treks and are listened to respectfully by the young leaders in community discussions, but they very rarely participate in formal gatherings. Instead, the older people wield their influence behind the scenes through grumbling and complaining if they are unhappy about decisions reached by younger leaders. Three elected chiefs represent the community legally and settle all disputes both within the community and between most community members and outsiders. Chiefs were originally recalled by new elections, held whenever a sufficient number of individuals are unhappy with the status quo. Recently, however, Catholic missionaries have pushed the Ache to set formal five-year terms for chief. Candidates are asked to stand in a certain spot, and Ache men, women, and children line up behind the candidate of their choice. The candidate with the longest line of followers wins the election. Some elections have been won primarily by the children's vote, which does not necessarily match that of their parents. In all elections, the two most important qualities of the winning candidates are competence dealing with outsiders and kindness (fairness) to fellow Ache. Those who make blatant economic gain from chieftainship, or who rule with an authoritarian manner, are usually quick to be removed by community vote.

Residence patterns have also changed through time. In the early days, the settlement consisted of one large cluster of families in small huts living in close proximity. The entire Chupa Pou colony lived in a village area of about 100 by 40 m in 1979. By 1989 families had spread out and built solid permanent houses of wooden boards. Some families moved 3–4 km from the center of the settlement, where the school, store, and soccer field were located. These families often sent their children to live with relatives near the school and visited the center of the settlement only once or twice a month. Because families live so far apart, food sharing in 1989 was often limited to only a few nearest neighbors and relatives. This contrasted sharply with early days at the settlement, when gigantic communal meals were often prepared and the entire population ate their meals together each day.

Mission evangelical activities have produced some permanent changes in Ache behavioral patterns as well. About a quarter of the Chupa Pou settlement, mainly women, attend church for an hour once a week, and occasionally attend mid-week for a song session. Preachers are young Ache men who exhort their listeners in stern tones to follow the rules laid out by Jesus. Many of the rules advocated, however, are interpretations, patterns convenient to the preacher himself, or Euroamerican cultural patterns taught by well-meaning missionaries. The preachers generally advocate a set of sociobehavioral patterns that is extremely biased toward serving male interests (e.g., women should unhesitatingly and obediently follow the commands of the men in the society; women should not engage in extramarital affairs; women should stay home and take care of the children) and the audience, which is partially coerced (by verbal prodding) into attendance, is mainly female. The impact of Christianity was due initially to the influence of the American Protestant missionaries at the Cerro Moroti reservation, rather than the Catholic missionaries at Chupa Pou. More recently, however both Catholics and Protestants have been involved in evangelical activities at every Ache reservation, and missionaries come from a variety of Latin American countries as well as the United States and Europe. Finally, although the Ache preachers stress the importance of Christian fundamentalist (and occasionally Euroamerican) values in their weekly sermons, it seems doubtful that the preaching alone (without the other social and economic changes) has seriously influenced the Ache lifestyle, and the preachers themselves often violate their own teachings (which generally leads to installation of a new preacher, who begins the cycle all over again).

Despite the religious teachings, the Ache continue to engage in frequent extra- and premarital sex; they sometimes commit infanticide; a few lie, steal, and cheat others out of money, gamble, and beat their wives. Despite discouragement from evangelical missionaries the Ache still share food communally, divorce each other frequently, drink alcohol and smoke tobacco, and commit a variety of other minor sins from the evangelical perspective. In other words, the Ache behave much like any other peasant or indigenous population that we have observed in South America. They are also acutely aware that other "Christians" who profess the same beliefs engage in the same "sins" as do the Ache. In fact, they comment openly about the shortcomings of their own missionaries, who sometimes berate them vigorously for particular sins but are just as guilty of committing others (from the Ache point of view). In addition, along with the acceptance of Christian religious beliefs, the Ache have increasingly become believers in the witchcraft and magic belief systems that characterize rural Paraguayan culture.

One sad effect of this exposure to organized religion has been the almost complete abandonment of Ache singing among all but the Ñacunday Ache. Evangelical missionaries taught the Ache that their "chants" were evil and should be abandoned. Catholic missionaries have used simple religious songs as a way to communicate with younger Ache and entice them on the road to Christianity. Neither group of missionaries has ever encouraged the Ache to sing in their own language. Even though these beautiful Ache songs have no spiritual content (the missionaries cannot understand the words in any case) and are often a form of spontaneous social expression, they have all but ceased to be heard in today's mission settlements. Instead they have been replaced by almost childlike translations of Protestant religious songs sung to western tunes. Ironically, the few verses are sometimes repeated hours at a time in a fashion which sounds much more like a "chant" than did the original spontaneously worded Ache singing.

Many social patterns have *not* changed much since first peaceful contact. The marriage system, one of frequent spouse switching during the early years of adult life, has remained relatively unchanged for the past twelve years. Residence after first marriage is still essentially matrilocal, and many children still have multiple recognized fathers (although mothers are more reluctant to admit this publicly). Men and women touch each other in public and flirt openly, despite the fact that Paraguayans and missionaries never engage in similar behaviors. Birth still takes place in a very public setting as described above, and the godparenting and naming systems are still active and important. The female puberty ceremony is still carried out, but without scarification. The male puberty ceremony, and club fights, however, have been completely abandoned.

Despite the changes that they have experienced in the past decade, most Ache adults seem happy and content on a daily basis, although recently they seem to be suffering from increasing nutritional stress and accompanying health problems. Since the abatement of the disastrous epidemics they have not had a difficult time adjusting to their new lifestyle, and they do not particularly regret the loss of many of their old cultural patterns. None of them expresses a desire to return to their forest lifestyle despite some naive attempts by well-meaning anthropologists and indigenous rights workers to convince them of the desirability of their former way of life. Their major concerns in life are keeping themselves and their children well fed and healthy, and maintaining high status *within the Ache community*. They show relatively little concern with their status in the larger Paraguayan society, nor do they seem to care much what most rural Paraguayans think about them or their lifestyle. Their biggest dreams are usually to acquire a shotgun, some new clothes, and perhaps a radio, and to have many healthy children grow to adulthood.

Although the Ache appear to be a typical semi-acculturated South American indigenous population we still note something slightly different. They are not like the half-dozen other South American native groups with whom we have worked or lived. The Ache, deep down, are still foragers. When they enter the forest they almost immediately slip into the old patterns of the past. They are the most competent forest people we have ever seen, and the most generous in sharing their food with each other in a band-level context. Their hunting and tracking skills and arboreal agility far surpass those of any other lowland South American population we have observed (including Ava Guarani, Piro, Machiguenga, Yaminahua, Hiwi, and Yanomamo). Their daily energy expenditure in the forest is truly phenomenal compared with that of the other groups we have observed. Despite the changes in their diet and activity patterns they continue to be characterized by an extremely robust and muscular body morphology. They generally shun figures of authority or the opportunity to "rule over" others. They smile and laugh constantly, and have an easy style of interpersonal interaction across all age and sex categories. They are very affectionate in public, with each other and with outsiders who are involved in their world. And although they are interested in bettering their standard of living when possible, they are not obsessed with materialistic gain or success. Instead they seem to value high-quality friendships and social interaction above all else.

SUMMARY

The Ache are a Tupi-Guarani speaking group of hunter-gatherers who may have lived in Paraguay for as long as 10,000 years according to archaeological data. They show many similarities to other trekking and foraging groups originally present in the Eastern Brazilian Highlands, and they differ culturally from their traditional enemies, the village-dwelling Guarani. The Ache had divided into four autonomous groups by the twentieth century. The Northern Ache roamed the previously depopulated primary forested regions of Eastern Paraguay, covering a home range area of about 18,500 km². The area is mainly mature forest with strong temperature seasonality and weak, unpredictable seasonal changes in rainfall. The forests of the Northern Ache are characterized by low species diversity and animal biomass relative to other South American tropical forests. Nevertheless, important Ache game animals are often exceptionally vulnerable to human hunters, and thus hunting is productive and contributes the majority of food in the Ache diet. The most important economic activities of women are extracting palm starch, fruits, and insect larvae. Important ritual events include birth purification, puberty ceremonies, and club fights. Club fights were an extremely important social event among the precontact Ache because they provided the only context in which the entire Northern Ache group would gather. The Northern Ache experienced first peaceful outside contact in the early 1970s. Shortly after that contact nearly one-third of the population died from contact-related respiratory disease. After contact in the 1970s the Ache began a transition to reservation life. Currently settlement life includes small-scale subsistence horticulture, some cash crop agriculture, and wage labor primarily by adolescent males. Ache social and political life is in a state of transition as well, with missionary and Paraguayan peasant influence increasing through time. Although the Ache are one of the poorest groups of people in the Americas they are generally content as long as their children are healthy and they maintain good relations with their neighbors.

NOTES

1.   The census figures presented in this chapter do not include Northern Ache who were captured and removed from the group but were still known to be alive. Our identification files show exactly 544 Northern Ache alive and not captured at the end of 1970. A small number of older individuals without surviving close relatives may not have been included in this count.

2.   Clastres (1972a) refers to the Ypety Ache as *Ache gatu* and the Yvytyruzu group he calls *irollangi*. Unfortunately we also used different names for these four Ache groups in previous publications. In Hill (1983a) and Hill and Kaplan (1988a) we called the Ypety group the "Yñaro Ache." Anyone concerned with this confusion should read the description of the home range carefully and refer to Figure 2.1 in order to determine which label applies to which group.

3.   Our census of this group acquired through informant interview shows twenty-six adults and ten children. Chase-Sardi (1971) also reports thirty-six individuals but with a

slightly different age composition, which may be due to different definitions of who is an adult. Melia et al. (1973:49) claim that forty-seven Ache were captured. Their report is erroneous, as is their claim that twenty members of the band died after contact. Demographic data that we collected show that thirteen individuals of Kuareijugi's band died at Cerro Moroti in 1971–1972 from contact-related respiratory infections.

Figure 2.1. Location of Ache groups reported during the seventeenth and twentieth centuries. The actual boundaries of groups 5 and 6 are unknown.

Members of the Ache band that first made contact in 1975 at the Manduvi Catholic Mission. Four individuals in this photo had died from contact-related respiratory disease within one year, and the fifth was taken by Paraguayans (photo by Miguel Chase Sardi, reproduced with permission).

3

Study Population and Sampling Methods

In this book we hope to describe the demographic parameters that characterized the Northern Ache during much of the past hundred years, from about 1890 to 1993. The Ache are of considerable interest because they are hunter-gatherers, but the patterns described in this book are not "representative" of hunter-gatherers. Instead, they represent demographic outcomes observed under certain conditions *specific to the recent Ache situation.* As such, our goal will be to use the Ache data to understand the relationship between ecological factors and life history patterns, not to project the Ache pattern by analogy to some other time or place in human or hominid history.

Ache life history could hypothetically be described by sampling the target population in a manner that does not introduce bias into the data set and then carrying out appropriate analyses. The procedure consists of first identifying the set of all individuals at risk of a particular life history event (e.g., a birth or death). This is called the risk set. Then we tabulate how many events took place during a unit of time (the risk unit) to individuals in the risk set and calculate the rate of the event (number of events divided by the number of individuals at risk). For example, in order to estimate the mortality rates for the forest Ache in the twentieth century we could randomly sample some proportion of all births that took place during that time, and then record how and when each individual died. All individuals born would be in the risk set until they died. In practice, however, the sample is much more complicated. First, it is impossible to sample randomly from all births during the twentieth century because we have not been observing the population directly during that entire time, and we cannot be sure that retrospective interviews would allow us to record all the Ache who lived or were born during this century. Indeed, most of the individuals born this century have already died, and we can only get information about them by interviewing living individuals. We must seriously consider what types of biases may be introduced in these interviews. Second, many individuals have not yet died, but excluding them from the sample will provide a very misleading picture of mortality. Third, the Northern Ache underwent radical demographic changes during the contact period and afterwards. Although the postcontact demographic patterns are of considerable interest, they must be kept separate from the patterns before contact. Finally, in order to describe a population, we must define who is included or excluded in the population and sample accordingly. Each of these problems will be discussed below, or in subsequent chapters.

STUDY POPULATION

The study population is composed of the group called Northern Ache, and our demographic sample spans the period from 1890 to the end of 1993. Our last complete census of the Ache was carried out in 1989, and reproductive histories of all Ache adults are complete to that year, but we have also collected demographic data on about half the population up through August 1994. We define Northern Ache as anyone who was born to a Northern Ache woman who was affiliated with an Ache reservation in 1989. Although the Yvytyruzu group split from the Northern Ache in the 1930s, they will not be included here because members of that group have not been systematically interviewed. From the time of this population split until 1971 the Northern Ache represent a closed breeding population: there was no marriage into or out of the group, and no migration into the group. The only outmigration consisted of children captured in warfare, who usually disappeared permanently and are counted as deaths in this study. Although it is very difficult to estimate the Northern Ache population size at the beginning of this century, by 1930 we have band reconstruction data that allow for an estimate of the population size at 241 individuals with perhaps some of the smallest children missing from the data base (Figure 3.1). By 1970, the year before first peaceful contact, the forest-living population can be estimated at 544 individuals. Thus, the forest population grew at 2% per year in the forty years prior to peaceful contact. The age and sex structure of the precontact population will be described in the next chapter.

After contact the Northern Ache population experienced great turmoil. By 1976 virgin soil epidemics had killed about 48% of the population that was living in 1970, and the population had only about 338 living members. Massive outmigration to live with Paraguayans claimed another 11% of the 1970 population during this same period. This "outmigration" was primarily due to Ache adults selling orphaned children, and Paraguayans forcibly removing Ache children and adolescents from the population, to be used as laborers or to exploit sexually. In addition, some Ache adults simply left to live with Paraguayans and never returned.

By 1977, when Hill first arrived in Paraguay, much of the contact turmoil was over. No additional Ache were forcibly removed from the population, and some of those children who had lived for a time with Paraguayan families began to return. Others were known to be dead, or married to Paraguayans and Guarani Indians, but many suffered unknown fates. The Ache who have returned are now called *berupuare*, or "those who came from the Paraguayans." They have, for the most part, readjusted to Ache life and become incorporated into the society. They have married Ache who never left the population, and often bring important new skills that are absent among the "naive" population. Nevertheless, because many of them grew up among rural Paraguayans, and because many of them began their reproductive careers as rural Paraguayans before returning to the Ache, the years that these berupuare lived with Paraguayans have been eliminated from the sample used to calculate fertility and mortality parameters. These years were not characterized by the same mortality and fertility conditions as those experienced by the remainder of the postcontact population, and their inclusion would only make the sample more complicated than it already is. The berupuare represented 4.3% of the 1987 adult female population and 5.0% of the adult male population. These individuals were removed from the risk set when they began living with Paraguayans and are only reentered in the risk set after they have come back to live in an Ache settlement for one year.

After 1971, Northern Ache adults also began to intermarry with Ache from other groups. Because we have defined children as Northern Ache if their mother belonged to that group, this does not lead to further complications in the sample; however, the rate of intermarriage is of some interest. Surprisingly, in 1989 no Northern Ache adult, male or female, was married to any non-Ache.[1] In the 1987 census, marriages by Northern Ache women to Ache men of the various groups were as follows: Northern Ache men, 94; Yvytyruzu men, 12; Ypety men, 4. The marriages recorded for Northern Ache men to women of the various groups were as follows: Northern Ache women, 94; Yvytyruzu women, 14; Ypety women, 3. The data thus indicate that about 15% of all Northern Ache are married to Ache from another group, mainly from the closely related Yvytyruzu group. Children of Northern Ache men whose mothers come from another group are by definition not members of the sample and have been excluded from all analyses except in the chapters where we examine male fertility patterns.

THE SAMPLE AND METHODS OF DATA COLLECTION

Anthropological demographers have recently become aware that too little attention is often paid to the methods that have been used to arrive at particular conclusions (see Chapter 2 in Pennington and Harpending 1993). This issue is critical since anthropological demographers see their enterprise as essentially scientific rather than interpretative. The reputation of the specialty is frequently undercut by shoddy methods or, even worse, methods that are left unspecified. Often only a few short sentences vaguely describe field and analytic methods, and the reader is supposed to be assured by statements like "the data were extensively cross-checked and the authors have high confidence in their accuracy." Superficial reporting of methods provides very little insight into potential sampling bias, relies heavily on collegial trust, and ultimately decreases the chance that significant mistakes will ever be detected or corrected. Thus, in the spirit of collective research it is essential that methods in anthropological demography be detailed despite the space required for the publication of such details. We dedicate the remainder of this chapter to specifying the characteristics of our sample, how information was obtained, and why only some of it was used for particular questions. The next chapter explains how we dated events that happened during unobserved periods of time.

At the end of 1989 the study population consisted of 537 living Northern Ache who resided at Ache settlements. Of these, 144 were females ten years of age or older and 194 were males at least ten years old. Complete reproductive histories of these individuals and a handful of adults who died between 1980 and 1989, plus reproductive histories of their deceased children, siblings, parents, grandparents, and parents' siblings, are the basis of most of the analyses presented in this book and comprise most of the MASTERIDENTIFICATION (master ID) file used for computer analyses. This data base is derived from six different types of interviews conducted at least once (and often several times) with almost all living adults. These interviews were about the reproductive history and offspring survivorship of: ego, ego's offspring, ego's siblings (maternal), ego's parents, ego's parents' parents, and ego's parents' siblings. A few additional individuals are listed in the master ID file who were identified in interviews about precontact band composition. Data from all six types of interviews were used only in the calculations of adult mortality rates; appropriate subsets of the master ID file are used for other analyses in this book.

In each interview type mentioned above, all offspring were listed in birth order along with the parents as well as information about year of birth, year of death, and cause of death for each child. Hypothetically this information could be used to estimate fertility and mortality rates over most of the study period. Systematic inspection for reporting bias, however, suggests that only subsets of the data are appropriate for estimating some demographic parameters (see below).

Reproductive histories were thus obtained either by direct observation and frequent censuses with prospective interview data (from 1977 to 1994) or through retrospective interviews conducted between 1981 and 1992. The entire data set consists of eight different classes of data obtained by three different methods: (1) direct observation/repeated census of the study population from 1977 to 1994; (2) six classes of interviews about reproductive histories of kin before 1977; and (3) interviews about family genealogies and band compositions prior to 1971. Direct observation/census data are commonly employed in small-population demographic research to describe patterns during a period of observation, and ego reproductive history interviews are used to identify patterns prior to the observation period. The other classes of interview data we employed are not commonly collected, but they provide a more complete and unbiased sample of the past and allow for analyses of trade-offs between life history traits. Several classes of data are briefly described below in order to provide more specific information about how and why they were collected.

Direct Observation

We began to work with the Ache in 1977 and had spent 51 months living with them by early 1995. Field periods were as follows:

January 1978–March 1979	15 months
March–July 1980	5 months
September 1981–April 1982	8 months
September 1984–February 1985	6 months
July–November 1987	4 months
June–July 1989	2 months
July–August 1990	1 month
July–August 1992	2 months
June–July 1993	2 months
March 1994	1 month
May–August 1994	3 months
January–March 1995	2 months

During each field session we took a complete census of the Chupa Pou and Arroyo Bandera colonies, recording all births and deaths that had taken place since the last field period and estimating the date of the event. By 1980 many Ache knew the western calendar system and kept careful track of birth dates, which were celebrated with a feast given by the parents of each child. In addition, missionaries from two of the Ache colonies kept records of births and deaths, which were generously provided to us. In 1993 and 1994 data were collected by an Ache research assistant, Martin Achipurangi. This data base provides a complete record of demographic patterns during the past seventeen years for the study population with very accurate information on dates and ages. Individuals whose entire reproductive careers took place during this time were generally not interviewed directly, except during the process of taking the census. This data base is not a sample, rather it is a *complete description* of fertility and mortality rates for the entire study population during the time period.

Interview about the Reproductive History of Living Adults

Seventy-nine of the *living* Northern Ache women began their reproductive careers before 1977. Sixty-three were interviewed directly and information for the remaining sixteen was obtained from a sister or daughter (see below). Eighty-six living men began their reproductive careers before 1977. Fifty-nine of them were interviewed directly, and information about the remainder came from a living brother or sister. Several of the men and women were interviewed more than once (a maximum of four times) in order to check the reliability of the interviews (described below). Despite carrying out interviews over an eleven-year period, we were unable to interview all the living adults in the population because of their very high mobility. For example, we might leave one settlement to visit another in hopes of collecting reproductive histories from several women there. When we arrived, one would be out in the forest, and of the remaining two, one might pack up and leave the next day to visit the settlement from which we had come. Thus, our original goal of interviewing all living adults was not achieved. In any case, information obtained from siblings and offspring is very reliable (see below) and there is little reason to be concerned about the fact that reproductive histories were not collected directly from all men and women.

Interviews with individual women and men were structured around a format of questions and were taped. They were conducted in the Ache language by one of the two of us working alone with a single informant. Both of us had extensive personal knowledge of all informants and had spent time living in the houses of more than a dozen different Ache families. Kim had known personally every single adult in the Northern Ache population since 1980, and he had a long-term personal relationship with about half the study population. He also knew the complete genealogies of more than half the adult population before data collection began and thus could immediately spot any gross errors or misunderstandings during the formal interview. By 1987 Kim knew by memory the genealogies of all living Northern Ache back at least two generations, the marital histories of more than half the adults, and detailed information about several hundred deceased Ache. Both of us also used computer printouts with brief genealogical information and reproductive histories while conducting interviews. This detailed prior knowledge allowed for extremely interactive interviews. For example, we could say "Your sister must have had another child before she died because we know that her last husband carried a young son on his shoulders when he made first outside contact." Such cross-examination and requests for clarification made the interviews more fun for informants (they felt that we cared about them personally since we knew many details of their lives and their kin), and it encouraged them to be as accurate as possible.

All informants also knew endless details about our lives and work and had already been informed through the gossip network about our interview format before we began to work with them. Many of them asked for clarification of our own reproductive histories during the interview about theirs (e.g., "Now Kim, did you ever have a child who died before you met your current wife?"). No potential informant ever refused to be interviewed (we provided refreshments and yerba mate tea during the interview), and most appeared to enjoy talking about their reproductive histories as long as the interview did not last too long. However, after 1985 the interview format had to be changed because Ache community leaders (heavily influenced by evangelical missionaries) requested that we no longer ask questions about extramarital sexual relations and "multiple paternity" of *recently* born children (see Chapter 9). We agreed to discontinue data collection on these topics, and interviews continued with no additional objections. Some informants cried during interviews when discussing dead kin, but none were reluctant to talk about deceased individuals, and many went into great detail about the death of loved ones despite their obvious grief. Our overall impression is that Ache informants were extremely candid with us when compared with other groups from whom we have collected demographic data. This is due partly to Ache cultural norms, which stress public knowledge and honesty, and partly to our intimate knowledge of the people, their kin, and their history. The detailed nature of our data base became widely known among the Ache, and by 1991 they were coming to us with questions about genealogical connections and past demographic events. In March 1994, one Ache man asked Kim to recount the entire history of his father's and mother's relatives, who they were and how they had died. He had been orphaned in childhood and had wanted to verify rumors about who his half-cousins might be.

Demographic interviews were generally conducted in a private setting (e.g., a mission building, or our camp tent) but were occasionally conducted in public settings. Most interviews lasted about two or three hours before we quit for the day, and we generally took a break every hour to socialize for five or ten minutes. Incomplete interviews were continued the next day. When collecting reproductive histories we worked with a previously constructed list of ages and an Ache event calendar, which allowed us to place all events in a known time sequence that was later converted to a series of absolute dates (see Chapter 4). Thus, the interview was structured around a rather loosely defined life history calendar (see Freedman et al. 1988). Each individual was asked to place himself/herself in a relative age list. Women were asked about when they had reached menarche, and men were asked about their age when their lip was pierced. We then elicited a listing of all spouses in chronological order. For each spouse an individual was asked to list all pregnancies and the outcome of each. The date for each live birth was ascertained using the relative age list, and all dates and causes of death were recorded. A series of informal and friendly probes were used to insure that events were unlikely to be forgotten. For example, at the end of some period of time we often asked women "Are you sure you didn't have another husband before that child was born?" or "Are you sure you didn't have another child who died very small?" Probes (*sensu* Freedman et al. 1988) were used frequently and were particularly effective because we already knew a good deal about the reproductive histories of informants before the interviews were started. Thus, for example, we were often able to cross-examine informants when various versions of the same reproductive history did not agree. Although these ad libbed probes occasionally uncovered previously unreported events, they seemed crucial for conveying our interest in the absolute accuracy of the data and for keeping our informants interested and alert. Occasionally we would even repeat events incorrectly in order to evaluate informant concern for accuracy. For example we might say "so your second daughter died from diarrhea before she could stand" when in fact the informant had reported that the child died from respiratory disease after she was able to walk. If informants did not immediately correct us we would cross-examine previously recorded data from the same interview and generally take a short break to tell jokes, consume refreshments, and regain the informant's attention. Data from direct observation, regular censuses, and retrospective interviews were all pooled to calculate age-specific mortality and fertility rates that will be reported in later chapters.

Interview about Ego's Offspring and Siblings' Reproductive Histories

Interviews conducted only with living men and women do not provide a satisfying data base for several reasons. First, nothing is learned about the fertility of individuals who died before the interview period, or about the survivorship of their offspring. This could be critical if reproductive patterns and subsequent mortality are linked. Imagine, for example, that women who are likely to die younger also have lower fertility and higher offspring mortality. This scenario, in fact, is exactly what we might expect to find for women who are poorly nourished or sickly. Under such conditions, a sample of reproductive histories from currently living women will result in an incorrect estimate of past demographic parameters in the population. Indeed, under these conditions, data derived from interviews with living individuals would overestimate the fertility of the past population and underestimate child mortality (just the opposite bias could result if women who have higher fertility and higher child survivorship are more likely to die, perhaps because of their greater reproductive effort). Since there is good reason to suspect that many life history parameters (e.g., age at first reproduction, fertility rates, age at last reproduction, mortality rates) are interrelated and correlated (see Chapter 3 in Clutton-Brock 1991), it would be unwise to estimate past demographic parameters using only the currently living members of a cohort. Retrospective data may contain unwanted bias, but data collected from direct observation and censuses do not present this problem since women in any cohort who will eventually die early are represented in proportion to their contribution to the population.

The second problem with a data base that includes only the reproductive histories of living individuals is that such a data base does not provide the information necessary to examine the effects of parental death on the survivorship of offspring, or to examine the life history parameters (such as high or low fertility, birth spacing, or early menarche) that lead to higher mortality of reproductive-aged individuals. Since our goal is to understand variations in demographic parameters, and assess both their causes and consequences, we must expand the data base to include men and women who have not survived as long as others in their same cohort. Ideally, we should analyze entire cohorts, or a random sample of individuals from each cohort. In a population that does not keep records this is almost impossible since it requires a complete census of all individuals who lived at some point in time during the past, and accurate information about the reproductive histories of deceased individuals from some third party. Thus, a perfect solution to the shortcomings of using only interviews from living women is difficult to achieve. Nevertheless, a partial solution is simple and useful.

In order to include reproductive data on deceased men and women, we decided to collect reproductive histories on all the offspring and siblings of all surviving individuals using an interview similar to that used for ego. In these interviews age at puberty and a list of all spouses during the lifetime was not obtained since pilot studies showed such information to be unreliable. The remainder of the interview was identical to that administered to all adults who could be contacted. The sample produced from these interviews, while considerably larger than that obtained from living adults alone, still does not include all individuals in each cohort, since any individual who did not survive to the present, *and* has no surviving parents or siblings, will not be included in this sample of reproductive histories.

Interview about Ego's Parents' Reproductive Histories

Although interviews provide a good deal of information about recent demographic patterns, the time depth of the information is limited by the age of the oldest individuals in the population. For fertility studies this is not a serious problem, since many men and women will be past the age of reproduction. Unfortunately, mortality rates in anthropological populations are usually calculated from the outcomes of each birth listed in reproductive histories of living women. Although these data are useful, they retain an unfortunate limitation since the oldest individuals at risk of death in the sample will be the children of *living* women. This means that the sample of deaths to individuals older than about thirty-five years of age is extremely small (e.g., Chapter 4 in Howell 1979), and it is difficult or impossible to estimate the age-specific mortality rates for older individuals. A much larger sample of individuals at risk of death in older age can be obtained by systematically including all siblings of living adults in the risk set. We acquired such a list by obtaining complete reproductive histories of each living adult's parents.

It is important to remember that a data base including parental reproductive histories will result in a biased sample of fertility and childhood mortality because only men or women who have produced surviving adult offspring will be included in this sample. For this reason, data generated from these interviews are used only to calculate adult mortality rates. Most individuals know their own parents' reproductive careers well (see below) and they know particularly well the fate of all siblings who survived to adulthood. The mortality information gained from parental reproductive histories of every living individual will result in a nearly unbiased sample of adults at risk of death and will include the deaths of adult siblings. The adult mortality rates can thus be calculated from a risk set of all living adults and all of their siblings who survived to adulthood. This greatly increases the sample size for calculating mortality rates in the age classes 35–60.

Interview about Ego's Grandparents' Reproductive Histories

Because of the importance of accurately estimating adult mortality rates, it was considered useful to acquire an even larger sample of older adults at risk than would be available from the four interview types described above. The parental reproductive history interviews described above might normally result in a good deal of information about older individuals for most human populations, but because of the high mortality among the Ache at contact, this data base alone did not result in a large enough sample of information on individuals who reached (or had the opportunity to reach) old age in the forest before contact. In order to supplement the sample, interviews about the fate of siblings of the parents of living adults (i.e., their aunts and uncles) were conducted. In these interviews the informant was asked to list all the siblings of each parent (i.e., grandparental reproductive histories), place them in the relative age list, and report the date and cause of death for each. The results clearly showed that individuals could not reliably list siblings of their parents who had died young (see below), but parental siblings *who survived to adulthood* were generally listed consistently and completely. There remained some doubt, however, about whether parents' siblings who died in young adulthood and might never have been seen by ego would be reliably listed. For this reason, the data collected from these interviews is used only to assess causes and rates of mortality for individuals who survived to greater than fifty years of age. In no case did we ever discover a mother's or father's sibling who survived to an estimated age of fifty and was not recalled by our informants.

Interview about Ego's Parents' Siblings' Reproductive Histories

Some very important questions in human biology require information *only* about offspring who survive to adulthood (this is a rough measure of individual reproductive success or fitness). Preliminary investigation suggested that most adults could accurately and reliably list all their first cousins who survived to adulthood (see below). Thus interviews about the reproductive histories of aunts and uncles were obtained for all living adults. These data are used in Chapters 12 and 13 along with the data from previously described interviews to investigate factors associated with high and low reproductive success and to examine effects of kin help on demographic parameters.

Precontact Band Composition Interviews

Between 1980 and 1992 we collected a good deal of information about pre-contact bands and their composition. The composition of Ache bands on particular days was determined by asking an informant to list all the people with whom he or she lived when a particularly memorable event took place (e.g., the day you were bit by a snake, the day you killed a jaguar, the day your sister was killed by lightning). These data will not be analyzed here, but individuals ascertained in these censuses who were not mentioned in any of the other interview types listed above have also been included in the master ID file. The use of band composition interviews allows us to compile a data base that includes almost every Ache who survived to adulthood in the twentieth century (see below). Since inclusion is dependent only upon survival to a specific and arbitrary point in time, these individuals can be considered at risk of death from that point onward, and as such are included in the adult mortality calculations for advanced ages beginning in 1960 (well after most of them have been identified through precontact censuses). The use of these left-censored data will be described in Chapter 6.

Thus, the final data base for analyses is a joint file that includes individuals directly observed since 1977 and ascertained using any of the interviews described above. Some individuals may be included in the risk set for many analyses, and some individuals may only be included in a risk set used in analyses of adult mortality rates (i.e., they are left-censored for mortality analyses). Each data base used for analyses will be specified in subsequent chapters; most analyses are carried out with only a subset of the entire data base. That subset must include an unbiased sample of those whose life histories as we know them can provide information about the question of interest.

The master ID file contains 1,563 entries. Each entry includes the name, ID number, sex, year of birth, month of birth, year of death, mother's ID number, and father's ID number for all individuals ascertained as mentioned above (month of death is also recorded for most individuals who died since contact). Each adult in the data base is assigned to a data category depending on how that individual's reproductive history data was obtained and how that individual was ascertained. The master ID file contains information on 1,563 Northern Ache born before 1994, 1,463 of whom were born after 1890 and 798 of whom lived to at least ten years of age. Forty-one of these individuals were identified during the band composition interviews, and the remainder through the reproductive history interviews listed above, or direct observation.

Extensive band composition interviewing and discussions with informants lead us to conclude that the master ID file currently contains very close to every single Northern Ache who was born after 1890 and reached adulthood in the forest, as well as all Ache of any age who survived past 1970. This conclusion is supported by capture/recapture analyses of adults in our band censuses. Capture/recapture is a common technique used in biology to determine the number of individuals of a particular species in a particular area. As individuals are captured and identified they are released. After a certain number of captures, new individuals are increasingly unlikely to be captured, and the total population number can be estimated as the asymptote of the census curve. We have collected information on the adult composition of 163 precontact bands using the interviews described above. Figure 3.2 shows the cumulative total number of adults (born between 1910 and 1940) in the population accounted for (ascertained) in the first sixty band censuses. It is readily apparent that fewer and fewer new individuals show up in each additional band census. In fact, the first sixty censuses include every single Ache adult who was alive in 1977, and all but four adults who were known to be alive in 1970. Since we have entered all adults mentioned in 163 interviews into our master ID file, we conclude that it would be highly improbable for any Ache adult to escape ascertainment in our band censuses. The MASTERIDEN-TIFICATION data base thus represents very close to the complete universe of Northern Ache adults during most of this century rather than just a sample of the adult population. Some type of reproductive history interview (described above) was conducted on nearly every adult mentioned in the data base.

RELIABILITY OF INTERVIEW DATA

Anthropologists collecting demographic and genealogical information often express confidence that their data from reproductive history interviews are reliable, since they were "extensively cross-checked." What "extensively cross-checked" means exactly, and how one decides how much cross-checking is adequate and whether the cross-checking indicates reliability, is generally not specified.

In order to examine the reliability of the data from various classes of interviews mentioned above, we repeated interviews on a number of individuals several times between 1981 and 1989. In addition, data from different siblings provide a cross-check on the accuracy of the parent, grandparent, and sibling reproductive history interviews. Table 3.1 shows a sample of the female reproductive histories that were cross-checked. The number of interviews of each type and the number of checks performed on each interview are indicated. The sample includes data from 435 different interviews on 219 living and deceased women's reproductive histories. This sample includes all women whose fertility data is reported in Chapter 8, and also the set of women whose offspring contribute to the at risk population in the child mortality data presented in Chapters 5 and 6. One-third of this data base is derived from interviews with ego herself, 35% comes from interviews about the reproductive history of a sister or daughter, 21% from reproductive history interviews about a mother, and 11% from other individuals (niece, first cousin, etc.). About 27% of the interviews were cross-checked two or more times, 34% were cross-checked once, and 39% were not cross-checked at all.

Cross-checked interviews allow for an assessment of interview reliability. Data concerning the reliability of five different categories of cross-checks are presented in Table 3.2. Percent reliability was calculated as the number of agreements in a category divided by the total number of events reported in that category. Thus, for example, two siblings might each report on their own mother's reproductive history. The first sibling lists seven children born, and the second sibling lists eight children born, one of whom is not listed by the first sibling. The percent agreement is calculated as $7/8$ or 88%.

Several interesting trends emerge from the reliability data. First, and most important, information gained from ego, sibling, and mother's reproductive history interviews generally show high reliability (between 90% and 100% reliability for most categories). The lowest reliability was for *cause* of death of offspring when mothers were repeatedly interviewed about their own children. This may seem surprising, but in almost all cases of disagreement the child died very young. The mother often first claimed that the child died of cough, and in a later interview would claim that it simply died at birth for no reason, or that it died of fever right after birth. Our impression from direct observation confirms that there is often confusion about the cause of death for very young infants. Certain symptoms seem relevant or irrelevant to the death depending upon who is asked. Mothers themselves are sometimes confused about the true causes of infant death and often reconstruct the event in their minds to minimize (perceived) blame upon themselves. There were almost no disagreements about cause of death for children over one year of age.

Second, and also very important, information derived from mother's and sibling reproductive history interviews appears to be almost as reliable as an interview with ego herself (also see below). This is probably because the Ache are very open with information and generally live in close proximity with kin. We believe that most women learn the details of their mother's reproductive histories as children, in casual conversation. Several times during the course of our fieldwork we heard mothers discussing the details of their earlier reproductive careers with their children. Later, sisters and brothers seem to take a similar interest in each other's reproductive histories. The third trend in the reliability data is that information *about* a male's reproduction, whether gathered from ego or from a sibling, is less reliable than information about a female's reproduction. This is not surprising, especially given the difficulties of assessing paternity in Ache society. Information that is collected *from* males is also less reliable than that which females provide (see below).

Finally, although this is not shown in the table, the sex of the interviewer made no difference in the completeness of the data collected from women or men. This is almost certainly because the communication barrier between the sexes is less pronounced among the Ache than it is among any other group of people with whom we have worked. Indeed, the only noticeable observer effect was that increasing linguistic competence provided more accurate information. Several interviews conducted early in the 1980s by individuals who had only a few months of experience speaking the Ache language had to be thrown out entirely because of their inaccuracy. In one particularly enlightening case, Kim re-interviewed an informant the day after a colleague had carried out an interview with the same person. As Kim surveyed the data collected by the colleague, at the beginning of the interview, he commented to the informant that the data seemed erroneous and asked him what had happened. The Ache informant replied, "I know, I just made it up because Buachugi [the colleague] didn't know the difference [implying also that the informant was not well understood]. You know the Ache, so I will tell you the truth." This disconcerting event was very atypical of the usual Ache frankness, but it provided an important lesson. We only caught the problem because we had prior knowledge of the genealogies. If informants believe that there is very little chance of the researcher discovering incorrect information, they may have little motivation to be accurate.

The reliability data from Ache interviews allow us to be comfortable using parent and sibling reproductive history interviews for some purposes. They also suggest that very little additional information was gained from extensive cross-checking and re-interviewing. It is important to caution that this conclusion is relevant to the Ache study only. Reliability of interviews about sensitive topics is likely to vary greatly across anthropological studies, depending on the group of people being studied and the history and abilities of the interviewer. However, any complete study should include some sample of reliability checks on interview data in order to provide a reasonable estimate of confidence in the data. Our experience suggests that linguistic competence is crucial for obtaining accurate information, and we believe that any researcher with less than 12–24 months of language experience should use a translator when possible.

SAMPLE BIAS

Despite the fact that it is possible to acquire information on the reproductive histories of a large number of deceased adults through extensive interviewing of living individuals, the data produced by such interviews may contain important biases owing to incomplete reporting. In particular, there is a danger that some individuals will fail to report births of infants who died at an early age and were subsequently forgotten or perhaps never known in the first place. This type of error is especially likely when the individual being interviewed is either younger than the individual whose reproductive history is being obtained or lived apart from that individual for periods of time. Such errors will lead to underestimates of fertility and infant mortality rates for the study population. However, it is possible to detect categories of data that contain such biases by comparing fertility and mortality rates obtained from suspect sources with the rates obtained from best sources.

In order to determine which types of reproductive history interviews lead to unreliable estimates of fertility and infant mortality, we have compared estimates derived from interviews with living individuals and estimates of the same parameters derived from interviews with individuals of varying degrees of decreasing relatedness to the target individual in the risk set. The results are shown in Table 3.3 and Figures 3.3 and 3.4.

It is useful in this type checking to have some idea about the expected reporting biases. Experience with the Ache led us to believe that small infants would be systematically underrepresented if they died young and if they were female (the Ache place much more emphasis on having male children). For this reason, sex ratio of all offspring born and mortality rates of offspring between birth and one year of age were compared for each category of interview. If small infants who die are often unreported, infant mortality from such interviews should be exceptionally low. Cumulative fertility rates for individuals over age forty-five were also calculated for each reproductive history interview type and compared with that reported by adults who were interviewed directly. Again, failure to report dead infants would lead to low cumulative fertility for a particular subsample. Although cumulative fertility of individuals who were deceased might be low for reasons unrelated to reporting bias, *there is no obvious reason why deceased individuals should produce offspring characterized by exceptionally high infant survivorship or high sex ratio.* Thus, reproductive histories from certain categories of deceased individuals which show low fertility as well as significantly *lower* infant mortality and higher offspring sex ratio than is found among the offspring born to living individuals of the same cohort are almost certainly incomplete.

Table 3.3 shows information from the reproductive histories of men and women as a function of the source of information and the sex of the individual in the risk set. Categories 2–10 and 12–20 represent male and female reproductive histories that have come from individuals increasingly more distantly related or further away in age from the target individual in the risk set. Each target individual was characterized by only one reproductive history interview. The closest kin category from which an individual's reproductive history was obtained was considered to be "the category" of that interview data. Thus, if we had information about a woman from herself, her sister, and her mother, we would code one reproductive history (even though it was taken three times) in the category "taken from a living woman about that living woman" (category 1). In our hierarchy, sister interviews took priority over interviews about daughters, and interviews about daughters were considered "closer" than interviews about a mother's reproduction. This reflects our impressions about which categories of kin knew most about each target person's reproductive history, but these impressions are also consistent with the statistical analyses presented in the table. The table can be read by following the referential sequences concerning the interviewee and the subject. For example, data in category 8 are taken from living women about the dead sisters of their dead mothers, or in other words their aunts. If the mother had been living in this case, the closest interview would have come from a living woman about her dead sister (the aunt) or data category 2.

The data suggest that interviews about Ache women's reproduction are generally complete if acquired by ego, her sister, her brother, her mother, or her daughter (Figure 3.4). Women's reproductive histories obtained from a son, a niece, a nephew, or some other less closely related individual show significantly lower infant mortality and a trend toward lower fertility and higher sex ratio of live-born offspring.[2] Thus, these data categories probably include an incomplete sample of offspring who died at an early age and cannot be used for analyses of fertility or infant mortality. The data also suggest that interviews about Ache men's reproduction are only complete if obtained by ego, his brother, his sister, or his daughter. Other interviews show unreasonably low infant mortality, high offspring sex ratio, or both. Note that in both cases daughters, but not sons, provided accurate information about their parents' reproductive histories. The fact that not all reproductive histories are equally accurate is taken into account when choosing the appropriate sample for all fertility and mortality analyses presented in this book and will be discussed again in later chapters.

Despite the fact that small children who die are often omitted in reproductive histories obtained from kin, the analyses suggests that other biases may be absent from or insignificant in the data base. For example, women and men living in the forest who survived to 1970 show the same sex ratio and mortality rates of offspring between ages two and ten regardless of the source used to obtain their reproductive history (Figure 3.5). This means that children who survive to age two are probably all reported regardless of whether the reproductive history is obtained from ego, siblings, offspring, nieces and nephews, or other less closely related individuals. Such a result is not surprising in light of the fact that the population is small and closed to migration; interaction between members is frequent and intimate; and information is shared widely through daily gossip. The analysis suggests that data elicited from more distant kin *are* useful for measuring mortality later in life as well as the number of children that are raised to adulthood. Reproductive history data from indirect sources will therefore be included in subsequent analyses when appropriate to the type of analysis being carried out, and individuals ascertained in such analyses will enter the risk set at ages above two years, the age at which all individuals truly at risk are likely to be reported (see Chapter 6).

Since both fertility and mortality parameters of the Ache in the precontact period will be estimated using a sample that is derived from one of the interview types described above, it is useful to consider who will be eliminated from our sample, and how much this might affect the results. Infant and child mortality (ages 0–9) will be calculated from risk intervals contributed by individuals mentioned in interviews with ego, ego's siblings, or ego's parents (data categories 1–5 and 11–15 in Table 3.3). Interviews with daughters also provide complete information but include a bias that must be disallowed since by definition these interviews can only take place if a daughter has survived (thus biasing the mortality rate of the sample). Juvenile and early adult mortality (ages 10–49) will be estimated from all individuals who are ascertained through any of the reproductive history interviews (all data categories on Table 3.3). Adult mortality over age fifty will be derived from the entire at risk population in the master ID file, including those ascertained through band censuses rather than reproductive histories. Individuals will only be included in this analysis if born after 1890, and if ascertained through census prior to the risk interval (see Chapter 6). This will result in maximum sample sizes at advanced age. This selection of data sets will provide a good sample for calculating infant and child mortality, and inclusion of almost the entire Ache population in the risk set used for calculating adult mortality. For example, an individual would not be included in the juvenile and young adult mortality sample of his cohort only if neither he nor any sibling, parent, offspring, aunt, uncle, niece or nephew, or first cousin survive to the interview date. In the 1989 population, only one living individual out of 395 living adults meets these criteria. If this individual had died before we interviewed him, his death would not be included in the sample, nor would the years at risk of mortality that he contributed to the sample.

The fertility sample is more limited. A complete record of all live births is derived from interviews with ego, ego's siblings, and ego's parents (data categories 1–5 and 11–15 in Table 3.3). Again, Table 3.3 shows that interviews with daughters are complete but will provide a biased estimate of fertility since they could only take place if a daughter is born (and survives). Thus, an individual's fertility will not be included in the sample if neither ego nor any sibling or parent survives to the interview date. Of the 265 Ache women in the master ID file who were born after 1920, thirty-five are excluded from the fertility sample by these criteria. We can only guess at their fertility, since the previous analysis suggests that reproductive histories obtained from more distant kin are generally incomplete. Thus, while the criteria for exclusion from the adult mortality sample are probably rarely met for most individuals and must represent only a very small fraction of the past population, the likelihood of being excluded in the fertility sample is higher and should be taken into account for comparative purposes.[3]

The samples used for fertility and mortality analyses in Chapters 5–9 are summarized in Table 3.4.

THE CONTACT PROBLEM

Thus far, we have described how the data base that will be used for fertility and mortality analyses was obtained. These data provide information about the Northern Ache population between 1890 and the end of 1993. During this time the Ache experienced dramatic changes in their lifestyle. Until December 1970, all Northern Ache lived as forest hunter-gatherers. Between 1971 and 1977 most of them made first peaceful contact and massive epidemics swept the population. From 1978 to the present, most of the Ache have lived mainly at reservation and mission settlements, spending about a quarter of their time on foraging expeditions. Because there is good reason to expect differences in mortality and fertility rates before and after first peaceful contact, the data are subdivided into three study periods for all analyses presented in this book. The first period, called the *forest period*, includes all data on fertility and mortality before 1971. The second period we call the *contact period*, from January 1, 1971, through the end of 1977. The final or *reservation period* encompasses the time after the contact-related epidemics ended, beginning January 1, 1978, and ending on the last day of 1993, a period covered by our own observation and by mission records. All analyses will divide the data base into these three periods. Individual adults will contribute to the data in each of the three time periods if they grew up in the forest and have survived to the present. The first two periods will be described using interview data, whereas the last period can be described using data from direct observation and censuses. Many readers will be particularly interested in the demographic parameters from the first period. During this time *all* Northern Ache lived completely from hunting and gathering with no outside trade or peaceful interactions with any neighboring people. Although demographic parameters were certainly influenced by outsiders (particularly through warfare), the first period can be taken as the best possible estimate of the demographic parameters that characterized this particular group of hunter-gatherers in the twentieth century. Data on later time periods allow us to examine subsequent changes resulting from contact and increasing acculturation.

SUMMARY

This study is designed to investigate demographic parameters that characterized the Northern Ache between 1890 and 1993. The group grew from around

240 individuals in 1930 to about 540 individuals in 1970, the last year before first peaceful contact with the outside world. It then underwent rapid depopulation owing to contact-related epidemics, but has since grown to about 590 individuals. The data thus show a population growing at about 2% per year before contact followed by a disastrous period of epidemics and a subsequent growth rate of 3.6% per year after contact. These data support Thornton et al.'s (1991) suggestion that Native American populations usually recover rapidly and completely after virgin soil epidemics and that previous assumptions about long-term population reduction that are built into estimates of precolumbian population size are unwarranted and frequently lead to gross overestimates of population size. In fact the Ache rebounded to their original population size in only sixteen years after a disastrous contact event that killed almost half the population! This is because most of the survivors of the contact period were individuals of high reproductive value—men and women in their early reproductive years.

In order to collect information on mortality and fertility in a systematic and unbiased fashion, we attempted to obtain reproductive histories of all adults of any particular sibship regardless of whether they had survived. This led to reproductive history interviews with living individuals and interviews about the reproductive careers of their deceased offspring, siblings, parents, grandparents, and parents' siblings. Such interviews provide a large but potentially problematic data base for estimating fertility and mortality. Reliability checks showed that information provided by close kin about each other's reproductive histories was generally reliable. However, interview data on more distant kin showed biases indicative of systematic underreporting of infants who died young, particularly female infants. Reproductive histories from daughters about their parents appear to be accurate but include mortality and fertility bias by definition since only individuals with a surviving daughter can be included in this sample. Information concerning older children appears accurate, even when reproductive histories are obtained from children, aunts and uncles, or nieces and nephews, and data about offspring who survive to adulthood appears reliable in all interview types. Because of these characteristics associated with each reproductive interview type, subsequent analyses in this book will use only data collected from appropriate sources that appear to be both complete and unbiased.

NOTES

1. A few of the *berupuare* women had previously been married to Paraguayans and two or three Ache men had married Guarani Indian women temporarily and then left them. In 1994 no Northern Ache in our census was married to a non-Ache.

2. Number of children born before 1970 who survived to age one or died during their first year was calculated for each reproductive history data category and compared with

that obtained from living women in interview category 1. Women in category 1 had 22 offspring who died during and 121 offspring who survived the first year of life. Results of chi-square or Fisher's exact tests (one-tailed) are as follows:

> Women—category 2, 16 die, 124 survive, $p = 0.21$; category 3, 4 die, 42 survive, $p = 0.19$; category 6, 33 die, 249 survive, $p = 0.18$; category 7, 1 die, 118 survive, $p < 0.01$; category 8, 2 die, 3 survive, $p = 0.19$; category 9, 0 die, 22 survive, $p = 0.03$; category 10, 0 die, 46 survive, $p < 0.01$.

> Men—category 11, 23 die, 125 live, $p = 0.97$; category 12, 7 die, 62 live, $p = 0.30$; category 13, 7 die, 53 live, $p = 0.49$; category 16, 33 die, 282 live, $p = 0.13$; category 17, 4 die, 122 live, $p < 0.01$; category 18, 0 die, 31 live, $p = 0.01$; category 19, 0 die, 16 live, $p = 0.06$; category 20, 3 die, 29 live, $p = 0.29$

3.   Precise estimates of the percentage of each cohort that will be excluded from the data base using interviews with living individuals can be calculated by plugging in the relevant values for mean fertility and survivorship rates, and calculating the probabilities of having no living relatives of the relevant classes. These estimates are based on the assumption that all individuals experience the same average fertility and mortality rates. If this were true, there would be no need to correct for the bias introduced by using only interviews from living individuals.

Table 3.1. Source and Number of Cross-checks for Each Type of Female Reproductive History Interview. About 60% of all female reproductive histories were cross-checked at least once, and some were cross-checked as many as five different times.

	Number of cross-checks							
Best source	*0*	*1*	*2*	*3*	*4*	*5*	*n*	*%*
ego	31	23	12	5	1	1	73	33.3
sister	14	13	7	2	0	0	36	16.4
brother	3	15	10	0	1	0	29	13.2
mother	11	1	0	0	0	0	12	5.5
child	10	22	10	2	1	0	45	20.5
other	16	1	3	3	1	0	24	11.0
n	85	75	42	12	4	1	219	
%	38.8	34.2	19.2	5.5	1.8	0.5		

Table 3.2. Percentage agreement of data reported in reproductive histories when crosschecked as specified.

Subject of reproductive history	*Type of check*	*Number of checks*	*Percentage agreement across informants*			
			Number of live births	*Sex of offspring*	*Cause of death*	*Age at death*
female ego	ego × ego	20	96	100	77	
male ego	ego × ego	15	85	100	97	98%
mother	offspring × offspring	18	89	98	94	for all
female sibling	sibling × sibling	26	91	97	89	combined
male sibling	sibling × sibling	22	82	98	86	

The type of check lists first source, then second source in cross-check. Thus if a reproductive history of a deceased sister is acquired by a living brother and sister, the percent agreement of the two interviews is shown in the fourth row of the table (female sibling checked sibling × sibling).

Table 3.3. Demographic Parameters Calculated from Interviews with Living Women and Men about Individuals Specified in Each Category

Data category	Interviewee	Subject of interview	Number of reproductive histories	Offspring born before 1971			Adults over age 45		
				sex ratio	% die at age 0	Fisher's exact* (p)	n	mean offspring born	s.e.
Females									
1	living women	those living women	164	1.18	0.179	—	23	6.870	0.591
2	living women	dead sisters of 1	49	1.33	0.114	0.212	6	8.667	0.494
3	living men	dead sisters of 11	20	1.75	0.087	0.186	2	9.000	—
4	living women	dead daughters of 1	3	—	—	—	0	—	—
5	living men	dead daughters of 11	0	—	—	—	0	—	—
6	living women	dead mothers of 1	37	1.05	0.117	0.179	25	8.160	0.409
7	living men	dead mothers of 11	22	2.61	0.008	0.000	17	5.471	0.610
8	living women	dead sisters of 6	5	—	0.400	0.185	1	1.000	—
9	living men	dead sisters of 7	6	1.30	0.000	0.034	5	4.000	1.100
10	living women	other females	18	1.94	0.000	0.001	9	3.333	0.730
Males									
11	living men	those living men	239	1.500	0.155	0.97	41	5.800	0.620
12	living women	dead brothers of 1	70	1.428	0.101	0.30	3	6.670	1.760
13	living men	dead brothers of 11	20	1.069	0.116	0.49	4	6.000	1.780
14	living women	dead sons of 1	3	—	—	—	0	—	—
15	living men	dead sons of 11	0	—	—	—	0	—	—
16	living women	dead fathers of 1	37	1.026	0.104	0.13	34	8.230	0.559
17	living men	dead fathers of 11	22	2.205	0.031	0.00	21	5.050	0.410
18	living women	dead brothers of 16	5	2.875	0.000	0.01	7	3.570	0.322
19	living men	dead brothers of 17	6	1.667	0.000	0.06	4	0.350	1.660
20	living men	other males	18	1.133	0.107	0.29	11	2.090	0.513

* Statistical test described in note 2 at end of this chapter. The tests compare the parameter estimate generated from living women's or men's reproductive histories with the parameter estimate generated from reproductive histories from other categories of kin. Shaded categories contain incomplete reproductive histories and were generated from interviews about more distantly related kin.

Note the low mortality and high sex ratio that characterize the offspring reported in interviews about more distantly related kin. Shaded categories contain incomplete reproductive histories and were not used for calculating fertility or infant mortality rates in subsequent chapters.

Table 3.4.   Sources of Data for Analyses Reported in Chapters 5–9

Analysis	Data type	Data categories	Categories on Table 3.3
mortality age 0–9	reproductive interviews	with ego, siblings, and parents	1–5, 11–15
mortality age 10–49	reproductive interviews	with ego, siblings, parents, offspring, nieces and nephews	1–9, 11–19
mortality age 50+	reproductive interviews and band censuses	with ego, siblings, parents, offspring, nieces and nephews, and grandchildren	1–20, and census data
fertility	reproductive interviews	with ego, siblings, and parents	1–5, 11–15

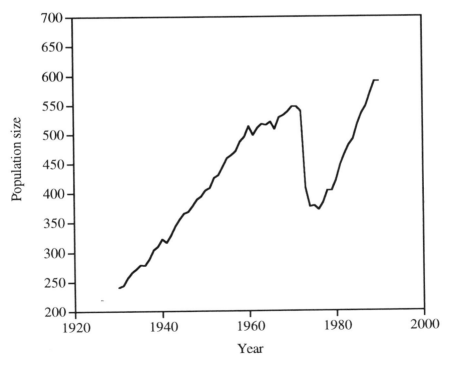

Figure 3.1.   Number of individuals in the Northern Ache population from 1930 to 1990.

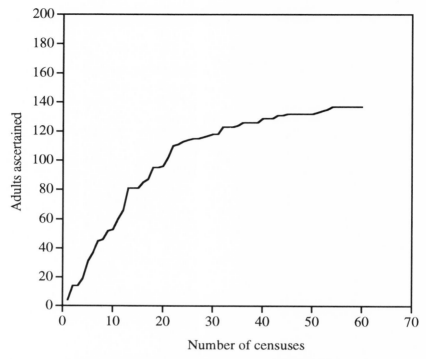

Figure 3.2. Capture-recapture analysis of the actual number of Ache born between 1910 and 1940 who survived to adulthood. New individuals mentioned in each census are added into the total population count. The cumulative number of individuals mentioned in the censuses increases until most individuals have already been mentioned, at which point the curve flattens out. The asymptote defines the total number of individuals that would be ascertained if an infinite number of censuses were carried out (i.e., the true population size). The data suggest that our 163 precontact band censuses would be sufficient to ascertain every adult in the population; thus our master ID data base probably contains every Northern Ache adult alive during the time period covered by band censuses (approximately 1950 to 1970).

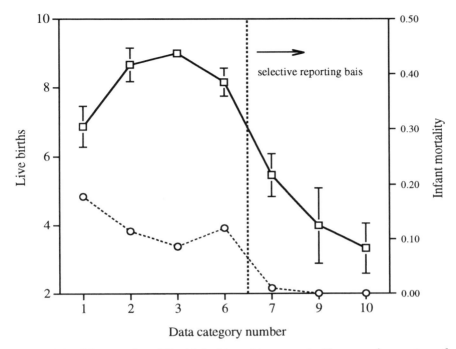

Figure 3.3. Mean number of live births ($\pm$ s.e.) to women $\geq$ 45 years and percentage of offspring who died before one year of age, by data category defined in Table 3.3. Note that categories 7–10 show very low fertility and infant mortality, indicative of incomplete reporting of infants who died.

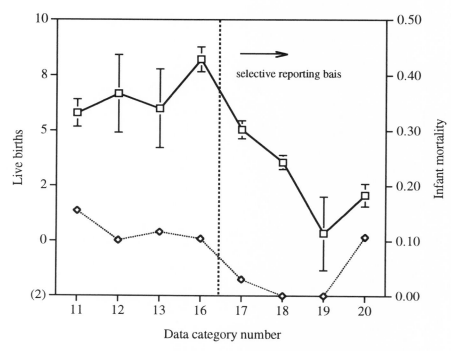

Figure 3.4.   Mean number of live births (± s.e.) to men ≥ 45 years, and percentage of offspring who died before one year of age, by data category number defined in Table 3.3. Note that categories 17–20 show very low fertility and infant mortality, indicative of incomplete reporting of infants who died.

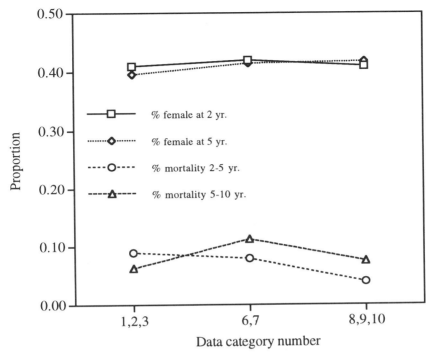

Figure 3.5. Proportion of offspring who reach age two or five that are female (the child sex ratio), and the mortality rate from ages 2–5 and 5–10 derived from different categories of female reproductive interviews. Sex ratios and mortality rates are the same for all interview categories, suggesting no selective bias in reporting children at these ages regardless of interview source.

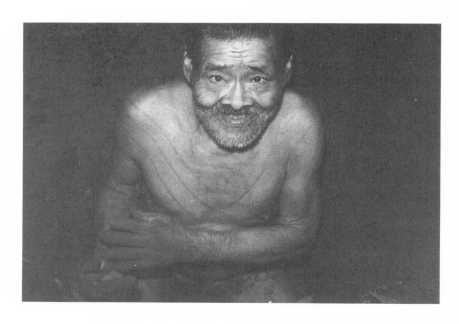

Old grandfather Japegi in 1982, when he was about sixty-eight years old, digging out an armadillo.

4

Age and Sex Structure
of the Study Population

Accurate and verifiable age estimates are necessary in any useful study of life history. In studies based on retrospective data, age estimates are used both to place individuals in appropriate age categories and as a basis for estimating elapsed time over which demographic processes are measured. Mortality rates are calculated as deaths per year lived for different age classes, and fertility is measured as births per year lived as a function of age. Many important life history events, such as menarche, first marriage, birth of first and last child, and menopause are compared between populations by looking at the distribution of ages at which the event took place. In short, the accuracy of the age estimates for a population is a critical determinant of the value of any life history study.

Keeping this in mind, small population demographers must be realistic about the limitations of their sample. Some important demographic outcomes may not be detectable with certain types of data. For example, a one-year difference between two populations in the age at menarche, first birth, last birth, or menopause is an important biological difference. Nevertheless, a one-year difference in population mean for a specific parameter cannot be reliably detected using data sets that are based on age estimates accurate within a range of 2–5 years.

The importance of accurately assessing age presents a dilemma to those who wish to work with small, isolated, technologically primitive populations. These groups provide an important opportunity to measure demographic parameters across a range of conditions that resemble those under which the genetic basis for those traits evolved. But the inability to age populations accurately in the absence of written records can invalidate any interesting patterns which might be discovered. This is especially problematic when aging techniques are developed ad hoc or are not verifiable. For this reason, demographers need to investigate whether methods can be developed that will lead independent investigators to the same age estimates for each individual in a population, and to age estimates that are likely to be correct. Although in some cases the estimates themselves may not be absolutely verifiable (if there are truly no written records), the methods should be. Most important, care must be taken in all demographic studies to specify the techniques used to derive age estimates. This information must be available in order to assess the importance of various reported patterns.

DIFFICULTIES ESTIMATING AGES FOR THE ACHE

The Ache represent an extreme challenge for any researcher hoping to develop a method of deriving age estimates from a population that doesn't keep records. First, the Ache are not particularly age conscious and do not use terms of address that denote whether the speaker is younger or older than the person being addressed. Age does not determine relative status, limit associations and friendships, or restrict marriage partners. There are no formal age grades or cohorts who pass through ritual events together. Thus, age is not considered as important a personal characteristic as it is in many other societies, and accordingly it receives less attention.

Second, eastern Paraguay is not characterized by well-marked and regular seasons, and people do not name or count years. In fact, the Ache simply designate any number greater than three as *tana* or "many." No regular events (such as ceremonies) take place on an annual or multi-annual basis. Third, there are no datable events in eastern Paraguay before 1965 that the Northern Ache can use as a point of reference. Fourth, massive epidemics during the contact period have altered the current age structure of the population in ways that make it unlikely to fit any stable population model (discussed in detail later).

Small-population demographers faced with similar problems in the past have employed a variety of solutions. Some have simply made "guesstimates" of age based on their own personal experience and a variety of genealogical clues (e.g., Chagnon 1974:159; Dyson 1977; Neel 1978:372; Melancon 1982:34). Among the Ache, this could be quite misleading. Our experience suggests that most fieldworkers consistently underestimate the age of children in the Ache population, and overestimate the age of old people, relative to what our methods now suggest are their true ages. Ache children characteristically show weights and heights about the same as American children two to three years younger. For example, the average eight-year-old Ache girl is the same height and weight as the average American girl only five years old (1,147 mm, 22.1 kg). Ache children also smile and laugh more than American children of the same age, which, combined with their small size, leads to an underestimation of their age. In 1994 when we took a five-year-old boy to the hospital, the reception nurse registered him as "about three years old." Such errors are typical. Some older men also appear younger than they are because of their exceptional physical conditioning. In 1994 a group of visiting American biologists who accompanied the Ache on a hunt commented how one man "in his forties" seemed to be capable of such vigorous hunting. According to our data, the man was actually 64 years old and had a son already in his forties. On the other hand, the physical condition of reproductive-aged women and elderly people of both sexes seems to deteriorate rapidly, leading to age estimates often ten years greater than their true age. When they died the oldest Ache man and woman that we knew in early years of fieldwork were about 78 and 72 years old, respectively, according to the absolute ages calculated later in this chapter. Most fieldworkers in our team who knew them estimated them to be well into their eighties. Currently the two oldest men are 84 and 76 years old, and the two oldest women are 78 and 77 years old. Most Americans would guess these people to be in their eighties or nineties.

Two recent anecdotes further illustrate the problems with using unsystematic age estimates for the Ache. Tykuarangi is an Ache woman who lives in Virginia. She was adopted as a child by an American family and taken to the United States after her parents died in 1972. When her birth certificate and passport were issued, her age was estimated at five years. When I met her in 1993 I explained that my data showed that she was really seven years old when she was adopted and that her age had been underestimated because she was small. She smiled and recounted how she had always thought that she was older than other kids in her school classes, and that now it made sense to her why she had reached menarche at nine years of age. She was really eleven! The second anecdote comes from an article in the *Nature Conservancy* magazine. It was written by a journalist who spent about two weeks with the Ache. In that article the author writes: "In his late thirties but with the body of a much younger man, Juancito carried only his old 36-gauge shotgun and a machete" (Homer 1992). The author would have been much more impressed, indeed, if he had realized that Juancito was actually fifty-six years old at the time and already had a daughter in her mid thirties.

Other researchers have gone beyond eyeball estimates of age. They have, for example, used dental examinations, event calendars, relative age lists, age sets, polynomial regression and interpolation, or a combination of these techniques (e.g., Blurton Jones et al. 1992; Borgerhoff Mulder 1989a; Leslie and Fry 1989; Wood, Johnson, and Campbell 1985) to derive age estimates for individuals in their study populations. Some researchers have used demographic events and parameters of their study population in order to estimate age by creating a "chain" (e.g., Early and Peters 1990), and some (e.g., Harpending and Wandsnider 1982; Pennington and Harpending 1988) have avoided the age problem altogether by simply reporting achieved fertility of postreproductive women, or survivorship to adulthood, loosely defined. Howell (1979) reports probably the most elaborate and well grounded method used to age a small, isolated population to date, and her study is often cited in the methods section of subsequent studies of small-population anthropological demography (e.g., Eder 1987; Goodman et al. 1985). Since this method has been somewhat confusing, we will describe it here.

HOWELL'S METHOD FOR ESTIMATING !KUNG AGES

In composing a reasonable age structure for the !Kung population, Howell (1979) followed a procedure pioneered by Rose (1960). She began by compiling a relative age list of the living !Kung population in 1968. This list ranked every member of the population relative to others, from oldest to youngest. Because the !Kung use kin terms that designate relative age, this procedure appears to have been relatively straightforward. Howell then assumed that at any point in time the !Kung population age structure should be the result of the fertility and mortality patterns over some preceding recent time interval (see next section). This is the logic used in all stable population theory (Coale and Demeny 1966; Lotka 1907).

The application of a stable population model allows one to estimate the age structure of a population, and the fertility and mortality rates experienced by its members, if any two of these three parameters are known. Thus, with appropriate information, a population age structure can be derived without knowing in advance the ages of individuals in that population. To do this one must estimate mortality and fertility rates in a way that does not require age estimates for individuals (otherwise it would be tautological).

Howell used the following procedure to devise the !Kung age structure: First, she estimated what percentage of children ever born survive to one year of age from interviews with postmenopausal women (Howell 1979:28). This allowed her to pick an appropriate *mortality level* for the !Kung from the model life tables published in Coale and Demeny (1966). Each life table shows expected mortality in standard age intervals, so Howell simply picked a model life table with a mortality rate between birth and one year of age that matched the one she had observed for the !Kung population.[1] A rough approximation of the percentage of children who survive to one year of age does not require any additional assumptions about ages for members of the population, and the value is not too sensitive to small errors.

In order to pick the appropriate *stable population model*, Howell calculated the proportion of the living population that was represented by the 0–4 and 5–9 year olds. This was simple since total population size can be determined from a census, and the exact ages of most !Kung children under age ten were known from direct observation during the 1960s. Each stable population model provided in Coale and Demeny (1966) consists of (1) a mortality level, (2) a fertility level, and (3) the corresponding age structure expected from the mortality and fertility rates. The !Kung mortality rate in the 0–1 year interval suggested to Howell that the West female (mortality) level 5 model life tables (which were derived in a manner described below) were most appropriate. These tables assume an infant mortality rate of 25.5%. For each stable population model, Coale and Demeny have tabulated the proportion of the population at any specified age expected from different fertility levels. Howell simply chose the column that most closely matched the percentage of individuals aged 1–4 and 5–9 in the real population. The tables can then be used to project the percentage of the population that should be found in each age interval from 0 to 80 years. As an alternative to the census data Howell could have used an estimate of the Gross Reproductive Rate (mean number of female children ever born to women who are now post-reproductive) in order to choose the correct age structure column.

Information on the expected proportion of the population in each age interval can be applied directly to a relative age list of the population in order to assign probable ages to each individual. For example, if the tables show that 3% of the population should be in the interval from 0 to 1 years old, and the relative age list contains six hundred individuals, the youngest eighteen individuals (3% of 600) on the list should be assigned ages corresponding to the first age interval. If the table shows that 10% of the population should be in the next interval (1–4 years), the next sixty individuals (10% of 600) on the list should be assigned to that interval. The process continues until the last individuals have been placed in an age interval. In the stable population model that Howell chose, only 0.4% of the population is expected to be over eight years of age, which is about two or three individuals in a population of six hundred.

Although there are likely to be some errors in age estimates for specific individuals, the aggregate average of age estimates for individuals in the population should be correct, if the mortality and fertility parameters used in the estimate represent those that produced the population, and if those parameters have been approximately constant through time. Thus, using this procedure, Howell was able to estimate dates of birth for the 244 age-ranked women in her resident population. Age estimates for other individuals (men and nonresidents) were obtained by noting their position in a relative age ranking composed of the women whose ages had been assigned, and assigning them the appropriate ages based on the age of nearby ranked individuals. Her resident population of 454 individuals shows estimated ages from newborn to 82 years.

SOME PROBLEMS USING STABLE POPULATION MODELS

Despite the elegance with which Howell was able to derive age estimates for the !Kung population, there are a few disadvantages associated with this method for estimating age. These drawbacks can be divided into three categories: (1) The possibility that the study population is not stable. (2) The possibility that the population is characterized by mortality and fertility patterns that are not represented in currently employed stable population models. (3) The possibility that the investigator used the wrong fertility or mortality levels to choose a stable population model to fit the study population. Each of these drawbacks will lead to the use of inappropriate age estimates. This in turn will result in incorrect estimates of virtually all demographic parameters of interest and, in the worst cases, may diminish or eliminate our ability to recognize populations that show unique mortality and fertility schedules relative to those commonly reported in large modern state societies.

Stable population models are mathematical constructs. They describe something that is expected to be observed in real populations when those populations meet certain assumptions. Specifically they describe the obligatory relationship between fertility, mortality, and population age structure if parameters *remain constant* through time. Populations characterized by certain birth and death rates will reach an equilibrium age structure, regardless of the initial age structure of the population. Only one possible age structure can result from any given set of age-specific fertility and mortality rates (but many combinations of fertility and mortality may produce the same age structure). Likewise, for a given age structure and known fertility rate, there is only one possible mortality schedule that can produce that age structure, and so on.

The logic of stable population theory is simple and has been proven mathematically (Sharpe and Lotka 1911). The main problem in its practical application has always been the fact that stable population distributions are only expected when mortality and fertility remain constant, are accurately described by predefined functions, and there is no migration in or out of a population. These conditions are probably always violated in human populations. Epidemics come and go and mortality rates rise and fall. Droughts and famines may affect mortality, fertility, or both. Usually, however, these fluctuations are not problematic because they tend to even out over time.

Since demographic parameters are generally measured over multiyear intervals, real populations may still show a fairly smooth population structure similar to that predicted by the models. Serious deviations may be expected if fertility and mortality change suddenly or consistently in one direction. This means, for example, that if contact with the outside world results in rapid decreases in mortality or increases in fertility, population structure is unlikely to fit any stable population model very well. Unfortunately, this is precisely the situation that characterizes many isolated populations of interest to anthropological demographers.

The Ache data presented in the next few chapters will illustrate just how severe the changes experienced at contact may be. How serious is this problem for demographers? Only a series of simulations could determine exactly, but there is considerable potential for misleading results. Artificially smoothing an age structure that is not represented by a stable population model will result in miscalculations of age-specific fertility and mortality and blur the distinction between the different rates that characterize different age intervals, and lead to incorrect estimates of how much each age interval is affected by conditions that abruptly change. The concern that changing demographic parameters might invalidate the use of stable population models has been commonly expressed by anthropological demographers (e.g., Howell 1979). Less concern has been shown over the question of whether *currently employed* stable population models are appropriate for traditional societies, however, even when mortality and fertility rates do not change through time.

In 1966 Coale and Demeny described four different types of mortality patterns in human populations. These four patterns resulted from a search to determine how many different categories of mortality curves were represented by the "reliable" data available at that time. Coale and Demeny culled their original data set considerably to choose those studies they deemed appropriate for constructing model life tables. Undoubtedly, they were correct in their concern for carefully collected data, but their criteria were certain to eliminate studies that might have shown the most deviant patterns. In fact, some data sets were eliminated specifically *because* they deviated from the most commonly observed patterns (Coale and Demeny 1966:14).

The most commonly observed pattern in modern western technological societies exhibits moderate mortality in the 0–9 age interval and lower mortality in adulthood, followed by an increase in mortality rates later in life. This pattern produces a set of mortality curves that represent differing levels of mortality but all having the same shape. In other words, the relationship between the mortality rates in infancy/childhood, adulthood, and old age remains the same in the models, but the absolute level of mortality differs. These curves are called the "West" mortality schedules. Although these mortality curves fit the observed data from many human populations, for two reasons it is unclear whether they should be considered universal.

First, no biological reason has yet been specified to explain why infant and adult mortality should be strictly proportional. The West models assume that an increase in infant mortality in any society is always associated with a specific proportional increase in the mortality rate *at every age*. Very different factors often lead to infant, juvenile, and adult death, and even when infectious diseases attack all age categories, susceptibility need not necessarily be equal or proportional across age classes and from one disease type to another.

Second, many human populations do not appear to fit the West mortality pattern. For example, Coale and Demeny discovered that in some northern European populations, infant mortality and mortality in old age were considerably lower than they are in the standard pattern. In contrast, some southern European populations show infant and old age mortality rates that are higher than the standard pattern. This might make biological sense if pathogens were more prevalent in warm climates and if these pathogens were relatively more lethal for the young and old than for prime aged adults. Given this possibility we must ask, "Could there be even greater deviations from the standard mortality pattern, and are such deviations likely to be detected using standard stable population models as a basis for assigning age structure to a population?"

Whether or not some human mortality patterns differ significantly from the model life tables commonly used for modern populations is a topic of considerable importance in biological anthropology (e.g., Howell 1982; Lovejoy et al. 1977; Pennington and Harpending 1993; Weiss 1973). Certainly, some populations must differ from the standard model life tables because of the restrictions placed on the data set used to construct them. For example, Coale and Demeny eliminated all data sets from countries that were involved in a major war. Since warfare is common and important in many traditional societies, it is hard to imagine that the mortality curve for males in these societies will ever match a data set that has artificially culled the effect of warfare.

The issue of variation in mortality and fertility rates among human populations is unlikely to be resolved by any single study. However, we must continue to be concerned about the more important question: *Would currently employed methods allow us to detect deviant patterns if they existed?* Although the conditions under which assigning an incorrect age structure to a population will obscure unfamiliar mortality patterns can best be determined mathematically or through a series of simulations, we can examine the !Kung case to illustrate why we should be concerned with the stable population model methodology of estimating age structure. A short exploration of this problem is presented in Appendix A at the end of this book.

The exercise shown in Appendix A suggests that the use of stable population models might lead to biologically important misinterpretations of demographic patterns. We do not mean to imply that Howell's analyses of the !Kung data are flawed. On the contrary, Howell's !Kung analyses probably represent the most complete small-population demographic study available. Instead, we hope to stimulate a more rigorous inspection of the methods that small population demographers have used, and greater concern about the limitations of those methods. The example presented in Appendix A also provides some practical suggestions for the future. Since it is easy to fit a few "measured" parameters into a variety of stable population models, perhaps demographers should use more parameters when they pick a stable population model. For example, it is not difficult to estimate survivorship to age fifteen and to age forty-five for females without knowing exact ages in a population. These are the approximate ages of menarche and menopause in many technologically primitive and subsistence-level societies. If a researcher can determine from interview data what percentage of females ever born survive to menarche and menopause, as well as the percentage that survives the first year of life, inclusion of this information will result in a much better idea about the true shape of the mortality curve. Such techniques are quite robust and insensitive to small differences in age at menarche and menopause because yearly mortality is fairly low around these ages relative to expected cumulative mortality.

Using this technique on the !Kung data, for example, one could immediately eliminate many of the model life tables (shown in Appendix A) that fit the survivorship parameter to age one year, as well as the proportion of the population under age ten. In addition, any extreme deviations from the standard model life tables (such as that reported in Lovejoy et al. 1977) will immediately be noted, and there is no great risk of obscuring a unique mortality profile by assigning an inappropriate population age structure. Undoubtedly many other improvements can be made in the method of determining the age structure for a population. In the next section of this book we describe a new method that does not use stable population models. Eventually we may discover a precise molecular or physiological marker that will enable determination of exact age in any human. Unfortunately, such a discovery may not take place until after isolated traditional populations have ceased to exist. At present, even the best biological techniques for estimating age of adults result in a standard error of at least ten years from known ages (e.g., Drusini et al. 1991; Ericksen 1991; Konigsberg and Frankenberg 1992; Richards and Miller 1991). Thus, we must continue to search for improvements or risk confirming the pessimistic conclusion summarized by Coale and Demeny twenty years ago.

The question of what is the pattern of mortality in a population of an underdeveloped area is essentially unresolvable, because there exists no way to determine exactly the age of an illiterate person who does not know it himself. . . . By the time a population has reached the stage where age-specific mortality rates can be measured with confidence, the level and age pattern of mortality during the underdeveloped period may never be known (Coale and Demeny 1966:29).

DERIVING AGE ESTIMATES FOR THE ACHE

Because the age structure of the Ache population, and fertility and mortality rates, were all severely altered by contact-related epidemics and other changes in lifestyle (including lessening of residential mobility) before a complete census could be carried out, methods of aging based on stable population assumptions are unlikely to be successful. For this reason we decided to explore alternative methods of assigning ages to the individuals in the study population who were born before the period of direct observation and missionary records (before 1971). Many of the techniques we considered were quickly shown to be inadequate or unfeasible. Ultimately, we settled on a method that used averaged informant rankings of age and informant estimates of absolute age differences between a large set of individuals, with a polynomial regression to fit the data set (cf. Blurton Jones et al. 1992). This technique is independent of any stable population model or assumptions about reproductive parameters such as mean birth interval and age at menarche or menopause and can be partially verified by comparing results obtained by this method with known dates. The method is generally employed only to provide ages for a subset of the population. The remaining individuals are then incorporated into the age structure based on information about their ages with respect to those individuals of "known age." We began by constructing a master relative age list of the entire living study population, and many deceased individuals who were well known by living informants.

The Relative Age List

Constructing a relative age list for an illiterate and dispersed population of about five hundred individuals is not straightforward. Two types of problems are commonly encountered. First, individuals may not have sufficient exposure to other individuals during key periods of their life to assess relative age. For example, when we asked individual informants if they were younger or older than another individual (who was obviously close in age), about one out of five times they would reply that they weren't sure because they "didn't see that individual well until they were fully adult." These answers ranged from "I never saw him" (before he died) to "I saw her when she had a child and I had one too, but I don't know who was older." In these cases, lack of an opinion was simply treated as missing data.

The second problem encountered in the construction of a master relative age list was more complicated. Not all informants agreed about relative age even though they claimed to have "seen each other well." These disagreements ranged from simple contradictions (A says he is older than B; B says he is older than A) to logical inconsistencies (A says he is older than B; B says he is older than C; C says he is older than A). As a result of these problems, we decided to construct a relative age list that was an *average* of many individual opinions. Thus, if A and B disagreed about their relative ages, the issue would be settled statistically by asking the opinions of several other individuals, and treating the most common opinion as the correct one. The disadvantage of this method is that the most common opinion is not necessarily correct, but it is difficult to see how else an objective observer can settle an issue that is apparently not verifiable.

A statistical approach to constructing a relative age list is also useful because it allows for some measure of the degree of validity in the data set, and an estimate of the range of likely error. For example, if twenty informants all rank A older than B, we can be fairly certain that A is older than B, and also that our ability to distinguish across the age range that is represented by individuals A and B is very good. If A and B are about five years apart in age, we might conclude that our data is very reliable for making five-year distinctions in age. If A and B are thought to be only one year apart in age, either we have very good time resolution or we have underestimated the age difference of the two individuals. Finally, if twenty informants give opinions about the relative ages of A and B, such that A is considered older by eleven informants and B is considered older by nine informants, we will conclude that A is older, but without the same level of confidence in our conclusion. In this case if A is thought to be about one year older than B, we might infer that our method does *not* allow for a reliable estimate of age within the range of one year. If the same twenty informants all agree that A is older than C, who is thought to be about five years younger, we might conclude that our method provides good resolution for differences of about five years but poor resolution for differences of one year. Such procedures allow us to evaluate the implications of demographic parameters that we measure with any data set.

In light of these points, a master relative age list was constructed for the Ache by eliciting multiple opinions of the relative age of various individuals and then averaging those opinions. The final list contains 462 individuals born before 1977 and is the result of 1,930 individual rankings of age from 166 informants. The procedure used to construct the final list is as follows:

1. Between 1982 and 1985 approximately five independent relative age lists were produced for each sex, and finally for both sexes combined. These lists were generally derived in informal interview settings and included input from two to ten individuals. These "group consensus" relative age lists were averaged to yield one final list that contained about two hundred living individuals and was used as a guide for subsequent steps.

2. The informal consensus relative age list was used as a guide to break the data into sixteen manageable blocks. New names of deceased but well-known individuals were added to the list in order to produce a reasonable-sized sample of individuals in each age block. Each block ultimately contained about 20–30 individuals who were believed to show a maximum age range of about three to ten years.

3. Individuals more than twenty years old were asked to rank themselves relative to every other individual in their age block (either older, younger, or the same). The ages of individuals who are under twenty years of age were ranked by their parents. Individuals also ranked themselves relative to a subset of individuals in the next older or younger block in order to determine if they (and the other individuals in their age block) had been assigned to the correct block. These interviews resulted in between four and nineteen sets of opinions for each age block, and each individual was generally ranked with respect to a dozen or so other individuals.

4. A final age ranking was produced from the opinions concerning each age block. The ranking that *minimized the number of contradictions of opinion* was chosen as "most correct." Theoretically, the number of opinions is $n(n - 1)$ for the n individuals in the block. Thus, with three individuals, if each ranks himself relative to the other two, the data set consists of six opinions. A perfect ranking with no contradictions is possible, but if some individuals disagree or give

rankings logically inconsistent with those of other individuals, the ranking will contain contradictions. The ranking that minimizes the number of contradictions is accepted as the "correct" ranking. For example, if the ranking from oldest to youngest in the order A,B,C results in three contradictions, and rank order A,C,B results in only one contradiction, whereas all other rankings result in four or more contradictions, we accept A,C,B as the "correct" ranking.[2] In practice, some of the individuals on the master relative age list are deceased (but ranked relative to those interviewed), some were not interviewed, and some could not rank themselves relative to certain others in their block. Thus, the true number of opinions in each block is often considerably less than $n(n - 1)$. Appendix B shows an example of these rank opinions for individuals in two adjacent blocks.

5.   When the data indicated that individuals had been placed in an incorrect age block, those individuals were moved into the adjacent block and placed in the age rank so as to minimize the number of contradictions about their correct age rank.

6.   Each block was ranked by this procedure, starting with the youngest block of individuals who were born between about 1975 and 1977 (exact ages are known for *all* individuals born after 1977, and for most individuals born after 1971). The youngest person in the next oldest time block was ranked immediately above the oldest person in the previous time block when the data indicated that neither belonged in an adjacent block.

7.   The procedure was continued for each earlier time block until finally there was only one informant who could rank other members of his or her time block. Ranking of individuals born before this time block is based either on the opinion of a single old person or on the collective opinions of many younger persons who saw older individuals as mature adults. The rankings of people born before 1900 are considered extremely rough estimates owing to the small number of opinions that produced that ranking.

This block-ranking procedure resulted in a final master relative age list, which is the most correct version of the true relative ages of the Ache that can be produced if each individual's opinion is given equal importance, and given the current data set. The rankings for two age blocks between 1936 and 1942 are shown in Appendix B. Although the *absolute* accuracy of the final ranking cannot be verified using any currently known method, an analyses of informant consistency is useful for assessing the value of the data set.

First we examine a small data set collected in 1987 on individuals with known dates of birth. In the process of having mothers rank their own children, we occasionally asked them to rank children whose birth dates were known and recorded. This resulted in data on sixty pairs of living and deceased individuals born between 1978 and 1981 whose absolute ages were known to the day. The rankings showed that 19% of the opinions about the relative age of individuals less than one year apart in age were incorrect, but that 0% of the rankings for individuals who differed by more than one year in age were incorrect. The largest error found was the incorrect ranking of a child who died at birth relative to a living nine-year-old who was born seven months later than the deceased infant. Between currently living children the largest error was a incorrect ranking of two children born four months apart. Of course it is possible that Ache women at current reservations have better knowledge of children's true ages than they did in the forest, so we must be cautious about our interpretation of these data.

In order to evaluate the master relative age list for all Ache, it is useful to consider what percentage of the opinions elicited were contradictory as a function of the age difference between ranked individuals, and how the probability of contradiction changes as we examine time blocks further back into the past.[3] The results of this analysis, shown in Table 4.1, indicate that although contradictions are common when ranking individuals thought to be less than a year apart in age (16.7% in all decades), they are quite rare when ranking individuals thought to be between two and five years apart in age (only 7.5% of opinions in all decades were contradictory). No contradictions were found when informants ranked individuals thought to be more than five years apart in age by the methods described below, even though some of the individuals being compared were born before 1910. The data seem to indicate that relative age distinctions between individuals born more than two years apart are consistently reported by Ache informants. Thus, although the Ache appear to be relatively unconcerned about age rank and have no formal cultural mechanisms for keeping track of such information, they do recount relative ages of members of their population consistently.

The Absolute Time Scale

Although the relative age list is a necessary step in the process of estimating ages, most investigators are likely to have few problems producing a reasonable and reliable ranking. The next step, matching the relative age list to an absolute time scale, is a formidable task given current techniques and methods. Nevertheless, it is critical to obtain age estimates as accurately as possible in anthropological demography, since small errors can accumulate in a manner which ultimately produces erroneous estimations of most demographic parameters of interest. The technique that we used relies on a subset of aged individuals who are used to produce a regression equation that is then fit to the relative age list. First, we produced a "temporary estimate" of year of birth for some individuals in the master age-ranked list using a variety of techniques. Second, we used a polynomial regression of the temporary estimate of year of birth on rank in the relative age list to derive an equation that could be used to assign the "statistical estimate" of year of birth for each individual in the master relative age list. Other individuals not in the original age ranking were later assigned a year of birth equal to that of someone in the relative age list reported to be their same age.

Temporary Estimate of Year of Birth.   The assignment of a temporary year of birth to individuals born before 1971 in the relative age list for the Northern Ache was accomplished using three procedures: (1) a calendar of dated events that could be used to place certain individuals born between 1965 and 1977; (2) early photos of children at first contact, which could be used to place some individuals born between 1960 and 1977; and (3) estimates of age difference between an informant and a younger individual, which could then be used to create an "age-difference chain" of birth dates back into the early 1900s. With each method individuals were assigned a year (but not month) of birth. Data on month of birth were elicited from mothers who identified prominent resources in season at the time a child was born. These assignments were judged unreliable because of the erratic seasonal weather patterns in Paraguay, however, and were not used for any subsequent analyses.

Dated events are often useful for aging specific individuals in a population. For example, if an earthquake was known to have struck an area in 1950, and certain individuals were born near that time, they can be assigned a birth date of 1950. In some areas of the world study populations have a long history of contact, and this technique can be especially useful (e.g., Borgerhoff Mulder 1989a; Wood, Johnson, and Campbell 1985) for assigning years of birth. Unfortunately, the Northern Ache had only sporadic and hostile contact with Paraguayans prior to 1970, and very few events that affected the Ache prior to that time can be dated. Because of constant warfare between the Ache and the Paraguayan peasant population, massacres and kidnappings of the Ache and destruction of Paraguayan fields, livestock, and houses were common events during the past century. Many peasants can recall the details of specific raids which the Ache also describe accurately. Even though we spoke Guarani (the language of Paraguayan peasants) well and had extensive experience interacting with Paraguayan peasants, we were unable to date these events reliably because the local peasants generally keep no written records and are unable to date most events that took place in the area. Asked when he built the house he currently lives in, a Paraguayan peasant might answer, "Well I don't really know. I think it was just before my son was born." The man's wife would then enter the discussion, but neither would be sure of the age of their son. Finally, the father would answer that his son was eleven, only to have the boy counter that he was actually thirteen.

The only event that is remembered by the Ache population and can also be securely dated is the construction of the Curuguaty-Saltos de Guaira road that bisects the Northern Ache traditional home range. This road was built over a period of several years, but the stretches that crossed important Ache trails and foraging territory were generally initiated in 1965 and completed in 1968. During those years there were also a number of skirmishes between Ache hunters and road construction crews. In one case, a girl's father was killed when she was not yet born, but her mother was about eight months pregnant. The man who was killed was surprised by workers who were just beginning construction on the new road, and the event can be dated with confidence to the year 1965. Thus, for example, several children who were born at this time, or whose mothers were in an advanced stage of pregnancy when this event happened, have been assigned birth dates in 1965.

Early photographs of Ache children at contact have also proven useful in assigning year of birth for some individuals. Photographs were taken by the news media, missionaries, and interested onlookers throughout the 1970s, often when an Ache band was first contacted in the forest. Because we now have a large collection of identification photos for children whose exact ages are known, and because we have collected a good deal of data on heights, weights, and developmental rates of children, most full-body photographs of Ache children at first contact can be used to assign an age that is thought to be accurate with an error range of ± 1 year. This "photo-comparison" technique of aging consists of lining up all the photos of children of known age in ranked order and then deciding where the photograph of an individual of unknown age would fit into the ranking. Figure 4.1 shows an example of how this comparison procedure works. The oldest individual aged by this method is a girl who was photographed at contact in August 1973. Her development, when compared with that of Ache girls of known ages, suggests an age of 13–14 years, and additional information on her size in 1965 suggested that she was probably born in 1960. Dates assigned through the photo-comparison technique show high internal consistency and agree well with informants' estimates of their own children's ages at the time of contact. For example, one girl was estimated by the photo-comparison technique to be thirteen years old in April 1978 when outsiders made first contact with her. In a 1987 interview her mother estimated that the daughter in question, at first contact, was the same age as a girl at the reservation who was known to be just over thirteen (13.1 years old). Later, in a 1988 interview it was discovered that the girl was born during the same year that the 1965 road had been built. All three of the estimates (photo-comparison, mother's guess, calendar event) suggest the girl was born in 1965. In another case a girl in a 1978 photograph was judged to be seven years old. Later we discovered that she had been born within a few weeks of an event that was dated to 1971. Many other similar cases led to considerable confidence in the photo-comparison technique within an error range of about one year.

Most adult members of the Ache population could not be assigned birth dates by using an event calendar or the photo-comparison technique. These individuals were first assigned birth dates by using a method that we term the "age-difference chain." The method consists of questioning individuals about their own age at the time that a younger individual (whom they know well) was born. In private interviews informants were asked specifically to pick an individual in the reservation population (whose age was known) who was about the same age as the informant when the birth of a known younger individual took place. Thus informants matched their age at an event (birth) to the age of a child they knew, and whose exact age we knew. This procedure should hypothetically provide an estimate of the *age difference* between the two individuals. In using this technique, we focused on births that occurred when the informant was sufficiently young to minimize error in assigning age based on body size. On the other hand, the informant had to be old enough to remember the birth accurately, and his or her own size at the time. Trial and error led us to focus on births that took place when the informant was about 10–15 years old. Births that took place when informants were less than ten years of age were not reliably remembered, and births that took place when informants were more than fifteen years old allowed for greater error in assigning the age of the informant at the birth of the younger individual. The information acquired through the age-difference chain can be used to assign birth dates to many individuals in the relative age list simply by working back through time systematically and creating a list of assigned years at birth. As individuals in each cohort are assigned birth dates, those dates are used to assign the birth dates of the next older cohort.

Statistical Estimate of Year of Birth. With the age-difference chain, years of birth for 63 individuals in the master relative age list were temporarily assigned between 1907 and 1959. Years of birth for an additional 34 individuals born between 1960 and 1973 were temporarily assigned using the photo-comparison technique. The precontact sample in the data base then consisted of 443 age-ranked individuals and temporary estimates of year of birth for 97 of those individuals. The oldest ranked individual had estimated her own year of birth at about 1907 using the age-difference chain method. The youngest individual in the ranking was the first person in the population with a birth certificate, born in 1973. In order to assign final ages to the ranked age list a fifth-order polynomial regression was applied to the data, with rank age as the independent variable and temporary estimate of year of birth as the dependent variable. The polynomial regression (Figure 4.2) fit the 97 temporary estimates of year of birth very closely ($r^2 = 0.996$). The regression equation was then used to assign a statistical estimate of year of birth for all 443 individuals in the master relative age list. The statistical estimate of year of birth is used as the final estimate for year of birth for all individuals on the relative age list. Thus, year of birth for all individuals born before contact is based on the *trend* in temporary estimates of year of birth of the 97 individuals interviewed by their position in the relative age ranking. This technique has the advantage of assigning years of birth without any preconceived notions or assumptions about the age structure of the population (Blurton Jones et al. 1992). The procedure also maintained the integrity of the master relative age ranking, since the slope of the polynomial function was positive along the entire curve. Figure 4.3 shows a close-up of the regression that was used to assign ages to the individuals born between 1936 and 1943 (their relative age ranking is listed in Appendix B).

Since the ages of more than half the population born between 1973 and 1977 were known, the remaining individuals in that segment of the relative age list were assigned dates of birth by linear extrapolation between the two nearest individuals of known age. Birth dates for individuals born after 1977 were obtained from written records. Once the statistical estimate of year of birth was assigned for all individuals in the relative age ranked list, any new individual who was mentioned in a subsequent interview was placed in the relative age rank and assigned a date of birth.

Results from the age-difference chain and polynomial regression technique are easy to obtain, but they must be used with caution. In order to have confidence in the absolute ages produced with this technique, some verification is crucial. In addition, even if the method were shown to be approximately accurate, errors in the age-difference chain might be additive such that a small error in each short time period could result in large errors for the birth dates of the oldest individuals in the population. Because of this, we must examine whether there is a consistent systematic bias in the age difference estimates rather than normally distributed variance around the mean, which would tend to balance out through time. Absolute verification of dates in the distant past may be impossible for many populations. For example, among the Northern Ache we cannot be positive of the true age of any individual in the population born before 1971. Ages of individuals born between 1960 and 1971 are based on photos and dated events and likely to contain little error. But indirect methods of verification are essential in order to support the use of the age-difference chain method for assigning year of birth back to the beginning of this century.

Verification. As in the case of the relative age verification, we employed two methods to test for the utility of the age-difference chain technique. The first was to compare the age estimates obtained by this procedure with actual ages using individuals with known birth dates. Preliminary questioning showed almost no error when younger individuals (15–20 years old) were questioned about recent births (i.e., informants stated their size/age at the birth of the younger individual in the population with almost no error). For this reason we decided to interview only the oldest individuals of known ages about births that took place when they were about 10–15 years old.[4] Ten individuals of "known" age between twenty and thirty years were asked to point out an individual in the population who was the same size/age that they had been when a specific child (also with a known birth date) was born. The true age of the study subjects at the time of the birth in question ranged from 10 years to 14.9 years (mean 12.5 years), and the estimates (by assigning the age of the person they picked as being the same as they had been at the time of the birth) ranged in error from 1.5 years too young to 2.8 years too old. The *mean* error of the sample, however, was only ±0.52 years (Table 4.2), not significantly different from 0 ($n = 10$, s.d. $= 1.2$, $t = 1.33$, $p = 0.22$). Because of the small sample size and the fact that reservation-living Ache may be more age conscious than their predecessors, this verification must be interpreted with caution. However, we tentatively conclude that either the age-difference chain procedure *on average* results in correct ages for the population or, at worst, it overestimates ages by about 0.5 years in every 12.5-year interval. Since the Ache relative age list relies on this procedure for absolute ages from 1960 back to 1907, this could mean that the individuals born in the 1910s may have been assigned accurately estimated years of birth, or at worst they might be estimated to be about two years older than they really are.

The second procedure used to test the validity of the age-difference chain method is a check on the agreement between different informant reports of age difference. The procedure allows for a measurement of the magnitude and direction of disagreement between the age estimate for ego derived from his or her own age-difference chain interview and the age estimate derived using the polynomial regression curve from all individuals. The average differences, calculated for each decade, ranged from +.75 years to .69 years with no consistent trend across time (Figure 4.4). The largest differences observed from single individuals deviated 3 years and +2 years from the estimate obtained in the regression. The data indicate that there is generally good agreement between the age estimate derived from an interview with a single individual and the age estimate extrapolated from the opinions of others ranked near him in the relative age list. In other words, individuals of about the same age independently estimated their respective ages to be very similar through the age-difference chain technique. In addition, individuals who were placed in exactly the same year of birth in the final age assignment showed very high levels of agreement when estimating their own ages individually (mean difference of estimates = 1.6 years, s.d. = .96, $n = 29$). Thus, while the accuracy of the age estimates could not be checked against an absolute standard, *the consistency of age estimates between individuals was very high.*

A third check on the consistency of age estimates from the age-difference chain was repeated in 1989 using a new and independent set of opinions. All individuals had already been age-ranked and assigned dates of birth prior to the 1989 field session. Sixteen adults from thirty to sixty years old were asked to estimate their age at the birth of children who, according to our statistical age estimates, were born when the informants should have been between ten and fifteen years old. The informants were carefully questioned about events surrounding the birth of each child in order to determine that (1) the birth was observed and (2) the informant had a good memory of the event. Then they picked a person (of known age) at the current reservation settlement that they believed was the same age as they were when the specified birth had taken place. This independent data set showed substantial agreement between the new informant opinions and the years of birth that had been previously assigned based on the age-difference chain and polynomial regression (Table 4.3). The mean difference between the elicited opinions of ego's age at the birth of a specific child and the difference in age between the two, as determined from the statistical estimate of year of birth assigned via polynomial regression, was 0.2 years ($n = 37$, s.d. = 2.4). *Thus, the new and independent age-difference opinions were highly consistent with the absolute ages that had previously been assigned to individuals in question.*

This verification essentially provides data on informant consistency in reporting time elapsed between events. We cannot obtain a measure of informant opinion relative to real time elapsed since no actual birth dates can be obtained for the precontact population. If all informants generally tend to overestimate or underestimate their ages when they are adolescents, we could obtain a very high measure of *consistency* but still produce an *inaccurate* time scale and assign incorrect ages at birth for much of the population. If such a trend existed, however, it would result in an expanding or contracting time line. In other words, if informants consistently overestimate their age, and the ages of each cohort are built on the past cohort, the error between actual age and estimated age will increase through time such that the age of the oldest cohort might be seriously overestimated.

For this reason it is desirable to devise a method to detect an expanding or contracting time line. Although random error in individual age estimates will tend to average out and not affect a demographic study, systematic error in one direction is a serious problem, even if estimates can be shown to be consistent. One way to detect this problem might be a plot like that used by Howell (1979:32) to assess the !Kung age estimates. Howell plotted the mother's age at the birth of her first five children for each cohort of women in order to show that no serious discrepancies are found across time using the age estimates from the stable population model. This type of plot should allow us to detect systematic expansion or contraction of the absolute time scale.

For example, if the age-difference chain method results in a consistent two-year overestimation of ego's age at the birth of the reference child, the absolute time scale should be expanding at a rate of about two years every 12.5 years (since the dated events rely on estimates when ego is between 10 and 15 years old). By the time a woman was 37.5 years old, the method should overestimate her age by six years. This could be detected by plotting ages of women at the birth of their own children. In the example given above, we would expect higher ages at specified parity for women who had all their children during the age-difference chain period (pre-1960) and lower ages at specified parity for women who had their children during the time period when age estimates are accurate (post-1960). The plot of age at first five births for Ache women as a function of decade of mother's birth is shown in Figure 4.5. The results suggest that the absolute time scale assigned using the age-difference chain method does not systematically result in overestimates or underestimates of age through time.

Finally, we can look at real family composition in order to gain an intuitive feel for the results of our aging procedure. Appendix C shows genealogies of five individuals we estimate were born between 1895 and 1907. Genealogy 1 is that of Kanegi, our earliest born informant, a woman we estimate was born in 1907 and who died in 1985. When we first met her in 1977 she was already so old that she would often fall far behind the rest of the band when camp was moved during the day. Occasionally she even slept alone along the trail because she could not catch up before nightfall. By 1985 she was almost completely blind and rarely ventured more than 20 m from her hut. Had the Ache still lived in the forest she would have either been carried or left to die. Kanegi died in 1985, but by 1990 her descendants included five living offspring, fourteen living grandoffspring, eighteen living great-grandoffspring, and one living great-great-grandoffspring. In addition, two of her female great-grandoffspring were pregnant in 1990.

Genealogy 2 is that of a man, Kanjegi, who informants claimed was just barely older than Kanegi (above). We estimate that Kanjegi was born in 1905 and we know that he died at contact in 1975. Kanjegi was reported to be very old and feeble at the time of his death. Photographs taken of his entire family in 1975 show that Kanjegi's oldest son already had five grandoffspring at that time and was undoubtedly more than fifty years old himself. By 1990 Kanjegi's descendants consisted of 4 living offspring, 27 living grandoffspring, 48 living great-grandoffspring, and 3 living great-great-grandoffspring.

Genealogy 3 is that of a woman, Buachugi, who died of contact-related respiratory disease in 1973 when her husband and his brothers refused to be taken to the Cerro Moroti reservation and instead hid deep in the forest. Older informants reported that Buachugi was a few years older than Kanegi (above). Two of Buachugi's children survived contact and have been important informants throughout our research. Buachugi is particularly useful for testing the accuracy of our aging procedure because her firstborn offspring (a daughter) survived to have a firstborn offspring (a daughter) who survived to have a firstborn offspring (a daughter) who survived to have a firstborn offspring we observed at a few months of age. The last two generations have birth dates that are known almost exactly. According to the final age estimates, the birth dates of Buachugi and the surviving firstborn offspring in each generation are 1901, 1920, 1938, 1957, and 1976. The age at first birth for each generation is therefore 19, 18, 19, and 19 years. Clearly Buachugi's actual year of birth cannot be much more recent than the year we assigned without implying unreasonably early ages at first birth for her and her descendants (the median age at first birth for all Ache women living in the forest is 19 years with a standard error of 0.44 years; see Chapter 8). We know that Buachugi died in 1973, and we estimate that she died at 72 years of age. Buachugi's descendants in 1990 included 2 living offspring, 13 living grandoffspring, 34 living great-grandoffspring, and 14 living great-great-grandoffspring.

Genealogy 4 is that of a woman, Cherygi, who was left behind to die when her band was hit by the contact epidemic. We estimate that she was born in 1895 and died in 1972. She reached menarche when Kanegi (above) was a small child (Cherygi already had two children by the time Kanegi remembers her well). Her second son was still alive in 1990 and is now the oldest living Northern Ache man. In 1990 Cherygi's descendants consisted of 1 living offspring, 18 living grand offspring, 48 living great-grandoffspring, and 12 living great-great-grandoffspring.

Genealogy 5 is that of a man, Kajagi, who was the father of an important current leader of the Northern Ache. Kajagi had two wives throughout most of his adult life and produced many children. He was reported to be extremely old when he was bitten by a snake and died the year before first contact (1970). Kanegi (above) said that she was too young to remember well when Kajagi underwent his lip-piercing ceremony. We estimate that he was born in about 1895 (12 years before Kanegi) and died in 1970. By 1990 Kajagi's descendants included 4 living offspring, 21 living grandoffspring, and 26 great-grandoffspring.

One of the most striking features of the ages we obtained using the age-difference chain technique is the fact that many individuals live to advanced ages. Howell (1979) emphasized this same point when she analyzed !Kung data, but it seems to be underappreciated by many anthropologists who believe that traditional populations are characterized by a life that is "nasty, brutish, and short." High mortality and short life span have also been emphasized in some recent paleodemographic studies, which suggest that Native American populations did not contain any individuals older than age fifty until fairly recently (e.g., Lovejoy et al. 1977). This viewpoint is inconsistent with data on observed populations as well as the delayed senescence rate that has evolved in humans. A variety of problems with paleodemographic methods, such as biased recovery and inaccurate aging techniques of older adults (see Buikstra and Konigsberg 1985 for a useful discussion of paleodemographic methods), have probably led to this erroneous conclusion about life span. The Ache show high rates of adult death from accidents and violence, yet many adults survive into their seventies and eighties. *While life may be difficult, it is not always short.* Several of the individuals we estimate to have lived into their seventies could not possibly have been much younger, because lowering their age at death would result in unreasonably early ages at reproduction for them and their descendants.

Both the age ranking and the age-difference chain methods have been the subject of verification and consistency checks, which demonstrate that informant estimates, *on average,* lead to internally consistent conclusions. In this analysis we find no evidence that the absolute ages assigned are systematically biased; however, more powerful methods of absolute verification would be extremely useful. The methods described for assigning ages will be most useful for aggregate-population-level analyses. The method does not assure that the date of birth for any one particular individual is necessarily accurate. This limitation is unfortunate for those who wish to test hypotheses about differences between small classes of individuals on some parameter of interest. The smaller the sample size, the more likely that errors in individual age estimates may affect the outcome of any specific test.

However, the age-difference chain and polynomial regression method has several advantages over the use of stable population models for assigning absolute ages to a relative age list. First, the population age structure derived from the methods we used is independent of any assumptions about age-specific mortality or fertility rates in the study population. Thus, when we use ages of individuals to estimate vital rates we do not have to be concerned about the circularity of the procedure. A stable population model, for example, assumes a certain shape of the mortality curve in order to assign ages to individuals, and then uses the age estimates generated in order to estimate the shape of the mortality curve.

A second advantage of the age-difference chain and polynomial regression method we employed is that the population age pyramids produced by this method (see next section) are not always widest at the base and narrower in each successive age class. Stable population models always result in decreasing proportions of individuals in each successive age class because they assume that no temporary changes in fertility and mortality rates can take place. Age pyramids that result from the method we used for aging the Ache are more likely to reflect the true population age structure in a fluctuating environment. As an example we show the age structure of the Ache population in the 1987 census (Figure 4.6) using ages assigned by the method described above. This is compared to the expected proportions in each age class according to the stable population model in Coale and Demeny (1966) that best fits the "known" population parameters of the Northern Ache after contact.[5] The current population age structure of the Ache could not be produced using any stable population model, and it is significantly different from the West male 5 model to which it comes closest.[6] This is primarily because of the demographic changes that took place as a result of first contact. The age class of individuals who were small children at the time of contact is greatly underrepresented, and those who were young adults at contact are overrepresented in the current age structure. The reasons for this will become clear in Chapter 6.

The most important advantage of the age-difference chain and polynomial regression method of assigning age is that it enables us to discover combinations of vital rates and population age structures that lie outside the commonly employed models *if such variants exist*. An assessment of the universality of human demographic parameters as they are reported in large modern societies is one of the most important contributions of small-population demography. We must employ techniques that will allow us to discover patterns, if they exist, that are not represented by modern state societies.

AGE-SEX STRUCTURE OF THE NORTHERN ACHE

Age-sex structure of the Northern Ache population at four points in time is shown in Figures 4.7–4.10. Each was tabulated from the master ID file of all Northern Ache ever mentioned in any interview during the previous ten years. Raw counts are presented along with a lowess smooth of the data that is more useful for detecting patterns in the population structure (see Pennington and Harpending 1993 for discussion about smoothing of age-sex data). The 1960 population shows an age pyramid (Figure 4.7) that suggests rapid population growth since the early 1930s, and slower growth before that time. This coincides with the time when the Northern and Yvytyruzu populations split and the Northern Ache moved northeast into their present home range. The 1960 population pyramid shows evidence of two bottlenecks, which affected females more than males. These may represent exceptionally difficult years in which child mortality was high and females suffered differentially. The 1960 population also shows a general excess of males up to about age thirty. Since analyses in Chapter 3 suggest that reporting bias is likely only for children under two years of age, the observed sex ratio is probably real and a function of (1) a male-biased sex ratio at birth; (2) higher mortality rates among females through childhood; and (3) preferential female infanticide/child homicide. These factors will be discussed in later chapters.

The 1970 population pyramid (Figure 4.8) shows essentially the same thing as the 1960 pyramid. 1970 was the last year that all Northern Ache bands lived as full-time uncontacted forest hunter-gatherers. The data show continued rapid population growth between 1960 and 1970, with a continued male bias in the sex ratio of younger age classes.

The 1980 population pyramid (Figure 4.9) shows the devastating effect of first contact. A comparison with the 1970 population suggests that contact-related epidemics killed many children of both sexes under the age of ten, and a high proportion of adults of both sexes over the age of forty. In addition, adult females of reproductive age appear to have been more susceptible than their age-matched male counterparts (or were more likely to "outmigrate" at contact). These trends, confirmed in Chapter 6, make possible a detailed description of the way contact affected different age-sex categories of individuals.

The 1989 population pyramid (Figure 4.10) shows the rapid recovery after the devastation of contact. This resulted in a larger population in 1989 than the precontact population of 1970 despite the horrendous toll of first contact. It is important to realize that this type of rapid growth following a population crash is likely because those who are most likely to survive contact are precisely the individuals of highest reproductive value. A similar pattern is reported for survival during periods of catastrophic death in other human populations (e.g., Grayson 1993) and other large mammals (e.g., Clutton-Brock et al. 1991, 1992). Estimates of precontact population size will be greatly exaggerated if they assume that the precontact population must necessarily have been considerably larger than the postcontact population (see Thornton et al. 1991 for discussion). The 1989 population pyramid suggests an extremely high population growth rate in the past ten years along with an increasingly female-biased sex ratio. The shift at contact from a male to female biased sex ratio in the junior age grades is particularly intriguing and will be discussed in a later chapter.

COMPARISON WITH THE !KUNG AND THE YANOMAMO

The age-sex structure of the precontact (1970) Ache population in Table 4.4 can be compared with that reported for !Kung hunter-gatherers in 1968 (Lee 1979:45) and a sample of Yanomamo in the 1960s analyzed by Neel and Weiss (1975:28). The Ache precontact population was significantly younger than the !Kung and has more individuals in older age classes than are reported for the Yanomamo. The differences between the Ache and the !Kung age structure are primarily due to higher fertility among the Ache (see Chapter 8). The difference between the Ache and the Yanomamo may be due to underestimation of the age of Yanomamo older adults (age estimates for the Yanomamo were assigned based on the ethnographer's visual assessment and genealogical clues). In addition to age *structure* differences, the Ache sex ratio is significantly more male-biased than that of the !Kung for both juveniles and adults. The sex composition of the Ache population is not significantly different from the similarly male-biased sex ratio found among the Yanomamo (Table 4.4).

The dependency ratios for the Ache (number of individuals under 15 or over 65 years divided by the number between 15 and 65 years) in 1970 and 1987 can be calculated for the population before contact and in recent years. In both cases the dependency ratios are high (0.79 for 1970, and 0.92 for 1987), indicating a very young population with high fertility. This contrasts sharply with the low dependency ratio (0.51) reported by Howell (1979:43) for the independently living !Kung groups in 1968. The Yanomamo dependency ratio is similar to that for the Ache, again suggesting a rapidly growing population.

SUMMARY

Accurate estimates of individual ages are crucial to any demographic study. Previously employed methods are problematic because they make specific assumptions about demographic parameters that are often not met, or constitute the topic of the investigation (and therefore should not be assumed). Anthropological demographers have been extremely lax about aging methods and often adopt a "trust me" approach to assigning ages. Vague statements about "multiple cross-checks," "internal consistency," or the researcher's "confidence in the age estimates" are not useful. Studies should provide an assessment of the accuracy of their aging technique by using known-aged individuals or by providing statistical analyses of data reliability. Verification is absolutely crucial if the field is to be considered scientific rather than interpretive. Very few studies in anthropological demography have met this challenge, and many results should be considered tentative given the lack of clarity on how accurate the age estimates are. We have tried to provide information on the likely accuracy of our aging technique and thus leave the reader in a better position to evaluate subsequent results.

We also hope to stimulate future researchers to develop even more adequate methods of age verification than those reported here. Ultimately, we may have a precise laboratory or field method for assigning exact chronological age in populations without written records, but until that time greater methodological concern is appropriate. Eyeball estimates are inappropriate for all but the most general age categories (e.g., infant, child, adult). Construction of a relative age list will often be a necessary first step, but the validity of such lists should be assessed by the researcher. Claims that age can be assigned by matching births to dated events should be verified, and some estimate of error should be provided. Claims that age can be assigned by examining dentition or some other morphological trait should be verified for all age classes, through blind comparison. Because dental aging techniques show considerable error for individuals over age twelve, age at menarche when reported for a population of women whose ages have been assigned through dental examination, for example, may easily show errors of greater than one year. Such samples are not appropriate for comparison when differences of less than two years are expected. Age at first birth, last birth, and menopause reported in such studies should be considered rough estimates unless a clear assessment of the aging technique is provided.

The technique that we use to estimate year of birth is based on a relative age list and informant reports about age differences between themselves and younger individuals. When the youngest individuals have known birth dates, a chain can be constructed that provides year of birth for individuals in the distant past. The age estimates thus derived are independent of any assumptions about such demographic parameters as age at specified parity, but they do require that individuals reliably report differences in age. The expected error in single estimates does constitute a serious problem unless it results in consistent over- or underestimates of age differences for the entire population. Our data suggest that Ache informants can remember and accurately report other population members who were born when the informant was between ten and fifteen years old; thus we were able to obtain a large sample of age-difference estimates for the living Ache population. Systematic bias in age-difference estimates was not found, and with a large sample of age-difference estimates it was easy for us to assign absolute ages to our relative age list using a polynomial regression. Such a technique allows the age structure of the population to take any shape and is not dependent on assumptions such as those built into stable population models.

After ages were assigned to every individual on our relative age list, and newly reported individuals were placed into the list and assigned an appropriate year of birth, we were able to examine the age-sex structure of the Northern Ache population through time. Our master ID file, which contains the sex and years of birth and death for every Ache who has ever been mentioned during our ethnographic research since 1977, was complete by 1986. Since that time only one new individual who was not already in the file has been mentioned in our interviews (a girl who died in her teen years and had no other living close relatives). Thus, we believe that our database contains a complete list of every adult Northern Ache who lived in the twentieth century, and probably every individual who survived at least to age five since 1940.

The master ID file was used to "census" the population in 1960, 1970, 1980, and 1989. The resultant age-sex pyramids show a rapidly growing population with a male-biased sex ratio before contact and an increasingly female-biased sex ratio since contact. Several "bottlenecks" are apparent before and at contact, suggesting periods of stress which resulted in high juvenile mortality. The contact-related epidemics also appear to have resulted in unequal mortality across different age-sex categories, a topic that will be discussed again in Chapter 6.

Finally, the age-sex composition of the precontact Ache population was radically different from that recorded for the !Kung in the 1960s. The Ache are a much younger population (probably due to higher fertility) and show a tendency toward a male-biased sex ratio across most age categories whereas the !Kung show a slightly female-biased sex ratio in all age categories. The Ache age-sex structure is much more similar to that reported for the Yanomamo in the 1960s, with both populations showing evidence of rapid growth and male-biased sex ratios. These patterns will be discussed again in later chapters.

NOTES

1.   Howell limited her choice to the West regional life tables, the derivation of which is discussed later in this chapter.

2.   Some possible rankings were disallowed if we had "strong" information that they were incorrect. For example, if an informant swore that he saw two children born, that A was older than B, and that he knew that because he had cut the umbilical cord of both, we took this into consideration. If an informant further backed a claim with additional detailed information, we used this to disallow some rankings. For example, we were told a story in which Chachugi, who could already walk, hit newborn Kanjegi with a stick, almost causing Kanjegi to lose his eye. Any ranking that had Kanjegi older than Chachugi would therefore be disallowed even if it resulted in the lowest number of contradictions.

3.   Age differences were determined using the aging procedure described in a later section. Therefore, the test of consistency was done after the final assignment of absolute age.

4.   These individuals' ages were derived from dated calendar events, or the photo-comparison method, and are probably accurate ±1 year.

5.   The stable population model is chosen to fit the percentages of the current population in the 0–5 and 5–10 age intervals (19.6% and 18.3%, respectively), and the mortality rates to age 1 (.18), age 15 (.39), and age 45 (.33), which are crude estimates that do not require exact age of any individual. The data best fit the West male 5 model when $R = 25$.

6. Goodness-of-fit test, df $= 15$, $\chi^2 = 40.28$, $p = 0.0004$.

7. Cochran-Mantel-Haenszel chi-square analyses (SAS 1985:403) for 2×3 tables (group $\times$ age) show that the Ache population is significantly younger than the !Kung population ($\chi^2 = 19.3$, $p < 0.001$, $n = 1,004$) and significantly older than the Yanomamo population ($\chi^2 = 52$, $p < 0.001$, $n = 3,169$). Fisher's exact test shows that for the interval between 0 and 15 years of age the differences in the sex ratio between the Ache and the !Kung are significant [p (one-tailed) $= 0.0001$, $n = 360$] and for the interval between 15 and 60 years of age these differences are borderline [p (one-tailed) $= 0.073$, $n = 574$].

Table 4.1.   Rate of Disagreement across Informants in Relative Age Assessment

Age difference between individuals‡	Percent disagreement in age rankings by block†							Percent Disagreement: All Decades
	Known age	1970s	1960s	1950s	1940s	1930s	1910–1920s	
<1 yr	19 [45]	5 [87]	22 [332]	12 [100]	20 [104]	22 [138]		16.7
1–2 yr	0 [15]	5 [19]	17 [83]	14 [49]	11 [36]	13 [70]		10.0
2–5 yr			5 [43]	10 [31]	9 [20]	6 [54]	7 [29]	07.5
5–10 yr						0 [7]	0 [52]	00.0

† The number in brackets indicates the sample size of opinions that could be contradicted
‡ Age differences were based on the "statistical year of birth" assigned as described in the text

Table 4.2. Verification of Age-difference Chain Method with Known Dated Events

Current age of informant	True age* at event	Age-difference chain** estimate of age at event	Error in age estimate
23	13.0	13.0	0.0
23	14.9	14.2	−0.7
21	12.2	13.0	0.8
24	13.9	14.2	0.3
26	14.0	16.0	2.0
22	10.0	12.8	2.8
25	12.0	12.5	0.5
30	13.0	13.0	0.0
27	13.5	12.0	−1.5
20	12.0	13.0	1.0
		Mean error	**0.5**

* As determined from calendar of events or photo-comparison. Some ages could only be determined to the nearest year with available data.

** Ego's estimate of own age when the event took place, by matching with another person in the current reservation population who is now the same age as ego was when the event took place.

Table 4.3. Consistency Check on Age-difference Chain Estimates before Contact

Current age* of informant	Statistical age* at event	Age-difference chain** estimate of age at event	Error in age estimate
42	11	12.8	1.8
42	12	13.0	1.0
40	12	13.0	1.0
46	13	13.0	0.0
46	9	12.5	3.5
42	12	10.5	−1.5
42	12	12.7	0.7
42	12	7.9	−4.1
41	14	14.0	0.0
41	11	12.5	1.5
33	15	16.0	1.0
46	10	10.8	0.8
46	12	8.5	−3.5
46	13	8.5	−4.5
46	13	10.8	−2.2
46	17	13.0	−4.0
49	11	15.0	4.0
49	15	13.0	−2.0
50	14	10.6	−3.4
50	17	19.0	2.0
52	11	11.5	0.5
52	12	11.5	−0.5
52	13	16.0	3.0
49	15	14.0	−1.0
52	17	18.0	1.0
52	15	16.0	1.0
31	10	8.0	−2.0
31	14	13.0	−1.0
58	11	10.6	−0.4
58	14	10.6	−3.4
58	15	17.0	2.0
58	16	10.6	−5.4
58	9	10.6	1.6
58	12	10.6	−1.4
56	10	13.0	3.0
56	10	12.5	2.5
56	12	13.0	1.0
		mean error	**−0.2**

* As determined from polynomial regression. Some ages could only be determined to the nearest year with available data.

** Ego's estimate of own age when the event took place, by matching with another person in the current reservation population who is now the same age as ego was when the event took place.

Table 4.4 Age-sex Composition of Ache, !Kung, and Yanomamo Populations (see note 7 for statistical tests)

Age	Male	Female	*n*	Percent
Ache 1970				
0–15	140	89	229	41.9
15–60	160	128	288	52.7
60+	16	14	30	5.5
total	316	231	547	100.0
Kung 1968*				
0–15	58	73	131	28.7
15–60	141	145	286	62.6
60+	17	23	40	8.8
total	216	241	457	100.0
Yanomamo 1960s**				
0–15	682	508	1190	45.4
15–60	738	667	1405	53.6
60+	11	16	27	1.0
total	1431	1191	2622	100.0

* From Lee 1979:45
** From Neel and Weiss 1975:28

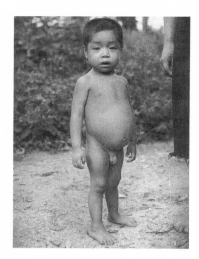

Figure 4.1. The use of photo comparison to assign birth dates. Two individuals of unknown age (left) were matched with photos of similar individuals of known age (right) to assign final ages. The top row shows Payvagi (upper left) near the date of his first peaceful contact with non-Ache in August 1975; the photo of Jakuchangi (upper right), age 32 months, was used to assign Payvagi's birth date. The bottom row shows Chachugi (lower left) in August 1975 at first contact, and the photo of Piragi (lower right), age 56 months, used to assign Chachugi's birth date.

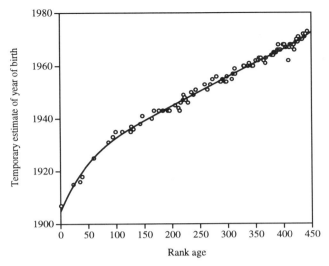

Figure 4.2. A fifth-order polynomial regression of temporary estimate of year of birth by age rank for 97 individuals between 1907 and 1973 ($r^2 = 0.992$). The regression function was used to assign statistical year of birth to each of the 443 age-ranked individuals in the population.

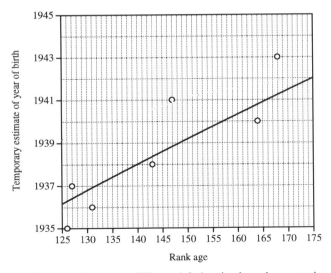

Figure 4.3. A close-up of a portion of Figure 4.2 showing how the regression function is used to assign statistical year of birth to ranked individuals. Open circles are temporary age estimates derived from the age-difference chain. Statistical age was assigned to each individual based on the *y* value of the function at any particular age rank. The raw data on age rank corresponding to this section are shown in Appendix B.

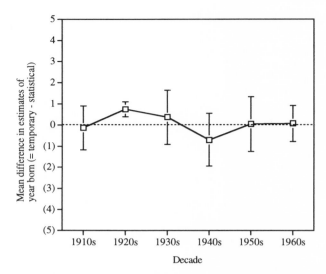

Figure 4.4. The difference between temporary age estimate (from the age-difference chain method) and statistically assigned age estimate (from the polynomial regression) in each decade. The mean measures consistent trends when over- or under-estimation of age occurs, whereas the standard deviation shows the mean difference per individual estimate.

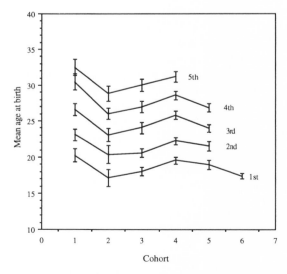

Figure 4.5. Mean age (± s.e.) at first five births for Ache women by ten-year cohort. The figure does not suggest systematic bias in the age-difference chain technique of estimating year of birth.

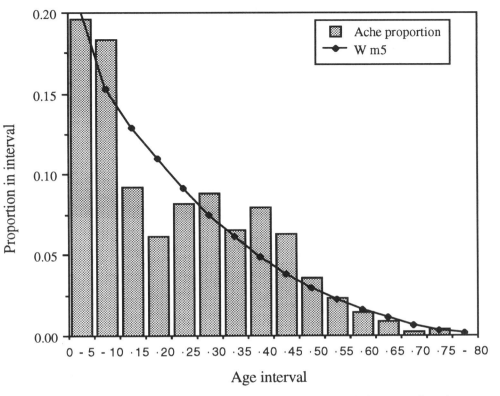

Figure 4.6. Age structure of the 1987 Northern Ache study population. Bars show the proportion of individuals in each age interval and the line shows the expected proportion if the best-fitting stable age population from Coale and Demeny (1966) is applied to the rank age list (see note 5).

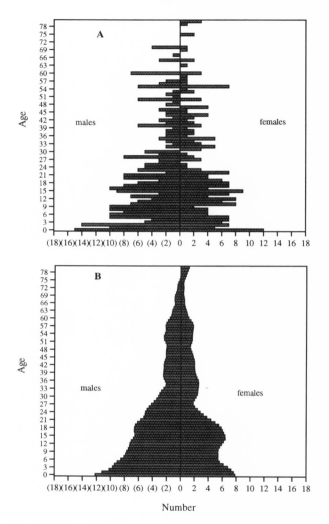

Figure 4.7.   Age-sex pyramid of Northern Ache in 1960 (A) and a running average, binomial smooth of that pyramid (B). Note the excess of males in juvenile age classes and the waves of apparent high female mortality.

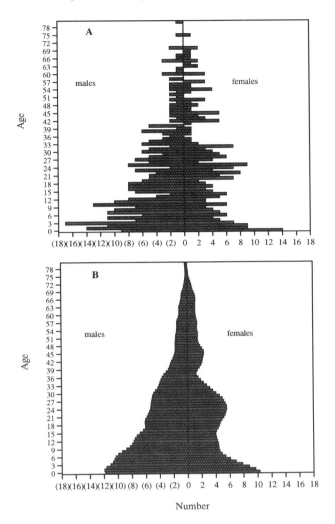

Figure 4.8. Age-sex pyramid of the Northern Ache in 1970 (A) and a running average, binomial smooth of that pyramid (B). Note the excess of males in the juvenile age classes and the waves of apparent high female mortality.

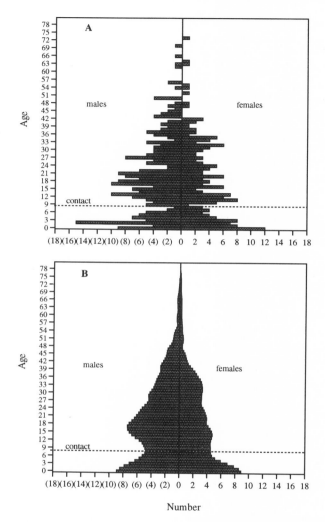

Figure 4.9.   Age-sex pyramid of Northern Ache in 1980 (A) and a running average, binomial smooth of that pyramid (B). The year of first peaceful outside contact is shown. Note that both young and old individuals are underrepresented owing to contact-related mortality.

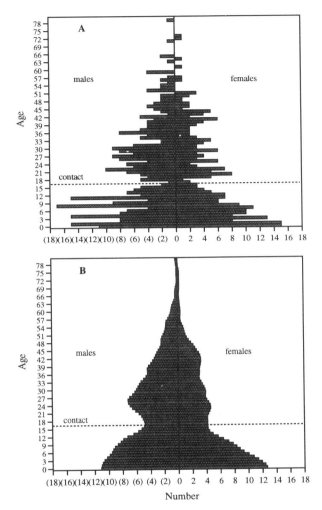

Figure 4.10. Age-sex pyramid of Northern Ache in 1989 (A) and a running average, binomial smooth of that pyramid (B). The year of first peaceful outside contact is shown. Note the male-biased sex ratio among contact survivors, but an increasingly female-biased sex ratio since that time.

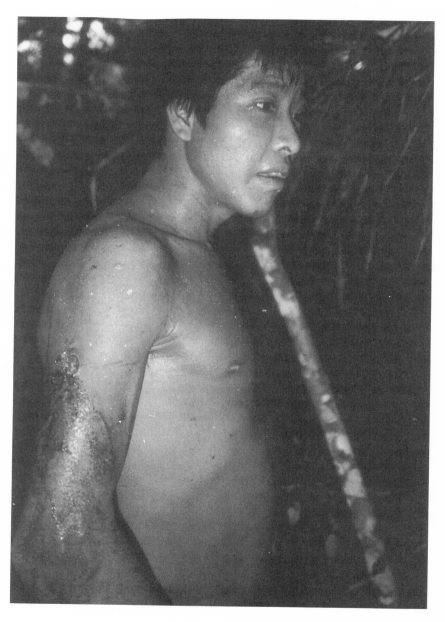

Ache man in 1980 who had been bitten by a coati.

5

Causes of Mortality

Understanding the causes and rates of death for different groups of individuals in any society provides a great deal of information on both their lifestyle and the types of conditions to which they must adapt. Most members of modern western societies have become so accustomed to relatively low mortality rates through most of their life that they have a difficult time imagining the lives of our recent ancestors, let alone those in our distant human past. This has led to two extreme characterizations of life and death in primitive society. The pessimists have viewed primitive life as essentially "nasty, brutish, and short" (as Hobbes wrote in 1651), while the romantics have suggested that primitive peoples can often be characterized as living in an "original affluent society" (Sahlins 1972) in which needed resources are easy to acquire and people live in happy harmony with nature and each other. Neither view is accurate, but romantic notions about the ease of primitive life are probably furthest from the truth and reflect the greatest lack of understanding about the difficulties of life in the past. Mortality, health, and growth data are objective measures of the many hardships of life in traditional societies and do not support romantic assertions that native populations enjoyed exceptionally good health before contact exposed them to modern health hazards. Some cultural anthropologists, unaware of the vast literature showing that these measures can be used to assess nutrition, work load, and environmental hazards of life accurately, continue to argue naively that their study population is an example of the "original affluent society" just because adults are observed to spend few hours per day in the food quest. This is equivalent to suggesting that the American homeless are really affluent because they work few hours per week, despite the fact that objective health measures would clearly show otherwise.

The Ache data presented here reflect conditions of life in one particular case and thus cannot be taken to typify human experience in technologically primitive societies. In combination with other similar studies of isolated small human populations, however, the Ache data can provide some idea of the range of and variation in mortality rates and causes experienced in primitive societies. In addition, the Ache data are particularly useful because the methods that we employed to study adult mortality provide a much larger sample of adult deaths than is usual for studies in anthropological demography. Finally, the mortality data in combination with other information about the environment and social system may ultimately provide us with an ability to predict approximate mortality parameters for other societies under specified conditions.

MORTAL DANGERS IN THE FOREST
AND ON THE RESERVATION

Life-threatening conditions that confront single individuals are brought on by the physical environment, and by interactions with other biological organisms, whether predators, competitors, parasites, or even prey. In eastern Paraguay, the abiotic environment can bring unexpected death in the form of lightning or windstorms, which can knock down towering trees or branches from the forest canopy. Floods have apparently killed enough Ache in the distant past that they figure importantly in Ache mythology. Generally, however, the physical environment is only hazardous when individuals are forced to expose themselves to it for long periods in order to acquire resources.

One form of environmental hazard that rarely kills outright, although it may be indirectly responsible for a very high percentage of deaths, especially in recent years, is exposure to cold. On even the coldest and wettest days, an Ache who stays in a hut and near a fire is in little danger. However, individuals who leave camp to search for food may be exposed to levels of cold that, in combination with rainfall and high humidity, can kill even an adult man if he is unfortunate enough to get lost without fire. Several days each year the temperatures fall below freezing and frost whitens the treetops, killing the uppermost leaves in the canopy. One day in July 1980 we measured the early morning temperature at −4 degrees centigrade. An old man who had gotten lost the day before and not returned to the band that night was feared dead because he had no way to make a fire (the Ache carry firebrands but do not have firemaking technology or techniques). Men and women commented that many of the capuchin monkeys must have frozen to death during the previous night, and the band spent the entire morning tracking the old man to learn his fate. Luckily, he had encountered another foraging band and was safe, but the lesson was not lost on the young boys who were learning to hunt for themselves.

Another time, one of us spent two days sitting cramped in a tiny leaky hut in the rain. On the third straight day of rain, the Ache decided to forage, as the band was extremely hungry. We walked about two hours in pouring rain with the temperature around 8 degrees centigrade. When the men finally stopped to build a fire, several individuals (including the anthropologists) were numb from the cold, almost to the point of delirium. Exposure to cold almost certainly plays an important part in susceptibility to respiratory infections, which have been a major killer of the Ache population in the twentieth century and are the most common medical complaint that we have treated in the field.

Most dangers in the Paraguayan environment, however, are the result of other biological organisms. Most important are conspecifics, and parasites in their role as disease vectors. In distant third place is the danger of death from the other animals, insects, and plants of the forest environment. Nevertheless, because Americans are unaccustomed to jaguar attacks, snake bites, and other jungle dangers, we tend to overestimate the probability of these rare events, and exotic dangers have generally concerned the members of our own research team (and their relatives) more than other hazards of fieldwork which are actually more common. These dangers also place important constraints on the lives of Ache foragers, and they permeate Ache mythology. Jaguars, for example, seem to be a serious threat even though they have killed only twelve Northern Ache during the past century. During the time we spent living in the forest, we saw jaguars only twice. Both times we were with an entire band, and individuals were clearly alarmed but not panicked. Later, however, when the man Kim had chosen for a focal follow study was attacked by a jaguar only a few meters from where he was searching for peccary tracks, all the individuals in the band became extremely concerned and cautious. The hunter had managed to hit the jaguar squarely on the head with a machete and it ran off, bleeding profusely. On another occasion, Hilly Kaplan was only meters behind his focal man when a jaguar jumped out of a tree on the man. The hunter managed to knock the jaguar off with his bow, but he was visibly shaken. The women of the band cried for a half an hour after the event, and all band members proceeded cautiously for some time.

Poisonous snakes are another common danger in eastern Paraguay. Our data show that thirty-four individuals were killed by poisonous snakes in the past century. We saw a half dozen or so bites in the field, some of which led to complete destruction or paralyses of an extremity. One strong adult man died from a *Bothrops* sp. (fer-de-lance, bushmaster) bite in 1981. We also killed many snakes ourselves and saw the Ache kill numerous more. Most individuals survive snake bites after a few days of intense pain. Occasionally, the victim will lose a limb from the toxin, which destroys all the flesh near the bite, and the wound may become severely infected. Most adult males in the study population have been bitten at least once by a poisonous snake, and after they survive a bite they are called *paje,* which roughly translates as "magic." The most common circumstance, which Kim only narrowly avoided because a companion yelled to him, is for a person to be bit after stepping on a snake while looking up into the canopy in search of arboreal game.

Insect pests are ubiquitous in eastern Paraguay. Stinging ants, bees, and wasps are endured on almost a daily basis. One wasp, which is particularly aggressive in the early wet season, has a sting that induces dizziness and vomiting, even in adults. Men who extract honey *always* get stung while removing the honeycomb. Army ants can bite viciously and invade a campsite day or night, as we learned at two o'clock in the morning in one forest camp in 1984. Another stinging ant is so painful that even eight hours after the sting, the affected part aches and burns. Spiders bite, particularly at night, and produce a tender swollen wound that often becomes seriously infected. Kim received a caterpillar sting on the upper arm that was so painful he was unable to speak for almost eight hours. Finally, a certain flying beetle, when startled, excretes a liquid that burns like acid and can temporarily blind a person for 48 hours. All these insects are dangerous enough that they leave little doubt an infant or small child would not survive long if left unattended on the forest floor. Forest camps are constantly interrupted by the cry of some child who is learning the hard way about which insects to avoid.

Other insect pests are more subtle but also represent a long-term threat to health and well being. Small fleas burrow in the feet and lay their eggs, which grow just under the surface of the skin and can lead to serious infections. Botflies also lay their larvae under the skin, resulting in an ever-growing and painful wound which can contain a worm of alarming proportions. Mosquitoes are generally not too bad, but in the peak of the warm-wet season they are very unpleasant. For example, on December 13, 1981, the focal men and women we followed slapped themselves an average of 17 times *per minute* ($n = 38$ one-minute samples, s.e. $= 16.2$) to ward off mosquitoes. Smaller forest gnats are even more unpleasant. They can barely be seen, but their bite is hard enough to draw blood and itches horribly. Ticks have to be removed several times a day in thick forest settings, and tiny ticks sometimes infest clothes and skin by the hundreds. Every night, after the evening meal, women and children check for ticks on the bodies of the hunters using a burning bamboo twig as a torch. Although the bites are not painful or serious, they often become infected and can lead to a painful wound, which may fester for months. Leeches are similarly unpleasant after a day of fishing in a lagoon. Lice are almost universal among children, and adults fight a never-ending battle to keep the number of lice in their hair to a minimum.

Microorganisms may be even more dangerous than insect pests. Despite the fact that the Ache move their camps almost every day, minimizing the accumulation of waste products and parasite populations, the wet tropical forest is an ideal environment for a variety of dangerous infectious vectors. Fungal infections, scabies, and other skin problems are found among 100% of the individuals in the population and generally pester anthropologists even months after leaving the field. Leshmaniasis and Chagas disease are both common and have led to hideous disfigurement of a few individuals. Malaria has come and gone several times from eastern Paraguay during the twentieth century, and it is extremely debilitating. During a particularly bad malarial year (1986–1987) we observed seizures from cerebral malaria that resulted in severe burns when affected individuals fell uncontrollably into fire hearths.

Finally, the forest lifestyle itself is dangerous simply because accidents happen and, until recently, medical treatment was nonexistent. In the short period of our lives that we spent in the forest, we have seen Ache foragers bitten by coatis, pacas, monkeys, and piranhas; torn open by thorns; shot by arrows; hit by falling trees; accidentally cut by machete or ax; burned in campfires; and fall out of fruit trees. Although none of these accidents was fatal during our field period, each contributed to a lowering of the overall health of individuals whose bodies were almost certainly fighting off the daily onslaught of disease and parasite vectors to which the Ache are exposed. While the accidents themselves may not be lethal, they may result in reduced performance by an adult caretaker or food provider, which ultimately endangers the life of a dependent child.

Threats to life and good health are considerably reduced at the current reservations. Areas of forest have been cleared down to bare dirt, eliminating many insect and animal pests. The occupational hazards of planting and weeding fields seem tame in comparison to the hunting-gathering lifestyle (both to us and to the Ache). Warfare and homicide rates have been effectively reduced to zero because of state and missionary intervention, and medical treatment is often available in mission-sponsored clinics. In conjunction with the reduction of some dangers, however, other health problems have become more common. Respiratory infections are now a serious problem and affect almost the entire population between May and August during the cold season each year. Tuberculosis, which was completely absent in the forest population and was not seen on reservations until the mid 1980s, has now become common. This may be due to increased population density (and rapid spread of disease vectors), use of fire hearths inside walled houses, communal sharing of yerba mate tea (each participant sucks from the same straw), generally poor nutrition at permanent settlements, or some combination of these factors. Gastrointestinal problems also plague the entire population from time to time. Amebiasis and giardiasis are endemic, and most small children experience frequent bouts of diarrhea. Intestinal parasites are common and can become serious. Several times, mothers brought their children to us for treatment because they had seen worms crawling out of the nose or mouth when the child was sleeping. Other new health problems have also arisen. Venereal disease is now endemic, though rapidly treated and apparently not affecting population fertility (see Chapter 8). Asthma has been reported for a few children and may be increasing in frequency. In short, the Ache have traded one set of health hazards for a new set, but overall survivorship has increased greatly as we will see. Nevertheless, harsh conditions of past and present life have weeded out all but the most hardy individuals. In the 1987 population there were only one blind and one partially blind individual, no deaf persons, no partial or complete cripples, and only one individual who was mildly retarded. No major body deformities were found. All obviously defective children that were born between 1977 and 1987 died before their third birthday. One boy born with a mild pelvic deformity has survived in recent times owing in part to missionary intervention and a series of operations.

CUSTOMS CONCERNING SICKNESS AND DEATH

Traditionally, the Ache expressed an extremely "biological" view of illness and death compared with what we have witnessed in other isolated traditional societies. Although the Ache did believe that consumption of certain food items could lead to fevers caused by an evil spirit entering the body, witchcraft was unknown, and accidental death or illness was usually attributed to chance rather than the design of some deity or evil spirit. Revenge, in the form of a club fight, was extracted when someone was thought to be to blame for a particular unfortunate event (such as the death or kidnapping of a child), but for the most part misfortune was the concern of only the affected party and his close kin.

In combination with their "biological" view of the causality of poor health, the Ache also did not have a well-developed system of native medicine or shamanism. There were no shamans, no special healers, and very few natural remedies were believed to be effective against most ailments. Occasionally, smoke from a fire would be blown on an injured part (such as a snakebite) or perhaps shavings from the bark of a certain vine would be mixed with water and rubbed on the body to cure headaches, fevers, and colds. They commonly tied a vine tightly around the waist, chest, or head to relieve some unwanted symptoms. Fat from insect larvae would be rubbed into skin infections; ectoparasites were removed manually if possible. Any person could perform these acts. Most injuries and illnesses were not treated at all, however, and the elaborate medicinal plant system employed by the neighboring Guarani tribes was unknown to the Ache. The victim would simply rest by a fire until he or she felt well enough to continue with daily activities.

The traditional Ache view that health problems were due to the vagaries of chance, and that little could be done to alleviate any suffering, resulted in minimal attempts to help the sick and injured. Several times we witnessed gravely ill individuals in the corner of a hut, completely ignored by other residents. The Ache describe a sick person as *mano* or "dead," and sometimes it appears that they resign themselves to the inevitable death of an individual long before he or she is "beyond help" according to our own medical standards. In many instances individuals were buried alive. For example, Bertoni (1941) relates an incident of a man who was buried alive but was able to crawl out of his grave, only to be burned to death by the other members of his band, who believed that it was his spirit returning to take revenge. We saw a case in 1978 where a woman completely ceased to care for or feed her spouse when he became gravely ill with pneumonia, even though we assured her that he would live (and he did thanks to penicillin). She left him alone in their hut to fend for himself and returned to her relatives. Since he was too weak to sit or stand at that point, he clearly would have died without our intervention. Later, after he recovered in a nearby hospital, he did not seem to hold a grudge against her for having given up on him, and in fact the couple was still married in 1994.

In the forest, when the Ache were highly mobile, a cruel fate fell upon anyone who could not keep up with the band. Many were simply left behind and never seen again. Others were left on trails near the houses of Paraguayans in the hope that these "enemies" would take pity on and care for the disabled. Still others were buried alive, in order to save them the hideous fate of being devoured by vultures while still conscious. Although such events were relatively rare before contact, they were extremely common during the period of contact when epidemics swept rapidly through the population. Old and sick individuals were simply left behind. Relatives often broke wide, well-marked trails, hoping that their loved ones would catch up later, and sometimes they did, even managing to crawl on their hands and knees from one camp to another until they were able to walk.

Despite this rather harsh treatment of the disabled, occasional examples of great sacrifice are also found. Several blind individuals were led around for years by others who helped them follow the band's trail (all, however, were ultimately abandoned in times of stress). One boy who had lost his leg below the knee from a snakebite was carried piggyback by his father and other relatives. (He was later left with Paraguayans at first contact.) Older children who couldn't walk for whatever reason were sometimes carried by their parents for years (again, all were ultimately abandoned, however).

When an individual died, he or she was buried in a hole, and a palm-thatched hut was built above the grave. The band then moved away from the site and did not return for some time. A particularly important individual was often accompanied in the grave by a small child who was sacrificed for the occasion. Sacrificed individuals were usually small girls but could be from almost any age-sex category under the right circumstances. This is discussed in more detail in a later chapter. The cadaver of an individual who had been particularly "mean," "angry," or "disliked by many people" was sometimes burned after death, rather than buried. Since old women and men were generally thought of as "mean or angry," many were burned rather than buried. This was based in a belief that revengeful spirits could linger in the place where a person was buried and could only be destroyed if the cadaver was burned. These spirits were thought to enter the body of someone who had consumed certain food items and cause lethal fevers (*juvy*).

Health care at the current reservations has changed dramatically. Most important, many Ache now believe that the sick and injured will generally recover if treated and cared for. Because the reservation Ache are no longer mobile, disabled individuals are no longer left behind or abandoned no matter how old or feeble they become. Although some individuals remain overtly callous to the misfortunes of others, many others are now intensely devoted to caring for their sick or disabled relatives.

ANALYTICAL METHODS AND CHOICE OF SAMPLE

Because we only witnessed a small number of deaths directly, most causes of death were obtained from interviews in the Ache language. An informant was asked "How did he die?" each time a death was reported. In some cases we followed up by asking for a description of symptoms just prior to the reported death. Informant categories generally agree with the categories that we could assign based on our own limited knowledge of tropical medicine and given the lack of laboratory and diagnostic facilities. Almost all the causes of death elicited from informants were biological in nature and made "medical sense." Only two of the seventy-one causes of death that Ache informants listed would not be considered likely ultimate causes of death by members of most western societies: two classes of supernaturally caused fevers and headache, or *juvy*. One class of juvy comes from touching human blood without undergoing purification, and the other class comes from eating certain foods. Regardless of our doubts about how these fevers were caused, the Ache may be correct in their assessment of the symptoms (headache and fever) that presaged death.

Ache informants were careful to distinguish between when they were speculating and when they were sure about the cause of death for a particular individual, but in this analysis we treat all reports equally. In any case, recorded causes of death are highly consistent across informants (see Table 3.2). In a small percentage of cases, more than one cause was listed. For example, an informant might say "that child died of cough because its parents neglected it" or "she was buried alive because she was sick." In these cases, the actual cause of death (cough, or buried alive) was recorded as the primary cause, with the additional factors (neglect, illness) recorded as secondary causes. Because secondary causes of death were not elicited *systematically*, the sample size of such "mitigating factors" is small and the patterns from our present data may not be particularly meaningful, so we have chosen to analyze only primary cause of death. Undoubtedly, many primary causes of death were also accompanied by some secondary relevant factor, but such issues are not addressed in most anthropological demography.

CAUSES OF MORTALITY DURING THE FOREST PERIOD

We have calculated the proportion of different causes of death for all individuals listed in the master ID file, since there is no reason to expect that *cause* of death will influence the probability of being included in the data set. Of the 1,423 Northern Ache born since 1890, 881 have died, and cause of death was reported for 843 of them (95%). Causes of mortality differ greatly among different age and sex categories in most human populations, so analyses specific to these age-sex groupings are informative. In the Ache population, causes of death have also changed considerably between the forest, contact, and reservation periods. For this reason the data are broken down into several age-sex categories and analyzed separately for the three time periods.

Percentages of reported deaths in the forest from each of the reported causes are shown in Table 5.1. These 382 deaths took place before 1971 when the individuals reported were unweaned infants (0–3 years), children (4–14 years), adults (15–59 years), or old people (60+ years) at the time of their death. The causes of death are divided into four major categories: illness/parasitic disease, degenerative/congenital/miscellaneous health problems, accident, and conspecific violence. The precise cause of death given by the informant is listed by these categories to facilitate cross-cultural comparison. The age-specific death rate from any cause can be estimated by multiplying the percentage of total deaths from a specific cause in an age-sex category by the mortality rates given in the next chapter.

The data indicate that conspecific violence was by far the most important cause of death in the study population during the past century, accounting for just over half of all deaths experienced in the forest. Violence initiated by the Ache themselves (homicide) is the most frequent cause of death to very young children and accounts for about 40% of the deaths due to violence. For other age categories the main cause of violent death was being killed (or captured and never seen again) in external warfare with Paraguayan peasants and Guarani indigenous groups, accounting for about 60% of the violent deaths.

The second major cause of death in the forest was illness and disease, which accounts for about a fourth of all deaths. Illnesses cause death in all age groups but are less likely to be lethal among weaned children, who are probably the healthiest age group in the population and are mainly killed by accidents and violence. Accidents are the third most common cause of death and account for about one death in eight. Accidents are important causes of death in every age group except the smallest children, who are probably carefully watched by their mothers or caretakers. Most accidents are associated with food acquisition activities and could be avoided by simply not foraging. In this light it is interesting to note that the percentage of deaths from accidents increases across the four age classes. This may indicate that individuals are willing to expose themselves to greater risks as they become older in order to acquire food. Such a pattern would be consistent with life history theory and the increasing extrinsic death rate owing to senescence.

Finally, degenerative and congenital diseases account for about one death in fifteen. They mainly affect the very young, who die immediately if they are abnormal, or the very old, who ultimately must succumb to the aging process itself. In addition, childbirth represents a special hazard for reproductive-aged women. Each category of deaths is discussed in more detail below.

Illness and Parasitic Disease

Illness and disease can strike any individual in the population regardless of age or sex. Despite our findings that since 1977 respiratory disease has been the major killer (see below), the precontact forest-dwelling Ache seem to have been relatively unaffected by respiratory infections compared with other causes of death. Instead, Ache children primarily succumbed to gastrointestinal problems whereas adults died primarily from the fevers that the Ache call *juvy*. The Ache believe that many of the gastrointestinal problems which kill children are associated with weaning and beginning to eat solid food. Young children seem to experience stomach pain and diarrhea frequently, and they often ultimately succumb to dehydration. This may be why parents often delay giving children any solid food until they are well over a year of age, and mothers who encourage their children to eat solid food at too young an age are scolded. The Ache attribute the fevers to eating bad (uncooked) meat, too much honey or too many insect larvae, and a variety of other "dangerous" foods. When describing the illness, however, they are quick to point out that it is the symptoms, intense fever and headache, that actually kill those who are affected. Our own experience treating the category of illnesses called *juvy* suggests to us that this category includes a variety of viral infections similar to what Americans call the flu, but also including symptoms of diseases such as malaria, dengue, and amebic dysentery. Malaria has been uncommon in the past few decades, but indications are that it was more common in the past. During the forest period several women apparently had seizures brought on by cerebral malaria, which also had a major effect on the Ache population in 1986–1987.

Other important diseases include skin and staphylococcal infections. Individuals of all age-sex categories are susceptible to, and die from, infection. The Ache call these diseases *eche ipe* or "body pus." Members of our research team were constantly taking oral antibiotics to fight these infections, which start as a small insect bite, cut, or scratch and rapidly become a large festering open sore in the tropical heat and humidity. Not infrequently we were called on to drain pus from wounds on the arms, legs, trunk, or head of Ache children and adults. Staphylococcal infections are sometimes internal, but the Ache recognize them as essentially the same thing as the more common surface infections. Internal infections can grow into large pockets of pus that are extremely painful and cause high fever before finally draining through a surface opening. The Ache lump other cases of "internal body swelling" with infections, but they are more likely to be some type of cancer. Several individuals were described as "growing a large ball" in a particular part of their body, which eventually killed them. Finally, Leshmaniasis, caused by a microorganism that produces open ulcerous wounds, was responsible for the deaths of a handful of individuals. In these cases the wound becomes larger and larger until the individual ultimately becomes hideously disfigured and dies of infection. In one case a teenage girl was stabbed to death by two men because "she had lost her nose to Leshmaniasis and was ugly."

In addition to the deaths tabulated above in our systematic sample, we have collected a variety of stories about illness and disease-related deaths that provide important insight into life in the forest. In one story a man died because he ate too much honey without mixing it with water. The Ache insist that eating pure honey in large quantities can cause death, and several times they chastised members of our research team for not mixing their honey with water. Several individuals died of fevers after holding a newborn child or a girl at her puberty ceremony. These deaths were said to be from exposure to human blood, which is always dangerous. One man's stomach bulged out bigger and bigger over a period of months until it looked like he had swallowed a watermelon. One child died of diarrhea, which his mother insisted was due to a short interbirth interval and the fact that the boy was weaned too early. Several children were completely covered by sores in a manner that evokes images of smallpox but was more probably due to some kind of systemic infection. One entire family died together of "shaking." We believe that the symptoms described probably refer to malaria (fever and chills).

Degenerative/Congenital Diseases

The degenerative/congenital disease category is composed of a variety of causes that do not fall easily into the other three categories. Deaths in this category were reported only for small children and people over sixty years of age, or women who died in childbirth. The children mainly died from difficult births, deformations, or prematurity. Many of these children simply died soon after birth from unknown causes but were not reported to be ill. The Ache have a strong aversion to raising any child that appears weak or defective and almost always kill such children soon after birth. Although many infanticides were reported (see below), we believe that some of the children reported to have died of defects at birth were actually killed and are coded incorrectly because we were not careful enough to ask whether the child was dead before it was buried. In many interviews, when we asked how a child died the mother would simply reply that it was *pura* or "defective." This category includes infants who are born feet first, those born deformed, and those born without hair (the Ache believe all infants born without hair on the head are defective), or those born prematurely. The Ache believe that many children are born defective and simply will not survive. They have undoubtedly learned this collectively through generations of observation, and the number of deaths of pura children who were not killed at birth suggests that they are correct.

About one-fifth of the deaths of old people could not be attributed to any cause other than "old age." Most of these individuals died in their sleep, or while sleeping in camp during the day. There were no cases of individuals complaining of chest pains or suddenly falling over dead. This suggests that heart attacks and strokes must be very rare in the population.

Specific examples of degenerative/congenital defects are sometimes found in Ache stories. One boy was born albino ("All white with white hair. Whiter than you.") and died or was buried alive soon after birth. Several children were born with clubfeet or "short fingers" and were killed or later died. Several children were born without an ear (or with only part of their ear) but were not killed. One boy was born without foreskin on his penis, and another without testes. Both survived to adulthood, but neither ever had a spouse.

Finally, deaths in childbirth represent a special risk for reproductive-aged women. In our data set four women are reported to have died in childbirth in the forest. This accounted for about 8% of the deaths to women between 15 and 60 years of age. Between 1940 and 1970, when most births and all deaths in childbirth would have been recorded, we estimate 4 deaths out of 597 children born, for a maternal death rate of approximately 1 per 150 births.

Accidents

Accidents are common and an inevitable consequence of the hunting-gathering lifestyle. Accidents account for about twice the proportion of male deaths as female deaths (17% vs. 7%), and the data strongly support the suggestion that hunting is more dangerous than gathering since during the active food-acquiring years (childhood and adulthood) 24% of all male deaths were due to accidents whereas for females the percentage of deaths from accidents is only 8%. Poisonous snakebites were the single most common lethal accident, accounting for about 6% of all deaths reported. More than 80% of the snakebite deaths were to males, and among *adult* males, snakebite accounts for 14% of all deaths. Getting eaten by a jaguar, lost, or hit by lightning each accounted for about 2% of all deaths. Again, more than 80% of the cases of being eaten by a jaguar were recorded for males, and this category accounted for 8% of all adult male deaths. Other less frequent accidents include a wide variety of mishaps such as drowning, being accidentally suffocated during sleep (for two newborns), falling from a tree, and being hit by a falling tree (that was being chopped down by another Ache).

Stories of accidental death are sometimes told in the evening when band members relate the day's events to things that happened in the past. Children are fascinated by these stories and probably learn invaluable lessons about the dangers of the forest, which aid in their own survival. One boy died when he forgot to pinch the head of a palm larva before swallowing it. The jaws of the larva clamped on to his throat and he choked to death. Several times an adolescent boy strayed too far from the adult men while hunting and was either never seen again or found dead several days later. One hunter who was digging an armadillo burrow fell into the hole head first and suffocated. Another fell out of a tree almost 40 m to his death while he was trying to recover an arrow that he had shot at a monkey. One small girl fell into a hole left by a bottle tree that had rotted away and broke her neck. Several men were attacked by jaguars. Some of their remains were found and others simply vanished. A boy was bitten on the head by a poisonous snake in the camp at night while he slept. He died the next day. One old woman was killed by a falling tree chopped by a adolescent girl for firewood. Henceforth the girl became known as "Falling Firewood," a nickname that reminded her daily of her misdeed. One man was bitten by a coati and later died of the wound. In a similar incident a hunter was bitten on the wrist in 1985. His main arteries and veins were punctured and he certainly would have died if he had not received modern medical attention. A small girl fell in a river while crossing on a log bridge and was swept away. An adolescent boy died of infection after his lip was pierced during his puberty ceremony. An infant's mother laid on top of it during the night (Ache mothers usually sleep sitting up with an infant in their lap) and smothered it. Another infant died after hitting its head on the ground while being born. A woman bled to death during a spontaneous abortion (several women aborted spontaneously after falling from fruit trees, and one woman aborted after falling to the ground while carrying firewood). Finally, in an event that seems a stroke of truly random bad luck, six people in one band were killed when a lightning bolt struck the camp during a storm.

Conspecific Violence

Death at the hands of another human being was by far the most common cause of death to forest-dwelling Ache. Important age-sex patterns emerge that cannot be detected when the entire sample of deaths is aggregated. First, as mentioned above, most deaths, except those among unweaned children, were caused by non-Ache in warfare and raids that were common until first peaceful contact. Among the deaths from warfare we have included individuals who were captured and never seen again. Only one of the individuals captured alive was over fifteen years of age, and very few of those captured are known to have survived. Among infants and children, being captured accounted for about one-fourth of all the "deaths" to both sexes. Individuals in all age-sex categories were shot and killed by non-Ache enemies; however, males were about twice as likely to be shot as females (20% vs. 11% of all deaths to each sex). Among the adult males, *external warfare accounted for 36% of all deaths.*

Killings within the group include infanticide, geronticide, child homicide (often in order to accompany an adult in the grave), and club fights. Death at the hands of another Ache accounted for about 22% of all deaths in the forest sample. Only four cases of "adult" homicide (unsanctioned by the social group) took place in the past century. We have also included two cases of extreme child neglect since the Ache treat this category as equivalent to infanticide (and biologically it produces the same result). We have observed parental neglectful behavior that the Ache label *pianjambyre* or "neglected by its provider (after a parent initiates sexual relations with a new partner)" directly after a man abandoned his wife and newborn child, and there was little doubt that the intention was for the child to die (which it did in about two weeks).

In-group killings consist of more female deaths in infancy and childhood and slightly more male deaths in adulthood. In the youngest age category, all types of infanticide/child homicide show only a slight sex bias (38% of male infant deaths, 41% of female infant deaths). In later childhood (4–15 years), however, homicide is a much more common cause of female death than it is for males (28% of female child deaths, 6% of male child deaths). In accordance with informant statements, most children killed to accompany an adult in the grave are female (80% of all children buried with a deceased adult).

In-group killings among adults account for 10% of all adult female deaths and 11% of the adult male deaths. Club fights were the single most important cause, accounting for about 8% of the deaths to males over fifteen years of age. Only one person (a teenage boy) in the twentieth-century population was shot with an arrow. This is in keeping with a strongly demonstrated aversion to uncontrolled in-group violence. Although the Ache killed all outsiders on sight before peaceful contact, club fights were the *only* sanctioned form of violence between men within the population itself. Other adult deaths from conspecific members of the Ache population included being buried alive because of old age or sickness, and being left behind to die (because of illness or blindness).

Stories about conspecific violence are probably more common topics of conversation than anything else, except current affairs and sexual gossip. Two women were stabbed to death by their husbands, who used an unstrung bow as a spear. A teenage boy was shot by a man who "was angry because he had a penis infection from having sex with a woman who was menstruating." A wife who was gravely ill asked her husband to bury her and her newborn child alive rather than leave them behind when the band moved its campsite. A boy was tied up on a Paraguayan road and left to be captured or die because he had a "paralyzed hand." A middle-aged woman was left behind by her band because she was blind and could not keep up. A middle-aged man was left behind because he was too sick to keep up. He was so weak that vultures came right down to the branches just above his head to wait for him to die. He managed to drive away the vultures and recovered from his illness. When he returned to his band they gave him the nickname "Vulture Droppings" because he was covered with feces from the birds who had perched above him. A woman reported that her first child was killed because the older men in the band didn't want a girl. Another woman mentioned that her first child was killed because the father of the child had abandoned her. A man killed the small boy of another couple because he was "in a bad mood and the child was crying." The brother of the victim, who witnessed the event, admitted that his own father did nothing to defend the child because "he was scared to death of the murderer." Another child was buried by a man because "it was funny looking and the other children laughed at it." A man named Tatu challenged another man to a club fight because Tatu's son had died and he wanted to take revenge on someone. Tatu was killed by his opponent in the fight. A middle-aged woman who was very ill asked to be buried alive with an old man who had died. One girl had extremely bad hemorrhoids so the men buried her alive. Another girl died of neglect (bad skin infections) because her stepmother did not care for her. A man reported that a brother who was born only a year and a half after him was stepped on and killed because the birth interval was too short. A woman and her two daughters were all buried alive when her husband died. Dozens of men women and children were shot by Paraguayans who raided their camps to capture slaves or in retaliation for the theft of a cow or horse. Lucky individuals describe how they survived. One man was shot twice in the arm and the chest but still managed to carry off his six-year-old son and run away. The man's father, however, was killed in the same incident. Another man was shot in the face and couldn't remove the shotgun pellets. A friend dug them out with his teeth, leaving a large scar on the man's face. The details of such deaths provide important insights into the lifestyle summarized in Table 5.1.

COMPARISON WITH THE !KUNG AND YANOMAMO

The causes of mortality among forest-living precontact Ache can be compared with data from the best-known hunter-gatherer and native South American populations to assess the similarity or differences in mortality patterns across traditional populations. Causes of death for the Ache, !Kung, and Yanomamo are compared in Tables 5.2 and 5.3. Howell (1979) broke down the !Kung causes of death into three major categories, which are reported here by sex for three age groupings. Since Howell provides only proportions for each cause of death, the actual number of deaths was approximated by multiplying the total sample size of deaths (342; Howell 1979:48) times the proportion reported by Howell (1979:68) and assuming an equal number of total deaths to each sex. The Yanomamo causes of death were not reported for different age categories, but they are divided by sex (Melancon 1982:42). Differences in proportions of deaths due to illness, degenerative diseases, accidents, and conspecific violence are highly significant between the Ache and both the !Kung and Yanomamo populations.[1]

The most obvious result from these comparisons is that conspecific violence is a much more important cause of death among the Ache than among either of the other two groups. Despite that fact that the Yanomamo have been called "the fierce people" (Chagnon 1968) and the !Kung have been called "the harmless people" (Thomas 1959), both groups show about the same levels of in-group killings of adults prior to state-level intervention. The Ache are much more likely than either the !Kung or the Yanomamo to die from something other than illness. Violent deaths, including accidents, account for about 11% of !Kung deaths,

20% of Yanomamo deaths, and approximately 70% of all Ache deaths. Conversely, illness accounts for only 24% of all Ache deaths before contact, but it accounts for 74% of Yanomamo deaths and 80% of !Kung deaths. We suspect that this difference is partially due to the fact that the Ache sample is the only one of the three that describes a group prior to peaceful contact with the outside world. Thus, forest-living Ache were not exposed to a variety of modern pathogens and experienced no state-level interference to mediate rates of violence within the society. The lack of permanent contact with members of the state society is also associated with the constant warfare that was the major killer of Ache adults during the twentieth century. Other smaller differences are also apparent but should be interpreted cautiously given the possible differences in age structure of the sample of deaths, and the difficulties of determining the true cause of death when an accident or conspecific violence is not implied. Respiratory disease is very common among the Yanomamo, and it results in a mortality pattern very similar to that seen among the postcontact (rather than precontact) Ache population. The lack of violence among the Yanomamo relative to that among the Ache may surprise many readers. It should be noted, however, that many of the violent deaths among the Ache are due to infanticide, child homicide, and external warfare against peasant colonists. Infanticide is also common among the Yanomamo, and it may be underreported in the cited study (cf. Early and Peters 1990). Child homicide does not appear to be common among the Yanomamo, and external warfare is very rare.

CAUSES OF DEATH DURING THE CONTACT PERIOD

For the Northern Ache the years immediately preceding permanent contact were characterized by extremely high mortality resulting from infectious diseases against which the Ache apparently had very little immunological defense. Ultimately, the cause of death in almost every case was respiratory infection; however, many times an individual first contracted another disease, such as measles, and then in a state of weakness fell ill with pneumonia. Many children who were not initially affected by virgin soil epidemics later died because their parents were unable to feed or care for them. A similar situation has been described for the Yanomamo, who also suffered high mortality during late 1950s and early 1960s after initial peaceful contact with outsiders (see Early and Peters 1990; Neel et al. 1970).

Causes of death during the period of first peaceful contact (1971–1977) are shown in Table 5.4. Contact-related illness accounts for about 85% of the adult deaths and 40% of the deaths of children during this time. Conspecific violence is the second most prevalent cause of death during this period, particularly among children, who were often buried alive with their deceased parents. We calculate that 168 of the 544 Northern Ache (31%) who were alive in 1970 died directly from contact-related diseases. Of these, 66 died in the forest, 92 at the Cerro Moroti government reservation/Protestant mission, 19 at the Manduvi Catholic mission, and 16 at Paraguayan houses near Curuguaty while waiting for transportation to a mission settlement. Experience with Ache bands contacted later (see Chapter 2) suggests that almost all these deaths could have been avoided if antibiotics against pneumonia had been administered, and food provided to the sick population (especially children) during the epidemics. Our data do not suggest that missionaries did not want to help the Ache, only that they failed to focus their help effectively during this time period. In the next chapter the age-sex pattern of contact-related deaths will be described along with some suggestions on how to avoid such a disaster in the future.

CAUSES OF DEATH DURING THE RESERVATION PERIOD

Levels of mortality and causes of death have changed radically since the Ache made first recorded peaceful contact. This contrast is primarily due to increased medical care, safer living and working environments, and an elimination of homicide and warfare as a result of state intervention. Because violent causes of death and accidental death rates have been greatly reduced, most individuals now die from illnesses. In addition, higher fertility rates, earlier weaning, and living in permanent settlements that concentrate parasitic and pathogenic organisms have probably increased the susceptibility and exposure to disease in the modern population.

Causes of death since 1978 are shown in Table 5.5. The number of adult deaths during this time period is so small that any conclusions should be cautiously drawn. One band made first contact during this time, and two small children in that band died from respiratory disease. For the most part, however, the overall pattern for all age-sex groups combined is almost identical to that reported for the !Kung (Howell 1979:68). About 80% of all deaths are due to illness, 10% to degenerative diseases, and 10% to accidents and violence. However, closer inspection of the Ache and !Kung data reveals some interesting differences. The Ache show higher rates of infanticide than the !Kung, and few if any cases of degenerative disease in the small sample of adult deaths. Recent studies of a similarly acculturated Yanomamo population show a very similar distribution of mortality causes (Early and Peters 1990). For the most part, we believe that the distribution of deaths in the different categories during the reservation period is very similar to that found in the surrounding peasant population. Rates of mortality, particularly in the youngest age classes, continue to be quite high, however, as will be seen in the next chapter.

SUMMARY

Tabulation of cause of death suggests that conspecific violence (death at the hands of another human) was the most common cause of death in the forest-living Ache population during the twentieth century. Infanticide was the most common cause of death of unweaned infants, whereas external warfare against Paraguayan colonists was the major cause of death for all older age categories. The data suggest that warfare with members of the Paraguayan society expanding into Ache territory was a prominent feature of twentieth-century Ache life. The Ache themselves mention their desire to avoid such warfare as a major motivating factor in their willingness to "be taken" to reservations.

Observations of Ache deaths from precontact warfare with non-Ache in the 1970s prompted some observers (e.g., Arens 1976, 1978; Melia et al. 1973; Munzel 1973, 1974) to insist that the Ache were victims of genocide. These old reports have recently resurfaced (Survival International 1993) despite the fact that we have presented a detailed critique of the genocide claim, including concrete demographic data contradicting the basis of that claim (Hill 1983a, 1983b). The data do not suggest that the Ache population was ever in danger of extinction from external warfare before 1970 (in fact the population was growing rapidly during the time they were allegedly being exterminated), nor is there evidence that any group of people (government, corporation, military, etc.) ever intended to exterminate the Ache. On the other hand, many peasants have indicated to us that their intention was to occupy the Ache land and use the Ache as low-paid laborers. The Ache contact situation also resulted in extremely high mortality, but this was due to carelessness and incompetence rather than intention, and the contact history is not particularly different from any of hundreds that have taken place in the Amazon over the past few centuries. Since the reports of Ache genocide have been published widely, we feel that it is important to correct erroneous information and to shed some light on the complicated issue of whether the Ache were victims of intentional or de facto genocide.

The Ache were killed in precontact warfare at an alarming rate. However, the situation cannot possibly be compared to examples of genocide such as the attempted extermination of the European Jews in the mid twentieth century. Individuals who initially alerted the world to the possibility of Ache genocide, or those who reacted to such reports, were undoubtedly well meaning but were poorly informed about the Ache situation. During the latter half of the twentieth century, when the Ache population was alleged to have been nearly exterminated, it was actually growing at a rate of 2.5% per year. During the same century but before contact, about 1.5% of the adult population died each year and about one-third of those deaths were a result of external warfare. Thus, we can estimate that *about 0.5% of the adult population was killed by Paraguayans each year.* Our data suggest that 61 Northern Ache were killed by Paraguayans during all of the twentieth century. The largest number of Ache ever killed in one raid was four, near the Naranjito ranch in 1971. About 67 children disappeared during the twentieth century, presumably captured by raiders. This contrasts with Munzel's (1976:37) estimate of 900 Northern Ache killed or kidnapped between 1968 and 1972 and reports of huge massacres in which whole bands were exterminated. Indeed, Munzel's number is almost twice the size of the entire Northern Ache population in 1968!

Our data indicate a significant mortality rate but probably not one that should be labeled "genocide." The Ache themselves killed dozens of Paraguayans during skirmishes and raids over the same time period. It is the Ache's best guess that *none* of the raids they experienced were ever carried out by the Paraguayan military (contrary to Munzel's and Arens's allegations) because perpetrators wore no uniforms and used only crude weapons (shotguns and pistols). No chiefs were ever tortured, and no Ache were ever killed in the process of capturing them for the government reservation (cf. Arens 1976). All Ache killings took place in small-scale raids before the reservation period. In a variety of cases the killers were known to be local ranch hands who organized a retaliatory raid after the Ache had killed and eaten their horses and cattle. Most killings took place after the Ache had stolen manioc from fields belonging to peasant families living on the forest frontier. Road building crews, who were government employees, killed no Ache despite the fact that they were often the targets of Ache arrows during the mid 1960s while constructing the Saltos de Guaira road.

In summary, the situation in the twentieth century was one of small-scale war between the Ache and invading peasants. We have heard similar reports of homicide and child capture among every other native group with whom we have worked in South America. This was a classic case of conquest, but not a case of genocide, and certainly not a unique case that deserved to be singled out among all the unfortunate histories of South American Indians. It should instead be described within the context of the slow conquest of the Americas that has been going on for more than five hundred years. Perhaps that entire process could be labeled genocide, given the all too frequent extermination of small tribal populations, but the Ache themselves were not the subjects of a policy of genocide. All the governments of North and South America have been involved in gross violations of indigenous rights and a long-term trend of displacing native peoples from their traditional lands. All these governments deserve to be condemned equally. Certainly nothing about the Ache situation provides a moral impetus for singling out Paraguay uniquely as being involved in "genocide," nor is there any moral justification for equating the Ache history to that of the Jews during the Second World War. Such loose analogies simply dilute the significance and horror of actual genocide when it is observed.

Other important causes of death among the Ache living in the forest include accident and illness. Snakebite was the most common lethal accident, and fevers as well as uncategorized illness were the most common causes of death from infectious agents. Surprisingly, to us, respiratory disease, which has been the major killer of the Ache population since contact, was very rarely a cause of death in the forest-dwelling population.

The contact period was devastating to the Ache population, and almost all deaths during the contact years (1971–1977) are due to contact-related respiratory disease. Deaths that are indirectly the result of contact were also common. Particularly important among indirect effects are homicide of orphaned children and deaths of children who were malnourished because their sick or dead parents could not provide adequate food and child care. Government officials and even some missionaries were clearly negligent during this time period and did little to ensure the survival of this fragile, newly contacted population. Nearly all these deaths could have been avoided by diligent administration of antibiotics and food supplementation during the periods of major illness. We hope that the Ache contact mortality data will provide an impetus to government and missionary organizations working with native peoples around the world. Indeed, through clear statistical documentation of the problem we should be able to bring strong political pressure to bear on all organizations currently involved in working with newly contacted native peoples.

In the past sixteen years, at reservation settlements, most deaths have been to children who are unweaned or in the process of weaning, with respiratory and gastrointestinal infections being most prominent causes of death. Adult deaths have occurred so rarely that it is difficult to categorize the major health hazards to the reservation adult population, but illness rather than accident has been the major cause of adult death. Recent observations suggest that tuberculosis is rapidly becoming a major Ache health problem. Programs to improve reservation nutrition and sanitation would probably address this problem most effectively. Because infant mortality is the most important cause of death on the reservations, a serious program of infant support and health monitoring on a regular basis would have the greatest impact on reservation mortality rates.

NOTE

1.   Statistics for differences in proportions of deaths between the Ache and the !Kung or Yanomamo from Tables 5.2 and 5.3 are as follows: Ache vs. !Kung 0–14 years, $\chi^2 = 167.3$, df = 2, $p < 0.001$; Ache vs. !Kung 15–59 years, $\chi^2 = 69.9$, df = 2, $p < 0.001$; Ache vs. !Kung 60+ years, $\chi^2 = 27.6$, df = 2, $p < 0.001$; Ache vs. Yanomamo all ages, $\chi^2 = 98.6$, df =3, $p < 0.001$.

Table 5.1. Causes of Death during the Forest Period

Reported cause	Number of deaths (children aged 0–3 years)					
	Female	Male	All	Category	n	%
respiratory	0	1	1	respiratory	1	0.8
diarrhea	4	3	7			
stomach problems	3	4	7	gastrointestinal	14	10.7
fever after eating buchu larvae	1	0	1	fever	1	0.8
skin infection	2	1	3			
swollen body/systemic infection	1	0	1			
sick (unspecified)	7	6	13			
too skinny	1	2	3	other	20	15.3
				all illness	**36**	**27.5**
mother had no milk	0	1	1			
no hair (premature?)	0	1	1			
unspecified newborn death	8	5	13			
defective	0	3	3			
born arm first	0	1	1	**congenital/**		
				degenerative	**19**	**14.5**
hit by lightning	0	1	1			
accidently suffocated	1	1	2	**accident**	**3**	**2.3**
sacrificed with adult	7	4	11			
mother died	1	1	2			
child homicide	9	15	24			
infanticide (father)	3	0	3			
infanticide (mother)	3	1	4			
neglect	1	1	2			
buried	0	1	1	homicide/		
left behind	2	3	5	neglect	52	39.7
shot by Paraguayan	0	1	1			
captured by Paraguayan*	9	11	20	warfare	21	16.0
				violence	**73**	**55.7**
All causes	**63**	**68**	**131**		**131**	**100.0**
	Number of deaths (juveniles aged 4–14 years)					
sick in lungs	1	0	1	respiratory	1	1.0
diarrhea	1	1	2			
stomach problems	1	0	1	gastrointestinal	3	3.0
fever after eating peccary	0	1	1			
fever after eating armadillo	0	1	1			
fever after eating pichu larvae	1	0	1			
fever after eating honey	0	1	1	fever	4	4.0
skin infection	1	1	2			
swollen body/systemic infection	1	1	2			

(continued)

Table 5.1.   *(continued)*

	Number of deaths (juveniles aged 4–14 years)					
sick (unspecified)	2	1	3	other	7	7.1
				all illness	**15**	**15.2**
snakebite	0	3	3			
hit by lightning	0	3	3			
drowned	1	0	1			
lost	0	3	3			
hit by falling tree	0	1	1	**accident**	**11**	**11.1**
sacrificed with adult	10	1	11			
child homicide	3	0	3			
left behind	1	2	3	homicide/		
				neglect	17	17.2
shot by Paraguayan	1	9	10			
captured by Paraguayan*	26	20	46	warfare	56	56.6
				violence	**73**	**73.8**
All causes	**50**	**49**	**99**		**99**	**100.0**

	Number of deaths (adults aged 15–59 years)					
sick in lungs	0	1	1	respiratory	1	0.8
stomach problems	1	0	1	gastrointestinal	1	0.8
fever after eating pichu larvae	3	5	8			
fever after eating kracho larvae	0	5	5			
fever after eating honey	3	3	6			
fever after eating palm starch	0	1	1			
fever after eating corn	1	0	1			
malaria	0	2	2			
fever after touching blood	1	2	3	fever	26	20.6
skin infection	0	1	1			
sores on neck	0	1	1			
swollen body/systemic infection	0	3	3			
liver problems	0	1	1			
sick (unspecified)	0	1	1	other	7	5.6
				all illness	**35**	**27.8**
old age	1	0	1	**congenital/**		
childbirth	3	0	3	**degenerative**	**4**	**3.2**
eaten by jaguar	1	7	8			
snakebite	3	12	15			
hit by lightning	1	2	3			
fell from tree	0	1	1			
lost	0	1	1			
hit by falling tree	1	0	1	**accident**	**29**	**23.0**
buried alive	1	0	1			
left behind	1	0	1			
club fight	0	6	6	homicide/		

Table 5.1.   (continued)

	Number of deaths (adults aged 15–59 years)					
homicide, killed by Ache	2	1	3	neglect	11	8.7
shot by Paraguayan	15	31	46			
captured by Paraguayan	1	0	1	warfare	47	37.3
				violence	**58**	**46.0**
All causes	**39**	**87**	**126**		**126**	**100.0**

	Number of deaths (adults aged 60+ years)**					
diarrhea	2	1	3			
sick (unspecified)	0	2	2	**all illness**	**5**	**18.5**
old age	2	4	6	**congenital/ degenerative**	**6**	**22.2**
eaten by jaguar	0	1	1			
snakebite	1	2	3			
lost .	3	0	3	**accident**	**7**	**25.9**
buried	1	0	1			
left behind	0	2	2			
club fight	0	2	2			
shot by Paraguayan	2	2	4	**violence**	**9**	**33.3**
All causes	**11**	**16**	**27**		**27**	**100.0**

* Some of these children may not have died, but information suggests that most died soon after capture.

** Includes some individuals born between 1880 and 1890.

Table 5.2. Ache and !Kung Causes of Death

Category	Ache before 1971				!Kung before 1973*			
	All	%	Female	Male	All	%	Female	Male
Children under 15 years of age								
all illness	51	**22.2**	27	24	144	**87.8**	70	74
degenerative	19	**8.3**	8	11	6	**3.7**	3	3
accident	14	**6.1**	2	12				
and					14	**8.5**	7	7
violence	146	**63.5**	76	70				
total	230	100.0	113	117	164	100.0	80	84
Adults between 15 and 59 years of age								
all illness	35	**28.0**	9	26	101	**79.5**	55	46
degenerative	4	**3.2**	4	0	4	**3.1**	2	2
accident	29	**23.2**	6	23				
and					22	**17.4**	5	17
violence	57	**45.6**	19	38				
total	125	100.0	38	87	127	100.0	62	65
Adults aged 60 +								
all illness	5	**18.5**	2	3	27	**51.9**	15	12
degenerative	6	**22.2**	2	4	21	**40.5**	12	9
accident	7	**25.9**	4	3				
and					4	**7.6**	2	2
violence	9	**33.3**	3	6				
total	27	100.0	11	16	52	100.0	29	23

* Data from Howell 1979 (Table 3.2) multiplied by 342 deaths listed on 1979:48.

Table 5.3. Ache and Yanomamo Causes of Death

Category	Ache before 1971				Yanomamo 1970 to 1974*			
	All	%	Female	Male	All	%	Female	Male
respiratory	3		1	2	24		11	13
gastrointestinal	21		12	9	6		3	3
fever	31		10	21	7		4	3
other	36		15	21	45		21	24
all illness	91	**23.8**	38	53	82	**73.9**	39	43
degenerative	29	**7.6**	14	15	7	**6.3**	4	3
accident	50	**13.1**	12	38	8	**7.2**	6	2
homicide	84		44	40	5	4.5	4	1
warfare	128		54	74	9	8.1	1	8
violence	212	**55.5**	98	114	14	**12.6**	5	9
total	**382**	100.0	**162**	**220**	**111**	100.0	**54**	**57**

* Data from Melacon 1982 (Table 3.1).

Table 5.4. Causes of Death during the Contact Period (1971–1977)

Reported cause	Female	Male	All	Category	n	%
				Number of deaths (children aged 0–14 years)		
respiratory	5	6	11	respiratory	11	8.6
vomiting	1	0	1	gastrointestinal	7	5.5
diarrhea	1	2	3			
stomach problems	2	1	3			
skin infection	0	1	1	other	6	4.7
sick (unspecified)	1	4	5			
				all illness	**24**	**18.8**
no hair (premature?)	0	4	4			
unspecified newborn death	5	4	9			
birth complications	0	1	1			
pura	0	1	1	**congenital/**		
born arm first	1	2	3	**degenerative**	**18**	**14.1**
snakebite	0	2	2	**accident**	**2**	**1.6**
sacrificed with adult	7	4	11			
mother died	0	1	1			
child homicide	1	3	4			
infanticide (father)	1	0	1			
infanticide (mother)	1	0	1			
buried	0	1	1	homicide/		
left behind	3	3	6	neglect	25	19.5
shot by Paraguayan	1	0	1			
captured by Paraguayan	2	2	4	warfare	5	3.9
				violence	**30**	**23.4**
sick at contact, forest	5	5	10			
sick at contact, Cerro Moroti	9	23	32			
sick at contact, Manduvi	3	3	6			
sick at contact, Paraguayan house	2	4	6	**contact epidemic**	**54**	**42.2**
All causes	**51**	**77**	**128**		**128**	**100.0**
kidnapped by Paraguayan*	12	26	38	**forced out-migration**	**38**	

(continued)

Table 5.4.   (continued)

Reported cause	Number of deaths (15+-year-old adults)					
	Female	Male	All	Category	n	%
	Number of deaths (15+-year-old adults)					
respiratory	1	2	3	respiratory	3	1.8
fever after eating peccary	0	1	1			
fever after eating honey	0	1	1			
fever after eating buchu larvae	1	0	1	fever	3	1.8
sick (unspecified)	1	0	1			
too skinny	0	1	1	other	2	1.2
				all illness	**8**	**4.8**
childbirth	1	0	1	**degenerative**	**1**	**0.6**
eaten by jaguar	0	1	1			
snakebite	2	4	6	**accident**	**7**	**4.2**
sacrificed with adult	1	1	2			
buried	1	0	1	**homicide/**		
left behind	1	0	1	**neglect**	**4**	**2.4**
shot by Paraguayan	3	4	7	**warfare**	**7**	**4.2**
sick at contact, forest	30	26	56			
sick at contact, Cerro Moroti	31	29	60			
sick at contact, Manduvi	7	6	13			
sick at contact, Paraguayan house	6	4	10	**contact epidemic**	**139**	**83.7**
All causes	**86**	**80**	**166**		**166**	**100.0**
kidnapped by Paraguayan	0	6	6	**forced out-migration**	**6**	

* Only about a fourth of these individuals can be currently located.

Table 5.5. Causes of Death at Reservations (1978–1993)

Reported cause	Female	Male	All	Category	n	%
	Number of deaths (children aged 0–14 years)					
respiratory	13	10	23	respiratory	23	27.4
diarrhea	1	1	2			
vomiting and diarrhea	2	0	2			
stomach problems	9	1	10	gastrointestinal	14	16.7
malaria	0	1	1	fever	1	1.2
tetanus	0	1	1			
leukemia	1	0	1			
swollen body/systemic infection	2	0	2			
sick (unspecified)	2	6	8			
too skinny	2	0	2			
anemia	0	1	1	other	15	17.9
				all illness	**53**	**63.1**
congenital defect	3	0	3			
no hair (premature?)	3	2	5			
unspecified newborn death	3	4	7			
birth complications	0	1	1	**congenital/**		
born arm first	0	1	1	**degenerative**	**17**	**20.2**
fell in hole	1	0	1			
drowned	1	0	1			
exposure to rain	1	0	1	**accident**	**3**	**3.6**
child homicide	2	1	3			
infanticide (father)	0	2	2			
infanticide (mother)	1	1	2	**homicide/**		
neglect	2	0	2	**neglect**	**9**	**10.7**
sick at contact, Manduvi	1	0	1			
sick at contact, Mboi Jagua	1	0	1	**contact epidemic**	**2**	**2.4**
All causes	**51**	**33**	**84**		**84**	**100.0**
	Number of deaths (adults aged 15+ years)					
respiratory	4	4	8			
tuberculosis	2	0	2			
internal problem	1	6	7			
cancer	0	1	1			
sick (unspecified)	0	1	1	**all illness**	**19**	**86.4**
snakebite	0	1	1			
falling tree	1	0	1			
fell in hole	0	1	1	**accident**	**3**	**13.6**
all causes	**8**	**14**	**22**		**22**	**100.0**

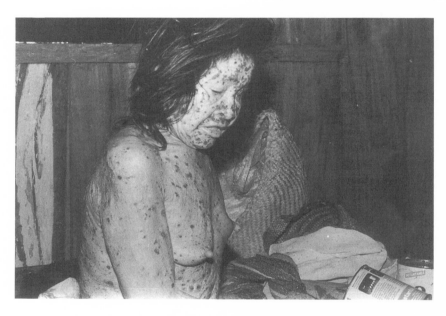

An Ache woman during a chicken pox epidemic in 1991 (photo by Bjarne Fostervold, reproduced with permission).

6

Rates of Mortality

Mortality rates through the lifespan represent the most fundamental of all life history constraints that affect living organisms. This is true for two reasons. First, rates of survivorship are often determined to a great extent by factors that are extrinsic to the organism and difficult to eliminate no matter what behavioral tactics are adopted or what genetic strategies evolve. Thus certain levels of mortality become baselines from which other life history parameters evolve. Second, those causes of death that are avoidable with appropriate behavioral, physiological, or genetic responses probably represent the major constraining factors of the environment through much of the lifespan since the organism *must survive* in order to reproduce. Because survival is critical to subsequent reproduction, feeding strategies and strategies of avoiding predators, parasites, and abiotic dangers become the primary constraints in the biology of living organisms. For these reasons, life history theory suggests that many life history traits, from body size to reproductive rate, are ultimately associated with the variation in mortality rates between different age periods in the lifespan and are ultimately most dependent on extrinsic levels of adult mortality (Berrigan et al. 1993; Harvey and Nee 1991).

THE LIFE TABLE/MORTALITY HAZARD APPROACH

Although crude rates of births and deaths in a population can be specified for any human group, these rates are not particularly useful biological measures because they are sensitive to the age and sex structure of populations and can vary for a multitude of reasons that will not be easily identified without detailed analyses of each population. Instead, age- and sex-specific rates are best used for comparative purposes and biological modeling. Age- and sex-specific life history variables of most living organisms, including humans, are generally expressed in the form known as a life table. Recent advances in statistical modeling of time to event data or hazard rate (Allison 1984; Blossfeld et al. 1989; Kalbfleisch and Prentice 1980; Tuma and Hannan 1984) provide more sophisticated ways to calculate survival parameters, but *discrete-time* hazards models are all closely related to the general concept of life table analyses (Blossfeld et al. 1989). Life tables express the probability of some life history event taking place (death, birth, marriage, etc.) to individuals who can be considered at risk of such an event during some specified time interval. Life tables and hazards models that express the probabilities of events taking place as a function of age, or parameters other than age, such as parity, marital duration, and sex, can be employed to examine specific biological hypotheses. Although life history theory generally treats changes in the life course through time, some important hazards may vary independently of age and yet still fall under the general topic of life history traits. For example, life tables displaying variables as a function of body size rather than age have been productively employed in biology to model a variety of behavioral trade-offs (e.g., Werner and Hall 1988).

For small human populations, the probability of mortality or survivorship in some time interval can be calculated using mathematical formulas that take into account the number of individuals at risk of death, and the number that actually experience death during some period of risk. Individuals who do not experience the event during an observation period or who are lost to observation are censored at the point when they are no longer in the risk set of people for whom a death could be recorded. In practice, censoring can be done manually during coding or automatically using software packages designed for use with censored data.

In the Ache study we have chosen risk intervals of one year and generally assume that all individuals are born at the beginning of the year and all deaths are tallied at the end of the year. This means that individuals who are born and die in the same year are scored as zero years old at death, individuals who die in the year following their birth are scored as one year old, etc. Individuals who die in a given interval are assumed to contribute a full year at risk. Thus, data from individuals used in Ache life table calculations or logistic regression discrete-time hazards models are generally censored at the end of the year in 1970, 1976, or 1993 depending upon whether the forest, contact, or reservation period is being examined (logistic regression requires all individuals to complete or fail to complete each interval; thus half intervals are not possible). Individuals born during a year that is included in the analysis thus contribute at least one year at risk before they are censored. In Kaplan-Meier analyses, however, censored individuals automatically contribute only one-half of a year at risk before they are withdrawn. These differences in censoring practice do not significantly alter the mortality hazard estimated from the two procedures.

Because observation periods have defined endpoints and few individuals were ever lost to observation, most individuals living during a period of observation are known to have either survived, died during, or been censored at the end of the observation period. Since no individuals migrated out of the population before contact or during the reservation period, or were lost to observation (captured individuals are counted as deaths), the probabilities of death in an interval and other related parameters can be calculated directly and simply for the forest and reservation periods. The contact period did include some "emigration," which leads to right-censoring of some individuals after they are lost to observation.

In this chapter we will be concerned with three life history parameters that are critical to understanding the biology of mortality of living organisms. First, we calculate the probability of death, which is estimated for each one-year interval. The age-specific probability of death from age x to age $x + 1$ (also called the mortality hazard or the conditional probability of death) when all individuals are assumed to complete an interval before being censored is generally calculated as:

$$q_x = \frac{d_x}{n_x} \tag{6.1}$$

where q_x is the yearly probability of death (or the mortality hazard), n_x is the number of individuals who begin the interval, and d_x is the number who die in the interval. This estimate of q_x is useful when many individuals are in the risk set and few individuals are censored after each interval. We use equation 6.1 to estimate mortality rate in our study because we record births and deaths by year of event and assume that all births take place on the first day of the year whereas deaths and censoring are assumed to take place on the last day of the year and in that order (first deaths, then censoring). This convention is adopted so our life tables will agree closely with the logistic regression models presented later (which also assume that death or censoring take place only after individuals contribute a full year at risk).

The q_x measure is important because it is a good indicator of comparative risk of death across different age and sex groups. When q_x is low, danger of death is relatively low. When q_x is high, the individual has a high probability of dying before completing the interval. Most important, whether or not q_x can be affected by behavior or other biological adjustments is critical to understanding the selection pressures that constrain an organism.

Unfortunately the age-specific mortality rate in small samples is very unstable for any particular interval, since small fluctuations in the number of deaths that occur can drastically alter the estimation of the hazard. For this reason it is often more useful to examine the survivorship function. The probability of surviving from live birth to age x, or l_x, is calculated as the product of one minus the mortality hazard from time 0 to time x. Since q_x is the probability of surviving from time x to $x + 1$, we can express survival to age x as:

$$l_x = \prod_{i=0}^{x-1} (1 - q_i) \tag{6.2}$$

The l_x values are interpreted as probabilities of survivorship to some specified age. The l_x curve is relatively smooth and does not show the instability of the q_x

function. However, since l_x is essentially a cumulative measure of q_x over several intervals, l_x values from different age categories are not independent. This makes it more difficult to isolate variables statistically that affect mortality when l_x is the dependent variable of analysis. Nevertheless, the l_x measure is biologically important because it indicates the probability at birth that an organism will survive to some later point in time when other important events may take place (such as mating and giving birth). The slope of the l_x curve in any time period gives an indication of how likely individuals of a particular age are to survive to that time period, and the slope of the log of the survival function is in fact equal to the instantaneous mortality rate at any age. The probability of surviving to some future time is critical in determining what is the best strategy in the present, and whether it would be advantageous to trade current potential gains in fitness for those that could be expected after some interval of time has passed.

A third useful life history parameter associated with mortality is mean expected remaining years of life for individuals of some age, or e_x. This can be calculated as

$$c_x = \left(\frac{1}{l_x} \sum_{i=x+1}^{\infty} l_i \right) + 0.5 \tag{6.3}$$

or the sum of all probabilities of surviving each extra year from age x plus a correction factor that allows dead individuals to contribute a half year of life in the year they die.[1] This measure of expected years of future life is particularly useful for modeling life history trade-offs between strategies that result in a current fitness benefit and those that can be expected to provide higher fitness benefits at some later point in time. Because expenditure of effort on reproduction at any point in time is expected to be sensitive to e_x, and because selection on genes that affect fertility is a function of future survivorship (Charlesworth 1980), measurements of this variable at key points in the lifespan are expected to correlate with many aspects of the fertility and reproductive investment pattern of living organisms.

The q_x, l_x, and e_x values for different age intervals are commonly reported in both human and animal demographic studies. Continuous and discrete-time hazards models can also be employed, which provide standard errors for these measures, confidence intervals, and comparisons of statistical significance across stratified independent variables (Allison 1984; Blossfeld et al. 1989; Kalbfleisch and Prentice 1980; Tuma and Hannan 1984). Standard software packages such as SAS (which we use) include a variety of canned procedures that calculate these statistics automatically for appropriate longitudinal and interval data (SAS 1985). More important, however, is the fact that techniques of discrete-time analyses using logistic regression enable easy estimation of covariate effects on the hazard of mortality even when independent variables are continuous and time variant.

MORTALITY PARAMETERS OF THE FOREST-LIVING ACHE

The life history parameters mentioned above were calculated for the precontact Ache using the reproductive history data described in Chapter 3 and a cutoff date of December 31, 1970. Since evidence suggested that only some interviews were appropriate for estimating infant and early childhood mortality (Chapter 3), but that most interviews could be used to provide accurate data on adult mortality, we constructed a synthetic life table using left-truncated partial lifetimes (cf. Pennington and Harpending 1993) to increase our sample of individuals at risk for older age intervals. Left truncation occurs when years at risk prior to some cutoff are excluded from the analyses. For example, individuals in the forest period who were ascertained in reproductive interviews that were not judged complete (Chapter 3) did not enter the risk set until the tenth year after their birth, and those ascertained by census do not enter the risk set until age fifty.

The hazard of mortality during the forest period was estimated for each interval using appropriate data. Synthetic survivorship curves for the forest-dwelling Ache were calculated according to equation 6.2. The number of individuals at risk in each age interval is shown in Figure 6.1. The sudden increases in the effective population at risk are due to the inclusion of left-truncated partial lifetimes at ages ten and fifty years. The population at risk was chosen as follows:

1. Age 0 to 9. The population at risk consists of all children ever born mentioned in ego, parent, or sibling interviews of categories 1–5 and 11–15 in Table 3.3. These interviews provide accurate and unbiased estimates of child mortality that do not differ significantly from those obtained from the reproductive histories of living women (Chapter 3).

2. Age 10 to 49. The population at risk consists of all children ever born mentioned in any reproductive history interview with kin from categories 1–9 and 11–19 in Table 3.3.

3. Age 50 to 75. The population at risk consists of all individuals included in the master ID file who were born after 1890.

Age-specific mortality rates and survivorship for each sex are shown in Figures 6.2 and 6.3. The tabulations of the mortality hazard and survivorship functions are shown in Table 6.1. The mortality hazard in Figure 6.2 was smoothed using logistic regression, with the yearly hazard as a dependent variable and first through fourth orders of age entered as independent variables (see Efron 1988; Pennington and Harpending 1993). This procedure produces a smooth age-varying hazard which retains local features.

The mortality hazard for forest-living Ache (Figure 6.2) shows the common U-shaped pattern that indicates high mortality early and late in life. We have cut off the curve at seventy years of age, since the number of individuals at risk for older ages is so small that mortality rate estimates are not reliable. The curves suggest higher mortality among females than among males early in life with a crossover at about age ten, followed by higher male mortality through the remainder of the lifespan.

In order to examine sex differences in mortality further it is useful to employ techniques of logistic regression (Aldrich and Nelson 1984). The logit transform is a technique that turns a probability such as the hazard of death, with values constrained to between 0 and 1, into a measure that can vary on a continuous scale from $-\infty$ to $+\infty$. This is done by converting the probability of an event into the log of the "odds" that an event will happen. If h_t is the probability that an individual will die in a specified interval of time from t to $t + 1$, then the odds of death is the probability of dying in the interval divided by the probability of living through the interval $[h_t/(1 - h_t)]$. The odds of an event happening can take any value from 0 to $+\infty$, and the log of the odds (or logit) will thus vary from $-\infty$ to $+\infty$. The logit is appropriate for use in regression models in which independent variables may also take values from $-\infty$ to $+\infty$. This procedure has the added property of turning an S-shaped probability function into straight lines, and it allows us to model nonlinear monotonically increasing or decreasing relationships using a form of linear regression. More complicated relationships can be modeled using polynomial functions of the logit, or other parametric models (see Wood 1990 for anthropological examples).

A regression model of the logit transformation (λ) of the mortality hazard (h_t) for discrete time units enables estimation of variation through time in the mortality hazard as well as permits an assessment of the effects of multiple covariates on the hazard (Allison 1982, 1984). The discrete-time logistic regression model is both practical and easy to use. For example, to examine infant mortality each individual who entered the interval 0 to 1 year is entered as a single case. All individuals must either complete the interval or die. Censoring takes place after the interval is complete (before the next interval). Regression coefficients measure the effect of a covariate (such as sex) on the log of the odds of death. The associated coefficient error can be used to determine confidence intervals for the relationship between the covariate and the hazard. The form of the equation is as follows:

$$\lambda = \log \frac{h_t}{1 - h_t} = a + \sum_{i=1}^{n} \beta_i x_i \qquad (6.4)$$

where h_t is the probability that an individual dies in the specified interval, λ is the logit transform of that probability, a is the intercept, there are n independent variables x, and the logit changes at rate β_i with respect to the values of each independent variable. The model does not assume any particular form of the hazard (e.g., parametric), and it is particularly flexible because a variable can be categorical or continuous and entered at any order of polynomial or some other transform (analogous to ordinary least-squares regression). This allows the hazard to vary in any possible way with a covariate. The logit regression model is estimated with a maximum likelihood procedure which calculates the values of β_i most likely to produce the observed result. As independent variables are added, the change in the -2 log likelihood of each model approximates a chi-square distribution, and in combination with the change in the degrees of freedom as more variables are added, provides a statistic used to determine which independent variables are significantly associated with changes in the logit. The coefficient β_i gives the change in the logit for each one-unit change in x_i. A negative parameter estimate ($\beta_i < 0$) indicates that increasing values of the covariate x_i are associated with a decreasing hazard of the event. A positive coefficient indicates a positive association between the value of the covariate and the hazard. Any number of polynomial or interaction terms can be entered in a model with signs interpreted as they are in linear regression. Standard errors of the coefficients also provide a test of significance in the final model for each variable. Finally, the effect of the covariate on the logit can easily be converted to estimate the effect on the hazard itself:

$$h_t = [1 + e^{(-\lambda)}]^{-1} \tag{6.5}$$

It is important to note that while the logistic regression models linear relationships between the logit and an independent variable, such relationships will generally not be linear when converted to the underlying probability hazards. When the hazard time interval chosen is one year, the hazard (h_t) is a good estimate of q_x or the probability of death from age x to age $x + 1$.

The effect of both categorical and continuous independent variables on the hazard of an event can be examined using logistic regression. Most analyses convert β_i values for categorical variables into a measure of the effect of that covariate on the *odds ratio* of an event [odds ($X_i = 1$)/odds ($X_i = 0$)], or on the *risk ratio* for subsamples characterized by different values for a particular covariate [$h_{(X_i=1)}/h_{(X_i=0)}$]. These ratios are measures of how much a particular state for a covariate (e.g., male) increases or decreases the odds or the risk that an event will take place. For example, an odds ratio of 2 means that when the covariate takes state 1 the odds of the event taking place are twice as great as when the covariate takes state 0. When the probability of an event is low in the two groups being compared (under 0.05) the odds ratio and the risk ratio are nearly identical. In this book we report the risk ratio for most independent variables when no interaction effects are present (the risk ratio for a single variable that interacts with another is not a meaningful measure of that variable's effect on the outcome variable).

In our analyses of sex differences we divide the lifespan into several groups as appropriate for the questions being asked. Juvenile mortality is modeled from 0 to 9 years when mortality rates are rapidly decreasing, and adult mortality is modeled separately from 10 to 80 years when mortality rates generally increase with age. The discrete-time logistic regression model for the mortality hazard during the forest period shows a significant difference between the sexes among both juveniles and adults (Table 6.2). Males show significantly higher survivorship than females throughout childhood after the first year of life (Figure 6.4). Indeed the risk of mortality for males during childhood is only .71 times as high as the female mortality risk. Of those individuals who survive to age ten, however, females show higher survivorship from age twenty onward, with the differences between the sexes exceeding two standard errors from the survivorship estimates across much of the adult lifespan (Figure 6.5). In adulthood males are characterized by a mortality risk 1.47 times that experienced by females.

The higher adult mortality rate for males is found almost universally in human populations and indeed is the standard mammalian pattern, which is most likely the direct or indirect result of sexual selection (Darwin 1871; see Trivers 1985 and Chapter 12 of this volume). The higher female mortality rate found among the Ache infants and children is not typical of humans, but this pattern is also found in other societies that tend to favor male children in some way and practice sex-biased infanticide, neglect, or preferential treatment. The Ache pattern contrasts with most modern developed countries in which female survivorship is higher than that of males in all age categories. The significance of the higher male survivorship in the junior age grades will be discussed in detail in a later chapter.

Although infant mortality (age 0–1) from all precontact cohorts aggregated is about 12% for both sexes, analysis of infant mortality rates by year of birth provides an interesting result. Our data show cohort fluctuations in the male mortality rate during the first year, consistent with changing mortality conditions through time, but no consistent increase or decrease in the mortality hazard from 1935 to 1970 (Figure 6.6). Female infant mortality, on the other hand, increases steadily throughout the entire time period. These results suggest a tendency to underreport infant female deaths in earlier cohorts and probably means that we have underestimated female mortality rates in the first year of life. Indeed, the female infant mortality rate during the last ten years before contact (1960–1970) was about 18%, which is probably closer to the mean female infant mortality rate prior to peaceful contact. Adult mortality rates during the twentieth century do not show evidence of underreporting, but they do show a tremendous increase at contact and a decrease during the reservation period, which will be discussed below.

A second interesting observation about forest mortality is that the Ache population shows an age-specific mortality profile with minimum mortality rates later in life than those reported in most other human demographic studies. The Ache data suggest lowest mortality rates around twenty years of age, whereas most standard life tables are built on the assumption that risk of mortality is lowest around ten years of age. The Ache show relatively higher mortality rates in late childhood and early adolescence primarily because individuals of that age were often killed in child homicide or warfare, or captured in warfare and counted as deaths.

The plot of survivorship from birth (Figure 6.3) reflects the differences already mentioned. Females show an initially steep drop in survivorship followed by a smaller steady decline in survivorship to about age seventy, where the curve once again shows a precipitous drop. Males are characterized by a survivorship curve that is remarkably unbending relative to most stable population models.

Age-specific hazards of mortality from specific causes can be analyzed using a model of competing risks (Kalbfleisch and Prentice 1980:163–187). This allows the investigator to focus on a single cause of death with individuals censored (and withdrawn from the risk set) if they die from any other cause. Individuals censored in any given year (because of death from a competing cause) contribute one-half year at risk to the sample. Among the Ache, the rate of death from accidents shows a sharp peak near age twenty for males and increases slowly with age for females (Figure 6.7). This pattern is quite similar to that found in modern state societies (Preston 1976), where accidental deaths are primarily due to automobiles. The similarity of the age-sex patterns of accidental death rates around the world suggests a common pattern of risk-taking behavior that differs between the sexes and through the lifespan.

Surprisingly, death from conspecific violence is highest for both males and females during the first ten years of life (Figure 6.8). Our data suggest that female children were much more likely to be killed than male children among the forest-dwelling Ache. This finding will be discussed in a later chapter. Young adult females also show rates of death from violence as high as those of males, although later in adulthood males are characterized by a higher violent death rate than females.

COMPARISON WITH THE !KUNG AND YANOMAMO

Whether or not isolated, technologically primitive populations are characterized by similar mortality rates across the lifespan, and how different those mortality rates are from the rates measured in modern societies, is a fascinating topic in human biology. Age-specific hazards of mortality for the forest-living Ache, a bush-living sample of !Kung, and a recent, more acculturated sample of !Kung are shown in Figure 6.9. The comparison of the Ache with the bush-living !Kung shows significantly higher infant mortality among the !Kung, but similar mortality rates throughout childhood and the middle adult years.[2] Bush-living !Kung are also characterized by higher mortality rates across the entire lifespan than !Kung observed in recent times. The large increase in bush-living !Kung mortality in the last measured age interval, however, is probably an artifact of the extremely small sample size of individuals at risk during that interval. A sample of !Kung adults observed more recently shows an age-specific mortality hazard similar to (but slightly lower than) that measured for Ache females (Howell 1979:96).

Two independent studies that provide good estimates of Yanomamo mortality have been carried out in recent years. The Yanomamo data in Figure 6.10 were collected by Chagnon between 1970 and 1974. The extremely low mortality rate reported for the first interval is almost certainly an artifact of underreporting children who died as infants. Neel and Weiss (1975:32) note the same problem for a Yanomamo data set. After the first interval, however, the Yanomamo mortality hazard is remarkably similar to that which we estimate for the Ache before peaceful contact.[3] The second study of Yanomamo mortality was carried out by Early and Peters (1990) using mission records and retrospective interviews that cover much of the twentieth century. This study provides estimates of sex-specific mortality by age categories (Figures 6.11 and 6.12), which are very similar to those we measured for the forest-living Ache population.

THE CONTACT PERIOD

The period between 1971 and 1977, when most Ache made first contact with the outside world, was characterized by large-scale virgin soil epidemics leading to the death of nearly 40% of the precontact population. Most deaths were due ultimately to respiratory infections, which were sometimes themselves the secondary complications of primary infections of diseases such as measles. Very young children often died simply because their parents were not able to care for them. We calculated the hazard of mortality by including only years at risk *during the contact period* in the denominator, and deaths during the contact period in the numerator for each age category (left-truncated partial lifetimes of all individuals begin at 1971 and right-censoring takes place at 1978). A discrete-time logistic regression model of the effects of contact on the mortality hazard is shown in Table 6.3. A separate model was run for each sex in both childhood and adulthood in order to avoid the complications of three-way interactions between age, sex, and contact.

In our analysis the contact period is coded as 1 and the forest period as 0. Thus a positive coefficient in the model indicates higher mortality in the contact period. If the age × period interaction term is positive, the difference between forest and contact mortality increases with age. Likewise a negative coefficient for the interaction term indicates a decreasing disparity between forest and contact mortality rates with increasing age. The interaction effects are best illustrated graphically, and the results of the logistic models provided in Table 6.3 are plotted in Figures 6.13 and 6.14. The contact period was characterized by significantly higher mortality in all age classes for both sexes. Among males, the probability of death during the contact period is 5–7 times as high as that estimated in the forest for most age categories and there are no significant period × age interaction terms. Among females, period × age interaction terms are significant and the analyses show a tendency for the mortality increase at contact to be disproportionately higher among the youngest and oldest individuals relative to their hazard of death in the forest. For example, the female infant mortality rate is 4 times as high at contact, dropping to about 1.5 times higher at age ten and then increasing to 16 times higher by age sixty. Indeed, only a handful of women over the age of fifty survived the contact period, yet most young women of high reproductive value survived.

The implications of these data for models about virgin soil epidemics and immune response are complicated. Young children died at higher rates during contact than in the forest—in many cases, according to informants and missionaries, because parents were sick or dead, not because young children themselves were severely affected. In fact, Ache informants insist that many of the young people did not succumb to any introduced disease but simply starved to death or were abandoned. Older people of both sexes fared poorly during contact, and females of high reproductive value were least likely to die at contact. Some of the age-sex patterns of increased mortality appear similar to those of other studies of catastrophic death (Grayson 1993) or those reported for large mammals that undergo periodic cyclical population crashes (Clutton-Brock et al. 1991, 1992). The data have obvious practical implications for any future contact situations. Older individuals are at highest risk, and young children must be cared for and provisioned while their parents are ill. Neel et al. (1970) draw the same conclusion based on the Yanomamo reaction to a measles epidemic, but unfortunately this information has not been incorporated into most modern contact situations.

Two other related phenomena should be mentioned because they provide information about the population response to contact epidemics and have implications for the current Ache age-sex structure. First, age-specific infanticide rates increased dramatically during the contact period. This increase is primarily due to the custom of killing children who are orphaned (see Chapter 13). Second, because of an Ache aversion to supporting orphaned children, and the Paraguayan custom of Indian slavery/servitude which persisted into the second half of the twentieth century, we also find substantial forced outmigration of children from the Northern Ache population during the contact years.

Figure 6.15 shows the percentage of individuals in each age-sex class who survived the contact years but subsequently left the Ache population during that period. Almost all the emigration was forced or coerced, with Ache adult survivors and Paraguayan peasants sometimes collaborating in the sale of orphaned children; however, a few Ache teenagers and adults clearly left of their own volition. The willingness of Ache survivors to sell orphaned children is much easier to understand in the context of the increased infanticide/child homicide rates during the contact period. Orphaned children traditionally fared poorly in

Ache society, and after contact the Ache discovered a ready market of willing buyers in the Paraguayan countryside. It should also be mentioned that during this confusing period of social upheaval, many Ache children were also forcibly taken from relatives who *were* willing to care for them. This problem has been discussed in some detail by various authors (e.g., Hill 1983a, 1983b; Melia et al. 1973; Munzel 1973, 1974). In recent years, primarily through the efforts of the Catholic church, about one-third of those children who were taken by Paraguayans during the contact period have been reintegrated into the Ache reservations and now comprise the population called *berupuare* (see Chapter 3).

THE RESERVATION PERIOD

Age- and sex-specific mortality rates at the reservations since 1978 can be compared with forest period mortality rates in order to evaluate some of the consequences of missionary indoctrination, state intervention to eliminate violence, change in diet, and access to western medicine. The measured rates of mortality, survivorship, and the size of the population at risk are shown in Table 6.4. Only years lived between 1978 and 1994 are included in the analyses. The number of individuals at risk is small in many categories, so estimated levels of mortality should be interpreted with caution. The results of the logistic regression discrete-time hazards model of mortality in the forest vs. that on reservations are shown in Table 6.5. The corresponding age-specific mortality hazards are shown in Figures 6.16 through 6.19. Again, significant interaction effects of the reservation period × age (note the crossover of the risk ratio during the juvenile period) make illustration of the results very useful. The logistic regression model shows that mortality is significantly higher on the reservations than in the forest for both sexes during the first year of life. A more detailed examination shows that most of these deaths take place in the first few months of life (Figure 6.20). After the first year of life, mortality rates are consistently and significantly lower on the reservations than they are during the forest period regardless of age.

The results dispel any romantic notion that life was easy in the forest relative to the current reservation situation. They also support the suggestion that one reason why groups like the Ache do not return to the bush after contact is because living on reservations leads to higher survivorship. The results also indicate that the benefits of reservation life are unevenly distributed across age categories, with improvements in infant health still lagging behind.

Despite the changes associated with reservation life, sex differences in survivorship have persisted to some extent. Males still show slightly higher survivorship than females during childhood, but later in life females show higher survivorship than males, just as was observed in the forest-living population (Figure 6.21). Nevertheless, so few deaths have taken place to individuals over three years of age that we cannot make statements about sex differences in mortality on reservation settlements with much confidence. Infant survival (from age 0–1), however, is higher among females than males during the reservation period (Figure 6.6). Since *all* deaths and person-years lived on the reservation are included in the data, this finding is not strictly speaking a sample-based statistic, but an empirical fact.

A final observation concerns the differences in mortality rates between the largest Catholic and Protestant mission settlements. In 1977 Richard Arens visited both missions and declared the Protestant mission to be "a death camp" whereas the Catholic mission was described in very favorable terms (Arens 1978). We previously criticized this and other publications by Arens as extremely inaccurate and misleading (Hill 1983a, 1983b). Arens had a strong personal bias against the American fundamentalist Protestant missionaries (New Tribes) and was undoubtedly influenced by his dislike of that organization. Since we have identified the mission at which each Ache child was born and where they grew up, the data allow us to estimate any mortality differences between the reservations quantitatively. We tested the hypothesis of differential mortality at the two missions during the first five years of life (there are too few deaths at later ages to perform a meaningful test) using a discrete-time logistic regression hazards model (Table 6.6). The results (plotted in Figure 6.22) contradict Arens and clearly indicate that survivorship was higher on the Protestant mission than at the Catholic mission during the eleven-year sample. In fact, Protestant missions have about one-fourth the death rate of Catholic missions for children of the mean age in the sample (1.77 years old). This difference is probably due to the better economic status, sanitary conditions, housing, and more frequently available health care at the Protestant mission. The results should not be taken as a demonstration that Catholic missionaries are less effective than Protestants, however. The Protestant mission was established ten years earlier than the Catholic mission, and the Ache at the Protestant mission are much more acculturated and incorporated into the national economy. Many of the differences in standard of living between the two missions are a direct result of the time since their establishment. Nevertheless, the difference between continuously available medical care at the Protestant mission and sporadic medical care at the Catholic mission may partially account for the results. These results also illustrate the importance of collecting demographic data in order to make assessments about the health and well-being of native peoples that are free of political agendas.

Despite their increased access to health care, the Ache at the Protestant mission asked the New Tribes missionaries to leave in 1990. The Ache were extremely unhappy with the missionaries' attitudes and behaviors, especially their unwillingness to treat the Ache respectfully and as equals. These traits overshadowed the value of their services (which continued on a visitor basis until 1993 when the Protestants were asked to end their work with the Ache permanently). This indicates that improvements in standard of living alone will not necessarily ingratiate outsiders with native populations. Nevertheless, we believe that analysis of mortality rates in missions and non-missionized villages of native populations is one of the most objective ways of assessing the effectiveness of missionary activity in improving the health and lives of native peoples. The Ache data show that some activities (e.g., health care, economic help, education) on both missions have improved the survivorship of all Ache age groups (except infants) above what it was in the forest. Members of the Ache community are aware of this and mention it as one reason why they would not want to return to their "old way of life."

SUMMARY

The rates of mortality among the forest-living Ache during this century can be compared with those reported in other studies of traditional and modern populations in order to detect similarities and differences in the human experience. Demographers have often assumed that the shape of human age-specific mortality patterns are universal, and that only the levels of mortality vary across populations. Even some anthropological demographers have agreed with this assessment (e.g., Howell 1979). Other demographers have shown discomfort with this position or have suggested that the conclusion is premature given the paucity of high-quality studies of mortality from populations not subsumed by modern nation states. Weiss (1973), for example, proposed a set of life tables for anthropological populations that differ from the standard life tables for state-level societies. Others have suggested that some African societies are characterized by adult mortality significantly different from that found in any European population (e.g., Gage 1989; Pennington and Harpending 1993).

Ache age-specific mortality curves differ considerably from any regional model life table developed from studies of modern nation-state populations (Figures 6.23 and 6.24). Specifically childhood and early adult mortality is higher among the Ache than is shown on model life tables with the same infant mortality rates. We suspect this difference is due to the reduction in deaths from accidents and conspecific violence in modern state situations. Model life tables were derived from a sample that specifically excluded any population involved in warfare (Coale and Demeny 1966). Accident rates may also be considerably lower in state societies owing to the removal of serious environmental hazards that threaten traditional peoples (snakes, jaguars, etc.).

When violence and accident hazards are stripped away, what is left is a profile of mortality from congenital abnormality, infectious disease, and senescence. If our goal is to study the mortality profile of these causes, model life tables are useful.[4] They may not be useful, however, if we wish to understand the mortality factors that have been important in the evolution of our species. Deaths from senescence appear to contribute disproportionately to the shape of the model life table curve in modern societies, causing an increasing mortality hazard from age twenty onward. Among the Ache (and other traditional societies free of state intervention) the high rate of deaths from accidents and violence may overwhelm the much lower rates resulting from senescence early in adulthood, leading to a relatively flatter mortality hazard through adulthood until late in life. Likewise, violent and accidental death rates in primitive societies may overwhelm child-hood disease rates after the first few years, leading to a much shallower decline in childhood mortality up to age ten.

We should not make the mistake of thinking that accidental and violent deaths are somehow less a part of the biology of mortality (the apparent assumption behind the attempt to cull some of these factors from modern life tables). Cer-tainly animal biologists would never think of removing deaths due to predation and studying only the impact of disease if they were concerned with major evolutionary forces acting on that species. Conspecific competitors, and preda-tors, are just as much a part of the biological context of an organism as its pathogens and parasites. Recent state intervention has radically reduced the level of conspecific violence in most areas of the world (Jones and Wrangham 1989; Knauft 1987; Manson and Wrangham 1991). The mortality experience described by modern model life tables will *not* necessarily provide the information that we need in order to evaluate models of the evolution of human characteristics. Most recent models of mammalian life history see adult mortality rates prior to senes-cence as the prime causal factor in the evolution of almost all other traits from developmental rates to reproductive parameters (Harvey and Nee 1991). Given the Ache data, we might provisionally conclude that conspecific violence rates are the strongest determinant of early adult mortality and therefore are most responsible for the evolved human life history.

Despite the Ache evidence for higher adult mortality rates relative to infant mortality than are commonly assumed by demographers of modern populations, the Ache study provides no support for the mortality profiles commonly reported in paleodemographic studies. Interpretations of remains from past populations have often suggested that virtually no adults survived beyond age 45–50 among our distant human ancestors (e.g., Trinkaus and Tompkins 1990) and even in recent aboriginal populations (e.g., Lovejoy et al. 1977; Whittington 1991). No living human population has ever been observed with such high adult mortality rates, and studies of the Ache, !Kung, and Yanomamo reported here, as well as other recent mortality studies of isolated primitive peoples (e.g., Blurton Jones et al. 1992; Headland 1989), should make us increasingly skeptical of such inter-pretations. Even the best paleodemographic methods of aging are characterized by standard errors of at least ten years (e.g., Drusini et al. 1991; Ericksen 1991; Richards and Miller 1991), and all paleodemographic studies make a series of assumptions about skeletal recovery and population stability that need to be examined carefully (Buikstra and Konigsberg 1985).

The Ache data contradict a widely held notion that life in primitive societies is nasty, brutish, and *short*. Although levels of violence are high relative to modern societies, and the situation might appear "brutish" to some observers, life was not necessarily short. An Ache woman who survived to age twenty could expect on average to live until age sixty, and an Ache man at age twenty could expect on average to live until age fifty-four. About a third of all Ache ever born lived to age sixty. Thus our data fit well with Howell's (1979) conclusion that hunter-gatherers did not necessarily have short lifespans.

One of the most interesting findings is the crossover in sex-specific mortality rates in the forest period. Males show much higher survivorship rates until age ten, and lower survivorship from age twenty onward. This type of pattern characterizes societies with a preference for male children and is indicative of female infanticide, homicide, or neglect during childhood. Sex ratio manipulation is an important area of study in evolutionary biology, and the Ache provide a good opportunity to test particular theories about the conditions under which offspring of one sex will be favored. This is examined further in Chapter 13.

The data presented in this chapter also allow us to examine changes in age-specific mortality with contact and subsequent settlement of Ache hunter-gatherers. We found that mortality rates increased dramatically during the six years following first peaceful outside contact but have since dropped to below the forest rates. Young and old females were more susceptible to contact-related diseases than teenage females or males. This may reflect the overall status of these age-sex groups in Ache society, since those most neglected during the epidemics were more likely to have died. Interestingly, females of highest reproductive value were least likely to die in the contact epidemics and the most likely to have been kidnapped by Paraguayans during the contact period. It is also important to note that the remaining population of survivors had high reproductive value, which allowed the Ache to recover their precontact population size in only seventeen years despite a massive epidemic.

Finally, the data dispel any romantic notions about life in the forest being somehow easier or more attractive. Mortality rates during the past fifteen years at reservations have been much lower than those experienced in the forest. Indeed, only twenty Ache between the ages of ten and sixty have died since 1978. Thus, current adult mortality compares favorably with that seen in any rural area of Latin America. The Ache are aware that death rates are lower on reservations than prior to contact and emphasize this as a benefit of having given up their forest lifestyle. If mortality during the first two years of life could be decreased to about 3%, the Ache population would have a life expectancy at birth of around sixty years and a mortality profile that differs little from those of other rural populations in developing countries around the world. These data should help missionaries and Indian rights groups to focus clearly on that goal.

NOTES

1.   The convention of counting dead individuals as contributing a half year of life in the year they die is common among demographers, and we adopt it here in order for our life expectancy values to be comparable with other published numbers. Additional corrections such as unequal weighting of survival probabilities in the first few years of the life table produce only minuscule changes in the life expectancy, which are much smaller than other sources of error expected from mortality estimates.

2.   In the age interval 0 to 1 year the !Kung data show 96 children who died in the interval and 475 who survived (Howell 1979:81). The Ache show 75 dead and 575 surviving the same interval ($\chi^2 = 7.021$, df $= 1$, $p = 0.008$).

3.   Use of the survivorship curve derived from the Yanomamo mortality hazard rates would (in conjunction with the reported fertility pattern shown in Chapter 8) lead to a much greater proportion of the population over age sixty than was reported by Neel and Weiss (1975:28). The rapidly tapering age pyramid (see Chapter 4) previously reported for the Yanomamo was probably due in part to underestimation of age in the older categories.

4.   This is only true, however, when susceptibility to violence or accident is independent of susceptibility to disease and other "natural" causes of death.

Table 6.1. Age and Sex-Specific Mortality of Northern Ache Living in the Forest

	Females					Interval	Males				
Interval	Enter (n_x)	Die (d_x)	Mortality (q_x)	Survivorship (l_x)	Expected life (e_x)		Enter (n_x)	Die (d_x)	Mortality (q_x)	Survivorship (l_x)	Expected life (e_x)
0	292	34	0.116	1.000	37.1	0	358	41	0.115	1.000	37.8
1	247	17	0.069	0.884	40.9	1	310	8	0.026	0.885	41.6
2	221	7	0.032	0.823	42.9	2	288	5	0.017	0.863	41.7
3	206	7	0.034	0.797	43.2	3	274	9	0.033	0.848	41.4
4	192	9	0.047	0.770	43.7	4	249	4	0.016	0.820	41.8
5	179	6	0.034	0.734	44.9	5	238	2	0.008	0.807	41.5
6	169	6	0.036	0.709	45.4	6	227	3	0.013	0.800	40.8
7	157	7	0.045	0.684	46.1	7	218	4	0.018	0.789	40.4
8	146	0	0.000	0.653	47.2	8	203	4	0.020	0.775	40.1
9	144	2	0.014	0.653	46.2	9	189	4	0.021	0.760	39.9
10	211	2	0.009	0.644	45.8	10	313	6	0.019	0.743	39.8
11	204	1	0.005	0.638	45.3	11	294	2	0.007	0.729	39.5
12	200	1	0.005	0.635	44.5	12	282	3	0.011	0.724	38.8
13	196	3	0.015	0.632	43.7	13	271	2	0.007	0.717	38.2
14	188	4	0.021	0.622	43.4	14	265	2	0.008	0.711	37.5
15	178	1	0.006	0.609	43.3	15	261	1	0.004	0.706	36.8
16	173	2	0.012	0.605	42.6	16	253	3	0.012	0.703	35.9
17	168	2	0.012	0.598	42.0	17	242	1	0.004	0.695	35.3
18	162	1	0.006	0.591	41.5	18	233	3	0.013	0.692	34.5
19	158	0	0.000	0.588	40.8	19	223	8	0.036	0.683	33.9
20	156	1	0.006	0.588	39.8	20	210	7	0.033	0.659	34.2
21	148	3	0.020	0.584	39.1	21	199	3	0.015	0.637	34.3
22	140	0	0.000	0.572	38.8	22	191	2	0.010	0.627	33.8
23	133	4	0.030	0.572	37.8	23	185	3	0.016	0.620	33.2
24	125	0	0.000	0.555	38.0	24	175	0	0.000	0.610	32.7
25	118	1	0.008	0.555	37.0	25	173	3	0.017	0.610	31.7

26	108	0	0.000	0.550	36.3	26	162	3	0.019	0.600	31.3
27	106	0	0.000	0.550	35.3	27	154	3	0.019	0.589	30.9
28	102	0	0.000	0.550	34.3	28	144	0	0.000	0.577	30.5
29	96	1	0.010	0.550	33.3	29	139	0	0.000	0.577	29.5
30	90	0	0.000	0.544	32.7	30	136	4	0.029	0.577	28.5
31	86	2	0.023	0.544	31.7	31	127	1	0.008	0.560	28.3
32	81	2	0.025	0.532	31.4	32	121	1	0.008	0.556	27.5
33	72	2	0.028	0.519	31.2	33	118	1	0.009	0.551	26.8
34	69	0	0.000	0.504	31.1	34	111	3	0.029	0.547	26.0
35	68	0	0.000	0.504	30.1	35	105	0	0.000	0.542	25.2
36	67	0	0.000	0.504	29.1	36	99	3	0.031	0.526	24.9
37	67	1	0.015	0.504	28.1	37	97	1	0.011	0.526	23.9
38	66	0	0.000	0.497	27.1	38	91	0	0.000	0.510	23.7
39	64	0	0.000	0.497	26.5	39	84	2	0.024	0.504	22.9
40	63	1	0.016	0.497	25.5	40	83	0	0.000	0.504	21.9
41	63	1	0.016	0.489	24.5	41	76	0	0.000	0.492	21.5
42	61	2	0.036	0.481	23.9	42	76	0	0.000	0.492	20.5
43	55	0	0.000	0.463	23.3	43	74	2	0.027	0.492	19.5
44	50	0	0.000	0.463	23.1	44	73	3	0.043	0.492	18.5
45	48	1	0.023	0.463	22.1	45	70	1	0.015	0.479	18.0
46	43	2	0.049	0.452	21.1	46	66	2	0.032	0.458	17.8
47	41	1	0.026	0.430	20.6	47	63	1	0.017	0.451	17.0
48	38	0	0.000	0.419	20.6	48	59	0	0.000	0.437	16.6
49	35	1	0.024	0.419	20.2	49	56	4	0.065	0.429	15.8
50	42	1	0.026	0.409	19.2	50	62	4	0.071	0.429	14.8
51	38	0	0.000	0.398	18.6	51	56	1	0.020	0.402	14.8
52	37	0	0.000	0.398	18.1	52	51	1	0.021	0.373	14.9
53	37	0	0.000	0.398	17.1	53	48	1	0.022	0.366	14.2
54	36	2	0.063	0.398	16.1	54	46	3	0.070	0.358	13.5
55	32	1	0.034	0.373	15.1	55	43	1	0.026	0.350	12.8
56	29	1	0.037	0.361	15.1	56	38	1	0.029	0.326	12.7
57	27				14.6	57	35			0.317	12.1

(continued)

Table 6.1. (continued)

| | Females | | | | | | Males | | | | |
Interval	Enter (n_x)	Die (d_x)	Mortality (q_x)	Survivorship (l_x)	Expected life (e_x)	Interval	Enter (n_x)	Die (d_x)	Mortality (q_x)	Survivorship (l_x)	Expected life (e_x)
58	23	0	0.000	0.347	14.2	58	34	2	0.059	0.308	11.4
59	23	0	0.000	0.347	13.2	59	30	1	0.033	0.290	11.1
60	23	1	0.043	0.347	12.2	60	29	4	0.138	0.280	10.4
61	19	0	0.000	0.332	11.7	61	23	1	0.043	0.242	11.0
62	19	1	0.053	0.332	10.7	62	21	2	0.095	0.231	10.5
63	18	2	0.111	0.315	10.3	63	18	0	0.000	0.209	10.6
64	14	0	0.000	0.280	10.5	64	18	1	0.056	0.209	9.6
65	13	0	0.000	0.280	9.5	65	17	2	0.118	0.198	9.1
66	11	0	0.000	0.280	8.5	66	12	0	0.000	0.174	9.3
67	10	0	0.000	0.280	7.5	67	11	0	0.000	0.174	8.3
68	9	1	0.111	0.280	6.5	68	10	0	0.000	0.174	7.3
69	7	0	0.000	0.249	6.2	69	10	0	0.000	0.174	6.3
70	6	1	0.167	0.249	5.2	70	10	1	0.100	0.174	5.3
71	3	0	0.000	0.207	5.2	71	7	0	0.000	0.157	4.8
72	3	0	0.000	0.207	4.2	72	7	0	0.000	0.157	3.8
73	3	1	0.333	0.207	3.2	73	7	3	0.429	0.157	2.8
74	2	0	0.000	0.138	3.5	74	4	0	0.000	0.090	3.5
75	2	0	0.000	0.138	2.5	75	4	2	0.500	0.090	2.5
76	1	0	0.000	0.138	1.5	76	2	0	0.000	0.045	3.5
77	1	1	1.000	0.138	0.5	77	2	0	0.000	0.045	2.5
78				0.000		78	2	0	0.000	0.045	1.5
						79	2	2	1.000	0.045	0.5
						80				0.000	

Table 6.2. Logistic Regression Model of Sex Differences in Mortality among Forest-living Ache

Independent variable	Cases coded	Mean value	Coefficient	χ² p	Risk ratio†
Forest mortality rate (age 0–9)					
−2 log likelihood for variables = 95.56					
df = 3					
intercept	5031		−2.0430	0.0001	
age	5031	4.55	−0.5213	0.0001	
age squared	5031	31.55	0.0357	0.0001	
sex (male = 1)	5031	0.57	−0.3468	0.0215	0.707
Forest mortality rate (age 10–80)					
−2 log likelihood for variables = 70.86					
df = 3					
intercept	11074		−4.4159	0.0001	
age	11074	28.04	−0.0379	0.0670	
age squared	11074	988.89	0.0009	0.0003	
sex (male = 1)	11074	0.59	0.3842	0.0219	1.468

† Ratio of the mortality hazard when the covariate takes value 1 divided by the mortality hazard when the covariate takes value 0, and all other variables are set at their mean value.

Table 6.3. Differences in Mortality between the Forest and Contact Periods

Independent variable	Cases coded	Mean value	Coefficient	$\chi^2 p$
Female mortality rate (age 0–9)				
−2 log likelihood for variables = 134.36				
df = 4				
intercept	2326		−2.0905	0.0001
age	2326	3.87	−0.4729	0.0001
age squared	2326	23.30	0.0334	0.0135
contact period	2326	0.16	1.6951	0.0001
contact × age	2326	0.62	−0.1608	0.0353
Female mortality rate (age 10–80)				
−2 log likelihood for variables = 207.079				
df = 4				
intercept	5557		−4.7640	0.0001
age	5557	27.29	−0.0081	0.7900
age squared	5557	945.22	0.0005	0.2000
contact period	5557	0.14	1.2614	0.0039
contact × age	5557	3.78	0.0329	0.0047
Male mortality rate (age 0–9)				
−2 log likelihood for variables = 203.894				
df = 4				
intercept	3005		−2.3363	0.0001
age	3005	4.00	−0.6178	0.0001
age squared	3005	24.42	0.0487	0.0001
contact period	3005	0.15	2.0150	0.0001
contact × age	3005	0.64	−0.0029	0.9600
Male mortality rate (age 10–80)				
−2 log likelihood for variables = 197.806				
df = 4				
intercept	7918		−4.0863	0.0001
age	7918	27.06	−0.0341	0.0896
age squared	7918	932.70	0.0009	0.0003
contact period	7918	0.14	1.7411	0.0001
contact × age	7918	3.68	0.0037	0.6807

Table 6.4. Age and Sex-specific Mortality of Northern Ache Living on Reservations (1978–1993)

	Females					Males				
Interval	Enter (n_x)	Die (d_x)	Mortality (q_x)	Survivorship (s_x)	Expected life (e_x)	Enter (n_x)	Die (d_x)	Mortality (q_x)	Survivorship (s_x)	Expected life (e_x)
0	188	25	0.133	1.000	45.6	182	28	0.154	1.000	50.4
1	157	15	0.096	0.867	51.5	150	7	0.047	0.846	58.5
2	133	2	0.015	0.784	55.9	136	1	0.007	0.807	60.3
3	122	2	0.016	0.772	55.7	126	2	0.016	0.801	59.8
4	107	1	0.009	0.760	55.7	115	0	0.000	0.788	59.7
5	104	3	0.029	0.753	55.2	100	0	0.000	0.788	58.7
6	93	2	0.022	0.731	55.8	96	0	0.000	0.788	57.7
7	84	0	0.000	0.715	56.0	95	0	0.000	0.788	56.7
8	73	0	0.000	0.715	55.0	93	0	0.000	0.788	55.7
9	71	0	0.000	0.715	54.0	76	0	0.000	0.788	54.7
10	68	2	0.029	0.715	53.0	75	0	0.000	0.788	53.7
11	67	0	0.000	0.694	53.6	79	0	0.000	0.788	52.7
12	64	1	0.016	0.694	52.6	70	0	0.000	0.788	51.7
13	60	0	0.000	0.683	52.4	77	0	0.000	0.788	50.7
14	61	0	0.000	0.683	51.4	75	0	0.000	0.788	49.7
15	62	1	0.016	0.683	50.4	78	0	0.000	0.788	48.7
16	55	1	0.018	0.672	50.2	70	0	0.000	0.788	47.7
17	51	0	0.000	0.660	50.2	73	0	0.000	0.788	46.7
18	49	0	0.000	0.660	49.2	72	0	0.000	0.788	45.7
19	51	0	0.000	0.660	48.2	70	0	0.000	0.788	44.7
20	45	0	0.000	0.660	47.2	72	2	0.028	0.788	43.7
21	45	0	0.000	0.660	46.2	72	0	0.000	0.766	44.0
22	50	0	0.000	0.660	45.2	72	0	0.000	0.766	43.0
23	52	1	0.019	0.660	44.2	69	1	0.014	0.766	42.0
24	51	0	0.000	0.647	44.0	70	1	0.014	0.755	41.6
25	50	0	0.000	0.647	43.0	73	0	0.000	0.744	41.2

(continued)

Table 6.4. (continued)

Interval	Females					Males				
	Enter (n_x)	Die (d_x)	Mortality (q_x)	Survivorship (s_x)	Expected life (e_x)	Enter (n_x)	Die (d_x)	Mortality (q_x)	Survivorship (s_x)	Expected life (e_x)
26	44	0	0.000	0.647	42.0	76	0	0.000	0.744	40.2
27	44	0	0.000	0.647	41.0	70	0	0.000	0.744	39.2
28	44	0	0.000	0.647	40.0	70	0	0.000	0.744	38.2
29	51	0	0.000	0.647	39.0	68	0	0.000	0.744	37.2
30	48	0	0.000	0.647	38.0	72	0	0.000	0.744	36.2
31	51	0	0.000	0.647	37.0	67	0	0.000	0.744	35.2
32	51	0	0.000	0.647	36.0	65	0	0.000	0.744	34.2
33	53	1	0.019	0.647	35.0	63	0	0.000	0.744	33.2
34	45	0	0.000	0.635	34.7	61	0	0.000	0.744	32.2
35	46	1	0.022	0.635	33.7	57	0	0.000	0.744	31.2
36	45	0	0.000	0.621	33.4	55	0	0.000	0.744	30.2
37	43	0	0.000	0.621	32.4	51	1	0.019	0.744	29.2
38	40	0	0.000	0.621	31.4	52	0	0.000	0.730	28.2
39	38	0	0.000	0.621	30.4	51	0	0.000	0.730	27.7
40	37	0	0.000	0.621	29.4	48	0	0.000	0.730	26.7
41	34	0	0.000	0.621	28.4	46	1	0.022	0.730	25.7
42	33	0	0.000	0.621	27.4	44	0	0.000	0.714	25.3
43	35	0	0.000	0.621	26.4	39	0	0.000	0.714	24.3
44	30	0	0.000	0.621	25.4	40	1	0.025	0.714	23.3
45	25	0	0.000	0.621	24.4	36	0	0.000	0.696	22.9
46	24	0	0.000	0.621	23.4	33	0	0.000	0.696	21.9
47	20	1	0.050	0.621	22.4	27	1	0.037	0.696	20.9

48	17	0	0.000	0.590	22.6	31	0	0.000	0.670	20.6
49	13	0	0.000	0.590	21.6	31	0	0.000	0.670	19.6
50	14	0	0.000	0.590	20.6	27	0	0.000	0.670	18.6
51	10	1	0.100	0.590	19.6	23	1	0.043	0.670	17.6
52	8	0	0.000	0.531	20.7	21	0	0.000	0.641	17.4
53	11	0	0.000	0.531	19.7	16	0	0.000	0.641	16.4
54	10	0	0.000	0.531	18.7	18	0	0.000	0.641	15.4
55	8	0	0.000	0.531	17.7	17	0	0.000	0.641	14.4
56	5	0	0.000	0.531	16.7	18	0	0.000	0.641	13.4
57	4	0	0.000	0.531	15.7	13	0	0.000	0.641	12.4
58	4	0	0.000	0.531	14.7	12	1	0.125	0.641	11.4
59	5	0	0.000	0.531	13.7	11	0	0.000	0.641	10.4
60	5	0	0.000	0.531	12.7	8	0	0.000	0.561	9.4
61	5	1	0.200	0.531	11.7	9	0	0.000	0.561	9.7
62	3	0	0.000	0.425	13.5	8	0	0.000	0.561	8.7
63	4	0	0.000	0.425	12.5	8	1	0.200	0.561	7.7
64	4	0	0.000	0.425	11.5	5	0	0.000	0.561	6.7
65	3	0	0.000	0.425	10.5	5	1	0.250	0.449	7.3
66	3	0	0.000	0.425	9.5	4	0	0.000	0.449	6.3
67	3	0	0.000	0.425	8.5	4	0	0.000	0.337	7.2
68	3	0	0.000	0.425	7.5	4	0	0.000	0.337	6.2
69	2	0	0.000	0.425	6.5	4	0	0.000	0.337	5.2
70	2	0	0.000	0.425	5.5	3	0	0.000	0.337	4.2
71	3	0	0.000	0.425	4.5	3	1	0.333	0.337	3.2
72	3	0	0.000	0.425	3.5	1	0	0.000	0.337	3.5
73	2	0	0.000	0.425	2.5	2	0	0.000	0.224	2.5
74	2	0	0.000	0.425	1.5	2	0	0.000	0.224	1.5
75	3	1	0.333	0.425	1.5	2	0	0.000	0.224	1.5

Table 6.5. Differences in Mortality between the Forest and Reservation Periods

Independent variable	Cases coded	Mean value	Coefficient	χ² p
Female mortality rate (age 0–9)				
−2 log likelihood for variables = 78.495				
df = 4				
intercept	2842		−2.1588	0.0001
age	2842	3.77	−0.3792	0.0015
age squared	2842	22.39	0.0209	0.1631
reservation period	2842	0.31	0.0906	0.1462
reservation × age	2842	1.11	−0.0679	0.0152
Female mortality rate (age 10–80)				
−2 log likelihood for variables = 27.186				
df = 4				
intercept	6203		−3.8147	0.0001
age	6203	27.50	−0.0741	0.0208
age squared	6203	956.56	0.0014	0.0009
reservation period	6203	0.23	−0.1332	0.4899
reservation × age	6203	6.44	−0.0012	0.8150
Male mortality rate (age 0–9)				
−2 log likelihood for variables = 133.885				
df = 4				
intercept	3541		−2.2156	0.0001
age	3541	3.92	−0.8133	0.0001
age squared	3541	23.58	0.0736	0.0001
reservation period	3541	0.28	0.6132	0.0167
reservation × age	3541	1.07	−0.5572	0.0062
Male mortality rate (age 10–80)				
−2 log likelihood for variables = 78.003				
df = 4				
intercept	8798		−4.0401	0.0001
age	8798	27.62	−0.0372	0.0943
age squared	8798	963.66	0.0009	0.0007
reservation period	8798	0.23	−0.5010	0.0113
reservation × age	8798	6.57	0.0062	0.1512

Table 6.6.   Differences in Mortality between the Catholic and Protestant Missions

Independent variable	Cases coded	Mean value	Coefficient	$\chi^2\ p$
Both sexes (age 0–5)				
-2 log likelihood for variables $= 83.8$				
df $= 4$				
intercept	1047		-1.4191	0.0000
age	1047	1.77	-0.4792	0.2479
age squared	1047	5.18	-0.1748	0.2820
Protestant	1047	0.43	-0.8608	0.0226
Protestant $\times$ age	1047	0.81	-0.3069	0.4888

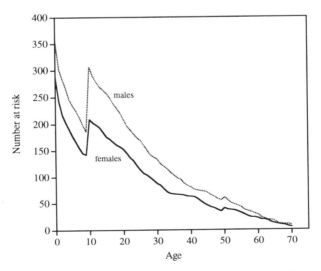

Figure 6.1.   Number of individuals at risk used in estimating the mortality hazard among forest-living Ache. Note the increase in the numbers at risk at ages ten and fifty resulting from the use of left-truncated partial lifetimes.

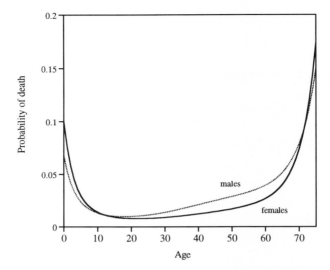

Figure 6.2.   Age-specific probability of death per year for forest-living Ache smoothed with logistic regression. The hazards show a crossover, with higher female mortality occurring before age ten and higher male mortality in adulthood.

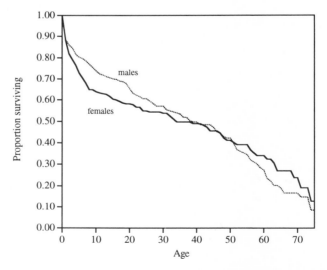

Figure 6.3.   Product-limit estimate of survivorship to a specified age for forest-living Ache.

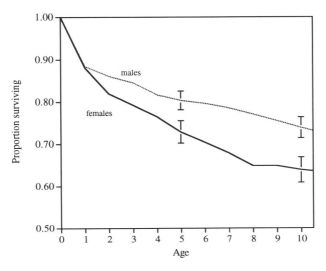

Figure 6.4. Product-limit estimate of survivorship in the forest period from birth to age ten for males and females. Bars show one standard error (Kaplan-Meier estimator).

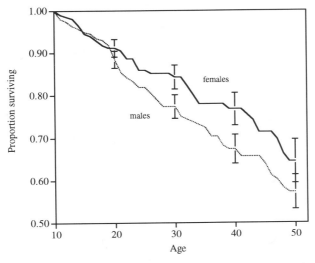

Figure 6.5. Product-limit estimate of survivorship in the forest period from ages ten to fifty for males and females who survive to age ten. Bars show one standard error (Kaplan-Meier estimator).

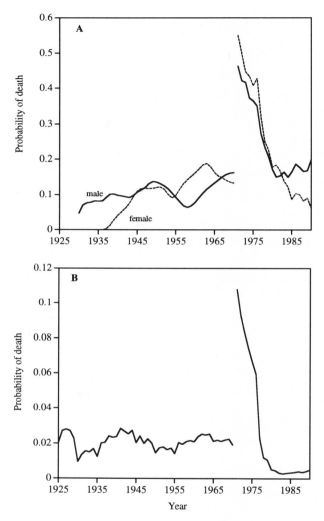

Figure 6.6.   Yearly infant (A) and adult (B) mortality rates during the twentieth century (nine-point running average truncated smooth). Note the increase in all mortality at contact, followed by lower adult but not infant mortality during the reservation period. Increasing mortality for infants during the forest period suggests selective reporting bias against infants who died, especially during the early twentieth century.

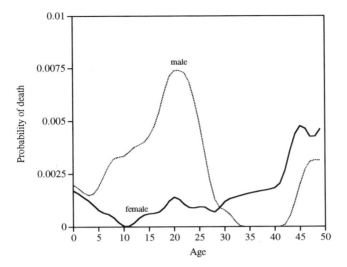

Figure 6.7. Age-specific yearly death rates from accidents for Ache males and females in the forest period (nine-point running average smooth).

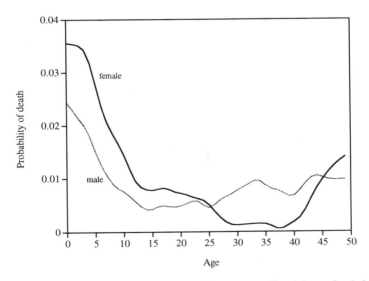

Figure 6.8. Age-specific probability of death from conspecific violence for Ache males and females in the forest period (nine-point running average smooth).

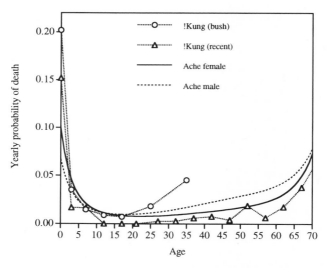

Figure 6.9. Comparison of age-specific mortality for Ache males and females and !Kung foragers of both sexes during an early and a more recent period (Howell 1979:81, 96).

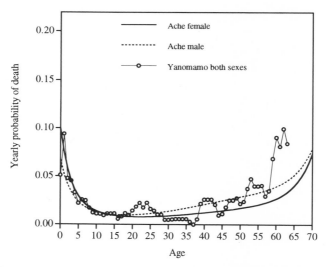

Figure 6.10. Comparison of age-specific mortality for Ache males and females and Yanomamo of both sexes (five-point moving average smooth; Melancon 1982:63).

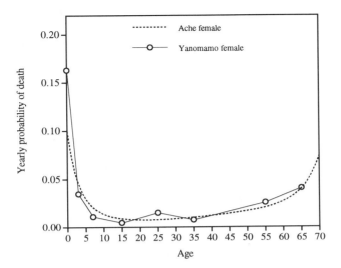

Figure 6.11. Comparison of age-specific mortality for Ache and Yanomamo females (Early and Peters 1990:73).

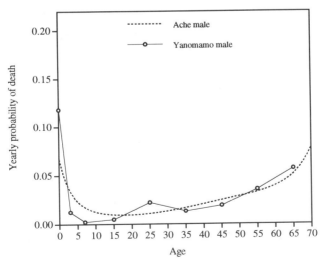

Figure 6.12. Comparison of age-specific mortality for Ache and Yanomamo males (Early and Peters 1990:73).

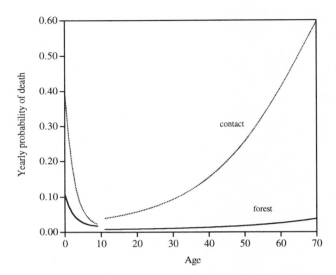

Figure 6.13.   Age-specific mortality of Ache females during forest and contact periods. Mortality hazard is derived from logistic regression in Table 6.3.

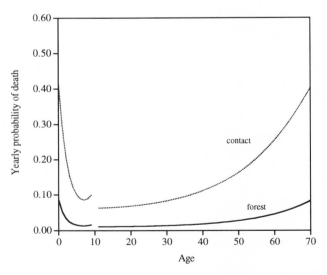

Figure 6.14.   Age-specific mortality of Ache males during forest and contact periods. Mortality hazard is derived from logistic regression in Table 6.3.

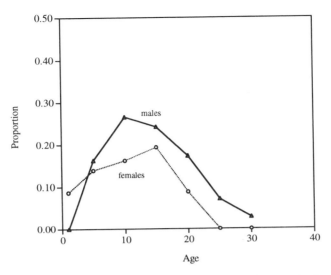

Figure 6.15. Proportion of all Northern Ache individuals who survived contact and subsequently left the population, by age and sex categories. Most individuals were sold by Ache adults or kidnapped by Paraguayan colonists.

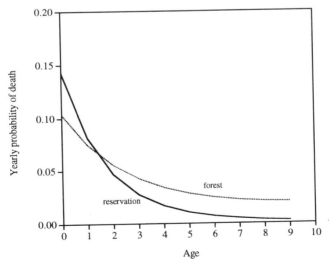

Figure 6.16. Comparison of age-specific mortality rates for Ache females in the forest and on reservations (from logistic regression in Table 6.4).

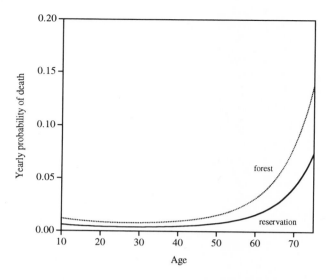

Figure 6.17.   Comparison of age-specific mortality rates for Ache females in the forest and on reservations (from logistic regression in Table 6.4).

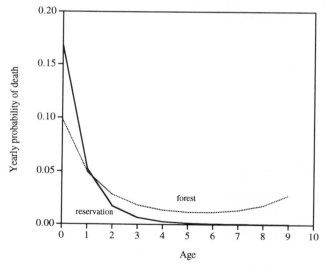

Figure 6.18.   Comparison of age-specific mortality rates for Ache males in the forest and on reservations (from logistic regression in Table 6.4).

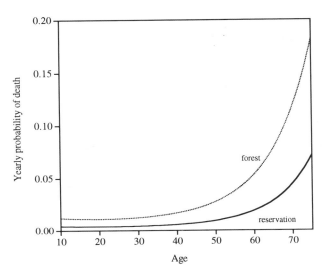

Figure 6.19. Comparison of age-specific mortality rates for Ache males in the forest and on reservations (from logistic regression in Table 6.4).

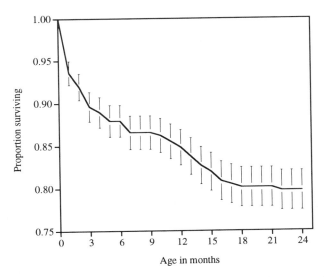

Figure 6.20. Product-limit estimate of survivorship during the first twenty-four months of life for Ache children born on reservations between 1978 and 1990. Bars show one standard error.

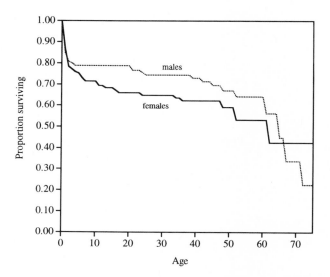

Figure 6.21.   Sex differences in survival for Ache living on reservations.

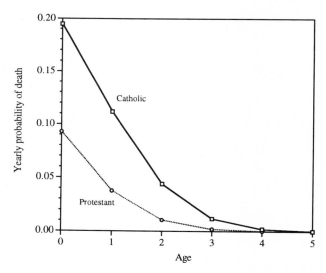

Figure 6.22.   Comparison of age-specific mortality for Ache children living at Catholic or Protestant missions (from logistic regression in Table 6.6).

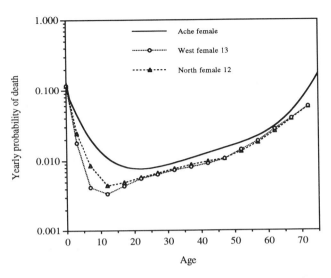

Figure 6.23. Comparison of female Ache mortality in the forest and two model life tables with the same infant mortality rate (Coale and Demeny 1966). Note higher Ache mortality in childhood and early adulthood.

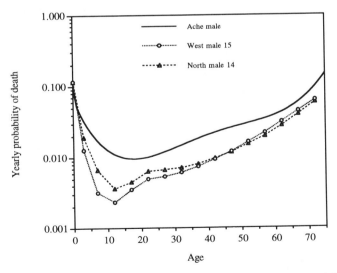

Figure 6.24. Comparison of male Ache mortality in the forest and two model life tables with the same infant mortality rate (Coale and Demeny 1966). Note higher Ache mortality in childhood and early adulthood.

A young girl is washed with scrapings from a vine by her father and grandmother in 1987 after her mother has given birth to a new child (photo by Bjarne Fostervold, reproduced with permission).

CHAPTER

7

Development, Marriage, and Other
Life Course Events

Now that we have examined the chances of survival for each sex through the life course, and the major causes of death, let us consider the chronological development of those individuals who survive. The major life history events for males and females show some biological similarities but many important differences. Individuals are nursed and weaned; develop through childhood, becoming increasingly independent; reach reproductive maturity; form mating pair bonds; reproduce; dissolve pair bonds; and ultimately cease reproducing and die. Although these events are almost universal, they vary considerably in timing between individual members of the population, and particularly across the sexes. Some of these differences are flexible behavioral patterns that differ between individuals or differentiate groups from one another. Other aspects of life history, such as the differences between the sexes, appear common to all human groups and in fact most other mammals. In this chapter, the life course of forest-dwelling Ache is described in detail and then we briefly discuss current trends at reservation settlements.

CHILDHOOD DEVELOPMENT

Ache infants at birth are about the same size as American children (mean = 3.39 kg, $n = 7$) and gain weight quickly during the first twelve months of life. They are almost always born with a full head of hair (infants who are born without hair, or feet first, were killed at birth) and are generally healthy and robust. Traditionally Ache infants spent the first year of their life in close proximity to their mother, suckling at will and sleeping in their mother's lap at night. Indeed, scan sampling and focal infant follows suggest that, in the forest, infants under one year of age spend about 93% of their daylight time in tactile contact with their mother or father, and they are never set down on the ground or left alone for more than a few seconds (Hurtado et al. 1992). Given the dangers of forest pests described in Chapter 5, it is likely that a mother's behavior is highly

219

constrained by the requirements of keeping her infant alive in a hostile environment. The need for complete devotion to high-quality child care apparently overrides other competing needs, so mothers with young infants spend significantly less time collecting food than do other women in the population, even when mothers of young infants have more dependent children to feed (Hurtado 1985; Hurtado et al. 1992)!

After about one year of age Ache children still spend 40% of their daylight time in their mother's arms or lap, but they sit or stand on the ground next to their mothers 48% of the day. It is not until about three years of age that Ache children begin to spend significant amounts of time more than one meter from their mother. Even still, Ache children between three and four years of age spend 76% of their daylight time less than one meter away from their mother and are monitored almost constantly (all data from Hurtado et al. 1992). Some parents went to even greater extremes to protect their children. "We used to tie our children. We tied our children (with a vine) around the ankle so that they wouldn't fall into the fire. When the arrows were being shot [in a nearby hunt] we would tie them [so they wouldn't be hit by a falling arrow]" (translated from an interview with Javagi taped in February 1985).

During early childhood Ache children grow slowly, and they rapidly fall behind their American counterparts in weight and height (Figures 7.1–7.4). Comparisons of weight for age between Ache children and modern American children (Frisancho 1990) show that Ache girls are right at the lowest fifth percentile of weight for age among American children, and Ache boys are just above the American fifth percentile. Both sexes of Ache children are below the American fifth percentile of height for age through their entire lives, beginning at about eighteen months of age. These anthropometric data suggest chronic low levels of malnutrition since most variation in height around the world has been shown to be the result of nutritional intake (Eveleth and Tanner 1976). Although we once thought that the Ache might be short because of natural selection operating against taller individuals, the rapid secular trend in increased height for Ache children suggests that short stature is nutritional rather than genetically determined. In addition, we have observed several Ache children who were adopted into American families during the 1970s, and they are all much taller than other Ache children of their age. One boy, who was adopted at four years of age and grew up in Los Angeles, California, is the tallest Ache male in the entire population and at age twenty-two stands a full 10 cm taller than the average for boys of his age who grew up in the reservation settlements.

Ache children generally continue nursing on demand until their mother is pregnant with her next child, and then they are weaned, although they may begin eating some solid foods such as armadillo fat or insect larvae (sucking out the soft inner parts) as early as 6–12 months. Informants report that women began to wean their children in the second or third month of the next pregnancy during the forest period, and they currently follow the same practice even though they now become pregnant much more quickly after a previous birth. Because Ache mothers wear little clothing and carry or sleep with children resting on their bare chest, nursing is frequent throughout the day and night (see Chapter 10). Weaning is an extremely unpleasant experience for mothers (and apparently for their children), with children screaming, hitting, and throwing tantrums for several weeks. The parent-offspring conflict of interest over interbirth interval and lactational investment (Trivers 1974) is an obvious and important life history event. During this time a woman will often apply some bitter plant substance to her nipples in order to discourage her child from trying to sneak a suckle when she is resting or sleeping. On one occasion we observed a sixteen-year-old boy tying palm leaves to the nipples of an unrelated woman who was trying to wean her 26-month-old girl because she was already three months pregnant. The mother tolerated this form of teasing because she had been trying to wean the girl for weeks without success.

Weaning is generally a gradual process when plotted for a population of women, since they may become pregnant at different intervals after the previous birth and occasionally children are weaned if their mother becomes seriously ill. In addition, informants report that some mothers who became pregnant very soon after the birth of a child simply continued to breast-feed that child all the way through their next pregnancy, and then, if the interbirth interval was too short (i.e., less than two years), would simply kill the newborn child and continue nursing the first. Figure 7.5 shows the proportion of each six-month age class of children who were still nursing in a sample of 56 children who spent time with us on forest treks in 1981–1982, and 30 children born between 1987 and 1990 who were living at the Chupa Pou settlement in 1990. A probit analysis of the data indicates the median age of weaning in the sample is 24.9 ± 2.7 months. Thus, the data suggest that about half the Ache children in the reservation situation are weaned by about two years of age. Unfortunately, we have no way at present to determine the age at weaning in the precontact situation.

Not only do Ache children physically develop at a different rate from American children, they also show differences in linguistic and motor development. Standardized developmental tests were applied to children in 1984–1985 in order to detect differences between young Ache children and their American age mates (all data from Kaplan and Dove 1987). Ache children show food awareness and request food at an earlier age than American children, but the developmental rate of other social skills is equivalent. Fine motor skills develop more slowly among the Ache, as does language acquisition. Gross motor skills are significantly delayed among the Ache, with children of 3–4 years being approximately seventeen months delayed in gross motor development relative to American children. A most striking example of delayed motor development is the fact that Ache children first walk independently at 21–23 months, nine months later than the mean for American children and a full year later than that reported for !Kung children (Konner 1976). Finally, the evidence suggests that Ache boys may develop more rapidly than girls during infancy and early childhood. Kaplan and Dove (1987) point out that these differences may be due to culturally variable parental behaviors, genes, or some other factors, but nevertheless they suggest that perhaps the dangerous Ache environment makes it most adaptive for parents to discourage exploration at a young age and for children to delay their environmental exploration (and hence motor development) until they are less vulnerable.

Young Ache children spend most of their time in camp, playing with objects, pets, and other children and seeking the attention of their mothers. When camp is moved infants are carried in a sling with their head resting on the mother's chest. At about eighteen months of age children are taught to ride on top of their mother's carrying basket, holding on to her head and ducking to one side when branches and vines obstruct the path. Children between three and five years of age will often be carried piggyback by their father, a grandparent, or other relative if mother has a younger child. During this time they begin to learn a good deal about the forest, recognizing stinging animals and plants, vines with sharp thorns, and a variety of different edible fruits. Between five and six years of age Ache children experience their second major life crisis (after weaning). At that age children weigh about 13–14 kg, and they are encouraged and sometimes even forced to walk by themselves when adults forage or when camp is moved. Campsites are generally about 3–5 km apart. Figure 7.5 shows the proportion of children in each six-month age class who walked alone between campsites in a sample of 56 children who spent time with us on forest treks in 1981–1982. A probit analysis shows the median age for walking between camps is about 64.4 months (95% confidence interval: 57.8–76.1 months). Thus about half the children are no longer carried by about five and a half years of age.

Walking through the dense tangles and thorns of the Paraguayan forest can be quite difficult for a five-year-old child. Children scream, cry, hit their parents, and try everything they can think of to get adults to continue carrying them. Often, they simply sit and refuse to walk, prompting older band members to leave them behind. This tactic leads to a dangerous game of "chicken" in which parents and children both hope the other will give in before the child is too far behind and may become lost. We observed one small boy to be lost for about half an hour during a parent-child transportation conflict. When the boy was finally located it was unclear whether he or his parents were more frightened. A small child cannot survive long in the Paraguayan forest, and if not found within one day is unlikely to survive. In any case, the boy's tactic paid off temporarily, since he was carried for the remainder of the day.

Later childhood is a time of exploration and learning for Ache children. During the day they remain with the adult women's group, foraging for fruits, insect larvae, and small animals. Both boys and girls spend a good deal of time in the trees at this age, either collecting fruits for themselves or knocking down fruits for the adult women to collect below. There is no segregation of play or foraging parties by sex, and children spend most of their time within 50 m of the adult women in mixed age-sex groups. Both sexes also learn to follow the signs indicating that Ache have walked through an area. These signs, which are almost invisible to the untutored, consist of bent leaves, twigs, and shrubs that the Ache call a *kuere* or "trail." Following these trails is one of the most important forest skills, and most children are successful by about eight years of age. This enables children to navigate between camps without always being within sight of adults, and it allows boys to begin small hunting forays without getting lost.

Boys may get their first bow as young as two years of age, but sometime around 10–12 years old they begin to carry one constantly. They do not usually know how to make bows or arrows until mid adulthood, so these tools are made by an older relative or friend. Girls spend a good deal of time baby-sitting for their mothers or other women and running errands, such as fetching water or bringing a tool to someone. Girls generally don't begin to carry a burden basket until after they are married, and they don't usually learn how to make baskets or other tools until that time. About 8–12 years of age individuals of both sexes become very independent of their parents, sometimes sleeping at a neighbor's hearth or even going off with another band for short periods. On one forest trip we observed a mother admonishing her ten-year-old daughter to sleep at another fire hearth because there were too many individuals sleeping at the nuclear family hearth. Boys are often encouraged to fend for themselves at an even earlier age; many girls reside with their parents until marriage, whereas no boys were ever observed to do so. Residing with some other relative or neighbor for lengthy periods of time seems particularly common among children whose biological father is no longer living with their mother, or has died. Indeed, in late childhood, many Ache children spend most of their time with a godparent or a man who "helped to create their essence" by providing meat to their mother when she was carrying them in the womb. These men are also very often listed as secondary fathers of the child (i.e., they had sexual relations with the mother when she was pregnant). During the reservation period, the pattern is similar, with teenagers of both sexes frequently sleeping in a different residence from their biological parents, and boys especially making extended trips to other reservation settlements and sometimes not returning for years.

ADOLESCENCE

As Ache children enter their early teen years the lives of boys and girls begin to diverge. Between ten and twelve years of age Ache girls may produce as much food as the average adult woman, especially during the fruit season (Hill and Kaplan 1988a). Boys continue to increase their daily food production levels throughout their teenage years and do not reach adult male levels of food production until they are in their mid-twenties. Nevertheless, boys are already producing more food than girls or adult women by the time they are about sixteen years old. Girls begin a rapid growth spurt several years before boys, and they are heavier than age-matched boys between eleven and twenty years of age (Figures 7.3 and 7.4). Ache women reach peak weight just before first reproduction and decline in weight throughout their reproductive years. This pattern of somatic depletion associated with reproduction is commonly seen in mammals but has been less often reported in human populations (but see Tracer 1991).

Ache females are also taller than males between about 11.5 and 15 years of age. Girls sometimes seem to change from a child to a reproductively capable adult in a single year. Several times during the course of our fieldwork we returned to the Ache after a year of absence and were unable at first to recognize some of the girls who had undergone this transition to womanhood. Not only were the girls larger and more physically developed, but their faces had become rounder and fatter during adolescence. In any case, teenage girls become women, and soon become the object of the attention of older men, whilst boys of the same age are still small, thin, and immature relative to the adult men. Both boys and girls begin experimenting with sex around twelve years of age, however, in a manner very similar to that described for the !Kung (Shostak 1981). Boys, who will not attain adulthood for several years, spend most of their teen years visiting other camps and trying to form friendships and alliances with their same-sex age mates and older men. It is quite common to see these boys intimately joking, tickling, and touching each other or the adult men who have chosen to befriend them.

When an Ache girl first menstruates she tells her mother or other band members and the female initiation ceremony is carried out as described in Chapter 2. All men who have had sex with the girl before that time are required to undergo ritual purification as well. A sample of 26 women born before 1955 who could date their menarche to the year a known child was born shows a mean age at menarche in the forest of 15.3 years (s.e. = 0.4 years). Age at menarche since contact is drawn from a larger sample and is much easier to estimate because of a recent events calendar and known dates of birth. Our sample of 56 women who have reached menarche during the reservation period shows a mean age at menarche of 14.0 years (s.e. = 0.2 years). The product-limit estimates for cumulative proportion of women at each age who have undergone menarche are shown in Figure 7.6. Menarche is significantly earlier in the reservation sample of women.[1] The change in age at menarche begins to show up in women who were born around 1960 and were thus about 11–12 years old at contact. The trend toward decreasing age at menarche is ever more evident in cohorts who were born and raised on reservations (Figure 7.7). This secular trend shows no signs of flattening out, and the Ache themselves have noticed the change. Several informants in 1987 explicitly stated (without prompting) that girls at the current reservations reach menarche at a younger age than they did in the forest. "Now girls are so small they reach menarche before they even have pubic hair. In the forest we all had pubic hair before we reached menarche. These girls develop too fast because they are hot (sexually excited) all the time" (translated from a conversation between four women in August 1987).

Every woman we interviewed who had reached menarche before contact reported that she had engaged in sexual intercourse with at least one adult man prior to menarche, and most of the women had already had two to four sex partners before menarche. In a small sample ($n = 26$), 85% of the women interviewed had also been married before menarche, although a handful of women reported that their fathers strongly discouraged them from marrying that early. "Our fathers were stingy with us, they didn't want us to marry when we were small" (translated from a conversation between four women in August 1987). "Our fathers said: 'Don't walk around at night.' Then we slept nearby our fathers" (translated from an interview with Chevu taped in December 1984). Despite their precocious sexual activity by western standards, adolescent Ache girls are generally reluctant and sexually reserved with most males most of the time. Indeed the best description of their behavior would be aggressively flirtatious but sexually coy to the point of causing frustration anxiety among most of their suitors. One of the most common complaints we heard from men and boys is that the *daregi* (postmenarcheal nulliparous women) were *pranja* (mean) or *pere mella bucha* (stingy with their genitals). The major activity of girls at this time is walking around in small groups laughing and giggling and carrying on in any manner that will attract attention. They frequently spend much of the day visiting from hearth to hearth and are fed abundantly wherever they go.

Puberty in boys is less well marked and is generally delayed several years relative to that of girls. This pattern is found in virtually all mammals and is undoubtedly related to sexual selection and male-male competition (e.g., Alexander et al. 1979; Shine 1989). Ache boys who began to take on adult characteristics were required to undergo an initiation ceremony before they were allowed to have sexual relations or take a wife. Even boys who were just beginning to flirt with girls and women were often forced to have their lip pierced although they strongly objected. After the lip-piercing ceremony, initiated males became fair targets in club fights. Boys who did not pursue sexual relations with women were generally initiated when their fathers, or other adult members, thought they were ready. Usually a few boys of about the same age were brought together for the initiation, or single boys would be initiated when a child was born or a girl in the band menstruated for the first time. Several men reported that their fathers withheld them from the initiation ceremony because they didn't want them to leave home or marry. The mean age of initiation in our small sample ($n = 20$) is 15.3 years (s.d. = 1.5, minimum = 13, maximum = 18). After the lip-piercing ceremony adolescent boys would often temporarily leave their parents to reside with other boys who had been initiated with them and/or a man who would "raise" them to full maturity. Many of the personality traits that seem common among western teenage boys are also seen among Ache adolescent males. In particular, males of this age appear extremely insecure and often engage in obnoxious or high-risk behavior in order to gain attention. Although they often swagger in an exaggerated manner when among age mates or women and children, these adolescent boys also show clear signs of intimidation when fully mature adult males are present. Nevertheless, interactions between adolescent males and fully adult men are usually relaxed and heavily embedded with joking and physical intimacy, which often seems to result in strong cross-generation alliances among men who are sometimes not close kin.

MARRIAGE AND DIVORCE

Marriage, according to the Ache usage of the word *breko* (spouse), implies that the partners cohabit openly, reside together at the same fire, share food and possessions, engage in sexual intercourse, and that the wife carries her husband's belongings in her burden basket. The Ache also recognize a form of relationship prior to marriage which is called "imitating marriage" (literal translation) and is roughly equivalent to courting in our own society except that partners often sleep and eat together without having sexual intercourse during this period. "Imitating marriage" is a mating phase that is only practiced by very young women (girls) and their suitors. Although many ethnographers might object to using the terms *marriage* to describe Ache unions and *divorce* to describe union dissolution, we think that the essence of a male-female long-term partnership for purposes of reproduction (among other things) is implied by the Ache word *breko* and is biologically equivalent to other forms of pair-bonding referred to as "marriage" around the world. The words *union* and *union dissolution* can be substituted wherever we refer to marriage and divorce.

Although young men and women begin experimenting with sex in their early teens, they might not actually marry for several more years. According to Ache informants, marriage generally takes place when a man asks a woman if he can stay at her hearth and she allows him. "We encountered her band and then I began to follow her. I joined her band and began to follow in order to marry her. Finally I slept with her at her father's fire. She had been married several times before but had left them all [her prior spouses]. She was not a girl, she was a postmenarcheal woman" (translated from an interview with Membogi taped in 1987). On other occasions a woman would simply follow a man and "stay with him" at the end of the day if he did not object. "She sat down next to me at night and wanted to sleep at my fire. I told her to go away but she refused. Then we were married. She followed me everywhere and refused each time I told her to leave me" (translated from an interview with Bepurangi in 1985). Recently, at the Ache reservations, gift giving has become an important part of the courtship period (some informants also stated that men and women gave small gifts of food in the forest). One man described the implications of gift giving: "Chejugi sent her brother to ask me for a chicken. She is married to Bepegi, yet she asked me for a chicken. Why does she want to ask me for a chicken? Then I gave it to her. I will steal her now, I will make her hide with me" (translated from an interview with Chachugi taped in November 1984, one week before he took Chejugi away from her husband Bepegi).

Although young women seemed generally willing to experiment with early trial marriage (they could always break it off the next day), young men were more reticent. Older men discouraged the young men from marrying or having sex, and boys would become targets in club fights when they began to "have" women openly. One informant described it this way: "We (young men) didn't have many lovers in the forest. The old men got mad. If you have sex you will become weak, you will become *pane* [unlucky in the hunt] they would say. Sometimes a man who 'walked around a lot' [messed around] was clubbed. Why are these newly initiated boys having women? (they would say)" (translated from an interview with Membogi and Japegi taped in 1984). Almost every male informant whose father was alive during his teen years stated that his father strongly discouraged him from marrying at a young age. Some Ache women also stated that their fathers discouraged them from marrying young. Informant descriptions suggest that this form of parent-offspring conflict was generally motivated by the parents' desire to "use" their children to help raise younger siblings (but see Chapter 13).

During the precontact period the marriage system of the Ache was characterized by extreme flexibility. There were no prescribed marriage partners, and only parents, siblings, first cousins (cross and parallel), and godparents were excluded as potential partners. Subsequent spouses were often chosen from the unmarried close relatives of a previous spouse. For example, various informants had been married at different times to a father and his son, a mother and her daughters, several brothers, and a half-dozen different sisters. One man had been the father of at least one child from three different sisters, and another man had fathered a child from a woman and her oldest daughter. No marriages were arranged; instead, men and women chose their own partners with very little influence or input from other adult relatives (see below for rare exceptions). Mate desertion was extremely common, and girls, even at a young age, seemed to exercise a very high degree of choice about potential partners, and they were able to make and dissolve relationships according to their own criteria. This is in stark contrast to other South American groups we have visited, where adults and particularly adult men are heavily involved in arranging the marriages of their younger kin. Only three times in sixteen years did we hear any evidence of an Ache parent trying to influence the marriage decisions of a child (it may have happened in private conversations when we were not present, but we have never heard any Ache claim this to be the case). In the first instance, an Ache mother complained to us that her eighteen-year-old daughter had abandoned the man that the mother wanted her to marry in order to live with another man who was not the mother's choice. The mother told us that she had discussed this with her daughter, but to no avail. In the second case, a woman stated that she left one of her husbands because "my father disliked him." Finally, another woman claimed that she left her husband because "his mother was mean to me."

Marriage preferences seem to indicate that women were quite choosy about their male partner. When asked what type of man they preferred, women often giggled and mentioned that he should be "handsome" and "kind." Men were much more serious about what they thought women were seeking in a mate, as the following conversation indicates:

Kim Hill: Achipura, what kind of man could get many women, what
               kind did women love, the kind who could easily find a wife?
Achipuragi: He had to be a good hunter.
       KH: So if a man was a good hunter he could easily find a wife.
        A: No, not just a good hunter. A good hunter could find a wife,
               but a man needed to be strong.
       KH: When you say strong, do you mean a man who could beat
               up others in a club fight?
        A: No, women don't like those men. Women don't like men
               who love to hit others. I mean a strong man. One who would
               walk far to hunt, one who would carry heavy loads. I mean a
               man who would work hard when everyone was tired, or
               build a hut when it was cold and rainy, a man who would
               carry his children and get firewood at night. I mean a man
               who was strong. A man who could endure and would not get
               tired.
       KH: Did women love big men then [i.e., men of large body
               size]?
        A: No, they would love a small man or a large man, but he had
               to be strong.
       KH: What other men would be able to acquire a wife easily?
        A: A man who was "a good man."
       KH: What does that mean, "a good man"?
        A: A good man is one who is handsome [attractive face]. One
               whom women love. One who is nice and smiles and tells
               jokes. He is a man who is handsome. A "good man" is a
               man whom women love.

Although most Ache marriages were monogamous unions, plural marriage was common as a transition state. Unfortunately, the detailed marriage interviews we conducted were not designed to elicit whether each marriage was strictly monogamous throughout its duration, so it is not possible to quantify rates of polygyny and polyandry. Marriage interviews in which informants volunteered additional information about each marriage suggest that virtually every adult woman over age thirty-five had been in a polygynous union at least once in her life. Most of these polygynous marriages were very short-term, however, generally leading to the abandonment of the marriage by one of the two co-wives within a matter of days or weeks. In this sense, such marriages are probably best considered transitional rather than permanent mating arrangements. Long-term polygynous marriages were much less common. Reconstructions compiled from informant interviews of band composition at fifty-six various events that took place before contact indicate that 15 out of 367 marriages for men were polygynous (4.1%), with no man ever having more than two wives simultaneously. Only 1 out of 375 marriages for women was polyandrous.

Males interviewed about all their marriages before contact were much less likely than females to mention involvement in a polygynous union. This is probably due to the age structure of the population interviewed (most men and women interviewed were under age forty at first contact) and the fact that it was primarily older Ache males (who all died at contact) who were involved in the polygynous marriages that were reported. Surprisingly, eleven out of eighteen men who were more than thirty years old at contact and were interviewed in detail about their marriages in the forest mentioned having been involved in a polyandrous marriage for some time period. Again, most of these marriages were very short lived and ended when one of the two co-husbands abandoned the relationship. At least two of them were known to have lasted more than six months, however. Polyandrous mating arrangements are rarely reported among human societies, although previous ethnographers working with the Ache have also mentioned frequent occurrence of polyandry as a characteristic feature of Ache society (e.g., Clastres 1972a).

In addition to polygyny and polyandry, one woman described a type of polygynandrous marriage during an interview. In that marriage she had been the first wife of a man who had a second wife, and that second wife also had a second husband. All four adults slept together at the same fire.

All adults involved in plural marriages as co-spouses initially insisted that they were not angry at or jealous of their co-spouse. Detailed questioning revealed that most of them believed that the other co-spouse was angry with or jealous of them, however, and that fighting between co-spouses was generally the reason why the relationship dissolved. Women were more likely than men to admit sexual jealousy in such relationships. For example, one woman stated, "At first I wasn't resentful, but then I did get a little mad when the young wife had intercourse. When she had intercourse I was mad" (translated from an interview with Chejugi taped in October 1984). "I wasn't happy as the second wife. We are angry when men have two wives. The old women (first wives) are angry when their husbands have sex with us. They don't sleep at night, they just scold us a lot. When the old women were enraged we were afraid" (translated from an

interview with Membogi taped in February 1985). In contrast, a man in a polyandrous marriage insisted, "When we (husbands) slept with her (our wife) we
would see each other have intercourse at night. We weren't annoyed. We men
weren't bad tempered" (translated from an interview with Kuaregi in July 1990).
These denials of male jealousy are similar to conversations we have had with
many Ache men, who claim that when their wives have affairs with other men
they are not angry at the man who cuckolded them, but they are upset with their
spouse. Ache men often beat their wives under such circumstances, but they
never directly confront her lover. We believe that such denials provide more
information about the character of male alliances and confrontation than they do
about differences between the sexes with regard to jealousy.

Between 1984 and 1987 we interviewed most living Ache adults about their
prior marriages. In these interviews adults were asked to list all their marriages in
order from first to last. In 1989 and 1990, thirty individuals of each sex were
interviewed in more detail about when the marriages took place, how long they
lasted, with whom the new couple resided, which spouse abandoned the relationship, and why the relationship ended.

From this sample of precontact marriages, important differences between men
and women are evident. Women are characterized by earlier age at first marriage
(15.2 vs. 20.2 years) and the age spread between spouses is larger for women's
first marriages than for men's first marriages (5.3 years vs. 1.1 years).[2] There are
also large but not significant (owing to small sample size) differences in duration
of first marriage, with women having shorter-duration first marriages (7.7
months vs. 14.3 months). In fact, first marriages for both men and women
always ended in divorce and were usually followed by a rapid series of
marriages.

Figures 7.8 and 7.9 show the cumulative number of spouses as a function of
age for men and women interviewed in the Northern Ache population. Women
and men who spent some portion of their adult lives in the forest before contact
(born before 1960) have many more cumulative marriages than those who have
only been married at missions and reservations. Our data suggest that this is
because marital dissolution rates were higher in the forest than on reservations
(see below) and that many marriages of the older cohort ended in death during
the contact period. Despite the fact that the number of marriages seems high,
these marriages are not just short romances but often result in offspring. Indeed,
most adult women have borne children fathered by several different men (Figure
7.10).

Detailed marital histories from thirty men and women who reached adulthood
before contact, along with data on the marital histories of all adults since 1977,
enable us to discriminate between divorce patterns in the forest, during the
contact upheaval, and on the current reservations. The data suggest that women
married at an earlier age and had experienced many more spouses than men of
their own age during early adulthood in the forest period (Figure 7.11). Presum-

ably the mean number of marriage partners would be close to the same for men and women over a lifetime, suggesting that men, but not women, continue to marry new partners in old age. Marriages in this sample were often of short duration, with women showing a mean of ten marriages by age thirty.

Marital dissolution can be examined further using techniques of event history analyses discussed in Chapter 6. A discrete-time logistic regression model of the hazard of marital dissolution because of divorce (rather than death) was developed in order to estimate the hazard (conditional probability) of dissolution as a function of marital duration, observation period, and age at marriage.[3] Results are shown in Table 7.1 and Figure 7.12. In all three periods, the probability of divorce per married year is highest in the first few years of a marriage and drops rapidly. Absolute divorce rates are notably higher than those reported for most modern populations, with the probability of divorce during the first year of a marriage being about 61% in the forest period and 26% in the reservation period. Age is not a significant predictor of divorce rate in the model but the coefficient is negative, as expected (e.g., older people probably have more stable marriages at any duration, just as reported for other human populations).

The differences between the three periods in overall divorce rate, or the shape of the divorce rate with marital duration, are highly significant. Specifically, divorce rates were higher during contact (at all but the shortest marital duration) and are lower on reservations (for the first several years of marriage) than they were in the forest period. The apparent decrease in marital stability during the contact period supports Ache claims that acculturated Ache men often stole the wives of newly contacted men during the period from 1971 to 1975. Interestingly, significant interaction terms reflecting the correlation between observation period and marital duration suggest that divorce rates increased mainly in longer-term marriages during the contact period but in the reservation period have decreased mainly in the early years of marriages. An in-depth examination of the trend in divorce rates during the period of direct observation (1977 to the present) shows steadily declining divorce rates during the reservation period (Figure 7.13).[4] Indeed, the most recent estimate of 10% marital dissolution in the second year of marriage is not too different from that observed in many western societies. The declining divorce rate in recent times also supports Ache claims that men no longer abandon their wives as readily as was customary in the forest. This seems to be at least partially due to the influence of Paraguayan neighbors and missionaries, both of whom strongly discourage divorce. The Ache have incorporated some of these ideas, and in August 1987 we observed a pantribal Ache meeting in which the primary topic of discussion was how to discourage frequent spouse switching. Changes in the Ache economy since contact have probably also led to increasing stability of marriages in recent years.

Marital dissolution in the forest was informal although occasionally accompanied by sadness on the part of the individual who was abandoned. Both men and women admitted to having cried after certain marriages ended.

Kim Hill: Why did you leave Tykuaragi?
Kuchingi   :I just left her. [Laughs.]
     KH: Did she have other men or what?
       K   :Yes, but that is not why [I left her]. We went on the trail. I sat
there by the fire straightening arrows and I told her to go on
ahead on the trail. "Here, take these arrow canes" I told her. As
I was thinking, my brother-in-law Japegi said "I am going to
hide" [go in a different direction from the band that just left].
Then I went with him. I left my wife. She went on with the
other Ache. When they told her she cried a lot. She cried. "He
has women badly," they said. "Why does he have women so
badly?" . . . Later, I left Puaagi for Pirajugi. She (Pirajugi) was
my lover while I was married to Puaagi. I had sex with her
when we went to steal manioc [from a Paraguayan settlement].
Puaagi went with many other Ache. I went alone with Pirajugi
and her brother. Some other man tickled my wife (Puaagi). I
thought, why is he tickling her—I wasn't afraid [jealous].
"Let's go steal manioc" said the man (to my wife Puaagi).
"Let's go." He pulled on my wife's basket. She went—they
went during the day with some other women. Then I also went
with a woman (Pirajugi). . . . I cried too when I was left. "I
am very hurt," I said when grandmother scolded me (for
crying). "I am very hurt by a woman." Then I went up into the
foothills far away (translated from an interview with Kuchingi
taped in October 1984).

Assessing causes of divorce, and determining which of the marriage partners
abandoned the relationship, is extremely complicated. Often, for example, one
spouse will leave the other, even though the first may already have clearly
abandoned commitment to the relationship. In fact, many spouses reported leaving their mate *because of clear signs that the other partner was no longer
committed to the marriage.* In 1994 several Ache men were overheard speculating on the divorce of a European friend who had come to visit without his wife.
"First she stopped letting him tickle her. She didn't say anything, she was quiet.
She just wouldn't let him touch her. Then she wouldn't have sex with him. She
never got mad; only men get mad before they leave. She just quit looking at him.
Then one day she ran off with a policeman and left him all alone. She never said
anything, she just left."

Despite the difficulties of deciding who is responsible when a marriage breaks
up, in our detailed interviews we asked both men and women to tell us who had
initiated the divorce and what was its major cause. Both sexes generally claimed
credit for having been the first to abandon the relationship. Men reported that
they abandoned their wives in 60% of the marital breakups, whereas women also

reported that they abandoned their husbands in 60% of all marital dissolutions. The impetus for divorce was quite different, however, depending on whether or not the person interviewed claimed that it had been the male or female partner that abandoned the other (Table 7.2). First, about half of all marriages were reported to have ended because one partner simply "wanted someone else." When wives abandoned the marriage they were reported as being actively "taken away" by another man. When men abandoned the marriage they simply "went to another woman." Females were reported to be the partner who had usually abandoned the marriage after "fights" or "unhappiness with plural marriage." Males were more likely to abandon a marriage because they "didn't want their spouse," for "no reason," or for "sexual infidelity." Miscellaneous causes of divorce included "I left her after she gave birth," "I left her because she didn't get pregnant," "I left her because she didn't love me," "I left him because his mother was mean to me," and "I left him because he was dark-skinned like me" (dark-skinned Ache prefer not to be married to a dark-skinned partner). Several men stated in informal interviews that they left women after they gave birth: "In the forest we didn't marry new mothers [women who had recently given birth]. 'They had an odor,' said the old men. Because they smelled like milk we were afraid (to marry them)" (translated from an interview with Javagi taped in February 1985).

A final characteristic of Ache marriage is the high variation across individuals in marital duration for both sexes. This means that for any particular age-sex category, some people's marriages were very short while other people's marriages lasted a long time. The longest marriage we recorded lasted forty-seven years and the shortest that we observed lasted only a few hours. In general, however, marriage turnover has been very high during the study period. Of the fifty-nine women who were married at the time of contact and who have survived to the present, only seven are still married to the same man.

Age differences between spouses can also be calculated from the detailed interviews. These data are plotted in Figure 7.14 for 675 marriages in the forest period. Figure 7.15 illustrates the standard deviation for one age cohort of women. Since many men in the population are not married, the age difference patterns need not be symmetrical. Indeed, the results show sexual dimorphism in the age disparity of partners. For example, the maximum age disparities range from the husband being thirty-nine years older than the wife to the husband being eighteen years younger than the wife (in 1994, after this analysis was complete, we observed a case of a husband twenty-eight years younger than his wife). The plot of age disparity as a function of age suggests that women were generally married to men about five or six years older than them, although there is a good deal of variation. The data suggest that women were most likely to be married to a man near their own age when they were in their early twenties, and that women in their late thirties and forties show high variation, with some women being married to men much younger and other women married to much older men.

Late in life, women are as likely to be married to a younger man as they are to an older one.

On the other hand, men generally reported being married to women about their own age or two years younger from the time they were fifteen to about thirty-five years old. Between ages thirty-five and fifty most men are married to women ten or more years younger, with no real increase in the variance around the mean age disparity. In old age the disparity for men shows extremely high variance, with some men being married to young women and others to women close to their own age.

Ache informants often stated that young women preferred to marry older men, and young men were sometimes forced to marry older women or stay single.

> *Kim Hill:* Why did you young girls have these older men for husbands?
> *Chevugi:* "They (older men) really know how to give," it was said. Newly initiated men [those who have recently had their lip pierced] don't give to their wives. Older men know how to give. "Don't marry teenage boys," that's the way they talked in the forest.
> *KH:* Do the teenage boys hit their wives a lot?
> *C:* No, they just don't know how to feed their wives. We think that they don't bring anything to their wives. Adult men really bring things. They really know how to bring to their children (translated from an interview with Chevu taped in December 1984).

Informants also state that women prefer men not too far from their own age. "Young women customarily love young men, and middle-aged women love middle-aged men. Our lovers are our own age. We middle-aged men can't attract those young (newly menstruating) girls. It was the same when we lived in the forest" (translated from a conversation with Achipura in 1990, commenting on which women at the reservation could be his lovers).

Postmarital residence for early marriages was primarily matrilocal in our limited sample on residence patterns. In sixteen of twenty first marriages for women and men, the new couple slept next to the wife's parents, in two cases they slept next to the husband's parents, and in two cases they slept near some other friend or relative. Later marriages show a residence pattern that is difficult to quantify because the couple often lived a few weeks with one set of in-laws, then a while alone, and finally some time with the other set of in-laws. Without a day-by-day accounting of residence (which is very difficult to obtain for the precontact period), we can only generalize that older married couples often spent time with close kin of either partner and also lived with friends, godparents, people who participated in their puberty ceremonies, and distant kin of varying relations. There were no stated residence rules, and band membership was extremely flexible. Almost every adult who had reached the age of forty before contact had spent some time in a band with almost every other adult in the population (about 250 adults total). During the reservation period the pattern seems similar. Almost all new marriages are characterized by matrilocal residence and behavior that might be called bride-service. After a few years, or if a child is born, some of these couples move to be near the husband's kin, whereas many remain near the wife's parents. Some have even moved to reservations where neither set of spousal parents reside, but instead where an older brother or sister are living.

OLD AGE

Because very few Ache over the age of forty survived the contact period, our knowledge of forest life in old age comes from limited observation plus informant accounts of the lives of their parents and grandparents. Women cease reproducing and go through menopause in their late forties. Although the Ache have a word for menopause, and describe some women as postmenopausal, most Ache women will not admit in an interview to being postmenopausal until they are quite old. This may be partially due to the fact that their menstrual cycles are irregular even when they are young, and missed cycles for several months do not necessarily indicate that a woman has ceased cycling permanently. Several women in their thirties and early forties went through periods of time longer than a year without menstruating, only to resume later. In one case, a woman conceived a child at forty years of age after experiencing irregular cycles for several years. Ache women use these examples to justify why they are not yet willing to say they are postmenopausal even when they probably are.

In any case Ache women ultimately cease reproducing and their youngest children grow up and become independent. Last-born children that survive are often very spoiled, and the Ache themselves recognize that mothers who are unlikely to have another child invest disproportionately in their last born: "Chachugi hasn't weaned her son even though he is almost five years old now. She knows she will not have another child, so why wean him?" (translated from an interview with Javagi in July 1990).

After a woman's youngest child is independent, the mother spends most of her time visiting her grown offspring and helping them in whatever way possible. It is our impression based on a very small sample that these women spend considerably more time living with their youngest children than they do with older ones. Postmenopausal women appear to go through two phases of assistance to their offspring. First, when they are still relatively young and strong (e.g., 45–60 years old), they spend a good deal of time collecting food and doing housework in order to ease the burden of their daughters or their sons' wives. Later, when they are too old to engage in physically taxing activities, they baby-sit grand-children and enable their daughters or daughters-in-law to work unencumbered.

Because men do not cease reproduction, they often continue on with family life well into their sixties. At that time they become unable to hunt successfully and often cease carrying bow and arrows. This marks the transition to old age, which is associated with a rapid decline in their ability to keep a younger wife and maintain high political status. These older men often break a path for the band when the camp is moved, and they spend much of the day foraging for small game, fruits, honey, and palm products near the women and children. They also spend a good deal of time making tools for younger men. Finally, grand-fathers, like grandmothers, become dedicated baby-sitters, freeing up younger individuals to forage far away from camp, often on short overnight trips.

> *Then the Ache hunted in a different area in order to bring armadillo. Then the Ache brought armadillo to the new camp to be eaten. Grandpa was left at the camp. Grandma is with him. They (parents) didn't take their children, they left them at camp (with the grandparents). . . . Where has father gone? To get insect larvae. . . . They took their wives with them. Grandpa was left at camp. I picked philo-dendron fruit for grandma's basket. . . . Father went hunting in the woods. . . . His wife went with him. The kids were left; they are with grandpa (Sammons 1978:00).*

Finally, when individuals of either sex became extremely old and unable to keep up with the band as it moved from place to place, they were simply left behind or killed. Interestingly, it appears that only old women were killed out-right by band members, whereas older men were simply left to die or were taken to a nearby "white-man's road" where they would walk toward a Paraguayan peasant's house and never be heard from again. The older women were generally hit over the head with an ax when they were not looking, a form of euthanasia that was sanctioned by the entire band (see Clastres 1972a).

> *In the forest after I hit [killed] old women I was cut with a rock; I was given the scars that mark a killer. After killing old women I was sliced up with a (sharp) rock, when we lived in the forest. I customarily killed old women. I used to kill my aunts [classificatory] when they were still moving (alive), I was not Ache [state of not being a person when someone kills another]. I had a big beard then; when they were still moving (alive) I would step on them, then they all died, there by the big river. I would kill old women when they were still moving, I didn't used to wait until they were completely dead to bury them. When they were still moving I would break them [their backs or necks]. The women were customarily afraid of me. As an Ache (before contact) I used to customarily kill old women. Now, here with the whites (non-Ache) I have become weak. I used to kill many old women, they were really afraid. I used to stick them there with my bow sometimes, then other Ache would grab my bow [to stop him from killing]. I wouldn't care for old women; all by*

myself I would stick them [with his bow] (75-year-old Piragi recounting stories of his youth, taped in 1985 and translated by the authors).

SUMMARY

Ache children living in the forest spent most of their early years in close proximity to their mother and developed slowly. They were weaned at around two and a half years old, usually because their mother became pregnant again. They grew slowly in comparison with American children and almost certainly experienced chronic low levels of nutritional stress. They became much more independent at around age five when they were forced to walk between camps and began to spend time on the periphery of the camp playing with other children. Children of both sexes began acquiring food during later childhood and obtained about half their daily caloric consumption levels by age 13–14. Boys continued to acquire more and more food until their mid twenties. Girls did not increase food acquisition levels much after age fourteen; instead they got married, reached menarche at around age fifteen, and lived with a series of spouses before experiencing first birth about three years later. Boys underwent a puberty initiation about age fifteen and generally married for the first time around age twenty. Marriages were often of short duration, with women and men experiencing a half dozen or more marriages by the time they were thirty years old. On average, women were married to men about five years older than them, although there is a good deal of individual variation. Men were married to women near their own age until their late thirties, at which time they often married women ten or more years younger. Women ceased reproducing in their early to mid forties, whereas some men had children into their fifties and sixties. In old age men and women spent most of their time engaged in useful tasks, especially baby-sitting. Very old individuals were often abandoned or killed when they became too great a burden on the residential band.

Patterns of events through the life course have changed somewhat since contact. On the reservation Ache children spend less time in close proximity to their mothers, are weaned somewhat earlier, and may grow slightly larger. Age at menarche has decreased rapidly since first contact, and marriages, particularly at young ages, are more stable on the reservations than they were during the forest period. Age differences between spouses do not show a sharp increase for men in their late thirties and forties on the reservations, suggesting that switching to a younger wife is no longer as common. Old people still spend much of their time baby-sitting or performing other useful tasks and are never killed outright, though some are neglected and probably suffer higher mortality as a result.

Compared on a large scale (i.e., relative to other primates or modern human groups), the patterns of development through the life course are not too different from those described in other traditional societies, such as the !Kung or Yanomamo (e.g., Chagnon 1968; Draper 1976; Howell 1979; Melancon 1982; Shostak 1981). Specific details do vary significantly, however, and should be the focus of further research on flexible life history adaptation. The high rates of marital instability among the Ache are particularly striking and may be uncharacteristic of traditional societies. This is difficult to assess, however, since so little quantitative data on marital stability are available. But surely other authors would have noted if spouse switching were as common as we found among forest-living Ache, since the number of different fathers of a woman's children gives a quick indication of marital stability. The lack of frequent spouse switching in other groups suggests that the Ache may be extreme in the continuum from high to low marital stability.

Explanations for the high Ache divorce rate can be sought in the demographic parameters themselves. Theoretical models of mate desertion (e.g., Lazarus 1990; Maynard Smith 1977) suggest that the ability of fathers to affect their offspring's survivorship and well being, as well as the availability of alternative fertile mating partners, should influence whether or not men decide to remain in a mated pair-bond or abandon the relationship. Women, too, should be influenced by the importance of biparental care and the ease of acquiring a new mate. Some of these ideas have been incorporated into explanations of large-scale differences in mating patterns (e.g., Draper and Harpending 1982; Harpending and Draper 1986) and should be examined further. We have explored these ideas elsewhere (Hurtado and Hill 1991) and conclude that this theoretical approach may offer some insight into high Ache divorce rates relative to those observed in other traditional societies. Nevertheless, Ache fathers do have a major impact on the survivorship of their children (see Chapter 13), and their willingness to abandon many children throughout their reproductive career, or the willingness of women to abandon the father of their children with such high frequencies, is still puzzling.

NOTES

1.   Kaplan-Meier product-limit estimate, test by strata of forest vs. age, log rank test, $\chi^2 = 8.458$, df = 1, $p = 0.004$ (SAS 1985).

2.   Kaplan-Meier analysis of age at first marriage for individuals born before 1960: mean age for women = 15.18 years, s.e. = 0.22, $n = 39$; mean age for men = 20.18 years, s.e. = 0.40, $n = 57$; log rank test, $\chi^2 = 73.76$, df = 1, $p = 0.0001$.

Kaplan-Meier analysis of duration of first marriage for individuals born before 1960: mean duration for women = 7.71 months, s.e. = 2.82, $n = 7$; mean duration for men = 14.25 months, s.e. = 3.91, $n = 12$; log rank test, $\chi^2 = 1.50$, df = 1, $p = 0.22$. Mean age difference between spouses in first marriage (male-female) for women's first marriage =

5.26 years, s.d. = 5.52, n = 39; for men's first marriage = 1.07 years, s.d. = 4.99, n = 57, t = 3.865, p (two-tailed) = .0002.

3. Marriages that ended because of spousal death were censored, and each marriage was coded as surviving or failing in each yearly interval. Because very short duration unions were not systematically elicited (and informants often failed to mention them), marriages were only coded if they lasted one month, and marriages were considered to have failed if a separation of more than one month included cohabitation of either partner with a member of the opposite sex. Some of these "failed marriages" were later reformed and contribute subsequently to the at-risk population once again. One thousand single-year intervals from 63 women were analyzed.

4. Discrete-time logistic regression model, n = 663 intervals from 1976 to 1989: dependent variable = marriage failure; independent variables, X1 = marital duration in years, X2 = (marital duration)^2, X3 = year that marriage was at risk of dissolution. Model χ^2 = 54.62, df = 3; Intercept β = 271.475, s.e. = 71.325, χ^2 = 14.49, p = 0.0001; X1 β = −0.238, s.e. = 0.084, χ^2 = 7.95, p = 0.0048; X2 β = 0.006, s.e. = 0.006, χ^2 = 0.83, p = 0.3620; X3 β = −0.138, s.e. = 0.036, χ^2 = 14.60, p = 0.0001.

Table 7.1. Yearly Hazard of Marital Dissolution as a Function of Marital Duration, Age, and Time Period

Independent variable	Coefficient	p
intercept	0.7690388	0.005
duration	−0.70161894	0.000
duration squared	0.0101608	0.023
age	−0.01350827	0.231
Forest	control	−
Contact (1971–1975)	−0.016807	0.959
Contact × duration	0.3725575	0.012
Reservation (1976–1989)	−1.48303002	0.000
Reservation × duration	0.38141973	0.005

n = 1000 person-years in marriage between 1940 and 1989; model χ^2 = 239.91, 7 df, p = 0.0001

Table 7.2.   Reported Causes of Divorce

	Male	Female
Reason	*Sex of number of cases reported divorce initiator*	
informant wanted another spouse	34	13
informant didn't want spouse	5	0
spouse stolen by competitor	1	21
fighting between spouses	4	10
unhappy as co-spouse	4	10
sexual infidelity	8	1
no reason	10	0
after child born	1	0
he was dark skinned	0	1
she didn't get pregnant	1	0
his mother was mean	0	1
she didn't love him	1	0

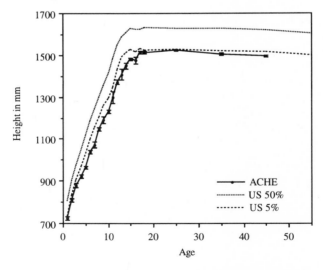

Figure 7.1.   Mean height of Ache females by age in 1980–1990 compared with a U.S. standard (white Americans, fifth and fiftieth percentiles; Frisancho 1990). Bars show one standard error.

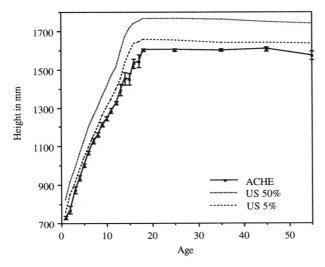

Figure 7.2. Mean height of Ache males by age in 1980–1990 compared with a U.S. standard (white Americans, fifth and fiftieth percentiles; Frisancho 1990). Bars show one standard error.

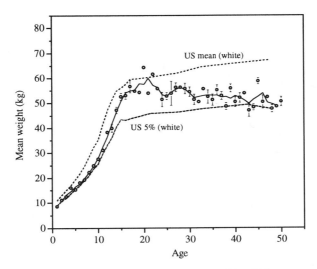

Figure 7.3. Mean weight of Ache females by age in 1980–1993 compared with U.S. mean and fifth percentile (white Americans only; Frisancho 1990). Bars show one standard error.

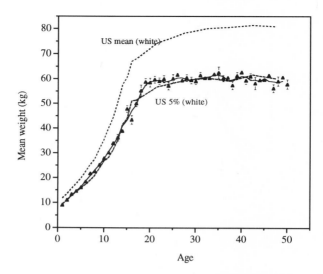

Figure 7.4. Mean weight of Ache males by age in 1980–1993 compared with U.S. mean and fifth percentile (white Americans only; Frisancho 1990). Bars show one standard error.

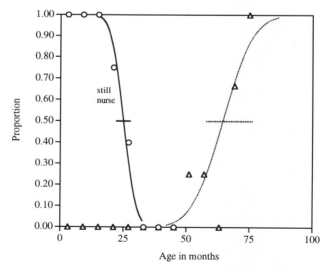

Figure 7.5. Probit regression (lines) of the proportion of Ache children still nursing and walking between camps. Bars show 95% confidence interval at fiftieth percentile; symbols show observed proportions at each age.

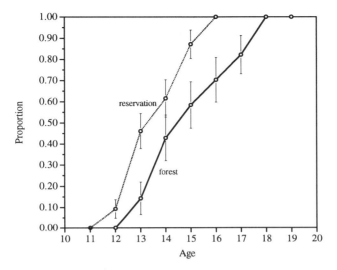

Figure 7.6. Product-limit estimate of proportion of Ache women who have reached menarche by a specified age in the forest and on reservations. Bars show one standard error.

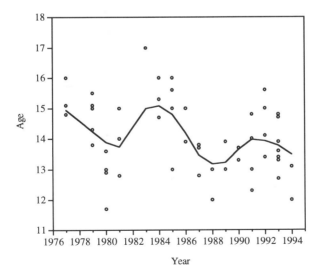

Figure 7.7. Age at menarche by year of observation for 56 women who reached menarche during the reservation period (line is three-year moving average). Each data point represents one woman who was observed to reach menarche during the specified year. Note that the average age of women reaching menarche in each year has been decreasing during the reservation period.

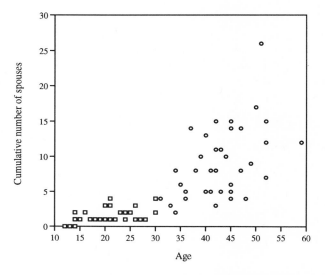

Figure 7.8. Cumulative number of spouses reported by living women in 1990. Squares represent women born after 1960 whose marriages all occurred on reservations.

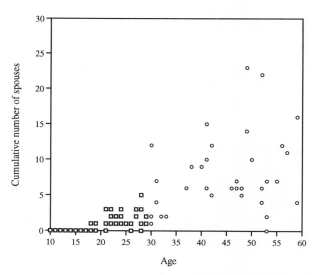

Figure 7.9. Cumulative number of spouses reported by living men in 1990. Squares represent men born after 1960 whose marriages all occurred on reservations.

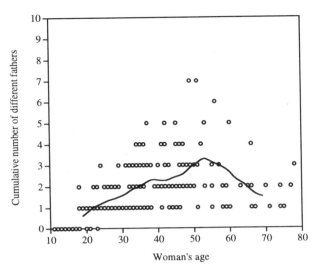

Figure 7.10. Cumulative number of different fathers of women's offspring reported by women of a specified age (lowess smooth). Note that most women have children with two or more men.

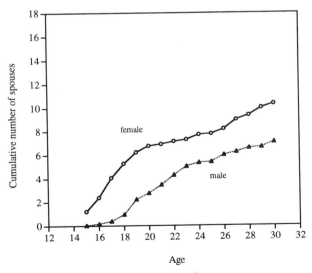

Figure 7.11. Mean cumulative number of spouses in the forest by age for Ache men and women.

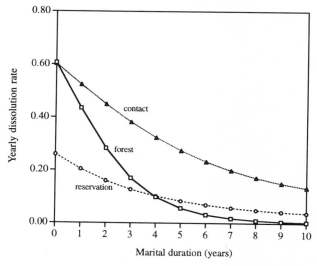

Figure 7.12. Hazard of marital dissolution during the first ten years of marriage for three time periods (from logistic regression model in Table 7.1).

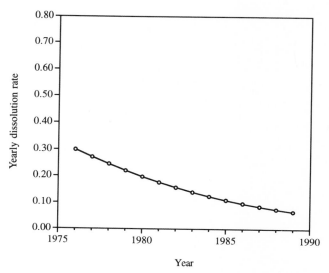

Figure 7.13. Hazard of marital dissolution during the second year of marriage on reservations (from logistic regression model; see note 4).

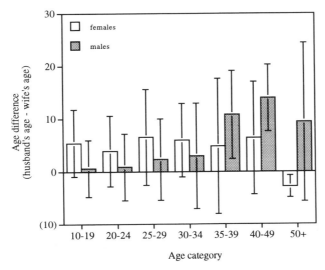

Figure 7.14. Mean age difference between spouses in five- or ten-year age categories for Ache men and women married in the forest period. Bars show one standard deviation.

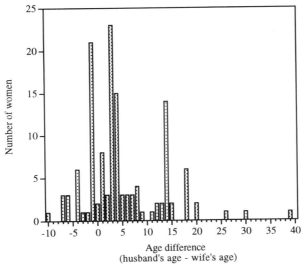

Figure 7.15. Distribution of spousal age difference for Ache women ages 20–29 in the forest period.

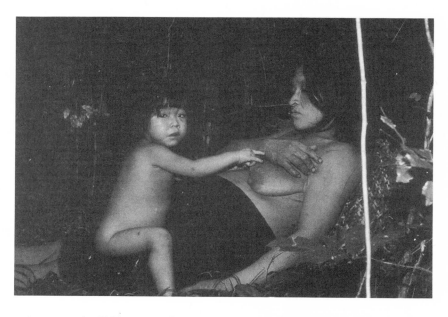

A woman in 1981 resting during early stages of labor while her youngest child demands attention.

CHAPTER

8

Female Fertility

Almost all females who reach adulthood ultimately give birth. Female fertility is not constant through the adult life span, however, nor is it uniform across all women. Differences in fertility across age and other categories of women may be considerable, and these differences have important implications for other evolved female traits, as well as for patterns of social interaction between women and other members of society.

PREGNANCY AND BIRTH

The Ache are aware that women must menstruate to be fertile, and that sexual intercourse is necessary in order for women to conceive. They avoid sexual intercourse during menstruation, citing a concern for "penis infections" (as they call them), but are not overly concerned about "polluting" effects of menstrual blood (there is some ritual concern about exposure to any type of human blood, however). Women discuss their menstrual cycling openly in the presence of men, and perhaps not surprisingly for a group that did not wear clothes until recently, whether or not a specific female is menstruating at any point in time is common knowledge. The Ache do not recognize conception as a single event, but rather as a process in which several individuals may contribute differentially through time to the creation of a new child.

A man (or men) who was frequently having intercourse with a woman at the time when "her blood flow ceased to be found" is considered to be the real father of her child, or "the one who put it (the baby) in." These primary fathers are most likely to be the ones who take on a serious parenting role and are generally identified as the father for any specific child if an interviewer insists on knowing who the "real" father is. Secondary fathers are also generally acknowledged and can play an important role in the subsequent care of a child, particularly if the primary father dies or refuses to provide paternal care himself. Secondary fathers include all those men who had sexual intercourse with a woman during the year prior to giving birth (including during pregnancy), and the man who is married to a woman when her child is born. Such men are referred to as "fathers" of the child in everyday conversation, and the child will call all such men by the same term as they use for their primary father. Only a request for clarification about these fathers will reveal which is the primary father and which are secondary fathers. Finally, when a woman has a long-standing relationship with more than one man, several men may be candidates for the primary father as well as being secondary fathers of the child. Paternity is essentially probabilistic to the Ache, and they treat it as such.

During pregnancy Ache women are subject to a small number of food taboos, and pregnant women are believed to have special healing powers, but they generally continue daily life as they did before conceiving. Ache women are anxious to have many children and are generally happy to be pregnant. However, women are very reluctant to admit that they are pregnant during the first trimester and will coyly avoid confirmation of the fact until it is rather obvious. It was our impression that this reluctance to admit pregnancy was primarily due to the heartbreak and embarrassment of spontaneous abortion, which is common in early stages of pregnancy, but there may also be some tendency for women to be treated differently once they have announced they are pregnant (men may provide more favors for women who are not pregnant). In any case, women recognize that they may be pregnant after missing a menstrual period, and men also recognize that these women may be pregnant.

I might be the father of Tykuara; my brother might also be his father. My brother took her (my wife) to the forest for many sleeps. When she came back to me I had her too. She never bled again after returning to me. I don't know who put it [the child] in. Was it my brother or was it me? (translated from an interview with Bepuragi taped in October 1984).

Some women mentioned becoming nauseous in the early months of pregnancy, and several claimed that women "know they are pregnant when their teeth begin to hurt." It was also reported that the man responsible for the pregnancy will often become nauseous during the pregnancy and his teeth may hurt as well. Nevertheless, during pregnancy Ache women continue to forage, carry young children, and move camp daily with the band. Many women told stories of spontaneous abortions after accidents (e.g., falling from a tree), illness, or general stress. Early abortions may not be easily detected, but abortions after the first trimester are noted by most women in the population. Figure 8.1 shows the cumulative mean number of abortions reported by women as a function of their age.[1] The data suggest that on average adult women experience several spontaneous abortions in a lifetime. These numbers should be taken as minimal estimates since many women probably failed to mention (or know about) every abortion they had experienced.

About the time that women publicly admit they are pregnant, they also begin weaning their previous infant (if one exists). This leads to an unpleasant mother-child conflict that was described in the previous chapter. As the time of birth approaches, most women that we observed continued their normal daily activities. When a woman begins to feel labor pains she is joined by a variety of helpers who stay with her throughout the delivery. Ache births are usually semi-public, and a variety of kin and nonkin are involved. For this reason we were able to observe several dozen births during fieldwork with the Ache. The father of the child often leaves the mother and goes off to hunt in the forest if labor takes place during the day, but in other cases (especially at night) the father of the child was the main helper. All births have at least two major helpers—a woman who will care for the child in the first few days after its birth, and a man who will cut the umbilical cord. These two main helpers are usually joined by a handful of secondary helpers, who will wash the child and hold the mother during delivery.

As contractions become regular and strong, pregnant women assume a semi-reclined seating posture, with a helper behind them providing a back rest and massaging their abdomen (see photos in Clastres 1972a). If this phase of labor lasts longer than a half an hour, various helpers take short turns holding and massaging the pregnant woman. Other individuals may massage her arms and legs, wipe sweat from her body, or give her short sips of water. Interestingly, many of the support personnel are men, and often they are unrelated to the pregnant mother and are not candidates for primary or secondary father of the child. Since the job of supporting and massaging the pregnant woman can be extremely strenuous, we were curious how these men were chosen. A few women reported that the men volunteered to help, and that they were "friends" (men who did not normally have sexual relations with the woman questioned) who simply enjoyed each other's company. Later the Ache men asked Kim if American men have female "friends" and described a nonsexual relationship based on the enjoyment of each other's company. They reported that such relationships are common among the Ache.

As the child is expelled, it is caught by the woman who has been designated to be its "godmother" (see Chapter 2). This woman holds the child and gently pushes on its head to reshape it after the elongation from passing through the birth canal. If the decision has been made to kill the child, or if it is defective, premature, one of a set of twins, or breach, it is not held by anyone but simply pushed into a hole and buried. After a few minutes the placenta is expelled and a predesignated man ties and cuts the umbilical cord with a bamboo knife about 10 cm from the child's abdomen. A bystander or the new mother usually buries the placenta on the spot. After the cord is cut, additional onlookers take turns holding and touching the newborn child. It is washed in warm water, and then the "godmother" holds it on her lap and remains near the new mother for the next few days. The new mother is generally ignored. She spends a few minutes to a few hours recovering from the delivery before holding the baby and encouraging it to suckle. In one case we observed the new mother continue on with a band move, walking at least a kilometer, within 15–20 minutes after the birth.

Some time after birth (minutes to days), the new mother chooses a name for the child. Mothers occasionally change their mind and give the child a different name after a week or two. The Ache give the name of an animal (e.g., armadillo, tapir) to each child; most names can be used for either male or female children. The name chosen is an animal that was given to the mother to cook during her pregnancy, often the largest or rarest animal or one eaten in particular abundance during the pregnancy. Immediately after the birth, all men who are potential fathers of the child enter a state of "attraction," in which living things are believed to be powerfully drawn to them. This state supposedly increases their hunting success (owing to increased encounters with game) but also makes them vulnerable to jaguar attacks. Many men that we interviewed insisted that their hunting success increased dramatically at this time. We believe that men hunt more intensively following the birth of a child. Men who are not successful hunters during their state of "attraction" are often the subject of derisive gossip.

About three days after the birth the new mother, the baby's fathers, and all individuals who touched the baby soon after birth are supposed to undergo a ritual purification (sometimes the child's siblings will also be purified). Segments of a large vine (the same one used by Guarani Indians for poisoning fish) are cut, and bark shavings are scraped off and collected in a pot of water. The bark water (which causes a tingling sensation on the skin) is used to wash each participant, and dry bark shavings are rubbed on the skin after the bath. Until this ritual is carried out none of the participants is supposed to touch water, or it is believed that the rivers will flood. Despite these supernatural dangers, during all the time that we lived with the Ache we only saw this ritual carried out two or three times, even though Catholic missionaries at Chupa Pou encouraged rather than discouraged participation in birth rituals.

After the birth of a child, women refrain from sexual intercourse for many months. Although there appears to be a good deal of individual variation in the length of abstinence, most women claimed that they did not have sexual intercourse until their child was more than a year old. During this time women also sleep sitting up rather than lying down. The infant lies on its back in its mother's lap, and the new mother sits cross-legged, leaning over the child (often partially resting on her sleeping husband) all night long. This is done in order to keep the child warm and protect it from exposure to dangers on the forest floor.

FERTILITY DURING THE FOREST PERIOD

Data on fertility of Ache women during the forest period are derived from 167 women born before 1959 and for whom we have what are likely to be complete and unbiased reproductive histories (categories 1–5, Table 3.3). Living in the forest as full-time foragers before peaceful contact with the outside world, Ache women show high fertility levels relative to those reported for most other traditional peoples. The cumulative number of live births reported by women of different ages prior to first contact (1971) is shown in Figure 8.2. The mean completed family size of twenty-seven women over age forty-five at first contact was 8.15 offspring (s.e. = 0.36). Only three of 107 women who reached age thirty in the forest had borne no children by that age; thus primary sterility was rare in the forest population.

More useful and precise measures of fertility can be obtained when data on women are divided into age categories. Fertility is then measured only for the woman-years at risk in a particular age interval. For example, each Ache woman in the forest who reached age thirty before contact will contribute one woman-year to the risk set for each age interval less than thirty years. Age-specific fertility (m_x) of a group of women who are at risk during a specific age interval x, $x + 1$, is defined here as the number of women who gave birth at age x divided by the total number who complete that age interval. Thus m_x is essentially a measure of the yearly probability of giving birth for women of a specified age. In this analysis we scored twins as a single birth event since only seven cases of twins were reported out of 1,384 births that we recorded between 1900 and 1990. Age-specific fertility for Ache women who probably reported all live births in the forest (categories 1–5, Table 3.3) are shown in Table 8.1 and Figure 8.3. The Total Fertility Rate (TFR), which is calculated as the sum of all the age-specific fertility across the reproductive span, is 8.03. This calculation of expected mean cumulative fertility for women who survive to the end of their reproductive span agrees well with the mean number of offspring (8.15) reported above for women who were more than forty-five years old before first contact.

Several traits of the Ache female age-specific fertility profile in the forest are striking. First, the maximum fertility levels observed are quite high, with almost one in three women giving birth each year during the years from age twenty to age thirty-nine. Second, fertility peaks at an older age than is reported for many other human groups. The highest fertility observed was for women from thirty to thirty-four years. Most natural fertility populations show fertility peaks from twenty to twenty-five years of age (Wood 1990), but a few other traditional populations have been observed to show a late fertility peak (e.g., Blurton Jones and Phillips 1991; Wood 1987). This finding might be due in part to errors in estimates of year of birth, but these errors would imply even higher age-specific fertility rates earlier in the reproductive span, since there is little doubt that all children listed were indeed born. Finally, not only does Ache female fertility peak at a later age than most populations, but the peak fertility years cover a greater percentage of the reproductive span than is often encountered, with Ache women showing fairly high fertility even in their early forties. This results in a higher lifetime achieved fertility than in most other traditional populations that have been studied. Nine of the women who completed their reproductive careers prior to contact have a surviving first and last child who we observed directly. The age estimates of these offspring are probably quite accurate and allow us to calculate a mean reproductive span of 25.2 years for those nine women. This suggests that female fertility was indeed high when they were in their early forties, as we have reported.

The frequency distribution of closed interbirth intervals (measured to the nearest year) for births that took place in the forest before contact is shown in Figure 8.4. The intervals are those reported between all Ache children born in the forest and their previous sibling when the births of both individuals could be dated to a single year using the relative age list and procedures described in Chapter 4. The mean interbirth interval (IBI) in this sample is 37.6 months (s.e. $= 0.95$ months, $n = 418$), the median is 36 months, and the mode is 36 months. These measures must be taken as rough estimates since age estimates show considerable random error in the range of ± 2 years (Chapter 4).

The final measurement of female fertility that is important for understanding overall population dynamics and female life history is the length of the reproductive span. Mean, median, and modal statistics for life course events provide slightly different information about the sample. All are appropriate for some but not other biological questions, so we report all three. Figure 8.5 shows the frequency distribution of ages at first birth for Ache women born before 1950. The mean age at first birth in this sample is 19.5 years (s.e. $= 0.44$, $n = 129$); both the median and mode are 19.0 years. The values for estimated age at first birth range from twelve to thirty-four years, with three women in this sample not experiencing first childbirth until after they were thirty years old. Two of these women gave birth to only one child in their life, and the third had only two live births.

Information on age at last birth in the precontact situation is limited to a small sample of women who were old enough to have finished their reproductive careers before leaving the forest (Figure 8.6). The mean age at last birth for women born before 1925 is 42.1 years (s.e. $= 0.63$, $n = 34$) with the median and mode at 43 years. The values for age at last birth ranged from 34 years (the same women who gave first birth at 34 years) to 48 years. The difference between the mean ages at last birth and first birth is 22.6 years, which is therefore approximately equal to the mean reproductive span of Ache women living in the forest. Dividing this reproductive span by the mean closed birth interval of 36 months suggests that Ache women should in general have experienced about seven closed intervals in a lifetime, which would then result in eight live births, a number that is quite close to the TFR and completed family size reported above.

COMPARISON WITH THE !KUNG AND YANOMAMO

Comparative data on female fertility for the Ache, the !Kung, and the Yanomamo are shown in Figure 8.7 and Table 8.2. Both the Ache and the

Yanomamo show high fertility relative to that of the !Kung. The comparison with the Yanomamo is complicated by the fact that most estimates of Yanomamo fertility are hampered by methodological problems. Neel and Weiss (1975) compare their estimate derived from the population age structure, physical examines, and urine tests with a previous much lower fertility estimate by Neel and Chagnon (1968). Subsequent researchers also admit that their studies underestimate births of infants who die young (e.g., Melancon 1982), and all research to date has been conducted in a population that has not been adequately aged. Not surprisingly, published values for completed family size range from 3.8 to 8 (Salzano 1988). In order to remain consistent with earlier chapters we compare our Ache results with those reported by Melancon (1982:97); however, Early and Peters's (1990) estimate of 7.9 live births in the Mucajai Yanomamo is probably the most accurate to date because of the extraordinary attention they paid to the problems of infant underreporting and the fact that many of the births were recorded by missionaries over a long time span. Whether or not the reported fertility variation among the Yanomamo is real cannot be determined until more attention is given to the details of methodology, particularly the use of retrospective interviews and problems of recall bias in populations with high infant mortality.

The data suggest that both the Ache and the Yanomamo show TFRs around seven or eight live births whereas the TFR for the bush-living !Kung is only about five (Howell 1979:124). The age-specific fertility profiles of the three groups suggest that the Ache generally have higher fertility, and that the fertility of older Ache women is particularly elevated when compared with that of their peers in the other two societies (Figure 8.7).

Differences in age-specific fertility were assessed statistically using a discrete-time logistic regression hazard model. Birth was the dependent variable, with the three age classes (15–24, 25–39, and 40–49 years) and groups as independent stratified variables. The differences between the Ache and the !Kung are statistically significant, with the Ache showing higher fertility across all age categories.[2] The Yanomamo show higher fertility than the Ache in the first age class and lower fertility in the subsequent two classes.[3] The high fertility observed among Yanomamo women from ten to twenty years old is curious and could indicate a real difference between the groups, or an error in assigning ages. The differences in fertility are supported by data on birth intervals showing that both the Ache and the Yanomamo have around three years between births whereas the !Kung interval in the bush is closer to four years (Howell 1979:134).

Finally, while ages at first birth are similar for the three groups, the Ache show a later age at last birth than either the !Kung or the Yanomamo by several years. Statistical tests cannot be performed since raw data for the comparison groups are not published. In any case, the possibility that this difference is partially caused by errors in age estimation of adult women should be considered along with possible explanations of real difference in reproductive span. If age estimation errors are responsible, it would imply even greater differences in age-specific fertility than reported above.

FERTILITY DURING THE RESERVATION PERIOD

Anthropologists have shown considerable interest in the issue of fertility and mortality changes among hunter-gatherers as they become sedentary. In Chapter 6, the data on mortality rate among the Ache after contact suggests that life is "easier" at the reservation settlements than it was in the forest, since mortality was considerably reduced in most age categories after the initial contact period ended. Ache data on fertility are consistent with the suggestion that overall health has improved on the reservations relative to the difficulties of forest life. During the contact years, when respiratory epidemics raged out of control, age-specific fertility rates in the older age intervals were significantly lower than they were in the forest (Figure 8.8).[4] The fact that only one birth was reported to a woman age forty or above during the contact period (at risk = 56 woman-years) may not be surprising, since older Ache women also suffered disproportionately higher mortality during contact and must have been in poor health during that time period.

Currently (since 1977), most fertility indicators suggest that Ache women may be enjoying improved health if such differences are reflected in birth rates. The cumulative fertility distribution of all currently living Ache women is shown in Figure 8.10. Only one woman in the current population appears to suffer from primary sterility; all other women who are in their middle or later childbearing years ($n = 72$ women aged 30+ years) have experienced at least one live birth. The age-specific fertility rates of women between 1977 and 1989 are shown in Table 8.3 and Figure 8.9. The age-specific fertility curve for reservation women is significantly different from the fertility curve of forest-living women, with women on the reservation showing higher fertility in their early years.[5] The fertility crossover in later years is provocative but not statistically significant. The difference may be due to chance, errors in age estimation, or the possibility that older women in the current population experienced premature secondary sterility as a result of the biological trauma of first contact and the associated epidemics. In any case, the current age-specific fertility profile is almost identical to that reported for the Yanomamo (shown in Figure 8.7) except that the Ache fertility rates are slightly higher in every age class, leading to a TFR of 8.5 live births.

Because all births since 1978 have been recorded by our team or by missionaries who provided us with the data, birth intervals have been measured to the nearest month for all closed intervals since 1978. A frequency distribution with IBIs collapsed into one-month intervals is shown in Figure 8.11. Not surprisingly, replacement intervals, in which the first child born dies before the second is conceived, are generally shorter (mean = 20.9 months, s.e. = 1.78, n = 43) than closed intervals, in which the first child survives to the conception of the second (mean = 33.9 months, s.e. = 0.85, n = 213). Second, a plot of IBI by women's ages (Figure 8.12) shows that decreasing age-specific fertility is partially due to increasing birth interval with age, as well as the ever-increasing number of older women who fail to close an interval altogether. Interestingly, closed birth intervals after a surviving child get progressively longer through the lifespan (from a mean of 28 months for fifteen-year-old women to about 34 months for forty-year-old women). This means that low age-specific fertility at young ages is primarily due to girls who have not yet begun to reproduce, whereas in older age, low fertility is due to both lowered fertility and an increasing proportion of women who have undergone secondary sterility.

Other reproductive parameters of Ache women also suggest higher overall fertility on the reservations than during the forest period. Mean birth intervals have become shorter (mean = 31.5 months, s.e. = 0.8, median = 29 months, n = 249) during the reservation period, and the mean age at first birth is significantly lower in the reservation population (mean = 17.7 years, s.e. = 0.36, median = 17.0 years, n = 66).[6] The age at first birth throughout the twentieth century is shown in Figure 8.13. The secular trend toward earlier first birth is clear and is present *within* the twelve-year reservation period as well, though the trend is only marginally significant in a univariate regression.[7] On the other hand, mean age at last birth is lower on the reservations but not significantly different from that reported before contact (mean = 38.5, s.d. = 6.5, n = 20).[8] This finding is consistent with the important life history generalization that age at first birth is more responsive to ecological conditions than is age at last birth.

A final observation about reservation fertility that is quite interesting but cannot be compared with any precontact data concerns birth seasonality. Almost every study of birth seasonality in human populations has found important seasonal differences in the monthly rates of live birth (see Leslie and Fry 1989). Figure 8.14 shows the number of births reported during each month for the Northern Ache from 1977 to 1989, when all births were recorded by missionaries. The data suggest a birth peak in the months of March and April. The significance of this finding will be discussed in more detail in Chapter 10.

SUMMARY

The Ache are characterized by high fertility relative to most other noncontraceptive populations (see Wood 1990). Completed family size in the forest was about eight live births. The Ache fertility is clearly higher than that reported for the !Kung. The comparison with the Yanomamo is more difficult because most estimates of Yanomamo fertility include some methodological problems. Ache forest fertility is not particularly high in adolescence, nor is first birth exceptionally early, taking place most often about age nineteen. Thus, the mean lag time between menarche and first birth in the forest is about four years, suggesting a period of adolescent subfecundity. On the other hand, fertility seems to peak later in the lifespan than it does for many other traditional populations, and fertility after age forty may be considerably higher than that found in most other traditional populations. The significance of higher fertility later in life is unclear since this pattern has been only rarely observed (see Blurton Jones and Phillips 1991).

Why Ache fertility in the twentieth century prior to first peaceful contact is so high is essentially a historical question. There is little doubt that Ache fertility must have been much lower during most of the past 10,000 years. At the observed growth rate of 2.5% per year, the Ache population would have grown from two individuals to 106 billion in 1,000 years! Historical records indicate that the Ache probably expanded into an empty niche after the local Guarani horticulturist population was decimated by Brazilian slave raiders in the seventeenth and eighteenth centuries. In addition, changes in the forest structure resulting from the rapid spread of Old World plants and insects (especially oranges and European bees) might have greatly increased the available food base in the past few hundred years. Oranges, which were dispersed by birds and monkeys, spread rapidly through all the Paraguayan forests and may have increased the densities of important game animals, such as monkeys, paca, and peccaries, which feed heavily on wild oranges. Perhaps none of these factors are important, and instead the Ache population simply experienced periodic crashes which eliminated long-term growth. Indeed, given the high growth rates observed in most traditional populations, we might speculate that much of human history is characterized by rapid population growth followed by catastrophic crashes. If growth phases are long and crashes are of short duration, the short sample periods typical of most demographic studies would usually only "observe" the population during a growth cycle. Whatever the historical explanation for high Ache fertility, the proximate cause of the recent population explosion must have been a local temporal increase in the food supply. The impact of food on fertility and mortality rates is examined in further detail in Chapter 10.

Fertility during the contact years decreased sharply, and subsequently it has increased on the reservation settlements. Ages at menarche and first birth in particular are decreasing so rapidly that the Ache themselves have commented on this trend. This is probably related to the worldwide secular trend in age at menarche that has been widely reported in the twentieth century and is believed to be caused by diet and health factors (Cumming et al. 1994). The increased adolescent fertility and decreased age at menarche have marked social consequences, which are just being appreciated by the Ache community. These changes thrust females directly from childhood to motherhood without adequate psychological or emotional development and will ultimately pose a serious challenge to Catholic missionaries working with the Ache, who are adamant about prohibiting the use of contraception but seem to be ineffective in discouraging early sexual activity.

Finally, the variation in fertility across individual females is pronounced. Ignoring women who never give birth, our data from the twentieth century concerning women whose reproductive histories are complete (categories 1–5 in Table 3.3) include postreproductive women with a minimum of three and a maximum of twelve live births (Figure 8.15). Although this fertility variation is not as great as that seen among males (Chapter 9), it has important evolutionary consequences. The variation within the society also allows for testing of models that will be the focus of later chapters and are designed to explain fertility patterns both within and between noncontraceptive societies.

NOTES

1. This number does not include most stillbirths, which were generally not easily distinguishable from cases in which a child was born live and then died at birth.

2. The logistic regression model is birth = intercept + !Kung + period2(25–39yr) + period3(40–49yr) + !Kung × period2 + !Kung × period3. The overall model chi-square is 162.93 with 5 df and $p = 0.0001$.

Independent variable	β	β s.e.	χ^2	p
Intercept	−1.349	0.070	372.63	0.0001
!Kung	−0.573	0.154	13.89	0.0002
period2	0.499	0.101	24.52	0.0001
period3	−0.322	0.168	3.67	0.056
!Kung × period2	−0.123	0.200	0.37	0.54
!Kung × period3	−1.256	0.387	10.51	0.0012

3. The logistic regression model is birth = intercept + Yanomamo + period2(25–39yr) + period3(40–49yr) + Yanomamo × period2 + Yanomamo × period3. The overall model chi-square is 162.93 with 5 df and $p = 0.0001$.

Independent variable	β	β s.e.	χ^2	p
Intercept	−1.349	0.070	372.63	0.0001
Yanomamo	0.332	0.131	6.41	0.0114
period2	0.499	0.101	24.52	0.0001
period3	−0.322	0.168	3.67	0.056
Yanomamo × period2	−0.608	0.181	11.34	0.0008
Yanomamo × period3	−1.478	0.370	15.97	0.0001

Because of the crossover, period2 was tested alone and shown to be significant:

Independent variable	β	β s.e.	χ^2	p
Yanomamo	-0.277	0.124	4.95	0.0261

4.   Because of a crossover in age-specific fertility, each period was analyzed separately. A logistic model was used to obtain confidence intervals as well as significance levels.

Independent variable	β	β s.e.	χ^2	p
Intercept	-1.349	0.070	372.63	0.0001
period1 (15–24yr), Contact	0.075	0.169	0.20	0.66
period2 (25–39yr), Contact	-0.123	0.151	0.67	0.42
period3 (40–49yr), Contact	-2.337	1.02	5.24	0.022

5.   Because of a crossover in age-specific fertility, each period was analyzed separately. A logistic model was used to obtain confidence intervals as well as significance levels.

Independent variable	β	β s.e.	χ^2	p
Intercept	-1.349	0.070	372.63	0.0001
period1 (15–24yr), Reservation	0.471	0.138	11.73	0.0006
period2 (25–39yr), Reservation	0.072	0.118	0.37	0.54
period3 (40–49yr), Reservation	0.377	0.282	1.79	0.181

6.   Kaplan-Meier test for age at first birth in forest and on reservations: log rank chi-square $= 4.82$, $p = 0.028$.

7.   An OLS regression with age at first birth as the dependent variable and year of observation as the independent variable gives the following result: $y = 576.3 - 0.281x$, $r^2 = 0.08$, $p = 0.08$.

8.   Kaplan-Meier test for age at last birth in forest and on reservations: log rank chi-square $= 2.58$, $p = 0.108$.

Table 8.1. Age-specific Fertility of Ache Women Living in the Forest

Age	Women-years at risk	Number born	Yearly probability of birth (m_x)	5-year mean m_x
10	173	0	0.000	
11	171	0	0.000	
12	167	1	0.006	
13	163	2	0.012	
14	156	4	0.026	
subtotal	**830**	**7**		**0.008**
15	147	13	0.088	
16	143	13	0.091	
17	139	19	0.137	
18	133	23	0.173	
19	129	36	0.279	
subtotal	**691**	**104**		**0.151**
20	127	33	0.260	
21	119	37	0.311	
22	112	31	0.277	
23	105	35	0.333	
24	98	18	0.184	
subtotal	**561**	**154**		**0.275**
25	91	30	0.330	
26	81	27	0.333	
27	79	24	0.304	
28	75	18	0.240	
29	70	19	0.271	
subtotal	**396**	**118**		**0.298**
30	65	23	0.354	
31	61	22	0.361	
32	58	13	0.224	
33	51	13	0.255	
34	48	19	0.396	
subtotal	**283**	**90**		**0.318**
35	47	11	0.234	
36	46	18	0.391	
37	46	12	0.261	
38	44	11	0.250	
39	43	11	0.256	
subtotal	**226**	**63**		**0.279**
40	42	9	0.214	
41	42	9	0.214	
42	40	9	0.225	
43	36	11	0.306	
44	32	4	0.125	
subtotal	**192**	**42**		**0.219**

(*continued*)

Table 8.1. (*continued*)

Age	Women-years at risk	Number born	Yearly probability of birth (m_x)	5-year mean m_x
45	31	6	0.194	
46	27	1	0.037	
47	26	1	0.038	
48	24	1	0.042	
49	22	0	0.000	
subtotal	**130**	**9**		**0.069**
total	**3309**	**TFR =**	**8.031**	**8.081**

Table 8.2   Comparative Fertility of Ache, !Kung, and Yanomamo Women

	Ache	!Kung	Yanomamo
Mean yearly probability of birth (15–24 yrs)	0.206	0.189	0.266
Mean yearly probability of birth (25–39 yrs)	0.299	0.158	0.245
Mean yearly probability of birth (40–49 yrs)	0.158	0.044	0.056
mean age at first birth	19.5	18.8	18.4
mean age at last birth	42.1	34.4	37.9
Total Fertility Rate (TFR)	8.03	4.69	6.86*
interbirth interval (months)	37.6	49.4	34.4

Sources: !Kung data from Howell 1979 (Table 6.1), Yanomamo data from Melancon 1982 (Table 4.2)
*Probably underestimated because of underreporting of deceased infants.

Table 8.3.   Age-specific Fertility of Ache Women on Reservations, 1978–1989

Age	Women-years at risk	Number born	Yearly probability of birth (m_x)	5-year mean m_x
10	46	0	0.000	
11	43	0	0.000	
12	41	0	0.000	
13	36	0	0.000	
14	35	1	0.029	
subtotal	**201**	**1**		**0.005**
15	35	4	0.114	
16	33	6	0.182	
17	32	10	0.313	
18	34	11	0.324	
19	36	12	0.333	
subtotal	**170**	**43**		**0.253**

Table 8.3. (*continued*)

Age	Women-years at risk	Number born	Yearly probability of birth (m_x)	5-year mean m_x
20	34	10	0.294	
21	34	12	0.353	
22	35	11	0.314	
23	36	12	0.333	
24	35	13	0.371	
subtotal	**174**	**58**		**0.333**
25	37	10	0.270	
26	35	15	0.429	
27	35	10	0.286	
28	37	11	0.297	
29	38	16	0.421	
subtotal	**182**	**62**		**0.341**
30	38	17	0.447	
31	37	11	0.297	
32	39	12	0.308	
33	40	15	0.375	
34	35	8	0.229	
subtotal	**189**	**63**		**0.333**
35	35	12	0.343	
36	34	11	0.324	
37	33	6	0.182	
38	32	5	0.156	
39	32	10	0.313	
subtotal	**166**	**44**		**0.265**
40	32	7	0.219	
41	28	4	0.143	
42	23	5	0.217	
43	21	0	0.000	
44	17	3	0.176	
subtotal	**121**	**19**		**0.157**
45	13	1	0.077	
46	13	0	0.000	
47	11	0	0.000	
48	9	0	0.000	
49	8	0	0.000	
subtotal	**54**	**1**		**0.019**
total	**1257**	**TFR =**	**8.468**	**8.529**

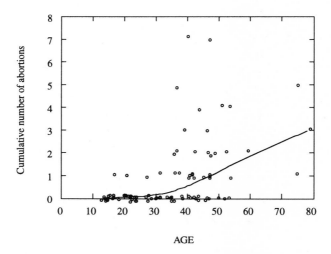

Figure 8.1.   Cumulative number of abortions reported by age for living Ache women (lowess smooth).

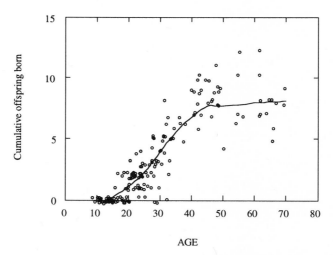

Figure 8.2.   Cumulative number of live births by age for 174 Ache women during the forest period (lowess smooth).

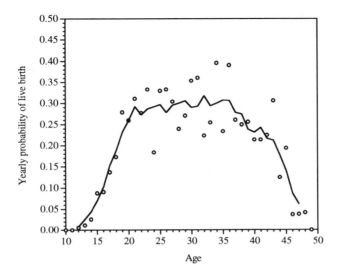

Figure 8.3. Age-specific fertility for Ache women during the forest period. Line shows five-point moving average.

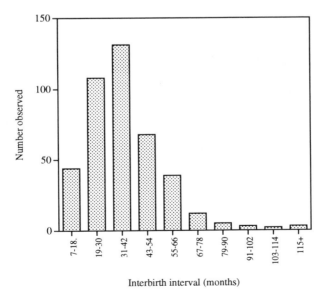

Figure 8.4. Frequency distribution of closed birth intervals in the forest period.

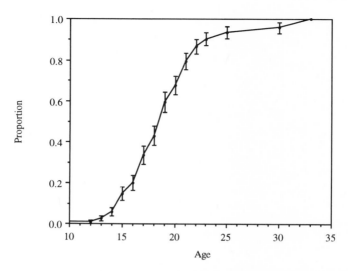

Figure 8.5. Proportion of Ache women during the forest period who experienced first birth by the specified age. Kaplan-Meier product-limit estimates (bars show probability s.e.), *n* = 129.

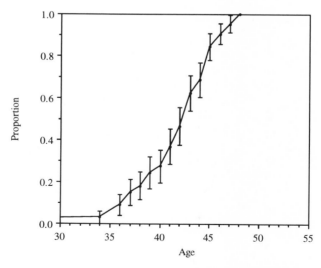

Figure 8.6. Proportion of Ache women during the forest period who experienced last birth by the specified age. Kaplan-Meier product-limit estimates (bars show probability s.e.), *n* = 34.

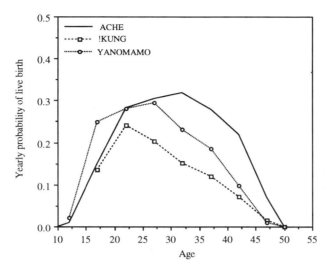

Figure 8.7. Female age-specific fertility (five-year mean) among forest-living Ache, !Kung, and Yanomamo.

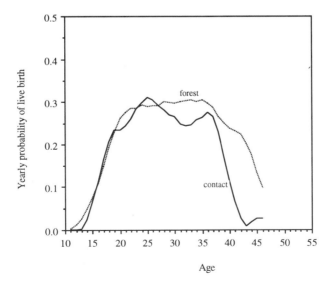

Figure 8.8. Comparison of age-specific fertility of Ache women at contact and during the forest period (five- and three-point running averages).

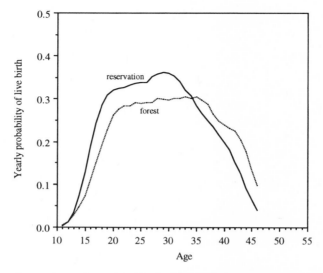

Figure 8.9. Comparison of age-specific fertility of Ache women on reservations and during the forest period (five- and three-point running averages).

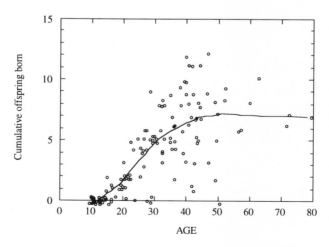

Figure 8.10. Cumulative number of live births by age for 137 Ache women living on reservations in 1989 (lowess smooth).

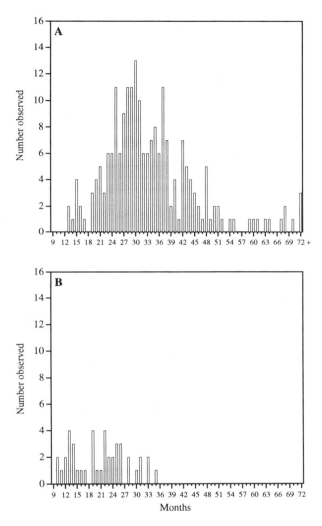

Figure 8.11.   Frequency distribution of all closed birth intervals observed between 1978 and 1993 when the first child of the pair (A) survives to the conception of the second or (B) dies before the conception of the second. Replacement intervals after a child has died are clearly much shorter.

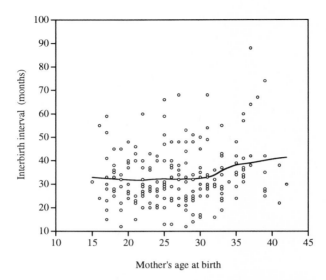

Figure 8.12. Scatterplot of closed birth intervals recorded between 1978 and 1990 by mother's age when the child beginning the interval was born (lowess smooth). The sample only contains cases in which the first sibling in the pair survives at least to the conception of the second (nonreplacement intervals). Note that fertility following a surviving infant is lower for older women, who are approaching but have not yet experienced secondary sterility.

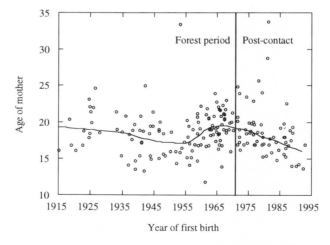

Figure 8.13. All first births recorded from the forest and postcontact (contact and reservation) samples. Note that in recent years the first births are taking place in younger and younger women (lowess smooth).

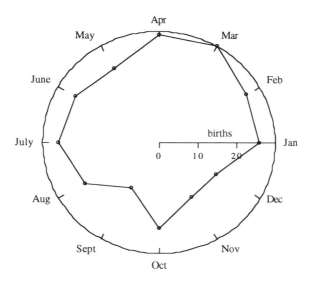

Figure 8.14. Birth seasonality on Ache reservations. The conception peak corresponds well with seasonal fluctuation in weight (discussion in Chapter 10).

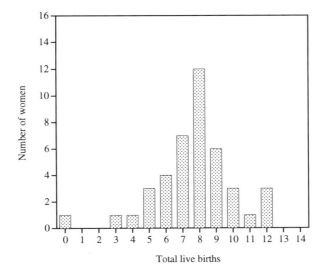

Figure 8.15. Completed parity distribution for all Ache women in the twentieth century who reached age fifty and for whom we are likely to have complete and accurate reproductive histories (categories 1–5, Table 3.3).

An Ache man with traditional lip plug ornament, 1980.

9

Male Fertility

Male fertility is poorly studied relative to female fertility for a variety of reasons, which are almost all ultimately derived from the fact that paternity is difficult to assess in many sexually reproducing organisms, including humans. In this chapter we examine male reproductive patterns among the Ache as far as they can be illuminated by taking informant reports of paternity and possible paternity at face value. As is the case for other organisms that are characterized by internal fertilization, we will probably not truly understand male reproductive patterns until assumed paternity can be reliably related to actual paternity. Paternity verification has become possible only in the past few years through DNA finger-printing, but such techniques have not yet been applied in scientific studies of remote human populations, and they may not be common for some time given current logistical and ethical problems concerning their use. Nevertheless, because many important problems in human biology and life history research require estimates of male fertility patterns we have examined them as completely as possible given the data available.

PATERNITY

Ache men realize that sexual relations must take place in order to father a child, and they also believe that those men who had sexual intercourse with a woman in the month prior to her first missed menstrual cycle are most likely to be the "real" father of a child. Nevertheless, the Ache also recognize the partial paternity of any man who has engaged in intercourse with a woman several months prior to discovering her pregnancy, and throughout her pregnancy right up to the day of birth. Because sexual relations with multiple men before the birth of a child was a common occurrence among the Ache, paternity is sometimes uncertain even when the diligent interviewer tediously attempts to untangle probable from improbable fathers. This problem is highlighted by examining a subset of individuals who reported all their own possible fathers. Between 1980 and 1989, 321 Ache adults interviewed about their own parents reported 632 fathers for an average of 1.97 fathers per individual (s.e. = 0.06; median = 2; mode = 2; maximum = 10).

In this study three different sources of information were taken into account to assign paternity: the opinion of the mother and her close kin, the opinion of putative fathers and their close kin, and the opinion of the offspring (who relies mainly on the first two sources). Comparing these three sources of information we found many cases of omission (a potential father of a child was forgotten by some individuals), but no cases where reported possible paternity was denied. If a woman identified a man as the father of her child or if a man claimed to have fathered a child, there was never any denial of this possibility by the corresponding partner. Thus a list of potential fathers of a child from a variety of different kin will provide a minimal estimate of the number of possible fathers, and if a sufficient number of individuals are interviewed they will probably provide a fairly complete list of potential fathers. In the sample used here, the fathers of all children were ascertained independently from at least two sources and sometimes from as many as six sources. Offspring usually provided the most complete list of possible fathers, whereas men were most likely to forget about possible offspring they had fathered, and women were somewhat less likely to forget about possible fathers of their children. The pattern makes sense since children seemed anxious to claim paternal investment from as many men as possible while men sometimes preferred to deny paternal responsibility.

Male fertility patterns in this chapter are reported for two types of paternity. The man who had most frequent sexual intercourse in the month prior to a woman's first missed period, and who is named as the "real father" or the "one who put (the child) in," is referred to here as the *primary father* (*apa eche, apa miare,* in Ache). He is probably in most cases the genetic father of the child in question. When there was disagreement about the identity of the primary father, we chose the man reported by the greatest number of informants. Analysis of male fertility using data on primary fathers is methodologically similar to use of male fertility data reported from most other populations, in which informants name a single man as father of a child. In this chapter all male fertility analyses refer only to primary fatherhood unless otherwise specified.

The *secondary fathers* (*apa peroare, apa momboare,* in Ache) of a child are also considered here, and age-specific rates of secondary fatherhood are described in this chapter. Secondary fathers include all men who had sexual intercourse with the mother, the timing of which indicates to informants that they were probably not the "real" father. Nevertheless, they did copulate with the mother near the time she became pregnant and *might* be the real father. Secondary fathers also sometimes include men who copulated with the mother late in her pregnancy and couldn't possibly be the biological father of the child in question. In some ways primary vs. secondary fatherhood may represent the outcome of two different male reproductive strategies, since most primary fathers are men who are involved in a long-term, recognized marriage and mating relationship with the mother of a child, whereas secondary fathers tend to be men who have temporary and/or hidden relations (premarital or extramarital) with the mother of a child. Not surprisingly, the age structure of men pursuing these two reproductive strategies is somewhat different (see below).

Finally, the Ache word for father is used to refer to all of father's brothers as well. This custom is common among tribal peoples, but demographers should be keenly aware of such a tendency if they collect data from censuses of groups of people they do not know personally. Ache children who lose their primary father in death almost always report a paternal uncle as their father. Only with good linguistic skills and a knowledge of the potential problem can this misunderstanding be avoided. It should also be noted that the linguistic lumping of brothers as potential fathers probably has some biological basis. During our data collection many cases were reported in which two or even three brothers were all candidates for primary or secondary father of a particular child, and in one case an older man and his son were both reported to be the father of a particular child (many men also reported fathering children by two or more sisters, and in a few cases men fathered children by a woman and her daughter). The same patterns were seen among successive children (e.g., the fathers of two successive children of a single woman were often brothers). These data suggest a tendency towards levirate and sororate mating and marriage practices, although the Ache do not recognize such a bias formally.

FATHERHOOD

Most Ache men approach fatherhood with a good deal of anticipation and obvious pride. They readily point out that their wives are pregnant even when the woman herself is still reluctant to admit the fact. They do not (as far as we could tell) change their behavior toward their pregnant wives in any way in order to alleviate their work load, pamper them, or provide them with a special diet. In fact, a good number of men admitted abandoning a female partner during pregnancy, only to return several months after birth had taken place (or sometimes not returning at all). As the birth nears, some men prepare to help in the delivery whereas others make it clear that they will not be around to participate. We were unable to ascertain how this decision is made, but we suspect that it was sometimes related to paternity confidence.

When a man's wife goes into labor he often goes off to hunt in the forest. Several hours later he may return, but he might not approach his own hut to inquire about the outcome of the birth until a substantial delay, during which he may feign disinterest. Such a response seemed to us more common among young fathers than among older, more experienced men. New fathers are expected to hunt long hours and also pound and extract palm fiber for their wives, although again we observed a good deal of variation in compliance with this rule.

Upon birth of a child, the primary father enters into ritual relationships with all the men and women involved in the birth, as described in Chapter 2. These special relationships between a man and the "godparents" of his children last as long as the child is alive and entail mutual obligations of care and aid. Several times we observed gift giving between unrelated men (especially between older and younger men); when we inquired about the exchange, we were told that one was a "godparent" to the other's children. For example, in one case we observed a man receiving a particularly desirable piece of meat. It was explained that he was the "godfather" of one of the children who lived at the house we were visiting. In another case we saw a man buy a shirt from a small Paraguayan store and give it to another man, explaining "he is the godfather of my child." These types of relationships between men might partially explain the help that women receive from unrelated male "friends" during the delivery of their children.

After the birth of a child the couple should not engage in sexual relations "until the child walks." Women sleep sitting up for several months and generally avoid any intimate contact with their husbands (they never lie down next to them at night during this period). This often results in men seeking out new sex partners during the first year after a child is born, but many men also admitted to us that they broke the taboo against intercourse after only a few months. Still, the temporary conjugal abandonment of new mothers was commonly observed by us and is probably a traditional pattern.

> *In the forest we didn't marry [stay married to] new mothers. Their bodies smell, the old men said. . . . The smell of milk was the only reason we were afraid (to be married to them). . . . I didn't touch [have intercourse with] new mothers . . . well, maybe only a little. It was bad (translated from an interview with Javagi taped in 1985).*

Some men in our sample never had any children (see below) and others never acquired a wife. One category of men in Ache society opts out of the male mating pool altogether. These men, called *panegi,* take on a female socio-economic role (the word *pane* means unsuccessful or unlucky at hunting). Men who are *panegi* generally do not hunt, but instead collect plant resources and insect larvae. They weave baskets, mats, and fans, and make tooth necklaces, bowstrings, and other female handicrafts. They spend long hours cooking, collecting firewood or water, and caring for children. Most informants stated that "panegis" did not ever engage in homosexual behavior (oral or anal) prior to first contact. A few informants said they were not sure, but had never heard of such behavior. These men were generally accepted by other members of the society as a natural part of the social group. Occasionally they participated in club fights but often were not hit by other men. Some also hunted certain animals but not others. One *panegi* of the southern Ache had children early in his life and then later became *pane.* On the reservation settlement these men grow their hair long and act overtly effeminate. In 1970, the year before first contact, there were 150 men over age twenty. Three of those men (2%) were panegi. Only one Northern Ache panegi survived the contact period, and he is currently the smallest man in the population (41.4 kg).

Our observation of two Ache "panegis," as well as stories we have heard, suggest that they were low status and not always treated well. They were forced to do menial chores and often did not receive much food (or good pieces) in the sharing network. Nonetheless, they were clearly accepted as members of the society who were generally recognized as providing useful services. Other band members (of both sexes) occasionally showed open affection to them, but they were also often the butt of jokes and off-color sexual humor. In one case, a very high status hunter told us a story of how a panegi had saved his life during the contact period. When all of his band had become ill, the healthy band members had fled, leaving the sick behind. A panegi stayed with the sick and provided them with collected foods for a few weeks until some recovered from the illness. The hunter told us the story with tears welling in his eyes, and he clearly had strong positive feelings toward the unrelated panegi who had nursed him back to health.

As men grow older they may increase in political power but often decline in hunting prowess (particularly after age fifty). Thus, their attractiveness to women may both increase and decrease with age in complicated ways. This change affects individual men differently and leads to three common patterns of reproduction through the lifespan. First, many middle-aged men abandon older wives to marry younger women (serial monogamy) and subsequently have several children with at least two women. Second, a few men acquire and maintain two wives (polygyny) in late middle age and may have two complete families or several smaller "partial families" with a variety of women. Third, and probably most common, many men stay married to women near their own age (long-term monogamy) and thus do not have significantly longer reproductive careers than do women. These men have the potential for longer reproductive spans than women, but that potential is not realized. Finally, some men never acquire a reproducing wife during early adulthood and by middle age are marked with a poor reputation so they are unlikely to acquire a wife for very long and may ultimately father no children. The combination of these patterns leads to slightly higher variance in lifetime fertility among males than that observed for females (Figure 9.1, and see Figure 8.15).

FERTILITY DURING THE FOREST PERIOD

Data on fertility of Ache men during the forest period are derived from 204 men born before 1955 and for whom we are likely to have complete and unbiased reproductive histories (categories 11–15, Table 3.3). Forest-dwelling Ache men sometimes began engaging in sexual behavior in their late teens but often didn't have their first child until their mid twenties or later. Figure 9.2 shows the cumulative probability of age at birth of first child for men born before 1950. The median age at first parenthood is a more useful statistic here since a significant proportion never fathered a child before they died or were right-censored (reached the contact period). The median is 24 years ($n = 202$; Kaplan-Meier product-limit estimate) and age at first birth ranged from age fifteen (probably an error in aging) to age fifty. In our precontact sample, 12.5% of all men age forty or above had never experienced primary fatherhood ($N = 80$).

The cumulative fertility of Ache men living in the forest whose ages in 1970 or at death were known is shown in Figure 9.3. It is evident that the variance in cumulative fertility for men is much higher at each age than that observed in women (cf. Figure 8.2). Indeed, the mean number of live births in the forest for twenty-five women who were between fifty and seventy years of age by 1970, and for whom we are likely to have complete and unbiased reproductive histories (categories 1–5; Table 3.3) is 7.84 with a standard deviation of 1.89 births. The mean number of live births for forty-eight men in the same age interval is 6.40 with a standard deviation of 3.88. The lack of a fertility asymptote in this sample should not be interpreted to mean that male fertility does not generally decline with age (see below). Instead, our sample suggests a positive relationship between fertility and the probability of a man surviving to old age, which is confirmed in Chapter 12.

An analysis of age-specific fertility rates provides more details on the male fertility pattern for the forest-dwelling Ache. In order to calculate male age-specific fertility we considered men as being at risk of fatherhood if they survived to the year *before* the birth could have taken place (e.g., all men who survive to age 29 are counted in the denominator as being at risk of fatherhood at age 30). This is because males, unlike females, can become parents after they are dead, and our calculation allows for this. Also males, unlike females, can produce children from two or more births in one year; thus male age-specific fertility in theory can be higher than 1.0.

Figure 9.4 shows the age-specific fertility of primary fatherhood for forest-dwelling Ache men between fifteen and seventy-five years of age. The data used to plot age-specific fertility are shown in Table 9.1. The total fertility rate (sum of all age-specific probabilities of fathering a child) for men up to age sixty-five is 8.47 live births. This number should not necessarily match the TFR for women since it pertains only to men who survive to age sixty-five, and it is also affected by the adult sex ratio.

The age-specific fertility curve suggests that male fertility in the forest peaks around forty years of age. Fertility in the early adult years lags behind females by only about five years, unlike some traditional populations where men are unable to acquire sexual access to women until they reach middle age (e.g., Hart et al. 1988). Peak fertility is about 0.3 offspring per year, no higher than that calculated for women in their most fertile years. Although men as a population do not show a higher age-specific fertility peak than do women, some individual men do achieve higher age-specific fertility than any individual women. Thus, some men had two or more children born in a particular year, particularly men under the age of forty.

The yearly probability of secondary (possible) fatherhood is shown in Figure 9.5. The curve must be taken as a minimal estimate of secondary paternity for reasons discussed above. Nevertheless the data are useful for estimating the *shape* of the age-specific fertility profile from secondary fatherhood since the shape of the curve is drawn from an unbiased sample of man-years at risk, and there is no reason why the secondary children from one age group of men should be underrepresented. The height of the paternity rate may be underestimated, owing to unreported cases of secondary paternity, but in any case, actual genetic paternity must be only a fraction of these reported cases. These patterns should not be the result of preferential reporting of older powerful men as primary fathers, since by the time the reproductive histories were collected most of the older men were dead and the men who had been younger during the sample period were much older. The data show a secondary fertility peak much earlier than the primary fertility for the same group of men living in the forest. While primary fertility is twice as high at age forty-five as at age twenty, secondary fertility shows the opposite trend, being about twice as high at age twenty as at age forty-five. This suggests that Ache men use a strategy of short-term hidden matings during their young adult years and later become involved in more open, long-term mating relationships. This same pattern, in which young immature males use "sneaky" copulation tactics, is often described for other sexually reproducing organisms from insects to mammals (e.g., Alcock et al. 1977; Howard 1978; Le Boeuf 1974; Gross and Charnov 1980).

COMPARISON WITH THE !KUNG AND YANOMAMO

Because we have already shown in the previous chapter that female fertility differs somewhat between the Ache, the !Kung, and the Yanomamo, comparisons of the level of fertility would be redundant (e.g., !Kung men are likely to have lower fertility than Ache men since !Kung women have lower fertility than Ache women). Also, mean male fertility is sensitive to the adult sex ratio, and Chapter 4 suggests some significant differences in this parameter between the Ache, the !Kung, and the Yanomamo as well. Nevertheless, although the absolute level of fertility for males in these groups may not be of interest, the shapes of the fertility curves provide some additional information about male reproductive patterns. A comparison of the age-specific fertility of the three groups is shown in Figure 9.6. Two important conclusions appear warranted. First, the

Ache and Yanomamo men show virtually identical fertility profiles, given the small sample sizes and sources of aging error in the two studies. Both groups show increasing fertility beginning in the late teen years and peaking in the mid thirties to early forties. Fertility declines slowly thereafter and remains significant well into old age. Second, although !Kung men show lower fertility than the two South American groups, they also seem to show a shorter reproductive span, with men beginning reproduction later and finishing earlier than among the Ache or Yanomamo. If these trends are real they may suggest higher levels of serial monogamy/polygyny among the South American groups than for the !Kung.

FERTILITY DURING THE RESERVATION PERIOD

Male fertility (primary paternity only) since 1978 can be estimated from the 154 men who were over age fifteen during this time period and at risk of fathering a child. All children born to these men were the offspring of Ache women (no man fathered a child with a non-Ache woman during the study period). Cumulative fertility by age is shown in Figure 9.7. Some of the older men in this cumulative fertility figure had already completed their reproduction during the forest and contact periods. Nine men in the current population have fathered more than ten children but none has produced more than fifteen. Five out of sixty-six men over age forty have never fathered any children. The age-specific rate of primary fatherhood on the reservations between 1978 and 1989 is shown in Table 9.2 and Figure 9.8. The data suggest higher fertility early in the reproductive lifespan and much lower fertility after age thirty-five on the reservations than was reported during the forest period. The total fertility rate for men has also declined since contact despite the fact that fertility has increased for Northern Ache women. This is probably due to an increase in the adult sex ratio (more males per female), and a prevalence of hypergyny in which the more-acculturated Ypety and Yvytyruzu Ache men have monopolized Northern Ache women to the exclusion of less-acculturated Northern Ache men.

The shift in male age-specific fertility after contact is consistent with a variety of social changes the Ache have reported and we have observed. Before contact, middle-aged men between thirty-five and fifty-five years old were politically powerful and monopolized many fertile women in the population. Younger men were afraid of these "fully grown adult men" because of their strong alliances and the fact that they sometimes killed younger men in club fights (never in the twentieth century did a young man kill a man in the "powerful" age category). Older men were directly responsible for most band-level food redistribution and often directed young men to hunt farthest from the women and children during the day and to sleep in the middle of the camp where they could be watched at night (so they would not engage in sexual relations with women).

After contact, teenage boys and men in their early twenties rapidly learned to communicate with missionaries and other outsiders, master new techniques and technology, and manipulate the national market economy and missionaries in ways that older men were unable or unwilling to do. Club fights and polygyny were prohibited, and younger men acquired shotguns, improving their hunting success and giving them the upper hand in any violent confrontation. Younger men were quickly favored by reservation administrators, were given first access to outside resources for redistribution, and thus acquired economic leverage over the older men. In addition, younger men were assigned (later elected) to be the "chiefs" of the Ache communities by missionaries and government officials, and when they converted more rapidly to Christianity they were favored economically by mission personnel.

An extreme example of these trends is drawn from one group of southern Ache that made contact in 1979. At that time Chimbegi, who was about forty-four years old, had four wives, aged 38, 24, 23, and 22. Chimbegi was recognized as a great hunter and a man who was "very very strong." After a few weeks on the reservation he was left with only the 38-year-old wife. The 23-year-old wife was stolen by an older, acculturated Ache man from a different group. The other two young wives were "given up" to men 17 and 24 years old who had had no wives in the forest. All three of the younger wives continued to reproduce for years; thus, Chimbegi, had he lived in the forest, would have experienced very high fertility in his forties and fifties. Instead, he has fathered no new children since leaving the forest.

All of these factors resulted in a substantial shift in age-specific fertility among Ache men. First, age at first birth is earlier (median = 23 years) on the reservation than it was for men in the forest.[1] The proportion of men who have experienced first birth also increases much more steeply on the reservations: almost all men father their first child by age thirty (see Figure 9.2). In the forest, fertility peaked around forty years of age and was high until age fifty. On the reservations fertility is currently highest around age twenty-seven and drops rapidly in older age. Eventually we might expect to see older age categories regaining relative fertility as the most acculturated young men move into middle age and the gap in ability to deal with outsiders decreases between the younger and older men in the population. Currently, however, many older men in the reservation population are unmarried and have little prospect of attracting a fertile wife.

SUMMARY

Ache informants provide data on two types of paternity. We define *primary fatherhood* according to criteria that suggest a high probability of biological paternity. The term *secondary fatherhood* encompasses several linguistic categories of "father" in the Ache language that are likely to indicate lower probabilities of biological paternity. The median age of first primary fatherhood is twenty-four years in the forest and about twenty-three years in reservation settlements. There is high variation in completed family size among older men living during the forest period, with some individuals producing more than fifteen offspring and others never having fathered a child. The age at last reproduction is theoretically dependent only on lifespan or age at censoring in males (since males can continue to reproduce until they die), but for those Ache males who survived to at least age sixty in the twentieth century and for whom we probably have complete reproductive data, the mean age at last reproduction is 48.1 years (Figure 9.9). Thus, the average male reproductive span (24 years) for males who survive to old age is almost exactly the same as the average reproductive span (23 years) of females who survive to old age, despite much greater variance among males.

The reproductive span of some Ache males is longer than that of females because males can continue to reproduce into late middle age. The pattern of longer reproductive span for some males relative to that of any female is the opposite of that found in most other mammals (see Clutton Brock 1988). The relatively shorter human female reproductive span is the result of menopause, a characteristic in mammals that may be unique to humans and perhaps toothed whales (Hill and Hurtado 1991; also see Chapter 12). The life history implications of the potentially longer male human reproductive span have not yet been well explored, but study of this pattern may lead to a good deal of insight about conflict between the sexes concerning levels of parental investment at any point in time (e.g., males may invest less per unit time over a much longer time period and females may always appear to invest more in their offspring at any point in time).

Patterns of primary and secondary paternity suggest a dual mixed reproductive strategy that varies in character through the life course. Fertility through secondary fatherhood is higher when Ache men are young, and fertility through primary fatherhood is more important at a later age. Younger Ache men may find it difficult to attract a permanent mate and thus make the best of a bad situation by sneaking copulations whenever possible. This results in many short-term sexual relationships that are unlikely to produce genetic descendants, but may occasionally result in offspring. Older men often have one or more steady mates and may devote less time to acquiring sneak copulations. Although this pattern is intriguing, it will be difficult to study in more detail because of the sensitive nature of information about the topic. Significant research on the topic would clearly require DNA fingerprinting techniques for assessing paternity.

Age-specific fertility of Ache men in the forest is very similar to that reported for the Yanomamo but different from that of !Kung men, who seem to start reproducing at older ages and cease reproduction at a younger age. It is likely that the !Kung pattern is partially the result of early secondary sterility among

!Kung women, but it may also reflect differences in the abilities of older men to provide resources either directly or through political alliances. In recent years the age-specific fertility peak of Ache men has shifted substantially toward younger ages, a pattern congruent with Ache reports concerning shifts in political and economic power since contact. In fact the fertility peak of reservation Ache men near twenty-seven years of age may be one of the youngest male fertility peaks reported for a traditional society and can only be understood in the context of rapid acculturation and political upheaval that has favored young men.

NOTE

1.   Kaplan-Meier product-limit estimate of age at first birth for 202 men born before 1955 and 81 men born since 1955. Test of equality, forest vs. reservation: $\chi^2 = 3.46$, df = 1, $p = 0.063$.

Table 9.1. Age-specific Fertility of Ache Men in the Forest Period

Age	Man-years at risk	Number born	Probability of birth (m_x)	5-year mean m_x
15	202	1	0.005	
16	195	5	0.026	
17	187	5	0.027	
18	176	7	0.040	
19	168	14	0.083	0.034
20	160	14	0.088	
21	152	12	0.079	
22	145	27	0.186	
23	138	26	0.188	
24	129	23	0.178	0.141
25	125	30	0.240	
26	118	26	0.220	
27	112	28	0.250	
28	103	25	0.243	
29	96	22	0.229	0.236
30	93	26	0.280	
31	88	17	0.193	
32	81	19	0.235	
33	79	21	0.266	
34	73	15	0.205	0.237
35	67	22	0.328	
36	63	14	0.222	
37	60	21	0.350	
38	57	16	0.281	
39	50	15	0.300	0.296
40	50	12	0.240	
41	45	17	0.378	
42	45	16	0.356	
43	45	12	0.267	
44	45	6	0.133	0.274
45	43	12	0.279	
46	41	7	0.171	
47	36	3	0.083	
48	33	7	0.212	
49	31	0	0.000	0.158
50	30	6	0.200	
51	28	5	0.179	
52	28	3	0.107	
53	25	3	0.120	
54	24	3	0.125	0.148
55	22	4	0.182	
56	20	0	0.000	
57	18	3	0.167	
58	17	3	0.176	
59	14	1	0.071	0.121
60	13	1	0.077	
61	11	1	0.091	
62	9	0	0.000	
63	9	1	0.111	
64	7	0	0.000	0.061
65–75	29	1	0.034	0.034
10 to 65	4086	TFR =	8.467	8.878

Table 9.2. Age-specific Fertility of Ache Men Living on Reservations (1978–1989)

Age	Man-years at risk	Number born	Probability of birth (m_x)	5-year mean m_x
15	48	0	0.000	
16	48	0	0.000	
17	51	1	0.020	
18	54	4	0.074	
19	56	7	0.125	0.047
20	57	7	0.123	
21	57	13	0.228	
22	55	6	0.109	
23	52	18	0.346	
24	47	5	0.106	0.183
25	48	17	0.354	
26	50	16	0.320	
27	51	15	0.294	
28	50	17	0.340	
29	49	13	0.265	0.315
30	48	12	0.250	
31	46	11	0.239	
32	43	16	0.372	
33	44	7	0.159	
34	45	11	0.244	0.252
35	45	7	0.156	
36	46	7	0.152	
37	42	8	0.190	
38	39	4	0.103	
39	36	6	0.167	0.154

Age	Man-years at risk	Number born	Probability of birth (m_x)	5-year mean m_x
40	33	6	0.182	
41	33	5	0.152	
42	32	4	0.125	
43	28	5	0.179	
44	28	4	0.143	0.156
45	27	4	0.148	
46	25	1	0.040	
47	21	4	0.190	
48	22	1	0.045	
49	20	1	0.050	0.096
50	18	2	0.111	
51	16	1	0.063	
52	16	0	0.000	
53	12	0	0.000	
54	12	1	0.083	0.054
55	11	0	0.000	
56	10	0	0.000	
57	8	0	0.000	
58	7	0	0.000	
59	7	1	0.143	0.023
60+	35	1	0.029	0.029
10 to 65	1628	TFR =	6.533	6.823

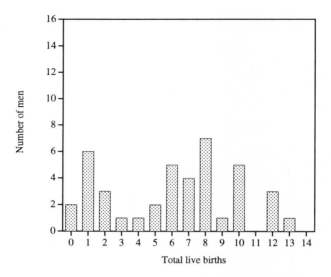

Figure 9.1.   Completed parity distribution for all Ache men in the twentieth century who reached age fifty and for whom we are likely to have complete and accurate reproductive histories (categories 11–15, Table 3.3). Note that males show much higher fertility variation than females (cf. Figure 8.15).

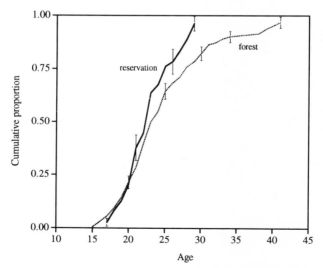

Figure 9.2.   Product-limit estimate of proportion of men having fathered their first child for Ache men born before 1955 (forest) and after 1955 (reservation). Bars show one standard error.

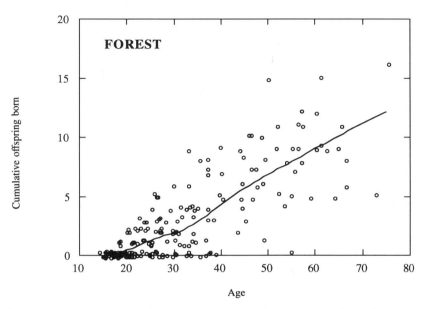

Figure 9.3. Cumulative fertility for Ache men prior to contact (n = 204, lowess smooth).

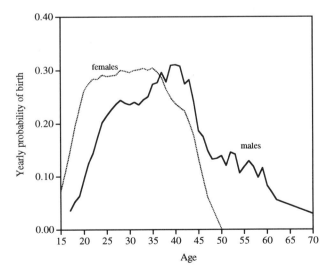

Figure 9.4. Age-specific fertility for Ache men living in the forest (five-point moving average) compared with female fertility.

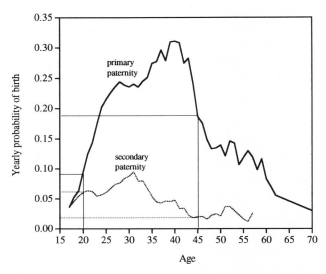

Figure 9.5. Age-specific rates of primary and secondary fatherhood (five-point moving average) for Ache men living in the forest. Note that primary fertility is twice as high at age forty-five as at age twenty, but secondary fertility is twice as high at the earlier age.

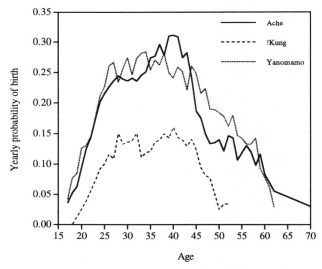

Figure 9.6. Age-specific fertility for Ache men living in the forest, compared with !Kung and Yanomamo men.

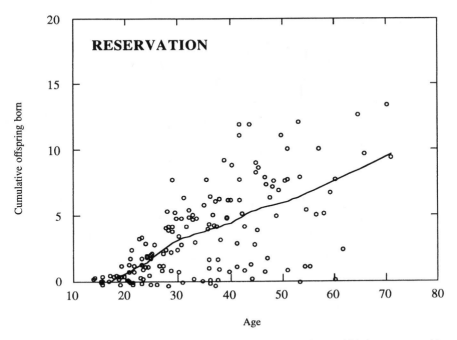

Figure 9.7. Cumulative fertility for Ache men living in 1990 (*n* = 154, lowess smooth).

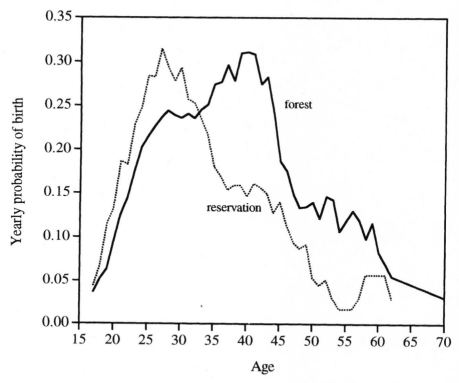

Figure 9.8. Age-specific fertility for Ache men living on reservations (five-point running average) compared with that of men during the forest period.

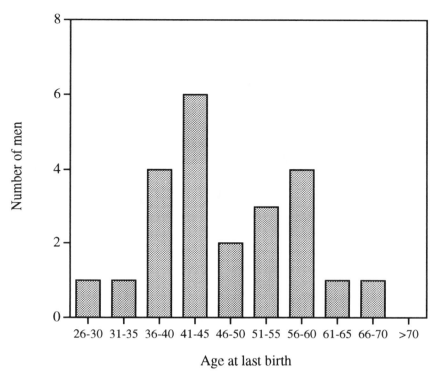

Figure 9.9. Age at last birth for twenty-three men who survived to at least sixty years of age and for whom reproductive data are likely to be complete (categories 11–15, Table 3.3). The mean age at last birth is 48.1 years (s.d. = 10.3), with a median of 45 and mode of 43 years. Note that last reproduction for many men occurs as early as it does for women, but that some men reproduce when they are much older.

An Ache girl of twenty months in 1980 suckles
while her mother makes a palm mat.

10

Resource Availability, Intrinsic Variation, and Life Cycle Constraints

---

The lives of biological organisms are a constant struggle to acquire resources in a competitive environment and turn those resources into a genetic contribution to future generations. In Chapter 1 we suggested that increased resource availability would generally lead to higher fertility rates as well as higher juvenile survivorship. There is good theoretical reason to expect this. First, the only reason living organisms should care about acquiring resources at all is if energy and other limiting components of life can be turned into greater genetic contribution. Second, natural selection should have operated to produce efficient physiological and behavioral mechanisms for converting resource advantage into reproductive advantage, since organisms without such mechanisms would have been replaced quickly on the scale of evolutionary time. There is abundant evidence that organisms are indeed designed to convert resources into surviving offspring effectively and that those with greater resource access generally have more surviving offspring (Chapter 1, Tables 1.1 and 1.2). However, a demonstration of significant association between resources and fitness is only marginally instructive because at some point increased resources will likely produce ever-diminishing fitness returns. Thus, an important goal for life history studies should be the characterization of the *shape* of the relationship between resources and life history traits, rather than a simple demonstration of significant associations. Mathematical functions describing the relationship between estimates of resource availability and vital rates are critical to developing quantitative, testable models about life history traits. The shape of these relationships ultimately determines the fitness implications of alternative life history responses, and thus provides the basis for explaining rather than describing life history patterns. In this chapter we provide some estimates of resource impact on fertility and mortality rates, and then in the next chapter we examine the shape of those relationships and use those estimates to test a mathematical model of one life history trait.

MEASURES OF INDEPENDENT VARIABLES
IN LIFE HISTORY MODELS

Throughout this chapter and those that follow we examine the relationship between specified independent variables and some life history trait. The independent variables have been chosen based on theoretical principles that suggest they should affect life history traits. However, the variables derived from theory are sometimes difficult or impossible to measure, and we are forced to used methods that provide indicators of the actual variable of interest. In statistical terminology, the independent but unmeasured variable that we believe should affect the dependent variable is called the *latent variable*. Traits that we expect to be indicators of the latent variable are called *manifest variables*. Some manifest variables may be tightly correlated with latent variables whereas others may be only weakly correlated. The use of manifest variables in statistical analyses is quite common but often unacknowledged. It does have important implications for the interpretation of results derived from theoretical expectations, however. If the correlation between the manifest variable and the latent variable derived from theory is low, a very strong relationship between the latent variable and the dependent variable will be required in order to detect a significant effect. Thus, one should be careful when interpreting the inability to reject the null hypothesis as evidence that no relationship exists between the latent variable and the dependent variable.

Latent variables derived from theory and discussed in the following chapters include total resources available to individuals, parental investment received by offspring, kin investment received, and inherent ability to convert resources into survival or fertility. Most of them can only be measured through the use of manifest variables that provide a crude measure of the variable of interest. However, several independently measured manifest variables can provide good estimates of the value of the latent variable. In statistics the use of such measures to infer the relationship between the latent variable and the dependent variable is referred to as *latent variable analysis* and is somewhat complex (Loehlin 1987). Although we do not employ latent variable analysis in this book, we will on occasion provide correlations between multiple manifest variables used in our analyses. If we make the simplifying assumption that each measure is independent and equally correlated to the latent variable, the correlation between two manifest variables should be the square of the correlation of each to the latent variable. We employ such a simplifying assumption on occasion in this chapter in order to consider the true relationship between a theoretically derived latent variable and a particular life history outcome. If the actual correlation between the manifest and latent variables is low, a strong association between the latent variable and the dependent variable and/or a large sample size would be necessary in order to detect significant effects; thus, many of our tests that use manifest variables to determine the effect of latent variables will be overly conservative. We will remind the reader of this problem at times in both the results and discussion sections when analyses do not allow us to reject the null hypothesis and yet we are not inclined to accept it either without further research.

INFANT AND CHILDHOOD MORTALITY

At a proximate level all causes of mortality are biological, and any less direct cause of increased mortality must work through biological mechanisms. This realization has led to the "proximate determinants" model of mortality (Mosley and Chen 1984), which is commonly employed in demography and public health. Specifically, factors can affect the mortality rate via either the probability of exposure to health insults or the probability that an exposure will end in death rather than recovery. With this framework of proximate determinants we may also develop a framework to organize less direct factors that will determine either exposure to or severity of health insults (and sometimes both). In this chapter we examine the way in which differential resource availability may affect mortality rates among the forest- and reservation-living Ache.

The strength of the impact of resource availability on mortality rates is expected to depend on the ecological context of each human group and their ability to use resources to affect the proximate determinants of mortality mentioned above. In general we expect parents to use available resources to improve the probabilities that their offspring will survive. However, Ache parents are often fatalistic about the difficulties of keeping any single child alive. They recognize that many causes of death are simply beyond their ability to control. Indeed, from the point of view of a parent making strategic decisions, the dangers of the world can be divided into hazards that can be affected by parental investment and those that (realistically) cannot. The second category of variables represent environmental constraints to which parents must react. The first category provides a major biological challenge, as parents grope to develop a pattern of optimal parental investment that makes the best use of their limited resources.

Mortality Variation Not Susceptible to Short-Term Parental Investment

Extrinsic Mortality Hazards. In theory parents can lower offspring mortality by locating their children in environments that contain fewer potential environmental and biological health insults. Conversely, they can actively eliminate health hazards in small areas or eliminate contact with such hazards. The Ache are particularly sensitive to these factors, and women's daily activities appear strongly constrained by the contingencies of high-quality child care (Hurtado et al. 1992) designed to reduce the probability of exposure to health insults. Indeed, focal follow and scan sample data suggest that small children spend nearly 100% of their time in contact with or in extremely close proximity to their mothers. Nevertheless, some mortality hazards are not easily affected by parental resource allocation.

One might expect that the forest environment would be more hazardous than the reservation environment. Data on childhood and adult mortality rates confirm this expectation (Figures 6.16–6.19). Death rates for most ages were several times higher in the forest than on current reservation settlements. However, infant mortality (birth to age 1), which contributes by far the greatest total number of deaths in the population, has until recently been at least as high on reservations as it was in the forest period (Figure 10.1). We suspect this is probably due to poor hygiene at reservations, and a greater frequency of contacts with infected individuals. Infants on reservations are generally wrapped in several layers of dirty clothes or blankets for the first few months of their lives. The unavailability of soap means that people and clothing are rarely washed. Houses are smoke-filled to the point of near suffocation for those not accustomed to it, and numerous visitors come in physical contact with the child as it is admired, touched, and held. All these factors make exposure to infectious and aggravating agents more likely, especially since most infant deaths are due to respiratory disease.

As discussed in Chapter 6, the Protestant reservation was characterized by lower infant mortality than the less-developed Catholic reservation (Figure 6.22). Again, we suspect most of this difference was due to improved sanitation and its effect on exposure hazard. Effective parental investment can alleviate some of the exposure to these hazards, but some of them are not avoidable *within the range of resource expenditure available to an Ache parent*. These hazards may be considered extrinsic constraints when modeling life history adaptation.

Ache parents at Chupa Pou also reported that seasonality has a significant impact on infant survival. Children born just before the cold months of the year are frequently exposed to respiratory infections as tiny infants and quickly perish. Maternal sickness during these months is also common and probably leads to negative health consequences for new infants. Logistic regression analyses confirm the Ache conjecture. Infants born at reservation settlements just prior to the cold season, or during it, were three times as likely to die as those born just after the cold season (Figure 10.2).

Genetically conferred differences in ability to resist parasites and pathogens may also be common in human populations because disease microorganisms evolve rapidly, often not allowing for host allelic fixation or equilibrium to be reached. In general, continual parasite-host coevolution is expected to result in perpetual adaptive change, which means that at any point in time some individuals in the population will be more genetically resistant to pathogens and parasites than are others. In order to determine whether genetically based differences in disease resistance do characterize a population, however, we need a way to detect individuals who are likely to show high heritable disease resistance.

Intrinsic Disease Resistance. Recent mate selection theory in biology suggests that in many species individuals are able to detect proximate indicators of differences in genetically based disease resistance and use such indicators as a basis for choosing a mate (see Hamilton and Zuk 1982; Read 1988). This mate selection for "good genes" should confer higher disease resistance on the offspring of those who chose mates with resistant alleles. Thus, in theory, offspring of individuals who are attractive to the opposite sex because of traits that indicate parasite and pathogen resistance should themselves be more resistant and show higher survivorship.

Recent evidence suggests that display characters making individuals attractive to the opposite sex are often indicators of parasite/pathogen resistance (for reviews see Møller 1990a; Read 1990) and thus may represent a natural manifest variable for the latent variable "disease resistance." Brighter colors on birds and fish are often evidence of freedom from micro parasites (Houde and Torio 1992; Milinski and Baker 1990; Zuk et al. 1990), as are longer tail feathers, more vigorous song patterns, attractive-smelling pheromones, and a host of other characters. Most important is the suggestion that susceptibility to fluctuating asymmetries in body morphology is partially heritable, and that those asymmetries may be an accurate indicator of pathogen stress during development (Leary and Allendorf 1989; Palmer and Strobeck 1986; Parsons 1990). Fluctuating asymmetries, which are common to all bilaterally organized species, are random deviations from perfect bilateral symmetry that are due to stressors during development. Insects and birds have been shown to prefer more symmetrical individuals for mates (Møller 1988, 1990b; Thornhill 1992; Thornhill and Sauer 1992).

Recent work on humans also suggests that facial asymmetries may reflect pathogen stress. Faces characterized by low levels of fluctuating asymmetry are most attractive to the opposite sex (see Jones 1993; Jones and Hill 1993; Thornhill and Gangestad 1993). In addition, faces with features near the population average are generally judged to be more attractive. Feature averageness is believed to be associated with genetic heterozygosity, protein heterozygosity, and ultimately parasite resistance (Jones 1993; Thornhill and Gangestad 1993). Whatever the connection to parasite resistance, the evidence clearly shows that symmetrical faces with features near the population mean are found quite attractive by members of the opposite sex (Langlois and Roggman 1990; but see Perrett et al. 1994), that individuals and populations around the world generally agree about who is attractive (Alley and Hildebrandt 1988; Jones and Hill 1993), and that facial attractiveness is a major criterion of mate choice worldwide (Buss 1989). If facial symmetry and feature averageness are indeed indicators of genetically conferred pathogen resistance, we might expect the offspring of attractive individuals to show higher pathogen resistance and ultimately better survivorship than the offspring of less attractive individuals. Because we collected attractiveness rankings for a subset of Ache men and women in 1990, this idea can be tested with Ache data.

Previous studies show that American opinions of attractiveness agree well with those of the Ache (Jones 1993; Jones and Hill 1993). These results are partially based on ratings of a sample that included eighty-three Ache faces. In order to expand attractiveness ratings to include all the women in the Ache population, facial attractiveness was scored on an arbitrary scale from 0 to 10 by Hill for all living Ache women in 1990. Age effects were controlled by ranking women in five-year cohorts relative to each other. Data from a smaller sample of women rated independently by Ache men (on a scale of 1 to 9) show that the mean attractiveness rating of women provided by Ache men correlates well ($r = 0.583$) with the values that Hill assigned (Figure 10.3). Thus we conclude that Hill's assessment of attractiveness is a good estimator of the Ache's opinion of female attractiveness. When age-controlled attractiveness (Hill's rating) is entered into a logistic regression model of infant and child mortality that also controls for the effect of age, however, we find no significant association between a mother's attractiveness and the juvenile mortality rate of her offspring on reservations or in the forest.[1] Thus we cannot show from our data that more attractive individuals are characterized by heritable disease resistance.

As mentioned in the above section, our causal path here is Hill's assessment of attractiveness → attractiveness → disease resistance → mortality rate, which implies three correlations in the pathway. Thus our measurement of attractiveness is a very indirect estimate of the latent variable "disease resistance," which itself will be imperfectly correlated with mortality rate. We might estimate that the first correlation in the path is positive and approximately equal to 0.76 (the square root of the correlation between the two independent measures of attractiveness). Since the product of the three correlations in the reservation sample is -0.002675, the measured standardized parameter estimate (see below), one of the other two relationships in the path (attractiveness with disease resistance or disease resistance with mortality) must be very weak.

Other Factors.   Finally, it is expected that a woman's age will have an impact on offspring survival that cannot be easily countered through variation in parental investment. Young women are inexperienced and often make errors of judgment in raising their offspring. As they grow older they gain experience and are likely to be more competent mothers and achieve higher offspring survival, even with the same resource availability. Among the Ache, older women frequently scold younger women and give them advice about how to raise their children. We never heard a single case of a younger woman arguing against such advice; instead, young mothers often immediately adjusted their behavior to conform to an older woman's suggestions. On the other hand, near the end of the reproductive span women often experience high child mortality rates. Currently available evidence suggests that older women often produce children who are inherently less viable owing to increasing genetic abnormality and deteriorating uterine environment (Kline et al. 1989). This fact, in combination with the lack of experience in child rearing by younger women, leads to the expectation that the fetal and infant mortality curve as a function of mother's age in most human populations will be mildly U-shaped. Ache data on forest and reservation period mortality rates by age of mother confirm this expectation.[2]

Resources and Juvenile Mortality

Background. Data from a variety of sources suggest that resources can be, and are, used by parents either to lower their offspring's rate of exposure to health hazards or to lower the severity of outcomes after an exposure. In much of the developing world, the association between mortality and poverty is thought to be mainly due to sanitation and nutrition, and a strong association is found between parental socioeconomic status and juvenile mortality (Williams 1990). Although parents on Ache reservations can, to some small extent, use resources to affect sanitation, most of the differences we expect to find in child mortality are nutritionally based and the result of differential food intake by children. Since some anthropologists working among traditional peoples apparently believe that foragers obtain all the food they "need" and that small body size does not necessarily indicate nutritional stress, or poor health and higher mortality (e.g., Lee 1979), it is important for us to examine this assumption carefully.

A number of studies have shown that food intake affects juvenile mortality rates in societies whose members show approximately the same growth rates, body size, and food intake levels as the Ache. For example, comparative studies consistently show a positive relationship between body size, food intake, and survivorship in developing regions of the world (Table 10.1). An equally large literature shows that bone growth is greater among survivors than among those who do not survive in age-matched samples of children and subadults (Saunders and Hoppa 1993). The causal link between food intake and survivorship has been clearly established with intervention studies, and results consistently show an increase in survivorship with greater food intake. Comparative and intervention studies also show a clear relationship between food intake and growth rates (Gopalan et al. 1973; Graham et al. 1981; Kielmann et al. 1978; Martorell et al. 1976; Mora et al. 1981; *Nutrition Reviews* 1983), which are known to correlate with mortality rate (Table 10.1). The positive effect of increased food intake in all these studies is probably due to an increased ability to fight health insults (such as improved immune response) rather than a decreased exposure to health hazards. Finally, intervention studies have also shown a positive effect of food intake on birth weight (Adair and Pollitt 1985; Christiansen et al. 1980; Garn 1982; Metcoff et al. 1981; Prentice et al. 1987). Since low birth weight is the single most important predictor of infant mortality around the world (Kline et al. 1989), the cumulative evidence from all these studies can leave little doubt that more food would lead to higher juvenile survivorship in most societies of the world.

At what point does higher food intake no longer lead to favorable biological outcome? We are aware of only one study that has addressed this topic quantitatively. Bairagi et al. (1985) show that weight-specific survivorship continues to improve among one- to four-year-old children of Bangladesh until they reach about 70% of the U.S. standard of median weight for age. Although Ache children are on average above this level, many individual children fall below the threshold. In addition, it is unclear whether the 70% threshold apparent in Bangladesh is generalizable to other ecological and social contexts around the world, since other studies have suggested that survivorship increases with body size across the entire spectrum of observed body sizes (references in Table 10.1). Much more work will need to be done before we can estimate at what point further growth is not associated with higher survivorship.

Juvenile Mortality in the Forest.   Ache data collection allows for a variety of tests to examine the relationship between resource availability and juvenile mortality rates. Again, we will be forced to use manifest variables as independent estimates of the latent variable of interest, parental resources. No one could monitor resource acquisition during the forest period, but informant data enable us to estimate two important variables for each child at risk: father's hunting skill and mother's body weight. Since a high proportion of all food consumed in Ache society was traditionally acquired by men, and since nuclear families often went off by themselves for several days, during these times offspring were often dependent on parental provisioning rather than band-wide food sharing. For these reasons father's hunting skill is probably the best variable for indicating differential food consumption. Mother's body size may also crudely correlate with a child's resource availability, and among mammals, female body weight does often correlate with offspring survival rate (Chapter 1). Larger females generally acquire more energy from the environment and thus have more total energy to invest in offspring. Among humans, large females have larger offspring, may produce more milk calories during lactation, and may be better able to absorb temporary weight loss in order to redistribute food shares to offspring.

We first examine the relationship between father's hunting skill, mother's body weight, and juvenile survival in the forest period, using logistic regression. Age is controlled in these regressions in order to isolate the effects of interest. In order to maintain sample size in multiple regressions so the effects of age are adequately controlled, all cases with missing values for a particular independent variable are coded with the mean value for that variable. Trials with univariate models show that this procedure does not affect the parameter estimate or the significance of variables of interest but does more accurately control for the effect of age-specific mortality in multivariate models. The same procedure also allows for more complete multivariate modeling without excessive loss of sample size owing to missing values.

Male hunting skill and female body size during the forest period were estimated by informant ranking. Informants who had known each man or woman in a particular age cohort were asked to rank them in order of hunting skill or body size. Both parameters are known to be consistent through time relative to the observed range of variation between individuals (Kaplan and Hill 1985b; Chapter 12). First, ten adult males or ten females adjacent to each other in the relative age list (i.e., born within two years of each other) were compared pairwise by informants. Whichever member of the pair "won" the comparison (better hunter or larger body) was scored as 1, and the "loser" as 0. In comparisons with nine other age-matched individuals the highest possible score is $9/9$ and the lowest possible score is $0/9$. These scores were then entered as the relative ranking for each parent in question. Thus men who were ranked by informants as the best hunters in their age cohort were scored as 1.0, and women who were ranked the largest in their age cohort were also scored as 1.0. The rank score is simply the percentage of age-matched peers ranked lower on the measure of interest.

The actual measured difference in hunting acquisition rates (kilograms of meat per hour) for a subset of the men in our forest sample who survived to the present shows a tenfold range, and women's body weight is characterized by a 25 kg range for those who survived to be weighed by us. The measurements were taken in the 1980s whereas the rank scores pertain to hunting skill and body size in the forest period, some ten to thirty years earlier. Remarkably, there is a good correlation between the two assessments. Figures 10.4 and 10.5 show that hunting rank assigned by informants correlates strongly with observed measures of hunting skill ($r = 0.506$), and size rank is highly correlated with body weight ($r = 0.716$) for a sample of women who were both ranked by informants and observed directly by us. Interestingly, female body size rankings correlated more strongly ($r = 0.824$) with Body Mass Index (kg/m^2) than it did with weight alone. This agrees with the Ache translation of the researchers' request: informants were asked to rank which woman "had the most meat on her body" and "was the most robust or biggest." We conclude that the informant rankings and measures of hunting skill or body size do provide reasonable estimates of the intermediate latent variables *paternal food production* and *maternal somatic resources* in this sample. How well each of these variables correlates with resources available for parental investment is less clear, but nevertheless we wish to examine whether these manifest variables can be shown to be associated with offspring mortality.

The results from the analysis of mortality rate during childhood in the forest period are shown in Table 10.2. Independent variables representing parental resource availability include both measured hunt rate and body weight as well as the rank score for each individual parent. Three categories of age are examined separately, and within category age effects are controlled through multiple re-gression. The sign of the parameter estimate indicates whether the independent variable is associated with increased (positive) or decreased (negative) mortality. The magnitude of the parameter estimate is heavily influenced by the scale of measurement. For this reason the standardized estimate is more useful for com-parisons across alternative independent variables when they are entered one at a time into a model that controls for other effects (e.g., age). The standardized parameter estimate measures the impact on the dependent variable in standard deviation units of changes in the independent variable also measured in standard deviation units and can thus be used to compare the effects of alternative inde-pendent variables directly. Thus, the difference between the parameter estimate and the standardized parameter estimate is analogous to the difference between regression and correlation coefficients in least-squares regression. With maxi-mum likelihood estimation, the change in -2 log likelihood of a model when a particular independent variable is added or left out approximates a chi-square distribution with degrees of freedom equivalent to the number of variables added or subtracted from the model. This statistic is the best for estimating the signifi-cance of the variable of interest.

Our results do show evidence that men who were better hunters achieved higher survival of older juvenile offspring in the forest, but there is no evidence that large women were characterized by lower offspring mortality than small women. The relationship between hunting skill or body size and mortality is expected to be negative. While this expectation largely holds true for the effect of father's hunting skill on child mortality, it is not at all true for the relationship between mother's body size and child mortality rates. The lack of a relationship between maternal size and child mortality may indicate that the manifest vari-ables are a very poor measure of maternal resources available for parental invest-ment or that parental investment has no effect on child mortality in the Ache forest ecology. The relationship between a man's hunting skill and the survival of his offspring is highly significant for older children but becomes increasingly less significant among younger children. The fact that the correlation is stronger with measured hunting skill (-0.1788) than with the ranked hunting data (-0.0056) suggests that the rank data are a less accurate estimate of paternal food produc-tion than are the measured hunting return rates. Still, it is curious that the impact of father's food production should be greatest on older rather than younger children. Because mortality rates are low in general for older children, however, the decrease in *relative risk* for older children of better hunters would result in a very small risk difference (number of surviving children) between good and poor hunters, and thus would have little impact on the fitness of Ache men.

Juvenile Mortality on Reservations.   Parental resource availability during the reservation period can be measured in several ways. We used data on father's observed hunting rate, mother's mean body weight, and the socioeconomic status

(SES) of a child's nuclear family in order to assess the impact of parental resources on juvenile mortality during the reservation period. Although SES is a concept originally developed to characterize people in industrialized societies, it has been modified here to suit the conditions and lifestyle of the Ache. Nuclear family SES was rated on a five-point scale of material well-being by Hill in 1990 for all Ache families. Although the SES rank is probably only a rough estimate of available resources for parental investment, subsequent measures of net worth in which the value of all personal property was tabulated for a subsample of 67 Ache families shows that Hill's SES estimates are indeed correlated with actual net worth ($r = 0.341$, Figure 10.6). Thus, Hill's estimates of SES for *all* Ache families can be used as a weak manifest variable for analyses of resource availability and life history traits. Interestingly the measured net worth of nuclear families varied over a fivefold range for adult individuals, thus providing a likely source of mortality variation in the population.

Results of logistic regression analyses to examine the relationship between juvenile mortality at the reservation settlements and measures of resource availability are shown in Table 10.3. Only ages 0 and 1–4 years are examined, since there have been very few deaths to children between ages five and nine on reservation settlements. The results show a significant negative relationship between father's SES rank and infant mortality rate, with a slightly weaker and nonsignificant negative relationship between father's SES rank and early childhood mortality. Father's return rate from hunting is positively associated with the childhood mortality rate (but not quite significant). This puzzling finding is not due to an association between SES and hunting rate ($r = 0.0$) or hunting rate and age (which is controlled). Because the infant mortality rate is much greater than the child mortality rate, the analyses suggest that a man's SES is a strong predictor of his offspring's survival to adulthood.

Mother's SES and body weight are also negatively associated with infant mortality, as expected, but in neither case can we be statistically confident of rejecting the null hypothesis that there is no relationship between the manifest variables and offspring mortality.

The data suggest that parental resources do have a fairly strong effect on offspring mortality. SES is probably only weakly correlated with the latent variable of interest. Indeed, if SES and net worth are independent measures of parental resources, the correlation between SES and the latent variable may be about 0.58 (the square root of the correlation between the two manifest variables). This might suggest correlations of about -0.3 and -0.2 for paternal resources and infant or early childhood mortality, respectively (the standardized estimates of SES on mortality divided by the estimated correlation between SES and the latent variable paternal resources) and correlations of -0.2 to -0.25 for maternal resources and offspring mortality. These values for the latent variables would all be significant, even though three of the four tests using only the manifest variables (SES score) failed to reach significance.

ADULT MORTALITY

In theory, many of the same factors that affect juvenile mortality should impact adult mortality as well. For example, adults who invest few resources in their own condition and immune system may experience high mortality rates. In practice, however, it seems that adults often prioritize their own survival as part of their own life history strategy, and only in times of extreme stress is adult mortality affected by resource availability. Models suggest that such a pattern will be common in iteroparous organisms (Charnov 1986) and will result in low variation in adult mortality rates across resource-stratified subsets of the population. It may be that factors beyond the control of adults (extrinsic mortality hazards) cause most of the significant patterned mortality variation after childhood and before senescence begins. Some mortality variation might also be expected because of increased risk taking as reproductive value declines, or as part of the male reproductive strategy. Thus, extrinsic hazards of the environment and those associated with age- and sex-specific risk taking, neither of which can be avoided by increased resource allocation, may be responsible for most observed adult mortality variation prior to the onset of senescence.

Extrinsic adult mortality hazards include accidents, pathogen prevalence, and conspecific violence. Observed differences between forest- and reservation-living Ache in adult mortality appear to be entirely the result of accidents and conspecific violence. There is no indication that the Ache adult population allocated fewer resources to their somatic maintenance in the forest than they do on the reservations. Indeed, photos at contact show that the Northern Ache adults were as fat and well-nourished living in the forest as they are on the current reservations (unlike children, who grew much slower in the forest than they do on the reservations).

While differences in adult mortality from variation in resources may not be easily derived from life history theory, differences between age and sex classes are clearly expected. Sexual selection results in high levels of competition between males for mates, which is generally associated with higher male mortality during adulthood than that which characterizes females. Older individuals should show higher mortality from senescence as well as increasing allocation to genetic reproduction (through offspring and kin) rather than maintenance, repair of their own soma, and storage.

The rejection of a connection between resource availability and adult mortality among the Ache is based on theoretical arguments that assume all adults should allocate abundant resources to somatic maintenance and repair as a life history priority. This suggestion can be tested with data on forest-living Ache. Logistic regression analyses designed to examine the relationship between adult male mortality (ages 15–60) and hunting skill rank, or adult female mortality and body size rank, suggest no significant relationship between either hunting skill or body size and age-specific mortality for men or women.[3]

VARIATION IN FEMALE FERTILITY RATE

Questions about fertility variation have generally focused on cross-cultural and individual differences in completed family size (CFS) measured in post-reproductive women or on the Total Fertility Rate (TFR), which is a sum of all age-specific fertility. For example, the Ache had a mean CFS of around eight live births, both in the forest and on reservation settlements. Groups like the !Kung of Botswana, the Gainj of New Guinea, or the Batak of the Philippines show mean CFSs closer to four live births (Eder 1987; Howell 1979; Wood, Johnson, and Campbell 1985). Since none of these groups employs contraception, what could account for these differences?

In recent years, anthropological debate on this question has focused on two likely causes of fertility variation. First, a good deal of work has shown that nursing patterns can influence fertility among study populations with significant variation in weaning time (see below). Second, some demographers have suggested that sexually transmitted diseases (STDs) and secondary sterility patterns may explain much of the observed variation in TFR among natural fertility populations (e.g., Caldwell and Caldwell 1983; see also Harpending 1994 and the reply by Blurton Jones 1994). Finally, as we suggested in Chapter 1, resource availability (e.g., nutrition) should influence human fertility, since it seems to affect the fertility of other mammals with similar reproductive physiologies. These three possible explanations of fertility variation are not mutually exclusive, but they do provide important test implications that can be examined with Ache data. We have no data on STDs among the Ache, and there is no evidence that they play an important role in limiting Ache fertility. For this reason, we focus here on the effects of nutrition and nursing patterns.

As in the case of mortality, variation in fertility rates must work through proximate causes. This has led population studies researchers to focus a good deal of attention on these proximate causes and develop sophisticated "proximate determinants" models of fertility variation (Bongaarts 1978, 1983; Wood 1994). Models of ultimate causality in fertility variation must complement what is known about proximate causation by explaining why populations vary with respect to the relevant proximate determinants that affect fertility and why women are designed to respond to proximate factors in the way that they do. One of the best ways to examine the impact of independent variables on fertility has been through the use of hazards models (Wood 1990, 1994) like those we have employed in this book. The explicit focus on changes through time in the fertility hazard has led to methodological complications and occasional misinterpretation of research results, however, because the independent variables that have the greatest effect on the fertility hazard of women when all periods of time are considered in the risk set may not be the variables that account for the observed variation in fertility rate between women or across populations. In addition, the major determinants of variation in fertility between individuals in populations in which a subset of individuals employs artificial nursing technology may tell us little about fertility variation in populations whose members uniformly feed infants only by natural lactation.

The hazard of conception leading to live birth may vary through time as a function of life cycle variables, or other intrinsic and endogenous factors that affect women. In humans, some life cycle stages are associated with near zero probability of conception. These time periods include pregnancy and early post-partum lactation, and the premenarcheal and postmenopausal periods of a woman's life. For any sample of women followed longitudinally, these periods will be the most important determinants of the conception hazard per risk unit when risk units cover short periods of time (e.g., a day, a week, a month). If women are in one of these reproductive stages, the conception hazard will be low, and if they are not, it will be much higher. Since all women go through the same life cycle and generally experience each of these stages, however, the impact of these variables on long-term fertility variation among women may be small. Other factors that do vary between women and among populations over longer time frames must therefore account for the observed variation in fertility rates of individuals or populations over time scales that include many reproductive events.

In the rest of this section we examine the impact of stages of the reproductive cycle on the hazard of conception, and then, having controlled for those effects, we examine whether there are intrinsic or environmental factors affecting women that lead to variation in fertility rate over longer time spans. In particular we examine the effects of nursing patterns, resource availability, and signs of pathogen resistance on the probability of conception (leading to live birth) during a specified time period.

Effects of the Reproductive Cycle

As women progress through their lives, the probability of producing a live birth changes. Prior to menarche, that probability is essentially zero. It is possible, however, for a woman to begin ovulatory cycling and conceive on her very first cycle, thus never menstruating prior to first birth. Precisely that seems to have happened at least twice in our Ache sample, once to a woman who first gave birth in the 1940s and again to a girl in 1993 who had not yet reached menarche in our August 1992 census, but gave birth to a child in the following April. Several Ache women, obviously amused with the situation, explained to us that she had gotten pregnant before menarche because she was "horny all the time."

After menarche, women generally experience a period of adolescent subfecundity. During this time ovarian cycles may be irregular or nonfunctional so the young women can be sexually active but not conceive. Such a pattern clearly characterizes Ache girls (see below), and Ache informants commented to us that postmenarcheal girls were not likely to get pregnant because "they are still small."

Once Ache girls have established themselves as fertile (by a first conception), they are characterized by fairly high and stable fertility rates until they reach age thirty (Figure 10.7). Indeed the pattern of age-specific fertility for *parous* Ache women suggests that the population-level age-specific fertility curve (Figure 8.3) increases in the teen years primarily because many young women have not yet begun regular and complete cycles. The Ache data provide no evidence that a woman who produces an offspring in her teen years becomes more fertile in her twenties. After age thirty, fertility rates begin to decline until menopause. In this case, however, evidence suggests that the population decline in fertility is not simply due to some women becoming infertile (which is true) but also to all women becoming less fertile with age. This is clearly illustrated by examining closed interbirth intervals. The interbirth intervals of young women are the same length as women at ages of peak fertility, but the mean interbirth interval of older women is longer (see Figure 8.12).

During their active reproductive span women experience increases and decreases in the probability of conception as a function of their immediate reproductive state. When pregnant, they cannot conceive again (and are removed from the risk set in our hazard model). While nursing a small infant, their probability of conception decreases tremendously (see below).

Reproductive State. The impact of reproductive state on the hazard of conception cannot be easily examined in our forest sample because of the difficulties of establishing the timing of events with necessary precision (i.e., to the nearest month). But because we were able to observe women between 1978 and 1993 directly, reservation fertility can be analyzed in considerable detail. Months of birth are known for all children, so dates of conception leading to live birth can also be estimated. Since we cannot accurately assess all pregnancies ending in spontaneous abortion, we examine *only conceptions leading to live birth.* The probability of such a conception is referred to as the conception hazard throughout this chapter. We first examined time to conception for all women ages twelve to fifty after four types of initial reproductive events: menarche; birth of a child who survived; birth of a child who died within five days of birth; and death of a woman's youngest infant (five days to five years old). The data were analyzed using a Kaplan-Meier product-limit estimate, and women were censored at death, at July 1993, or when they reached fifty years of age. Results (Figure 10.8) suggest that the waiting time to conception after a woman gives birth to a child who dies immediately is almost identical to that after a child dies in infancy (there is a slight depression of fecundity immediately following birth that is not seen immediately following the death of an infant). In both cases half of the women had conceived by eleven or twelve months from the time of the infant's death. We have collapsed these two categories into a single one (after youngest child dies) for subsequent analyses.

Waiting times to conception after menarche and after the birth of a child who survives differ significantly from each other and from the waiting time to conception after the youngest child dies (Figure 10.8). Waiting time to conception after the birth of a child who survives is about twice as long as that after the birth of a child who immediately dies. The reservation data show that 50% of women experienced a conception leading to live birth within twenty-four months after the birth of a prior surviving child. This is almost identical to the mean age at weaning in the reservation sample (see Chapter 7) and provides supporting evidence of the effect of lactation on suppression of fecundability among the Ache (although women reported that they wean their infants *after* they become pregnant rather than vice versa). Waiting time to conception after menarche was even longer, with 50% of the women in our sample conceiving their first child within thirty months after they reached menarche. Since most Ache women are sexually active throughout their adolescent years, this indicates a period of postmenarcheal subfecundity that is commonly reported in other human groups as well (e.g., Apter et al. 1978; Lipson and Ellison 1992).

Logistic regression illustrates the impact of different reproductive states on conception even more clearly because it allows us to examine the probability of an event taking place to those who have not yet experienced that event but who are at risk. We developed a conception hazard model that would enable us to measure the effects of these three reproductive states on the conditional probability of conception. The data were analyzed using a discrete-time logistic regression model of the quarterly conception hazard. Births are recorded by month, but many time-varying covariates reported later are recorded to the nearest two or three months (e.g., body weights, parental deaths) so we chose yearly quarters as the unit of analysis. Conception times were calculated backward from the date of live birth (-9 months). Women entered one of the three risk sets when they reached menarche, gave birth to a liveborn child, or experienced an infant death. They left the risk set if they became pregnant, if they died, if they changed reproductive state (e.g., their youngest child died), or if they reached age fifty. The sample consists of 4,069 quarterly intervals resulting in 347 conceptions that led to a live birth.

The probability of conception after menarche begins quite low and then peaks at about fifty months, slowly tapering off after about sixty months (Figure 10.9). Much to our astonishment, we still had conceptions leading to first births taking place more than 200 months after menarche among women who had been sexually active since before menarche. Why these women did not conceive earlier is unclear. The hazard of conception following birth of a child that survives is initially very low and then peaks at about thirty-four months in the reservation population (Figure 10.9). The hazard of conception after infant death, however, begins high and increases only slightly (it is almost constant) in the first year after an infant dies, peaking at about fifteen months. The difference in the conception hazard in the first twenty-four months following the birth of an infant who lives and one who dies provides clear and strong evidence for lactational suppression of fertility.

Nursing Patterns and Fertility.   The impact of nursing patterns on conception has been extensively studied in recent years. The results of these studies suggest that women's bodies have evolved physiological mechanisms to monitor whether they are currently encumbered by an infant and, if so, to delay reproduction. This general response to lactation is universal, and it is unclear to what extent the response will help to explain the variation in mean fertility rates within and between traditional societies.

Some researchers have been very enthusiastic about the possibility that nursing patterns explain not only the long delay between births generally found in natural fertility populations, but also the variation observed among them. For example, Campbell and Wood (1988) present data suggesting that the *period of lactational anovulation* is the primary determinant of variation in TFR around the world, and then suggest that this variation is due to nursing patterns, stating: "most of the variation in TFR among traditional societies is attributable to differences in *breast feeding practices,* age patterns of marriage, and fecundability" (1988:39; emphasis added). A more cautious conclusion about nursing patterns is advocated by Lesthaeghe (1987:171): "Our knowledge of the link between breast feeding and lactational amenorrhea does not go beyond the existence of a statistical tool for converting the average (or median) duration of breast feeding into mean (or median) durations of amenorrhea." Data from numerous studies do show that populations or individuals who terminate breast feeding soon after birth have shorter periods of lactational amenorrhea than do those who breastfeed longer, and a great deal has been learned about the physiological mechanisms responsible for this distinction (see Wood 1994 for review). Most of these studies involve populations or individuals who use artificial infant feeding (baby bottles), thus introducing extremely high variance in the length of lactation, which may overwhelm other factors important in traditional populations. As is the case in all multivariate causality, if one variable is allowed to take extreme values, that variable is likely to be responsible for most of the observed variation in the dependent variable. Results from such observations may tell us little about the factors responsible for variation under more "natural" conditions, however. The factors that determine the length of lactational amenorrhea in populations in which all women nourish their infants exclusively by maternal lactation until traditional foods are introduced to the infant are not well established.

Certainly women in traditional natural fertility populations have birth intervals longer than twenty-four months because of lactational anovulation, but much variation between women and across groups remains to be accounted for. Do nutrition, health, energy expenditure, social stress, or other factors interact with nursing patterns to determine variation in the length of lactational amenorrhea? Why do some women have consistently shorter intervals and others consistently longer ones? Why do the Gainj, for example, show a TFR of 4.3 (Wood, Johnson, and Campbell 1985) and the Ache show a TFR of 8, even though both populations nurse their infants frequently and on demand? We are aware of no study showing that fertility in one traditional group is low relative to those of many other traditional populations *because* of differences in breast-feeding patterns. In fact, many studies of breast feeding do not measure potential confounding variables (e.g., healthy well-nourished women may show different nursing patterns than poorly nourished women, yet often only nursing is monitored). In order to establish that breast feeding patterns account for most of the observed fertility variation in traditional societies, investigators would need to collect data on nursing patterns *and* other variables likely to affect fertility (energy balance, pathogen stress, etc.) for several different groups along with their observed fertility patterns. The few data that exist suggest that many populations show nearly identical nursing patterns to the Gainj or the !Kung and yet have much higher fertility. For example, Fink et al. (1992) describe nursing patterns and prolactin levels among a group of Mayan women that are nearly identical to those reported for the Gainj, yet the Mayan women have a mean completed family size greater than eight. Similarly, Worthman et al. (1993) have shown that ovarian suppression associated with lactation is greatly reduced among the well nourished Amele of lowland New Guinea. The lack of information on interaction between nursing patterns and other factors that affect fertility is implicitly recognized by some researchers: "the pattern of suckling in relation to amenorrhea must be established separately for each society" (McNeilly 1993:396).

Because we monitored several focal mother-infant pairs between 1982 and 1987, we can look at age-specific nursing patterns and conception times for a small sample of individuals. All mother infant pairs were the subject of focal follows between 8 AM and 6 PM that ended when a nursing session ended. Generally, Hurtado would follow a mother-infant pair until three nursing sessions were completed. Since we sampled nursing sessions rather than periods of time, none of our nursing sessions or intervals between sessions are censored (i.e., all intervals were closed). We defined a nursing session as a series of nursing events separated by less than one minute (Vitzhum 1989). The mean lengths of sessions and intervals between sessions were calculated for ten mother-infant pairs and are shown in Figures 10.10 and 10.11. All women in the study were married and exposed to regular copulation after infants were about one year old. All but one of these infants survived to be followed by another pregnancy, and the time to conception following each infant is shown on the figures along with the relevant nursing parameters that were observed for each infant. Although the sample size is very small, it is immediately obvious that age-specific nursing patterns measured at one point in time during infancy do not predict differences between women in time to next pregnancy (we have observed a similar pattern in unpublished data on Hiwi foragers of Venezuela). The observed wait times to conception range from fifteen months to thirty-nine months, with the two extremes in conception wait time characterizing women whose infants were almost exactly the same age (15 months) and showed almost identical nursing patterns during the same month when one woman (but not the other) conceived. All women in the sample are between eighteen and thirty-nine, and the woman's age does not account for much of the variation in time to conception in this sample. For the two extreme cases mentioned above the mothers of the infants were twenty-seven and twenty-six years old, respectively. Given the similarity between Ache nursing patterns and those of other tribal groups (e.g., Wood, Lai, et al. 1985) with much longer birth intervals, we should be reluctant to accept the notion that differences in nursing patterns among tribal societies can explain the observed differences in fertility *across these groups* without further data.

Individual Differences in Fecundity?

Biological factors may lead to high intrinsic fertility, even with other variables held constant. Ellison (1995), for example, has shown considerable variation in reproductive hormone profiles across age-matched women in a single population. These levels are believed to correlate with fecundity, or the ability to conceive when reproductively cycling and exposed to intercourse. Inherent fecundity differences among adult women could be the result of factors that are mainly genetic, as well as developmental differences between individuals that might lead to inherent differences in health and the efficiency with which resources can be converted into offspring. This theoretically derived variable cannot be measured (it is latent) and thus we must search for ways to estimate this property for individual women. Recent mate choice models have pointed out that choice for good genes might be expected under such circumstances, and evidence suggests that humans may indeed exercise mate choice based on features that predict intrinsic health differences (Jones 1993; Jones and Hill 1993; Thornhill and Gangestad 1993). As mentioned in the mortality section of this chapter, "good genes" mate choice is likely when appreciable genetic variation is present in a population, and offspring stand to gain fitness benefits by inheriting particular traits from exceptionally fit parents. Most of these mate choice models are designed to explain female choice and assume that disease resistance leading to higher offspring survival is a major fitness benefit of exercising choice. Among humans, however, male investment is high in mating and/or parenting, and males may spend considerable periods of time in exclusive mating relationships. Thus, males are also likely to be choosy about their female partners. Males might be expected to choose females primarily based on cues associated with maternal condition and resource availability. Curiously, however, recent empirical studies of human males around the world suggest that "attractiveness" is an extremely important mate choice criteria (Buss 1989, 1994). The importance of facial attractiveness in mate choice by males suggests the possibility that facial attractiveness may be a proximate indicator of intrinsic fertility differences among females.

A discrete-time logistic regression model allowed us to examine the association between facial attractiveness rating (described in the previous section) and the quarterly hazard of conception for the reservation population. Since our measure of attractiveness is not expected to vary systematically with a woman's age (the attractiveness scores we use are controlled by age cohort), this important source of fertility variation was not included in the model. Attractiveness may covary to some extent with the three reproductive states—nulliparous, last born child alive, after death of last child (unattractive women may be more likely to experience a child death or be nulliparous)—or duration in each state, so they are entered into a multivariate model as dummy variables. Results (Table 10.4) suggest that attractiveness is indeed positively associated with fertility in the Ache population. The positive association between attractiveness and fertility is statistically significant in the reservation sample but is not significant in the forest sample, in which attractiveness of women could only be established for those who survived to the present. Nevertheless, both show the same standardized parameter estimate, which is high enough to imply a real relationship between the latent variable of interest (inherent health and reproductive efficiency) and fertility. Women who were rated to have the most attractive faces showed fertility 1.16 times as high as those of average attractiveness. Note here that we do not infer causality; that is, we do not know whether high fertility might also lead to attractiveness, or if some third factor (such as health) is positively associated with both. However, the evolutionary significance for understanding the basis of attractiveness (i.e., that traits signaling high fertility are attractive to males) is the same in any case.

Resource Availability and Fertility

Resource availability can be shown to influence reproductive rates in a wide variety of organisms (Chapter 1). Importantly, resource availability has been shown to affect fertility among many primates (e.g., Dunbar 1987; Mori 1979; Robinson 1988; Sadlier 1969). This connection is believed to represent an adaptation in which offspring production is curtailed when resources are limited. Among humans, food intake and energetic balance have been shown to affect reproductive hormone profiles that may be linked to fecundity (Ellison 1995). Thus, not only does it make sense that natural selection should design fertility mechanisms that are sensitive to maternal condition and the available food supply, but studies of the proximate mechanisms of fertility in humans suggest that such mechanisms do in fact exist. Nevertheless there is still some debate about the extent to which human reproduction is sensitive to naturally occurring variation in the energy balance (see Peacock 1990).

Given the strong theoretical expectation of a link between food and fertility, and the demonstration that energetic balance affects reproductive hormone levels, it is surprising that many demographers have denied the existence of an association between food and fertility rate. In our view, this denial is primarily due to an inappropriate generalization regarding the relative contribution of nursing and nutrition on absolute fertility levels from studies in populations in which length of lactation varies tremendously and nutritional intake varies less. Since lactational periods have extremely powerful effects on fertility in such studies, demographers have assumed that different lactational patterns around the world must account for most of the worldwide variation in fertility rate even among societies that do not use artificial infant feeding (e.g., Campbell and Wood 1988).

Also important seems to be a political agenda denying the food-nutrition link (Bongaarts 1980; Scott and Johnston 1985), which is well illustrated by Bongaarts's assessment of the implications of finding a connection between nutritional and fertility. In an important article examining the determinants of differential fertility, Bongaarts states in the introduction: "A strong link between nutrition and fecundity would have important implications, especially for food aid programs for the developing world. If improving nutrition in those countries increased their birthrates, it would exacerbate an already serious population growth problem" (1980:564). After examining available evidence and concluding that "Breast-feeding is the principal determinant of postpartum amenorrhea" (1980:568), Bongaarts then concludes: "Concern about the effect on fertility of food aid to poor nations (provided that this aid does not include large quantities of infant formula) appears to be unwarranted." While we agree that food supplementation would probably have a minuscule effect on fertility rates in many areas of the world, this does *not* imply that food is not the major determinant of observed variation in fertility within and between many populations, including traditional societies, that use no contraception.

Recent food intervention studies in traditional populations seem to leave little doubt that better nutrition leads to higher fertility. For example, Lunn et al. (1984) show that variation in nutritional intake resulting from food supplementation in Gambia affects the prolactin levels and the period of lactational anovulation despite the fact that women breast-feed infants upon demand for a prolonged period of time. Delgado et al. (1978) also show that increased nutritional intake due to supplementation in rural Guatemala was associated with shorter lactational amenorrhea. Comparative studies also support the conclusion that energy balance is related to fertility. Lewis et al. (1991) show that a sample of modern Australian women had extremely short periods of lactational anovulation despite breast-feeding patterns nearly identical to those of the !Kung, who show long periods of lactational anovulation. A multitude of other studies show relationships between fertility and anthropometric measures or self-selected food intake, again suggesting an energy balance–fertility link (e.g., Bongaarts and Delgado 1979; Carael 1978; Chowdhury 1978; Huffman et al. 1978, 1980). Most important, recent studies using complete samples of women at risk of resuming ovulation after birth, and appropriate hazards analyses to isolate the effects of nutritional covariates when other effects are controlled, show even stronger associations between the period of lactational anovulation and energy balance in both nursing and nonnursing women (e.g., Huffman et al. 1987). Finally, Worthman et al. (1993) have recently published hormonal analyses among the Amele of New Guinea, suggesting that maternal nutritional status may attenuate the mother's pituitary response to her infant's suckling. This is exactly the type of mechanism relating food to fertility that we might expect to be favored by natural selection, balancing physiological input concerning the presence of a dependent infant with maternal resource supply in "decisions" regarding optimal timing for the next birth.

The relationship between resources and fertility rate for Ache women can be explored by examining the association between mean body weight, body size rank (precontact), or SES level for Ache women during the forest and reservation periods. Size rank during the forest period, acquired as described earlier in this chapter, correlates well with measured body weight. Mean body weight is the average of all weights taken between 1980 and 1993 for women over 18 years of age. Data presented in the next chapter show that body weight differences between women are generally much greater than fluctuations through time in single women. SES was determined as described earlier in this chapter and correlates with measured net worth in 1992.

Discrete-time multiple logistic regression controlling for age, reproductive state, and time since last birth shows that indicators of differential resource access do associate with differential fertility in the Ache sample (Table 10.5). Although size rank in the forest period and body weight or SES during the reservation period are all positively associated with fertility, only results from the reservation period achieve statistical significance. According to the model of the timing of first birth presented in the next chapter, the relationship between mean adult weight and fertility should be positive only among parous women. This relationship is expected since the model we develop of age at first reproduction suggests that larger nulliparous women sometimes become larger because they are not reproducing. Therefore, women who end up larger in adulthood should show low fertility during their adolescent years, whereas large parous women should have high fertility (owing to increased energy availability). Further analysis supports this prediction since the relationship between weight and fertility among only parous women is much stronger than that for all women combined, and it shows an extremely low significance value ($p = 0.0002$).[4]

Finally, when all three significant predictors of reservation fertility (attractiveness, SES, and weight) are entered in a multivariate model along with age, both body weight and attractiveness are found to be significant.[5] SES, on the other hand, is not associated with fertility once the effects of the other variables have been controlled. This means that both weight and attractiveness have independent effects on fertility and that SES effects are primarily a result of the correlation between SES and the other two variables ($r = 0.42$ between SES and attractiveness, $r = 0.246$ between SES and weight, $p = 0.0001$ for both) in our sample of women.

Some of the best evidence relevant to variation in fertility and resource availability across an individual woman's reproductive lifespan comes from studies of seasonal patterns of conception. Although some of the available data has been interpreted by demographers to support the position that lactational patterns are the major determinants of fertility variation (e.g., Wood 1990:234), the data generally support a direct energy balance model of fertility better than a lactational frequency model (e.g., Cantrelle and Leridon 1971; Leslie and Fry 1989; Paul et al. 1979). For example, Becker et al. (1986) show that in Matlab, Bangladesh, the period of the rice harvest and the few months following (November–April) correspond with the period of highest probability of resumption of menses among lactating women, highest probability of conception among menstruating women, highest probability that births will be live rather than dead, and highest neonatal survival. The low food period (August and September) is associated with lowest fecundability per copulation, lowest risk of conception per month, and highest probability of stillbirth. The low food period is also the time of *highest probability of terminating breast feeding, or initiating solid food supplementation* (Becker et al. 1986:471). Thus women were least likely to resume ovulation or conceive during the period when weaning was most likely. Exactly the same pattern has been described for Senegal (Cantrelle and Leridon 1971). Finally, we found in another group of South American hunter-gatherers that seasonal food intake and weight change is a strong predictor of fertility (see Hurtado and Hill 1992).

The seasonal effect on fecundability among the Ache can be examined by calculating the conception hazard during each month of the year for the entire sample of reservation-living women. The results suggest that the hazard of conception is closely related to seasonal changes in weight in the Ache population (Figure 10.12). In particular, the months with lowest conception rates (January, February, March) are also the months with the lowest body weights, and we previously showed that these same months are characterized by lowest food intake through the year on foraging expeditions (Hill et al. 1984). This pattern is probably not explained by seasonal changes in nursing patterns since the same pattern is found (with a marginal significance level) among nulliparous women and among women who have no living infant (i.e., nonlactating women).[6] The seasonal pattern could possibly be due to patterns in coital frequency that change with temperature since the conception peak occurs during the coldest months of the year and the conception valley occurs during the hottest time of the year (also the period with the highest density of insect pests). Nevertheless, we have never heard any gossip to suggest that coital frequency varies with temperature. Finally, the fact that mean body weight is also significantly associated with fecundability leads us to conclude that seasonal conception patterns are probably driven by energy balance directly rather than by some other confounding variable.

VARIATION IN MALE FERTILITY RATE

The age-specific patterns of male fertility were described in Chapter 9. Given these patterns we would like to know whether resource-related factors are associated with an increase or decrease in the fertility rates of males in our sample. This can be accomplished through multiple regression in which age effects are controlled. Thus, if we take reported primary paternity at face value, male fertility prior to contact can be examined in a manner similar to that described for females. In our analysis, however, we set the risk interval at six months rather than a year in order to allow for multiple births assigned to the same man in a single calendar year (i.e., two births in a single year were coded as one in each six-month period). No man in our sample fathered more than two children in a single year. In addition, we have less information on male attractiveness than we do for females, so we are not able to examine the effects of that variable on male fertility. Instead, we concentrate on three resource-related variables: male hunting rate, male body size, and (on reservations) male socioeconomic status.

During the forest period men between the ages of eighteen and sixty were considered at risk of producing a child as long as they had not died more than a year prior to the interval being analyzed. The sample includes 5,556 intervals at risk from 176 men born between 1890 and 1952, resulting in 538 births. Since very few men produce offspring after age fifty on the reservation settlements, we looked at the variation in male fertility from eighteen to fifty years. The sample consists of 157 men born between 1928 and 1975 and contributing 3,266 intervals at risk that resulted in 331 live births. Hunting skill before contact was estimated using the ranking procedure described earlier in this chapter. Hunting return rates were measured directly between 1980 and 1985 for a large sample of men. Male body size was estimated as the mean of all the body weights recorded for men who exceeded eighteen years of age between 1977 and 1993. Socioeconomic status was estimated by assigning a rank score from 1 to 5 as described earlier in this chapter.

Results of logistic regression do show an association between resource acquisition and fertility of Ache men both prior to contact and during the reservation period. The relationship between hunting ranks obtained from informants and forest fertility rate is positive and highly significant (Table 10.6). The relationship is also positive and highly significant when measured hunting return rate rather than hunting skill is used as the independent variable.[7] The relationship between forest fertility and mean adult body weight (measured during the reservation period long after the period represented by the fertility risk intervals) is also positive and marginally significant. Reservation fertility rates show highly significant positive associations with both SES and mean adult body weight, but no relationship with measured hunting return rates (Table 10.6).

SUMMARY

The results of statistical tests designed to examine the relationship between resources and mortality or fertility rates are mixed, but they do suggest that in general improved access to resources leads to higher offspring survival and fertility for both sexes (Table 10.7). Several patterns emerge when the results are considered together. First, the hypothesis that resources can be used either to increase offspring survival or to increase fertility is supported by the data. The sign of independent tests of this hypothesis is in the predicted direction (negative for resources and mortality, positive for resources and fertility) in twenty of twenty-eight tests. Second, the results are stronger when manifest variables and outcomes from the reservation period are used than they are for the forest period. Twelve of the sixteen tests that were unable to reject the null hypothesis were carried out on data from the forest period, using very rough indicators of the independent variable. Third, resources appear to affect fertility more than mortality in the Ache case. Fertility was the dependent variable in only two of the sixteen tests that clearly failed to reject the null hypothesis, and in both of those cases the sign of the parameter estimate was in the predicted direction. Five of the seven tests that showed a clear association between the manifest variable and a life history trait included fertility as the dependent variable. Fourth, resources appear to be more strongly associated with male variation in life history than female variation. Tests for associations between resources and male fertility or offspring mortality provided five of the seven significant results with the manifest variables, and the highest standardized parameter estimates as well as the lowest p-values. Taking all results together, then, we find the strongest associations between resources and a life history trait in our tests of male fertility during the reservation period.

The association between resources and fertility should be interpreted cautiously. As is the case for many other studies of this relationship, the direction of the causal arrow was often unclear to us. Do men with more resources obtain greater access to females, or females with higher fertility? Do they use their resources to increase a female partner's fertility, or do they simply work harder and produce more goods *because* they have larger families to support? Anecdotes from the Ache suggest that both patterns are responsible for the result. In addition there is a tendency for single men with no children to give away their resources, whereas men with families retained more of their production and thus had higher SES scores when we observed them. Thus, further research will be required to disentangle the meaning of the association between resources and fertility.

The lack of strong associations between parental resources and offspring survival could mean several things: (1) we have not been able to obtain very good measures of variation between adults with regard to resource availability in our forest and reservation samples; (2) there is very little variation in resource availability among the Ache; or (3) variation between adults in resource availability has little impact on offspring survival in the Ache socioecological context. We consider 2 and 3 to be unlikely, but note that in recent times missionaries have frequently intervened on reservation settlements in order to dampen mortality differences between Ache families. Sick children were often temporarily taken in by missionaries, fed, and nursed back to health.

The fact that paternal resources affect mainly infant survival on reservations but late childhood survival in the forest is somewhat puzzling. We believe that the reservation effect is mainly due to improved sanitation and protection from exposure to hazards. Most infants on reservations died of respiratory disease, and housing construction and ventilation, number of blankets, and availability of clothing seem likely to be involved in exposure to health insults. On the other hand, forest mortality was primarily due to infanticide, child homicide, and warfare with Paraguayans. For some reason older children of men who were observed as good hunters between 1980 and 1985 were less susceptible to this violence than the children of men who were poor hunters during the same time period. Since our evidence suggests that hunting return rates for men are fairly stable through time, it is likely that children of good hunters in the forest were less susceptible to violence than children of poor hunters.

Other interesting associations between resources and life history traits were also uncovered. First, body weight of both men and women is associated with reservation fertility and body weight measured in the 1980s and is weakly but positively associated with forest fertility. In both cases the effect is stronger for males than for females. This condition is necessary for body size dimorphism to be explained by sexual selection (see Chapter 11). Second, across all dimensions measured, male fitness components are more strongly affected by resource availability than are female fitness components. These conditions are necessary in order for the expectation derived from the Trivers-Willard hypothesis (Trivers and Willard 1973) regarding sex ratio manipulation by parents to be met.

Third, male hunting rank score is strongly associated with forest fertility whereas SES, but not hunting return rate, is associated with reservation fertility. This suggests to us that Ache women have probably shifted mate choice criteria from favoring good hunters to favoring those who accumulate resources through farming and wage labor. This is clear evidence of the diminishing importance of the hunter-gather lifestyle among the current Ache population. During the forest period, however, good hunters had both higher fertility ·and better offspring survival to adulthood (ages 5–9 and probably ages 1–4) than poor hunters. This confirms earlier preliminary reports (Kaplan and Hill 1985b) in which we suggested that better hunters among the foraging Ache produced higher numbers of surviving offspring than did worse hunters.

Female attractiveness was associated with higher age-controlled fertility, but not with higher offspring survival in the Ache sample. This finding provides no support for the idea that traits are found to be attractive because they signal an ability to produce healthier offspring (i.e., offspring who are more likely to survive because of better disease resistance). Ache women are considered more attractive if their faces are more symmetrical, closer to average proportions, and neotonous (Jones 1993), but our data suggest that all these features may provide information about fecundity rather than heritable disease resistance among the Ache. Attractive women in the reservation period had higher fertility than unattractive women even when the model controlled for the age variable. This may be partially due to the fact that attractiveness is significantly correlated with SES ($r = 0.422$, $p < 0.0001$) in this sample. However, multiple regression with age, weight, SES, and attractiveness, shows that attractiveness is a strong predictor of fertility even when the other covariates are being controlled. As far as we know, no theory of female facial attractiveness has explicitly considered signals that indicate high inherent fecundity *with the age variable controlled*. Perhaps a more general theory of mate choice for disease resistance should include reproductive efficiency as well as heritable increased survival as a desired trait.

A more general anthropological implication of the analyses presented in this chapter is that the concept of the "original affluent society" (Sahlins 1972) as a characterization of hunter-gatherers is flawed. The Ache eat better than almost any other group of foragers ever studied (Hill et al. 1984), and they weigh considerably more than well-known groups such as the !Kung, yet data clearly indicate that they do not get "enough food to meet their needs." More food is shown to impact positively on fertility of both sexes and may also increase child survival (though the evidence is weak). Since individuals consistently voice a desire for high fertility, and high survivorship, and such a preference would be favored by natural selection under many conditions, there is no basis for the assertion that the Ache obtain all the food they need. Regardless of how many hours they work at acquiring food, neither the Ache nor members of any other foraging society can be shown to meet their food needs in any biological sense. Indeed, neither the Ache nor any other traditional people with whom we have worked in the past two decades agrees with the proposition that they obtain all the food they need. Instead they emphatically insist that they are hungry and would prefer more food (as do the !Kung, with their incessant begging from visitors).

This conclusion could easily have been predicted without the Ache data. Most nutritional anthropologists and world health workers have known for decades that small body stature universally signals undesirable conditions and, conversely, that unhealthy living conditions (nutrition, pathogens, disease, etc.) lead to small body size. No group of people in the world, except perhaps African pygmies, has ever been shown to be small for genetic reasons (Cavalli-Sforza 1986; Dietz et al. 1989; Frisancho 1981; Hasstedt 1986), and members of small traditional populations such as the Ache or the !Kung often grow as large as modern Americans when provided with equivalent nutrition and health conditions during childhood (Chapter 7; J. Bock, Department of Anthropology, University of New Mexico, personal communication). Most traditional peoples suffer mild food stress, and more food would result in greater body size, higher fertility, and probably better juvenile survivorship. If we believe that individuals universally care about health, survival, fertility, and the survival of their offspring, then we must recognize that a failure to meet optimal health, survival, and fertility levels indicates that they do not meet their food requirements. Indeed, food "needs" themselves can only be objectively assessed with reference to whether optimal health is obtained.

The "original affluent society" myth suggesting that our ancestors easily met their daily needs before we became greedy and began to desire more than that which is necessary is an idea that tells us more about late twentieth century anthropological thought than it does about the lives of foraging peoples. The "original affluent society" concept has no basis in empirical reality or biology, but it is also a cruel hoax because it leads members of modern societies to avoid the empathy or guilt that they should feel when considering the plight of people living under difficult conditions. Indeed, after seventeen years of working with foragers in three different countries and hearing the complaints of hunger, the cries of children, and having watched people suffering from less than desirable health, it is difficult for us to feel charitable towards those who have perpetrated this farcical myth in modern anthropology. Not surprisingly, the foragers with whom we have shared our lives feel the same way: "If he thinks that this is all the food we want, let him come down here and eat with us, and feed his children that which we feed ours" (Dawiya, a Hiwi forager, commenting in 1988 on our story about a man who claims that the Hiwi only work a few hours per day because they obtain plenty of food).

NOTES

1.   Logistic regression of forest child mortality hazard from age 0 through 4, by age of child and attractiveness score of mother gave the following results: intervals at risk = 2,637; mean age = 1.81 years, mean attractiveness score = 3.17; final model -2 log likelihood chi-square for covariates = 45.659 with 2 df, compared with 45.103 with 1 df

for the model excluding the mother's attractiveness term; p-value for model improvement with mother's age terms $= 0.48$; standardized parameter estimate for age $= -0.349359$, for mother's attractiveness $= 0.034697$.

Logistic regression of reservation child mortality hazard from age 0 through 4 by age of child and attractiveness score of mother yielded the following results: intervals at risk $= 1,294$; mean age $= 1.79$ years, mean attractiveness score $= 3.22$; model -2 log likelihood chi-square for covariates $= 46.8$ with 2 df, compared with 46.81 with 3 df for the model excluding the mother's attractiveness term; p-value for model improvement with mother's age terms $= 0.96$; parameter estimate for intercept $= -1.7021$, for age -0.9438, for attractiveness score -0.00358; standardized parameter estimate for attractiveness $= -0.002675$; partial chi-square probability for attractiveness $= 0.97$. Tests on infant mortality rate only gave similar results.

2. Logistic regression of forest child mortality hazard from age 0 through 4 by age of child, age of mother, and mother's age squared yielded the following results: intervals at risk $= 2,627$; mean age $= 1.81$ years, mean age of mother $= 27.18$; final model -2 log likelihood chi-square for covariates $= 51.389$ with 3 df, compared with 45.030 with 1 df for the model excluding the mother's age terms; p-value for model improvement with mother's age terms $= 0.043$; standardized parameter estimate for age $= -0.347059$, for mother's age $= -0.603175$, for mother's age squared $= 0.519249$.

Few deaths took place after age 1 in the reservation period. Logistic regression of reservation infant mortality hazard from age 0 to 1 by age of mother and mother's age squared yielded the following results: intervals at risk $= 363$; mean age of mother $= 28.18$; final model -2 log likelihood chi-square for covariates 4.935 with 2 df; p-value for model improvement with mother's age terms $= 0.085$; standardized parameter estimate for mother's age $= -0.133723$, for mother's age squared $= 0.303390$.

3. Logistic regression of adult female mortality rate by body size and controlling for age yielded the following result: intervals at risk $= 3,249$; mean age $= 29.7$; mean size rank $= 0.51$; final model -2 log likelihood chi-square for covariates $= 16.426$ with 2 df, compared with 16.137 with 1 df for the model with excluding the size rank variable; p-value for model improvement with size rank variable $= 0.65$; standardized parameter estimate for age $= 0.4213$, for size rank $= 0.0599$.

Logistic regression of adult male mortality rate by hunting skill rank with age controlled yielded the following result: intervals at risk $= 3,249$; mean age $= 29.7$; mean hunting rank $= 0.50$; final model -2 log likelihood chi-square for covariates $= 15.691$ with 2 df, compared with 15.499 with 1 df for the model excluding the hunting rank variable; p-value for model improvement with hunting rank variable $= 0.74$; standardized parameter estimate for age $= 0.2746$, for hunting rank $= 0.033$.

4. Logistic regression of the fertility hazard during the reservation period as a function of age, age squared, body weight, and other reproductive state variables was performed. Independent variables are age, age squared, previous offspring dead, nulliparous, duration in reproductive state, duration squared, and mean adult body weight. The multiple regression yielded the following result: intervals at risk $= 4,336$; mean age $= 29.9$; mean weight $= 53.6$; final model -2 log likelihood chi-square for covariates $= 296.935$ with 6 df, $p = 0.0001$ vs. -2 log likelihood chi-square for covariates of 282.834 with 5 df for the model without weight. Model improvement $p = 0.0002$.

5. Logistic regression of fertility hazard during the reservation period as a function of age, SES, body weight, attractiveness and other reproductive state variables was per-

formed: Independent variables are age, age squared, previous offspring dead, nulliparous, duration in reproductive state, duration squared, mean adult body weight, SES rank score, and attractiveness rank score. The multiple regression yields the following result: intervals at risk = 4,336; mean age = 29.9; mean weight = 53.6; mean SES = 2.99; mean attractiveness = 3.11; final model -2 log likelihood chi-square for covariates = 224.815 with 9 df, $p = 0.0001$. Standardized parameter estimates and partial p-values for the three independent variables of interest are: SES = 0.0111, $p = 0.76$; weight = 0.0795, $p = 0.02$; attractiveness = 0.0732, $p = 0.039$. Body weight has the greatest effect on reservation fertility with other variables controlled. SES has no impact after other variables have been controlled.

6. Logistic regression of conception hazard on reservation settlements for women who were nulliparous or had no living infant was performed Independent variables are age, age squared, and four seasonal covariates as dummy variables. The multiple regression yielded the following result: intervals at risk = 1,247; mean age = 26.6; mean (season1) = 0.245; mean (season2) = 0.272; mean (season3) = 0.257; season4 is the control; final model -2 log likelihood chi-square for covariates = 54.844 with 5 df, compared with 47.847 with 2 df for the model excluding the season variables; p-value for model improvement with the season variables = 0.076. The seasonal effect on conception hazard is marginally significant when only nonlactating women are in the risk set.

7. Logistic regression of fertility hazard during the forest period as a function of hunting return rate measured between 1980 and 1985. Independent variables are age, age squared, and hunting return rate (kg meat/hour). The multiple regression yielded the following result: intervals at risk = 5,556; mean age = 31.5; mean return rate = 0.496 kg/hr; final model -2 log likelihood chi-square for covariates 82.59 with 3 df, compared with 78.439 with 2 df for the model excluding the hunting rate variable; p-value for model improvement with size rank variable = 0.043.

Table 10.1. Comparative and Experimental Studies of the Effect of Growth and Food Intake on Juvenile Survivorship

COMPARATIVE

Place, sample size	Subjects' age (years)	Predictor	Outcome	Effect	Study design
Bengal *n* = 8292 Sommer and Low-enstein 1975	1–9	Midarm circumference/height	survivorship	+	longitudinal prospective 18 months
Bangladesh *n* = 2019 Chen et al. 1980	1–2	Weight/age Arm circumference/age Weight/height	survivorship	+ + +	longitudinal prospective 24 months
Bangladesh (Matlab) *n* = 1000 Bairagi et al. 1985	1–4	Weight/age Height/age	survivorship	+ +	longitudinal prospective one year
Guinea-Bisseau (Bandim) *n* = 2228 Smedman et al. 1987	0.5–5	Height/age	survivorship	+	longitudinal prospecitive 8–12 months
West Java *n* = 4000 Katz et al. 1989	birth–2 2–5	Height/age Weight/height	mortality	+ +	longitudinal prospective 18 months
Zaire (Kasongo) *n* = 4273 Kasongo Project Team 1986	0.5–4	Growth acceleration (wt/age; wt/ht; wt/age)	survivorship	+	longitudinal prospective 3 months

EXPERIMENTAL

N. Peru *n* = 1700 Baertl et al. 1970	1–5 birth–1	+ 250 calories + 12.5 g protein same supplement in pregnancy	survivorship perinatal survivorship	+ +	longitudinal prospecitive 6 years
India (Narangwal) *n* = 2900 Kielmann et al. 1978	1–5	+ 400 calories + 11 g protein	survivorship	+	longitudinal prospecitive 3 years

Table 10.2. Effect of Parental Resource Availability on Juvenile Mortality Rates during the Forest Period

	Independent variable	Age 0					Age 1–4					Age 5–9				
		Coded cases	Mean value	Parameter estimate	Stand. estimate	Partial p	Coded cases	Mean value	Parameter estimate	Stand. estimate	Partial p	Coded cases	Mean value	Parameter estimate	Stand. estimate	Partial p
logistic multiple regression	age	650	—	—	—	—	1987	2.4	-0.1239	-0.0763	0.27	1870	6.9	-0.0630	-0.0490	0.59
	father's hunt rank score	556	0.57	-0.0664	-0.0081	0.9	1666	0.57	-0.1488	-0.0181	0.79	1526	0.56	-0.0471	-0.0056	0.95
model comparison	Models age vs. age, hunt rank	change in -2 log likelihood for added covariates 0.014	1 df		χ² p **0.9**		change in -2 log likelihood for added covariates 0.069	1 df		χ² p **0.85**		change in -2 log likelihood for added covariates 0.004	1 df		χ² p **>0.9**	
logistic multiple regression	age	650	—	—	—	—	1987	2.4	-0.1225	-0.0749	0.28	1870	6.9	-0.0442	-0.0344	0.6
	father's hunt rate (kg/hr)	89	0.54	1.1634	0.0565	0.41	220	0.53	-2.3557	-0.0952	0.11	71	0.53	-5.9660	-0.1788	0.0006
model comparison	Models age vs. age, kg/hr	change in -2 log likelihood for added covariates 0.686	1 df		χ² p **0.41**		change in -2 log likelihood for added covariates 2.277	1 df		χ² p **0.18**		change in -2 log likelihood for added covariates 8.309	1 df		χ² p **0.003**	
logistic multiple regression	age	650	—	—	—	—	1987	2.4	-0.1241	-0.0764	0.27	1870	6.9	-0.0629	-0.0489	0.59
	mother's size rank score	552	0.53	-0.3451	-0.0519	0.44	1717	0.53	0.5318	0.0797	0.25	1615	0.53	0.6986	0.1047	0.25
model comparison	Models age vs. age, sizerank	change in -2 log likelihood for added covariates 0.586	1 df		χ² p **0.44**		change in -2 log likelihood for added covariates 1.323	1 df		χ² p **0.35**		change in -2 log likelihood for added covariates 1.336	1 df		χ² p **0.34**	
logistic multiple regression	age	650	—	—	—	—	1987	2.4	-0.1240	-0.0764	0.27	1870	6.9	-0.0630	-0.0490	0.59
	mo.'s weight kilograms	97	50.2	0.0755	0.0672	0.28	233	50.1	0.0755	0.0676	0.7	152	49.5	-0.0377	-0.0198	0.83
model comparison	Models age vs. age, weight	change in -2 log likelihood for added covariates 1.18	1 df		χ² p **0.29**		change in -2 log likelihood for added covariates 0.156	1 df		χ² p **0.77**		change in -2 log likelihood for added covariates 0.048	1 df		χ² p **0.87**	

Table 10.3. Effect of Parental Resource Availability on Juvenile Mortality Rates during the Reservation Period

		Age 0					Age 1–4				
	Independent variable	Cases	Mean value	Parameter estimate	Stand. estimate	Partial p	Cases	Mean value	Parameter estimate	Stand. estimate	Partial p
logistic multiple regression	age	363	0	–	–	–	1104	2.404	–0.9902	–0.6102	0.0001
	father's SES rank score	248	3.3	–0.373	–0.1765	0.038	681	3.3	–0.2526	–0.1188	0.263
model comparison	Models age vs. age, SESrank	change in –2 log likelihood for added covariates 4.463 1 df				χ^2 p **0.0346**	change in –2 log likelihood for added covariates 1.259 1 df				χ^2 p **0.357**
logistic multiple regression	age	363	0	–	–	–	1104	2.4	–0.9826	–0.6055	0.0001
	father's hunting rate (kg/hr)	123	0.56	0.2792	0.0209	0.8	368	0.55	2.917	0.2022	0.064
model comparison	Models age vs. age, kg/hr	change in –2 log likelihood for added covariates 0.065 1 df				χ^2 p **0.8**	change in –2 log likelihood for added covariates 3.375 1 df				χ^2 p **0.071**
logistic multiple regression	age	363	0	–	–	–	1104	2.4	–0.9863	–0.6078	0.0001
	mother's ses rank score	251	3.3	–0.2553	–0.1288	0.118	694	3.3	–0.2989	–0.1502	0.156
model comparison	Models age vs. age, SESrank	change in –2 log likelihood for added covariates 2.467 1 df				χ^2 p **0.116**	change in –2 log likelihood for added covariates 2.007 1 df				χ^2 p **0.224**
logistic multiple regression	age	363	0	–	–	–	1104	2.4	–0.9873	–0.6084	0.0001
	mother's weight kilograms	259	54.7	–0.042	–0.1162	0.169	722	54.6	0.0014	0.0003	0.997
model comparison	Models age vs. age, weight	change in –2 log likelihood for added covariates 1.941 1 df				χ^2 p **0.1635**	change in –2 log likelihood for added covariates 0 1 df				χ^2 p **0.997**

Table 10.4. The Relationship between Attractiveness Rating (age-controlled) and Fertility for Ache Women

			Forest period			
	Independent variable	*Cases*	*Mean*	*Parameter estimate*	*Stand. estimate*	*Partial p*
logistic	age	2581	26.6	0.3439	1.7480	0.0001
multiple	(age)^2	2581	794	−0.0057	1.7490	0.0001
regression	attractiveness score	343	3.02	0.0773	0.0227	0.4055
model comparison	Models age, (age)^2 vs. age, (age)^2, attractiveness	change in −2 log likelihood for added covariates 0.693 1 df				χ^2 p **0.458**
			Reservation period			
logistic	age	4336	29.9	0.3049	1.6160	0.0001
multiple	(age)^2	4336	989	−0.0062	−1.9897	0.0001
regression	nulliparous	586	0.135	−0.2421	−0.0456	0.33
	living youngest*	3089	0.713	control	control	control
	dead youngest*	661	0.152	0.7342	0.1455	0.0001
	time	4336	31.87	0.0622	1.5700	0.0001
	(time since last birth)^2	4336	3111	−0.0006	−2.9700	0.0001
	attractiveness score	3807	3.1	0.0931	0.0667	0.035
model comparison	Models age, age2, reproductive state vs. reprod. state, age, age2, attract. score	change in −2 log likelihood for added covariates 4.478 1 df				χ^2 p **0.037**

* Whether youngest child is alive or dead at beginning of interval at risk.

Table 10.5. The Relationship between Resource Availability and Fertility for Ache
Women

			Forest period			
	Independent variable	*Cases*	*Mean*	*Parameter estimate*	*Stand. estimate*	*Partial p*
logistic	age	2581	26.6	0.3434	1.7457	0.0001
multiple	age²	2581	794	−0.0057	1.7474	0.0001
regression	size rank score	2153	0.504	0.2062	0.0311	0.233
model	Models	change in −2 log likelihood				χ²
comparison	age, age² vs.	for added covariates				p
	age, age², size	1.424	1 df			**0.33**

			Reservation period			
logistic	age	4336	29.9	0.2958	1.5681	0.0001
multiple	age²	4336	989	−0.0060	−1.9237	0.0001
regression	nulliparous	4336	0.135	−0.2923	−0.0551	0.245
	living youngest*	4336	0.713	control	control	control
	dead youngest*	4336	0.152	0.7857	0.1557	0.0001
	time since last birth	4336	31.86	0.0635	1.6019	0.0001
	(time since last birth)²	4336	3111	−0.0006	−3.0579	0.0001
	adult body weight	3288	53.7	0.0257	0.0717	0.021
model	Models	change in −2 log likelihood				χ²
comparison	age, age², reproductive	for added covariates				p
	state vs. reproductive	5.244	1 df			**0.023**
	age, age², state, weight					

			Reservation period			
logistic	age	4336	29.9	0.2843	1.5073	0.0001
multiple	age²	4336	989	−0.0058	−1.8733	0.0001
regression	nulliparous	4336	0.135	−0.2728	−0.0514	0.277
	living youngest*	4336	0.713	control	control	control
	dead youngest*	4336	0.152	0.7191	0.1425	0.0001
	time since last birth	4336	31.86	0.0630	1.5902	0.0001
	(time since last birth)²	4336	3111	−0.0006	−3.0426	0.0001
	SES rank	3508	2.99	0.1023	0.0617	0.053
model	Models	change in −2 log likelihood				χ²
comparison	age, age², reproductive	for added covariates				p
	state vs. reproductive	3.745	1 df			**0.054**
	age, age², state, SES rank					

* Whether youngest child is alive or dead at beginning of interval at risk.

Table 10.6. The Relationship between Resource Availability and Fertility (age-controlled) for Ache Men

	Independent variable	Cases	Mean	Parameter estimate	Stand. estimate	Partial p
		Forest period				
logistic	age	5556	31.5	0.2630	1.5762	0.0001
multiple	age^2	5556	1107	−0.0036	−1.5455	0.0001
regression	hunting rank score	4958	0.524	0.7070	0.1002	0.0001
model comparison	Models age, age^2 vs. age, age^2, hunt rank	change in −2 log likelihood for added covariates 15.155 1 df				χ^2 p <**0.001**
logistic	age	5556	31.5	0.2663	1.5964	0.0001
multiple	age^2	5556	1107	−0.0036	−1.5595	0.0001
regression	mean adult body weight	1068	58.33	0.0368	0.0462	0.097
model comparison	Models age, age^2 vs. age, age^2, size	change in −2 log likelihood for added covariates 2.874 1 df				χ^2 p **0.093**
		Reservation period				
logistic	age	3266	31.7	0.3240	1.5960	0.0001
multiple	age^2	3266	3289	−0.0053	−1.7298	0.0001
regression	hunting return rate (kg meat/hour)	1153	0.552	0.1255	0.0101	0.76
model comparison	Models age, age^2, age, age^2, hunting return rate	change in −2 log likelihood for added covariates 0.097 1 df				χ^2 p **0.89**
logistic	age	3266	31.7	0.2733	1.3467	0.0001
multiple	age^2	3266	3289	−0.0044	−1.4440	0.0001
regression	SES rank	2826	2.65	0.3201	0.2031	0.0001
model comparison	Models age, age^2, age, age^2, SES rank	change in −2 log likelihood for added covariates 39.551 1 df				χ^2 p <**0.001**
logistic	age	3266	31.7	0.3080	1.5172	0.0001
multiple	age^2	3266	3289	−0.0050	−1.6446	0.0001
regression	mean adult body weight	2461	60.26	0.0300	0.0786	0.016
model comparison	Models age, age^2, age, age^2, weight	change in − 2 log likelihood for added covariates 7.599 1 df				χ^2 p **0.006**

* Number of cases with coded values; missing values were coded to the mean value.

Table 10.7. Summary of the Relationship between Resources and Life History Traits

Manifest variable	Estimated correlation with latent variable*	Latent variable	Dependent variable	Standardized parameter estimate**	p
Significant association between manifest variable and dependent variable					
Males		**Offspring Mortality**			
hunting rate (1980–1985)	0.71	paternal food prod.	forest offspring mortality (age 5–9)	**−0.1788**	0.003
SES	0.58	paternal resources	reservation offspring mortality (age 0)	**−0.1765**	0.034
Females		**Offspring Mortality**			
Males		**Fertility**			
hunting rank	0.71	paternal food prod.	forest fertility	**0.1002**	0.001
SES	0.58	paternal resources	reservation fertility	**0.0203**	0.000
mean weight (1980–1993)	0.85	paternal somatic resources	reservation fertility	**0.0786**	0.006
Females		**Fertility**			
mean weight (1980–1993)	0.85	maternal somatic resources	reservation fertility	**0.0717**	0.023
SES	0.58	maternal resources	reservation fertility	**0.0617**	0.054
Possible association between latent variable and dependent variable					
Males		**Offspring Mortality**			
hunting rate (1980–1985)	0.71	paternal food prod.	forest offspring mortality (age 1–4)	−0.0952	0.180
SES	0.58	paternal resources	reservation offspring mortality (age 1–4)	−0.1188	0.357
Females		**Offspring Mortality**			
mean weight (1980–1993)	0.85	maternal somatic resources	reservation offspring mortality (age 0)	−0.1162	0.164
SES	0.58	maternal resources	reservation offspring mortality (age 0)	−0.1288	0.116
SES	0.58	maternal resources	reservation offspring mortality (age 1–4)	−0.1502	0.224
Males		**Fertility**			
Females		**Fertility**			
mean weight (1980–1993)	0.85	paternal somatic resources	forest fertility	**0.0462**	0.093

(continued)

Table 10.7. (continued)

Manifest variable	Estimated correlation with latent variable*	Latent variable	Dependent variable	Standardized parameter estimate**	p
Null hypothesis (no association) cannot be rejected					
Males		**Offspring Mortality**			
hunting rate (1980–1985)	0.71	paternal food prod.	forest offspring mortality (age 0)	0.0570	0.410
hunting rank	0.71	paternal food prod.	forest offspring mortality (age 0)	**−0.0664**	0.900
hunting rank	0.71	paternal food prod.	forest offspring mortality (age 1–4)	**−0.0181**	0.850
hunting rank	0.71	paternal food prod.	forest offspring mortality (age 5–9)	**−0.0471**	0.950
hunting rate (1980–1985)	0.71	paternal food prod.	reservation offspring mortality (age 0)	0.0209	0.800
hunting rate (1980–1985)	0.71	paternal food prod.	reservation offspring mortality (age 1–4)	0.2022	0.071
Females		**Offspring Mortality**			
body size rank	0.85	maternal somatic resources	forest offspring mortality (age 0)	**−0.0519**	0.440
body size rank	0.85	maternal somatic resources	forest offspring mortality (age 1–4)	0.0797	0.350
body size rank	0.85	maternal somatic resources	forest offspring mortality (age 5–9)	0.1047	0.340
mean weight (1980–1993)	0.85	maternal somatic resources	forest offspring mortality (age 0)	0.0672	0.290
mean weight (1980–1993)	0.85	maternal somatic resources	forest offspring mortality (age 1–4)	0.0676	0.770
mean weight (1980–1993)	0.85	maternal somatic resources	forest offspring mortality (age 5–9)	**−0.0198**	0.870
mean weight (1980–1993)	0.85	maternal somatic resources	reservation offspring mortality (age 1–4)	0.0003	0.997
Males		**Fertility**			
hunting rate (1980–1985)	0.71	paternal food prod.	reservation fertility	**0.0101**	0.890
Females		**Fertility**			
body size rank	0.85	maternal somatic resources	forest fertility	**0.0311**	0.330

* Estimated as the square root of the correlation between two independently measured manifest variables of the same latent variable (see text).

** Values in bold print show predicted sign for hypothesized association.

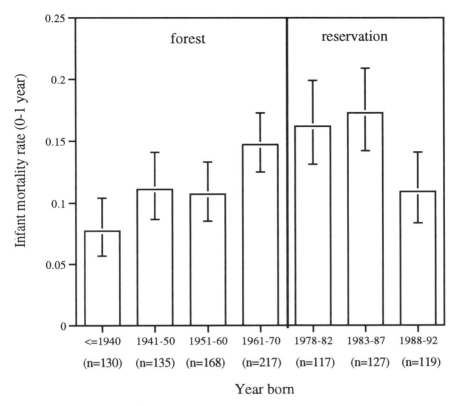

Figure 10.1. Infant mortality in the Ache population during the forest and reservation periods. Bars show one standard error of rate estimate for the intercept in each period from logistic regression. Infant mortality appears to be higher in the first ten years of the reservation period than it was in the forest period.

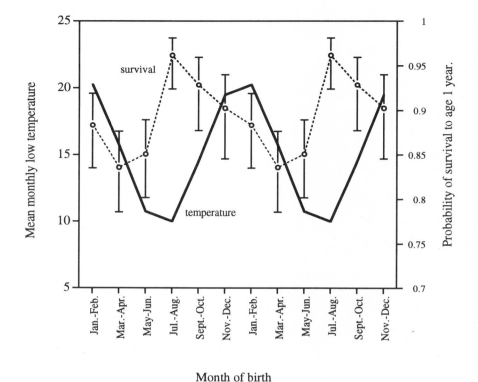

Month of birth

Figure 10.2.   Mean low temperature (solid line) and infant survival rate (dashed line) by
season of birth (pooled bimonthly) for children born during the reservation period.
Bars show standard error around the survival probability (from logistic regression).
The yearly cycle is duplicated for clarity of presentation. The data support the Ache
suggestion that survivorship is best for children born just after the cold period and
worst for children born just before the cold period each year.

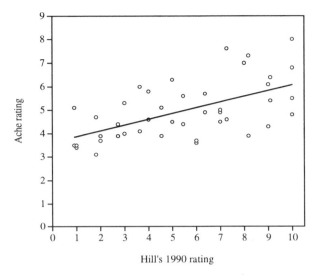

Figure 10.3. The relationship between the attractiveness rating that we assigned to Ache women and mean rating derived from the opinions of Ache men ($r = 0.583$).

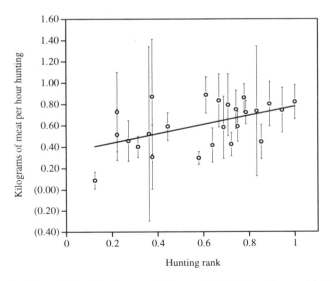

Figure 10.4. The relationship between informant-elicited hunting rankings and measured meat acquisition rates between 1980 and 1985 for twenty-five hunters. Bars show one standard error around the daily weighted mean of the hourly hunting return rate.

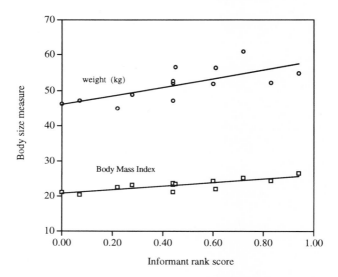

Figure 10.5.   The relationship between informant-elicited body size rankings and measured weight (*r* = 0.716) or Body Mass Index (BMI; *r* = 0.824) between 1980 and 1989 for twenty-three Ache women.

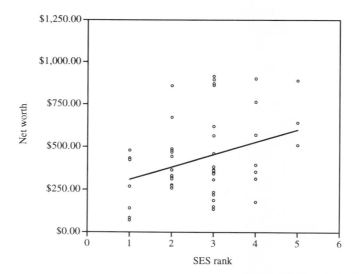

Figure 10.6.   The relationship between SES ranking and the measured net worth of Ache nuclear families in 1992 (*r* = 0.341).

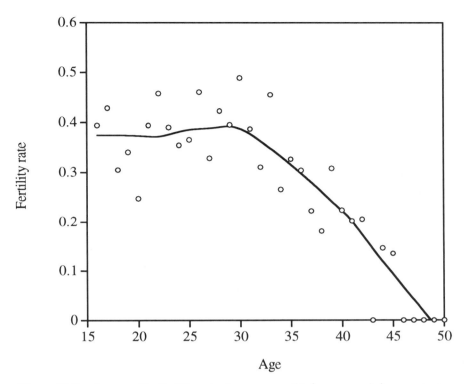

Figure 10.7. Age-specific fertility rate (lowess smooth) for parous Ache women on reservations. Fertility rate is calculated as probability of conception leading to live birth per twelve-month period. Parous women include all women who had given birth or experienced an abortion after the first trimester. Note the flat fertility rate for women between fifteen and thirty years of age.

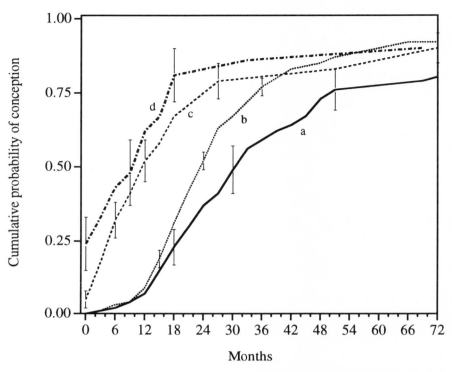

Figure 10.8. The cumulative probability (Kaplan-Meier product-limit estimate) of having conceived after four types of reproductive events: (a) menarche ($n = 48$); (b) birth of a child who survives to the interval at risk ($n = 285$); (c) birth of a child who dies within five days of birth ($n = 57$); and (d) death of a woman's youngest child ($n = 21$). Bars show the standard error at approximately each quartile. Conception after a child dies is rapid for most women. Time to conception after the birth of a surviving child is longer, and time to conception after menarche is longer still.

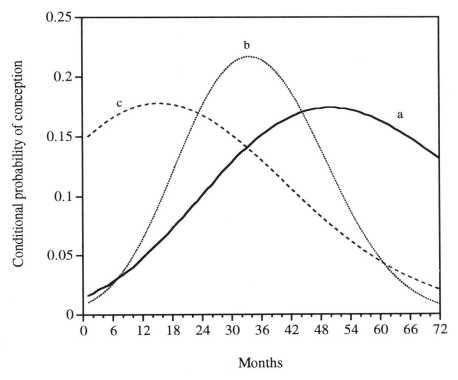

Months

Figure 10.9. The conditional probability of conception per three-month interval after (a) menarche; (b) birth of a child who lives to the end of the three-month interval of analyses; (c) death of a woman's youngest child. The conception hazard was smoothed using logistic regression and a third-order polynomial of elapsed time in months.

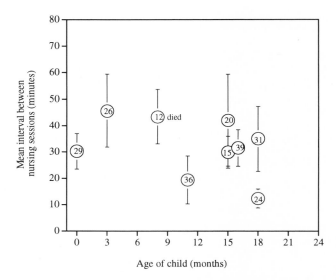

Figure 10.10. The relationship between time to the conception of the next sibling and the mean interval between nursing sessions for infants of known age. The number shown at the mean of session interval is the time in months to the conception of the next sibling. Bars show the standard error of the mean interval between nursing sessions for each child. There is no apparent relationship between age-specific nursing pattern of an infant and the observed time to the next conception.

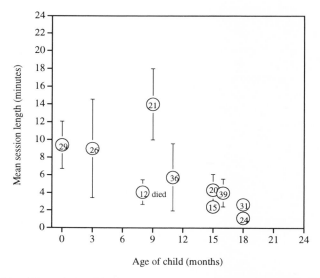

Figure 10.11. The relationship between mean nursing session length for infants of known ages and the interval to conception of the next sibling. The number shown at the mean session length for each child is the time (in months) to the next conception. Bars show the standard error of mean session length for each child.

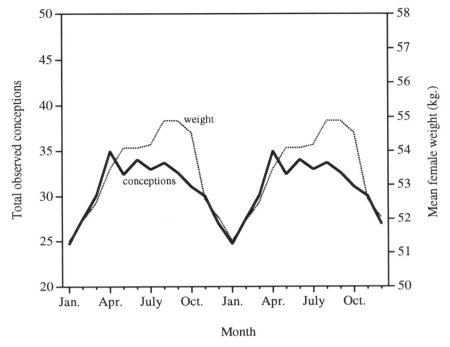

Figure 10.12. Total number of conceptions that led to a live birth during each month of the year from 1978 to 1992 (solid line) and mean monthly weight of adult women during the same sample period (dotted line). Data for monthly conception number and weight have been smoothed with a three-point moving average. Two full years are shown beginning in January in order to illustrate cyclicity. Note the strong seasonal correspondence between mean adult female weight and the number of conceptions that led to live births in the same month.

Two Ache girls about fourteen and a half years old who both reached menarche a few months after this photograph was taken in 1979.

11

Body Size and the Timing of Sexual Maturity

The development of children and whether or not they have become adults are topics that seem to fascinate humans. Ache mothers constantly gossip with each other about the growth of their children, and their passage through important developmental landmarks. "Chejugi knows how to sit"; "My child can walk now"; "She really knows how to talk"; "He is quite a grown up young man"; "She has almost reached menarche, she is sexually active now." These types of comments are important filler information in any casual conversation. Indeed, some of the first information that the Ache volunteer each year when we visit them is which girls have begun to menstruate, and which young people (males and females) have produced a first child while we were away.

In recent years Ache girls have begun to reach menarche at an earlier age than before (see Figures 7.6 and 7.7), and age at first birth has also decreased (see Figure 8.13). The Ache themselves are aware of these trends. They speculate on why girls at reservation settlements reach menarche earlier than those in the forest and connect this observation to an increase in individual growth rates on reservation settlements. Although they partially account for rapid maturity among the current cohort by claiming that "Girls nowadays are horny all the time. That's why they reach menarche so quickly," they have also observed that American women reach menarche even earlier than Ache girls and attribute the difference to diet. Indeed two men in 1993 asked us if our ten-year-old daughter had already reached menarche despite the fact that no Ache girl has reached menarche prior to thirteen years of age. They based their guess on the observation that the daughters of American missionaries seemed to mature rapidly, and because our daughter was much taller than any of the Ache children who were born in the same year. "Your women reach menarche very young don't they?" "That is because you have strong food."

The Ache have also noticed other aspects of development. In particular, they are quick to comment that girls always mature at a younger age than boys, and that this pattern has not changed at the reservation settlements. This pattern is universal to humans and indeed to almost all mammals. Demographers have described these patterns for more than a century, but an explanation of the pattern requires a biological theory of development. In this chapter we describe such a theory and show how it can explain, rather than just describe, the developmental patterns that capture the attention of the Ache as much as they puzzle the researcher. We begin with a short discussion of growth.

ALLOMETRY, DETERMINATE GROWTH, AND ACHE GROWTH PATTERNS

The mere fact that organisms grow presents an interesting puzzle to life history theorists. Growing takes time and energy. The energy put into growth could instead be used to produce offspring. The time spent growing delays sexual maturation and thus lowers the probability of surviving to reproductive age. Since growth is associated with these strong fitness costs, it can only make biological sense for an organism to grow if larger body size at sexual maturation is associated with some fitness advantage. That advantage is usually higher fertility and/or higher survivorship (self and offspring). This realization provides considerable insight into the biology of body size. Small organisms are small because they experience high (unavoidable) mortality rates. It takes time to grow, and they cannot afford to wait; they must reproduce quickly before they die. Large animals have lower mortality rates and can afford to grow for a longer period of time. But since mortality rates are often size dependent, mortality and growth must be locked together into combinations of possible rates that are interdependent and determined by the ecological niche of each species. Growth patterns, then, represent the solution to a trade-off between decreasing survival to reproductive age and increasing survival or fertility after maturity. This same general principle applies to all organisms, animal or plant: "When investment in the vegetative body is not completely paid back as future reproductive products, growth has been too great. Conversely, investment in vegetative machinery has been too small when the gain in current reproduction does not completely compensate for losses in future reproduction due to present vegetative allocation" (Kozlowski 1992:15).

Allometric Growth

The rate of growth that can be achieved is determined by the production of energy and the consumption of energy for activity and maintenance. The difference between these two is available for growth. For homeotherms, the consumption of energy is an increasing allometric function of body weight, with the power being less than one. This means that less energy is used per gram of weight as the size of organisms increases. Gross energy production is also a positive function of size within and across organisms. It, too, seems to increase monotonically as a power function of size, with the power being less than one but greater than the power associated with energy consumption. In plants this decreasing ratio of energy production to size is primarily due to self-shading and an increased proportion of structural components that do not produce energy. Among animals, the relationship between energy production and body size is less well understood. But in any case, net energy production among animals and plants is generally an increasing power function of body size with the power less than one (Sibly and Callow 1986).

Since all excess energy production is converted into growth by juvenile organisms, direct observations of growth show that most living organisms produce more energy as size increases, but that energy production does not increase linearly with body size. Instead, growth too is a power function of body size with a power of less than one. During the growth (juvenile) phase, animals generally grow allometrically such that

$$\frac{dW}{dT} = AW^b \tag{11.1}$$

where W is weight in kilograms, T is time, A is the growth coefficient with units in the reciprocal of time, and b is the allometric growth rate power. A variety of studies have suggested that b is about .75 for many animal groups (Case 1978; Lavigne 1982; Reiss 1989). This means that individual growth rates scale with the .75 power of body weight, and larger animals put on fewer grams of body weight per unit weight and time than do smaller animals. The growth coefficient is normally distinct for each phase of growth—that phase during which the organism is dependent on parental feeding (infancy), and the juvenile (postweaning) growth phase after independence from parental investment. Although almost all animal studies show b values between .65 and .85, the post-weaning values for A vary considerably across major phylogenetic groupings. Charnov (1993) has recently shown that while A is approximately 1.0 for most mammals, it can be estimated at only 0.42 for a sample of 72 primate species. This has a variety of implications for primate life histories, including the expectation that primates will have longer life spans and lower offspring production rates than other mammals of the same size (Charnov and Berrigan 1993). It also means that larger individuals produce more net surplus energy per unit time (that can be used for reproduction) than do smaller individuals. Since net energy can be converted to offspring, larger individuals should therefore be able to produce more offspring of a specified size than smaller individuals.

Using the discrete-time form of equation 11.1 we might expect that post-weaning Ache growth should conform to the equation

$$\frac{\Delta W}{\Delta T} = AW^{.75} \tag{11.2}$$

and thus body size at time x could be described by the recursion equation:

$$W_x = W_{x-1} + AW_{x-1}^{.75} \tag{11.3}$$

Figure 11.1 shows that Ache growth during childhood and early adolescence indeed fits this equation, with $A = 0.29$ for females and $A = 0.23$ for males, starting at 18 kg for six-year-old children. This is true despite the fact that Ache children are not truly controlling their own food intake rate after weaning because parents continue to provide food throughout childhood. The correlations between the body weights predicted by the equation and the observed mean body weights at each age are high for both sexes until the age at which some individuals begin to reproduce ($r = 0.996$, $p < 0.001$ for females from age 6 to 15 and $r = 0.987$, $p < 0.001$ for males from age 6 to age 18). The very low growth coefficients imply that the Ache should have even longer life spans for their body size than other primates (which is true). The low growth coefficients also imply that fertility rates should be extremely low for the Ache relative to other primates of the same size. This expectation is not supported, perhaps because of menopause (Hill 1993; also see Chapters 12 and 14 in this volume) or perhaps because the coefficient is determined by parental investment in offspring growth rather than a body size effect on net energy production.

Determinate Growth

Mammals, like many other organisms, are characterized by a pattern of determinate growth. Surplus energy (the difference between energy intake and respiration) harvested by mammals is converted into growth until sexual maturity, and then growth ceases and surplus energy is converted into reproduction. Figure 11.1 shows that the Ache grow at a constant and allometric rate until around the age of sexual maturation and then cease growth. Indeed, the growth equation fits the Ache extremely well until age fifteen for females and age eighteen for males. After that, growth of Ache adolescents tapers off and then ceases. These data represent the growth trajectory for the Ache as a population, however. The growth trajectories of single individuals show a much more abrupt halt in growth that is often linked closely to reproduction among females (Figure 11.2). Indeed the small sample that we have suggests little or no increase in body size after first birth for Ache women (Figures 11.2, 11.3, and 11.15). Since the Ache use no contraception, girls who reach the age where energy is shunted from growth to reproductive function should show a nearly simultaneous cessation of growth and beginning of reproduction (with perhaps a short lag). If girls in a cohort are approximately the same size and growing at the same rate, those who become reproductive first should end up smallest and those who reproduce later should be larger in adulthood. The view of determinate growth also predicts that size differences between women as adults should be approximately constant through time, and they should be related to the age at which those women became reproductive if childhood growth rates were not too different. This general view is consistent with available Ache data (Figure 11.3).

Women in modern societies also show determinate growth despite the fact that they may delay reproduction for many years. This suggests that humans are programmed to shunt energy from growth to reproductive function at a particular age regardless of whether offspring are actually produced at that age. Most of that extra energy would normally be used in pregnancy and lactation. Women in societies with artificial contraception probably store some of the extra energy designated for reproduction as fat until they begin to produce offspring. This may partially explain why weight gain continues past adolescence in modern societies but not among women in traditional societies (see Figure 7.3).

OPTIMAL AGE AT FIRST REPRODUCTION

The Problem

When should human females begin to reproduce, given the fitness costs (e.g., lower probability of surviving to each subsequent age) and likely benefits (e.g., greater energy production and stores, more experience) of delayed reproduction? The data suggest that humans show the typical mammalian pattern of determinate growth. Energy is used for growth during the juvenile period. At maturity, humans experience a switch point beyond which body physiological mechanisms cease promoting growth and allow (or channel) the use of surplus energy for reproduction and reproductive functions. At what age should women experience this switch?

The age at maturity is usually measured as the age of first reproduction in most organisms and is referred to as α in life history literature. Natural selection can presumably act on the growth-reproduction switch point in order to produce earlier or later ages of α (and larger or smaller adult body size). If reproductive value at some age is assumed to be proportional to size at that age, then optimal age of α can be conceptualized as a trade-off between survivorship and growth (Figure 11.4, following the logic of Roff 1986, Kozlowski and Wiegert 1987, and Charnov 1989). As individuals grow they increase in body size with a resultant greater net energy production which can be channeled into fertility or survivorship. But each time unit of delay before the onset of reproduction decreases the chances of surviving to reproductive age. Following Charnov (1989), if we estimate fitness as lifetime reproductive success in a stationary population, note that

$$R_0 = \Sigma \, l_x m_x \tag{11.4}$$

which can be simplified to

$$R_0 = l_\alpha V_\alpha \tag{11.5}$$

where l_α is the probability of surviving to maturity, and V_α is the reproductive value at maturity. If V_α is proportional to W_α (weight at age α), then R_0 is maximized when

$$\frac{-\mathrm{d}\log l_\alpha}{\mathrm{d}\alpha} = \frac{\mathrm{d}\log W_\alpha}{\mathrm{d}\alpha} \tag{11.6}$$

The optimal solution for age of first birth is shown in Figure 11.4. The solution is at the point where the proportional gain in body weight is balanced by the proportional loss in survival (or the instantaneous mortality rate). This model is a useful conceptualization of the survival-growth trade-off faced by living organisms. For most organisms, more biologically realistic models can be developed that measure fitness as the population growth exponent (r), and also measure the impact of body size on fertility or mortality rather than simply assuming that V_α proportional to W_α (see Chapter 6 in Stearns 1992; Chapter 7 in Roff 1992). Empirical data from the reservation period provide all the parameters necessary to develop and test a biologically realistic model of the optimal timing of first birth for Ache women (see below). We develop a simple model of age at sexual maturity in order to illustrate the power of the life history approach to explain rather than simply describe life history traits. The model assumes that the benefit from later reproduction is increased body size, which results in increased fertility, and that the costs of later reproduction are reduced survivorship to reproductive age, a shorter reproductive span, and a longer generation time. These assumptions are all supported with empirical data.

Methods of Analysis

Many estimates of fitness can be used to evaluate genetic or phenotypic alternatives of living organisms. When populations are growing, and fertility and mortality rates are density-independent, the best measure of fitness is probably r, the intrinsic population growth rate associated with a particular gene or trait (Charlesworth 1980). Although r can be solved analytically only when fertility and mortality can be described as functions, it is relatively easy to solve by iteration, if the life history associated with each trait can be specified precisely. Thus, if the fertility and mortality schedules associated with alternative traits (ages of maturity) are known, we can calculate the fitness value of each trait using the Lotka equation (Lotka 1907) and solving for r:

$$1 = \sum_{x=0}^{\infty} l_x m_x e^{-r(x+1)} \tag{11.7}$$

where l_x is the probability of survival from birth to age x, and m_x is the number of same-sex offspring produced at age x.

The Ache data suggest that we can predict Ache adult body size as a function of age at maturity from the allometric growth equation. Thus, for example, if Ache women kept growing until age nineteen, before shunting energy to reproduction, the allometric growth equation predicts that on average they would weigh about 77.5 kg as adults. If on the other hand they switch to reproduction at age twelve they should weigh only 38 kg as adults (see Figure 11.1). Thus, by empirically estimating the impact of increased body weight on reproductive value at maturity we can assess the expected fitness that would be achieved if females began reproducing at a variety of different ages. Analyses presented in Chapter 10 suggest that female body weight primarily affects fertility rather than adult or offspring survival among the Ache. If we assume that body weight affects only fertility, we can estimate the expected genetic contribution of Ache women as a function of different ages at first birth, α by using the following equation:

$$1 = l_\alpha \sum_{y=\alpha}^{\infty} \frac{l_y}{l_\alpha} m_y(W_\alpha) e^{-r(y-x+1)} \tag{11.8}$$

where l_α is survival from birth to age of maturity, l_y is survival from birth to age y, and $m_y(W_\alpha)$ is one-half of the expected fertility at age y as a function of body size at maturity, W_α. The sum term is the reproductive value of an individual at maturity given that maturity takes place at age α. Note that both juvenile survival and fertility are functions of α, the age at first reproduction. By estimating the relationship between m_y and W_α we can simply plug in the appropriate birth and survival rates associated with different values of α and solve for r in order to determine exactly what age of maturity will lead to the highest fitness.

We already have shown in the previous chapter that m_y is indeed a function of female body weight with a positive overall slope (Table 10.5), but here we need a good estimate of the actual shape of this relationship in order to solve for the optimal age at maturity among the Ache during the reservations period. Theory and logic suggest that the function relating fertility to weight should be positive, perhaps negatively accelerated, and monotonic. Thus, we first determine whether the relationship fits best as a linear equation or some other positive function with a decreasing slope. This can be accomplished using logistic regression. Note that the estimate must be derived from the fertility of *parous* women as a function of weight. The model assesses alternative phenotypic options by specifying an age at cessation of growth followed by reproduction. We wish to estimate the subsequent fertility consequences of that particular age at maturity (and associated adult body weight). Thus the appropriate shape of the fertility curve after the specified age at first birth will be that of parous women, which shows much less of an initial incline with age than does the populationwide fertility curve that includes in the risk set nulliparous women who have not stopped growing (see Figure 10.7).

In order to determine the expected fertility of Ache women as a function of body weight after they begin reproducing, we developed a logistic regression model that examines the hazard of live birth by age and weight for parous women. All women who had experienced a live birth after 1977 are in the risk set, and the risk interval is three months. The results of the logistic regression are shown in Table 11.1. In order to isolate the effects of weight on fertility we compared a basic model incorporating the three variables: (1) "age," (2) "age squared," and (3) "previous child dead" (to control reproductive state) with three models that included a woman's weight as an additional independent variable. Weight was entered alone, with a weight squared term, and (4) as a log transformed variable in order to allow for the possibility of a nonlinear but monotonically increasing relationship with fertility. Addition of the weight terms to all three fertility models resulted in significant model improvement, but the model with log transformed weight produces the greatest improvement in significance of the base model ($p < 0.03$ for model improvement with log weight as an independent variable). The outcome from the logistic regression allows us to estimate age-specific fertility as a function of body weight for parous women as:

$$\log \frac{m_y}{1 - m_y} = I + \beta_1(\text{age}) + \beta_2(\text{age}^2)$$

$$+ \beta_3(\text{prevoffdead}) + \beta_4(\ln \text{weight}) \qquad (11.9)$$

where the intercept and the coefficients are determined from the regression (Table 11.1) and all terms except the age and weight terms are constants set to the sample average ($K = I + \beta_3 \text{ prevoffdead} = -12.11 + 0.698 \times 0.176$). Thus, to estimate age-specific fertility at each age greater than or equal to α as a function of body weight we have:[1]

$$m_y = \frac{1}{1 + e^{-(K + \beta_1 \text{age} + \beta_2 \text{age}^2 + \beta_4 \ln W_\alpha)}} \qquad (11.10)$$

where W_α, the weight achieved by first reproduction and assumed throughout the adult lifespan, is calculated using equation 11.3 and starting with a weight of 18 kg at six years of age and a growth coefficient of 0.29/year. The values of β_1, β_2, and β_4 are taken from Table 11.1.

The logistic regression shows that fertility does increase with body weight among parous Ache women, and the relationship is monotonically increasing and almost linear across the observed weight range (see below and Figure 11.11). Since fertility increases with body weight, we can conclude that Ache women do indeed face a trade-off between the demographic advantages of early reproduction (longer reproductive span, higher survival to reproductive age, shorter generation time) and the demographic advantages of later reproduction (larger body size leading to higher fertility).

A Biologically Realistic Model of Optimal Age
of First Birth for Ache Women

In this section we develop a model of age at sexual maturity during the reservation period that takes into account decreasing survival and reproductive span, as well as increasing generation time, as costs of later reproduction. Increased fertility with body size is the only advantage of maturational delay in our model. We have assumed that the timing of reproductive senescence (menopause) is an independent life history trait that does not covary with age of first birth or adult body size. Thus, all women in the model are characterized by declining fertility and reproductive cessation by age fifty. The assumption of a fixed age at menopause regardless of age at first reproduction or body size cannot be verified with Ache data since we cannot assign ages with the necessary accuracy to women who have already reached menopause. Nevertheless, many other studies in natural fertility populations suggest no relationship between age at last birth (or menopause) and age at first birth or menarche (Borgerhoff Mulder 1989a and references therein).

Although these assumptions are straightforward, we must also decide how growth, age, and fertility are related. The logic of the model suggests that energy is shunted from growth to reproductive function at some point in time. We therefore assume that females cease growth at a particular age and can give birth the following year (the delay is the necessary gestation period). If fertility is assumed to be a simple function of age and weight, we can easily illustrate the model trade-off as shown in Figure 11.5. Estimating fertility directly from equation 11.10 thus provides us with a simple, testable model of optimal age at first birth (model 1). However, equation 11.10 is likely to provide a biased estimate of fertility at very young ages. We have shown in the previous chapter that elapsed time since previous birth has a strong impact on fertility among all women. It is also likely that time since previous birth is not distributed randomly with respect to age in the sample used to provide the values for equation 11.10. Instead, very young women in the sample, if they are parous, have usually only recently given birth and will therefore be more likely to be characterized by short time since last birth.

Because the logistic regression (Table 11.1) used to estimate the impact of weight on fertility (eq. 11.10) does not control for time since last birth, an upward initial slope of the age-specific fertility curve of parous women (see Figure 11.5) may be an artifact of this sample bias. It would be most useful to know what the age-specific fertility curve looks like for women who begin reproduction at age thirteen, fourteen, fifteen, and so on in order to model the consequences of first reproduction at those same ages, but our sample sizes are much to small for such analyses. Instead, we must determine whether fertility really does increase between ages fifteen and twenty-five for parous women when the time since last birth is controlled. A logistic regression on the hazard of conception of parous women that controls for time since last birth suggests no relationship at all between fertility and age between fifteen and twenty-five for these women.[2] Our data therefore suggest that peak age-specific fecundity is achieved as soon as women experience their first birth! This assumption is incorporated below into model 2.

Both models we examine allow body weight to influence age-specific fertility according to equation 11.7. The first model assumes that fertility is a probabilistic function of age and body weight following the end of the growth period (illustrated in Figure 11.5). The second model assumes that fertility is constant from the year following growth cessation to age twenty-five (similar to Figure 10.7) and determined by weight as shown in equation 11.7. From age twenty-five onward in model 2 fertility is equivalent to that shown in model 1.

The empirical estimation of all the relevant parameters described above using data on reservation-living Ache allows us to test our optimality model of the timing of first birth. The age-specific fertility values from equation 11.10 (as specified by models 1 and 2) are substituted into equation 11.8. Using Ache life tables to calculate juvenile survival and estimating the adult mortality rate at about 0.5% per year (see Chapter 6), we can solve for r as a function of various ages at first reproduction using an iterative goal-seeking function. This was done in MS Excel using the specified life table as the input, with the solution to the Lotka equation set to a goal value of 1 and r as the parameter that was allowed to vary. Figure 11.6 shows the instantaneous yearly growth rate that will be achieved by Ache women who begin reproducing between fourteen and twenty-three years of age according to the outcome of the two models. An example of the calculation for women who begin reproduction at age sixteen and assuming model 1 fertility is shown in Table 11.2.

One of the models seems to capture the essence of the maturational trade-off remarkably well. Model 1 predicts an age of first reproduction of nineteen years, about 1.5 years too late. A variety of other models (not shown) that differ only in the shape of the age-specific fertility curve give optimal ages of first birth between about seventeen and twenty. Model 2 results in an optimal age of first birth at eighteen years; the actual Ache mean is close to 17.5 years. This model also predicts cessation of growth at a body size of 63 kg, somewhat higher than the observed mean for newly parous women who have reached adult size in the past fifteen years (mean = 56.7 kg, s.e. = 1.0 kg, n = 46). This difference may be due to the fact that the model allows maximum growth until the year before first birth whereas actual growth slows 2–3 years before first birth among Ache women. If we use the upper and lower 95% confidence intervals from the logistic regression to estimate the impact of body size on fertility, the optimal ages of first birth from model 2 range from twelve to twenty-four. Thus, high confidence in the model can only be achieved with a tighter estimate of the effect of weight on age-specific fertility rates.

The optimal age of maturity in the models we developed is not sensitive to small changes in adult mortality rate. Values across a tenfold range (0.1% to 1%), encompassing most published estimates of adult mortality in traditional human populations, always lead to the same optimal ages at first reproduction shown in Figure 11.6. This is because the major cost of delayed reproduction in the model is a 5–7% decrease in lifetime total fertility by shortening the reproductive span one year with each year delay. This reduction is offset by about an 8% increase in weight each year, which impacts fertility positively. Adult mortality in the range around 1% adds very little to the cost of delay each year. Values of mortality outside the human range do, however, change the optimal solution. For example, assuming a chimpanzeelike adult mortality rate of 7% per year leads to a predicted optimal age of growth cessation of about fourteen years (using model 2), which is close to the age of first reproduction actually observed in wild chimpanzees (Goodall 1986).

Further Tests of Model Implications

The general model of age at maturation suggests that this parameter should be sensitive to growth rates. This feature of the model is important since demographers have clearly demonstrated a secular trend in age at maturity around the world, and the trend is believed to be primarily the result of improved nutrition (e.g., Chowdhury et al. 1977; Foster et al. 1986; Riley et al. 1993). Stearns and Koella (1986) have previously suggested that the age of maturity for human females should be characterized by a genetic reaction norm. This means that the observed phenotype for the trait should depend on an environmental characteristic and that natural selection should produce a "response pattern" which is adaptive rather than a single optimal phenotype. Stearns and Koella (1986) developed a simple model similar to that presented here but with some additional assumptions (growth rate was allowed to affect juvenile survival) and showed that the model could predict the secular trend in age of menarche observed in Europe during the past two centuries reasonably well. Their model suggested that modern women should reach menarche at earlier ages, but at larger body sizes, than women in previous centuries, who experienced slow growth due to nutritional stress.

The model we present above allows for two additional tests of its utility, one intragroup comparison and one cross-cultural comparison. First, according to the model, girls who grow faster should reach sexual maturity at earlier ages. This is because the proportional gain in fertility becomes smaller as women become larger and is ultimately balanced by reproductive losses from expected offspring mortality and from a decreasing reproductive span. Since we have body weight data for a variety of girls during the early years of our study period who were later observed to mature and give birth, we can test the proposition that fast-growing girls mature earlier.

Table 11.3 shows a logistic regression of the age-specific hazard of menarche and first birth as a function of the body weight of an Ache girl compared with the mean weight of girls at the same age. Mean body weights at each age are shown in Figure 11.1. The difference between the average weight for a particular age and that observed for any particular girl was calculated in units of one standard deviation for 64 girls between the ages of seven and thirteen. Most girls were weighed 2–5 times, and the average of the difference between their weight and the population mean weight (in standard deviation units) was used as the independent variable. The relationship between weight during childhood and the probability of reaching menarche at each age is positive but not significant, probably because of the small sample size. This analysis shows that fast-growing girls are also characterized by a higher probability of first birth for each year they are at risk. Time-to-event (Kaplan-Meier) analysis shows that heavier-than-average Ache girls reach both menarche and first birth at earlier ages than their lighter peers (Figure 11.7).

Second, we can apply our most successful model (model 2) to other human groups with different growth rates in order to see whether the model is appropriately sensitive to growth rate in its prediction of optimal age at first birth. Inappropriate sensitivity would be indicated by large variation in optimal age of first birth with only small changes in the growth rate or, conversely, no change at all in the optimal age of first birth across a wide spectrum of observed growth rates. We have chosen the !Kung for comparison since good anthropometric data exist as well as good records of age at first birth (Howell 1979:128, 195). We also examine the model's predictions about sexual maturity in modern America, where growth rates are the highest ever reported for any human population.

Figures 11.8 and 11.9 show the !Kung and American growth equations and their fit to the observed body weight data for females in each population. The !Kung grow much slower than the Ache, whereas (white) American girls grow slightly faster (cf. Figure 11.1). At age ten, !Kung girls weigh only 19.5 kg on average, whereas Ache girls weigh 27.6 kg and white American girls weigh 35.1 kg on average. When body weights for each group are plugged into equation 11.7 and the fertility assumptions of model 2 are used, we find that the model does a reasonably good job of predicting changes in age of sexual maturity (Figure 11.10). The results are summarized in Table 11.4. The faster growth rate of American women does lead to an earlier optimal age of first birth, and the slower growth rate of the !Kung leads to a later optimal age at first birth. The predicted age of first birth for American women cannot be tested directly because white American women generally use contraception and abstinence to avoid pregnancy during teen years. The prediction is congruent, however, with early age of menarche for American girls. The fit for the !Kung, however, is quite remarkable. Indeed the prediction of age at first birth for the !Kung matches the observed modal age (19 years) exactly. The model also does a reasonably good job of predicting adult body size differences in the three groups, and the age at which growth ceases. Because the optimality analysis results in a very flat curve describing the relationship between age at maturity and fitness, however, we should be cautious about our enthusiasm for the results. The analyses suggest that significant errors in age at first birth (such as five years too old or too young) will result in only about a 15% difference in number of descendants produced over one generation. Why the fitness curve is so flat, and whether an optimal reaction norm could evolve with such low selection coefficients favoring the optimum, needs to be examined more fully.

The success of the model suggests that much of the logic incorporated may be correct, even though some details may be incorrect and further modifications may be necessary. The success is also quite surprising given that the model assumes that the relationship between body size and fertility is the same for all three groups of women. This indicates that further research is appropriate in order to examine the fertility assumptions of models 1 and 2 as well as the relationship between weight and fertility among parous women in other natural fertility populations.

Sexual Dimorphism in Body Size

The model we presented above suggests that three factors most strongly affect the optimal age at first reproduction in traditional natural fertility populations: the growth rate, the length of the reproductive span, and the shape of the fertility × body weight function. Charnov (1993:109–112) has shown that differences between the sexes in one or more of these factors could explain observed sexual dimorphism in body size as well as the observation that males generally reach sexual maturity at a later age than females. In particular Charnov (1983) has shown that only very slight differences in the effect of body size on fertility are needed in order for selection to favor considerable sexual dimorphism in size. If males can gain slightly more fertility than females with larger body size it will often pay for them to have a slightly longer growth period than females, thus reaching sexual maturity at a later age and also attaining larger body size.

We can easily build a model of timing of sexual maturity and cessation of growth for males similar to that developed above for females. First we use logistic regression to establish the age-specific fertility curve of fully adult males and determine the effect of body size on male fertility. We have already established that body weight is positively associated with male fertility (see Table 10.6). Here we wish only to examine the shape of the association and determine whether the relationship is linear or nonlinear. However, males, unlike females, may expend considerable reproductive effort attempting to obtain copulations even when they produce no offspring. Thus, for males, the initiation of reproductive effort is not necessarily signaled by first birth (analogous to the sample of parous women above). But Ache growth data suggest that very few males gain any significant weight after age twenty-one (see Figure 7.4); thus we assume that most males have begun energetic investment in reproduction by that age, and the logistic regression sample includes only men aged twenty-one and older.

The results of three logistic regressions are shown in Table 11.5. The best-fit model is a second-degree polynomial regression by age and age squared, which also includes weight and weight squared terms as independent variables. The analyses suggest a stronger effect of body size on male fertility than we found on female fertility across much of the male weight distribution, but a negative relationship between weight and male fertility near the high end of the male weight distribution (Figure 11.11). The lower fertility of exceptionally large males is curious, but it may reflect a size effect on hunting returns. Although large men may be at an advantage in intrasexual competition, as hunters they are not as effective as intermediate-sized males (Figure 11.12) and they consume more energy, thus possibly leaving less energy for reproduction. In any case there is a sixfold range of age-controlled fertility as a function of male body weight, but less than a twofold range of fertility across female body weights. Thus, the effect of male body weight on fertility is much greater than the effect of female body weight on fertility, one of the requirements we mentioned above for the evolution of sexual dimorphism in body size.

An optimality model of male age at sexual maturation was developed by assuming that, prior to maturation, growth follows the allometric growth equation for males shown in Figure 11.1. The effect of body weight on male fertility is estimated using the logistic regression shown in Table 11.5, and the mortality schedule followed Table 6.4 with adult mortality set at 0.5% until age forty and doubling every ten years thereafter (see Figure 6.19). Fertility from age at first birth to age twenty-five was assumed to be constant and a function of body weight (as was assumed for females above), whereas subsequent fertility values were determined directly from the second-order logistic regression in Table 11.5. Male fertility was assumed to be zero after age sixty. In essence, then, the model is identical to model 2 for females except that male growth rates, male mortality rates, and male age- and weight-specific fertility values were used. In this case we solve for optimal *size* at maturation rather than age at first birth, since males who begin energy investment in reproduction will not always produce an offspring. The results of the model (Figure 11.13) are in rough agreement with observed body sizes for Ache men. According to the model, optimal body size is around 65 kg and males should stop growing around age nineteen. Observations on Ache men who matured during the reservation period show modal adult body size (for all men >21 years old) is about 60 kg (s.e. = 0.41, n = 178) and growth cessation takes place at about eighteen years of age (Figure 11.1).

The male and female models thus predict later age of maturity for males, and a body weight dimorphism ratio of 1.03 (male weight/female weight). Figure 11.14 shows the observed frequency distribution of body weights for all adult males and females during the reservation period. The ratio of mean male to mean female body weight is 1.11. The lack of agreement is primarily due to our incorrect prediction of female body weight and the fact that males grow slower than females. Why the male growth coefficient is only 0.23/year but the female coefficient is 0.29/year is a very important question that must be addressed in order to produce a complete explanation of body size dimorphism. Note also that the fitness curve for males is much more peaked, suggesting stronger selection against suboptimal body size than is the case for females. This leads to an expectation that there should be less variation in male body weight than female body weight despite the fact that females are smaller and variance in many biological traits is often related to size. This expectation of lower variance in body weight among males is clearly met for the Ache. The range of female weights (Figure 11.14) is much greater than the observed spread for male weights; in fact, adult females were both the lightest and heaviest individuals in our sample of adult body weights.

The body size and sexual maturity models also allow for some speculation. The Ache *fitness curve* as a function of male body weight decreases sharply after about 65 kg primarily because the curve relating *fertility* to body weight also shows a sharp decrease at about the same place. As we mentioned earlier, this may be due to the negative relationship between hunting returns and body size for large men, which we believe is related to the difficulties large individuals have with mobility in dense tropical forest. In any case, the shape of the curve relating body size to fertility among males should differ across human populations. This suggests that we might expect to find some differences in sexual dimorphism between human populations experiencing different ecological constraints. In particular, we would like to know whether tropical forest groups are generally characterized by lower sexual dimorphism than other groups, because the costs of mobility for large males may quickly override any advantages of larger body size in the context of intrasexual competition. For example, the male to female body size ratio among the !Kung is 1.20 (Lee 1979:285), higher than for the Ache despite the fact that the !Kung are smaller, and sexual dimorphism usually increases with body size among primates (Sailer et al. 1985) and across human populations (Wolfe and Gray 1982:212–213).

Despite these tantalizing results, we should be cautious in accepting adaptationist arguments for apparent variation in body size sexual dimorphism between human populations. The most thorough study to date of worldwide body size dimorphism in humans concluded that all observed variation might simply be due to sampling error (Gaulin and Boster 1985), and at least one theoretical study has suggested that body size dimorphism may evolve very slowly (Rogers and Mukherjee 1991). The models developed in this chapter, however, suggest that variation in the degree of sexual dimorphism across human populations might be adaptive as long as sex-specific growth rates vary, the relationship between weight and fertility varies, the length of the male reproductive span varies, or sex-specific adult mortality rates are highly disparate. Since we believe that some of these conditions are likely to be met in the sample of human populations currently and recently observed by anthropologists, we tentatively reject the conclusion that body size dimorphism is expected to be (or known to be) uniform among human populations. Of course none of our work addresses whether or not appropriate genetic systems exist to produce the reaction norms we suggest here.

SUMMARY

In this chapter we examine why the Ache begin reproduction when they do, and the related question about why they are the size that they are. A life history trade-off model is developed following the logic of many previous studies on plants, invertebrates, fish, and even mammals. The model assumes that since growth takes time and organisms are constantly at risk of death, selection can only favor an extended period of growth when important fitness gains are associated with body size. Most studies suggest that those gains are increased fertility and/or increased survival. Our empirical data show that larger body size is associated with higher fertility for Ache men and women. An optimization model was developed to examine the trade-off between decreased survival and reproductive span vs. increased fertility as a function of body size. The most successful variant of the model for females assumes that women give birth with some probability that is proportional to body weight every year after the year in which they cease growth. It further assumes that age-specific fertility is constant in the early years of a woman's life after she reaches maturity but declines steadily in the later reproductive span, terminating at age fifty.

The model we developed predicts an optimal age of first birth that is only one year older than the observed modal age at first reproduction. The same model also successfully predicts age at first birth for !Kung foragers, who grow more slowly. According to the model, (white) American women are expected to cease growth earlier than the Ache or !Kung and yet attain an equal or larger adult body size. These two expectations are met, but we cannot test the prediction about age of first birth directly (because American women use artificial means of avoiding conception). These predictions, while relying on formal mathematical modeling, are consistent with observed secular trends in maturation around the world that are thought to be due to nutritional changes.

The same logic used to develop quantitative models of the optimal timing of sexual maturity can be used to explain why Ache males are larger than Ache females. A model analogous to the one developed for females predicts that Ache males should grow two years longer and attain greater body size than females. This is because the effect of body size on fertility is greater for males, and because males have a longer reproductive span over which to exploit the fertility gains of increased body size. Indeed, the model for Ache males would predict much larger body size still were it not for the fact that the relationship between body size and fertility among males begins to decrease at high weights, and growth beyond some point is apparently disadvantageous.

In our optimality model of the timing of maturity (actually the optimal age for cessation of growth), some problems remain. This is true, even if we assume that the model is approximately correct and that the parameters have been accurately determined. First, despite the fact that we have established the relationship between size and fertility using logistic regression, we must explain the character of that relationship in order to have a complete explanation of why the Ache reach maturity at a particular age. Why is the relationship between size and fertility positive and close to linear for females, but declining at greater weights for males? Why isn't the slope steeper, or shallower? Second, why do the Ache grow according to the allometric equations shown in Figure 11.1? Why do humans grow so slow when faster growth rates would increase fitness and seem possible, judging from the adolescent growth spurt? Why do Ache males grow slower than Ache females?

We should also consider whether we have incorrectly measured some Ache parameters, or omitted significant fitness costs and benefits from the model. First, why is there no apparent relationship between female body weight and infant survival among the Ache? Just such a relationship is commonly observed in human populations and can shift the optimal age of first birth in the direction of later maturity. Finally, is there a relationship between age at first birth and subsequent adult survival or reproductive span? Such interactions are not included in the model, and we could find no evidence for them among the Ache, but our data may not be sufficient for detecting small effects of this type. Would such interactions change the optimal timing of maturity?

We are particularly concerned with two additional measures. First, we expect that the relationship between body weight and fertility among women should show diminishing returns, yet we found a linear association in our data. Had the relationship been concave, as we expected, earlier ages at maturity would be favored. Second, the allometric growth function does not accurately describe the growth trajectory of women who fail to reproduce between ages fifteen and twenty-five. Instead, late-reproducing women show dramatically slowed growth during this period (Figure 11.15). This may be due to the fact that their bodies have made the switch from allocating energy for growth to allocating energy for reproductive function, but we are concerned that the allometric growth equation might describe growth that would not be possible even if women delayed maturity for several years. Although cross-species studies may show a positive relationship between net energy production and body size, it seems likely that the ecological niche will ultimately limit the ability to harvest greater energy with greater body size. When metabolic demands equal the energy that can be extracted from the environment, an individual should cease growth, and this cutoff should be specific to the feeding ecology of the organism. If we assumed a slower growth rate after age fifteen in our models we would again find an earlier optimal age at maturity for Ache women.

Finally, there is good reason to believe that humans (and other organisms) can benefit in other ways from delayed reproduction. Many birds achieve full adult body weight several years before they begin to reproduce. Reproduction is probably delayed because other advantages can be accrued by waiting. One such advantage is experience. If humans could achieve full adult body weight at an earlier age, but not have sufficient experience for successful reproduction until a later age, our model would not adequately capture the life history trade-off. Perhaps alternative models that allow for the effects of age and learning on reproduction will be more useful and will be able to explain at least in part why humans and other primates grow so slowly (cf. Janson and Van Schaik 1993).

The most important contribution of this chapter is to point out the utility of life history theory for explaining demographic trends and observed human phenotypic variation. Studies that show proximate relationships between timing of maturity and some socioenvironmental factor may be useful but can never be considered explanatory. The fact that SES, for example, can be shown to correlate with age at menarche in some society, or across societies, does not constitute an *explanation* for the variation in age at menarche. It is simply a redescription of variation in timing of menarche showing its association with an independent variable. An explanation requires knowing why the observed association between the dependent and independent variable(s) exists, and why it takes the form that it does and not some other shape or slope. We have tried to show that demographic variables can be explained by using biological models and, more specifically, by recourse to functional explanations derived from evolutionary theory. Indeed, in the example given above, it is only by showing the relationship between SES, the age of menarche, and associated fitness outcomes that we can claim to have an explanation rather than a description of that relationship.

Regardless of the answers to the questions listed above, our aim has been to demonstrate the utility of life history theory to issues about the timing of maturity and adult body size. Indeed, to our knowledge, no other explanatory theory exists for explaining variation in these traits. In the next two chapters we examine other life history models that, although not as successful, also seem to provide explanations rather than descriptions of demographic parameters.

NOTES

1.   The logistic regression model of the fertility hazard was performed on a data set coded in three-month intervals. In order to convert these probabilities into yearly intervals we assumed that no more than one child could be born per year; thus the fertility hazard of a twelve-month interval (m_{12}) is equal to the 1 minus the product of the probabilities of not giving birth in each three-month interval, or $m_{12} = 1 - (1 - m_3)^4$.

2. A logistic regression on the quarterly hazard of live birth, controlling for time since last birth, was carried out on data from all parous women between the ages of fifteen and twenty-five. The variables in the base model are "time since last birth" and the squared term of the time variable. A model including age as the third independent variable increased the -2 log likelihood by only 0.282, which, with 1 degree of freedom, means a model improvement probability of approximately $p = 0.84$. The parameter estimate for the age variable was -0.0230, suggesting a slightly negative (if any) relationship between age and fertility. Thus, women in their teen years are not less fertile than women in their early twenties if they are parous, and if time since last birth is controlled.

Table 11.1. The Relationship between Weight and Fertility for Parous Women during the Reservation Period

Left panel

Independent variable	Cases	Mean	Parameter estimate	Partial p
Control				
age	3750	32	0.3322	0.0001
(age)2	3750	1097	−0.00643	0.0001
offsp. dead	3750	0.176	0.6538	0.0001
	−2 log likelihood for model covariates **105.181**			
model df	**3**			p **0.0001**
Model 2				
age	3750	32	0.3342	0.0001
(age)2	3750	1097	−0.0064	0.0001
offsp. dead	3750	0.176	0.6991	0.0001
Weight	3750	53.48	0.0701	0.646
(Weight)2	3750	2883	−0.0004	0.773
				model improvement p **0.097**
	−2 log likelihood for model covariates **109.874**			
model df	**5**			

Right panel

Independent variable	Cases	Mean	Parameter estimate	Partial p
Model 1				
age	3750	32	0.3346	0.0001
(age)2	3750	1097	−0.00641	0.0001
offsp. dead	3750	0.176	0.6954	0.0001
Weight	3750	53.48	0.0261	0.0309
				model improvement p **0.034**
	−2 log likelihood for model covariates **109.79**			
model df	**4**			p **0.0001**
Model 3				
age	3750	32	0.3344	0.0001
(age)2	3750	1097	−0.0064	0.0001
offsp. dead	3750	0.176	0.6978	0.0001
ln Weight	3750	3.975	1.4365	0.308
				model improvement p **0.032**
	−2 log likelihood for model covariates **109.85**			
model df	**4**			

Table 11.2.   Calculations of *r* When Growth Ceases at Age 16 (body weight = 57.87 kg) and Reproduction Starts at Age 17 According to Model 1 Fertility

Alpha age	l_x	m_x	$r = 0.03911$ $\exp[-r(x+1)]$	product $l_x m_x \exp[-r(x+1)]$
14	0.6852	0.0000	0.3779	0.0000
15	0.6817	0.0000	0.3542	0.0000
16	0.6783	0.0000	0.3320	0.0000
17	0.6750	0.1565	0.3111	0.0657
18	0.6716	0.1705	0.2916	0.0668
19	0.6682	0.1835	0.2733	0.0670
20	0.6649	0.1954	0.2561	0.0665
21	0.6616	0.2057	0.2400	0.0653
22	0.6583	0.2145	0.2249	0.0635
23	0.6550	0.2215	0.2108	0.0612
24	0.6517	0.2266	0.1976	0.0583
25	0.6485	0.2298	0.1852	0.0552
26	0.6453	0.2310	0.1735	0.0517
27	0.6420	0.2303	0.1626	0.0481
28	0.6388	0.2276	0.1524	0.0443
29	0.6357	0.2229	0.1428	0.0405
30	0.6325	0.2164	0.1339	0.0366
31	0.6293	0.2081	0.1255	0.0329
32	0.6262	0.1981	0.1176	0.0292
33	0.6231	0.1866	0.1102	0.0256
34	0.6200	0.1739	0.1033	0.0223
35	0.6169	0.1601	0.0968	0.0191
36	0.6138	0.1456	0.0907	0.0162
37	0.6107	0.1306	0.0850	0.0136
38	0.6077	0.1157	0.0797	0.0112
39	0.6047	0.1010	0.0747	0.0091
40	0.6016	0.0869	0.0700	0.0073
41	0.5986	0.0737	0.0656	0.0058
42	0.5956	0.0616	0.0615	0.0045
43	0.5927	0.0507	0.0576	0.0035
44	0.5897	0.0411	0.0540	0.0026
45	0.5868	0.0329	0.0506	0.0020
46	0.5839	0.0259	0.0474	0.0014
47	0.5809	0.0201	0.0444	0.0010
48	0.5780	0.0154	0.0416	0.0007
49	0.5752	0.0116	0.0390	0.0005
50	0.5723	0.0000	0.0366	0.0000
V_O				0.9999

Table 11.3. The Relationship between Weight during Childhood (standardized residuals from the age-specific mean) for Ache Girls (age 7–13) and the Age-specific Hazard of Menarche or First Birth

Independent variable	Cases	Mean	Parameter estimate	Partial p
Menarche				
age	282	11.6	1.1639	0.0001
Weight AVSDDIF*	282	0.012	0.3666	0.14
	change in −2 log likelihood			model
	for model with AVSDDIF			improvement
	2.188			p
model df	1			**0.19**

Independent variable	Cases	Mean	Parameter estimate	Partial p
First birth				
age	396	12.77	0.5938	0.0001
Weight AVSDDIF*	396	−0.011	0.6374	0.011
	change in −2 log likelihood			model
	for model with AVSDDIF			improvement
	6.784			p
model df	1			**0.009**

* Average difference between a girl's weight at age x and the population mean weight at age x, measured in units of standard deviation of the age-specific weight.

Table 11.4. Life History Trait Predictions Using Optimization Modeling (described in text) and Observed Values for Relevant Life History Traits from Three Populations

Women	Model predictions			Observed			
	Age cease growth	Age first birth	Adult body weight	Age cease growth*	Modal age first birth	Modal age menarche	Mean adult body weight
Ache	17	18	63.9	15	17	13	56.7†
!Kung	18	19	38.6	20	19	17	42.5
White American	15	16	62.9	14	**	12	62.1

Sources: Frisancho 1990:165; Howell 1979:128, 178, 195; Eveleth and Tanner 1976)
* Visual estimate from Figures 11.1 and 11.8
** Not relevant since these women avoid conception by using contraceptives or sexual abstinence.
† Mean weight of women who have reached adulthood in past 15 years.

Table 11.5. The Relationship between Weight and Fertility for Ache Men 21 Years and Older on Reservations

Independent variable	Cases	Mean	Parameter estimate	Partial p
Control				
age	2892	33.3	0.22	0.0032
(age)²	2892	1178	−0.00383	0.0006
	−2 log likelihood for model covariates			
	34.677			
model df	2			p 0.0001
Model 2				
age	2892	33.3	0.1946	0.0093
(age)²	2892	1178	−0.00344	0.0021
Weight	2892	60.35	0.4851	0.0408
(Weight)²	2892	3363	−0.00367	0.0547
	−2 log likelihood for model covariates			model improvement
	44.242			
model df	4			p **0.008**

Independent variable	Cases	Mean	Parameter estimate	Partial p
Model 1				
age	2892	33.3	0.2041	0.0063
(age)²	2892	1178	−0.00357	0.0014
Weight	2892	6035	0.0308	0.0198
	−2 log likelihood for model covariates			model improvement
	40.71			
model df	3		p 0.0001	p **0.016**
Model 3				
age	2892	33.3	0.2024	0.0068
(age)²	2892	1178	−0.00354	0.0016
ln Weight	2892	4.097	1.9897	0.0146
	−2 log likelihood for model covariates			model improvement
	40.692			
model df	3			p **0.016**

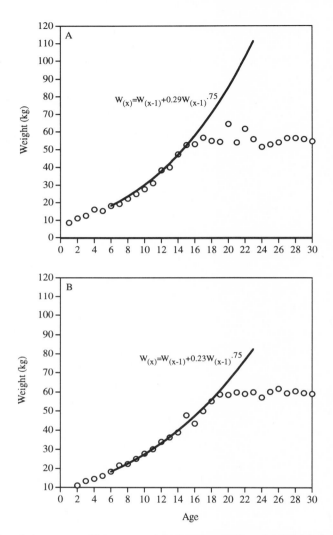

Figure 11.1.   Ache age-specific mean weight between 1980 and 1993 (circles) for females (A) and males (B) and the predicted weight from the allometric growth
equation using the best-fitted growth coefficient. Note the abrupt halt in growth
around age fifteen for females and age eighteen for males.

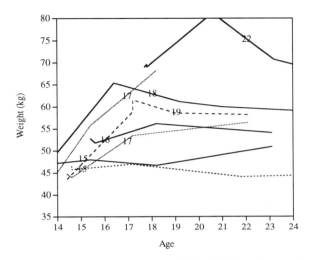

Figure 11.2. Longitudinal weight data from 1978–1993 for eight Ache women who experienced a first birth during that time. At age fourteen all women were nulliparous and weighed between 43 and 49 kg. The number on each line shows the age at first birth for each woman. Total growth and mean adult body weight are clearly related to age at first birth, and little or no weight gain is evident after first birth.

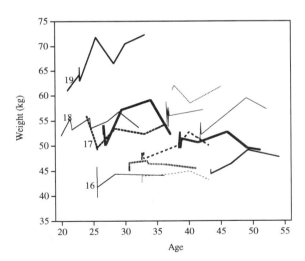

Figure 11.3. Longitudinal weight data for thirteen Ache women between 1978 and 1993. Age at first birth is shown (number next to the line) for the four youngest women. Note that adult weights vary much less through time for individual women than between them, and that adult weight appears strongly related to age at first birth. Heavy women in this sample were always heavy during the fifteen-year sample span, and light women were always light.

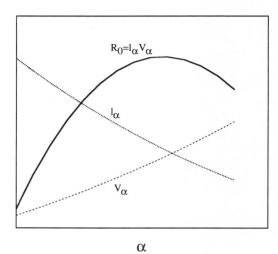

α

Figure 11.4. A conceptual model of the optimal age at first birth (α) when fitness is measured as lifetime reproductive success (R_0) and energy is diverted from growth to reproduction at maturity (after Charnov 1989). The product of survival to maturity (l_α) and reproductive value at maturity (V_α) defines R_0. The maximum value for R_0 is reached when $-d \log l_\alpha / d\alpha = d \log V_\alpha / d\alpha$. If we assume that V_α is proportional to weight at maturity ($V_\alpha = kW_\alpha$), the optimal age at first reproduction is the point at which the proportional yearly weight gain (growth rate divided by size) is exactly matched by proportional loss in survival (the mortality rate).

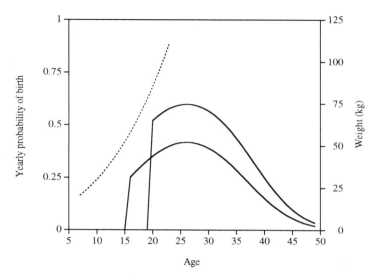

Figure 11.5. The expected weight of Ache women (dotted line) if they grow according to the allometric growth function in Figure 11.1, and the resultant age-specific fertility curves (solid lines) for women who cease growth and begin reproduction at age fifteen or age nineteen. The age-specific fertility curve is a function of body weight as determined empirically by logistic regression (Table 11.1). Ache data suggest that women who begin reproduction at age fifteen will end up smaller and have lower age-specific fertility throughout their lives than women who first reproduce at age nineteen.

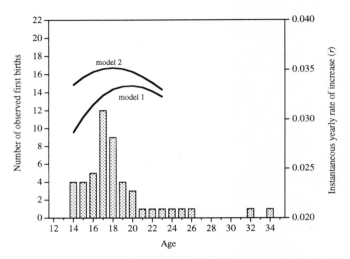

Figure 11.6.   Estimated fitness (*r*) from two models of age at first birth using Ache data, and the observed number of first births between 1978 and 1993. Both models assume age-specific fertility proportional to body weight, a fixed reproductive span, and a constant adult mortality hazard, but the two models differ in their early fertility assumptions (see text).

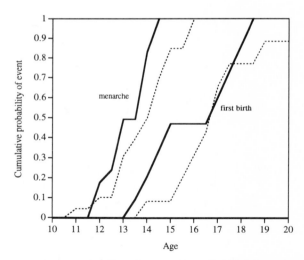

Figure 11.7.   Cumulative probability of menarche or first birth by a given age for Ache women who were on average heavier (solid lines) or lighter (dashed lines) than the mean observed weight for their age as measured when they were between seven and thirteen years of age. Women who were heavy for their age during childhood reach menarche and first birth at earlier ages (Table 11.3).

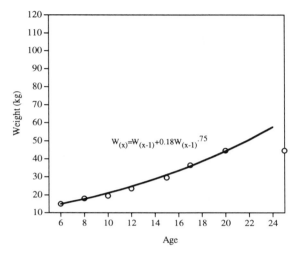

Figure 11.8. !Kung female body weight as predicted from the best-fitting allometric growth equation, and observed weights (from Howell 1979:195). Note that !Kung females grow much slower than Ache females (cf. Figure 11.1) and continue growing until a later age.

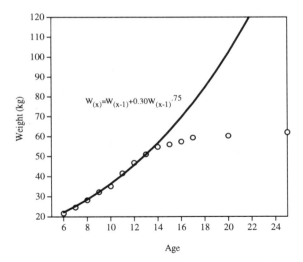

Figure 11.9. White American female body weight as predicted from the best-fitting allometric growth equation, and observed weights (from Frisancho 1990:165). Note that U.S. females grow faster than Ache females (cf. Figure 11.1) but cease growth at an earlier age.

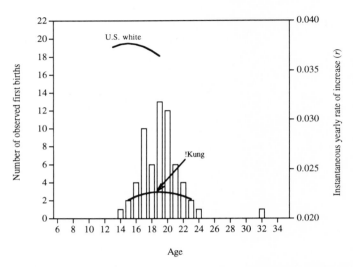

Figure 11.10. Estimated relative fitness (*r*) as a function of age at first birth using !Kung or U.S. growth data and assumptions from model 2 (see text). The observed frequency of first births among the !Kung (Howell 1979:128) is shown as a histogram. The model appropriately predicts earlier maturity for American women and later maturity for !Kung women, relative to Ache women.

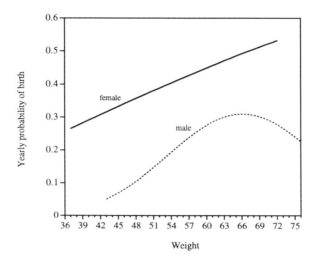

Figure 11.11. The relationship between body weight and fertility at age thirty for Ache men and parous women as determined by best-fitting logistic regression (Tables 11.1 and 11.5). Note that the relationship is much steeper for males over most of the weight range (only 6% of males weighed more than 67 kg). Overall higher fertility values for females come from a skewed adult sex ratio, asymmetrical outmarriage, and an age difference between spouses.

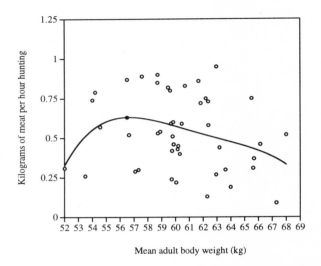

Figure 11.12. The relationship between body size and hunting return rate between 1980 and 1985 for forty-six adult men (polynomial smooth).

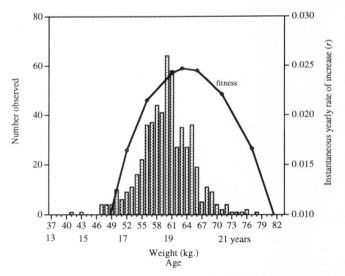

Figure 11.13. Predicted fitness (*r*) as a function of body size for males (solid line) using reservation data on growth rate, mortality, and the impact of body size on fertility. The *x*-axis also shows the age that corresponds to each body weight if growth follows the allometric equation shown for males in Figure 11.1. The histogram shows actual frequencies of body weights measured for Ache males who reached sexual maturity between 1978 and 1993. The model suggests males should stop growing between nineteen and twenty years of age near a body size of 65 kg.

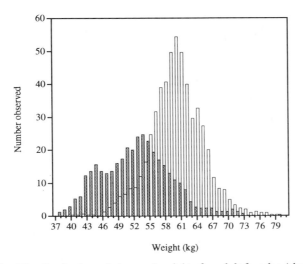

Figure 11.14. The distribution of observed weights for adult females (shaded bars) and adult males (open bars) between 1978 and 1993 (three-point moving average smooth). Males are heavier on average (mean = 59.95, *n* = 196) but show lower variance (s.d. = 5.3) than females (mean = 54.13, *n* = 171, s.d. = 7.3). Both the lightest and the heaviest individuals in the population were females.

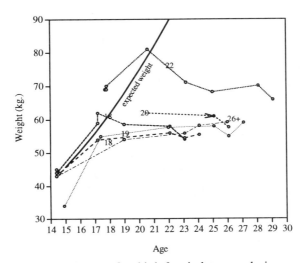

Figure 11.15. Weight and age at first birth for six late-reproducing women during the reservation period. The solid line shows expected weights if women continue to grow according to the growth equation used throughout this chapter until the year before their first birth. Although five of the six women were probably near the expected weight at age fifteen, only one continued to grow from age fifteen onward according to the determinate growth equation used in this chapter, and one has still not reproduced at age twenty-six despite cessation of growth.

An Ache woman with three children ages forty-seven months, twenty months, and two weeks in August of 1990. During the forest period all three of these children would have to be carried when the band moved camp. This woman is one of the young girls shown in the photograph before Chapter 11.

12

Life History Trade-offs and Phenotypic Correlations

In the previous chapter, we described how Ache women and men are faced with a trade-off between continued growth and reproduction. The solution to that trade-off determines the timing of sexual maturity and adult body size. Many other trade-offs are also common throughout the life course, and the Ache recognize some of these:

Women who reach menarche when they are small get old, we say. Those who reach menarche late are still new (young) maidens. The others have borne children and grow old, but those who reach menarche late are still new maidens (translated from an interview with Achipurangi in 1994).

The one who followed me [in birth order] was killed. It was a short birth spacing. My mother killed him because I was small. "You won't have enough milk for the older one," she was told. "You must feed the older one." Then she killed my brother, the one who was born after me (translated from an interview with Kuchingi in 1985).

Modern life history theory is based on the assumption that limited time, energy, and resources are available for expenditure. Resources expended on a particular life function cannot therefore be expended on an alternative function, and the entire life course is characterized by a sequence of allocation decisions that constitute life history trade-offs. Natural selection is expected to result in decision mechanisms to deal with these trade-offs. Such mechanisms should generally maximize contribution to the gene pool through optimal energy allocation to fertility and mortality. These evolved life history mechanisms may include DNA sequences that determine life history traits with little environmental input, or physiological design that is sensitive to environmental contingencies and a central nervous system that engages in conscious and unconscious decision-making about how to allocate resources through the life span. Many of the life history traits described in this chapter are considered to be the result of evolved reaction norms mediated through physiological or behavioral mechanisms rather than genetically based phenotypic differences. Reaction norms are genetically evolved response patterns that produce phenotypic variation keyed to relevant environmental variation. They result in adaptive life history variation in which the phenotypic variation itself has no genetic basis but is instead induced by key ecological variables.

Despite the fact that use of time and energy in mutually exclusive ways inevitably leads to life history trade-offs, our ability to measure such trade-offs in nature is extremely limited. This is because individuals vary considerably in their access to resources, body condition, access to stored resources, and ability to convert resources into offspring. Such variation will often result in positive phenotypic correlations, a situation in which higher apparent expenditure on one life history trait will be associated with higher apparent expenditure on another life history trait as well (see van Noordwijk and de Jong 1986). Since phenotypic correlations are likely to be common, life history trade-offs can only be detected with careful experimental manipulation or complex multivariate statistical analyses (cf. Bell and Koufopanou 1986; Pease and Bull 1988; Reznik 1985).

The difficulties of detecting life history trade-offs can be illustrated with a familiar example (van Noordwijk and de Jong 1986). People in modern societies face a trade-off in expenditure on housing vs. transportation. With the same money one can either buy a nicer house or a better automobile. It is difficult to demonstrate this trade-off with natural observations, however, because individuals with nice houses also tend to have more expensive automobiles. Thus the observed correlation between housing and automobile expenditure is often positive rather than negative. Such observations give the false impression that automobiles do not cost anything, since the ownership of an expensive vehicle does not seem to decrease the money that can be spent on housing. Only because most of us have experienced this trade-off are we not misled by the positive correlation.

We could, however, demonstrate that the house-automobile trade-off does indeed exist if we controlled levels of total resource availability experimentally, or manipulated some individuals of known income to induce them to spend more on housing than their equal-income peers do. We might also detect the trade-off if we analyzed the correlation between housing and automobile expenditures with multivariate statistics that controlled for the effect of differential income across individuals. These are precisely the types of tools available to biologists who wish to measure the true extent of life history trade-offs in living organisms. However, we must not be naive about the interpretation of results when such a complex set of interactions is expected. When both trade-offs and phenotypic correlations between life history traits are known to exist, the relationship between fertility and other life history components of fitness can be negative, neutral, or positive depending upon the relative strength of trade-offs vs. correlations and upon how well correlations are controlled for statistically.

THE COST OF REPRODUCTION

The principle of allocation suggests that individuals who engage in high reproductive expenditure at some point in time should have lower reproductive output or lower survival in subsequent time periods. The trade-off between current reproduction and future reproduction (including survival) is generally referred to as *the cost of reproduction*. In the disaggregated form of the reproductive value equation, this trade-off is nicely captured by the two terms that are summed on the right side of the equation:

$$V_x = m_x e^{-r} + \sum_{y=x+1}^{\infty} \frac{l_y}{l_x} m_y e^{-r(y-x+1)} \tag{12.1}$$

Resources can either be invested in fertility at age x, or in the residual reproductive value at that age, which is the sum of the product of future survivorship and fertility. The expenditure balance that maximizes genetic contribution should be favored by natural selection if variation in the mechanisms involved in the "decision" about the allocation are at least partially heritable.

Ache demographic data enable us to search for evidence of the cost of reproduction in a noncontracepting human population living under conditions that are likely to be similar to those under which fertility trade-off mechanisms evolved in humans. Unlike recent studies on the cost of reproduction in plants and nonhuman animals, however, studies of humans cannot involve experimental manipulations to increase or decrease their reproductive effort at convenient points in time. In their place, multivariate statistical modeling may be the best way to establish the character of reproductive trade-offs. The use of discrete-time hazards modeling is a critical analytical technique since it can incorporate the effects of time-varying covariates (previous reproductive output) in order to isolate the effect of concern (the impact on current survival and fertility). The ability of the logistic regression hazard model to incorporate a multitude of covariates is also important since the potential impact of resource access and resulting phenotypic correlations may be eliminated under some conditions.

Phenotypic Correlations

Phenotypic correlations between past fertility and current fertility or survivorship for Ache males and females during the forest and reservation periods are shown in Table 12.1. The probability of death or birth to an individual at risk are the dependent variables in the discrete-time logistic regression hazards models. Age is controlled in all models with a first- and second-order polynomial term. Factors known to have a strong effect on the reservation conception hazard and also likely to be related to previous fertility are statistically controlled in the model of female fertility on reservations. Independent variables for all models are (1) age at first birth; (2) number of live births experienced (or produced) up to the beginning of the risk interval; (3) percent offspring survival prior to the risk interval; and (4) number of living offspring at the commencement of the risk interval. These independent variables should enable us to determine whether men or women with high reproductive output or offspring survival in the past, or high numbers of currently surviving offspring, show higher or lower age-specific fertility and survival than their peers in subsequent time intervals. In other words, does natural variation in the population birth and death rates demonstrate a trade-off between past reproductive effort and subsequent reproductive value, or is there a phenotypic correlation between life history traits?

The results of the analysis (Table 12.1) show little effect of fertility on subsequent survival of Ache adults. For both sexes individuals with higher early fertility rates show lower mortality rates (the negative sign for parameter estimates in the table), but p values do not render the results convincing. Only the relationship between male mortality and number of living offspring that a man has fathered approaches statistical significance. According to the Ache data, men with more living offspring may show lower adult mortality rates. This result has also been reported in at least two other human populations (Friedlander 1993; Johnson et al. 1994).

The relationship between past reproductive effort and current fertility is much stronger and more consistent across both sexes. Females and males with high previous fertility show significantly *higher* age-specific fertility in each interval at risk during the reservation period. The negative relationships between past fertility or percent child survival and current fertility found for females during the forest period are probably due to differences between women in reproductive state. Women who have just lost a child will show low offspring survival (and high fertility). The reservation analysis controls for this effect by including reproductive state in the model. During the forest period, females with high previous fertility also show lower current fertility, but this effect is probably due to the fact that women with high cumulative fertility for their age at the beginning of a risk interval have usually just given birth. Thus, they are unlikely to conceive in the subsequent interval since they have a nursing infant. This effect is statistically eliminated in the reservation sample by including "time since last birth" as a covariate. In the reservation sample women with high cumulative age-specific fertility are much more likely to conceive again than women with low cumulative fertility when duration since last birth and reproductive state are statistically controlled. Males in all time periods are characterized by a strong positive relationship between past and present fertility rate. Such heterogeneity in fertility has been reported in other traditional populations as well (e.g., Borgerhoff Mulder 1992b; Pennington and Harpending 1993).

The results also indicate a relationship between age at first birth and adult fertility. For both men and women, early age at first birth is associated with higher subsequent age-specific fertility (although the pattern for females on reservation settlements is not close to significant and may not support this generalization). This result is similar to that reported by Borgerhoff Mulder (1989b) for the Kipsigis of Kenya. Finally, with the exception of women in the forest period, the data also show a positive relationship between cumulative offspring survival and fertility rate. Both men and women on reservations and men in the forest with higher previous offspring survival rates show higher current fertility probabilities in the hazard models. All of these phenotypic correlations are most likely an indication of differential resource access whereby some individuals are able to both produce more offspring at all points in time and also invest more in each offspring to increase health and survivorship. Indeed the relationships between life history traits may provide a better indication of the impact of resources on these traits than do the crude measures of resource availability that we use in Chapter 10.

The Trade-off between Current and Future Fertility

In order to eliminate the phenotypic correlations caused by variation in resource access or individual condition we repeated the analysis in Table 12.1 but added control variables to our hazards models. The control variables for the forest period were female size rank, male hunting rank, and mean male body weight between 1977 and 1993 (which can be extrapolated back to the forest period, as discussed in Chapter 10). The reservation period control variables were mean female body weight, SES rank, attractiveness score, male SES, mean hunting return rate, and mean male body weight. These covariates are all manifest variables that indicate different aspects of differential resource access and were shown (or suspected) in Chapter 10 to impact on fertility rates (since none of the variables can be shown to affect adult mortality we did not repeat the mortality analyses described in the previous section). By controlling for such variables we expect to cancel out at least part of the individual differences in the population with regard to the latent variables of interest that would lead to phenotypic correlation. This should allow for a direct measure of the cost of reproduction in terms of future fertility. The results of these "resources-controlled" analyses are shown in Table 12.2. *The analyses provide no new evidence of a cost of reproduction* when resource access or body condition are partially controlled. Instead the results are virtually identical to those from statistical models that do not control for differential resource availability. In general, men and women with high previous fertility or offspring survival are found to have high fertility in current risk intervals. Both sexes show a negative relationship between age at first reproduction and subsequent age-specific fertility.

OFFSPRING NUMBER AND OFFSPRING FITNESS

Interbirth Interval and Child Survivorship

Several researchers have recently suggested that the major cost of high reproduction in humans may not be lower subsequent fertility or adult survivorship but
instead lower offspring quality. If this speculation is correct, natural selection
might still favor intermediate fertility levels when the costs of reproduction to
adults are negligible. In life history terms, the lack of a cost of reproduction
means that high fertility must lead to lowered offspring reproductive value in
order for the optimal fertility rate to be less than the maximum possible (Kaplan
et al. 1995). Empirical support for this proposition seems to be available from
only one human study, that of Blurton Jones (1986) on the !Kung. Following the
logic of Lack (1947) and Smith and Fretwell (1974), Blurton Jones assumed that
the major cost of high fertility was lowered investment in each offspring and
subsequently increased offspring mortality. If the effect of increased fertility on
child mortality were high enough it could cancel out any fitness benefits of higher
fertility. Over the long run, natural selection should produce fertility-regulating
mechanisms that result in intermediate levels of fertility. In the simplest version
of this model,

$$w = nl_\alpha \qquad\qquad\qquad (12.2)$$

where *w*, fitness, is estimated as the number of offspring born, *n*, times their
survival to maturity, l_α. Since l_α is assumed to be a monotonically increasing
function of parental investment, and parental investment per offspring is assumed
to be equal to total parental resources, *R*, divided by number of offspring *n*, logic
suggests that l_α should be a monotonically decreasing function of *n*. This means
that an intermediate value of *n* will often maximize *w*, and that the optimal value
for *n* is primarily determined by the shape of the relationship between fertility *(n)*
and offspring survival (l_α).

Using this logic, Blurton Jones (1986) attempted to fit a monotonically decreasing function to raw data on mortality and interbirth interval (IBI) for the
!Kung. His analyses shows that several monotonically decreasing functions do fit
the data in a statistically adequate fashion. Given the survival rates predicted by
his function with the best fit, !Kung women could maximize their rate of production of offspring who survive to adulthood by spacing their children about forty-
eight months apart. This prediction matches the observed modal interbirth
interval of the !Kung study population precisely. Nevertheless, a few problems
with the analyses should make us cautious about accepting its conclusions. First,
Blurton Jones did not measure the effect of IBI on mortality but rather on the
probability of "success" of a pair of siblings. "Success" was counted when two
adjacent siblings survived to age ten, and an interval was considered a failure if

one or both siblings died in childhood. This manner of estimating child survival by success rate of pairs causes statistical complications, and success rate should not be taken as a direct estimate of survival rate (Harpending 1994). Second, the sample used by Blurton Jones to establish the relationship between fertility and survival is very small, thus leading to extremely wide confidence intervals around the predicted survival for the fertility values, and the ability of the raw data to fit any of a wide variety of functions equally well. A simple second-order polynomial model, for example, fits better than the backload model used by Blurton Jones and predicts an optimal IBI of fifty-four months rather than forty-eight months.[1] Third, the backload model that is fit to the IBI-mortality data is specific to mongongo nut harvesting during only one season of the year. Many other San groups have similar interbirth intervals yet do not exploit mongongos. It seems that the model is far too specific to a small portion of the San economy to account for a generally long interbirth interval among many San groups in a variety of different ecological settings. Finally, the analysis does not adequately correct for likely phenotypic correlation (all bush-living women are assumed to have the same somatic and extrasomatic resource availability), and thus it is unclear whether a trade-off is really expected. These and other problems have led to recent debate about the meaning of the !Kung study results (see Harpending 1994, and Blurton Jones's 1994 reply). Although the Blurton Jones study represents the first application of life history theory to the problem human fertility, additional studies will be required on other groups to determine whether the trade-off between survival and fertility generally leads to a predicted optimal fertility rate that matches the empirically observed modal fertility rate.

Ache data allow for a test of the proposition that decreasing survival associated with increased fertility results in an intermediate fertility rate that will maximize the rate of production of surviving offspring. Under those conditions we might expect that the optimal fertility rate (or interbirth interval) should match that most commonly observed in the population. We examine this trade-off by estimating first the impact of parental investment in other siblings on juvenile mortality, and then the impact of the parental fertility rate itself on juvenile mortality. Table 12.3 shows the relationship between parental investment in competing siblings and juvenile mortality of Ache children. Table 12.4 shows the same relationship when total parental resources are controlled. Independent variables are the number of juvenile siblings (those less than ten years old and from the same mother), and percent survival of siblings born prior to the risk interval. Early childhood mortality in the forest is not associated with either independent variable, but reservation mortality data suggest that children whose previous siblings experienced low mortality rates are also *less* likely to die at any particular age. The statistical significance of this phenotypic correlation is removed when variation in parental resources is statistically controlled.

In contrast to the results for early childhood, late childhood mortality in the forest is indeed positively associated with the number of juvenile siblings at the time of the risk interval (too few deaths took place after age five at reservation settlements to do meaningful analyses of reservation data). The result is strengthened when variation in parental resources is controlled. This seems to indicate that older children who had more competing juvenile siblings in the forest suffered higher mortality than age-matched children with fewer competing juvenile sibs. The result is the only evidence of a life history trade-off in these analyses, and the remainder of the results show either a positive or no correlation between parental investment in competing siblings and the age-specific mortality rates of Ache children.

The relationship between offspring number and offspring fitness can be estimated more directly by measuring the impact of IBI on age-specific juvenile survival. Again, the effect of parental resources on child mortality rate can be partially controlled using multiple regression in order to minimize the effect of phenotypic correlations. Results of the analysis are shown in Table 12.5. First we examined the impact of the IBI on the mortality rate of the second sibling in a pair. Only data of children whose previously born sibling had survived to the risk interval are included in the analyses (i.e., replacement intervals are excluded from analysis). The data suggest a *positive* relationship between length of the IBI and infant mortality rate (age 0–1) in the raw data set, but this effect is eliminated when parental resources and mother's age are statistically controlled (Figure 12.1). Thus infants born after a long IBI show lower than average survival but are generally the offspring of parents with few resources or perhaps older women, who generally show longer interbirth intervals and higher offspring mortality (Chapter 10).

Mortality of children from age one to age four, on the other hand, is associated with the IBI to the previous sibling (a second-order term of IBI was not significant), and the relationship is monotonically negative, as predicted when there is a trade-off between offspring number and quality. The negative relationship between IBI and age-specific mortality remains the same regardless of whether or not parental resources are statistically controlled (Figure 12.2). Subsequent analysis also shows a borderline significant and positive interaction effect between IBI and age on the child mortality hazard.[2] This means that the effect of IBI on child mortality becomes less as children get older in the range from one to four years. Most of the effect of IBI on mortality takes place between one and two years of age (results not shown).

The relationship between age-specific mortality and IBI to the next born offspring is more complicated to analyze. Very few young children have experienced the birth of a subsequent sibling, thus sample size is quite small until ages of three years and greater. We carried out two analyses on reservation mortality data. First we examined the effect of the birth of the next sibling on the age-specific mortality probability for all Ache children between ages one and four. If parental investment in a new sibling increases the mortality rate for the previously born sibling, that effect should be detected in this analysis. Second, for all children who did indeed experience the birth of a sibling during the interval at risk, we analyzed the impact of the length of the IBI to the next sibling on the age-specific probability of death. Results suggest that IBI to the next born sibling has virtually no impact on age-specific mortality at any age from one to four years even when parental resource variation is statistically controlled (Table 12.5). Children in the risk set who do not yet have a next born sibling show the same age-specific mortality profile as those who do have a next born sibling during the risk interval. Of those who have experienced a next born sibling before the risk interval is complete, a shorter birth interval to the next sib is not associated with a higher mortality risk. Among the Ache children from five to fifteen years of age only nine deaths have taken place in the reservation period; thus we did not attempt statistical analyses of IBI on mortality at later ages. However, the mean IBI to next sib for the nine children who died in this age range was 34.7 months, close to the population average. Thus, there is no evidence suggesting that IBI to next sibling has any impact on the survival of Ache children during the reservation period.

Parental Fertility and Offspring Fertility

In many societies child survivorship is high and yet parents invest a good deal in their offspring. It seems likely that this investment is motivated by parental desire to affect the status, health, and overall quality of their children rather than simply ensure that they survive. Such parental behavior could evolve if investment produced significant gains in offspring fertility during adulthood. In order to investigate reproductive trade-offs fully, we need to consider the effect of parental fertility on offspring fertility. Specifically, we want to determine whether high parental fertility (or short IBI) will lead to offspring who survive but have low fertility during adulthood because of an inability to acquire a mate, poor health, limited access to resources, poor overall body condition, or for some other reason. The results from the previous chapter suggest that if parents produce poorly nourished children with slow growth rates, those children will begin reproduction at a later age and will have lower reproductive value at maturity then well-nourished, fast-growing children.

In order to examine the impact of parental reproductive decisions on offspring fertility we developed discrete-time logistic regression hazard models with age-specific fertility rate as the dependent variable and maternal or paternal completed family size as independent variables. Results (shown in Table 12.6) suggest no relationship between parental fertility and the age-specific fertility rates of females (Figure 12.3). Male fertility, however, is positively associated with paternal fertility even when parental resources are statistically controlled. Thus, instead of a trade-off, there is a positive correlation between parental and offspring fertility. The relationship between father-son fertility rates is indeed quite high. For example, the data indicate a 57% greater age-specific fertility during the forest period for an average-aged man whose father had produced eight children vs. a man whose father had produced only two offspring. Thus, in the Ache society, men who father more children also produce sons who father more children (Figure 12.3). Some of this effect appears to be due to the fact that brothers help each other (see next chapter).

Regardless of the reasons for the association between paternal and male adult fertility performance, the results of these analyses do not suggest any significant negative impact of parental fertility on the ability of children to produce offspring of their own. Offspring of parents who produced many children show fertility rates just as high as those of parents who produced few children (Figure 12.3). This is true even when parental resource differentials are partially controlled (Table 12.6).

A Model of Optimal Interbirth Interval

Demographic data and analyses described in this chapter enable us to develop a fitness maximization model of fertility (or IBI) using Ache data. The model is static, since it predicts only the optimal constant fertility rate throughout the reproductive span. In essence, then, we are modeling the optimal IBI for Ache women under population-average conditions. We ignore population growth and assume that the expected fitness of an individual at age x can be estimated as:

$$w_{x,1} = V_{x,1} V_{0,2} \tag{12.3}$$

where $w_{x,1}$ is the fitness of an individual at age x in generation 1, $V_{x,1}$ is that individual's reproductive value at age x and $V_{0,2}$ is the reproductive value at birth of that individual's offspring (born in generation 2). In English, then, the fitness of an individual making a fertility decision at age x in the first generation ($w_{x,1}$) is equal to the expected number of offspring that will be born in a lifetime as a consequence of that reproductive decision ($V_{x,1}$) times the reproductive value of those offspring ($V_{0,2}$) given the fertility decision that is made at time x. This equation is similar to equation 12.2 because both terms on the right-hand side of the equality are functions of the fertility rate chosen at time x (and all subsequent times in this static model). Given the possibility of a cost of reproduction, we could further disaggregate this equation as follows:

$$w_{x,1} = [m_{x,1} + V_{x+1,1}] V_{0,2} \tag{12.4}$$

This form of the equation allows the decision about current fertility to affect both future survival and fertility as well as offspring survival and fertility. We will use this form to model the optimal average fertility rate (1/IBI). Tables 12.1–12.6

provide detailed empirical estimates of the impact of current fertility on residual reproductive value as well as offspring reproductive value at birth.

Ache empirical results enable us to simplify the calculation of fitness as a function of fertility shown in equation 12.4. No impact of fertility on subsequent survival or fertility could be shown from Ache data (Tables 12.1 and 12.2). Thus both terms in the brackets of equation 12.4 are directly proportional to the fertility rate and the reciprocal of the interbirth interval chosen (m_x = 1/IBI). Ache data also suggest no impact of parental fertility on offspring fertility (Table 12.6); thus, the only component of $V_{0,2}$ affected by the parental fertility decision is the juvenile survival rate. Parental fertility was shown to affect juvenile survival, but only between the ages of one and four (Table 12.5 and Figure 12.2). This means that we can simplify the entire calculation to measure the rate of offspring production who survive to age five, as a function of different fertility rates (or IBIs). This is directly analogous to the approach used by Blurton Jones (1986) and described above.

Figure 12.4 shows the results of calculations of offspring production rates (who survive to age five) as a function of an average IBI achieved by fertility "decision" mechanisms during the reservation period. The figure also shows the expected survival rate of offspring as a function of parental fertility. The calculations are derived from the logistic regressions in Table 12.5 showing the relationship between IBI and previous born sibling and age-specific mortality rates when parental resources are controlled. The results clearly show that *the fitness-maximizing fertility rate in the Ache sample is the same as the maximum fertility rate observed during the sample period.* Despite the fact that offspring survival is higher at intermediate fertility rates, the extra offspring produced by achieving short IBIs more than compensate for the increased rate of loss of those offspring. There is no apparent optimal intermediate fertility rate given the conditions experienced by the average Ache adult living at current reservation settlements. The shortest IBIs (about fifteen months) observed during the sample period result in highest fitness. This is true even when the effects of parental resource access (SES, hunting return rate, body size) are partially controlled through multiple regression. The model is therefore unable to predict the modal interbirth interval correctly during the reservation period. This interval is about thirty months when the first child of the interval survives to the birth of the second (Figure 8.11).

COMPONENTS OF REPRODUCTIVE SUCCESS AND INTERGENERATIONAL CORRELATIONS

The fact that Ache adults seem to pay almost no costs of reproduction in our sample leads us to examine the relationship between fertility and Lifetime Repro-

ductive Success (LRS), and the correlation between parental and offspring reproductive success. Figure 12.5 shows the frequency distribution of LRS by birth
cohort and sex for Ache adults who complete their reproductive careers (i.e.,
survive to age fifty). Members of the first cohort were born between 1890 and
1909 and were at least sixty years old at contact, if they survived to that event.
The second cohort was born between 1910 and 1929, and members were at least
forty years old at contact. Members of the third cohort, born between 1930 and
1940, were actively reproducing during the contact and reservation periods. LRS
is measured as the number of offspring produced who survive to age fifteen for
early cohorts and the number of offspring produced who survive to age five in the
recent cohorts (very few Ache children die after age five during the reservation
period). The sample includes all Ache ever born who survive to age fifty. Reproductive data are complete for all cohorts since virtually no offspring who survived to age fifteen was likely to be missing from our data base (see Chapter 3).

Because only individuals who survived to age fifty are included here, we
eliminate the effects of juvenile and early to mid adult survivorship on LRS. We
can thus examine the variance in LRS for individuals who survived through most
or all of their reproductive span. Mean LRS in our sample is lower for males in
general because of the male-biased sex ratio in the adult age cohorts (there are on
average only .67 females per male in this adult sample). The recent cohort shows
lower LRS for both sexes than that of earlier cohorts primarily because members
of the recent cohort were in the middle of their reproductive span during the
contact period, when fertility was low and offspring mortality was extremely
high. The analyses show that male variation in reproductive success is much
greater than female variation, with coefficients of variation for males ranging
from 1.5 to 2.1 times as high as those for females. Since survival through the
reproductive span is also lower for males (Chapter 6), there must be considerably
more variance in the LRS of males who reach sexual maturity than for females
who survive to maturity.

Figure 12.6 shows the relationship between fertility and LRS for the three
cohorts defined above. Figure 12.7 shows the relationship between offspring
survival and LRS for individuals who produced at least one offspring. Individuals who produced no offspring cannot be assigned an offspring survivorship rate
and thus were eliminated from the second regression. The analysis shows that for
both sexes fertility is a much stronger predictor of LRS than is offspring survivorship rate. For women in particular, offspring survival rate may be a very poor
predictor of LRS. In our sample this appears to depend on whether we consider a
cohort that finished reproduction in the forest period or a cohort that experienced
part of the reproductive span after contact. Other studies of traditional populations have suggested that either fertility or offspring mortality variation can be
the most important determinant of LRS among women, depending on ecological
contexts (e.g., Borgerhoff Mulder 1987). Studies of mammals suggest that fertil-

ity variation is almost always the most important component of male LRS (Clutton-Brock 1988).

Ache data also allow us to examine intergenerational correlations in LRS between parents and offspring. Results, shown in Figure 12.8, suggest that male LRS is positively correlated with the LRS of both a man's mother and his father, whereas a female's LRS shows no relationship to that of her parents. This result is not unexpected since we have already shown a positive association between parental fertility and the fertility of adult Ache men but not women (Table 12.6, Figure 12.3).

Finally, it is important to demonstrate that higher fertility and LRS in a single generation also lead to higher fitness when measured across several generations. This will allow us to assess the value of LRS as a measure of fitness, and to examine long-term life history trade-offs. Since we have not been able to show any costs of reproduction that outweigh the benefits of an increased number of offspring, we expect to find a monotonically increasing relationship between fertility in a single generation and some measure of fitness taken over several generations. In order to test this hypothesis we measure long-term fitness of ego at some point in time as the sum of all direct descendants produced by an individual, with each multiplied times his or her reproductive value at that point in time and discounted according to his or her genetic coefficient of relatedness (Hamilton's r) to ego. Thus fitness is estimated as

$$w_x = \sum_{i=1}^{n} V_{y,i} r_i \tag{12.5}$$

where w_x is fitness of ego at x years after ego's birth, n is the total number of direct genetic descendants of ego, $V_{y,i}$ is the reproductive value of the ith descendant who is y years old at x years after ego's birth, and r_i is the genetic coefficient of relatedness between ego and the ith descendant ($r = 0.5$ for offspring, 0.25 for grandoffspring, etc.). This procedure essentially calculates the average number of gene copies of an individual found in all descendants when the value of each is calibrated to that of a newborn (because V_0 is generally 1). For the analysis we have chosen to estimate long-term fitness (w_x) for individuals at 70–75 years after birth, depending on the cohort. Reproductive value of each descendant is determined by his or her age and sex and can be calculated using formula 12.1 and tables in Chapters 6, 8, and 9, which show survival and fertility rates by age for men and women.

Reproductive value for men and women in the forest period and on reservations is shown in Figure 12.9. The growth rates of the population (r) during the forest and reservation periods are determined directly from census data in the master ID file. Since these growth rates are not exactly the same as those implied by the life tables, reproductive value at birth is slightly off from the expected value of 1. Note also that during both time periods males show lower reproductive value at birth than females. In the forest, this difference is primarily due to the high male-biased sex ratio at birth, resulting in a male-biased adult sex ratio and higher average female fertility. During the reservation period the higher female reproductive value at age 0 is due to the extreme bias in the adult sex ratio after contact (many more males survived—thus they show low average fertility) and the fact that many Northern Ache women were married to men in the other two Ache groups during this time period (hypergamy). The significance of a male-biased sex ratio at birth will be examined in the next chapter.

For the analyses of fertility and long-term fitness we sample all Ache men and women born between 1890 and 1917. Since we are interested in the impact of fertility decisions on long-term fitness, we include only individuals who survived to age fifty. In order to minimize cohort effects, but obtain a large enough sample of individuals who were born at least seventy years before our last complete year of data collection, we divided the sample into two cohorts, 1890–1900 and 1901–1917. The fitness of the first cohort is measured at seventy years of age, which occurs before first contact for all individuals in the sample. The analysis of the first cohort is therefore relevant to long-term life history trade-offs during the "stable" forest-living period. The fitness of the second cohort is measured at age seventy-five, which is reached *after* the contact period for all individuals in the sample. Thus long-term fitness for the later cohort includes all effects of the contact period and is therefore lower than fitness numbers measured for the first cohort.

The results (shown in Figures 12.10 and 12.11) suggest that higher fertility during one's own reproductive span does generally result in higher genetic contribution when measured over a long period of time (nearly two generations later). There is, however, an indication that females with exceptionally high fertility (more than eight or nine live births) may produce lower-quality descendants and ultimately achieve lower fitness than females with completed fertility around eight live births. There is no evidence of a long-term fitness cost to exceptionally high male fertility. For both sexes the relationship between LRS and long-term fitness is positive and monotonically increasing. In three of the four analyses the relationship between LRS and long-term fitness is close to linear, suggesting that LRS is a good biological measure of fitness (long-term genetic contribution) in our sample. In both cohorts (at seventy or seventy-five years after birth) about two-thirds of the value of the genetic contribution of individuals (i.e., the summed reproductive value discounted by genetic coefficient of relatedness) was present in the soma of their grandchildren, about one-fourth in their adult children, and a small fraction (about 7%) in their great-grandchildren.

Both males and females show an average increase from one to about eight genetic copy equivalents (age 0) of themselves during the 70-year forest period, and from 1 to about 5.3 genetic copies of themselves during the 75-year period that spanned the forest, contact, and reservation periods. Despite the fact that females surviving to age fifty seem to have higher LRS than males surviving to age fifty (Figure 12.5), the average long-term genetic contribution of individuals who survive to age fifty appears to be about the same for both sexes. Again, however, the range is slightly greater for males, with the most successful male producing twenty-two genetic copies of himself and the most successful female producing only about seventeen genetic copies of herself.

MEN AND WOMEN WITH HIGH REPRODUCTIVE SUCCESS

In order to provide more insight into the lives and kin of biologically successful men and women, we present short sketches of the two men and women in the population over age fifty with the highest lifetime reproductive success (defined as children who survive to age five). Names have been changed to maintain confidentiality for these individuals and their families.

Bejyvagi was seventy years old in 1994 and had produced thirteen children with four different women; ten of them survived to age five or greater. He had never been in a polygynous marriage for more than a few months, but instead produced children with three successive wives in his younger years and then remained with his final wife for the last thirty-three years, producing six more children. He raised one of his children from a previous marriage rather than allowing the child to stay with its mother after a divorce. He is a very mild mannered and timid man with a pleasant smile and a easy laugh. He is quick to flirt with women and once proposed marriage (in earnest) to an American woman visiting the Ache. He hunts well but was generally disinclined to participate in club fights and is not known to be particularly strong or brave. He is average height and weight for an Ache man. He lost one brother to a club fight and told us on several occasions that those who organized the club fights were "really stupid." He was among one of the last groups of Ache to leave the forest and has always been a "traditionalist." He is a very adept storyteller but is difficult as an informant because he tends to stray from the topic of inquiry. Two of his sons are very successful Ache schoolteachers and have completely given up the forest way of life. His daughters have fared less well, one in particular being very low status with a difficult time holding on to a mate. His mother was the sister of several of the politically most important men in the forest period, and he is related in some form to about one-quarter of the entire Northern Ache population. His father left his mother when he was a small child, and his five surviving siblings were all fathered by his stepfather, who was killed in a club fight. His only surviving brother has produced no offspring in his entire life and is considered to have a very unpleasant personality as well as being a poor hunter. His three sisters are all married to well-liked men, and he has generally resided near them until recently. Now he shares his house with one son and lives next to another. He and his wife both have severe tuberculosis, and his wife is nearly blind. He has lost nearly ten kilograms in the past seven years and is not important in Ache society either politically or socially. The lack of care given to him by his close family members is a scandal according to local gossip.

Jukugi is fifty-five years old and has produced thirteen children, nine of whom are still alive. His children come from two marriages. His first wife died at contact but he had already abandoned her in the forest with his four children from that marriage. The two older boys from that marriage were raised by unrelated Ache, whereas the youngest daughter died and the other daughter was sold to Paraguayans by an unrelated Ache. The two sons now live next to him. One is the chief of an Ache reservation and the other is widely recognized as the best Ache hunter. Both sons learned to hunt with other unrelated men, and we observed them at a very young age killing large game. Both are very committed to a forest lifestyle and are sometimes the object of derisive gossip because they seem to prefer the forest to the reservation (they are "backward savages"). The other nine children all have the same mother, a woman seventeen years his junior with whom Jukugi has remained for twenty-one years. He is a very dedicated father to his children from his current wife and has many young children, including a two-year-old. He is one of the few Ache men that we have ever seen cry. This happened one day when he came to tell us that one of his small children had died. Jukugi has a very mild mannered personality and is especially liked by most anthropologists who have worked with the Ache. He is not now, nor has he ever been, politically important. He was our primary informant for checking genealogical data in the 1980s, and he has an immense store of knowledge about Ache history and relationships. He is an average hunter, but not aggressive or known for strength. He is quite short and noticeably small; he weighs about 5 kg less than the average Ache man his age. His father was perhaps the most important "big man" in the forest period of the twentieth century and had sixteen children, three of whom live with the Ache and three of whom disappeared with Paraguayans at contact. His mother was the first wife in a polygynous marriage for about five years and then was abandoned by his father. He has one surviving maternal half brother, who he rarely sees now, and one of his sisters is Pirajugi, the woman eaten by the jaguar in the story that begins this book. He is in good health and is known as a hard worker who owns many domestic animals.

Byvangi is fifty-six years old and gave birth to nine children, seven of whom survived to at least five years of age. She is the wife of Bejyvagi (above), but her first three children were from a different husband. She is known as a hardworking person, but with a rather dull personality. She seems to us to be exceptionally dedicated to her children and will endure untold suffering and hunger to improve her children's lives. She has been nearly blind for many years and quite sick, but often gives food that is meant for her (support from anthropologists and missionaries) to her children instead. One full brother was one of the largest Ache men of the forest period and generally feared in club fights. Her mother asked to be buried alive with this son (Byvangi's brother) when he died at contact. That man's two surviving offspring are the heaviest woman in the population and one of the largest men. Byvangi's other full brother was only married for three years during the postcontact period and produced one offspring. Her half brother was eaten by a jaguar but produced three offspring before he died. Her father sired five children but was left behind during the forest period when he was unable to keep up with the band because of old age.

Piragi is seventy-eight years old and gave birth to seven children, all of whom survived to adulthood and four of whom are still alive as of the mid-1990s. All her children were produced with one husband, who went blind in the forest period but didn't die until contact. Her two oldest children died from fevers in the forest. She has a very outgoing personality with a good sense of humor, but her surviving children are much more reserved. She has dedicated the past fifteen years of her life to taking care of her grandchildren, and during the 1980s would often carry the heaviest of her daughter's young children while on forest treks. She currently lives with her last born child, a daughter, and is well fed but has difficulty getting around. Nevertheless, we observed her walking several kilometers to collect oranges in 1994. Older Ache men were still attempting to woo her into marriage as recently as ten years ago. Her mother and father were both killed by Paraguayans in a raid when she was a teenager. Two of her sisters (but no brothers) survived to adulthood. One sister was bitten by a snake and died in her early twenties and produced no surviving offspring. The other sister had ten children, five of whom survived to adulthood and were famous "Paraguayan killers" who went out of their way to seek revenge for past murders of Ache relatives.

SUMMARY

This chapter presents analyses designed to describe phenotypic correlations between life history traits and then measure trade-offs between traits. The expectation of trade-offs between alternative life history functions that require energy is now a basic premise of life history theory, and logically flows from the laws of conservation of matter and energy. Nevertheless, many biologists have pointed out the difficulties of adequately measuring life history trade-offs, and this study reaffirms their cautionary statements. We attempted to eliminate the effects of differential resource access that would lead to positive correlations between life history traits by using multiple regression analyses. Nevertheless, for the most part we were unsuccessful in demonstrating that life history trade-offs do exist (Table 12.7). Interpretation of forest fertility analysis is complicated because reproductive state and duration since last birth could not be controlled. Thus, high fertility or high juvenile survival automatically leads to subsequent fertility reduction in the risk units immediately following a live birth, which confounds any attempt to measure long-term consequences of high fertility. Thus, analysis of forest data simply reaffirm well-established short-term life history trade-offs—women who are pregnant cannot conceive again until they give birth, and women with small infants are unlikely to conceive. However, high reproductive rates by adults were found to have no negative impact on their subsequent survival or fertility during the reservation period. Instead, early fertility was positively correlated with subsequent fertility even when we controlled for socioeconomic status, body size, and hunting return rate, factors which themselves were all shown to be associated with differential fertility in the Ache population (Chapter 10).

Results also show that men or women who begin reproducing at an early age have higher than average age-specific fertility, and again this is true even controlling for variables indicating access to resources. This result seems contrary to the expectations derived in the previous chapter, where the model we developed suggests that unless individuals are resource privileged (and fast growing), those who begin reproduction at early ages should end up smaller and as a result show lower fertility rates than those who begin reproduction at later ages. Of course only by controlling for adolescent body size could we definitively reject the predictions from that model, and perhaps most Ache who begin reproduction early do so because they grow fast in childhood.

The search for trade-offs in offspring quantity and quality fared slightly better. Although Ache children with more competing juvenile siblings generally do not show lower survivorship (with the possible exception of children 5–9 years old in the forest period), we were able to show that short interbirth intervals are associated with a higher mortality rate of children between one and four years of age. The result, however, applies only to the birth interval between a child and his or her previously born sibling. The interval to next sibling apparently has no impact on child survivorship among the Ache. We found it curious that the effect of the interbirth interval (IBI) on mortality is not evident in the youngest age class (birth to one year). We suspect that mortality in that interval is primarily due to factors that affect the intrinsic viability of children in the first month after birth, generally from poor household hygiene. It is somewhat troublesome, however, that SES has an effect on infant mortality but not on later childhood mortality (Tables 10.2 and 10.3). This indicates that the cost of short IBIs to Ache children is not equivalent to an SES difference between families (i.e., the cost of a short IBI is apparently not simply a reduction in parental resources).

Our attempt to measure other costs of high parental fertility to their offspring also failed. Children of high fertility parents who survive to adulthood seem to have just as much success finding their own mates as do children of parents with lower fertility. Indeed, male children who come from a large sibship seem to have even higher fertility than males who grow up in smaller families. Thus, our data provide no support for the notion that Ache parents who raise many children produce lower-quality children than parents who limit their reproductive output.

All these tests enable us to develop an explicit optimization model of parental fertility. Results show that Ache women who attain maximum fertility rates observed during the reservation period can expect to achieve maximum fitness under current conditions. There is no support for the notion that the modal interbirth interval is also the one that will maximize fitness in this population.

Finally, the lack of measurable trade-offs between reproduction and other aspects of life history led us to examine correlations between life history components and across generations. Higher fertility leads to higher lifetime reproductive success for both sexes and during all time periods in the Ache sample. Variation in completed fertility accounts for a greater proportion of the variation in LRS than does offspring survivorship rate for either sex. Parental LRS is unrelated to LRS among females but is positively correlated with LRS among males. The relationship is particularly strong between the LRS of fathers and sons. A multigenerational assessment of fitness allows for greater confidence in some of our conclusions, but it also introduces some problems. Long-term fitness for individuals born early in this century is measured as the summed reproductive value of all descendants at a particular time after their birth devalued by their genetic coefficient of relatedness to those descendants. Long-term fitness correlates very well with lifetime reproductive success, but there are hints that it is not a simple linear function of completed fertility, especially among women. This is curious since the relationship between fertility and LRS is linear (Figure 12.6), and the relationship between LRS and long-term fitness is nearly linear in our sample (Figures 12.10 and 12.11).

Thus, this final, somewhat puzzling result is the only evidence we have that an intermediate level of fertility might possibly lead to higher fitness than would the maximum fertility rate observed. The only obvious difference between an analyses of long-term fitness by fertility and the sum of all the component analyses presented earlier in the chapter is that the effects of fertility on grandchildren's well-being are incorporated into the measure of long-term fitness (most long-term fitness in our analyses was tied up in the soma of grandoffspring). Although high adult fertility could affect not offspring fertility but the survival of grand-offspring, we are somewhat doubtful that this effect would be large. The impact of fertility on offspring survival is small in our sample, and analyses presented in the next chapter suggest that the impact of grandparental investment on the survival of their grandoffspring is even smaller.

The results presented here have many implications beyond the scope of this short summary. First, it will be noted by most biologists that many more collateral kin effects need to be measured when the impact of fertility on true biological fitness is being assessed for a social organism. Perhaps adults with high fertility rates are not able to provide much kin help to siblings, nieces, nephews, grandoffspring, etc., and thus leave fewer genetic descendants than those with more moderate fertility. Perhaps high-fertility individuals are a resource drain on other relatives who subsequently have lowered fertility. In a small-scale society like the Ache, with widespread resource sharing and lifetime residence with close kin, such a possibility cannot be discounted.

Indeed, the incorporation of kin selection logic provides one of the best explanations for why we cannot seem to measure life history trade-offs in our sample. If individuals who "overproduce" offspring are subsequently helped by close kin with few dependents of their own, we might not measure a "cost of reproduction" (to adults or offspring) even when differential resource access is controlled using the measures that we have available. More problematic still (and congruent with this idea) would be the possibility that individuals only achieve high fertility if they "know" they have other close kin they can count on to help out. According to this hypothesis, the number of close kin in combination with their own dependent load would be one of the best predictors of fertility variation in the population, and that fertility variation may not be associated with any obvious life history trade-offs. Testing such an idea with the Ache data base is possible but requires some complicated programming and clearly thought out hypotheses. We begin an exploration of kin helping on life history in the next chapter.

Another possible explanation for why we haven't been able to detect many life history trade-offs using the Ache data is simply that we do not have good measures of individuals' resource availability and are thus unable to remove the effects of phenotypic correlations. We consider this explanation possible but somewhat unlikely, particularly for the reservation period. Net worth interviews conducted in 1992 are very complete and in combination with hunting return rate data give us a very good idea of resource flow into Ache households resulting from their own productivity. Again, however, considerable kin help that would not show up as a form of resource access by either of our two best measures is still possible. Continued monitoring of Ache economic variation in the next few years should enable us to determine if measurement insensitivity is a major weakness in our analyses.

A third possibility is that intrinsic variation between individuals in their ability to use resources for reproduction confounds the patterns that would indicate trade-offs. This problem is best illustrated with a thought experiment. Imagine that fertility is a function of two factors, resources and efficiency. *High efficiency* is an unobservable quality that enables individuals with the same income to have more *usable* resources (because of better pathogen resistance, more effective biochemical pathways, etc.). When resource income is held constant, more efficient individuals would achieve higher fertility, perhaps because fewer of their resources would need to be committed to offspring in order to ensure their survival (and could thus be allocated to reproduction) or perhaps because fewer of their resources would need to be dedicated to somatic maintenance (fighting parasites and pathogens). Now imagine we carry out a multiple regression with offspring survival as the dependent variable and interbirth interval as well as some measure of resource income as independent variables (just as we did in this chapter). The multiple regression will estimate the coefficient of income on survival, with IBI held constant, and the coefficient of IBI on survival, with income held constant. It does not, however, control for inherent efficiency. Thus, individuals with the same income who show short IBIs are likely to be those with high intrinsic efficiency. The shorter IBI with income held constant will not be associated with lower offspring survival (as would be expected in the cost trade-off model) but instead may be associated with no difference in survival or even slightly higher survival. Under these conditions, regressions of survival by IBI with income (SES) held constant (like those carried out in this chapter) will not be adequate for measuring life history trade-offs. Only experimental manipulation of reproductive effort would allow for a true measure of life history trade-offs, the costs of reproduction, and the offspring quality vs. quantity trade-off (thanks to H. Kaplan for bringing this point to our attention).

A final possibility is that we detect no trade-offs between life history traits in the Ache population because none existed during the sample period. Many individuals have suggested that life history trade-offs might be expressed primarily during times of stress and resource shortage. Empirical support for such a position is growing (e.g., Haukioja and Hakala 1978; Tatar and Carey 1995; Tinbergen et al. 1985; Tutor 1962). Perhaps during periods of high growth and resource abundance, such as the forest and reservation periods for the Northern Ache, resources are abundant and kin support ubiquitous, leading to a situation where individuals suffer no serious demographic consequences of early or high fertility. During the period of horrendous population crash these trade-offs might be readily observed, but in this chapter we have eliminated the contact period from all analyses. Testing this hypothesis would be simple with Ache data but will have to await future analyses.

In light of these considerations we must be cautious about conclusions such as the one presented above concerning optimal interbirth intervals. Our analyses suggested that the impact of short interbirth intervals on offspring survival was minimal and as a consequence, a fifteen-month interbirth interval would apparently lead to maximum fitness. There is good reason, however, to doubt this conclusion. Consistent adherence to a fifteen-month IBI by a population of Ache would probably lead to an impossible dependency load of juveniles that could never be adequately provisioned. In the Ache population currently the average adult female age is about thirty years. A thirty-year-old woman reproducing at a fifteen-month birth interval who had her first child at age eighteen could expect to have produced children that (if all survived) would be 12, 11, 10, 8, 7, 6, 4, 3, 2, and <1 years old. Of these ten children about half would still be alive given observed mortality (Figure 12.4). Studies of the production and consumption of food by Ache children show that these children would require about 9,850 calories of food per day during the forest period (Kaplan 1994).[3] While it is possible that parents might provide that many calories on top of their own consumption at reservation settlements, we find it unlikely. During periods in the forest, when our observations show that males provide more than 80% of the food consumed, and the mean male foraging return rate is about 2,000 calories per hour, men would have to work about seven hours per day, every day, in order to feed this "average" size family of five surviving offspring. Men near the end of their reproductive careers (e.g., age fifty) would have to either work ten hours per day on food production or obtain help from kin with lower dependency ratios. Thus, one problem with our conclusion is that we have never observed any women who consistently give birth at fifteen-month intervals so we are unable to measure the true costs of such a fertility pattern.

The most important implication of these results is the realization that no current models that adequately *explain* fertility variation in traditional societies have withstood empirical scrutiny. Instead we have some good ideas derived from sound theoretical logic but not exactly supported with a strong body of data. Better resource access probably leads to higher fertility in traditional human populations (see Chapter 10), but what determines the precise fertility level achieved by physiological mechanisms or the conscious decision making (or both) in these groups? Many human evolutionary biologists have assumed that traditional fertility patterns make biological sense, and that intermediate fertility levels result from straightforward trade-offs described in the "costs of reproduction" and the "offspring number vs. offspring fitness" trade-off. While these ideas are grounded in solid theory that has been quite successful for nonhuman organisms, and we know of no alternative theory that can provide an ultimate explanation for the precise levels of fertility observed, the specific models derived from this theory should be examined much more carefully given the difficulties of empirically validating them.

The assumption that fertility variation in traditional societies conforms in a straightforward fashion to evolutionary predictions needs to be reexamined. The fertility reduction after the demographic transition to levels that clearly do not maximize fitness (e.g., Kaplan et al. 1995) may not be a unique historical phenomenon. Fertility levels lower than those that would apparently maximize long-term fitness may characterize some (many?) traditional societies as well as modern industrial societies. If this is true, considerable theoretical development will be required to make sense of human fertility patterns. The assumption that low fertility in modern societies is due to strange new factors never historically experienced by human populations is in our opinion premature. The Ache seem to have lower fertility than would maximize their long-term fitness, yet no current model can explain why this is so. Men and women in modern industrial societies are opting for lower fertility still, and no available model can yet explain these phenomena. The problem is clear, but the solution is likely to be complex (see Kaplan 1994; Kaplan et al. 1995). We hope that the failures in this chapter will stimulate further research into this topic.

NOTES

1. The best-fit logistic regression model of the mortality hazard as a function of the IBI using the Blurton Jones data (1986:Tab. 1) shows the following parameters: Intercept = 5.3834, IBI = −0.172, IBI squared = 0.0011. It results in a sum of squares deviation of predicted survival and observed survival of 0.222, better than the .324 sum of squares deviation from the backload model used by Blurton Jones (1986:Tab. 4). The second-order polynomial model predicts an optimal IBI of 54 months if IBI is allowed to vary continuously.

2. The parameter estimate for the effect of IBI on age-controlled mortality on reservation settlements is −0.1763. The interaction effect (IBI × age) when added to the model shows a parameter estimate of 0.0611 and a partial p value of .106.

3. From Kaplan 1994 (Tab. 1C, net calories produced per day by Ache children) we can estimate food needs of a twelve-year-old that must be supplied by an adult at about 2,000 calories/day; for ten- and eleven-year-old children the amount is the same. The food needs of eight-, seven-, and six-year-old children that must be supplied by adults are about 2,150 calories/day. The food needs of four- and three-year-old children are about 2,050 calories/day, and the food needs of the two-year-olds (and younger) would be about 1,100 calories/day. Since only half these children would be expected to survive, the total daily caloric requirement is 9,850.

Table 12.1. Phenotypic Correlations between Adult Life
            History Traits

Independent variable	Parameter estimate	p
Adult mortality hazard		
(females age 20–70, forest period)		
age	controlled	—
(age)^2	controlled	—
age at first birth	−0.0377	0.345
number of live births	−0.0857	0.274
percent offspring survival	−0.6984	0.370
number of living offspring	−0.0916	0.384
Adult mortality hazard		
(males age 20–70, forest period)		
age	controlled	—
(age)^2	controlled	—
age at first birth	0.0517	0.470
number of live births	−0.0726	0.106
percent offspring survival	−0.2983	0.810
number of living offspring	−0.1007	0.076
Yearly fertility hazard		
(females age 15–50, forest period)		
age	controlled	—
(age)^2	controlled	—
age at first birth	−0.0645	0.0001
number of live births	−0.0683	0.0660
percent offspring survival	−0.8840	0.0001
number of living offspring	−0.1320	0.0010
Quarterly conception hazard		
(females age 15–50, reservation period)		
age	controlled	—
(age)^2	controlled	—
time since last birth	controlled	—
(time since last birth)^2	controlled	—
nulliparous	controlled	—
previous child living	controlled	—
previous child dead	controlled	—
age at first birth	−0.0097	0.8400
number of live births	0.2861	0.0001
percent offspring survival	0.2770	0.0001
number of living offspring	0.2901	0.0001

Table 12.1. (*Continued*)

Independent variable	Parameter estimate	p
Semiannual fertility hazard (males age 15–60, forest period)		
age	controlled	—
$(age)^2$	controlled	—
age at first birth	−0.0501	0.0001
number of live births	0.0956	0.0010
percent offspring survival	0.0928	0.8500
number of living offspring	0.0892	0.0020
Semiannual fertility hazard (males age 15–60, reservation period)		
age	controlled	—
$(age)^2$	controlled	—
age at first birth	−0.0693	0.0001
number of live births	0.1841	0.0001
percent offspring survival	0.4597	0.0230
number of living offspring	0.2291	0.0001

The table shows the parameter estimate and *p* value for model improvement when a single specified variable is entered into a model with the specified control variables.

Table 12.2. The Costs of Reproduction

Independent variable	Parameter estimate	p
Yearly fertility hazard (females age 15–50, forest period)		
age	controlled	—
$(age)^2$	controlled	—
size rank	controlled	—
age at first birth	−0.0648	0.0001
number of live births	−0.0730	0.0480
percent offspring survival	−0.8725	0.0001
number of living offspring	−0.1357	0.0010

(*continued*)

Table 12.2.   (*continued*)

Independent variable	Parameter estimate	p
Quarterly conception hazard		
(females age 15–50, reservation period)		
age	controlled	—
(age)²	controlled	—
time since last birth	controlled	—
(time since last birth)²	controlled	—
nulliparous	controlled	—
previous child living	controlled	—
previous child dead	controlled	—
weight	controlled	—
SES	controlled	—
attractiveness rank	controlled	—
age at first birth	−0.0074	0.8720
number of live births	0.2937	0.0001
percent offspring survival	0.2637	0.0001
number of living offspring	0.2900	0.0001
Semiannual fertility hazard		
(males age 15–60, forest period)		
age	controlled	—
(age)²	controlled	—
hunting rank	controlled	—
weight	controlled	—
age at first birth	−0.0501	0.0001
number of live births	0.0912	0.0010
percent offspring survival	0.0640	0.8790
number of living offspring	0.0846	0.0040
Semiannual fertility hazard		
(males age 15–60, reservation period)		
age	controlled	—
(age)²	controlled	—
SES	controlled	—
hunting rate	controlled	—
weight	controlled	—
age at first birth	−0.0373	0.0670
number of live births	0.1284	0.0001
percent offspring survival	0.5280	0.0100
number of living offspring	0.1678	0.0001

The table shows the parameter estimate and *p* value for model improvement when a single specified variable is entered into a model with the specified control variables.

Table 12.3. Phenotypic Correlations between Offspring Quality and Quantity

Independent variable	Parameter estimate	p
Juvenile mortality hazard		
(children age 0–4, forest period)		
age	controlled	—
age²	controlled	—
sex	controlled	—
mother's age	controlled	—
mother's age²	controlled	—
number of sibs <10 years old	−0.0314	0.887
percent sibling survival	−0.1349	0.874
Juvenile mortality hazard		
(children age 5–9, forest period)		
age	controlled	—
age²	controlled	—
sex	controlled	—
mother's age	controlled	—
mother's age²	controlled	—
number of sibs <10 years old	0.2605	0.085
percent sibling survival	−0.5701	0.433
Juvenile mortality hazard		
(children age 0–4, reservation period)		
age	controlled	—
age²	controlled	—
sex	controlled	—
mother's age	controlled	—
mother's age²	controlled	—
number of sibs <10 years old	−0.0156	0.897
percent sibling survival	−0.7630	0.055

The table shows the parameter estimate and *p* value for model improvement when a single specified variable is entered into a model with the specified control variables.

Table 12.4. Trade-offs between Offspring Quality and Quantity with Resources Controlled

Independent variable	Parameter estimate	p
Juvenile mortality hazard		
(children age 0–4, forest period)		
age	controlled	—
age²	controlled	—
sex	controlled	—
mother's age	controlled	—
mother's age²	controlled	—
mother's size rank	controlled	—
father's hunting return rate	controlled	—
number of sibs <10 years old	−0.0334	0.885
percent sibling survival	−0.1414	0.872
Juvenile mortality hazard		
(children age 5–9, forest period)		
age	controlled	—
age²	controlled	—
sex	controlled	—
mother's age	controlled	—
mother's age²	controlled	—
mother's size rank	controlled	—
father's hunting return rate	controlled	—
number of sibs <10 years old	0.2858	0.059
percent sibling survival	−0.4433	0.828
Juvenile mortality hazard		
(children age 0–4, reservation period)		
age	controlled	—
age²	controlled	—
sex	controlled	—
mother's age	controlled	—
mother's age²	controlled	—
mother's weight	controlled	—
father's hunting rate	controlled	—
father's SES	controlled	—
number of sibs <10 years old	0.0286	0.885
percent sibling survival	−0.6184	0.188

The table shows the parameter estimate and *p* value for model improvement when a single specified variable is entered into a model with the specified control variables.

Table 12.5. The Relationship between Interbirth Interval
(IBI) and Offspring Mortality

Independent variable	Parameter estimate	p
Juvenile mortality hazard		
(children age 0, phenotypic correlation)		
IBI to previous sibling	0.0309	0.049
Juvenile mortality hazard		
(children age 1–4, phenotypic correlation)		
age	controlled	—
IBI to previous sibling	−0.0716	0.060
Juvenile mortality hazard		
(children age 1–4, phenotypic correlation)		
age	controlled	—
next sibling born	−0.4715	0.590
IBI to next sibling	−0.0515	0.852
Juvenile mortality hazard		
(children age 0, resources controlled)		
mother's weight	controlled	—
father's SES	controlled	—
father's hunting rate	controlled	—
mother's age	controlled	—
mother's age^2	controlled	—
IBI to previous sibling	0.00276	0.886
Juvenile mortality hazard		
(children age 1–4, resources controlled)		
mother's weight	controlled	—
father's SES	controlled	—
father's hunting rate	controlled	—
mother's age	controlled	—
mother's age^2	controlled	—
age	controlled	—
IBI to previous sibling	−0.0647	0.081

(*continued*)

Table 12.5. (*continued*)

Independent variable	Parameter estimate	p
Juvenile mortality hazard		
(children age 1–4, resources controlled)		
mother's weight	controlled	—
father's SES	controlled	—
father's hunting rate	controlled	—
mother's age	controlled	—
mother's age^2	controlled	—
age	controlled	—
next sibling born	−0.4152	0.643
IBI to next sibling	−0.1087	0.411

For the models with IBI to previous sib, all children who were conceived when the previously born sibling was alive are included in the risk set. For analyses on IBI to next sibling, "next sibling born" is scored 0 (no) or 1 (yes). IBI to next sibling is analyzed only for children whose following sibling has been born before the end of the risk interval. The table shows the parameter estimate and *p* value for model improvement when a single specified variable is entered into a model with the specified control variables.

Table 12.6. Phenotypic Correlations and Trade-offs between Parental Completed Family Size and Offspring Age-specific Fertility during the Reservation Period

Independent variable	Parameter estimate	p
Female fertility hazard		
age	controlled	—
(age)^2	controlled	—
mother's offspring born	−0.0137	0.810
father's offspring born	0.0121	0.802
Female fertility hazard (parental resources controlled)		
age	controlled	—
(age)^2	controlled	—
mother's size rank	controlled	—
father's hunting rank	controlled	—
mother's offspring born	−0.0130	0.821
father's offspring born	0.1635	0.858
Male fertility hazard		
age	controlled	—
(age)^2	controlled	—
mother's offspring born	0.0205	0.463
father's offspring born	0.0637	0.000
Male fertility hazard (parental resources controlled)		
age	controlled	—
(age)^2	controlled	—
mother's size rank	controlled	—
father's hunting rank	controlled	—
mother's offspring born	0.0166	0.510
father's offspring born	0.0646	0.000

The table shows the parameter estimate and *p* value for model improvement when a single specified variable is entered into a model with the specified control variables.

Table 12.7.   Summary of Trade-offs between Reproductive Effort and Other Life History Variables for Ache Women

Independent variable	Dependent variable	Effect	p	Sample
Reproductive value immediately following birth				
Number of previous offspring born	Fertility	−	0.048	forest
Percent offspring survival	Fertility	−	0.000	forest
Own reproductive value				
Number of previous offspring born	Mortality	0	0.270	forest
Number of previous offspring born	Fertility	+	0.001	reservation
Percent offspring survival	Fertility	+	0.000	reservation
Offspring reproductive value				
Number of juvenile siblings	Mortality (0–4)	0	0.830	forest
Number of juvenile siblings	Mortality (5–9)	−	0.60	forest
Number of juvenile siblings	Mortality (0–4)	0	0.890	reservation
IBI to previous sibling	Mortality (0)	0	0.886	reservation
IBI to previous sibling	Mortality (1–4)	−	0.080	reservation
IBI to next sibling	Mortality (1–4)	0	0.410	reservation
Mother's total fertility	Fertility	0	0.820	reservation

Data are taken from Tables 12.2–12.6 when resources are controlled.

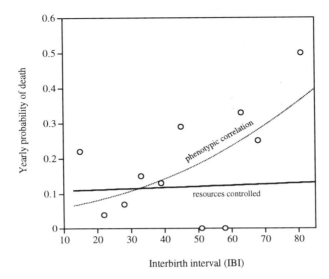

Interbirth interval (IBI)

Figure 12.1. The relationship between interbirth interval (IBI) and the probability of death from birth to age one. Only children who were conceived while the previously born sibling was alive (nonreplacement intervals) are included in the risk set. Infant mortality in each six-month class of IBI is shown by points. The dotted line is the best-fit logistic regression model from the raw data (see Table 12.5) and the solid line is the best-fit model when maternal weight, paternal SES, paternal hunting rate, and mother's age are controlled. The analysis suggests a phenotypic correlation due to parental resources, but no trade-off between IBI and infant survival when resource differences are statistically controlled.

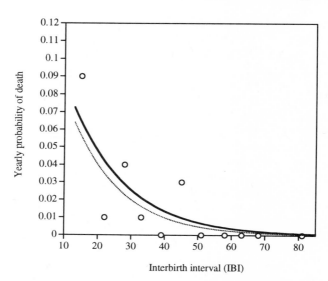

Figure 12.2.   The relationship between interbirth interval (IBI) and the probability of death from age one to age four. Only children who were conceived while the previous born sibling was alive (nonreplacement intervals) are included in the risk set. Juvenile mortality in each six-month class of IBI is shown by points. The dotted line is the best-fit logistic regression model from the raw data (see Table 12.5) and the solid line is the best-fit model when maternal weight, paternal SES, paternal hunting rate, and mother's age are controlled. The analysis suggests a trade-off between IBI and juvenile survival. When birth spacing is short between a child and a previously born surviving sibling, mortality is higher.

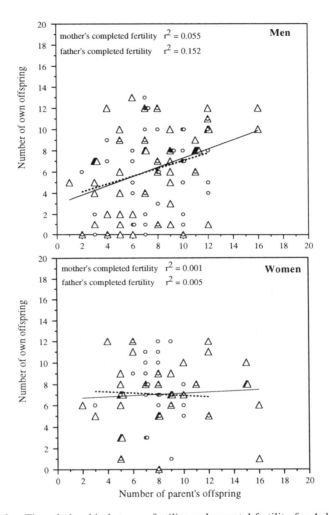

Figure 12.3. The relationship between fertility and parental fertility for Ache men and women over age forty-five living on reservations. Father's completed family size is shown with triangles (and solid line regression slope) while mother's completed family size is shown with circles (dashed line regression slope). Multiple observations are offset to the right. Only the relationship between men's completed fertility and that of their parents is significantly different from 0 (*p* = .005 for father, *p* = 0.098 for mother). This result is confirmed in Table 12.6.

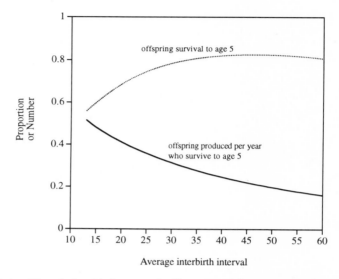

Figure 12.4.   The relationship between fertility rate and fitness or offspring survival for Ache women on reservations. Fitness is measured as number of offspring who survive to age five (see text). Note that interbirth intervals of about forty-five months maximize offspring survival, but the shortest interbirth intervals that we observed would be associated with highest parental fitness.

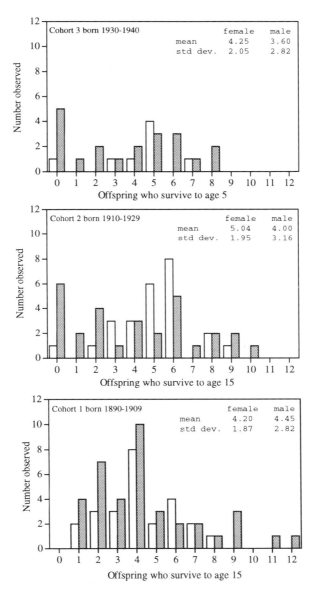

Figure 12.5. Lifetime reproductive success for three cohorts of Ache women (unshaded) and men (shaded). Note the higher variance in male reproductive success.

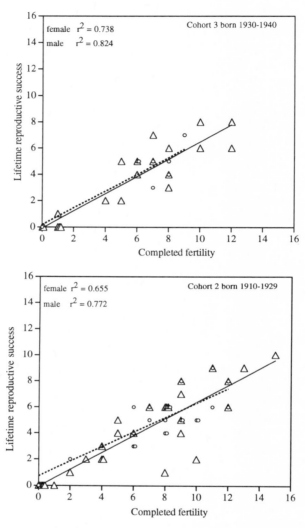

Figure 12.6.   The relationship between completed fertility and lifetime reproductive success (LRS) as defined in the text for cohorts of Ache men (triangles, solid line) and women (circles, dashed line). Multiple observations are offset to the right. Differential fertility predicts about 80% of the variance in LRS of men and about 70% of the variance in LRS of women who survive to age fifty.

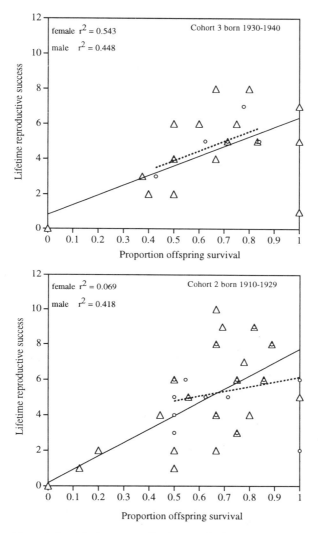

Figure 12.7. The relationship between offspring survival rates and LRS (as defined in the text) for Ache men (triangles, solid line) and women (circles, dashed line) who survive to age fifty. Individuals with no live births were excluded from the sample. Differential offspring survival predicts only about 40% of the variance in LRS for men who produce at least one offspring, and between 7% and 50% of the variance in LRS for women who produce at least one offspring.

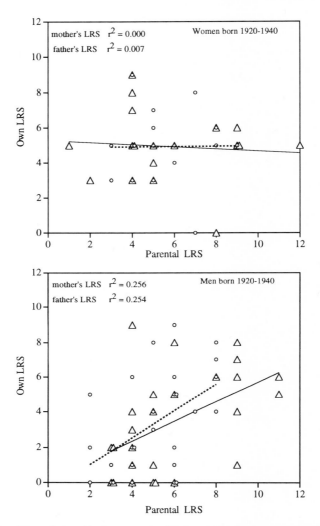

Figure 12.8.   The relationship between the lifetime reproductive success of Ache men and women who survive to age fifty and the LRS of their father (triangles, solid line) or mother (circles, dashed line). Multiple observations are offset to the right. While there is no relationship between the LRS of women and that of their parents, the relationship between male LRS and that of both parents is statistically significant (*p* = 0.007, 0.007).

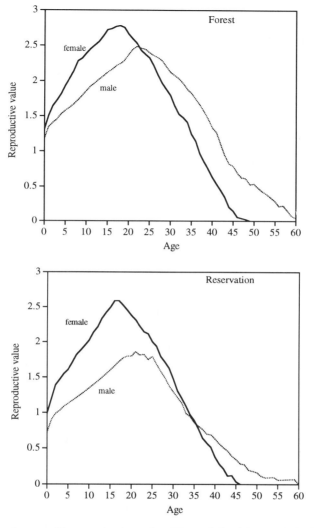

Figure 12.9. Age-specific reproductive value (V_x, as defined in eq. 1.1) of males and females during the forest and reservation periods. The instantaneous annual growth rate (r) was determined from census data from 1945 to 1970 (forest $r = 0.016$) and 1978–1989 (reservation $r = 0.035$). Survival and fertility rates are determined from tables in Chapters 6, 8, and 9. Note that males show lower reproductive value at birth in both time periods.

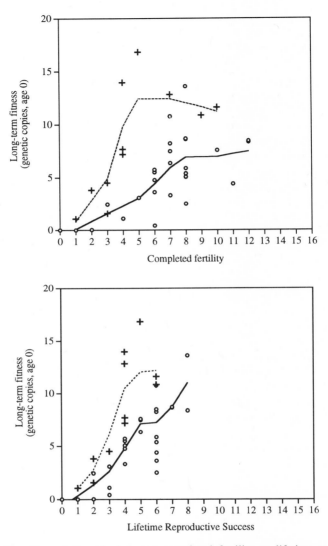

Figure 12.10. The relationship between completed fertility or lifetime reproductive success and long-term fitness for Ache women born between 1890 and 1900 (crosses, dashed line) or 1901–1917 (circles, solid line). Data are fit with a lowess smooth. Long-term fitness is calculated at seventy years for the early cohort (W_{70}) and seventy-five years for the later cohort (W_{75}) according to equation 12.5. Analysis of the early cohort measures fitness effects during the forest period only. Analysis of the later cohort measures the impact of the contact and reservation periods on long-term fitness. Note that fertility levels below the maximum may result in highest long-term fitness, whereas maximum LRS results in maximum long-term fitness.

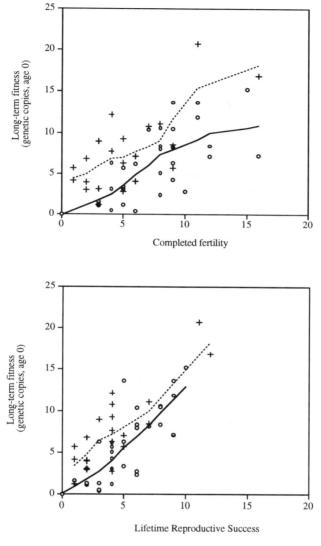

Figure 12.11. The relationship between completed fertility or lifetime reproductive success and long-term fitness for Ache men born between 1890 and 1900 (crosses, dashed line) or 1901–1917 (circles, solid line). Data points are fit with a lowess smooth. Long-term fitness is calculated at seventy years for the early cohort (W_{70}) and seventy-five years for the later cohort (W_{75}) according to equation 12.5. Note the higher fitness in the cohort that was measured before the contact period. Fertility and LRS appear to be good indicators of fitness measured through all descendants after three generations.

Grandmother Kanegi in 1982 when she was about seventy-six years old.

13

Kin Effects on Life History

Evolutionary biologists have realized for nearly thirty years now that natural selection is likely to produce patterns of resource investment that promote the spread of an individual's genes residing not only in offspring but also the bodies of other close relatives (Hamilton 1964). Indeed Hamilton's rule (Hamilton 1975) suggests not only that individuals will often invest in close kin, but that they should apportion their investment according to the way it will impact on the reproductive value of various individuals in the population, discounted by their genetic relatedness (see Rogers 1994). This means, for example, that an individual may invest some resources in a nephew rather than in one of his or her own offspring when two conditions are met. First, the impact on the nephew's reproductive value must be greater than it would be on the reproductive value of an offspring. And second, the nephew's gain in reproductive value must be greater, even when discounted by the proportionally lower genetic relationship with ego than that of an offspring. These conditions are not difficult to meet in a world where the vagaries of chance lead to extreme need among some and plenty for others. Thus, we might expect humans to invest in kin other than offspring quite frequently. The greater the need for investment (i.e., the greater its impact on reproductive value), the more likely it is that even distant kin may provide support.

If this logic is correct, we may have difficulty measuring costs of reproduction without experimental manipulation (as mentioned in the previous chapter), since individuals who make potentially costly life history errors (e.g., too high fertility) are likely to be helped by other close kin who are in a favorable position to do so. It also means that we should be able to measure the impact of close kin on each other's survival and fertility (if there is an impact), but again, the measurement of the impact through natural variation rather than experimentation will be complicated. The absence of a particular genetic relative who could provide support should lead to demographic changes that allow us to measure the impact of that relative's investment on ego. But at the same time, all kin may increase or decrease their own investment in proportion to that being provided by other remaining kin, thus obscuring the effect we wish to measure.

An example can help to clarify this problem. If we want to determine whether grandmothers invest in their grandoffspring and show that the support provided increases child survival, the best "natural" verification is to compare children whose grandmothers have died with children who have a living grandmother. According to the experimental design the difference in survivorship between the two groups of children could be attributed to the impact of grandmaternal investment. Unfortunately for the scientist, however, children have many other potential kin helpers who are also aware of the "experimental" conditions and should react appropriately. When a grandmother is investing in a child, other close kin may receive little fitness gain from their own investment in that same child and thus provide nothing. With grandmother absent, however, these same kin may be able to affect that child's reproductive value strongly by providing help, and thus might be expected to do so. In the worst case scenario (for the scientist), we may see no difference at all in child survival for children with and without grandmothers and conclude that grandmothers provide no consequential care or resources to their grandoffspring. This problem is partially eliminated by looking at multiple kin effects simultaneously. Since all resources will be expended on some kin, the absence of a grandmother should impact on somebody somewhere in the kin network. But with kin help spread among many needy relatives, slight changes in allocation will be difficult to detect.

Despite these complications the investigation of kin effects on life history is an important area of research that must be pursued. Biologists have been keenly aware of kinship and potential conflicts of interest between parents and offspring when developing theoretical models of fertility (e.g., Godfray and Parker 1991). Anthropologists and demographers need to be even more sensitive to kinship effects since humans are an extremely social species whose members generally live for long periods of time near many individuals who are all acutely aware of their genetic relatedness to each other. The use of verbal communication to keep track of genetic relatedness, as well as a long life span and a long postreproductive phase (for all females, and on average for most males as well), means that there is ample opportunity for complex kin investment patterns to emerge. Indeed, those investment patterns may be part of the explanation for the evolution of a postreproductive life span in human females (see below). This chapter is dedicated to examining whether kin investment patterns can be detected through their life history effects (kin investment ultimately must impact on survival or fertility to be of biological consequence), and to look at a few special topics that include investment by individuals other than parents to their juvenile offspring. Specifically, we will examine the effects of grandparents, collateral kin, and potential alternative fathers on patterns of reproductive senescence (menopause), sex ratio manipulation, infanticide, and mating.

KIN EFFECTS ON MORTALITY

In theory, any significant investment by close kin should on average increase the survival or fertility of the individuals receiving the help. If not, the investment is "wasted" in an evolutionary sense. The Ache recognize kin help in everyday conversation and believe it to be important. Grandmothers and grandfathers baby-sit small children, brothers and sisters often take in each other's children for extended periods of time (especially now on reservation settlements), and older siblings care for younger siblings. Widespread food sharing characterizes the Ache, but everyone seems especially willing to give up food to younger individuals who are close kin. Some excerpts from tapes about forest life recorded and published by missionary Ruth Sammons illustrate these patterns. Although these texts were translated into English by Sammons, we have retranslated from the original Ache in order to reflect our knowledge of the context of forest life (Sammons has never seen the Ache living in the forest):

Dad stayed out overnight in the forest. I would have gone with him but I didn't see him leave. I wonder where he went. He's in the forest. He'll come back tomorrow. Stay in camp (they said). Stay in camp with grandpa. Don't go out walking in the forest, a snake might bite you. Your father will be back. Don't cry. Mom went with him (dad). Mom will carry back in her basket the monkeys that he shoots. Grandma was also left in camp. Grandpa is often left in camp. Grandma stays with him. They (parents) don't take their kids, they leave them at camp. I didn't see dad leave (he went out hunting very early). He might come back around sundown. He took his wife with him. Grandpa is usually left in camp. Dad went off hunting in the forest. His wife went with him. The kids were all left with grandpa (Byvangi in Sammons 1978:8–9).

After that the guy who had recently had his lip pierced (teenage boy) went hunting in the forest. Then the peccary that the teenage boy had killed was carried to camp. All the Ache ate it all up. Grandpa is given the head, the head of the peccary killed by the teenage boy. Then I and the other kids eat (the head) with grandpa. [The head is considered the best piece of a peccary.] They say, "the jowl will not be given to anybody who is lazy. The jowl is not given to lazy people. That's what grandpa tells us kids" [implying that the kids should help out when asked]. Then we sit by grandpa and get some of the head that he is eating. Grandma is the one who cooks it [the parents are still not back yet] (Byvangi in Sammons 1978:10).

Grandpa shot a currasow. Grandpa gave me the leg of that which he killed. He didn't give to others. To us (kids) he used to give the leg of what he killed. Mom used to eat the breast meat of what grandpa killed. She didn't share the breast meat. "You should share breast meat with your kids. What, you are not going to share breast meat with your kids, you who eat so much of it?" That's what grandpa said to mom. Mother was mad at me. Then mother wouldn't speak to me. When grandpa shot a deer he carried it on his shoulders to the camp. I went over to where he was arriving. Then grandpa threw it down on my foot. Then I cried. I made fun of grandpa's big penis. Then mom said to me, "You who eat so much of what your grandpa brings in, why do you make fun of his penis?" That's what mom said to me (Baepurangi in Sammons 1978:43).

Mom cried a lot when her father died. Mom almost died when her father died, when grandpa died. "Don't cry a lot, that's what grandpa said to mom. When I die don't cry a lot." That's what grandpa said to mom. That's what grandma said to mom (before she died too). Mom took care of her little sister [when the speaker's grandparents died]. She raised her. She raised her on palm fiber starch pudding. Mom really used to pound palm fiber (Baepurangi in Sammons 1978:44).

Grandpa got mad at us. He got mad at us for trying to take away his meat (when he was sick). He scolded us. He wouldn't give to his grandchildren. Grandma really gave to her grandchildren. Grandma really shared a lot with her grandchildren. The one who held me on her lap when I was born (godmother) gave me some leg. She really knew how to share, the one who held me. The one who held me really would share with me, her grandchild, her godchild. [Here the grandmother is also in the ritual tapare-chave *or "godmother-godchild" relationship with the speaker] (Baepurangi in Sammons 1978:45).*

Grandpa raised us. Grandpa used to bring pichu larvae to his grandchildren so they could suck them. Grandma used to fill up her basket with pichu larvae and bring them. She used to hide them down deep in her basket for her grandchildren to eat. She would give the bad ones to mom. The ones grandma cooked she would give to her grandchildren to suck. She would pull her grandchildren over by her. Then they would suck larvae with grandma. The ones with the fat sucked out would then be given to grandpa. Grandpa would give them away to someone else. Grandma brought pichu larvae to her grandchildren. Grandma really brought lots of pichu to her grandchildren (Baepurangi in Sammons 1978:52).

Grandma didn't want anybody hitting us. She was very protective (jealous, stingy) of her grandchildren. Grandma would scold other kids. "You bad little kid, what are you doing hitting my grandchild?" Just like that grandma would talk to the other kids. Our grandma would send (push) us at them. "Hit them, why do you cry so much when the others hit." That's how our grandma would talk to us. Then we would hit the other kids too. Grandma would send her grandchildren to hit back, she would send us (Baepurangi in Sammons 1978:54).

My uncle used to give me armadillo leg. Armadillo leg he would share with us (kids). He didn't give it to anyone else. To us only he gave it, the one who cut my umbilical cord. Mother's brother cut my umbilical cord when I was born. I cried when the one who had cut my cord died. Mother said to me, "Why are you crying so much, you who ate so much of what he (the one who cut your cord) shot? Don't cry" (Baepurangi in Sammons 1978:50–51).

Other statements also suggest that male kin alliances during violent confrontation might be particularly important to adult survival and that both men and women are defended by their male kin.

Grandpa was a big strong man. Then my dad would get into club fights. Dad was a strong club fighter. He would bust open heads of other guys. (He was so strong that) then his wife would grab a hold of his bow (to stop him from killing). Then grandma would grab his bow. His father would defend him, my grandpa. Grandpa would defend (take revenge for) his son, if they hit his son, grandpa (would do it). Then when they were fighting we cried, when dad was hit. Dad almost died. Another guy hit him. It broke his head open. Then he called to his brother, to my uncle. Then he came to defend his brother, the guy who is my uncle. He sent them scurrying with his bow. Dad's brother was really strong. Dad was strong too. They were as strong as each other. All dad's brothers were big strong men. Dad was smaller. His own brothers were all really big. Dad didn't want people to hit his brothers. He would fight someone like that, he would fight with those enemies (Baepurangi in Sammons 1978:48).

One man used to hit his wife a lot. He stuck his wife with the point of a bow. Then her father defended (took revenge for) her. There are those who don't defend their daughters. There are those who really defend their daughters, they have club fights. Some women hit each other. They hit another woman. They don't want them having sex. If they eat his penis (have sex) they are mad. They are very jealous (stingy with their husbands). We say they are husband stingy, husband stingy. Another will say, "why are you flirting so much with the husband of one you know is going to be so jealous?" She is angry. She scratches up her husband's face. She really scratches it up. She is really mad. Sometimes the one who isn't the wife is jealous. When the one who is not the wife is jealous they fight. Another woman will defend her. Another woman will defend the one who isn't the wife.

When a woman scolds another sometimes a man will defend her. They really defend women. One guy really defended his sister. He always defended his sister. He was mean to his brother-in-law. . . . Grandpa was mean, he really fought with his wife. He would really scratch up her face. He would stick her with his bow. He would try to stick her with burning sticks in the genitals. She cried. Then her father defended her. Her father was the one who would customarily defend her. When her daughter was about to get in a serious fight the mother-in-law would grab the infant out of her lap and take it. Grandpa was mean (Tejugi in Sammons 1978:122–123).

The recognition that close kin help each other presents a challenge for demographers and life history researchers. Can we obtain a quantitative estimate of the impact of that help on the survival or fertility of the recipients? Such an estimate of kin help is required for testing a variety of hypotheses about social behavior in humans as well as life history theories about the postreproductive phase that characterizes females of our species.

Kin Help and Child Mortality Rates

In order to examine the impact of close kin on child mortality rates, we developed a set of univariate logistic regression models. Logistic regression is particularly useful here because it allows the incorporation of time-varying covariates, such as whether or not an individual's parents are alive or divorced or the number of aunts and uncles that an individual has. For example, in some of the intervals during which an individual is at risk of death the individual's parents are married and during other intervals the parents are divorced. Since each risk interval is a unit of analysis, logistic regression hazards modeling allows us to isolate the effect of parental divorce on the probability of death in a risk interval statistically. Similarly, comparison of death rates for individuals with and without certain classes of close kin should allow us to estimate the impact of help from that kin class on the survivorship of individuals in the study sample.

The analyses described below control for important variables known to covary with mortality rate or covary with both mortality and the number of potential kin helpers. These variables include age, sex, and mother's age. To this multivariate model we added each kin category (one at a time) to determine whether the presence of close kin in each category had any impact on the probability of death in a yearly interval. Results are shown in Tables 13.1 and 13.2. Independent variables are mother alive, father alive, parents divorced, number of living adult brothers (≥ 10 years old), number of living adult sisters, number of living grandmothers, number of living grandfathers, number of living aunts (mother's or father's full and half sisters), number of living uncles, total number of living close kin helpers (living parents, grandparents, aunts and uncles), and the ratio of total kin helpers to total living close kin competitors (siblings and first cousins). Half siblings, half aunts, half uncles, and half cousins were all scored as one-half of a relative in their respective classes. Note that for the last two categories, potential kin helpers are all in generations above ego whereas potential competitors are in the same generation.

The analyses suggest that parents, but not other kin, have a strong and unique influence on the mortality of Ache children living in the forest period (Table 13.1). Mother's death increases the age-specific mortality rate of children by about fivefold whereas father's death increases mortality about threefold. Even when both parents are alive, their divorce is associated with a threefold increase in the mortality of their offspring. Not surprisingly, mother's death in the first year of a child's life leads to mortality in 100% of the cases in our sample. However, other age effects of parental absence are not marked. In fact, a lack of significant interaction terms (parental death or divorce by age) in the models suggests that the proportional effects on mortality do not change with age through much of childhood (see note 2 below). Even older children who lose a parent are more likely to perish than those whose parents are alive and married. A good deal of this effect is due to child homicide (discussed below), but children who are orphaned are also reported to be treated worse and are probably more likely to die from a variety of causes.

The presence or absence or number of grandparents, aunts, uncles, and adult siblings seem to have little or no impact on child survival. These results fail to reach significance even when parental death and divorce are controlled in multivariate models (statistics not shown). As mentioned above, this does not constitute strong evidence that these kin provide no support to young children. In all but one case (aunts) the direction of the association is correct (i.e., more kin, lower mortality), suggesting that perhaps there is a helping effect from each single kin category but that many other things also affect child mortality, thus confounding the weak effect of grandparents, aunts, and uncles on child mortality. Although each kin category by itself might produce little change in survival, we might expect that the sum of all older kin helpers would be positively related to survival in our sample. This prediction is not met. Instead, we find that children with many other siblings and cousins have higher survival rates. Thus, the negative relationship between the variable "all older close kin divided by their alternative kin obligations (competitors)" seems to indicate a phenotypic correlation like that described in the previous chapter. We cannot show that those with more older potential kin helpers or fewer same-age kin competitors receive more kin help. Instead it seems that children born into kin groups that have produced many surviving young dependents are also more likely to survive themselves.

Parental effects on juvenile survival at the reservation settlements are considerably less striking (Table 13.2). Few small children in our sample had deceased parents, and no statistically significant impact of parental absence could be shown. In fact, only four children were at risk whose mothers were dead, and two of the four died during the observation period. Only a handful of children at risk were fathered by deceased men, and all of them survived the observation period. We were surprised (because the Ache insist that this effect is strong) that children of divorced parents did not experience *significantly* higher mortality rates than children whose parents were still living together. (Although the parameter estimate shows a 1.8-fold increase in mortality for this group, the effect is characterized by high variation and thus not significant.) There seems to be no patterned kin effect for the remaining classes of relatives. However, the ratio of all living helper kin combined divided by all potential kin competitors did strongly and significantly associate with child mortality. Those children with a higher ratio of helper/competitor kin showed significantly lower mortality. This is the kind of result one would expect if each individual received help from older close kin, but those older kin members spread their help across various junior recipients. This may mean that the ecology of the reservation situation is more amenable to kin help than was the forest period. The Ache themselves have mentioned to us that in the forest they spent more effort cultivating nonkin social relationships whereas on reservations many forms of help come only from close kin and residence patterns are now more strictly kin oriented. However, during the forest period close kin did influence the probability of child homicide, which was the leading cause of death (see below).

Kin Help and Adult Mortality

Because of the low number of adult deaths during the reservation period we analyzed only the forest data on adult mortality. Logistic regression shows no significant associations between the presence, absence, or number of adult kin in any category and the mortality rate of forest-living adult Ache (Table 13.3). The sign of the relationship was negative for both fathers and brothers but not for mothers or sisters; thus the data only weakly suggest that adult male kin have a stronger dampening effect on the adult mortality of their relatives than do adult female kin (as the Ache stories suggest). Clearly a much larger sample of adult deaths would be required in order to test this proposition adequately.

KIN EFFECTS ON FERTILITY

If kin help is provided in the form of food or care that releases parents from parental investment burdens, such help could ultimately increase the fertility of the individuals being assisted. In addition, through political alliances and perhaps access to resource-providing kin, males could be more successful in coercing or attracting additional female mating partners if they received significant kin help.

Kin Help and Female Fertility

Kin effects on age-specific fertility can be partially isolated through logistic regression. Each interval at risk takes place when certain relatives are alive and others are not. The difference between fertility rates when individuals have varying numbers of living relatives may be due to the helping effects of those relatives; logistic regression hazards analyses can give us an estimate of those effects, if they exist. Analysis of kin effects on female fertility in the forest and during the reservation period is shown in Table 13.4. The analyses reveal no relationship between number of living brothers and sisters or parents and the fertility of women during the reservation period. This result is discussed below. The data also show no significant impact of parents on the fertility of their adult daughters. Interestingly we find a negative relationship between number of living adult siblings and fertility for women living in the forest period. The relationship between fertility and number of brothers is negative and highly significant. The relationship between fertility and number of sisters is also negative and is about the same magnitude (parameter estimates are similar) but the relationship is less consistent and therefore not quite significant. Since sisters have a strong positive impact on the fertility of their brothers (see below), but brothers have a strong negative impact on the fertility of their sisters, one interpretation of this result is that sisters provide substantial kin help to their brothers at a fitness cost to themselves. If this is true, however, it is still unclear to us why sisters should produce a negative impact on each other's fertility. These negative effects may cancel out positive phenotypic correlation between daughters and parents, ultimately leading to no relationship between parental and daughter fertility, as we found in the previous chapter.

Kin Help and Male Fertility

In order to determine the relationship between adult close kin and male fertility we carried out two more sets of logistic regressions—one for the forest period and another for the reservation period. Both analyses control for age effects in order to isolate the impacts of kin presence or absence that might covary with a man's age. Results are shown in Table 13.5. Kin effects in the forest seem quite pronounced. The analyses show that men with more living adult brothers and sisters (age ten or greater) during a year at risk were characterized by higher probabilities of fathering a child. In both cases an additional sibling was associated with about 10% higher age-specific fertility. Men who had a living mother may also have experienced higher fertility than those whose mother was dead, but whether or not a man's father was alive seems to have no relationship to his age-specific fertility in the forest period.

Results of analyses for the reservation period suggest sibling effects on male fertility are still important and result in about 14% higher age-specific fertility per year. Parental effects appear completely unimportant. This agrees with our general impression that the new economic situation has rendered the older generation of Ache relatively powerless and economically unimportant. Younger males are more effective at manipulating missionaries, government officials, and neighboring Paraguayan *campesinos* (and even anthropologists). Older Ache do not speak any Spanish and usually only a bit of Guarani (the lingua franca of the Paraguayan countryside); they do not understand the monetary system; and they find that their skills (hunting and gathering) have become increasingly irrelevant to the reservation situation. Finally, because of their lack of economic power, they command little respect and no political power that can be used to help their adult offspring.

REPRODUCTIVE SENESCENCE

Ache women experience a complete cessation of all reproductive function about two-thirds of the way through their expected adult life span. Living under traditional forest conditions, all women experienced menopause before or around age fifty, and yet those who survived to menopause lived on average about twenty more years after reproductive termination (Table 6.1). These and other data from around the world indicate that women are characterized by a reproductive life history profile that is rarely found in mammals and probably unique among all the primates (Pavelka and Fedigan 1991). Human females and a few other mammals, such as toothed whales (Marsh and Kasuya 1986) and certain strains of laboratory mice (Festing and Blackmore 1971), experience termination of reproductive function well before the end of the typical adult life span.

In contrast to the human pattern, other large mammals and our nearest ape relatives show no termination of reproductive function even though they may enjoy long life spans. For example, the maximum age of reproduction for female chimpanzees is considerably greater than the mean life expectancy at sexual maturity (Figure 13.1). Similarly, although only 5% of all elephants born reach fifty-five years of age, female fertility at that age is still about 50% of the maximum observed age-specific fertility (Crooze et al. 1981:306). Baleen whales may live to age ninety or more and yet females still continue to reproduce at these advanced ages (Mizrooh 1981).

The pattern of human female reproductive senescence begins long before its termination with menopause. Although this reproductive decline has sometimes been described as just a special form of general senescence (e.g., Wood 1990), the fact that reproductive senescence does not coincide with all other forms of somatic senescence (Figure 13.2) presents a special problem for life history theory. Two specific hypotheses have been proposed to account for this observation. First, some authors have proposed that menopause is essentially an artifact of a recently increased life span among humans (e.g., Washburn 1981; Weiss 1981). This hypothesis was based primarily on the observation that traditional human populations are often characterized by much shorter mean life spans than are modern populations. The comparison primarily relies on data concerning life expectancy at birth. The hypothesis seems unlikely to be correct given evidence from studies such as those presented in Chapter 6 and Howell's (1979) study of the !Kung, which show that despite high infant mortality rates, traditional human populations have probably often enjoyed reasonably long *adult* life spans. For example, by the age of first reproduction Ache women during the forest period had a life expectancy of sixty years (see Table 6.1). To our knowledge there are no demographic studies showing low life expectancy of human females near the age of menopause. If most females who survived to sexual maturity could also expect to survive long past the age of menopause, then selection should strongly favor continued reproductive function during the expected adult life span. The fact that senescence occurs much later for all other body functions is also a problem for the recent-long-life-span hypothesis. If all other body systems have had time to evolve to new conditions and a longer life span, why hasn't reproductive span evolved as well?

The second and more frequently proposed hypothesis for human menopause we refer to as the "grandmother hypothesis." First proposed by George Williams (1957), the grandmother hypothesis suggests that as women age, greater fitness benefits may be gained through investing time and resources in existing offspring and grandoffspring than could be expected through continued investment in the production of additional new offspring (Alexander 1974; Gaulin 1980; Hamilton 1966; Hawkes et al. 1989; Trivers 1972). The proponents of the grandmother hypothesis have not been explicit about why humans but few other organisms would commonly reach a point in the life span where the fitness gains from investment in existing kin would outweigh the gains from further reproduction. The proponents of this hypothesis have also relied heavily on the assumption that death rates are high among older women, and thus the production of new dependent offspring, which might die if mother herself dies, could be an imprudent use of available resources. This is somewhat problematic since female yearly mortality is not much higher in the late forties than it is in the twenties (Table 6.1). Nevertheless, a switch to kin investment rather than direct reproduction could be favored under other conditions (e.g., an increasing number of kin with age, and a negatively accelerated relationship between resource investment and impact on reproductive value among aging women), and thus the grandmother hypothesis must be taken seriously and subjected to careful empirical testing.

The Ache present an ideal situation for testing the grandmother hypothesis. First, the Ache are hunter-gatherers who, through the 1970s, lived in a manner that is probably similar (but not identical) to their traditional lifestyle for the past 10,000 years (see Chapter 2). Thus, the data base may represent some relationship between ecological and demographic parameters that have characterized this group during a long period of time during which the trait of menopause was presumably maintained by natural selection. Although the Ache are not an appropriate model for testing ideas about the *origin* of menopause, we can test the proposition that the grandmother hypothesis accounts for the maintenance of menopause in this group. Second, we have a good deal of information about kin effects on relevant demographic parameters in the Ache and thus can develop and test a very explicit mathematical model of kin selected menopause using empirical data. Here we develop and test a model of reproductive termination using data on fertility, mortality, and kin effects during the forest period.

In order to test the grandmother hypothesis we must first specify the alternatives that we believe have been available to the retention process of natural selection and then calculate which alternative phenotype (of the specified possibilities) would lead to highest fitness. Here we assume that aging women are faced with an allocation problem. *They can either allocate time and resources to helping their existing offspring reproduce and increasing the survival of their grandoffspring, or they can produce new children of their own and provide less help to existing kin.* Our model explicitly allows only investment in kin or in own reproduction. In reality, however, older women do not have this second option any longer since according to the hypothesis natural selection has already resulted in the obligatory termination of reproductive function at some age. Currently living postmenopausal women therefore must invest all their resources in already existing kin.

It has been noted in several recent studies that older females do appear to work hard and contribute resources to their close kin in traditional societies (e.g., Hawkes et al. 1989; Hurtado and Hill 1987; Kaplan 1994). Kin investment by older women must have resulted in a significant impact on the fitness of those kin in the past, or there would be no selective force favoring any postreproductive life span at all. Indeed, if women truly did nothing to increase genetic representation after menopause, natural selection would not act on the postreproductive life span and we would expect rapid postreproductive senescence (Charlesworth 1980; Hamilton 1966). Any slight gain in fitness earlier in life that would be costly in the postreproductive period would be favored by natural selection. Thus, in the formulation of the hypothesis that we wish to test, we must estimate the impact that mothers have on their children's survival and fertility, as well as the effect that grandmothers have on the survival of their grandoffspring. We must then estimate how many offspring a woman could produce if she were able to continue reproducing in the post menopausal years, and finally, determine whether the kin-helping effects more than outweigh the expected genetic contribution from continued reproduction, if it were possible.

The model we propose to test examines the trade-off between kin help and continued reproduction. Since analysis in the previous section suggests that women have no impact on the survival of adult offspring, we consider only effects on the fertility of adult offspring and on the survival of grandoffspring. Despite the fact that some of these effects are not statistically significant, we will use the parameter values from the logistic regressions as the best estimates of the effects in the Ache population. Since women are expected to continue to invest in their own juvenile offspring regardless of which reproductive strategy is chosen, the impact of women on the survival of their juvenile offspring is ignored here. The genetic contribution from each of the alternative strategies must be measured in a common currency for adequate comparison. Here we choose the currency of newborn offspring (reproductive value = 1, genetic relatedness coefficient = .5). If we examine alternative genetic contribution during a yearly interval, the contribution from kin help must be greater than the expected genetic gain from reproduction for menopause to be favored. We can express this condition mathematically as:

$$r \sum_{i=\alpha}^{\infty} \{S_i(fs_i^* - fs_i) + D_i(fd_i^* - fd_i)\} + r \sum_{j=0}^{9} G_j(S_j^* - S_j)V_{j+1} > m_x^* V_0^* \quad (13.1)$$

where a woman of age x has a fertility of m_x^*, S_i sons and D_i daughters at various ages i, and G_j grandchildren at various ages j. The terms f^*s_i and f^*d_i represent the fertility of sons and daughters with the help their mother can provide if she doesn't reproduce, and fs_i and fd_i are the age-specific fertility of sons and daughters without their mother's help. Thus, the first sum term represents a mother's impact on her adult children's fertility if they get the help she provides by not reproducing. More specifically, it is the number of additional grandchildren produced per year because of the help a woman of age x provides her offspring. This is multiplied by r, the proportional relatedness of the new grandoffspring produced compared with that of a woman's own offspring ($r = 0.5$).

The second term sums the effects of increased survivorship of grandoffspring across all ages from 0 to 9 discounted by their relatedness compared with that of an offspring. G_j is the number of grandoffspring of age j, S_j^* is the survival of those offspring with grandmothers help, and S_j is the expected survival without grandmother's help. V_j is the reproductive value of grandoffspring at age j. This term is necessary because the genetic impact of grandmother's effect on grand-offspring survival depends upon the reproductive value of the grandoffspring if it lives. Helping a newborn grandoffspring to survive one year is not worth as much (in genetic contribution) as helping a six-year-old child survive a year, because the six-year-old has a higher reproductive value.

On the right side of the inequality m_x^* is the number of offspring that a woman of postmenopausal age x could produce per year if she were reproductive and V_0^* is the reproductive value of the offspring that she will produce. Those offspring will not have a reproductive value equivalent to those produced by younger individuals (whose $V_0 = 1$). Instead, a slight difference in reproductive value of children born to older women is expected because young children without a mother are unlikely to survive (see above section) and older women are more likely to die each year than younger women. The difference in maternal survival during the first year is in fact a good estimate of the ratio of reproductive value since virtually no children survive the death of their mother in the first year. The fivefold difference in child mortality with or without a mother in subsequent years could also lower the reproductive value of children born to older mothers, but actual data show that this effect is minuscule because (1) older women survive at almost the same rates as younger women and (2) juvenile mortality is so low after the second year of life (about 2%) that a proportional increase in the mortality rate still has little effect on reproductive value.

All but one of the values for the variables in inequality 13.1 have been determined in this or earlier chapters: m_x^* is a hypothetical value that cannot be determined in any current human population (since all women now undergo menopause and have no fertility late in life). Fertility rate just prior to menopause could be used here, but that rate is extremely low and represents the very thing we are trying to explain, namely reproductive senescence. Instead we will ini-tially estimate m_x^* as a fraction of maximal fertility that is determined by the survival curve. If, for example, 70% of all women survive from their mid twenties to the age of menopause, we will assume that fertility rates at meno-pause could be 70% of those experienced during their twenties if women did not undergo rapid reproductive senescence. This is the same thing as allowing repro-ductive senescence at the same rate as the senescence observed for other body functions (Figure 13.2). Finally, if the right side of inequality 13.1 is greater than the left side, conditions for menopause are not met. In order to explore this trade-off further we will reduce the value of m_x^* until we reach equality, thus allowing us to determine how low fertility would have to drop for older women in order for kin selection to favor menopause.

Since menopause generally takes place between forty-five and fifty years of age around the world and there is very little variance in that age (Pavelka and Fedigan 1991), we will solve for m_x^* in a way that will balance the left side and right sides of inequality 13.1 when women are fifty years of age. The left side of the inequality requires an estimate of how many sons and daughters as well as grandchildren of each age are likely to be alive when a woman is fifty years old, and then an estimate of a woman's impact on the fertility of her sons and daughters as well as the survivorship of her grandoffspring. The impact on fertility, and mortality has been determined by logistic regression and is reported in Tables 13.1, 13.5, and 13.6. We use data from the forest period since we are primarily concerned with the maintenance of menopause under traditional conditions.

The mean number of kin in each category that a fifty-year-old woman can expect to be available for her help is calculated using real data rather than a life table composite. Table 13.6 shows the total number of living adult sons and daughters when a woman reaches age fifty, the mean ages of the sons and daughters, and the total number of grandchildren of each age for a sample of Ache women who reached age fifty in the forest. The sample includes all women born between 1900 and 1920 who reached fifty years of age in the forest period. The sample shows that fifty-year-old women could expect on average to have about 1.7 adult sons and 1.1 adult daughters, and that both sex offspring will be a mean age of around twenty-three years old. A fifty-year-old woman could also expect on average to have a total of about 3.2 grandchildren, about half of whom will be under three years of age. This number of descendants at age fifty for real women is considerably lower than expected using the product of the average forest fertility and mortality life tables presented in Chapters 6 and 8. That product would result in closer to five surviving offspring at age fifty. This means that women who reached age fifty before contact showed considerably lower fertility and/or offspring survival than were experienced in the sample of person years we used to create the life tables.

Table 13.7 shows the calculations of inequality 13.1 for fifty-year-old Ache women in a spreadsheet format. The calculations suggest that *menopause cannot be favored by kin selection with the assumptions in this particular model unless female fertility drops to about one-sixth of its peak value* as women approach the age of menopause. At that point, if the same resources that are used to achieve this extremely low fertility rate could instead be channeled into close kin, having the demographic effects on those kin that we estimated using logistic regression, natural selection might indeed favor menopause. Note that the model requires a tremendous drop in female fertility (unaccounted for by the model) in order to favor the ultimate permanent cessation of reproductive function.

The results of this analysis suggest to us that female reproductive senescence is not maintained by kin selection as envisioned by the grandmother hypothesis, or that we have incorporated erroneous assumptions and parameter estimates into our model. We came to this same conclusion in an earlier analysis (Hill and Hurtado 1991) which used very different analytical techniques, a subset of the same data, and slightly different model assumptions. Continued exploration of the model, changing assumptions and parameters, suggests to us that small changes in the values used for each variable have little effect on the conclusion, except for changes in the values we used to estimate the kin-helping effect. The assumption that older women should cease reproduction because they may die soon and their children will not survive maternal loss is notably incorrect. The mortality rate of fifty-year-old women in our sample is only 2% per year. Since the mortality rate of twenty-year-old women is 1% per year, the difference in maternal survival for children born to mothers of the two ages is trivial and cannot lead to reproductive cessation.

The model fails primarily because there are not many close kin alive that a fifty-year-old woman can help (only about 2.7 offspring and 3.2 grandoffspring), and because she has little impact on close kin (and virtually no impact on more distant kin). Even with a doubling of the number of living offspring and grand-offspring, fertility would have to drop to a third its maximum value before reproductive termination would be favored. The model assumes just over a 20% increase in sons' fertility and in grandoffspring survival at each age owing to the help of a postmenopausal mother or grandmother. If mother's effect on her daughters' fertility were also equivalent to the effect on sons' fertility, a woman's fertility would still have to drop to about one-fourth that of peak fertility in order to favor menopause at age fifty. Only if the impact on offspring fertility were about triple what we measured, or the impact on grandoffspring survival were markedly greater in the early years of a child's life, could inequality 13.1 favor menopause for women with only a slight senescence of their reproductive function. Rogers (1994) has presented a different model but shows a similar result, namely that the effect of older women on the survival and fertility of their close kin must be quite dramatic in order for menopause to be favored by kin selection.

We believe there are a variety of other reasons to doubt the grandmother hypothesis, ranging from the inflexibility of the age at which menopause occurs (cf. Wood 1994) to important details about the reproductive system and the character of its deterioration with age. In reality, reproductive senescence starts long before menopause in most women, and oocytes lose their viability. If true, the grandmother hypothesis suggests that natural selection would favor maximum fertility until kin helping began and then a sudden termination of reproductive function. Most important, the impact that older women can have on close kin is likely to vary tremendously with ecological context and from woman to woman within a society. In our sample, for example, several women had few or no close kin in whom to invest when they reached age fifty. Others had multitudes of close kin long before they ceased reproducing. In an ideal adaptationist world, menopause should be phenotypically plastic and sensitive to these factors if it were maintained by kin selection. Indeed, a cultural rule that mimics this expected plasticity is found in some societies. Among the Nyakyusa and many other West African populations, women are required by taboo to cease reproduction when their first grandchild is born (Wilson 1957:137). The fact that the age at menopause is insensitive to factors that would change the costs and benefits of reproductive cessation as envisioned by the grandmother hypothesis suggests to us that some other functional explanation of reproductive senescence should be sought.

INFANTICIDE AND CHILD HOMICIDE

Killing of infants and small children is common among many organisms and human societies (Hrdy 1995). Child homicide is generally expected when it can increase the fitness of the perpetrator and when countermeasures to defend the offspring are difficult or ineffective. This is particularly likely when parents themselves are involved in the killing, or when unrelated males have something to gain by killing a juvenile, and the father of the victim is absent or dead. Causes and patterns of infanticide among mammals and especially primates have been widely investigated in recent years (Hausfater and Hrdy 1984). Child homicide among humans has also been recently examined from an evolutionary perspective (Daly and Wilson 1988). Among humans, child homicide is most likely when (1) the child is of low reproductive value, and additional investment is unlikely to significantly increase that reproductive value (e.g., deformed children, those without a parent to help raise them, children who are small, unhealthy, twins, or firstborns); (2) the child is of the wrong sex (when sex ratio manipulation is advantageous to the killer); (3) the child is not related to the killer, who is in a long-term mating relationship with the child's parent (owing to the killer's reluctance to invest in the child, or the killer's reluctance for his or her spouse to invest in the unrelated child instead of producing and investing in new offspring that will be related to the killer). Among the Ache, child homicide also seems common when unrelated individuals are being coerced into providing resources for a child who does not receive sufficient parental investment (i.e., orphans). Again, the following are our translations:

> It's like this, when other people leave their kids (behind in camp) other Ache scold them (the kids). "Hurry up and follow your father, nobody will give you anything (to eat) if you stay here (with others)." Then the kids who are left behind say "I

didn't see my father leave." Other Ache won't share with the kids of others who are left behind in camp. Because of that Ache don't leave their kids in camp with others. But only when they go to steal manioc (from outsiders) then they usually leave the kids behind. Like this, the Ache will say "stay here with grandpa." If the kids cry they say "(your parents) are still looking for manioc" (Byvangi in Sammons 1978:15).

We really hate orphans (from an interview with Bepurangi taped in 1978).

I have lots of fathers. Another woman took my dad, then I was born with a different father. My father took my mother back again. The old Ache used to say "Lots of orphans were left behind. (They were left) where arrows had been shot (during a hunt). Because they laughed a lot (played around a lot) they were left." (The orphans said) "We are always playing, who is going to wait for us, why do we play so much? Why don't their mothers wait (stay) with them?" Their mothers all ran off (and left them) (Kajagi in Sammons 1978:110).

[From a female informant whose mother had died when she was young] Grandma said, "Little white-skinned girl, come here, sip that grease." Then we got to sip the palm starch (mixed with grease) soup. Grandma said, "Why do you treat her as if she still has a mother? Don't scold the little orphan when she wants to sip some grease soup" (Tejugi in Sammons 1978:125).

[After having recently seen large jaguar tracks] "Don't cry now. Are you crying because you want your mother to die? Do you want to be buried with your dead mother? Do you want to be thrown in the grave with your mother and stepped on until your excrement comes out? Your mother is going to die if you keep crying. When you are an orphan nobody will ever take care of you again." That's what they say. "Throw all my children in the grave on top of me." "You guys are really killers." "When we throw your kid in the grave with his father don't you cry" (people say). "Who is going to cry? You guys talk too much." We (are the ones who) should be crying, you take such bad care of it (the child). You take such bad care that it is still crying. Its grandma takes better care than you, why are you crying? (Brikugi in Sammons 1978:188).

The Ache pattern of child homicide is heavily associated with a belief in the importance of companions after death. But since the children sacrificed are almost always orphans (or in some cases defective), it can easily be argued that the belief functions more as a justification than a cause of the behavior. During the forest and contact periods children were often thrown in the grave alive or killed and then placed on the chest of important men who died. Some women were also accompanied in the grave by small children. Although young children were generally preferred, sometimes children as old as 10–13 years would be killed (see Clastres 1972a for accounts). Older children who were sacrificed were usually female, although boys as old as 6–8 were occasionally killed and many were dragged to the edge of the grave only to be saved by relatives. Indeed, a large number of Ache adults that we interviewed could recall having been taken to the edge of a grave at least once in their life with a threat of sacrifice, only to be rescued by some close relative. The trauma of such events seems etched in the minds of all who experienced it.

> *My father died when I was only about twenty-two days old [it is unclear how the informant came up with this precise age, which was given in Spanish]. Then my mother told the Ache to throw my brother Bejyvagi and I in the grave [Bejyvagi was about four years old], to be sacrificed with our father. There was a big fight. Some Ache dragged us to the grave site and others pulled us back out again. There were those who defended me. They were not all relatives, some of them were just my "defenders." They liked me. They threatened my mother, "If you don't take back your sons and care for them we will shoot all your daughters with arrows" [the informant had two sisters aged seventeen and twelve at this time]. They tugged and pulled for a long time. Finally my defenders won. They said to me, wow you must have been strong. Why didn't you get torn apart when we were pulling so hard on your arms and legs [some children were literally torn apart this way]. Then my mother took care of me. Later she married Kanjegi. When he died, they sacrificed my little sister [who was about one or two years old]. She didn't have any defenders. My mother gave her up. My brother Bejyvagi and I held on tight to her but they pulled her away from us [the two boys here are about four and eight years old]. We tried to defend her, but some big men pulled her away [informant states that he can't recall who these men were]. My brother and I cried a lot. Our sister screamed. They didn't kill her, they just buried her alive. They put dirt on her real fast and just buried her alive with her father, Kanjegi (translated from an interview with Kuachingi in 1994).*

Other Ache, who were children at the time their peers were killed, seem to have blocked out the memory altogether. For example, in 1991 Hill interviewed a man about several children he had killed in 1973 during the contact epidemic. The man recounted a horrifying story of coming upon a dead woman and her healthy thirteen-year-old daughter after a band had dispersed in the forest because of an epidemic. After digging the hole and placing the woman's body in it, he turned to the girl. She ran shrieking in the forest, crying and begging that he not kill her. He caught the girl, dragged her to the grave, and strangled her to death. His own thirteen-year-old daughter was present at the time and witnessed the entire event, according to his account. That daughter, who was also present during our interview, denied having any recollection of the event and was visibly shocked by the account. The man told the story with tears welling up in his eyes and explained that it was the Ache custom to kill children after their parents died. We were distressed by the interview and couldn't help berating the man for what seemed like inhumane behavior (we had heard many tales of child homicide and had even been present in Ache camps when some small children were suffocated, but we had never heard such gruesome details of the sacrifice of an older child who was described as beautiful, healthy, and happy). The killer asked for our forgiveness and acknowledged that he never should have carried out the task and simply "wasn't thinking." He finally explained that "the old powerful men told us we had to kill all the orphans, and we did as they said without thinking."

Ache data enable us to examine the impact of a variety of factors on the probability of being killed during childhood. These effects are shown in Table 13.8. Data suggest that age, sex, and presence of both parents as well as their continued marriage to each other are the most critical variables determining the probability that a child will be killed. Young children are much more likely to be killed than are older children. This is consistent with logic suggesting that low-reproductive-value individuals will be considered more expendable by close kin (Daly and Wilson 1988) and also the realization by nonkin who are being coerced into investing in them that young children are likely to require much more investment to reach adulthood than are older children (see Kaplan 1994). In our data set 5% of all children born were killed in their first year of life, yet only about 2% of children between ages five and nine were killed per year. Multiplying infanticide rates at each age by the number who survive to that age, we can calculate that about 14% of all male children and 23% of all female children born in the forest were victims of infanticide before they reached age ten (Table 13.9). Females in general were killed at a rate 1.67 times as high as males, but there was no difference by sex in the rate of infanticide during the first year of life.[1] As Ache children got older, child homicide was more and more likely to be directed toward females, a pattern that agrees with Ache statements about the preference of female children as companions in the grave. Young children of both sexes were often killed because they were defective, born breach, or had an absent father. Older children were invariably killed only in the context of being chosen as grave companions for an adult who had died.

The impact of parental absence on child homicide rates is quite astounding. Overall, children without mothers were 4.5 times as likely to be killed during each year of childhood. During the first year of life, however, children who lost their mother had a 100% probability of being killed by another Ache. The proportional effect of mother absence on child homicide steadily decreased during childhood.[2] Children without fathers were 3.9 times as likely to be killed in each year of childhood, but the proportional effect did not decrease significantly with age. Divorce also greatly increased the probability that a child would be killed. Children of divorced parents were 2.8 times as likely to be killed each year during childhood, and again the effect of divorce on child homicide did not decrease with age. Thus, the analyses of the interaction effects of parental status by age of child on the probability of child homicide suggest that *the loss of a mother impacted primarily on young children, whereas the loss of a father or parental divorce greatly increased the homicide rate of children at all ages.*

Although one might expect older women to be less likely to allow a child to be killed because of their low reproductive value and inability to recoup reproductive losses (Daly and Wilson 1988), we found no effect of mother's age on the probability that a child would be killed. We suspect that this is because younger women are more politically powerful than older women in Ache society owing to their mate value. They use this "power" to protect offspring from infanticide, whereas older women had less bargaining leverage. Finally, distant kin seem to have some impact on the probability that a child will become a victim of violence. Numbers of living grandmothers and grandfathers are both negatively associated with the probability of child homicide, but only the grandfather effect is statistically significant in a univariate model. However, when a multivariate model controls for the effect of both parental death and divorce, number of living grandparents *is* a significant predictor of the probability of being killed.[3] It seems that Ache grandparents could and did save their grandchildren from child homicide. Thus, children with more grandparents were less likely to be killed when other factors are controlled. Data show that aunts and uncles, on the other hand, have no statistical effect at all on the chances that a child will be killed, despite the fact that some Ache informants claimed otherwise.

I would have saved my sister's child from being killed if I had been there. He was a beautiful white-skinned boy (translated from an interview with Chachugi taped in 1984).

Finally, our results suggest that children with secondary fathers may be less likely to be victims of child homicide than those with only a single primary father, though the effect is not statistically significant in this sample.[4] This agrees with our general impression based on informant statements suggesting that father death or divorce is particularly likely to lead to child homicide if the child has no other possible genetic father. This observation will be discussed in detail in a later section.

The recognition that paternal help is critical to offspring survival also has strong implications for understanding Ache mating and parental investment patterns, and for explaining different rates of mate desertion (divorce). Indeed, both in the forest and on the reservation the Ache are likely to invoke the welfare of offspring as the main reason why a couple having marital difficulty should remain together.

[Father is about to leave mother.] Then grandma says to her daughter, "Why did you do it? You probably hit your husband in the face." Then mom cries when grandma is mad at her. Grandma is real mad. "Don't hit a man in the face, why did you hit your companion in the face?" Then Dad got angry. He got really angry and didn't have her (Mom) any more. He left her. He left her for another lover. Then grandma scolded mom. Why did you hit the one in the face who used to share with you big pieces of coati fat, do you want to be left? That's what grandma said to mom. We (kids) all cried then when our father left. When we all cried grandma brought dad back. Dad took mom back again. Grandma was the one who brought him back. She scolded him angrily. "Take back again the one you left and keep her

for good. What are you going to do, leave all your kids behind?" (Baepurangi in Sammons 1978:38).

My dad said to my mother, "Go over there to your lover, to the place of the one who will (wants to) have you." Then my dad said "I dreamed I was going to die. I dreamed that I was going to make dirt." Then after seeing the palm heart that my dad chopped out my mom said "You won't live anymore, this palm heart is not new (good edible shoot). This palm heart is rotten in the center." Then my dad said, "Go over there to the one who wants you (will have you). I am going to die." Then my dad also said to my mom, "When I die don't go whacking my kids. When I die don't leave my kids. Don't let my children yell when I die." Then dad also said to mom, "When I die be sure to instruct the kids (not to yell or they will be buried with him)" (Brikugi in Sammons 1978:92).

Since models of mate desertion derived from evolutionary theory generally emphasize the importance of parental impact on offspring well-being as a critical variable in determining the incidence of mate desertion (Maynard Smith 1977), these data have important implications for understanding divorce rates in Ache society. Indeed, a crude model of mate desertion based on the impact of desertion on offspring and the probability that males can find another fertile spouse is helpful for making qualitative predictions about relative divorce rates between the Ache and at least one other foraging society (Hurtado and Hill 1991).

SEX-BIASED INVESTMENT

Biased sex ratios in junior age grades is a commonly observed phenomenon among humans, and many explanations have been proposed for these observations (see Sief 1990 for review). Ache data show a strong male bias in the sex ratio of children born prior to contact (Figure 13.3), and significantly better survivorship of male children during the forest period (see Chapter 6). Informants have also clearly indicated to us that male children were preferred during the forest period (there may still be a preference among older people) and that male children were treated better and received more food from both their parents and other band members.

Upon seeing a deformed baby (or one born feet first) we say "Your baby is bad because you are mean, why do you think your baby was made so badly?" That's what we say when a baby is deformed (or born feet first). We say it's messed up. When it's born right we say born good. "Is it a boy? Yes, a boy." "Is it a girl? Yes, a girl." "Because you talked against your husband you didn't have a boy." Grandma scolds her. "Because you fought so much with your husband you had a baby with a big vagina" (Tejugi in Sammons 1978:124).

If the part around the vertebra of the monkey was really fat it wouldn't be shared with our sister. Then my sister would get really angry. Then she would yell to grandpa. When it wasn't shared with her our sister would yell to grandpa. "Grandpa, they are not sharing it with me," that's how my sister would talk to grandpa. Then dad would toss a monkey arm to his daughter. "What do you think, that you are a boy, crying so much for meat all the time?" That's what my father would say to his daughter (Baepurangi in Sammons 1978:45).

This general preference for male children is clear despite the fact that some individual Ache have indicated to us that they personally had either no preference or even a slight preference for female children. In particular, younger individuals at reservation settlements are more likely to express no sex preference, but some attitude is detected in some conversations about forest life as well.

[male speaker] When I almost died my sisters all cried. Then mom scolded my sisters. "You who hit your brother so much, why do you cry now young maids?" That's what mom said. She didn't usually scold her daughters. She never hit them. She really loved her female children. She had only a few daughters. Only two. She had many sons. We were many (us boys). Another old woman (their godmother) had said to mom, "You don't have many daughters, why do you hit them, why do you scold them?" (Baepurangi in Sammons 1978:40).

The number of children born between 1940 and 1970 to women for whom we have fertility data that probably includes every birth (see Chapter 4) is 313 males and 251 females. The data thus indicate a forest period sex ratio of 1.25 males for each female ever born. Because 70% of all males survived to age fifteen but only 60% of female children survived to that age (Table 6.1), the junior age grades show strikingly biased sex ratios (Figure 4.10b). Population waves like those shown in the age structure data in Chapter 4 can also be seen clearly in the sex ratio trends prior to contact (Figure 13.3). The waves do not correspond to each other, however, and there is no relationship between sex ratio in a particular year and the total number of children born that year, as might be expected if the sex ratio were biased in particularly difficult years (data not shown).

In a previous publication we suggested that the populationwide male-biased sex ratio could be the result of the lower cost of raising male children (Hill and Kaplan 1988b). More than a half century ago Fisher (1930) showed that if one sex were less costly to raise, more individuals of that sex should be produced. Others have expanded on Fisher's idea and shown that expected fitness gains by each sex as a function of investment in that sex should ultimately determine optimal offspring sex ratio (Charnov 1982). Since we know that males produce more food than females during their adolescent years (Hill and Kaplan 1988a), we reasoned that males might give back some food to their parents or younger siblings and thus be cheaper to raise, when all the costs of investment were calculated throughout the entire period of parental investment.

Subsequent analyses render the above argument unlikely. First, Kaplan (1994) has shown that Ache children are probably costly to parents throughout their entire lives. Children do not produce enough food to meet their own needs until late adolescence, and parents produce far more than they consume even in old age. Thus, food resources are generally flowing down from one generation to the next, and parents are generally providing help to children (and grandchildren) rather than vice versa. Second, females marry at younger ages than males and often bring an older male provider (their husband) into the family residence group. Adolescent males often leave their parents' band and thus provide nothing to their close kin. Third, data in Tables 13.1–13.5 do not support the idea that male siblings perform as "helpers at the nest." The survivorship rates of children are not higher if they have adolescent brothers who could help feed them (Tables 13.1 and 13.2). Parents with adolescent male children do not show higher fertility than parents with adolescent female children, and adult brothers do not increase the fertility of their siblings any more than adult sisters do.[5] Instead, men with more brothers or sisters show higher fertility, whereas women with more brothers or sisters experienced lower fertility in the forest period (Tables 13.4 and 13.5). Finally, calculations of reproductive value (Figure 12.9) show that female children have a higher reproductive value at birth than do male children. This is primarily *because of* the sex ratio bias in adulthood, but it leaves us puzzled. If males can be expected to produce fewer children on average than females, and if they provide no extra help to close kin beyond that provided by females, why should women give birth to more sons on average, and amplify the sex ratio bias even more through selective female infanticide and childhood neglect? Clearly more research will be necessary in order to make sense of the precontact sex bias among the Ache.

A second observation about Ache sex ratio trends might make more sense. During the postcontact period Ache sex ratios have rapidly dropped to parity or below (Figure 13.3). During this same period Northern Ache men experienced a severe reduction in their fertility rates relative to Northern Ache women. This can be seen directly by comparing the reservation TFR for males of 6.5 with that of females, 8.5. The difference is also noticeable in the widening gap of reproductive value between females and males during the reservation period (Figure 12.9). During the postcontact period Northern Ache men have experienced low fertility relative to Northern Ache women for two reasons. First, more women than men died during contact epidemics, and this left a skewed adult sex ratio with many available men who could find no wife. Second, more "sophisticated" members of the two other Ache ethnic groups, who were contacted 10–15 years earlier than the Northern Ache, made a point of taking as many Northern Ache women as possible. Thus, Northern Ache men lost wives and potential wives to members of other Ache groups who had more resources and more political power at the reservation settlements. This pattern has only recently begun to subside. Because of the low expected fitness value of male offspring under these conditions, a shift toward a more female-biased sex ratio is consistent with basic predictions of sex ratio theory (e.g., Trivers and Willard 1973; Charnov 1982). Whether these trends will continue, leading to a more female-biased sex ratio like that which has been found for other small populations experiencing frequent hypergamous marriages with outsiders (e.g., Cronk 1989), remains to be seen.

PATTERNS IN FEMALE MATING AND FEMALE MATE CHOICE

The fact that adult male mortality was high among forest-living Ache, and that children often died or were killed after the death of their father, provides special conditions likely to affect mate choice patterns of Ache women. This situation is likely to characterize other mammals who also experience high rates of infanticide or benefit from considerable paternal investment. In order to cope with these conditions one obvious tactic available to females is to spread paternity probability among several males so the death of a single man will not mean that a child is truly orphaned. This female reproductive tactic has been suggested for other mammals as well. Hrdy (1979, 1981), for example, suggested that female primates might engage in copulation with multiple males in order to reduce the chance that a particular infant would be killed if its father were not available to defend it. If many males believe that they have some probability of paternity, they may all be willing to take some risk to defend a juvenile (or at least be unwilling to kill it). The Ache have a complex system of paternity (discussed in Chapters 7 and 9) in which females frequently copulated with several males during their pregnancy and announced the multiple paternity of a child at its birth (often even changing their claims of primary paternity later as some potential fathers died or were not present). Thus, fathers of Ache children include the *miare* (one who put it in), the *peroare* (ones who mixed it), the *momboare* (one who spilled it out), and the *bykuare* (ones who provided its essence). This system of common secondary fatherhood resulted in a situation where the average number of total "fathers" reported for each child in a large subset of our forest sample was 1.93 men who had sexual relations with the mother directly before or during her pregnancy.

From the traditional Ache point of view, the production of offspring involved a mother, all men who copulated with her, and also men who provided "the essence of the child" by supplying its mother with meat. These men were particularly concerned about the child's survival and had the right to punish either the mother or the father of a child if it should die. Not surprisingly, men who regularly supplied meat to the mother were also likely to be her lovers, and thus a secondary father of the child in question. Statements made by Ache informants in the context of stories about forest life clearly show this type of connection, and the importance of the secondary fathers to the well-being of a child whose primary father dies. Stories also suggest the theme of never-ending conflict between men and women over spreading of potential paternity and the production of extra children outside the marriage.

My secondary father will take care of me if my father dies. Yes, my secondary father will take care of me if my father dies. He will make me feel good (console me). Another, an old woman, will generally say to us, "Your secondary father will make you feel better, why do you cry?" That's how an old woman will talk to us. If dad dies you cry. Those who have many fathers don't cry (Baepurangi in Sammons 1978:52).

[In the context of a newborn child's possible illness after its father had come back from hunting one day] The Ache gave meat to the child. Then a child vomited the meat that it had eaten. Then grandma scolded the one (father) for denying that he was the father of another child. "Another man's penis was eaten. [As if she were talking to the other woman], why do you deny it? Another woman's baby was made, why do you deny it, in order not to be scolded you deny it?" Then our grandma said, "Go over there (somewhere where there were other Ache) and ask if that isn't your secondary father." "You better go follow your grandchild before it dies," the husband scolded. Then grandma went off behind the trail of the grandchild she had sent out. [Note: it is somewhat ambiguous from this text whether the mother or father of the child is being scolded for denying another lover. The grandmother talks as if she is scolding both sexes yet then sends the child out to look for another father.] (Brikugi in Sammons 1978:89).

Then if the child for whom one has provided the essence (gave meat to the mother) dies, he will hit the father of the child with a club. Yes, there will be a club fight if the one he provided the essence of dies. Then other Ache will grab hold of the club and shout, don't hit so many times. Yes, and the mother of the child will also be hit by the one who provided its essence (Byvangi in Sammons 1978:17).

Dad killed an armadillo and brought it. It was to provide the essence for his sister-in-law's child. His sister-in-law was pregnant. Dad customarily provided the essence for his sister-in-law's children. My uncle's kids were provided. My uncle's kids. Dad provided them horse (meat), the same as my essence. My uncle was (also) the one who provided my essence, horse. It was my uncle. My uncle was the one who shot my likeness (horse) to provide my essence to his sister-in-law. Then my essence was created from horse. . . . Dad used to hit his brother. He didn't like his brother. My uncle was disliked [by the speaker's father]. My dad would split his brother open and knock him down with a bow. After some point in time my father never liked his brother any more. He hated him. (My uncle) would have sex with his (my dad's) wife. My father never liked again the one that used to have sex with his wife. He would club fight with a bow then. In the forest they would club fight with bows (Baepurangi in Sammons 1978:49).

Mom was mean. Mom hit me with the knot of a log (because the speaker wouldn't carry an armadillo). She hit me with the knot of that log. Then I called dad. "Dad,

dad, dad," I called him. He answered back, "What are you crying so much for?"
"Mom hit me." (Dad said) "you're going to have few children, why do you go
around hitting them?" That's what dad said to mom. Dad could get really mad. He
hit mom in the forest when she had sex with another. Mom used to have sex with
another (or several others). He hit mom. They would have a fight. They would
scratch faces. He would really scratch mom's face. Dad was really strong. Mom
was weak. Mom used to hit dad in the face. Then he would scratch up her face in
revenge (to defend himself). Then mom would cry. Dad was really strong. Now he
never hits her any more, here at the reservation. Before where we used to live he
would hit her a lot. Now he doesn't hit her anymore (Baepurangi in Sammons
1978:43).

The possibility that secondary fathers might provide protection for small
children in the common event of the death of a primary father can be tested with
the Ache data. About 63% of the children in our forest sample were reported to
have one or more secondary fathers. The results of logistic regression show that
highest survivorship of children may be attained for children with one primary
and one secondary father (Figure 13.4). The difference in mortality between
those with no or one secondary father is significant but the difference in mortality
between those with two or more secondary fathers and those with no or one is not
significant.[6] Our best estimate of the shape of the relationship between age-
specific mortality and number of fathers suggests an intermediate number of total
fathers is optimal for child survival. Those children with one primary and one
secondary father show the highest survival in our data set, and one secondary
father is also the most common number reported during our reproductive interviews. Presumably women who produced children with more than two fathers
greatly reduced the confidence of paternity for all the candidate fathers and risked
losing parental investment altogether. Probably for this reason children with
three or more fathers appear to have fared worse than those with only one or two
fathers.Informants have also suggested that some children were better treated
than others, and that some were killed flat out even when both their parents (and
some secondary fathers) were alive.

Bejaro-the-killer was really mean. Really really mean. He came back from hunting
and heard my brother crying. My brother was crying a lot and wouldn't shut up.
Then Bejaro slammed him against a tree. He slammed him and he was dead. My
mother was crying when my father returned from hunting. My father didn't do
anything. He was upset. He didn't do anything. He was really afraid of Bejaro-the-
killer. Bejaro was really strong (translated from an interview with Kravachi in
1984).

We expected that this type of difference between men might lead to a preference for the character of fathers as well as the number of candidate fathers.
Specifically we wondered if women would prefer strong men who could win club

fights and defend their offspring from potential abuse. However, a few informal interviews conducted in 1990 and 1991 did not support this conjecture. Instead, the women we asked were adamant that "club fight winners" were not desirable mates.

> *We don't like those men who love to club fight. "If they love to club fight they beat their wives," they say. "They don't know how to have women." That's what we say (translated from an interview with Javagi in 1990).*

> *Women don't love men who win club fights, they love men who are strong, men who work hard and endure uncomfortable conditions without complaining (translated from an interview with Achipurangi in 1994).*

Nevertheless, since we have data on each man who lived in the forest and whether or not he had ever killed anyone, we can examine the relationship between status as a "killer" and life history variation. In our sample 19.3% of all adult men had killed another person (Ache or outsider). Chagnon (1988) has shown that Yanomamo men who have killed have higher lifetime reproductive success than those who have never killed, and that this difference is primarily due to higher fertility through a greater number of wives (or greater probability of having a wife at each age). Ache data (Table 13.10) suggest that men who have killed do not have higher fertility than those who have never killed anyone, but they *are* characterized by higher offspring survival. This could be the result of a direct protective effect of strong fathers, or perhaps some inherited factor that makes both father and offspring healthier than the average Ache in the population (assuming that men who have killed are healthier than others).

SUMMARY

In this chapter we examine kin effects on mortality and fertility rates in the Ache population. Kin effects are estimated by looking at the relationship between presence and absence of certain kin, or the total number of living kin in a particular category during the interval at risk, and the probability of birth or death taking place. Obviously there are other explanations for positive or negative relationships that do not imply a causal connection between kin helping and the life history variable of interest. For example, if children with a living grandmother have a higher probability of surviving, one explanation could be genetically conferred disease resistance. Another explanation could be that the extended family had more resources available that were invested in both grandmother and grandchild. Despite these problems we believe the results of statistical analyses are interesting and should lead to improved research design for detecting kin investment in the future. The lack of a relationship between the presence of some living kin and a life history trait, and the strong relationship found when looking at other kin, is likely to eliminate some possible interpretations. For example, if living grandparents are positively associated with survival of children but number of living aunts and uncles has no relationship to child survival, both of the alternative explanations presented above become unlikely. Aunts and uncles are just as related to a child as are its grandparents (assuming 100% paternity confidence). Both categories of kin are also equally related to a child's parents, and family resources should be just as likely to be expended on aunts and uncles as on grandparents. In many cases, therefore, our interpretation of associations between kin presence and life history traits as a measure of "kin impact" on those traits may not be too far wrong.

The analyses suggest very strong impact of parental investment on child survival during the forest period. Both mother's and father's death led to a great increase in the mortality rate of children, as did divorce. The proportional impact of maternal presence on child mortality diminished with the age of the child, whereas the proportional impact on mortality due to paternal death or divorce did not diminish with age during childhood in the forest period. Parental impact on reservation child mortality rate is less pronounced but probably fails to achieve statistical significance only because very few children in our risk set were orphans (thus leading to a high standard error of the parameter estimate). Parameter estimates of parental impact during the reservation period were in the same direction as those in the forest sample, and generally close to the same magnitude. However, in recent years the services provided on reservation settlements by Catholic and Protestant missionaries to orphaned children are substantial. At the Chupa Pou mission, the missionaries have constructed a special house just for orphaned children, often allow them to eat meals with mission personnel, and in some cases have allowed small orphaned children to be temporarily adopted by members of the local Catholic community.

Interestingly, we can find little evidence that other close kin, such as adult siblings, grandparents, aunts, or uncles, have much of an influence on child mortality rates either in the forest or during the reservation period. Furthermore, in the forest period, children who would appear to be at a disadvantage for receiving kin help because of the presence of many other young kin competitors actually show higher survivorship that those with fewer kin competitors. This "phenotypic correlation" may be due to heritable disease resistance, differences in kin group resource access, or some other factor that we have not yet examined. The analyses of the impact of adult kin on adult mortality did not uncover any significant relationships. Again the interpretation of this result should not be construed to mean that we have shown that adult kin do not effect each other's mortality rates, only that we cannot show such effects in our Ache sample, which includes only 148 adult deaths. There is a hint that male kin (father and brothers) may impact more on adult survival than female kin, and this possibility should be examined in other data sets with larger samples.

The impact of close kin on age-specific fertility rate shows a very different pattern from what we found with mortality. First, adult siblings have more influence on each other's fertility than do parents. In the forest period, for example, the fertility of both sexes shows some relationship to the number of brothers or sisters that are alive during the risk interval. Second, the relationship between number of living sibs and fertility is more consistent for males than for females. Ache men living in the forest or during the reservation period had significantly higher fertility with each additional brother or sister who was alive during a risk interval. The magnitude of this effect is almost constant whether brothers or sisters are counted, and whether the fertility measurement takes place in the forest or during the reservation period. In all cases and additional adult sib results in a 10–15% increase in age-specific fertility.

The relationship between fertility and number of siblings for Ache women is erratic across time periods. Siblings do seem to impact on female fertility in the forest but not during the reservation period. Finally, the impact of siblings on female fertility during the forest period is negative rather than positive! Women with more brothers or more sisters were characterized by a 10% reduction in age-specific fertility during the forest period for each additional adult sibling living during the risk interval. This suggests that during the forest period Ache women increased the fertility of their brothers, but that those brothers somehow decreased the fertility of their sisters. Furthermore, sisters seem to have decreased each other's fertility during the forest period. Neither effect is easy to explain. If women are sacrificing to help their brothers, the analyses suggest they give up one child of their own for each child that they help their brothers produce. Since women are more related to their own children than to the offspring of their brothers, and because paternity confidence is always lower than maternity confidence, such a kin-helping pattern would not be evolutionarily stable. If sisters really do decrease each other's fertility, we are at a loss to provide a functional explanation for such a pattern unless this is a birth order effect (e.g., Hrdy and Judge 1993).

Measurements of kin impacts on fertility and survival allow us to develop explicit models to test hypotheses about kinship and life history traits. One of the most interesting is the "grandmother hypothesis" for explaining why human females experience menopause. This hypothesis suggests that women reach an age where greater fitness gains can be achieved by investing in already existing kin (offspring and grandoffspring) than by trying to produce new offspring. Ache data do suggest that postmenopausal women probably have a positive effect on the survival of their grandoffspring and the fertility of their sons. There seems to be no impact of mothers on the fertility of their daughters, however. In this chapter we developed a model that assumes that older women can use time and energy either to produce their own offspring (with some efficiency lower than that achieved by younger women) or to influence the fertility of their adult offspring and the survival of their grandoffspring.

Since all women do undergo menopause and cannot use any time and energy for their own fertility in old age, we assumed that the logistic regressions described in earlier sections concerning the impact of older women on their children's fertility or their grandchildren's mortality gave us a reasonable estimate of the fitness gains that can be achieved by diverting resources from reproduction. Such an assumption allows us to calculate that women would maximize fitness by producing their own offspring if the same resources could be used to achieve a fertility rate about one-sixth of maximal female fertility. Thus, the model suggested that only after a marked reduction in fertility "efficiency" would natural selection be expected to favor a switch from allocating resources in reproductive effort to allocating resources to help offspring and grandoffspring. Further modeling (not shown here) has demonstrated that this conclusion does not change when parameters are changed unless the measures of kin help we have employed are changed. Still, we are concerned that the removal of a specific kin from our model will not allow for an accurate measure of the demographic impact of kin help because other kin will adjust their investment accordingly. Substantial increases in the kin helping effects (offspring fertility and grandoffspring survival) could favor menopause in this model, but there are no empirical data on any human group to suggest that kin helping effects are likely to be much greater than those we estimate.

An increased impact of older women on the fitness of their close kin is most likely during periods of extreme stress. Perhaps the Ache data, which come from a period of high population growth, will not be relevant to selective pressures for reproductive senescence during population bottlenecks. This is discussed again in the next chapter. However, since the goal of the hypothesis is to explain the reduction in female fertility through time (eventually reaching zero), we tentatively conclude that the grandmother hypothesis is not likely to account for the human female fertility profile. We do note however that the grandmother hypothesis (in some form) *must* be the correct explanation for the existence of a postreproductive life span in women. If postreproductive women did not contribute significantly to the survival and fertility of other kin, there would be no selective pressure at all to counteract rapid senescence and death following menopause. Since men and women senesce at about the same rates in late adulthood, it must be the case that female genetic contribution during that time is about as high as male genetic contribution.

Infanticide and child homicide rates among the Ache during the forest period also seem to be strongly influenced by the presence or absence of close kin. Children with one or both parents dead, or those whose parents are divorced, show much higher rates of victimization than those whose parents are alive and married. The presence of a living grandfather seems to have a strong impact on the probability that a Ache child will be killed. Living grandmothers also decrease the homicide rate on their grandoffspring, but the magnitude of the effect is smaller and only attains significance when parental variables are controlled.

Our data show that the Ache were characterized by extremely high rates of child homicide during the forest period, when about 14% of all male children and 23% of all female children born were killed before the age of ten. Girls were killed more often than boys at all ages after the first year of life. Younger children were at much greater risk than older children, as predicted by their low reproductive value, but younger mothers were not more likely to have an offspring killed than older mothers, contrary to simple expectations from life history theory (Daly and Wilson 1988). Perhaps this pattern is complicated by the fact that the killer in most cases was an individual other than a child's own parents. Unfortunately we did not collect information systematically on the identity of every killer so this hypothesis cannot be examined with our current data set.

The sex ratio of children produced and raised is an interesting problem in kin investment. For the most part, parents are expected to invest in offspring of whichever sex will give the highest fitness return for investment. Since those returns are likely to vary with ecology, mating system, and other social variables, organisms might be expected to show male-biased, female-biased, or unbiased sex ratio under different circumstances. The Ache data suggest a strongly male-biased sex ratio during the forest period followed by an increasingly neutral or even female-biased sex ratio in the reservation period. Since kin investment patterns can also affect the cost of "raising" children of each sex, sex ratio is not only a manifestation of investment but can be a reaction to particular investment patterns. If, for example, male offspring were to provide more help to their siblings when they reached adolescence, natural selection might favor the production of more male offspring, or a greater investment in male offspring during childhood. Just such a scenario was proposed by us for the male-biased sex ratio observed during the forest period (Hill and Kaplan 1988b). Results of analyses presented in this chapter, however, do not support this hypothesis. Sisters had just as much of a positive impact as did brothers on their adult male siblings' fertility, and both sexes showed equally detrimental impacts on their adult sisters' fertility rates. Neither sex produced any significant impact on the survival of their younger siblings or on the fertility of their parents after they reached adolescence.

Thus, we still do not know what factor ultimately explains the male-biased sex ratio during the forest period. One possibility that we cannot absolutely rule out is that the high sex ratio is due to chance, or reporting bias, although we have taken every precaution to exclude the second possibility (see Chapters 3 and 4). The recent shift toward a more equal or female-biased sex ratio, if it is real, may indicate parental investment patterns under conditions of increasing outmarriage. Northern Ache men are lower status than Ache men of the other groups in their breeding population, and some Ache women may soon begin to mate with higher-status Paraguayan peasants, causing an even greater imbalance in the expected lifetime fertility of sons and daughters. Thus, the situation is somewhat similar to that described by Cronk (1989) for the Mukogodo of Kenya, where a female-biased sex ratio is found among a low-status group that commonly mates with neighboring high-status groups. Whether these trends will lead to a long-term female-biased sex ratio remains to be seen.

Finally, we examine the impact of potential paternity on the survival of Ache children. In many populations of primates and humans around the world, females engage in copulations with multiple male partners. This behavior has not been well studied in humans, perhaps because both sexes have their own reasons for not wanting to acknowledge its frequency. In any case, since such female "promiscuity" is reported to be common in some societies and not as common in others, human biologists need to consider alternative explanations for such patterns. In our view there are two likely reasons for females to engage in copulation with multiple males. First, they may be wishing to acquire "good genes" from some partners and "paternal investment" from other partners in a universe in which few males possess both traits, and those males are in short supply. Second, females may be primarily concerned only with paternal investment and recognize that spreading paternity probability is a way to increase total paternal investment or reduce the risk of very low levels of paternal investment (especially in the event of paternal death).

Since Ache data suggest that most offspring have at least two candidates for biological paternity, a functional approach would suggest that multiple paternity in the Ache case may result in higher offspring reproductive value than that which characterizes children with a single father. Ache results tend to support this view, although a larger sample size would leave less room for doubt. The positive (as well as negative) effects associated with multiple paternity are particularly likely to be observed among the Ache because of a strong cultural system that insists that all potential fathers should be identified (by a woman and by the men themselves). In our sample we found no cases where either sex made a paternity claim for a child that was denied by the other sex. Women and men interviewed generally agreed about who the potential fathers of each child were, and disagreement was usually due to omission through faulty recollection. In more than ten years of interviews we have found no cases where Ache men claimed to have had sexual relations with a woman who denied it, or where women claimed sexual relations that a man denied. This pattern is in contrast with that found in modern societies and may be due to the lack of privacy in Ache society.

In summary, the use of discrete-time logistic regression hazards models appears to be a powerful tool for measuring the life history impacts of investment by close kin. Some effects are clearly evident even with crude analyses, whereas others may require much more complete control of confounding variables. This chapter just begins to explore some of the many possibilities and is meant primarily to stimulate further research in this area. Particular attention should be paid to operationalizing variables of interest and assessing kin impacts through techniques more sophisticated than simply coding the presence or absence of a particular kin category during an interval at risk. In any case, since the life history of an organism is ultimately designed to maximize genetic representation through time, and since a good proportion of an individual's genes will often reside in bodies other than his or her offspring, the investigation of kinship effects on life histories of individuals must be incorporated as an integral part of the overall life history research agenda.

NOTES

1. Logistic regression was carried out on the hazard of child homicide for children aged 0 and with the independent variable of sex. The model chi-square was only 0.011 with a p of 0.91.

2. Multivariate logistic regression models with age, age squared, sex, father alive, mother alive, parental divorce, and each of the parental states (mother, father, divorced) as controlled covariates in turn, shows −2 log likelihood model improvements of 2.893, 0.05, and 0.928, respectively, with the interaction terms "mother × age," "father × age," and "divorced × age," respectively, added in, parameter estimates are 0.2473, −0.0227, and −0.0773, respectively and p values of 0.09, 0.89, and 0.42, respectively. Only the "mother × age" interaction term approaches significance.

3. A multivariate logistic regression model with age, age squared, sex, father alive, mother alive, and parental divorce as controlled covariates shows a −2 log likelihood model improvement of 3.587 with the variable "number of grandmothers" added in, parameter estimate = −0.2991, $p = 0.06$. The −2 log likelihood model improvement is 7.356 with the variable "number of grandfathers" added in, parameter estimate = −0.4283, $p = 0.007$.

4. A multivariate logistic regression model with age, age squared, sex, father alive, mother alive, and parental divorce as controlled covariates shows a −2 log likelihood model improvement of 1.87 with the variable "number of secondary fathers" added in, parameter estimate = −0.3252, $p = 0.24$.

5. A multivariate logistic regression model of female fertility in the forest with age and age squared controlled as covariates shows a −2 log likelihood model improvement of 1.0 with the variable "number of male children age ten years or greater" added in, parameter estimate = 0, $p = 0.5$.

6. A multivariate logistic regression model of mortality from age 0–9 with age, age squared, and sex as controlled covariates shows a −2 log likelihood model improvement of 3.769 with the variables "0 secondary fathers" and "2+ secondary fathers" added in, $p = 0.2$ for model improvement. For 0 secondary fathers, parameter estimate = −0.7189, partial $p = 0.058$. For 2+ secondary fathers, parameter estimate = −0.4426, partial $p = 0.326$.

Table 13.1. Kin Effects on Child Mortality Rates during the Forest Period: Age 0–9
    years

Variable	Mean value	Parameter	Change in −2 log likelihood	p
age	3.92	controlled	controlled	controlled
age²	23.59	controlled	controlled	controlled
sex	0.57	controlled	controlled	controlled
mother's age	27.23	controlled	controlled	controlled
mother's age²	802.27	controlled	controlled	controlled
mother alive	0.98	−1.6277	15.946	**.000**
father alive	0.95	−1.1146	12.999	**.000**
parents divorced**	0.14	1.0892	25.085	**.000**
adult brothers	0.72	0.1075	0.678	.460
adult sisters	0.60	−0.1038	0.406	.810
living grandmothers	1.25	−0.1924	2.392	.156
living grandfathers	0.96	−0.1715	1.914	.240
living aunts	2.70	0.0464	0.831	.430
living uncles	3.82	−0.0009	0	.990
total kin helpers†	12.15	−0.0147	0.3	.840
helpers/competitors‡	0.25	2.1608	4.175	**.043**

** analyses included only children whose parents were both living.

 † total number of parents, gransparents, aunts, and uncles alive during the risk interval.

 ‡ total number of parents, grandparents, aunts, and uncles, divided by total number of first cousins
   and siblings alive during the risk interval.

The *p* value is based on the chi-square distribution of change in −2 log likelihood of the model with
each new variable added independently to the model with control variables and an increase of 1 degree of freedom.

Table 13.2. Kin Effects on Child Mortality Rates at Reservation Settlements: Age 0–4 years

Variable	Mean value	Parameter	Change in −2 log likelihood	p
age	1.81	controlled	controlled	controlled
age²	5.29	controlled	controlled	controlled
sex	0.50	controlled	controlled	controlled
mother's age	29.70	controlled	controlled	controlled
mother's age²	937.24	controlled	controlled	controlled
mother alive	0.99	−2.2349	2.057	.210
father alive	0.99	*	*	*
parents divorced**	0.10	0.6286	1.808	.260
adult brothers	0.39	0.3171	1.889	.245
adult sisters	0.27	0.4123	1.913	.240
living grandmothers	0.38	−0.3238	1.457	.320
living grandfathers	0.43	0.1766	0.442	.510
living aunts	2.80	0.0614	0.524	.490
living uncles	3.34	−0.0729	0.676	.460
total kin helpers†	7.16	−0.0229	0.203	.860
helpers/competitors‡	0.24	−0.9924	6.418	**.012**

* conversion matrix singular, no statistics calculated (no child deaths to father = 0).

** analyses included only children whose parents were both living.

† total number of parents, gransparents, aunts, and uncles alive during the risk interval.

‡ total number of parents, grandparents, aunts, and uncles, divided by total number of first cousins and siblings alive during the risk interval.

The *p* value is based on the chi-square distribution of change in −2 log likelihood of the model with each new variable added independently to the model with control variables and an increase of 1 degree of freedom.

Table 13.3. Kin Effects on Adult Mortality Rates during the Forest Period: Age 15–60

Variable	Mean value	Parameter	Change in −2 log likelihood	p
age	29.10	controlled	controlled	controlled
age^2	969.80	controlled	controlled	controlled
sex	0.59	controlled	controlled	controlled
mother alive	0.67	0.1646	0.476	.496
father alive	0.57	−0.3021	1.741	.270
adult brothers	2.04	−0.0779	0.929	.416
adult sisters	1.34	0.0297	0.108	.870

The *p*-value is based on the chi-square distribution of change in −2 log likelihood of the model with each new variable added independently to the model with control variables and an increase of 1 degree of freedom.

Table 13.4. Kin Effects on Female Fertility Rate: Age 15–50

Variable	Mean value	Parameter	Change in −2 log likelihood	p
Forest				
age	26.63	controlled	controlled	controlled
age^2	794.38	controlled	controlled	controlled
mother alive	0.72	0.0367	0.0990	.880
father alive	0.61	0.0786	0.4870	.490
adult brothers	1.64	−0.1067	7.3950	**.007**
adult sisters	1.01	−0.0848	2.5840	.120
Reservation				
age	29.94	controlled	controlled	controlled
age^2	3290.17	controlled	controlled	controlled
mother alive	0.24	−0.0639	0.2280	.853
father alive	0.24	0.0525	0.1310	.870
adult brothers	1.59	−0.0434	0.7000	.456
adult sisters	1.20	−0.0210	0.2140	.856

The *p*-value is based on the chi-square distribution of change in −2 log likelihood of the model with each new variable added independently to the model with control variables and an increase of 1 degree of freedom.

Table 13.5. Kin Effects on Male Fertility Rates: Age 18–50

Variable	Mean value	Parameter	Change in −2 log likelihood	p
Forest				
age	31.45	controlled	controlled	controlled
age²	1107.00	controlled	controlled	controlled
mother alive	0.66	0.1928	3.2270	**.077**
father alive	0.50	0.0636	0.3800	.520
adult brothers	1.82	0.0950	5.0010	**.025**
adult sisters	1.30	0.0899	5.4010	**.021**
Reservation				
age	31.70	controlled	controlled	controlled
age²	1084.00	controlled	controlled	controlled
mother alive	0.14	−0.1030	0.3100	.530
father alive	0.22	−0.0228	0.0230	.870
adult brothers	1.59	0.1233	6.6170	**.010**
adult sisters	1.09	0.1451	6.2060	**.014**

The *p*-value is based on the chi-square distribution of change in −2 log likelihood of the model with each new variable added independently to the model with control variables and an increase of 1 degree of freedom.

Table 13.6. Adult Sons, Adult Daughters, and Grandchildren of Women in the Forest at Age 50

Woman			Adult children				Number of grandchildren by age									
ID	Born	Died	Sons	Mean age	Daughters	Mean age	0	1	2	3	4	5	6	7	8	9
2031	1900	1973	0	.	4	20.5	2	2	0	1	0	1	0	0	0	0
2032	1900	1972	3	21.7	2	20.0	1	0	2	0	0	0	0	1	0	0
2080	1900	1950	2	19.0	1	31.0	0	0	0	0	1	0	0	0	1	0
2083	1900	1968	1	16.0	0	.	0	0	0	0	0	0	0	0	0	0
2030	1901	1973	1	19.0	2	28.5	1	0	0	1	0	0	1	1	0	0
2035	1902	1972	2	16.5	0	.	0	0	0	0	0	0	0	0	0	0
2034	1903	1973	0	.	0	.	0	0	0	0	0	0	0	0	0	0
2069	1904	1972	0	.	1	26.0	0	1	0	0	0	0	1	0	0	1
2042	1905	1967	3	25.0	3	24.3	2	2	1	1	1	5	0	1	1	1
2071	1905	1972	2	21.5	1	26.0	1	0	0	0	1	0	0	1	0	0
2075	1905	1973	2	21.0	1	17.0	2	0	1	0	0	0	0	0	0	0
2078	1905	1961	0	.	2	23.0	0	1	0	0	0	0	1	0	1	0
2085	1905	1968	2	26.0	2	22.0	1	1	0	1	0	0	1	0	0	1
2090	1905	1960	2	25.0	0	.	0	0	0	0	0	0	0	0	0	0
2092	1905	1960	1	35.0	0	.	0	0	0	0	0	0	1	0	0	0
2046	1906	1972	4	24.0	0	.	0	0	1	1	0	2	1	1	0	0

3001	1907	1985	2	26.5	1	17.0	1	0	0	1	0	0	0	0	1	0
3002	1907	1972	1	32.0	1	19.0	1	1	0	1	0	0	0	0	0	0
2058	1910	1972	3	23.0	1	22.0	3	1	1	0	0	0	0	0	0	0
2064	1910	1972	0	.	0	.	0	0	0	0	0	0	0	0	0	0
4323	1910	1972	3	21.3	1	22.0	1	1	0	1	0	0	0	0	0	0
3019	1913	1972	3	20.0	1	24.0	0	1	0	0	0	2	0	0	0	0
3020	1913	1972	1	26.0	1	23.0	1	1	1	2	1	0	0	1	0	0
3021	1913	1972	2	21.5	1	27.0	0	0	1	0	0	1	0	1	0	0
4053	1914	1972	2	20.0	1	27.0	0	2	1	1	1	1	1	0	0	0
3025	1915	1972	2	24.0	1	25.0	0	1	0	0	0	1	1	0	1	0
3030	1916	1993	3	20.3	2	16.0	0	0	0	0	0	1	1	0	0	0
3031	1916	1972	3	24.3	1	.	0	1	1	1	0	1	0	0	0	0
3803	1916	1972	2	28.5	0	.	0	0	0	1	0	0	0	0	0	0
4297	1916	1971	1	25.0	1	20.0	0	0	0	1	1	1	0	0	0	0
3032	1917	1968	3	24.0	0	.	1	0	1	0	1	0	0	0	0	0
3035	1917	1993	0	.	2	21.5	1	1	0	2	0	0	0	0	2	0
3033	1920	1972	4	20.3	2	23.5	1	2	0	2	1	0	1	0	1	1
3047	1920	1971	1	17.0	1	19.0	0	0	0	0	0	0	0	0	0	0
4120	1920	1972	0	.	2	21.0	0	1	1	0	0	1	0	0	0	0
Mean values			1.74	22.98	1.09	22.61	0.57	0.57	0.31	0.40	0.17	0.43	0.20	0.23	0.23	0.09

Table 13.7. The Calculations for a Kin-selection Model of Menopause

Yearly impact on fitness through kin help if women stop reproducing at age 50

Increase in son's production of offspring

mean number of sons	mean fertility of sons	mother effect proportional fertility increase	mean extra offspring produced from all sons	genetic relatedness discount (0.50)
1.743	0.170	0.213	0.063	**0.032**

Increase in daughter's production of offspring

mean number of daughters	mean fertility of daughters	mother effect proportional fertility increase	mean extra offspring produced from all sons	genetic relatedness discount −0.500
1.086	0.260	0.037	0.011	**0.005**

Impact on existing grandchildren if women stop reproducing at age 50 to help grandchildren

age	mean number of grandchildren at age x	children without grandmother (mean mortality)	proportional mortality with grandmother alive	increase in number of grandchildren who survive at age x	reproductive value at age x	genetic relatedness discount (0.50)
0	0.571	0.115	0.825	0.013	1.000	0.007
1	0.571	0.045	0.825	0.005	1.149	0.003
2	0.314	0.024	0.825	0.001	1.228	0.001

3	0.400	0.033	0.825	0.002	1.280	0.002
4	0.171	0.029	0.825	0.001	1.347	0.001
5	0.429	0.019	0.825	0.001	1.415	0.001
6	0.200	0.023	0.825	0.001	1.472	0.001
7	0.229	0.029	0.825	0.001	1.535	0.001
8	0.229	0.011	0.825	0.000	1.614	0.000
9	0.086	0.018	0.825	0.000	1.655	0.000
					subtotal	0.015
						0.052

Total increase in reproductive value of kin measured in offspring equivalents

VS.

Yearly production of offspring if women continued reproduction at age 50

mean survival age 50–51	mean survival age 27–28	proportional reproductive value of children born to mother at age 50	required fertility rate in order to produce as many offspring equivalents as possible through kin help
0.983	0.992	0.991	**0.053**

maximum observed 5-year fertility rate	0.318
percent of maximum fertility that would favor reproductive termination	**16.55%**

Table 13.8.   Child Homicide among Forest-living Ache as a Function of Age, Sex, and Kin Help

Variable	Mean value	Parameter	Change in −2 log likelihood	p
Age 15–60 years				
age	3.92	−0.3138	17.08	**.000**
age²	23.60	0.0213	2.213	.130
sex (1 = male)	0.57	−0.5159	6.888	**.009**
age × sex	2.24	−0.0994	1.753	.240
With age and sex controlled, the effect of adding one additional variable				
mother dead	0.02	1.5029	9.229	**.003**
father dead	0.05	1.3728	16.554	**.001**
parents divorced	0.86	1.0244	19.714	**.001**
mother's age	27.20	−0.00115	0.008	.920
living grandmother	1.26	−0.2095	2.207	.190
living grandfathers	0.95	−0.3574	5.979	**.016**
living aunts	2.69	0.0354	0.59	.476
living uncles	3.80	0.00163	0.001	.990

The *p*-value is based on the chi-square distribution of change in −2 log likelihood of the model with each new variable added independently to the model with control variables and an increase of 1 degree of freedom.

Table 13.9. Age-specific Rates of Child Homicide During the Forest Period

Age	At risk	Killed	Probability of being killed at age x	Probability survive to age x	Percent born who are killed by infanticide*
Males					
0	358	18	0.050	1.000	0.050
1	310	7	0.023	0.885	0.020
2	288	2	0.007	0.863	0.006
3	274	7	0.026	0.848	0.022
4	249	3	0.012	0.820	0.010
5	238	0	0.000	0.807	0.000
6	227	3	0.013	0.800	0.011
7	218	3	0.014	0.789	0.011
8	203	2	0.010	0.775	0.008
9	189	2	0.011	0.760	0.008
				total	0.145
Females					
0	289	14	0.048	1.000	0.048
1	247	12	0.049	0.884	0.043
2	221	3	0.014	0.823	0.011
3	206	5	0.024	0.797	0.019
4	192	6	0.031	0.770	0.024
5	179	6	0.034	0.734	0.025
6	169	5	0.030	0.709	0.021
7	157	7	0.045	0.684	0.030
8	146	0	0.000	0.653	0.000
9	144	2	0.014	0.653	0.009
				total	0.231

* The percent killed at each age times the probability of surviving to that age from the forest life table (Table 6.1).

Table 13.10. The Relationship between Having Killed Another Person and Fertility or Offspring Mortality for Ache Men Living during the Forest Period

Variable	Mean value	Parameter	Change in −2 log likelihood	p
Fertility: Age 18–50 years				
age	31.45	controlled	controlled	controlled
age²	1107.00	controlled	controlled	controlled
has killed someone	0.20	−0.0997	0.755	.447
Offspring mortality: Age 0–9 years				
age	1.81	controlled	controlled	controlled
age²	5.29	controlled	controlled	controlled
sex	0.56	controlled	controlled	controlled
mother's age	27.18	controlled	controlled	controlled
mother's age²	799.60	controlled	controlled	controlled
father has killed	1.09	0.1451	4.986	**.026**

The *p*-value is based on the chi-square distribution of change in −2 log likelihood of the model with each new variable added independently to the model with control variables and an increase of 1 degree of freedom.

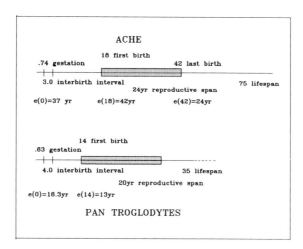

Figure 13.1. Comparison of some important life history variables for Ache women and chimpanzees *(Pan troglodytes).* Points along the bar mark gestation period, interbirth interval, age at first birth, reproductive span, age at last birth, and maximum lifespan (age at which 5% of all individuals born are still alive). Below the bar are life expectancies calculated at birth, at first reproduction, and at last reproduction (adapted from Hill and Hurtado 1991; chimpanzee data from Goodall 1986 and Nishida et al. 1990).

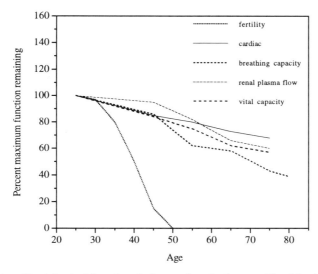

Figure 13.2. Physiological functions in human females by age. Physiological data from Mildvan and Strehler (1960) and fertility data from Wood (1990). Most body functions senesce at about the same time late in life, but female reproductive function is completely terminated by age fifty (adapted from Hill and Hurtado 1991).

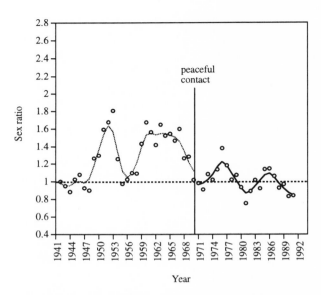

Figure 13.3.   Sex ratio (males/females) of offspring born to Ache women during a half century. Sample includes only children from women who were unlikely to under-report births (see Chapter 4). Data points represent a five-year running tabulation and generally include 40–50 children of each sex. The line is a binomial smooth of that data. Despite oscillations the sex ratio at birth seems to have decreased since contact.

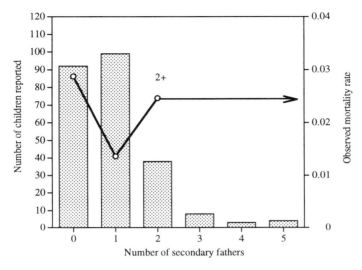

Figure 13.4. The relationship between number of secondary fathers reported for children in the forest period (age 0–9) and the yearly mortality rate (solid line). Also shown is the frequency distribution of children, with each number of secondary fathers reported in the forest sample (histogram). All children with two or more secondary fathers were lumped for analyses. The data suggest lowest mortality with one secondary father and higher mortality with zero secondary fathers (see note 6). The difference in mortality between two or more secondary fathers and the other categories is not significant. Note that the lowest observed mortality also corresponds with the most common category of children, those with one secondary father in addition to their primary father.

An Ache schoolteacher, his wife, and their youngest child in 1987.

14

Conclusions

LIFE HISTORY OF THE ACHE AND OTHER MODERN FORAGERS

Nancy Howell's 1979 study of the Dobe !Kung was a pioneering effort which placed a new emphasis on empirical demography among traditional small-scale societies. Because most of human history was spent in small-scale societies, and all of our current life history traits (and the reaction norms that produce them) evolved in such a context, we clearly need more information on mortality and fertility parameters in such societies in order to understand our own biology. In the time since Howell's study was published new works have emerged, but far too little is known about fertility and mortality rates in societies living under traditional economic regimes and with little or no western medical attention or state level interference in their lives. When we began our data collection in the early 1980s we fully expected to find a half dozen new demographic studies on modern foraging people by the time we had finished. Such a data base would provide a reasonable sample for valid scientific comparison. Instead, we discover that Howell's work remains the most complete demographic study of a foraging people to date, and that few good demographic studies on traditional peoples have emerged since that time. Our Ache study provides the most complete comparison available to date. This is unfortunate because the Ache study raises many more questions than it answers, and information from groups other than the Ache and the !Kung will be needed to answer those questions.

Because the Ache demographic patterns are so thoroughly documented it may be tempting to think of the Ache as "representative" of foraging people. Just such a view has commonly been applied to the !Kung for the past twenty years. Of course in the current academic political climate the !Kung are a more attractive model because they show apparent population control through low fertility and also exhibit low levels of violence. These traits that are congruent with the way many observers wish to portray our ancestors. Because of the appealing nature of !Kung demographic parameters and other aspects of their behavior and society (egalitarian conservationists living monogamously, sharing communally in a society where women are politically equal to men and do not depend on them economically), a new and romantic noble savage myth has been built around them, with widespread popular acceptance of the idea that they represent our ancestors. The Ache provide a counter image which is considerably less appealing to many, but clearly just as valid.

But, it would be a great mistake to replace the !Kung model with an Ache one. The Ache and the !Kung live in two different ecologies and have two different histories. Neither is representative of hunter-gatherers in general, because no one group can ever be representative of all of recent human history. The forest-living Ache were first studied during a century of explosive population growth. This may be due to the previous annihilation of competing native groups by Brazilian slave raiders in the seventeenth and eighteenth centuries. It could also be due to changes in the structure of the Paraguayan forest after the introduction of Old World resources (especially oranges and honeybees), which temporarily increased the forest food supply for the Ache and their important prey species. These topics are important areas of investigation, but in any case the Ache population as we studied it cannot have been representative of the Ache population over the past 5,000 years. At a growth rate of 2.5% per year, a small band of 20 Ache would grow in 5,000 years to a population of 3.9×10^{55} individuals! The Ache that we studied are therefore representative of foragers under very special and favorable conditions. Are the !Kung more representative of our past?

In Table 14.1 we summarize much of the information available on the demography of foraging peoples. Kelly (1995) has also recently summarized current knowledge of demographic parameters of foragers. There are huge gaps in our knowledge, and in truth we can say that we still know very little. Hopefully this book will stimulate more work and help other researchers to organize data collection around a set of comparative questions. The table shows that most people studied are small in size, but there is nearly a 1.5-fold difference in mean body size among females (Agta = 37 kg, Ache = 51.8 kg). This difference seems to be the result of very different growth rates, and if so, the model presented in Chapter 11 suggests that women in smaller body-sized groups should be characterized by either later maturation or higher adult mortality rates. The data are not sufficient to test either of these predictions. Infant mortality rates seem to vary between 10% and 20% and survival to adulthood is between 40% and 65%. Mean age at first birth ranges from about sixteen to twenty years, but the median rather than the mean is the appropriate measure here since some females never give birth and many are likely to be censored in any short study. Mean completed family size of women ranges from about 2.5 to more than 8, but many of the low numbers may represent populations experiencing high sterility as a result of sexually transmitted diseases. Birth intervals, where measured, range from about 24 to 48 months. Polygyny ranges from very common to totally absent. Homicide and infanticide also range from common to absent. Juvenile sex ratio ranges from very male biased (Hiwi = 1.63) to strongly female biased (!Kung = 0.81).

The most striking thing about this small and spotty sample is that the Ache and the !Kung are at opposite ends of the spectrum on many parameters. Ache women are the largest in the sample and !Kung women among the smallest. Ache women have among the highest fertility and !Kung women among the lowest. The Ache are characterized by high levels of mortality from violence and the !Kung among the lowest. The Ache have a very high male-biased juvenile sex ratio and the !Kung show a strong female-biased juvenile sex ratio. Clearly neither group is "representative" of foraging people. Instead, we find life history variation is the pattern, and that variation demands an explanation. Human life histories reflect the conditions of the study population rather than some rigid specieswide parameters.

The Ache data therefore represent an opportunity. Our goal as scientists is to describe and explain variation. A complete explanation of variation requires an understanding of why certain independent and dependent variables are linked the way they are. More specifically we need a theory to explain the shape of the function that relates any life history variable to the other variables that affect it. It is in this realm that the Ache data are invaluable, not as another analogy for some mythical ancestral past where all humans were characterized by the "typical" life history pattern.

HUMANS AS APES

An examination of the range of life history patterns that characterize modern foraging peoples suggests some important differences between humans and our primate relatives, particularly the great apes. Although gestation periods are nearly identical among the great apes, human babies are born larger and humans seem to wean their infants at earlier ages in many societies than do apes (Harvey and Clutton-Brock 1985). Humans gain weight at about the same rate as chimpanzees and orangutans, but grow for several more years and thus reach larger body size (see below).

Gorillas grow much faster and are larger; thus they should be able to produce more energy per unit time than the other great apes. Given that they produce similar sized offspring as the other apes, and that gorilla mothers should be able to produce more energy for reproduction than other apes, this should result in either higher fertility or faster infant growth for the species. The second seems to be true. Gorillas also seem to experience higher adult mortality, which may be due to their terrestrial habit. In any case the higher growth rate and higher adult mortality rate in gorillas would be expected to lead to an earlier age at maturity, which agrees with observations on the species (Harvey and Clutton-Brock 1985).

Comparisons between humans and orangutans are difficult because so little is known about orangutan life history. Surprisingly, orangutans but not chimpanzees or gorillas have been reported to experience higher fertility than traditional living humans. Other than that, the orangutan life history appears very similar to that of chimpanzees, but with slightly larger body size and considerably greater sexual dimorphism.

Human life history varies considerably from that of common chimpanzees. Humans live longer, are larger, begin reproduction at later ages, and develop more slowly during childhood than chimpanzees. Many of these traits are probably best understood as the consequence of radically different adult mortality rates (see below), but some are more complicated and are undoubtedly related to parental investment patterns that keep human juveniles dependent upon their parents almost until sexual maturity. Life history theory can be used to examine these patterns and make informed guesses about when hominid life histories began to diverge from those of the pongids. Some of these predictions will undoubtedly be testable by examining patterns of dental eruption and skeletal maturation in fossil hominids, and work in this area has already suggested that some early hominid life histories may be much more similar to chimpanzees than to modern humans (e.g., Smith 1991).

Human adults have exceptionally low mortality rates prior to senescence relative to other mammals with a similar body size and our nearest primate relatives. A simple regression model of log survivorship by weight suggests early adult mortality rates on the order of 0.14–0.2 per year for mammals of human body size (see Promislow and Harvey 1990). Chimpanzee data (Goodall 1986:112) provide a crude estimate of early adult mortality at around 0.07–0.1 per year, lower than the mammalian average for their size. Data from four studies of technologically primitive human groups show that early adult mortality (age 15–24) ranges from 0.007 for the Batak to 0.016 per year for the Yanomamo, with the !Kung and the Ache rates both around 0.012 per year (also see Chapter 6, this volume; Eder 1987; Howell 1979; Melancon 1982). A good estimate of the early adult mortality rate would be 1–2% per year. Thus, it is safe to say that even in foraging populations *Homo sapiens* does not experience mortality anywhere near that of other apes.

The fact that humans show a four- to tenfold decrease in adult mortality compared with that of chimpanzees has important ramifications for understanding hominid life history divergence. First, humans and chimpanzees grow at about the same rate through childhood (Gavan 1953; Kirkwood 1985). Using the optimal age at first reproduction model in Chapter 11, it is readily apparent that chimpanzees should begin reproducing at an earlier age and a smaller body size than are optimal for humans. This should change the entire developmental trajectory in order to ensure juvenile development is complete before reproductive age.

One might also predict that chimpanzees would have higher age-specific fertility rates than humans throughout the life span since they will not live as long. This turns out not to be the case. Instead human females generally reproduce at higher rates than chimpanzee females, perhaps because of exceptionally high levels of male provisioning. Given higher fertility and longer reproductive spans, one might also expect that humans would show higher juvenile mortality rates than chimpanzees (in order that both achieve zero population growth over the long run). This is not the case for recently studied hunter-gatherers. Humans also show exceptionally long periods of juvenile dependence that are again subsidized by male economic contributions. This allows offspring to develop at slow rates and remain relatively helpless until they are almost fully adult in size. Again, one might expect this to slow human reproductive rates relative to those of chimpanzees, but the opposite is observed. In summary, humans have longer life spans, longer reproductive spans, higher fertility, and higher offspring survival than chimpanzees. Chimpanzee populations are often near demographic equilibrium. Most traditional human populations (especially those not being heavily exploited by more powerful neighbors) that have been demographically described are growing rapidly. These observations lead to a puzzling question concerning how human populations maintained zero growth rates during most of our species' history.

HUMANS AS HOMINIDS

No natural fertility population yet observed is characterized by zero growth, as would be required over much of our species' history. A few groups may achieve nearly zero growth but show fertility profiles that suggest premature secondary sterility owing to sexually transmitted diseases (STDs). Natural fertility mechanisms seem to suggest that the maximum birth interval that can be attained in poorly nourished, noncontracepting populations with late weaning is about 48 months. This is considerably shorter than the 60-month intervals that characterize chimpanzees in the wild. A 48-month interval between births also implies six live births if reproduction begins at age twenty and ends at forty years of age. There is no evidence to suggest shorter reproductive spans except in populations that have STDs. And indeed, foragers not affected by STDs do show completed family sizes of around six live births. Most also show survivorship to adulthood around 50%. This leads to very high population growth that would be impossible to sustain. If maximum average IBI in humans really is around forty-eight months, then juvenile mortality must have been around 67% during most of human history. Such high mortality has never been observed in any traditional population.

An alternative view on human life history is that rapid growth has been a common characteristic of our species. Periods of growth could be interspersed with occasional population crashes in order to produce slow or no long-term population growth. These crashes could involve a percentage of each isolated population, or alternatively some populations might go completely extinct while others continued to expand. Population crashes that eliminated about 60% of the population every fifty years would produce stability through time if women bore six children and three survived to adulthood. Just such an event did take place in Ache history during the 1970s (first peaceful contact), but in this book we have treated that event as unrepresentative of most of Ache history. If such events were common in human history our species might be very "r-selected" (with traits that are favored under density-independent conditions) and our high fertility rate relative to those of the other great apes would then make sense. Given these considerations, we might conclude that humans have a derived live history that is very much more "r-selected" than those of any of our great ape relatives, despite our long life span. Humans might then be seen as a "colonizing species" of ape— probably not a bad description of our recent history.

This brief comparison suggests that events associated with a reduction in hominid adult mortality rates and the origin of male provisioning patterns are critical to understanding most differences in human and chimp life histories. Since the only good data on adult chimpanzee mortality in the wild comes from a site without predators (human or other), we are unsure exactly why chimpanzee mortality rates are so high. In the past several million years it is more likely that chimpanzee populations have indeed faced significant predation from carnivores and hominids (otherwise they should senesce at slower rates). One might speculate that mortality due to predation would be lower for hominids than chimps as soon as hominids began to forage socially (female chimpanzees probably spend larger portions of their time in solitary foraging than do human females) and would further decrease through time with the advent of weapon technology. Male provisioning of females and adolescents seems keenly tied to the transition from frugivore to carnivorous omnivore. Thus, particular key points in hominid evolution (social foraging, weapons, male provisioning) may represent the initiating conditions that led to the currently observed divergence of life history between humans and apes. If these points can be defined in the archeological record, life history predictions may be testable using fossil hominid remains.

The available data suggest that humans have a very different life history from those of the other apes. Since the divergence between these species is recent, we are compelled to wonder at what point the human life history pattern arose, and what other features are associated with such a pattern. Perhaps the very behavioral traits that set us apart from the other apes (pair bonding, male provisioning, predatory behavior, multi-male and multi-female social groups, complex communication, etc.) are all intricately linked to our life history shift (long life spans, menopause, high fertility) in a suite of traits that arose together and distinguish our species from the other apes. Perhaps only some of these traits arose together and others far antedate or postdate the life history shift. Identifying the time of such important changes would in some way be equivalent to identifying when we ceased being ape and started being human. The search for the "genesis" of our species as we know it is a very intellectually attractive and exciting enterprise. Can we recognize the human life history shift from the fossil record? Did it occur early or late in the evolutionary trajectory of hominids?

These questions are probably far from answerable given the data currently available, but they should continue to intrigue human biologists for some time. Recent analyses suggest that early hominids (Australopithecines) were probably characterized by a life history much more similar to chimpanzees than to humans (Smith 1991). For later hominids the answer is just beginning to emerge. In particular, we are beginning to obtain a sample of Neanderthal remains large enough to do meaningful demographic analyses on ages at death. Interpretation of such data is very complex because of a variety of problems, including the fact that age pyramids are more affected by fertility than mortality rates, aging techniques are not readily verifiable on populations that may differ biologically from modern humans, aging techniques show a good deal of error later in the life span, and many processes may lead to sample biases that are as yet poorly understood (especially social processes and differential preservation; Hill 1995). The dangers of such complications are well illustrated by the famous Libben site in North America (Lovejoy et al. 1977), which suggested a mortality curve much more like apes than modern humans for a recent Native American population (between AD 800 and 1100). The Libben mortality curve derived from 1,327 articulated individuals is almost certainly wrong. It shows no survivors beyond 50 years and implies an almost impossible fertility rate in order to achieve population stability (Milner et al. 1989). It implies (because of adult mortality) a much earlier age at first reproduction than seen among modern humans according to most life history models (see Chapter 11), and it also implies a very unlikely human social situation in which few children would ever be raised to adulthood by their parents (Howell 1982). Finally, Libben mortality rates are impossible for modern humans over any length of time because they would be associated with a different evolved senescence rate (there is no selection pressure on physiological function after the age at which nobody survives), and not enough time has passed for the descendants of Libben to have evolved the modern human rate of senescence.

Keeping these cautions in mind, Trinkaus (1995) has recently analyzed Neanderthal distributions of age at death. He concludes that Neanderthals may have been characterized by significantly lower adult survival than modern humans, but he also mentions most of the same problems that have concerned paleodemographers in general, and those who have commented on the Libben site. Trinkaus was unable to show significant differences between Neanderthal and Ache mortality distribution for any age class except young adults, however (the Neanderthals show much higher percentage of deaths than do the Ache). If Neanderthals really do have high young adult mortality, we might expect this to result in a life history more similar to that of other apes. This intriguing possibility should have many test implications. Alternatively, perhaps the Neanderthal adults in the 50+ age category are selectively missing from sites where remains have been found because of social behavior and spatial segregation by age. This and other possibilities have been discussed by Trinkaus (1995) and Hill (1995), and no immediate resolution of the issue is likely.

THEORETICAL IMPLICATIONS

The Ache study contributes to life history theory in an exploratory rather than a definitive manner. Very few previous studies of human demographic patterns have been carried out within a life history framework. We have emphasized that human demographers have made important contributions to the description of mortality and fertility patterns. Demographers have also developed important analytical tools (like the hazards models used throughout this book) and established many connections between a variety of social and ecological variables and demographic outcomes. But current demographic studies are doomed to be descriptive in nature because the field has no coherent body of theory that can offer *explanations* for the observed patterns. We have repeated several times throughout this book that a complete explanation must address why certain associations are found and why they take the character that they do. In our opinion, only life history theory meets this challenge. It does so because demographic parameters are the essence of the biological life cycle of an organism, with fertility and mortality being the two components of fitness. Only a theory grounded in modern evolutionary biology is likely to be able to explain mortality and fertility patterns in any living organism, human or nonhuman. This is because demographic parameters and the physiological mechanisms that produce them are subject to natural selection, and there is no way for them to escape natural selection regardless of whether they are genetically programmed or are the product of conscious thought, learning, or cultural constraints. Any tendencies, abilities, or desires that affect fertility and mortality profiles will always be derived from organic designs (the central nervous system) and subject to natural selection. If cultural practices act in ways disfavorable to genetic contribution, the ability and desire to adopt such practices will be extinguished through natural selection. The human brain, and all that flows from it, is and always will be a servant to the goal of genetic representation.

We can summarize the main theoretical contributions of this book in a few simple sentences. In fact they primarily constitute a series of questions rather than answers. First, why have we found so little evidence of a cost of reproduction in the Ache study? Is this because of methodological flaws in our study, or because the Ache represented in our sample experienced conditions where there were no significant costs of reproduction? An answer to this question will be crucial for explaining human fertility variation in traditional societies as well as the demographic transition to small family size in recent western societies.

Second, is our model of age at first reproduction basically correct? Ache data fit so well with the model that we are highly optimistic. But other studies on other populations will be required to assess whether there are major flaws in the model assumptions. Also, the model assumes important benefits with increased growth. If it is correct, a major challenge will be to understand why human growth rates are so low compared with those of other mammals. Charnov (1993) has recently pointed out that low primate growth rates are a key to understanding the unique nature of primate life histories. This is even more true for humans, who are characterized by a lower growth constant than most primates (about 0.25 for the Ache vs. 0.4 for most primates). Is it really true that larger body size will lead to higher net energy production in humans, or is there an optimal body size, beyond which net energy production begins to decline? This is a crucial question for modeling optimal age at which growth should stop and reproduction begin.

Third, what is the functional explanation for menopause? The fact that the female reproductive system senesces long before other body functions is a major life history mystery. Since there is very strong selection pressure on fertility, this trait cannot be simply ignored as a byproduct of general senescence or a recent increase in the human life span. Inclusive fitness benefits from diverting energy to children and grandchildren seem like they could favor the termination of direct reproduction, but the Ache data suggest that this is not true in the Ache situation. If kin selection has not maintained menopause in the Ache, what has? Are the Ache analyses generalizable to other groups, or did we sample a unique period when menopause was not favored by selection? Only further studies with other populations will clarify this issue.

Fourth, how important is the adult morality rate for determining the overall character of the human life history? We already mentioned that the growth rate is an important life history constraint that must be imposed by feeding ecology and perhaps the avoidance of predation (cf. Janson and Van Schaik 1993). Many life history theorists believe that extrinsic adult mortality is another key constraint in determining the overall life history of an organism (see Chapter 1). Our data suggest that humans in traditional societies are characterized by a 1% per year mortality rate in adulthood prior to the onset of senescence. This is by far the lowest mortality rate for any mammal or primate, except perhaps a few of the largest whales. Humans also have the longest maximum life span of any mammal. Indeed it is the low adult mortality rate that is probably responsible for the late and slow rate of human senescence (see Austad and Fischer 1991, 1992). Recent evidence from opossums strongly suggests that different rates of physiological senescence evolve when adult mortality rates change (Austad 1993). Is the origin of the low human mortality rate tied to other human traits, such as a large brain, the use of effective weapons, and changes in the mating structure.

A final theoretical contribution of the Ache study concerns a topic barely touched on directly. What role do rapid population growth and periodic population crashes play in human evolutionary history? Perhaps trade-offs were not detected, and menopause not favored by kin selection, because the Ache were in a period of resource abundance. Could many life history traits instead be adapted to survival through periodic population crashes? If so, then perhaps the Ache data presented in this book will tell us little about selective forces that have shaped our life history. Perhaps instead of focusing analyses on the precontact forest period and the recent reservation period, we should have spent more time examining the patterns of mortality and fertility during the seven-year contact period when half the Ache population died. Perhaps our species' high reproductive capabilities can only be understood in a context of frequent population crashes. We are indeed a colonizing species, having recently moved out of Africa and colonized nearly every land mass on earth. Maybe it should not surprise us to find that we are not the archetype K-selected species that many have assumed (because we have big brains, slow development, and long life spans) but that in fact many of our traits may have evolved under density-independent conditions and others may be adaptations designed to survive periodic, extreme population crashes. It will take a good deal of future work in human life history to sort out the answers to these questions.

APPLIED ANTHROPOLOGICAL DEMOGRAPHY

Although much of the work we present in this book is motivated by academic questions and theoretical issues, most workers, including ourselves, derive a good deal of personal satisfaction from using our studies to make a difference in the lives of our study subjects. The Ache study population that is the subject of this book also contains some of our closest friends. This work directly affects their lives in three ways. First, data collected and analyzed here can help to define some of the most serious problems that the Ache face both individually and as a people. These include health issues and the implications of long-term population growth. Second, this study is relevant to native human rights campaigns around the world, and claims that are made concerning policies that are beneficial or detrimental to native peoples. Third, the Ache, by consenting to this study, have chosen to participate in the worldwide scientific community in order to contribute to the search for solutions to questions about all humankind. Because the Ache have not hesitated to request the help that can come from modern science and technology, it is only fitting that they have also contributed to modern scientific progress. They need not be intimidated by scientific advancement—they are a part of it.

Two findings from this book are relevant to the Ache directly. First, current reservation mortality is primarily due to respiratory infection in children under two years of age. Reducing infant mortality to 2% in the first year of life and 1% in the second year of life would result in a life expectancy at birth over 60 years. Based on comparison with the Pto. Barra group of Ache, who experience considerably lower juvenile mortality, it is our impression that this problem could be solved by improved sanitary conditions at the other four Ache reservations. Most deaths take place in the cold season of the year, when adults are uniformly ill with the flu or some cold virus and small children quickly become infected and die. Houses at four of the Ache reservations are drafty but also excessively smoky, and people sit or sleep on bare dirt floors during the winter, exacerbating minor respiratory ailments. The Pto. Barra reservation, which has experienced no infant or child deaths in more than ten years, is characterized by small but well-built houses with wood board floors and wood-burning stoves that allow ventilation to the outside. Pto. Barra Ache also possess more clothing and blankets than Ache at the other reservations, and a continuous supply of soap to keep their clothing and bedding clean. We are pleased that we recently obtained a large grant to improve housing and sanitation on two of the Ache reservations.

The second problem for the Ache population is a fertility rate that cannot be long sustained and will ultimately lead to great suffering, poverty, and high infant mortality. The Ache are surrounded on all sides by politically dominant groups and have been progressively losing territory and resources. There are about 750 Ache now, but with a 23-year population doubling time, there will be nearly 5,000 by the time that many of today's small children reach old age. Currently available land and resources simply cannot support 5,000 Ache at anything near the standard of living that they all hope to attain within the next half century. Many Ache parents are already complaining that their families are too large and their children suffer as a result. Life history theory suggests that high fertility is generally balanced by high juvenile mortality. That is a price that the Ache (quite rightly) are not willing to accept. They, like most Americans, would prefer smaller families in which all children survive to adulthood. Unfortunately, the Ache perception of the problem may be at odds with the policies favored by Catholic missionaries who provide health care at two of the five Ache reservations. Because of this, young couples have begun approaching us to inquire discreetly about ways of obtaining birth control technology. In our view, everything about the Ache situation suggests that such requests will become more frequent, and the Ache will not be content to "let nature run its course" as they have been advised. Without a solution to the Ache fertility problem there is likely to be growing friction between the Ache and those who advocate uncontrolled fertility for the group. The suffering associated with a 20% infant mortality rate in order to reduce families to a manageable size will not be endured by the Ache for long.

The quantitative approach used in this study also has important implications for the design, implementation, and evaluation of programs that claim, but rarely show, protection of indigenous human rights. Serious human rights violations continue to be an unresolved and overlooked problem throughout the Americas. Sources of oppression and resistance are poorly understood from either theoretical or empirical perspectives, which makes the process of intervention a fortuitous game. Unfortunately, instead of embracing the benefits of the scientific process for improving knowledge in this area, the present trend in many branches of applied anthropology is antiscientific and relies on emotional or political advocacy fed by poor judgment and very little if any reliable or valid information. Just such a history characterized the Ache situation through the 1970s, where well-meaning emotional appeals concerning Ache "genocide" were backed with inaccurate, distorted, and even fraudulent information (Miguel Chase-Sardi, personal communication). Funds raised through such appeals were virtually never channeled back to help the Ache. Because these appeals were not based on careful and accurate documentation of the problem, and gross exaggerations quickly became apparent, a false picture of Ache suffering was created that ultimately did not serve the interests of the Ache themselves but instead seemed mainly designed to feed a gullible international audience. Despite the fact that good demographic data on the Ache have existed for nearly a decade (see Hill 1983a, 1983b), subsequent "debates" about the Ache situation relied entirely on emotional appeals and political advocacy and have degenerated into territorial disputes between agencies claiming to truly represent a concern for indigenous rights.

The antiscience trend in anthropology in recent years has, and continues to have, devastating effects on the lives of indigenous peoples throughout South America. It has created an adversarial atmosphere that makes it impossible to measure the morbidity and mortality outcomes of racist public policies and programs, racist resource allocation strategies, racist criminal justice systems, etc., or disasters and potential disasters. This atmosphere effectively keeps many truths from escaping the clutches of dishonest local and national government officials. Instead it focuses public attention on endless petty political debates generated by professional "rights advocates" who draw enviable salaries and have minimal understanding of the lives of indigenous peoples. The deaths, rapes, hunger, and psychological abuses that natives experience, as well as truth itself, always seem to be secondary issues in this political game.

Indeed some current anthropological schools of thought have completely abandoned the idea that truth exists at all, and instead insist that each version of history is equally valid. This "postmodernist" perspective has been widely adopted by both academic anthropologists and some human rights agencies. Although we sympathize with a perspective that much of history is actually propaganda that serves the interests of those who write it, the denial that any truth can be discovered or documented must be rejected as both naive and dangerous. Indeed, nothing could be more devastating to native peoples than a perspective that logically maintains that indigenous suffering can simply be considered another "version of history."

The antiscience trend also calls into question the true function of agencies whose livelihood depends upon the protection of indigenous human rights because it points to the dismal knowledge base used to guide decision-making and efforts to influence local and national indigenous policies. Without a sound scientific basis the steps necessary to ensure human rights protection cannot be specified. Minimally, requirements include a framework that identifies the independent variables necessary to produce favorable human rights outcomes among indigenous groups, the methodologies necessary to measure variables and outcomes, and a process to revise frameworks as new information is generated. Those who attempt to influence policy, and who propose or implement programs, should rely on systematic sources of information in order to monitor human rights abuses.

On the basis of our Ache study we can be very specific about our recommendations in this area. All programs designed to "help" indigenous peoples should result in measurably better health, higher juvenile growth rates, and lower mortality, or we should be skeptical that the "help" is of any significance to the target population. Evolutionary theory suggests that *all* humans, regardless of ethnicity, should care about these factors, and our experience confirms this expectation. These objective criteria of success should be applied to all development programs, in our opinion, and the cost effectiveness of each program in terms of outcome per dollar spent should be measured and evaluated. Individuals, organizations, and programs that attempt to circumvent such monitoring are in our view suspect. Too many development projects exist primarily in order to provide a salary for the director and a few subordinates, and too many organizations and institutions solicit public donations or government funding and assert (but never demonstrate) that they are helping native people.

Human behavioral ecologists working with small populations often have to play two roles: as investigator into the causes and consequences of selective processes and as human rights advocate. These roles need not be in conflict with each other. As investigators use scientific rigor to make the most reliable and valid inference, they also more likely to generate data that can be used to help avert disastrous outcomes among indigenous peoples over the long and short term. The latter objective is the most pressing and more likely to be obtained with unbiased findings, logical reasoning, sound research design, and appropriate analyses. In the absence of experimentation, these are the best tools we have for solving complex human problems in both basic and applied human evolutionary sciences. An antiscience trend in recent anthropology is robbing indigenous peoples of this basic human right.

Finally, this life history study points to other, more general areas of applied research. For decades, scientists have alluded to the relevance of "ancestral" conditions for understanding present-day demographic parameters, and much of human biology. Isolated groups of foragers and incipient horticulturalists are the closest human context to these presumed conditions. However, few have attempted to specify the causal linkages that need to be isolated in foraging populations in order to elucidate modern health profiles. Life history theory provides a powerful theoretical and quantitative modeling tool for working through linkages between ecological factors that prevail under ancestral conditions and behavior, biological mechanisms, and natural selection for biological, physiological, psychological, and immunological human traits. Initially, it provides organizing, qualitative, and quantitative principles for working out the details of how and why some human biological mechanisms were selected and maintained in early human history and why they result in negative health outcomes in the context of modern society. This logical process should help medical scientists tackle some baffling modern health problems, such as increasing rates of allergies and asthma, heart and circulatory problems, reproductive cancers, unhealthy dietary trends, obesity and diabetes, chronic fatigue syndrome, human immunodeficiency viral infections, and a variety of other "new" health problems. A collaboration between anthropologists and medical researchers will be required to make headway on such issues (e.g., Eaton et al. 1994).

We hope this work will stimulate new and increased interest in merging the social sciences, demography, and epidemiology with a theoretical perspective derived from biology about the timing of vital events in living organisms. In such a perspective, the study of *any* human group is relevant to understanding *all* human groups. If so, then we and the Ache have collaborated together on a useful project to learn about ourselves and generate knowledge that can benefit all of humankind.

Table 14.1. Comparative Life History Parameters from Modern Foraging Populations

Group	Male, fem weight (kg)	Infant mortality (0–1)	Juvenile mortality (0–15)	Woman's age at first birth	Woman's completed family size	Mean interbirth interval (months)	Polygyny (% married men)	Warfare (% killed)	Homicide (y/n) %	Infanticide (% killed)	Sex ratio (0–5 yr)
North America											
Inuit				15 to 20		40.9	none		yes	40% of girls	0.74
Nunamiut	72.8, 65.7					24–96	wife exch		yes		
Inupiat						24	wife exch				
Polar Eskimo					4	36	wife exch				
Washo							rare	yes			
N. Paiute					2.8			yes	yes		1
South America											
Macu	50.9, 41.0										
Yahgan					7 to 10						
Ayoreo			60%					high	yes high	16%	0.89
Ache	59.6, 51.8	21%	35%	18.5	8.1	37	4.1%	38% of adult males	8% of adult males	85% of all infants	1.22
Hiwi	56.0, 48.0		52%	young	5.13			high	high	common	1.63
Yuqui							some				1.12
Warao	53.0						none				
Yora	63.9, 49.5		49%		8.5	36	23.0%	no			0.97
Africa											
E. Hadza	53.1, 46.0		47.00%	30.9	6.15						
Efe	43.0, 39.4	12%			2.7					none	
!Kung	49.0, 41.0	20%	40%	19.96	4.7	48	6.0%		yes	1.20%	0.81

(continued)

Table 14.1. (continued)

Group	Male, fem weight (kg)	Infant mortality (0–1)	Juvenile mortality (0–15)	Woman's age at first birth	Woman's completed family size	Mean interbirth interval (months)	Polygyny (% married men)	Warfare (% killed)	Homicide (y/n) %	Infanticide (% killed)	Sex ratio (0–5 yr)
Southeast Asia											
Yumbri	48.8						yes				
Batek					2.67	36					
Birhor							yes	0	no	0	
Pandaram					6 to 7		yes	0	no	0	
Paliyan							<5%		no		
Agta	37.0		49%		6.53		20.0%		yes	0	
Batak	46.5, 40.5		45%	18	3.94	28					0.85
Onge	40.4, 37.4				2.8		0.0%				1.31
Penan	52.9, 37.9										1.23
Australia											
Gidjingali		>22%	>40%	15.9	6.4	44	39.0%	high	yes	5–11%	1.21
Alyawara					5.25		47.2%		yes		1.86
Walbiri	57.0, 45.0			17		18–24	42.5		yes		0.92
Groote Eylandt	60.0, 42.0	high			3.5		49.0%	0	yes	0	

References for Table 14.1

Inuit: Balicki (1970); Condon 1987
Nunamiut: Auger et al. 1980; Gubser 1965
Inupiat: Chance 1966
Polar Eskimo: Gilberg 1984
Washo: Powers 1877
N. Paiute: Steward 1933

Macu: Milton 1984
Yahgan: Gusinde 1961; Stuart 1972
Ayoreo: Bormida and Califano 1978; Bugos 1985
Ache: Hurtado et al. 1985
Hiwi: Hill and Hurtado 1987
Yuqui: Stearman 1989; Hewlett 1991
Yora: Hill and Kaplan 1989

E. Hadza: Barnicott et al. 1972; Blurton Jones et al. 1992
Efe: Bailey and Aunger 1989; Bailey and Peacock 1988; Dietz et al. 1989
!Kung: Lee 1979

Yumbri: Nimmanahaeminda (1984)
Batek: Evans 1937:27
Birhor: Sinha 1972
Pandaram: Morris 1982
Paliyan: Gardner 1965
Agta: Goodman et al. 1985; Bion Griffin and Griffin 1992
Batak: Eder 1987
Onge: Cappieri 1974:34
Penan: Avadhani 1975; Kedit 1982

Gidjingali: Hamilton 1981; Hiatt 1965
Alyawara: Elkin 1940
Walbiri: Abbie 1956; Meggitt 1962
Groote Eylandt: McArthur 1960; McCarthy and McArthur 1960; Rose 1960

Implications of Stable Age Models
for Deriving !Kung Ages

Howell (1979) used three "measured" parameters to pick an age structure for the !Kung population: (1) survivorship to one year of age (79.8%, 1979:81); (2) proportion of the population in the 0–4 year age interval (12.6%, 1979:32); and (3) proportion in the 5–9 year age interval (10.1%, 1979:32). These parameters suggested that the model life table "West female 5" and an age structure in the column defined by an annual rate of increase of approximately $R = 0$ best fit the !Kung data. However, several other model life tables from Coale and Demeny (1966) show equal or less deviation from the three "measured" parameters. Howell noted this fact but preferred to restrict herself to using the West model life tables. Some of these tables have very differently shaped mortality curves, as can be seen in Figure A.1a. These alternative models imply different annual rates of increase (from $R = 0$ to $R = 10$), but all fit the three "measured" parameters for the !Kung population closely.

In theory, almost any possible mortality curve with infant mortality at about 20% could approximately fit the observed proportions for the first two age categories, as long as the fertility rate was adjusted appropriately. Interestingly, however, the cumulative percent of the population below each age interval implied by fitting the "measured" !Kung parameters to the different possible model life tables is almost exactly the same regardless of the fact that the mortality curves are substantially disparate (Figure A.1). The *cumulative* percentage of the population up to age *x,* used to estimate ages for individuals in the relative age list, does not differ by more than 2% between the stable population model that Howell used and the model that is most divergent from that model but still meets the three "measured" parameters (Figure A.2). Thus, the difference between the age structures that might be derived from each of the different models that meet the "measured" parameters appears small. This difference however, may have important consequences.

Each age class in the stable population models described above usually contains less than 10% of the population, and less than 5% of the population is expected to fall in many of the older age intervals. This means that an error of ±2% of the total population in an interval that contains only 5% of the total population may constitute a major distortion in the data set. Take for example the age class 20–24 years. According to the model Howell used (West female 5) 48.6% of the population should be equal to or younger than that age. The North female 6 (Nf6) model however, which also fits the three "measured" parameters well, suggests that 50.9% of the population should be younger than twenty-five years. If Howell had chosen the Nf6 model to assign individual ages when in fact the West female 5 (Wf5) model was correct, she would have included in the 20–24 age interval the 2.3% of the population who were just older than twenty-five. Since only 8.6% of the total population should be in the 20–24 interval, and since 2.3% in that interval would actually belong in the next older interval, this means that *more than one-quarter of the people assigned to the interval would actually belong in the next older interval*. Thus, the relative proportion of individuals included in an interval who do not belong in that interval can be substantial if the wrong stable population model is chosen (Figure A.3).

Let's continue the hypothetical example of the !Kung age structure and consider the implications. Howell assigned the !Kung ages using the Wf5 model in conjunction with her relative age list. Based on the published !Kung mortality curve (1979:81) it appears that the South female 7 (Sf7) model fits the mortality data better than any other model in Coale and Demeny's tables (Figure A.1). This model produces an age structure (using the "measured" parameters) differing from that which Howell derived primarily in the older age classes (Figure A.2). If this model were correct, what would be the implications of the erroneous use of model West female 5 to assign !Kung ages?

Consider the interval from forty to forty-four years. The Sf7 model shows a lower cumulative proportion of the population to age forty-five. If the South model is correct, Howell will have included women in the 40–44 age category who should actually have been in the 45–49 age category . Specifically, we can calculate that if the Sf7 model is actually most appropriate for the !Kung, then 21% of the women included in the 40–44 year age interval in Howell's analyses actually should have been in the 45–49 age interval! Would the inclusion of women from the next older age category have an effect on the demographic parameters calculated for the !Kung? The answer is yes. If 21% of the oldest women assigned to the 40–44 age class should be in the 45–49 category, the inclusion of these older women will undoubtedly decrease the age-specific fertility calculated for the 40–44 age class, but the magnitude of the effect is difficult to calculate because the age-specific fertilities of the two adjacent age classes would also be distorted (and they must be correctly known to calculate the precise magnitude of the effect). A crude estimate suggests that age-specific fertility for the 40–44 age group would increase from .119 to about .127 (a 7% increase) if Howell had chosen the Sf7 model rather than the Wf5 model to assign ages to her study population.[1]

Although it is difficult to determine precisely the magnitude of the change in demographic parameters that might be expected due to choosing an inappropriate stable population model to estimate ages, the direction of those changes can easily be determined. In the example above, if the Sf7 age structure were actually the appropriate model to use, Howell's !Kung analyses represents an underestimate of fertility and an overestimate of mortality rates for older women. In addition, the median ages at menopause and last birth will have been under-estimated, and the interbirth intervals calculated by dividing total fertility by reproductive span are underestimated. The mean age at menarche will have been overestimated. All these differences would be expected simply because the age classes used in the analyses contain women from adjacent (older or younger) age classes. Use of the Sf7 model would essentially make the !Kung reproductive span look longer than Howell described it to be, but with fertility showing less of a peak during prime adult years. This characterization of the !Kung has serious biological implications. Emphasis might then be focused on explaining the low !Kung fertility during prime reproductive years rather than explaining the short reproductive span, late age of first reproduction, and the impact of secondary sterility in the population. Thus interpretation of the entire data set and its biological implications can be affected by the simple choice of a stable popula-tion model which is fit by eye to a few measured parameters.

NOTE

1.   Using linear extrapolation from Howell (1979:124) we calculate the age-specific fertility of women that Howell classifies as 40 years old to be 0.136 and the age-specific fertility of 45-year-old !Kung women to be 0.085. Eliminating the 21% of women in the interval which belong to the next higher interval, we calculate fertility of the remaining 79% in the 40–44 interval as: $0.119 = .79x + .21(.085)$, or $x = .125$. Adding in the 20% of the women from the 35–39 interval who actually belong in the 40–44 interval, we calculate the true fertility rate for women who should be in the 40–44 interval as $.8(.125) + .2(.136) = .127$.

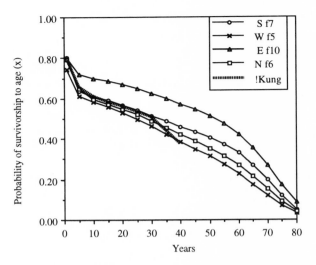

Figure A.1a.   Observed !Kung survivorship compared with four model life tables (from Coale and Demeny 1966) that closely fit the observed mortality rate in the first-year interval.

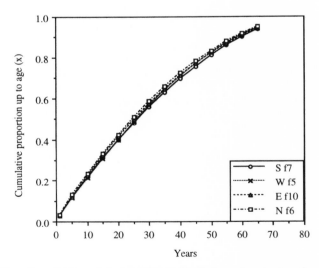

Figure A.1b.   Cumulative proportion of individuals in each age class from four model life tables that best fit the observed proportions in the first three age intervals in Howell's (1979) study of the !Kung. Note that while mortality profiles differ considerably in Figure A.1a, the proportion of individuals expected in each age category is much more similar.

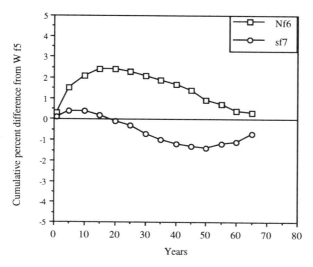

Figure A.2.   Percent difference in the cumulative proportion of individuals up to age x, between the Wf5 stable population model chosen by Howell (1979) for the !Kung and two other models that closely fit "measured" !Kung parameters.

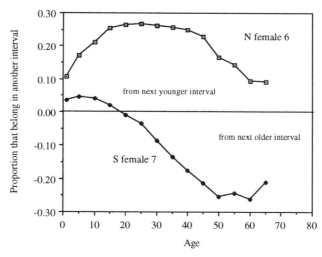

Figure A.3.   Proportion of individuals assigned to incorrect five-year age intervals according to the Wf5 stable population model in Coale and Demeny 1966 if in fact the Nf6 or Sf7 models actually characterize the population. The values above the midline show the proportion of individuals assigned to a five-year interval that actually belong in the next younger interval. Values below the midline show the proportion of individuals that actually belong in the next older interval.

Block Rankings of Relative Age

Example 1

ID	Temporary estimate* (year born)	Male initiation group**	Final age rank	Individual informants' opinions regarding age rank†												
From Earlier Block																
3104		1						+								
3110		2				+		+								
3111	1935(2)	2				+		+								
3112								+								
3113		3				+	−	+								
3114		3				+		+								
3115		4			+											
3116		4				+	+	+								
1936–1939 Block																
3118		5	120			+		+								
3119		5	121			+		+								
3120		6	122			+		+	+						+	
3121			123		0	+	+	=	+	+		+				+
3122		6	124		−	+	+		−				−			+

ID		n	Code													
3123		6	125	–	+	+	+	+	–				+	+	
3125	1935(1)	7	126	+	0	+	+	+	+						
3126	1937(1)	8	127	+	+	0		+	+		+	+	+	+	
3127		8	128	+			0	+	+						
3128		7	129	+		+	–	+			+	+	+	+	
3129			130	–	–	–	–	+							
3130	1936.2(6)	5	131	–	+	+		0	+	–	+	+	+	+	+
3131			132	–	–			–	0	+	+	+	+	+	+
3132			133		–		–	+	–	0					
3133			134		+	–	+	+	–	–	=	–			
3134			135		–		–			+					
3135			136		+			+	–			=	–	+	+
3136			137	+	+		–	+	–	–	0		–		
3137			138	+	+	–	+	+	–	+	–	0		+	+
3138		9	139		–		–	–	–			–	0	+	+
3139			140		–	–	–	–	–			+	–		
3140		9	141		–		+	–	–						
3141		9	142				–						0		
		10													

(continued)

Example 1 (continued)

ID	Temporary estimate* (year born)	Male intiation group**	Final age rank	Individual informants' opinions regarding age rank[+]										
3142	1937.5(2)		143			**0**	−	+	−	−	−	−	−	−
3143			144	+				−	+					−
3144		9	145	+	+	−		+	+	−	−		−	−
From Later Block														
3145				+	**0**	−	−	−	−	−		+		−
3146	1941(1)	11		**0**		+	+	−	+					−
3147		11				−								
3148		11				−		−						
3149		11				−		+	−	−	+			−
3150		10		+		+	+	−	+	−				
3151		10				−	−	−				−		−
3152		10				−								
3168												−		−

Example 2

ID	Temporary estimate* (year born)	Male initiation group**	Final age rank	Individual informants' opinions regarding age rank†																	
From Earlier Block																						
3121							+		+													
3131				−							+											
3132				+		+	+	+	+		+										+	+
3133						+	−				+											
3134				0										0	+							
3135				−		=	−	+			+											
3136				+	0		−							+								
3137		9									+											
3138				−		0	−	+	+	+	+			=	+							
3139		9				−	+	+	+	+	+	+										
3141		10					0					+										
3142	1937.5(2)			−		−	−	0			+			=							+	
3143				−	+					+	+			+								−

(continued)

Example 2 (continued)

ID	Temporary estimate* (year born)	Male initiation group**	Final age rank†	Individual informants' opinions regarding age rank†
3144		9		+ + + + + +
1940–1943 Block				
3145			146	− + 0 + + − +
3146	1941(1)	11	147	+ − + 0 + + + − + +
3147		11	148	− + + + +
3148		11	149	− + − +
3149		11	150	− + + + + + + +
3150		10	151	− + 0 + + + + +
3151		10	152	− + + − + + +
3152		10	153	− − +
3153		10	154	
3154		10	155	+
3155			156	− + + −
3156			157	0 + + + −

3157		12	158					+			+			−	−	−		−	−		−	+
3158		12	159																			
3159			160			−		+				=			−	+					−	
3160		?	161					+				=			−	−		−				+
3161			162									+										
3162			163	+		−	+	=			−		**0**	−		−						−
3163	1940(1)	?	164	+			+					**0**	−			−						
3164		13	165					+			+				−							
3165		?	166		+		+				+	−	−	+		−						−
3166		?	167		+			−			+			+	−							
3167	1943(1)		168			+		+		+	**0**	−	−	−	−	−						−
3168			169			−					−	−	−	−	−	+		−		−	−	
3169		?	170								−	=	−			−						−
3170			171			−	+	+			−	−		−	−	+		−				−
3171			172							**0**	+	−										
3172		14	173		+		−	+	+		−	=		+								
3173		14	174	=	−			+				−										
3174		13	175					+			−									−		

(continued)

Example 2 *(continued)*

ID	Temporary estimate* (year born)	Male initiation group**	Final age rank	Individual informants' opinions regarding age rank[†]								
3175			176	+	+	+	+	0	–	+	–	–
3176	1943(1)	?	177	+	+	0	+	–	–	–		–
3178		?	178									
3179		?	179	+	–	0	+	–	–	–		–
3180		14	180	–	–	0	–					
3181			181	0	–	–	–					
3182		?	182	+	–	+	–	–	–		–	
3183		?	183	+	–	+	–	–				

From Later Block

| 3184 | 1943(2) | 15 | | + | 0 | – | + | – | | | | – |

	Age											
3185	15				−				−			−
3186	15											
3187	15			−								
3188	?					−						
3189	16	+		−	−			+	−			−
3190	16	+		−	−							
3191			−		+							
3192				+	+							
3193 1943(3)	17	0	+	−	−	−						
3198	18		+	−	−							
3202			−		−							
3203			−		−							

*In parentheses is the number of men who provided absolute age difference estimates between themselves and the person mentioned.

**Men who were initiated as a cohort and had their lips pierced at the same time.

†Age rank opinions from each informant are shown in a column. **0** is informant, + means individual is ranked older than informant, − means individual is ranked younger than informant, and = means individual is ranked as same age as informant.

Five Genealogies with Multiple Generations

	Ego				Offspring				Grandchildren				Great-grandchildren				Great-great-grandchildren			
	ID	Sex	Born	Died	ID	Sex	Born	Died	ID	Sex	Born	Died	ID	Sex	Born	Died	ID	Sex	Born	Died
Genealogy 1																				
	3001	0	1907	1985	3060	1	1924	–	3241	0	1949	–	4231	0	1973	1973				
													3459	0	1974	–				
													3521	0	1979	1982				
													3601	0	1983	1983				
													3662	1	1985	–				
													4327	0	1989	1989				
									3247	0	1950	1975	3431	0	1970	–	4400	0	1989	–
													3457	0	1974	–				
													3877	1	1969	1969				
									3878	1	1952	1952								
									4227	0	1952	1952								
									3879	1	1954	1961								
									3305	1	1957	–	3535	0	1980	–				
													3600		1983	1983				
													3629	1	1984	–				

3673	1	1986	–
4382	1	1989	–
3700	0	1987	–
7070	1	1983	–
7071	0	1985	–
7099	1	1988	–
3666	1	1985	–
4383	1	1990	–
3880	0	1960	1960
3360	1	1962	–
3393	1	1966	–
3423	0	1969	–
3433	1	1971	–
3456	1	1974	–
3512	1	1978	–
3935	0	1962	1963
3800	0	1960	1960
3351	1	1961	–
3385	0	1964	–
4168	1	1989	–
4160	0	1981	1983
3808	0	1928	1928
3103	1	1933	1956
3125	1	1937	–
3145	0	1940	–

(continued)

Ego				Offspring				Grandchildren				Great-grandchildren				Great-great-grandchildren			
ID	Sex	Born	Died	ID	Sex	Born	Died	ID	Sex	Born	Died	ID	Sex	Born	Died	ID	Sex	Born	Died
3001	0	1907	1985	3145	0	1940	–	3385	0	1964	–	4162	1	1986	–				
												4368	1	1988	–				
								3410	1	1967	–	3694	1	1987	1987				
								3442	1	1972	1973								
								3482	0	1977	–								
								3584	1	1982	1982								
								3622	1	1984	1984								
				3175	0	1943	–	3801	0	1963	1971								
								3805	1	1976	1976								
								3590	0	1982	–								
				3225	0	1948	–	3806	0	1966	1966								
								3807	1	1970	1971								
								3445	0	1972	–	4395	1	1989	–				

Genealogy 2

2040	1	1905	1975	3050	1	1921	1975	3222	0	1948	–	4000	1	1965	–
												3417	0	1968	–
												4001	1	1971	–
												4002	1	1973	1975
												4003	0	1975	1975
												4004	1	1978	1978
												3529	1	1980	–
												3555	1	1981	–
												4005	1	1983	1983
												4157	1	1985	–
												4158	1	1988	–
								3993	1	1950	1969				
								3996	1	1952	1952				
								3995	0	1953	1972	4189	1	1971	1972
								3317	1	1958	1975				
								3997	1	1962	–				

(continued)

Ego				Offspring				Grandchildren				Great-grandchildren				Great-great-grandchildren			
ID	Sex	Born	Died	ID	Sex	Born	Died	ID	Sex	Born	Died	ID	Sex	Born	Died	ID	Sex	Born	Died
2040	1	1905	1975	3058	0	1924	1975	3869	0	1943	1944	3871	1	1963	1964				
								3205	0	1946	–	3872	1	1965	1965				
												3873	0	1967	1968				
												3426	0	1969	–	3676	1	1986	1987
																4179	0	1989	–
												3874	0	1972	1972				
												3875	1	1975	1975				
												3876	1	1977	1977				
												3520	0	1979	–				
												3573	0	1981	1982				
												3614	1	1983	1983				
												3682	0	1986	–				
								3247	0	1950	1975	3431	0	1970	–	4400	0	1989	–
												3457	0	1974	–				
												3877	1	1969	1969				

3478	1	1976	–
3527	0	1979	–
3581	1	1982	–
3637	1	1984	–
3701	1	1987	–
4385	1	1990	–
3259	1	1951	–
3314	1	1955	1972
3368	1	1963	–
3394	1	1966	–
3636	1	1984	1985
3687	1	1986	–
4397	1	1990	1990
3421	0	1969	–
3630	1	1984	1985
3668	0	1986	1987
4180	0	1988	–
3473	0	1976	–
3250	1	1950	–
4116	1	1950	1968
3268	1	1952	–
3914	1	1925	1945
3087	1	1930	–

(continued)

Genealogy 2 (continued)

Ego				Offspring				Grandchildren				Great-grandchildren				Great-great-grandchildren			
ID	Sex	Born	Died	ID	Sex	Born	Died	ID	Sex	Born	Died	ID	Sex	Born	Died	ID	Sex	Born	Died
2040	1	1905	1975	3087	1	1930	–	3289	1	1955	1971	4132	1	1980	–				
								3300	1	1956	–	7046	1	1979	–				
												7047	1	1981	–				
												7048	0	1982	–				
												7100	1	1988	–				
												7112	0	1990	–				
								3319	1	1958	–	7006	0	1983	–				
								3342	1	1960	–	7105	1	1986	–				
												8014	0	1985	–				
												8031	1	1989	–				
				3093	0	1932	–	3213	1	1947	1975								
								3881	0	1950	1972	3397	1	1966	–	4361	1	1988	–
												4414	0	1969	–				
								3285	1	1954	1978	3981	1	1977	1977				

3358 1 1961 1977
3375 0 1964 –

3588 1 1981 –
4150 0 1983 1983
4151 0 1985 1985
3693 1 1987 –
4370 0 1990 –

4393 1967 1967
3305 1 1957 –

3535 0 1980 –
3600 1 1983 1983
3629 1 1984 –
3673 1 1986 –
4382 1 1989 –

3880 0 1960 1960
3373 1 1962 –
3882 0 1965 –
3883 0 1970 1970
3344 1 1960 –

3121 0 1936 1971

3144 1 1939 –

3631 0 1984 –

(continued)

Ego				Offspring				Grandchildren				Great-grandchildren				Great-great-grandchildren			
ID	Sex	Born	Died	ID	Sex	Born	Died	ID	Sex	Born	Died	ID	Sex	Born	Died	ID	Sex	Born	Died
2040	1	1905	1975	3144	1	1939	–	3344	1	1960	–	3686	0	1986	–				
												4376	0	1989	–				
								3374	1	1963	–	7008	0	1986	–				
												7107	0	1988	–				
								3407	1	1967	–	7108	0	1988	–				
												7109	0	1990	–				
								4600	1	1969	1971								
								3866	1	1970	1975								
								3490	0	1977	–								

3176   1   1943 –

4326   0   1979   1979

3557   1   1981 –

3611   0   1983 –

3678   0   1986 –

3371   1   1963 –

3630   1   1984   1985

3668   0   1986   1987

4180   0   1988 –

3224   0   1948   1971

3400   0   1966 –

3598   0   1983 –

4429   1   1966   1966

3884   0   1968 –

Genealogy 3

Ego				Offspring				Grandchildren				Great-grandchildren				Great-great-grandchildren			
ID	Sex	Born	Died	ID	Sex	Born	Died	ID	Sex	Born	Died	ID	Sex	Born	Died	ID	Sex	Born	Died
2030	0	1901	1973	3033	0	1920	1972	3131	0	1938	1971	3309	0	1957	–	3475	1	1976	–
																3507	1	1978	–
																3540	0	1979	–
																4149	0	1981	1982
																3609	1	1983	–
																3653	1	1985	–
																3703	0	1987	–
																4369	1	1989	–
												3349	1	1961	–	3675	1	1986	–
																4167	0	1988	–
												3380	1	1964	–	3594	1	1982	–
												3399	0	1967	–	3658	1	1985	–
																4366	0	1988	–
												3861	0	1954	1956				

3141	1	1939	1961								
3197	1	1945	1972	4269	1	1967	1972				
				4270	0	1970	1971				
				3842	0	1972	1972				
3228	1	1948	1971	3397	1	1966	–	4361	1	1988	–
				4414	0	1969	–				
3262	1	1952	1973	4130	1	1969	1972				
3282	1	1954	1973								
3295	0	1955	–	3862	0	1975	1975				
				3491	1	1977	–				
				3545	0	1980	–				
				3597	1	1983	–				
				3665	0	1985	1985				
				3689	0	1986	–				
				4169	1	1989	–				
3306	0	1957	–	3460	0	1975	–	4607	0	1989	–
				3496	1	1978	–				

(continued)

Genealogy 3 (continued)

Ego				Offspring				Grandchildren				Great-grandchildren				Great-great-grandchildren			
ID	Sex	Born	Died	ID	Sex	Born	Died	ID	Sex	Born	Died	ID	Sex	Born	Died	ID	Sex	Born	Died
2030	0	1901	1973	3033	0	1920	1972	3306	0	1957	–	3559	1	1981	–				
												3654	0	1985	–				
												3705	0	1987	1988				
												4408	0	1990	–				
				3061	0	1925	1972	3860	1	1962	–								
								3183	1	1944	1960								
								3863	1	1948	1948								
								3258	1	1951	1963								
								3264	1	1953	–	8009	1	1974	–				
												8010	0	1978	–				
												8011	0	1980	–				
												8012	1	1983	–				
								3310	0	1957	–	3560	0	1981	–				
												4152	1	1983	1983				
												3634	0	1984	–				

(continued)

Genealogy 3 (continued)

Ego				Offspring				Grandchildren				Great-grandchildren				Great-great-grandchildren			
ID	Sex	Born	Died	ID	Sex	Born	Died	ID	Sex	Born	Died	ID	Sex	Born	Died	ID	Sex	Born	Died
2030	0	1901	1973	3130	1	1937	–	3584	1	1982	1982								
				3138	0	1939	–	3622	1	1984	1984								
				3179	0	1943	1978	3355	0	1962	–	3537	0	1980	1980				
												3566	0	1981	–				
												3644	1	1985	1988				
												4165	0	1988	1988				
												4164	0	1989	–				
								3389	0	1964	1965								
								3424	0	1969	–	3694	1	1987	1987				
								3448	1	1973	–	4166	0	1989	–				
								3867	0	1978	1978								
				3208	0	1946	1975	3865	0	1967	1968								
								3866	1	1970	1975								

Genealogy 4

2073	0	1895	1972
4017	1	1916	1972
3195	0	1945	–
4049	1	1964	1972

4050	0	1971	1972
3465	1	1975	–
3500	1	1978	–
3612	0	1983	–

4045	0	1948	1972
3381	1	1964	–

3676 1 1986 1987

4051	1	1967	1970
4052	0	1971	1972

3950	1	1951	1973
4069	1	1969	–

3353	0	1956	–
3667	0	1986	–
4398	1	1989	–

3327	1	1959	–
4030	1	1976	1976

3513	0	1978	–
3516	1	1978	–
3572	1	1981	–
3617	1	1983	–
3670	0	1986	–
4176	0	1989	–

(continued)

Genealogy 4 (continued)

Ego				Offspring				Grandchildren				Great-grandchildren				Great-great-grandchildren			
ID	Sex	Born	Died	ID	Sex	Born	Died	ID	Sex	Born	Died	ID	Sex	Born	Died	ID	Sex	Born	Died
2073	0	1895	1972	4017	1	1916	1972	4046	1	1962	–								
								4048	0	1966	1972								
								4047	0	1970	–								
				3039	1	1918	–	3869	0	1943	1944								
								3182	1	1944	–	3382	0	1964	–	3578	0	1982	1982
																3624	1	1984	–
																3685	0	1986	–
																4190	0	1988	–
																4387	1	1990	–
												3401	1	1966	–	4405	0	1988	–
																4406	1	1990	–
												3430	1	1970	–				
												4013	0	1973	1978				
												4014	1	1975	1975				
												4015	0	1976	1978				

3511	0	1978	–	
3549	0	1981	–	
3626	0	1984	–	
4016	1	1986	1986	
3692	0	1987	–	
4407	1	1990	–	
3871	1	1963	1964	
3872	1	1965	1965	
3873	0	1967	1968	
3426	0	1969	–	
3874	0	1972	1972	
3875	1	1975	1975	
3876	1	1977	1977	
3520	0	1979	–	
3573	0	1981	1982	
3614	1	1983	1983	
3682	0	1986	–	

3676 1 1986 1987

4179 0 1989 –

3205 0 1946 –

(continued)

| Ego | | | | Offspring | | | | Grandchildren | | | | Great-grandchildren | | | | Great-great-grandchildren | | | |
ID	Sex	Born	Died	ID	Sex	Born	Died	ID	Sex	Born	Died	ID	Sex	Born	Died	ID	Sex	Born	Died
Genealogy 4 (continued)																			
2073	0	1895	1972	3039	1	1918	–	3226	1	1948	–	3420	1	1968	–	4399	0	1989	–
												3440	0	1972	–	4361	1	1988	–
												3462	1	1975	–				
												3503	1	1978	1978				
												3534	0	1980	1980				
												3583	0	1982	1983				
												3623	1	1984	–				
												3698	1	1987	1987				
												4184	0	1988	1989				
								4135	1	1951	1960								
								3294	1	1955	–	3460	0	1975	–	4607	0	1989	–
												3496	1	1978	–				
												3590	0	1982	–				
												3709	1	1987	–				
												4391	1	1990	–				

4141 1 1921 1952

3190 1 1944 1965

4075 0 1942 1973

3446 0 1973 1978

3504 0 1978 –

3333 1 1959 –

4136 1 1960 –

4137 0 1963 1970

3421 0 1969 –

3630 1 1984 1985

3668 0 1986 1987

4180 0 1988 –

4174 1 1988 1989

4081 1 1963 1963

3386 1 1965 –

4082 0 1967 1967

4083 1 1968 1968

4084 0 1969 1971

4085 0 1972 1972

4086 1 1973 1973

3691 0 1986 –

4177 0 1989 –

(continued)

Genealogy 4 (*continued*)

Ego				Offspring				Grandchildren				Great-grandchildren				Great-great-grandchildren			
ID	Sex	Born	Died	ID	Sex	Born	Died	ID	Sex	Born	Died	ID	Sex	Born	Died	ID	Sex	Born	Died
2073	0	1895	1972	4142	1	1924	1928												
				4143	1	1928	1930												
				3840	1	1932	1972	3249	0	1950	–	3991	0	1971	1972				
												3461	0	1975	–				
												3992	0	1977	1977				
												3502	0	1978	–				
												3536	1	1980	–				
												3603	0	1983	–				
												3646	0	1985	–				
												3711	1	1988	–				

3287 1 1954 –

3515 0 1978 –

3526 0 1979 1979

3571 0 1981 1982

3643 1 1985 1985

3699 1 1987 1987

4392 0 1990 –

3986 1 1956 1965

3337 0 1960 –

3514 0 1978 –

3551 0 1981 1982

3595 0 1982 –

3672 0 1986 –

4386 0 1990 –

3354 1 1961 –

3415 1 1968 –

3987 0 1970 1972

4395 1 1989 –

4144 0 1935 1940

Genealogy 5

Ego				Offspring				Grandchildren				Great-grandchildren				Great-great-grandchildren			
ID	Sex	Born	Died	ID	Sex	Born	Died	ID	Sex	Born	Died	ID	Sex	Born	Died	ID	Sex	Born	Died
2029	1	1895	1970	3070	1	1925	1962												
				3073	0	1927	1972	3170	0	1943	–	3902	1	1965	1965				
												3903	0	1967	–				
												3435	1	1971	–				
												3904	0	1974	1974				
												3470	1	1976	–				
												3905	0	1978	1978				
												3547	1	1980	–				
												4171	1	1988	–				
								3221	0	1948	–	3899	1	1967	1967				
												3900	0	1968	1983				
												3438	1	1971	–				
												3901	0	1973	1973				
												3478	1	1976	–				
												3527	0	1979	–				
												3581	1	1982	–				

3637	1	1984	–
3701	1	1987	–
4385	1	1990	–
4476	0	1973	1973
3461	0	1975	–
3992	0	1977	1977
3502	0	1978	–
3536	1	1980	–
3603	0	1983	–
3646	0	1985	–
3711	1	1988	–
3616	0	1983	–
3661	1	1985	–
3707	0	1987	–
3518	0	1979	1980
3575	1	1981	–
3683	0	1986	–
4175	1	1988	–
3276	1	1953	–
3302	1	1956	–
3352	1	1961	–
3896	0	1963	1967
3898	1	1965	1972

Genealogy 5 (continued)

Ego				Offspring				Grandchildren				Great-grandchildren				Great-great-grandchildren			
ID	Sex	Born	Died	ID	Sex	Born	Died	ID	Sex	Born	Died	ID	Sex	Born	Died	ID	Sex	Born	Died
2029	1	1895	1970	3082	1	1929	1955	3813	1	1948	1952								
								3815	0	1952	1963								
								3814	0	1956	1977	3474	0	1976	–				
								3816	0	1958	1963								
				3102	1	1931	1965	4296	0	1959	1960								
				3090	0	1933	–	3250	1	1950	–	3473	0	1976	–				
								3289	1	1955	1971								
								3907	1	1958	–								
								3908	0	1964	–								
								3909	1	1967	1972								
								3910	0	1970	1970								
				3895	1	1936	1942												
				4232	0	1940	1972												
				3149	1	1940	1974	3334	1	1959	–	7039		1982	–				
												7040	0	1985	–				
												7096	0	1987	–				

| 7111 | 0 | 1989 – | |

3398	1	1966 –	
4217	1	1968 –	
4218	1	1970 –	
3541	1	1980 –	
7083	1	1979	1979
7080	1	1981 –	
7081	1	1983 –	
3674	1	1986 –	
4172	0	1988 –	
3562	1	1981 –	
3608	1	1983 –	
3690	1	1986 –	
3690	1	1986 –	
4241	0	1989 –	

4233	1	1943	1973
4146	0	1943	1943
4147	0	1945	1945
3209	0	1946 –	
4234	1	1949	1949
3281	1	1954	1973
3313	1	1958 –	
3376	0	1963 –	

References

Abbie, A. A. (1956) Metrical characters of a Central Australian tribe. *Oceania* 27:226.

Adair, L. S., and E. Pollitt. (1985) Outcome of maternal nutritional supplementation: a comprehensive review of the Bacon Chow Study. *American Journal of Clinical Nutrition* 41(5):948–978.

Albon, S. D., B. Mitchell, and B. W. Staines. (1983) Fertility and body weight in female red deer: a density-dependent relationship. *Journal of Animal Ecology* 52:969–980.

Alcock, J., C. E. Jones, and S. L. Buchman. (1977) Male mating strategies in the bee *Centris palida*, Fox (Anthophoridae: Hymenoptera). *American Naturalist* 111:145–155.

Aldrich, J. H., and F. D. Nelson. (1984) *Linear Probability, Logit and Probit Models*. Sage University Paper Series on Quantitative Applications in the Social Sciences. Beverly Hills and London: Sage Publications.

Alexander, R. D. (1974) The evolution of social behavior. *Annual Review of Ecology and Systematics* 5:325–383.

Alexander, R. D., J. L. Hoogland, R. D. Howard, K. M. Noonan, and P. W. Sherman. (1979) Sexual dimorphism and breeding system in pinnipeds, ungulates, primates and humans. In *Evolutionary Biology and Human Social Behavior*, N. Chagnon and W. Irons, eds., pp. 402–435. Belmont, California: Wadsworth.

Alley, T. R., and K. A. Hildebrandt. (1988) Determinants and consequences of facial aesthetics. In *Social and Applied Aspects of Perceiving Faces*, T. R. Alley, ed., pp. 101–140. New Jersey: Lawrence Erlbaum Associates.

Allison, P. D. (1982) Discrete time methods for the analyses of event histories. In *Social Methodology*, S. Leinhardt, ed., pp. 61–98. San Francisco: Jossey-Bass.

——— (1984) *Event History Analyses: Regression for Longitudinal Event Data*. Sage University Paper Series on Quantitative Applications in the Social Sciences. Beverly Hills and London: Sage Publications.

Altmann, S. A. (1991) Diets of yearling female primates predict lifetime fitness. *Proceedings of the National Academy of Science USA* 88:420–423.

Alvard, M. (1993) Testing the "ecologically noble savage" hypothesis: interspecific prey choice by Piro hunters of Amazonian Peru. *Human Ecology* 21(4):335–387.

Apter, D., L. Viinikka, and R. Vihko. (1978) Hormonal patterns of adolescent menstrual cycles. *Journal of Clinical Endocrinology and Metabolism* 57:82–86.

Arens, R. (1976) *Genocide in Paraguay*. Philadelphia: Temple University Press.

——— (1978) *The Forest Indians in Stroessner's Paraguay: Survival or Extinction?* Survival International Report. London: Survival International.

Auger, F., P. L. Jamison, J. Balslev-Jorgenson, T. Lewin, J. F. De Pena, and J. Skrobak-Kaczynski. (1980) Anthropometry of circumpolar populations. In *The Human Biology of Circumpolar Populations*, F. A. Milan, ed., pp. 213–256. Cambridge: Cambridge University Press.

Austad, S. N. (1993a) Comparative perspectives and choice of animal models in aging research. *Aging: Clinical and Experimental Research* 5:259–267.

———— (1993b) Retarded aging rate in an insular population of opossums. *Journal of Zoology* 229:695–708.

Austad, S. N., and K. E. Fischer. (1991) Mammalian aging, metabolism and ecology: evidence from the bats and marsupials. *Journal of Gerontology* 46(2):47–53.

———— (1992) Primate longevity: its place in the mammalian scheme. *American Journal of Primatology* 28:251–261.

Avadhani, P. N. (1975) A study of the Punan Busang. *Malayan Nature Journal* 28:121–172.

Baertl, J. M., E. Morales, G. Verastegui, and G. G. Graham. (1970) Diet supplementation for entire communities: growth and mortality of infants and children. *American Journal of Clinical Nutrition* 23(6):707–715.

Bailey, R., and R. Aunger Jr. (1989) Significance of the social relationships of Efe pygmy men in the Ituri forest, Zaire. *American Journal of Physical Anthropology* 78:495–507.

Bailey, R., and N. Peacock. (1988) Efe pygmies of northeastern Zaire: subsistence strategies in the Ituri forest. In *Coping with Uncertainty in the Food Supply,* I. de Garine and G. A. Harrisson, eds., pp. 88–117. Oxford: Clarendon Press.

Bairagi, R., M. K. Chowdhury, Y. J. Kim, and G. T. Curlin. (1985) Alternative anthropometric indicators of mortality. *American Journal of Clinical Nutrition* 42:296–306.

Balicki, A. (1970) *The Netsilik Eskimos: Adaptive Process*. American Museum of Natural History. Garden City, New York: Natural History Press.

Barnicott, N. A., F. J. Bennett, J. C. Woodburn, T. R. E. Pilkington, and A. Antonis. (1972) Blood pressure and serum cholesterol in the Hadza of Tanzania. *Human Biology* 44:87–116.

Becker, S., A. Chowdhury, and H. Leridon. (1986) Seasonal patterns of reproduction in Matlab, Bangladesh. *Population Studies* 40:457–472.

Bell, G., and V. Koufopanou. (1986) The cost of reproduction. In *Oxford Surveys in Evolutionary Biology*, R. Dawkins and M. Ridley, eds., pp. 83–131. Oxford: Oxford University Press.

Bellows, R. A., and R. E. Short. (1978) Effects of precalving feed level on birth weight, calving difficulty and subsequent fertility. *Journal of Animal Science* 46:1523–1528.

Belsky, J., L. Steinberg, and P. Draper. (1991) Childhood experience, interpersonal development, and reproductive strategy: an evolutionary theory of socialization. *Child Development* 62:647–670.

Bercovitch, F. B., and S. C. Strum. (1993) Dominance rank, resource availability, and reproductive maturation in female savanna baboons. *Behavioral Ecology and Sociobiology* 33:313–318.

Berrigan, D., A. Purvis, P. H. Harvey, et al. (1993) Phylogenetic contrasts and the evolution of mammalian life histories. *Evolutionary Ecology* 7:270–278.

Bertoni, G., and J. R. Gorham. (1973) The people of Paraguay: origin and numbers. In

Paraguay: Ecological Essays, J. R. Gorham, ed., pp. 109–140. Miami: Academy of the Arts and Sciences of the Americas.

Bertoni, M. (1941) *Los Guayakies*. Asunción: Revista de la Sociedad Cientifica del Paraguay.

Bion Griffin, P., and M. Griffin. (1992) Fathers and child-care among the Cayagan Agta. In *Father-Child Relations*, Barry S. Hewlett, ed., pp. 297–330. New York: Aldine de Gruyter.

Black, F. L. (1991) Reasons for failure of genetic classification of South Amerind populations. *Human Biology* 63(6):763–774.

Blossfeld, H. P., A. Hamerle, and K. U. Mayer. (1989) *Event History Analyses*. Hillsdale, New Jersey: Lawrence Erlbaum Associates.

Blurton Jones, N. (1986) Bushman birth spacing: a test for optimal interbirth intervals. *Ethology and Sociobiology* 7:91–105.

———— (1994) A reply to Dr. Harpending. *American Journal of Physical Anthropology* 93:391–396.

Blurton Jones, N., and J. Phillips. (1991) Fertility of older Hadza women. Unpublished manuscript, Department of Anthropology, UCLA.

Blurton Jones, N., L. Smith, J. O'Connell, K. Hawkes, and C. L. Kamusora. (1992) Demography of the Hadza, an increasing and high density population of savanna foragers. *American Journal of Physical Anthropology* 89:159–181.

Bongaarts, J. (1978) A framework for analyzing the proximate determinants of fertility. *Population and Development Review* 4:105–132.

———— (1980) Does malnutrition affect fecundity? A summary of evidence. *Science* 208:564–569.

———— (1983) The proximate determinants of natural marital fertility. In *Determinants of Fertility in Developing Countries*, R. Bulatao and R. Lee, eds., pp. 103–138. New York: Academic Press.

Bongaarts, J., and H. Delgado. (1979) Effects of nutritional status on fertility in rural Guatemala. In *Natural Fertility*, H. Leridon and J. Menken, eds., pp. 107–133. Liege: Ordina Editions.

Bonner, J. T. (1965) *Size and Cycle*. Princeton, New Jersey: Princeton University Press.

Borgerhoff Mulder, M. (1987) Resources and reproductive success in women, with an example from the Kipsigis. *Journal of Zoology* 213:489–505.

———— (1989a) Menarche, menopause, and reproduction in the Kipsigis of Kenya. *Journal of Biosocial Science* 21:179–192.

———— (1989b) Early maturing Kipsigis women have higher reproductive success than late maturing women and cost more to marry. *Behavioral Ecology and Sociobiology* 24:145–153.

———— (1991) Human behavioral ecology. In *Behavioural Ecology*, J. Krebs and N. Davies, eds., pp. 69–98. Oxford: Blackwell Scientific.

———— (1992a) Reproductive decisions. *In Evolutionary Ecology and Human Behavior*, E. A. Smith and B. Winterhalder, eds., pp. 339–374. New York: Aldine de Gruyter.

———— (1992b) Demography of Pastoralists: preliminary data on the Datoga of Tanzania. *Human Ecology* 20(4):383–405.

Bormida, M., and M. Califano. (1978) *Los Indios Ayoreo del Chaco Boreal: Informacion Basica Acerca de Su Cultura*. Buenos Aires: Fundacion Para la Educacion, la Ciencia, y la Cultura.

Boyce, M. S. (1981) Beaver life-history responses to exploitation. *Journal of Applied Ecology* 18:749–753.

——— (1988) *Evolution of Life Histories of Mammals*. New Haven: Yale University Press.

Bronson, R. T. (1981) Age at death of necroscopied intact and neutered cats. *American Journal of Veterinary Research* 42:1606–1608.

Brown, S., D. C. Gajdusek, W. Leyshon, A. Steinberg, K. Brown, and C Curtain. (1974) Genetic studies in Paraguay: blood group, red cell, and serum genetic patterns of the Guayaki and Ayore Indians, Mennonite settlers and seven other Indian tribes of the Paraguayan Chaco. *American Journal of Physical Anthropology* 41:317–344.

Brown, S., T. Tsai, and D. C. Gajdusek. (1975) Seroepidemiology of human papoviruses: discovery of virgin populations and some unusual patterns of antibody prevalence among remote peoples of the world. *American Journal of Epidemiology* 102:331–340.

Bugos, P. E. (1985) *An Evolutionary Ecological Analysis of the Social Organization of the Ayoreo of the Northern Grand Chaco*. Ph.D. Dissertation, Northwestern University.

Buikstra, J., and L. Konigsberg. (1985) Paleodemography: critiques and controversies. *American Anthropologist* 87:316–333.

Buss, D. (1989) Sex differences in human mate preferences: evolutionary hypothesis tested in 37 cultures. *Behavioral and Brain Sciences* 12(1):1–14.

——— (1994) *The Evolution of Desire*. New York: Basic Books.

Caldwell, J. C., and P. Caldwell. (1983) The demographic evidence for the incidence and cause of abnormally low fertility in tropical Africa. *World Health Statistics Quarterly* 36(1):1–34. Geneva: World Health Organization.

Campbell, B. C., and J. R. Udry. (1992) Mother's age at menarche, not stress, accounts for daughter's age at menarche. Paper presented at the 4th biennial meeting of the Society of Research on Adolescence, Washington, D.C.

Campbell, K. L., and J. Wood. (1988) Fertility in traditional societies. In *Natural Human Fertility: Social and Biological Mechanisms*, P. Diggory and S. Teper, eds., pp. 39–69. London: Macmillan.

Cantrelle, P., and B. Leridon. (1971) Breast-feeding, mortality in childhood, and fertility in a rural zone of Senegal. *Population Studies* 25:503–533.

Cappieri, M. (1974) *The Andamanese: Cultural Elements—Elements of Demogenetics, Physical Anthropology and Raciology*. Miami: Field Research Projects.

Carael, M. (1978) Relations between birth intervals and nutrition in three Central African populations. In *Nutrition and Human Reproduction*, W. H. Mosley, ed., pp. 365–384. New York: Plenum.

Caro, T., D. Sellen, A. Parish, R. Frank, D. Brown, E. Voland, and M. Borgerhoff Mulder. (1995) Termination of reproduction in nonhuman and human female primates. *International Journal of Primatology*. In press.

Case, T. J. (1978) On the evolution and adaptive significance of postnatal growth rates in the terrestrial vertebrates. *Quarterly Review of Biology* 53:243–282.

Cavalli-Sforza, L. L. (1986) African Pygmies: an evaluation of the state of research. In *African Pygmies*, pp. 361–426. L. L. Cavalli-Sforza, ed. New York: Academic Press.

Chagnon, N. (1968) *Yanomamo, the Fierce People*. New York: Holt, Rinehart and Winston.

——— (1974) *Studying the Yanomamo*. New York: Holt, Rinehart and Winston.

———— (1988) Life histories, blood revenge, and warfare in a tribal population. *Science* 239:985–992.

Chance, N. A. (1966) *The Eskimo of North Alaska*. New York: Holt, Rinehart and Winston.

Charlesworth, B. (1980) *Evolution in Age-Structured Populations*. Cambridge: Cambridge University Press.

Charnov, E. L. (1982*) The Theory of Sex Allocation*. Princeton, New Jersey: Princeton University Press.

———— (1986) Life history evolution in a "recruitment population": why are adult mortality rates constant? *Oikos* 47:129–134.

———— (1989) Natural selection on the age of maturity in shrimp. *Evolutionary Ecology* 3:236–239.

———— (1990) On the evolution of age of maturity and the adult lifespan. *Journal of Evolutionary Biology* 3:139–144.

———— (1991) Pure numbers, invariants and symmetry in the evolution of life histories. *Evolutionary Ecology* 5:339–342.

———— (1993) *Life History Invariants*. Oxford: Oxford University Press.

Charnov, E. L., and D. Berrigan. (1991) Dimensionless numbers and the assembly rules for life histories. In *The Evolution of Reproductive Strategies*, P. Harvey, L. Partridge, and L. Southwood, eds., pp. 41–48. Cambridge: Cambridge University Press.

———— (1993) Why do female primates have such long lifespans and so few babies? or Life in the slow lane. *Evolutionary Anthropology* 1(6):191–194.

Charnov, E. L., and J. R. Krebs. (1974) On clutch size and fitness. *Ibis* 116:217–219.

Chase-Sardi, M. (1971) The present situation of the Indians in Paraguay. In *The Situation of the Indian in South America*, W. Dostal, ed., pp. 173–217. Geneva: World Council of Churches.

———— (1989) Bibliographia de los Ache-Guayaki. Unpublished manuscript, Universidad Catolica, Asunción.

Chen, L. C., A. K. M. Alauddin Chowdhury, and S. L. Huffman. (1980) Anthropometric assessment of energy-protein malnutrition and subsequent risk of mortality among preschool aged children. *American Journal of Clinical Nutrition* 33:1836–1845.

Chowdhury, A. K. M. A. (1978) Effect of maternal nutrition on fertility in rural Bangladesh. In *Nutrition and Human Reproduction*, W. H. Mosley, ed., pp. 401–409. New York: Plenum.

Chowdhury, A. K. M. A., S. L. Huffman, and G. T. Curlin. (1977) Malnutrition, menarche and marriage in rural Bangladesh. *Social Biology* 24:316–325.

Christiansen, N., M. G. Herrera, J. O. Mora, and L. Navarro. (1980) Effects of nutritional supplementation during pregnancy upon birthweight: the influence of pre-supplementation diet. *Nutrition Reports International* 21(4):615–624.

Cieslak, D. G., V. D. Liebbrandt, and N. J. Benevenga. (1983) Effect of a high fat supplement in late gestation and lactation on piglet survival and performance. *Journal of Animal Science* 57:954–959.

Clastres, P. (1972a) *Chronique des Indiens Guayaki. Ce que Sevant les Aché, Chasseurs Nomades du Paraguay*. Paris: Pion.

———— (1972b) The Guayaki. In *Hunters and Gatherers Today*, M. Bicchieri, ed., pp. 138–174. New York: Holt, Rinehart, and Winston.

———— (1974) Guayaki cannibalism. In *Native South Americans: Ethnology of the Least Known Continent*, P. Lyon, ed., pp. 309–321. Boston: Little, Brown.

Clutton-Brock, T. H. (1983) Selection in relation to sex. In *Evolution from Molecules to Man*, pp. 457–81. D. S. Bendall, ed. Cambridge: Cambridge University Press.

———, ed. (1988) *Reproductive Success*. Chicago: University of Chicago Press.

——— (1991) *The Evolution of Parental Care*. Princeton, New Jersey: Princeton University Press.

——— (1994) Counting sheep. *Natural History* 103(3):28–32.

Clutton-Brock , T. H., D. F. Price, S. D. Albon, and P. A. Jewell. (1991) Persistent instability and population regulation in Soay sheep. *Journal of Animal Ecology* 60:593–608.

Clutton-Brock, T. H, O. F. Price, S. D. Albon. (1992) Early development and population fluctuations in Soay sheep. *Journal of Animal Ecology* 61(2):381–396.

Coale, A., and P. Demeny. (1966) *Regional Model Life Tables and Stable Populations*. Princeton, New Jersey: Princeton University Press.

Condon, R. G. (1987) *Inuit Youth: Growth and Change in the Canadian Arctic*. New Brunswick, New Jersey: Rutgers University Press.

Cromwell, G. L., T. J. Prince, G. E. Combs, C. V. Maxwell, D. A. Knabe, and D. E. Orr. (1982) Effects of additional feed during late gestation on reproductive performance of sows. *Journal of Animal Science* 55:268.

Cronk, L. (1989) Low socio-economic status and female biased parental investment: the Mukogodo example. *American Anthropologist* 91:414–429.

Crooze, H., A. K. Hillman, and E. M. Lang. (1981) Elephants and their habitats: how do they tolerate each other? In *Dynamics of Large Mammal Populations*, C. W. Fowler and T. D. Smith, eds. New York: John Wiley and Sons.

Crowl, T. A., and A. P. Covich. (1990) Predator-induced life history shifts in a freshwater snail. *Science* 247:949–951.

Cumming, D. C., G. D. Wheeler, and V. J. Harber. (1994) Physical activity, nutrition and reproduction. In *Human Reproductive Ecology: Interactions of Environment, Fertility and Behavior*, K. L. Campbell and J. W. Wood, eds., pp. 55–76. Albany, New York: New York Academy of Sciences.

Daly, M., and M. Wilson. (1988) Evolutionary social psychology and family homicide. *Science* 242:519–524.

Darwin, C. (1859) *The Origin of Species*. London: Murray.

——— (1871) *The Descent of Man and Selection in Relation to Sex*. New York: Appleton.

de Catanzaro, D. (1991) Evolutionary limits to self preservation. *Ethology and Sociobiology* 12:13–28.

Delgado, H., A. Lechtig, E. Brineman, R. Martorell, C. Yarbrough, and R. Klein. (1978) Nutrition and birth interval components: the Guatemalan experiences. In *Nutrition and Human Reproduction*, W. H. Mosely, ed., pp. 385–400. New York: Plenum.

Dietz, W. H., B. Marino, N. R. Peacock, and R. C. Bailey. (1989) Nutritional status of Efe Pygmies and Lese horticulturalists. *American Journal of Physical Anthropology* 78:509–518.

Draper, P. (1976) Social and economic constraints on child life among the !Kung. In *Kalahari Hunters and Gatherers*, R. B. Lee and I. DeVore, eds., pp. 199–217. Cambridge, Massachusetts: Harvard University Press.

Draper, P., and H. Harpending. (1982) Father absence and reproductive strategy: an evolutionary perspective. *Journal of Anthropological Research* 38:255–273.

Drusini, A., I. Calliari, and A. Volvpe. (1991) Root dentine transparency: age determination of human teeth using computerized densitometric analyses. *American Journal of Physical Anthropology* 85(1):25–30.

Dunbar, R. I. M. (1987) Demography and reproduction. In *Primate Societies*, B. Smuts, ed., pp. 240–249. Chicago: University of Chicago Press.

Dyson, T. (1977) The demography of the Hadza in historical perspective. *African Historical Demography*. University of Edinburgh: Centre for African Studies.

Early, J., and J. Peters. (1990) *The Population Dynamics of the Mucajai Yanomamo*. New York: Academic Press.

Eaton, S. B., M. C. Pike, R. V. Short, et al. (1994) Women's reproductive cancers in evolutionary context. *Quarterly Review of Biology* 69(3):353–367.

Eberhart, L. L. (1977) "Optimal" management policies for marine mammals. *Wildlife Society Bulletin* 5:162–169.

Eder, J. (1987) *On the Road to Tribal Extinction*. Berkeley: University of California Press.

Efron, B. (1988) Logistic regression, survival analysis and the Kaplan-Meier curve. *Journal of the American Statistical Association* 83:414–425.

Eisenberg, J. F. (1973) *Vertebrate Ecology in the Northern Neotropics*. Washington, D.C.: Smithsonian Institution Press.

Eisenberg, J., and R. Thorington. (1973) A preliminary analysis of neotropical mammal fauna. *Biotropica* 5:150–160.

Elkin, A. P. (1940) Kinship in South Australia. *Oceania* 10(3):295–399.

Ellison, P. (1995) Understanding natural variation in human ovarian function. In *Human Reproductive Decisions: Biological and Social Perspectives*, R. I. M. Dunbar, ed. London: MacMillan, in press.

Ellison, P. T., N. R. Peacock, and C. Lager. (1989) Ecology and ovarian function among Lese women of the Ituri forest. *American Journal of Physical Anthropology* 78:519–526.

Emmons, L. (1984) Geographic variation of densities and diversities of non-flying mammals in Amazonia. *Biotropica* 16(3):210–222.

Ericksen, M. F. (1991) Histologic estimation of age at death using the anterior cortex of the femur. *American Journal of Physical Anthropology* 84:171–179.

Evans, I. (1937) *The Negritos of Malaya*. Cambridge: Cambridge University Press.

Eveleth, P. B., and J. M. Tanner. (1976) *Worldwide Variation in Human Growth*. Cambridge: Cambridge University Press.

Festing, M. F., and D. K. Blackmore. (1971) Life span of specified pathogen-free (MRC category 4) mice and rats. *Laboratory Animal Bulletin* 5:179–192.

Fink, A. E., G. Fink, H. Wilson, J. Bennie, S. Carroll, and H. Dick. (1992) Lactation, nutrition, fertility and the secretion of prolactin and gonadotrophins in Mopan Mayan women. *Journal of Biosocial Science* 24(1):35–52.

Fisher, R. A. (1930) *The Genetical Theory of Natural Selection*. Oxford: Clarendon Press.

Foster, A., J. A. Menken, A. K. M. A. Chowdhury, and J. Trussel. (1986) Female reproductive development: a hazards model analysis. *Social Biology* 33:183–198.

Fowler, C. W. (1981) Density dependence as related to life history strategy. *Ecology* 62:602–610.

——— (1987) A review of density dependence in populations of large mammals. In *Current Mammalogy*, Vol. 1, H. H. Genoways, ed., pp. 401–441. New York: Plenum Press.

Fowler, K., and L. Partridge. (1989) A cost of mating in female fruitflies. *Nature* 338:760–761.

Freedman, D., A. Thornton, D. Camburn, D. Alwin, and L. Young-DeMarco. (1988) The life history calendar: a technique for collecting retrospective data. In *Sociological Methodology*, pp. 37–68. Washington, D.C.: American Sociological Association.

Friedlander, Nancylee J. (1993) *Reproductive Success, Postreproductive Health, and Survivorship in a Southern California Community*. Ph.D. Dissertation, Department of Anthropology, Harvard University.

Frisancho, A. R. (1981) *Human Adaptation: A Functional Interpretation*. Ann Arbor: University of Michigan Press.

——— (1990) *Anthropometric Standards for the Assessment of Growth and Nutritional Status*. Ann Arbor: University of Michigan Press.

Fundacion Moises Bertoni. (1987) *Mbaracayu Project. Technical Report*. Asunción, Paraguay.

Gage, T. B. (1989) Bio-mathematical approaches to the study of human mortality. *Yearbook of Physical Anthropology* 32:185–214.

Gardner, P. M. (1965) Paliyan social structure. Contributions to Anthropology: Band Societies. Proceedings of the Conference on Band Organisation. *Bulletin* 28:153–171. Ottawa: National Museums of Canada.'

Garn, S. M. (1982) Relationship of various maternal body mass measures and size of the newborn. *American Journal of Clinical Nutrition* 3694:664–668.

Gaulin, S. (1980) Sexual dimorphism in the human post-reproductive lifespan: possible causes. *Human Evolution* 9:227–232.

Gaulin, S., and J. Boster. (1985) Cross-cultural differences in sexual dimorphism: is there any variance to be explained? *Ethology and Sociobiology* 6:219–225.

Gavan, J. A. (1953) Growth and development of the chimpanzee: a longitudinal and comparative study. *Human Biology* 25:93–143.

Geronimus, A. (1987) On teenage childbearing and neonatal mortality in the United States. *Population and Development Review* 13(2):245–279.

Gilberg, R. (1984) Polar Eskimo. In *Artic,* D. Damas, ed., pp. 577–594. *Handbook of North American Indians,* Vol. 5. Washington, D.C.: Smithsonian Institution.

Godfray, H. C., and J. R. Ives. (1988) Stochasticity in invertebrate clutch size models. *Theoretical Population Biology* 33:79–101.

Godfray, H. C., and G. A. Parker. (1991) Clutch size, fecundity and parent-offspring conflict. *Philosophical Transactions of the Royal Society of London* B 332:67–79.

Good, K. (1989) *Yanomami Hunting Patterns: Trekking and Garden Relocation as an Adaptation to Game Availability in Amazonia, Venezuela*. Ph.D. Dissertation, University of Florida.

Goodall, J. (1986) *Chimpanzees of Gombe: Behavioral Patterns*. Cambridge, Massachusetts: Harvard University Press.

Goodman, M., A. Estokio-Griffin, P. Bion Griffin, and J. Grove. (1985) Menarche, pregnancy, birth spacing and menopause among the Agta women foragers of Cagayan Province, Luzon, the Philippines. *Annals of Human Biology* 12(2):169–177.

Gopalan, C., M. C. Swaminathan, V. K. Krishna Kumari, D. Hanumantha Rao, and K. Vijajaraghavan. (1973) Effect of calorie supplementation on growth of undernourished children. *American Journal of Clinical Nutrition* 26(5):563–566.

Graham, G. G., H. M. Creed, W. C. MacLean, J. Rabold, C. H. Kallman, and E. D. Mellits. (1981) Determinants of growth among poor children: relation of nutrient intakes to expenditure for food. *American Journal of Clinical Nutrition* 34(4):555–561.

Grayson, D. (1993) Differential mortality and the Donner party disaster. *Evolutionary Anthropology* 2(5):151–158.

Gross, M. R. (1985) Disruptive selection for alternative life histories in salmon. *Nature* 313:47–48.

Gross, M. R., and E. L. Charnov. (1980) Alternative male life histories in bluegill sunfish. *Proceedings of the National Academy of Science USA* 77:6937–6940.

Gubser, N. J. (1965) *The Nunamiut Eskimo: Hunters of Caribou.* New Haven: Yale University Press.

Gusinde, M. (1961) [1937]. *The Yamana: The Life and Thought of the Water Nomads of Cape Horn,* Vols. 1–5. New Haven: Human Relations Area Files.

Gustafsson, L., and W. J. Sutherland. (1988) The costs of reproduction in the collared flycatcher, *Ficedula albicollis. Nature* 335:813–815.

Hamilton, A. (1981) *Nature and Nurture: Aboriginal Child Rearing in North Arnhem Land.* Canberra: Australian Institute of Aboriginal Studies.

Hamilton, G. D., and F. H. Bronson. (1985) Food restriction and reproductive development in wild house mice. *Biology of Reproduction* 32:773–778.

Hamilton, J. B. (1965) Relationship of castration, spaying, and sex to survival and duration of life in domestic cats. *Journal of Gerontology* 20:96–104.

Hamilton, J. B., and G. E. Mestler. (1969) Mortality and survival: a comparison of eunuchs with intact men and women in a mentally retarded population. *Journal of Gerontology* 24:395–411.

Hamilton, W. D. (1964) The genetical evolution of social behavior. *Journal of Theoretical Biology* 7:1–52.

——— (1966) The moulding of senescence by natural selection. *Journal of Theoretical Biology* 12:12–45.

——— (1975) Innate social aptitudes in man, an approach from evolutionary genetics. In *Biosocial Anthropology,* R. Fox, ed., pp. 133–157. New York: Wiley.

Hamilton, W. D., and M. Zuk. (1982) Heritable true fitness and bright birds: a role for parasites? *Science* 218:384–387.

Harpending, H. (1994) Infertility and forager demography. *American Journal of Physical Anthropology* 93:385–390.

Harpending, H., and P. Draper. (1986) Selection against human family organization. In *On Evolutionary Anthropology: Essays in Honor of Harry Hoijer,* B. J. Williams, ed., pp. 37–75. Los Angeles: UCLA, Undena Press.

Harpending, H., and L. Wandsnider. (1982) Population structures of Ghanzi and Ngamiland !Kung. In *Current Developments in Anthropological Genetics,* J. H. Mielke and M .H. Crawford, eds., pp. 29–50. New York: Plenum Press.

Harris, M. (1979) *Cultural Materialism.* New York: Random House.

Hart, C. W. M., A. R. Pilling, and J. C. Goodale. (1988) *The Tiwi of North Australia,* 3rd ed. Fort Worth: Holt, Rinehart and Winston.

Harvey, P., and T. Clutton-Brock. (1985) Life history variation in primates. *Evolution* 39(3):559–581.

Harvey, P., and S. Nee. (1991) How to live like a mammal. *Nature* 350:23–24.

Harvey, P., L. Partridge, and L. Southwood, eds. (1991) *The Evolution of Reproductive Strategies*. Cambridge: Cambridge University Press.

Hasher, L., and R. T. Zacks. (1984) Automatic processing of fundamental information. *American Psychologist* 39(12):1372–1388.

Hasstedt, S. J. (1986) An analysis of the inheritance of height in the Pygmies of the Central African Republic. In *African Pygmies*, L. L Cavalli-Sforza, ed., pp. 311–318. New York: Academic Press.

Haukioja, E., and T. Hakala. (1978) Life history evolution in *Anodonta piscinalis* (Mollusca, Pelecypoda). *Oecologia* 35:253–266.

Hausfater, G., and S. Hrdy. (1984) *Infanticide: Comparative and Evolutionary Perspectives*. New York: Aldine.

Hawkes, K. (1987) How much food do foragers need? In *Food and Evolution: Towards a Theory of Human Food Habits*, M. Harris and E. Ross, eds., pp. 22–51. Philadelphia: Temple University Press.

———— 1990. Why do men hunt? Some benefits for risky strategies. In *Risk and Uncertainty in the Food Supply*, E. Cashdan., ed., pp. 145–166. Boulder: Westview Press.

———— (1991) Showing off: tests of another hypothesis about men's foraging goals. *Ethology and Sociobiology* 11:29–54.

Hawkes, K., and K. Hill. (1982) Porqué recolectan los cazadores? La explotación óptima de recursos entre los Aché del Paraguay Oriental. *Suplemento Antropologico* XVII:99–130. Asunción, Paraguay.

Hawkes, K., K. Hill, and J. O'Connell. (1982) Why hunters gather: optimal foraging and the Ache of Eastern Paraguay. *American Ethnologist* (2):379–398.

Hawkes, K., J. O'Connell, K. Hill, and E. Charnov. (1985) How much is enough? Hunters and limited needs. *Ethology and Sociobiology* 6:3–16.

Hawkes, K., H. Kaplan, K. Hill, and A. M. Hurtado. (1987) Ache at the settlement: contrast between farming and foraging. *Human Ecology* 15(2):133–161.

Hawkes, K., J. F. O'Connell, and N. Blurton Jones. (1989) Hardworking Hadza grandmothers. In *Comparative Socioecology of Mammals and Man*, R. Foley and V. Standen, eds., pp. 341–366. London: Basil Blackwell.

Headland, T. (1989) Population decline in a Philippine Negrito hunter-gatherer society. *American Journal of Human Biology* 1:59–72.

Henry, J. (1941) *Jungle People*. New York: Vintage Books.

Hester, J. (1966) Late Pleistocene environments and early man in South America. *American Naturalist* 100(914):377–388.

Hewlett, B. S. (1991) Demography and child-care in pre-industrial societies. *Journal of Anthropological Research* 47:52–73.

Hiatt, L. R. (1965) *Kinship and Conflict*. Canberra: Australian National University.

Hill, K. (1983a) *Adult Male Subsistence Strategies among Ache Hunter-Gatherers of Eastern Paraguay*. Ph.D. Dissertation, University of Utah.

———— (1983b) Los Ache del Paraguay Oriental: Condiciones Actuales e Historia Reciente. *Suplemento* Antropológico XVIII:149–178. Asunción, Paraguay.

———— (1988) Macronutrient modifications of optimal foraging theory: an approach using indifference curves applied to some modern foragers. *Human Ecology* 16(2):157–197.

———— (1993) Life history theory and evolutionary anthropology. *Evolutionary Anthropology* 2(3):78–88.

——— (1995) Paleodemography. Letter to the editor. *Evolutionary Anthropology*, in press.

Hill, K., and K. Hawkes. (1983) Neotropical hunting among the Ache of Eastern Paraguay. In *Adaptive Responses of Native Amazonians*, R. Hames and W. Vickers, eds., pp. 139–188. New York: Academic Press.

Hill, K., and A. M. Hurtado. (1989) Ecological studies among some South American foragers. *American Scientist* 77(5):436–443.

——— (1991) The evolution of reproductive senescence and menopause in human females. *Human Nature* 2(4):315–350.

——— (1995) Kin-selected menopause? In *Human Nature: A Critical Reader*, Laura Betzig, ed. New York: Oxford University Press, in press.

Hill, K., and H. Kaplan. (1988a) Tradeoffs in male and female reproductive strategies among the Ache, part 1. In *Human Reproductive Behavior*, L. Betzig, P. Turke, and M. Borgerhoff Mulder, eds., pp. 277–290. Cambridge: Cambridge University Press.

——— (1988b) Tradeoffs in male and female reproductive strategies among the Ache, part 2. In *Human Reproductive Behavior*, L. Betzig, P. Turke, and M. Borgerhoff Mulder, eds., pp. 291–306. Cambridge: Cambridge University Press.

——— (1989) Population and dry-season subsistence strategies of the recently contacted Yora of Peru. *National Geographic Research* 5:317–334.

Hill, K., K. Hawkes, A. M. Hurtado, and H. Kaplan. (1984) Seasonal variance in the diet of Ache hunter-gatherers in eastern Paraguay. *Human Ecology* 12:145–180.

Hill, K., K. Hawkes, H. Kaplan, and A. M. Hurtado. (1987) Foraging decisions among Ache hunter-gatherers: new data and implications for optimal foraging models. *Ethology and Sociobiology* 8:1–36.

Hill, K., H. Kaplan, K. Hawkes, and A. M. Hurtado. (1985) Men's time allocation to subsistence work among the Ache of eastern Paraguay. *Human Ecology* 13:29–47.

Hobbes, T. (1947) [1651] *Leviathan*. London: J. M. Dent.

Holmberg, A. (1969) *Nomads of the Long Bow*. Garden City, New York: Natural History Press.

Homer, S. (1992) Last hunt of the forest people. *Nature Conservancy* 18(November/December):7–14.

Houde, A. E., and A. J. Torio. (1992) Effect of parasitic infection on male color pattern and female choice in guppies. *Behavioral Ecology* 3(4):346–351.

Howard, C. (1991) *Navajo Tribal Demography, 1983–1986, in Comparative and Historical Perspective*. Ph.D. Dissertation, University of New Mexico.

Howard, R. D. (1978) The evolution of mating strategies in bullfrogs, *Rana catesbiana*. *Evolution* 32:850–871.

Howell, N. (1979) *Demography of the Dobe !Kung*. New York: Academic Press.

——— (1982) Village composition implied by a paleodemographic life table: the Libben site. *American Journal of Physical Anthropology* 59:263–269.

Hrdy, S. (1981) *The Woman That Never Evolved*. Cambridge, Massachusetts: Harvard University Press.

——— (1992) Fitness tradeoffs in the history and evolution of delegated mothering with special reference to wet nursing, abandonment, and infanticide. *Ethology and Sociobiology* 13:409–442.

——— (1995) Infanticide. In *Encyclopedia of Cultural Anthropology*, D. Levingston and M. Ember. Lakeville, Connecticut: American Reference, in press.

Hrdy, S., and D. Judge. (1993) Darwin and the puzzle of primogeniture: an essay on biases in parental investment after death. *Human Nature* 4(1):1–45.

Huffman, S. L., A. M. K. Chowdhury, J. Chakborty, and W. H. Mosley. (1978) Nutrition and postpartum amenorrhea in rural Bangladesh. *Population Studies* 32:251–260.

Huffman, S. L., A. M. K. Chowdhury, and Z. M. Sykes. (1980) Lactation and fertility in rural Bangladesh. *Population Studies* 34:337–347.

Huffman, S. L., K. Ford, H. Allen, and P. Streble. (1987) Nutrition and fertility in Bangladesh: breastfeeding and postpartum amenorrhea. *Population Studies* 41:447–462.

Hurt, W. R. (1964) Recent radiocarbon dates for central and southern Brazil. *American Antiquity* 30(1):25–33.

Hurtado, A. M. (1985) *Women's Subsistence Strategies among Ache Hunter-Gatherers of Eastern Paraguay*. Ph.D. Dissertation, University of Utah.

Hurtado, A. M., and K. Hill. (1987) Early dry season subsistence ecology of the Cuiva foragers of Venezuela. *Human Ecology* 15:163–187.

Hurtado, A. M., and K. R. Hill. (1990) Seasonality in a foraging society: Variation in diet, work effort, fertility and the sexual division of labor among the Hiwi of Venezuela. *Journal of Anthropological Research* 46(3):293–345.

——— (1991) Paternal effect on offspring survivorship among Ache and Hiwi nunter-gatherers: implications for modeling pair-bond stability. In *Father-Child Relations: Cultural and Biosocial Contexts*, B. S. Hewlett, ed., pp. 31–55. New York: Aldine.

Hurtado, A., K. Hawkes, K. Hill, and H. Kaplan. (1985) Female subsistence strategies among Ache hunter-gatherers of eastern Paraguay. *Human Ecology* 13:1–28.

Hurtado, A., K. Hill, H. Kaplan, and I. Hurtado. (1992) Trade-offs between female food acquisition and child care among Hiwi and Ache foragers. *Human Nature* 3(3):185–216.

Janson, C. H., and C. P. Van Schaik. (1993) Ecological risk aversion in juvenile primates: slow and steady wins the race. In *Juvenile Primates: Life History, Development and Behavior*, M. E. Pereira and L. A. Fairbanks, eds., pp. 57–74. Oxford: Oxford University Press.

Johnson, S., H. Kaplan, and J. Lancaster. (1994) The association between fertility and mortality differentials among men in an industrialized population. Paper presented at the Annual Conference for Cross-Cultural Research, Santa Fe, New Mexico. February.

Jones, D. (1993) *The Evolutionary Psychology of Physical Attractiveness: Results from Five Populations*. Ph.D. Dissertation, University of Michigan.

Jones, D., and, K. Hill. (1993) Criteria of facial attractiveness in five populations. *Human Nature* 4(3):271–296.

Jones, D., and R. Wrangham. (1989) Rates of lethal violence in non-state societies in relation to group size and population density. Paper presented at the Human Behavior and Evolution Society Conference, University of Michigan, Ann Arbor, June.

Jones, K. (1983) Forager archeology: the Ache of eastern Paraguay. In *Carnivores, Human Scavengers, and Predators: a Question of Bone Technology*, G. M. Lemoyne and A. S. MacEachern, eds., pp. 171–191. Calgary: Archeological Association of the University of Calgary.

——— (1984) *Hunting and Scavenging by Early Hominids: a Study in Archeological Method and Theory*. Ph.D. Dissertation, University of Utah.

Kalbfleisch, J. D., and R. L. Prentice. (1980) *The Statistical Analyses of Failure Time Data*. New York: John Wiley.

Kaplan, H. (1983) *The Evolution of Food Sharing among Adult Conspecifics: Research with Ache Hunter-gatherers of Eastern Paraguay*. Ph.D. Dissertation, University of Utah.

—— (1994) Evolutionary and wealth flows theories of fertility: empirical tests and new models. *Population and Development Review* 20:753–791.

Kaplan, H., and H. Dove. (1987) Infant development among the Ache of Paraguay. *Developmental Psychology* 23(2):190–198.

Kaplan, H., and K. Hill. (1985a) Food sharing among Ache foragers: tests of explanatory hypotheses. *Current Anthropology* 26(2):223–245.

—— (1985b) Hunting ability and reproductive success among male Ache foragers. *Current Anthropology* 26(1):131–133.

Kaplan, H., K. Hill, and A. M. Hurtado. (1990) Risk, foraging and food sharing among the Ache. In *Risk and Uncertainty in the Food Supply*, E. Cashdan, ed., pp. 107–144. Boulder: Westview Press.

Kaplan, H., K. Hill, K. Hawkes, and A. M. Hurtado. (1984) Food sharing among the Ache hunter-gatherers of eastern Paraguay. *Current Anthropology* 25:113–115.

Kaplan, H., J. Lancaster, J. Bock, and S. Johnson. (1995) Fertility and fitness among Albuquerque men: a competitive labor market theory. In *Human Reproductive Decisions: Biological and Social Perspectives*, R. I. M. Dunbar, ed. London: Macmillan, in press.

Kasongo Project Team. (1986) Growth decelerations among under-5-year-old children in Kasongo (Zaire). II. Relationship with subsequent risk of dying, and operational consequences. *Bulletin of the World Health Organization* 64(5):703–709.

Katz, J. K., P. West, I. Tarwotjo, and A. Sommer. (1989) The importance of age in evaluating anthropometric indices for predicting mortality. *American Journal of Epidemiology* 130(6):1219–1226.

Kedit, P. M. (1982) An ecological study of the Penan. *The Sarawak Museum Journal* 30:224–279.

Keel, S. (1987) Inventory of forest property owned by the World Bank. In *Proposal to the Nature Conservancy to Create the Mbaracayu Wilderness Area*, appendix. Centro de Datos par la Conservacion, Asunción, Paraguay.

Kelly, R. (1995) The foraging spectrum: Diversity in hunter-gatherer lifeways. Washington: Smithsonian Institution Press.

Kielmann, A. A., C. E. Taylor, and R. L. Parker. (1978) The Narangwal Nutrition Study: a summary review. *American Journal of Clinical Nutrition* 31:2040–2052.

Kirkwood, J. K. (1985) Patterns of growth in primates. *Journal of Zoology, London* 205:123–136.

Kirkwood, J. K., and M. Rose. (1991) Evolution of senescence: late survival sacrificed for reproduction. In *The Evolution of Reproductive Strategies*, P. Harvey, L. Partridge, and L. Southwood, eds., pp. 15–24. Cambridge: Cambridge University Press.

Kitcher, P. (1985) *Vaulting Ambition: Sociobiology and the Quest for Human Nature*. Cambridge: MIT Press.

Kline, J., Z. Stein, and M. Susser. (1989) *Conception to Birth: Epidemiology of Prenatal Development*. New York: Oxford University Press.

Knauft, B. (1987) Reconsidering violence in simple human societies: homicide among the Gebusi of New Guinea. *Current Anthropology* 28:457–500.

Kohrs, M. B., A. E. Harper, and G. R. Kerr. (1976) Effects of a low-protein diet during pregnancy of the rhesus monkey: 1. Reproductive efficiency. *American Journal of Clinical Nutrition* 29:136–145.

Konigsberg, L. W., and S. R. Frankenberg. (1992) Estimation of age structure in anthropological demography. *American Journal of Physical Anthropology* 89:235–256.

Konner, M. (1976) Maternal care, infant behavior and development among the !Kung. In *Kalahari Hunters and Gatherers: Studies of the !Kung San and Their Neighbors*, R. B. Lee and I. DeVore, eds., pp. 218–245. Cambridge, Massachusetts: Harvard University Press.

Kozlowski, J. (1992) Optimal allocation of resources to growth and reproduction: implications for age and size at maturity. *Trends in Evolutionary Ecology* 7:15–19.

Kozlowski, J., and R. G. Wiegert. (1987) Optimal age and size at maturity in the annuals and perennials with determinate growth. *Evolutionary Ecology* 1:231–244.

La Hitte, Ch. de, and H. Ten Kate. (1897) Notes etnographiques sur les Indies Guayakis et description de luers caracteres physiques. *Annales del Musue de la Plata*, Vol. 2. Argentina.

Lack, D. (1947) The significance of clutch size. *Ibis* 89:302–352.

Langlois, J. H., and L. A. Roggman. (1990) Attractive faces are only average. *American Psychological Society* 1:115–121.

Lanning, E., and T. Patterson. (1967) Early man in South America. *Scientific American* 217(5):44–50.

Lavigne, D. M. (1982) Similarity of energy budgets of animal populations. *Journal of Animal Ecology* 51:195–206.

Lazarus, J. (1990) The logic of mate desertion. *Animal Behaviour* 39:672–684.

Le Boeuf, B. J. (1974) Male-male competition and reproductive success in elephant seals. *American Zoologist* 14:163–176.

Leary, R. L., and F. W. Allendorf. (1989) Fluctuating asymmetry as an indicator of stress: implications for wildlife biology. *Trends in Evolutionary Ecology* 4:214–217.

Lee, R. B. (1979) *The !Kung San*. Cambridge: Cambridge University Press.

Lemenager, R. P., W. H. Smith, T. G. Martin, W. L. Singleton, and J. R. Hodges. (1980) Effects of winter and summer energy levels on heifer growth and reproductive performance. *Journal of Animal Science* 51:837–842.

Leslie, P. W., and P. H. Fry. (1989) Extreme seasonality of births among nomadic Turkana pastoralists. *American Journal of Physical Anthropology* 79:103–115.

Lessells, C. (1991) The evolution of life histories. In *Behavioural Ecology: An Evolutionary Approach*, 3rd edition, J. Krebs and N. Davies, eds., pp. 32–68. Oxford: Blackwell Scientific.

Lesthaeghe, R. (1987) Lactation and lactation-related variables: contraception and fertility, an overview of data problems and world trends. *International Journal of Gynaecology and Obstetrics* 25 (Suppl.):143–173.

Levi-Strauss, C. (1948) La vie familiale et sociale des indiens Nambikwara. *Journal de la Societe des Americanistes* (Paris) 37:1–132.

Lewis, P. R., J. B. Brown, M. B. Renfree, and R. V. Short. (1991) The resumption of ovulation and menstruation in a well-nourished population of women breastfeeding for an extended period of time. *Fertility and Sterility* 55:529–536.

Lipson, S. F., and P. T. Ellison. (1992) Normative study of age variation in salivary progesterone profiles. *Journal of Biosocial Science* 24:233–244.

Lodge, G. A., and B. Hardy. (1968) The influence of nutrition during oestrus on ovulation rate in the sow. *Journal of Reproductive Fertility* 15:329–332.

Loehlin, J. C. (1987) *Latent Variable Models. An Introduction to Factor, Path, and Structural Analyses.* Hillsdale, New Jersey: Lawrence Erlbaum Associates.

Lotka, A. J. (1907) The relation between birth and death rates. *Science* 26:21–22.

Lovejoy, C. O., R. Meindl, T. Pryzbeck, T. Barton, K. Heiple, and D. Kotting. (1977) Paleodemography of the Libben site, Ottawa County, Ohio. *Science* 198:291–293.

Lozano, P. (1873–1874) *Historia de la Conquista del Paraguay, Rio de La Plata, y Tucuman,* Vol. 1. Buenos Aires.

Luckinbill, L., M. Clare, W. Krell, W. Cirocco, and P. Richards. (1987) Estimating the number of genetic elements that defer senescence in *Drosophila. Evolutionary Ecology* 1:37–46.

Lunn, P., S. Austin, A. M. Prentice, and R. Whitehead. (1984) The effect of improved nutrition on plasma prolactin concentrations and postpartum infertility in lactating Gambian women. *American Journal of Clinical Nutrition* 39:227–235.

MacNeish, R. S., ed. (1973) *Early Man in America: Readings from Scientific American.* San Francisco: W. H. Freeman.

Manocha, S. L., and J. Long. (1977) Experimental protein malnutrition during gestation and breeding performance of squirrel monkeys. *Primates* 18:923–930.

Manrique Castañeda, L. (1966) Notas sobre la somatometría de los Guayaki. *Suplemento Antropológico de la Revista Ateneo Paraguayo* II(1):65–74.

Manson, J., and R. Wrangham. (1991) Intergroup aggression in chimpanzees and humans. *Current Anthropology* 32:369–390.

Marsh, H., and T. Kasuya. (1986) Evidence for reproductive senescence in female Cetaceans. *Report of the International Whaling Commission,* Special Issue 8:57–74.

Martorell, R. H., A. Lechtig, C. Yarbrough, H. Delgado, and R. E. Klein. (1976) Protein-calorie supplementation and postnatal physical growth: a review of findings from developing countries. *Archives of Latin American Nutrition* 26(2):115–128.

Matson, G., H. Sutton, J. Swanson, and A. Robinson. (1968) Distribution of blood groups among Indians in South America, II. Paraguay. *American Journal of Physical Anthropology* 29:81–98.

Maybury Lewis, D. (1967) *Akwe-Shavante Society.* Oxford: Clarendon Press.

Maynard Smith, J. (1958) The effect of temperature and of egg laying on the longevity of *Drosophila subobscura. Journal of Experimental Biology* 35:832–842.

———— (1977) Parental investment: a prospective analysis. *Animal Behaviour* 25:1–9.

———— (1982) *Evolution and the Theory of Games.* Cambridge: Cambridge University Press.

Mayntzhusen, F. (1912) Mitteilungen aus dem Gebiete der Guayaki. *Actas del XVII International Congress of Americanists, Buenos Aires 1910,* (1):470.

———— (1920) *Die Sprache der Guayaki. Zeitschrift für Eingeborenensprachen* X (1919/20): 2–22. Berlin: Hamburg.

———— (1928) Instrumentos paleoliticos del Paraguay. *Annals, 20th International Congress of Americanists* 2(II):177–180. Rio de Janeiro.

———— (1945) Los Guayaki y la "Civilizacion." *Boletin de la Junta de Estudios Historicos de Misiones* 5:8–11. Posadas, Argentina.

McArthur, M. (1960) Food consumption and dietary levels of groups of Aborigines living on naturally occurring foods. In *Records of the American-Australian Scientific Expedition to Arnhem Land,* Vol. 2, C. P. Mountfield, ed. Melbourne: Melbourne University Press.

McCarthy, F. D., and M. McArthur. (1960) The food quest and the time factor in

Aboriginal economic life. In *Records of the American-Australian Scientific Expedition to Arnhem Land*, Vol. 2, C. P. Mountfield, ed. Melbourne University Press.

McNeilly, A. S. (1993) Breastfeeding and fertility. *In Biomedical and Demographic Determinants of Reproduction*, R. H. Gray, H. Leridon, and A. Spira, eds., pp. 391–412. Oxford: Clarendon Press.

Meggitt, M. J. (1962) *Desert People.* Sydney: Angus & Robertson.

Melancon, T. (1982) *Marriage and Reproduction among the Yanomamo Indians of Venezuela.* Ph.D. Dissertation, Pennsylvania State University.

Melia, B., and C. Munzel. (1973) Ratones y Jaguares. In *La Agonia de los Ache Guayaki: Hisoria y Cantos*, B. Melia, L. Miraglia, C. Munzel and M. Munzel, eds. Centro de Estudios Antropológicos, Universidad Catolica: Asunción.

Melia, B., L. Miraglia, M. Munzel, and C. Munzel. (1973) *La Agonia de los Ache Guayaki: Hisoria y Cantos.* Centro de Estudios Antropológicos, Universidad Catolica: Asunción.

Menghim, O. (1957) El poblamiento prehistórico de misiones. *Anales de Arqueología y Etnología* 12:19–40. Facultad de Filosofía y Letras, Universidad Nacional de Cuyo, Mendoza, Argentina.

Metcoff, J., L. Bentle, C. E. Bodwell, J. P. Costiloe, W. Crosby, P. McClain, H. H. Sandstead, D. Seshachalam, and F. Weaver. (1981) Maternal nutrition and fetal outcome. *American Journal of Clinical Nutrition* 34(4):708–721.

Metraux, A. (1946) The Caingang. In *Handbook of South American Indians*, Vol. 1, J. Steward, ed., pp. 445–475. Washington, D.C.: Smithsonian Institution.

——— (1948) The Guarani. In *Handbook of South American Indians*, Vol. 3, J. Steward, ed., pp. 69–94. Washington, D.C.: Smithsonian Institution.

Milagres, J. C., E. U. Dillard, and O. W. Robison. (1979) Influences of age and early growth on reproductive performance of yearling Hereford heifers. *Journal of Animal Science* 48:1089–1095.

Mildvan, A. S., and B. L. Strehler. (1960) A critique of theories of mortality. In *The Biology of Aging,* B. L. Strehler, ed., pp. 45–78. New York: American Institute of Biological Sciences.

Milinski, M., and T. C. M. Baker. (1990) Female sticklebacks use male coloration in mate choice and hence avoid parasitized males. *Nature* 344:330–333.

Milner, G. R., D. A. Humpf, and H. Harpending. (1989) Pattern matching of age-at-death distributions in paleodemographic analyses. *American Journal of Physical Anthropology* 80:49–58.

Milton, K. (1984) Protein and carbohydrate resources of the Maku Indians of northwestern Amazonia. *American Anthropologist* 86(1):7–27.

Minchella, D. J., and P. T. Loverde. (1981) A cost of increased early reproductive effort in the snail *Biomphalaria glabrata*. *American Naturalist* 118:876–881.

Miraglia, L. (1969) Observaciones somaticas y serologicas en la raza Guayaki. *Suplemento* Antropológico *de la Revista Ateneo Paraguayo* IV(2):133–137.

——— (1973) Dos capturas de Aché-Guayakí en el Paraguay en Abril 1972. In *La Agonía de los Aché Guayakí: Historia y Cantos* B. Melia, L. Miraglia, C. Munzel and M. Munzel, eds., pp. 55–71. Asunción: Centro de Estudios Antropológicos, Universidad Católica.

Miraglia, L., and E. Saguier Negrete. (1969) Los Guayaki: Raza Trepadora. *Suplemento* Antropológico *de la Revista Ateneo Paraguayo* IV(2):139–159.

Mizrooh, S. A. (1981) Analyses of some biological parameters in the Antarctic fin whale. *Report of the International Whaling Commission* 31:425–434.

Møller, A. P. (1988) Female choice selects for male sexual tail ornaments in a monogamous swallow. *Nature* 332:640–642.

———— (1990a) Male tail length and female mate choice in the monogamous swallow, *Hirundo rustica*. *Animal Behavior* 39:458–465.

———— (1990b) Parasites and sexual selection: current status of the Hamilton and Zuk hypothesis. *Journal of Evolutionary Biology* 3:319–328.

Mora, J. O., M. G. Herrera, J. Suescun, L. de Navarro, and M. Wagner. (1981) The effects of nutritional supplementation on physical growth of children at risk of malnutrition. *American Journal of Clinical Nutrition* 34(9):1885–1892.

Moreno Azorero, R. (1966) Proyecto de Investigación. Estudios genéticos, demográficos, antropométricos y médicos de poblaciones indígenas de la República del Paraguay. *Suplemento Antropológico de la Revista Ateneo Paraguayo* II(1):315–319.

Mori, A. (1979) Analysis of population changes by measurement of body weight in the Koshima troop of Japanese monkeys. *Primates* 20:371–397.

Morris, B. (1982) Economy, affinity and inter-cultural pressure: notes on Hill Pandaram group structure. *Man* 17: 452–461.

Mosley, W. H., and L. Chen. (1984) *Child Survival: Strategies for Research*. Population and Development Review Supplement, Vol. 10. New York: Population Council.

Munzel, M. (1973) *The Ache Indians: Genocide in Paraguay*. International Work Group for Indigenous Affairs (IWGIA) Document 11. Copenhagen.

———— (1974) *The Ache: Genocide Continues in Paraguay*. International Work Group for Indigenous Affairs (IWGIA) Document 17. Copenhagen.

———— (1976) Man hunt. In *Genocide in Paraguay*, R. Arens, ed., pp. 19–45. Philadelphia: Temple University Press.

Myers, P., A. Taber, and I. Gamarra de Fox. (1995) Mammalogy in Paraguay. Unpublished manuscript, Museum of Zoology, University of Michigan, Ann Arbor.

Neel, J. V. (1978) The population structure of an Amerindian tribe, the Yanomamo. *Annual Review of Genetics* 12:365–413.

Neel, J. V., and N. Chagnon. (1968) The demography of two tribes of primitive relatively unacculturated American Indians. *Proceedings of the National Academy of Sciences* 59: 680–689.

Neel, J. V., and K. Weiss. (1975) The genetic structure of a tribal population, the Yanomama Indians. *American Journal of Physical Anthropology* 42:25–52.

Neel, J. V., W. R. Centerwall, N. A. Chagnon, and H. L. Casey. (1970) Notes on the effect of measles and measles vaccine in a virgin-soil population of South American Indians. *American Journal of Epidemiology* 91(4):418–429.

Nimmanahaeminda, K. (1984) The Mrabri language. In *Peoples of the Golden Triangle: Six Tribes in Thailand*, L. Lewis and E. Lewis, eds., pp. 179–183. New York: Thames and Hudson.

Nishida, T., H. Takasaki, and Y. Takahata. (1990) Demography and reproductive profiles. In *The Chimpanzees of Mahale Mountains*, T. Nishida, ed., pp. 67–89. Tokyo: University of Tokyo Press.

Nutrition Reviews. (1983) Nutritional supplementation and growth of children at risk of malnutrition. *Nutrition Reviews* 41(4):111–113.

Olesiuk, P. F., M. A. Bigg, and G. M. Ellis. (1990) Life history and population dynamics of resident killer whales *(Orcinus orca)* in the coastal waters of British Columbia and Washington state. *Reports of the International Whaling Commission*, Special Issue 12:209–243.

Olovson, S. G. (1986) Diet and breeding performance in cats. *Laboratory Animals* 20:221–230.

Palloni, A., and S. Millman. (1986) Effect of inter-birth-intervals and breastfeeding on infant mortality and early childhood mortality. *Population Studies* 40:215–236.

Palmer, A. R., and C. Strobeck. (1986) Fluctuating asymmetry: measurement, analysis, patterns. *Annual Review of Ecological Systems* 17:391–421.

Panter-Brick, C. (1991) Lactation, birth spacing and maternal workloads among two castes in rural Nepal. *Journal of Biosocial Science* 23:137–154.

Parker, G., and J. Maynard Smith. (1990) Optimality theory in evolutionary biology. *Nature* 348:27–33.

Parsons, P. A. (1990) Fluctuating asymmetry: an epigenetic measure of stress. *Biological Reviews* 65:131–145.

Paul, A., E. Muller, and R. G. Whitehead. (1979) The quantitative effects of maternal dietary energy intake on pregnancy and lactation in rural Gambian women. *Transactions of the Royal Society of Tropical Medicine and Hygiene* 73:686–692.

Paveleka, M., and L. M. Fedigan. (1991) Menopause: a comparative life history perspective. *Yearbook of Physical Anthropology* 34:13–38.

Peacock, N. R. (1990) Comparative and cross-cultural approaches to the study of human female reproductive failure. In *Primate Life History and Evolution: Monographs in Primatology*, Vol. 24, C. J. De Rousseau, ed., pp. 195–220. New York: Wiley Liss.

Pease, C. M., and J. J. Bull. (1988) A critique of methods measuring life history trade-offs. *Journal of Evolutionary Biology* 1:293–303.

Pennington, R., and H. Harpending. (1988) Fitness and fertility among Kalahari !Kung. *American Journal of Physical Anthropology* 77:303–319.

————— (1993) *The Structure of an African Pastoralist Community: Demography, History, and Ecology of the Ngamiland Herero*. Oxford: Clarendon Press.

Perrett, D. I., K. A. May, and S. Yoshikawa. (1994) Facial shape and judgements of female attractiveness. *Nature* 368:239–242.

Pookajorn, S. (1988) Archeological research of the Hoabinhian culture or technocomplex and its comparison with ethnoarchaeology of the Phi Tong Luang, a hunter-gatherer group of Thailand. In *Archeological Ventoria*, H. von Hansjurgen, ed., pp. 186–275. Cologne: Institut für Urgeschichte.

Powers, E. (1877) Centennial Mission to the Indians of Western Nevada and California. *Annual Report for 1876*, pp. 449–460. Washington, D.C.: Smithsonian Institution.

Prance, Ghillean, ed. (1982) *Biological Diversification in the Tropics*. Proceedings of the Fifth International Symposium of the Association for Tropical Biology, held at Macuto Beach, Caracas, Venezuela, February 8–13, 1979. New York: Columbia University Press.

Prasad, B. M., C. D. Conover, D. K. Sarkar, J. Rabii, and J. Advis. (1993) Feed restriction in prepubertal lambs: effect on puberty onset and on in vivo release of luteinizing-hormone-releasing hormone, neuropeptide Y and beta-endorphin from the posterior-lateral median eminence. *Neuroendocrinology* 57:1171–1181.

Prentice, A. M., T. J. Cole, F. A. Foord, W. H. Lamb, and R. G. Whitehead. (1987) Increased birthweight after prenatal dietary supplementation of rural African women. *American Journal of Clinical Nutrition* 46(6):912–925.

Preston, S. H. (1976) *Mortality Patterns in National Populations*. New York: Academic Press.

Promislow, D. E. L., and P. H. Harvey. (1990) Living fast and dying young: a comparative analysis of life history variation among mammals. *Journal of Zoology* 220:417–437.

Read, A. F. (1988) Sexual selection and the role of parasites. *Trends in Ecology and Evolution* 3:97–102.

———— (1990) Parasites and the evolution of host sexual behavior. In *Parasitism and the Evolution of Host Behavior*, C. J. Barnard and J. M. Behnke, eds., pp. 117–157. London: Taylor and Francis.

Reiss, M. J. (1989) *The Allometry of Growth and Reproduction*. Cambridge: Cambridge University Press.

Renshaw, J. (1989) Report to the Fundación Bertoni. Unpublished manuscript, Fundación Moisés Bertoni, Asunción, Paraguay.

Reznik, D. (1985) Costs of reproduction: an evaluation of the empirical evidence. *Oikos* 44: 257–267.

Richards, L. C., and S. L. J. Miller. (1991) Relationships between age and dental attrition in Australian Aboriginals. *American Journal of Physical Anthropology* 84:159–164.

Riley, A. P., J. L. Samuelson, and S. L. Huffman. (1993) The relationship of age at menarche and fertility in undernourished adolescents. In *Biomedical and Demographic Determinants of Reproduction*, R. H. Gray, H. Leridon, and A. Spira, eds., pp. 50–64. Oxford: Clarendon Press.

Robinson, J., and K. Redford, eds. (1991) *Neotropical Wildlife Use and Conservation*. Chicago: University of Chicago Press.

Roff, D. A. (1986) Predicting body size with life history models. *Bioscience* 36:316–323.

———— (1992) *The Evolution of Life Histories*. New York: Chapman and Hall.

Rogers, A. (1990) The evolutionary economics of human reproduction. *Ethology and Sociobiology* 11:479–495.

———— (1994) Evolution of time preference by natural selection. *American Economic Review* 84(3):460–481.

Rogers, A., and A. Mukherjee. (1991) Quantitative genetics of sexual dimorphism in human body size. *Evolution* 46(1):226–234.

Roosevelt, A. C. (1980) *Parmana*. New York: Academic Press.

———— (1991) *Moundbuilders of the Amazon*. New York: Academic Press.

Rose, F. G. G. (1960) *Classification of Kin, Age Structure and Marriage amongst the Groote Eylandt Aborigines*. Oxford: Pergamon Press.

Rose, M. R. (1984) Laboratory evolution of postponed senescence in *Drosophila melanogaster*. *Evolution* 38(5):1004–1010.

Sadlier, R. M. S. (1969) *Ecology of Reproduction in Wild and Domestic Mammals*. London: Methuen.

Saguier Negrete, E., M. Luigi, R. Juste. (1968) Caracteres primitivos y pigmoides de dos esqueletos Guayakí. *Revista de la Sociedad Científica Paraguaya* IX: 23–41. Asunción, Paraguay.

Sahlins, M. (1972) *Stone Age Economics*. New York: Aldine.

———— (1976) *The Use and Abuse of Biology: An Anthropological Critique of Sociobiology*. Ann Arbor: University of Michigan Press.

Sailer, L. D., S. Gaulin, J. Boster, and J. Kurland. (1985) Measuring the relationship between dietary quality and body size in primates. *Primates* 26(1):14–27.

Salzano, F. M. (1988) *South American Indians: a Case Study in Evolution*. New York: Oxford University Press.

Sammons, R. (1978) *Ache Texts*. Asuncion, Paraguay: New Tribes Mission.

SAS® (1985) *User's Guide: Statistics, Version 5 Edition*. Cary, North Carolina: SAS Institute.

Saunders, S. R., and R. D. Hoppa. (1993) Growth deficit in survivors and non-survivors: biological mortality bias in subadult skeletal samples. *Yearbook of Physical Anthropology* 36:127–151.

Schwartz, S. M., M. E. Wilson, M. L. Walker, and D. C. Collins. (1988) Dietary influences on growth and sexual maturation in premenarcheal rhesus monkeys. *Hormones and Behavior* 22:231–251.

Scott, E. C., and F. E. Johnston. (1985) Science, nutrition, fat, and policy: tests of the critical-fat hypothesis. *Current Anthropology* 26:463–473.

Seerley, R. W., R. A. Snyder, and H. C. McCampbell. (1981) The influence of sow dietary lipids and choline on piglet survival, milk and carcass composition. *Journal of Animal Science* 52:542–550.

Sharpe, F. R., and A. J. Lotka (1911) A problem in age-distribution. *Philosophical Magazine* 6(21):435–438.

Shine, R. (1989) Ecological causes for the evolution of sexual dimorphism: a review of the evidence. *Quarterly Review of Biology* 64:419–461.

Shostak, M. (1981) *Nisa: The Life and Words of a !Kung Woman*. Cambridge, Massachusetts: Harvard University Press.

Sibly, R. M., and P. Calow. (1986) *Physiological Ecology of Animals*. Oxford: Blackwell Scientific.

Sief, D. (1990) Explaining biased sex ratios in human populations. *Current Anthropology* 31:25–48.

Sinha, D. P. (1972) The Birhors. In *Hunters and Gatherers Today*, M. G. Bicchieri, ed., pp. 61–72. New York: Holt, Rinehart and Winston.

Skelly, D. K., and E. E. Werner. (1990) Behavioral and life history responses of larval American toads to an odonate predator. *Ecology* 7:2313–2322.

Smart, J. L., and E. Silence. (1977) Problems of undernutrition research with breeding mice. *Laboratory Animals* 7:165–168.

Smedman, L., G. Sterky, L. Mellander, and S. Wall. (1987) Anthropometry and subsequent mortality in groups of children aged 6–59 months in Guinea-Bisseau. *American Journal of Clinical Nutrition* 46:360–373.

Smith, B. H. (1991) Dental development and the evolution of life history in Hominidae. *American Journal of Physical Anthropology* 86:157–174.

Smith, C. C., and S. D. Fretwell. (1974) The optimal balance between size and number of offspring. *American Naturalist* 108:499–506.

Smith, E. A., and B. Winterhalder, eds. (1992) *Evolutionary Ecology and Human Behavior*. New York: Aldine de Gruyter.

Smith, R. J., and B. Melia. (1978) Genocide of the Ache-Guayaki? *Survival International* Supplement 21:8–13.

Sommer, A., and M. S. Loewenstein. (1975) Nutritional status and mortality: a prospective validation of the QUAC stick. *American Journal of Clinical Nutrition* 28:287–292.

Stearman, A. (1989) *Yuqui: Forest Nomads in a Changing World*. Orlando: Holt, Rinehart and Winston.

Stearns, S. (1992) *The Evolution of Life Histories*. Oxford: Oxford University Press.

Stearns, S., and R. E. Crandall. (1981) Quantitative predictions of delayed maturity. *Evolution* 35:455–463.

Stearns, S. C., and J. Koella. (1986) The evolution of phenotypic plasticity in life history traits: predictions for norms of reaction for age and size at maturity. *Evolution* 40:893–913.

Steward, J. H. (1933) Ethnography of the Owens Valley Paiute. *University of California Publications in American Archaeology and Ethnology* 33:233–350.

———, ed. (1946) *Handbook of South American Indians*, Vol. 1. Washington, D.C.: Smithsonian Institution.

——— (1949) *Handbook of South American Indians*, Vol. 5. Washington, D.C.: Smithsonian Institution.

Stuart, D. E. (1972) *Band Structure and Ecological Variability: the Ona and Yahgan of Tierra del Fuego*. Ph.D. Dissertation, University of New Mexico.

Sugiyama, Y., and H. Ohsawa. (1982) Population dynamics of Japanese monkeys with special reference to the effect of artificial feeding. *Folia Primatologica* 39:238–263.

Sunquist, M. E., and J. F. Eisenberg. (1993) Reproductive strategies of female didelphis. *Bulletin of the Florida Museum of National History, Biological Sciences* 36(4):109–140.

Survival International. (1993) *The Denial of Genocide*. London: Survival International.

Susnik, B. (1979–1980) *Los Aborígenes del Paraguay II. Etnohistoria de los Guaraníes*. Asunción: Museo Etnográfico Andrés Barbero.

——— (1983) El Rol de Los Indígenas en la Formación y en la Vivencia del Paraguay, Tomo I. *Etnohistoria de los Guaraníes*. Asunción: Instituto Paraguayo de Estudios Nacionales.

Tatar, M., and J. R. Carey. (1995) Nutrition mediates reproductive costs in the beetle *Calosobruchus maculatus*. *Ecology*, in press.

Taylor, B., and W. Gabriel. (1992) To grow or not to grow: optimal resource allocation for Daphnia. *American Naturalist* 139:248–266.

Techo, N. del. (1897) *Historia del la Provincia del Paraguay de la Compania de Jesus*. Madrid.

Thomas, E. M. (1959) *The Harmless People*. New York: Knopf.

Thornhill, R. (1992) Fluctuating asymmetry and the mating system of the Japanese scorpionfly (*Panorpa japonica*). *Animal Behavior* 44:867–879.

Thornhill, R., and S. Gangestad. (1993) Human facial beauty: averageness, symmetry, and parasite resistance. *Human Nature* 4(3):237–269.

Thornhill, R., and K. P. Sauer. (1992) Genetic sire effects on the fighting ability of sons and daughters and mating success of sons in the scorpionfly (*Panorpa vulgaris*). *Animal Behavior* 43:255–264.

Thornhill, R., and N. Thornhill. (1989) The evolution of psychological pain. In *Sociobiology and the Social Sciences*, R. Behl and N. Behl, eds., pp. 73–103. Lubbock: Texas Tech University Press.

Thornton, R., T. Miller, and J. Warren. (1991) American Indian population recovery following smallpox epidemics. *American Anthropologist* 93(1):28–45.

Tinbergen, J. M., J. H. van Balen, and H. M. van Eck. (1985) Density-dependent survival in an isolated great tit population: Kluyer's data reanalyzed. *Ardea* 73:38–48.

Tracer, D. (1991) Fertility related changes in maternal body composition among the Au of Papua New Guinea. *American Journal of Physical Anthropology* 85(4):393–406.

Trinkaus, E. (1995) Neandertal mortality patterns. *Journal of Archaeological Science* 22(1):121–143.

Trinkaus, E., and R. L. Tompkins. (1990) The Neandertal life cycle: the possibility, probability, and perceptibility of contrasts with recent humans. In *Primate Life History and Evolution*, C. J. De Rousseau, ed., pp. 153–180. Monographs in Primatology, Vol. 14. New York: Wiley-Liss.

Trivers, R. L. (1972) Parental investment and sexual selection. In *Sexual Selection and the Descent of Man*, B. Campbell, ed., pp. 136–179. Chicago: Aldine.

—————— (1974) Parent-offspring conflict. *American Zoologist* 14:249–264.

—————— (1985) *Social Evolution*. Menlo Park, California: Benjamin/Cummings.

Trivers, R. L., and D. E. Willard. (1973) Natural selection of parental ability to vary the sex ratio of offspring. *Science* 179:90–92.

Tuma, N. B., and M. T. Hannan. (1984) *Social Dynamics*. Orlando: Academic Press.

Turke, P. (1988) Helpers at the nest: childcare networks on Ifaluk. In *Human Reproductive Behavior*, L. Betzig, P. Turke, and M. Borgerhoff Mulder, eds., pp. 173–188. Cambridge: Cambridge University Press.

Tutor, B. M. (1962) Nesting studies of the boat-tailed grackle. *Auk* 79:77–84.

van Noordwijk, A. J., and G. de Jong. (1986) Acquisition and allocation of resources: their influence on variation in life history tactics. *American Naturalist* 128:127–142.

Vellard, J. (1939) *Une Civilisation du Miel. Les Indiens Guayakis du Paraguay*. Paris.

Verme, L. J. (1965) Reproduction studies on penned white-tailed deer. *Journal of Wildlife Management* 29:74–79.

Vitzhum, V. J. (1989) Nursing behaviour and its relation to duration of post-partum amenorrhea in an Andean community. *Journal of Biosocial Science* 21:145–160.

Washburn, S. L. (1981) Longevity in primates. In *Aging, Biology and Behavior*, J. March and J. McGaugh, eds., pp. 11–29. New York: Academic Press.

Watanabe, K., and A. Mori. (1992) Characteristic features of the reproduction of Koshima monkeys, a summary of 34 years of observation. *Primates* 33:1–32.

Weiss, K. (1973) *Demographic Models for Anthropology*. Memoirs of the Society for American Archaeology 27. *American Antiquity* 38 (2, part II).

Weiss, K. M. (1981) Evolutionary perspectives on human aging. In *Other Ways of Growing Old*, P. Amoss and S. Harrell, eds., pp. 25–58. Stanford: Stanford University Press.

Werner, D. (1983) Why do the Mekranoti trek? In *Adaptive Responses of Native Amazonians*, R. Hames and W. Vickers, eds., pp. 139–188. New York: Academic Press.

Werner, E. (1988) Size, scaling, and the evolution of complex life cycles. In *Size-Structured Populations*, B. Ebenmann and L. Persson, eds., pp. 60–81. Berlin: Springer-Verlag.

Werner, E., and D. J. Hall. (1988) Ontogenetic habitat shifts in bluegill: the foraging rate-predation risk trade-off. *Ecology* 69(5):1352–1366.

Whittington, S. L. (1991) Detection of significant demographic differences between subpopulations of prehispanic Maya from Copan, Honduras by survival analysis. *American Journal of Physical Anthropology* 85(2):167–184.

Willey, G. (1971) *South America. An Introduction to American Archeology,* Vol. 2. Englewood Cliffs, New Jersey: Prentice Hall.

Williams, D. (1990) Socioeconomic differentials in health: a review and redirection. *Social Psychology Quarterly* 53(2):81–99.

Williams, G. C. (1957) Pleiotrophy, natural selection and the evolution of senescence. *Evolution* 11:398–411.

———— (1966) *Adaptation and Natural Selection*. Princeton, New Jersey: Princeton University Press.

Williams, G. C., and R. Nesse. (1991) The dawn of Darwinian medicine. *Quarterly Review of Biology* 66:1–22.

Wilson, K. (1989) The evolution of oviposition behavior in the bruchid (*callsobruchus maculatus*). Ph.D. Dissertation, University of Sheffield.

Wilson, M. (1957) *Rituals of Kinship among the Nyakyusa*. Oxford: Oxford University Press.

Wolfe, L. D., and J. P. Gray. (1982) A cross-cultural investigation into the sexual dimorphism of stature. In *Sexual Dimorphism in* Homo Sapiens: *a Question of Size*, R. L. Hall, ed., pp. 197–230. New York: Praeger.

Wolfers, D., and S. Scrimshaw. (1975) Child survival and intervals between pregnancies in Guayaquil, Ecuador. *Population Studies* 29(3):479–495.

Wood, J. (1987) Problems of applying model fertility and mortality schedules to data from Papua New Guinea. In *The Survey under Difficult Conditions: Demographic Data Collection in Papua New Guinea*, T. McDevitt, ed., pp. 371–397. New Haven: HRAF Press.

———— (1990) Fertility in anthropological populations. *Annual Review of Anthropology* 19:211–242.

———— (1994) *Dynamics of Human Reproduction: Biology, Biometry, and Demography*. New York: Aldine de Gruyter.

Wood, J., and P. Smouse. (1982) A method of analyzing density-dependent vital rates with an application to the Gainj of Papua New Guinea. *American Journal of Physical Anthropology* 58:403–411.

Wood, J., P. Johnson, and K. Campbell. (1985) Demographic and endocrinological aspects of low natural fertility in Highland New Guinea. *Journal of Biosocial Science* 17:57–79.

Wood, J., D. Lai, P. Johnson, K. Campbell, and I. Maslar. (1985) Lactation and birth spacing in Highland New Guinea. *Journal of Biosocial Science* Supplement 9:159–173.

Worthman, C., C. L. Jenkins, J. F. Stallings, and D. Lai. (1993) Attenuation of nursing-related ovarian suppression and high fertility in well-nourished, intensively breastfeeding Amele women of lowland Papua New Guinea. *Journal of Biosocial Science* 25:425–443.

Zuk, M., R. Thornhill, and J. D. Ligon. (1990) Parasites and mate choice in red jungle fowl. *American Zoologist* 30:235–244.

Index